Okinawan-English Wordbook

I would like to express my best wishes on the publication of the *Okinawan-English Wordbook*.

It has been more than a century since the first Okinawans left here for the island kingdom of Hawai'i, sowing the seeds of a relationship that now produces a very special flower. The *Okinawan-English Wordbook*, like the island cultures that nurtured it, bears the traces of a wide variety of people and cultures.

For many years, the late Dr. Mitsugu Sakihara, who came to the United States from Okinawa in 1951, painstakingly matched the words of his youth to the words of his adopted home, eventually compiling an Okinawan-English dictionary with nearly 10,000 entries. After his death in 2001, his unpublished manuscript was studied extensively by linguistics scholars at the University of the Ryukyus, who shared their work with their colleagues at the University of Hawai'i. Two years ago, the Center for Japanese Studies at the University of Hawai'i, and the University of Hawai'i Press, took on the task of publishing Dr. Sakaihara's work in wordbook form, timed to coincide with the 4th Worldwide Uchinanchu Festival.

This work, the dream of an Okinawan immigrant to Hawai'i, was brought to completion through the efforts of people from two distinguished universities. Okinawa Prefecture would like to adopt the *Okinawan-English Wordbook* as a memento of the 4th Worldwide Uchinanchu Festival.

I hope that the *Wordbook* will form a bridge between the Okinawan immigrants overseas and the Okinawan people in this prefecture, and that this bond will be further strengthened to develop mutual contributions in the future.

In conclusion, I would like to express my deepest respects to all the individuals involved in this project.

    Keiichi Inamine
    Governor of Okinawa Prefecture
    January 2006

Okinawan-English Wordbook

A short Lexicon of the Okinawan Language
with English Definitions and
Japanese Cognates

Mitsugu Sakihara

Edited by Stewart Curry

Supervising Editors
Leon A. Serafim and Shigehisa Karimata

Consulting Editor Moriyo Shimabukuro

University of Hawai'i Press
Honolulu

© 2006 University of Hawai'i Press
All rights reserved
Printed in the United States of America
11 10 09 08 07 06   6 5 4 3 2 1

Library of Congress Cataloging-in-Publication Data
Sakihara, Mitsugu, 1928-
 Okinawan-English wordbook : a short lexicon of the Okinawan language with English definitions and Japanese cognates / Mitsugu Sakihara ; edited by Stewart Curry ; supervising editors, Leon A. Serafim and Shigehisa Karimata.
   p. cm.
 Includes bibliographical references and index.
 ISBN-13: 978-0-8248-3051-9 (hardcover : alk. paper)
 ISBN-10: 0-8248-3051-2 (hardcover : alk. paper)
 ISBN-13: 978-0-8248-3102-8 (pbk. : alk. paper)
 ISBN-10: 0-8248-3102-0 (pbk. : alk. paper)
 1. Ryukyuan language—Dictionaries—English.   I. Curry, Stewart, 1965- . II. Serafim, Leon Angelo. III. Karimata, Shigehisa, 1954-
 . IV. Title.
PL693.R9S256 2006
495.6'7095229—dc22
                                                        2006008731

Camera-ready copy for this book was
prepared by Stewart Curry

University of Hawai'i Press books are printed on
acid-free paper and meet the guidelines for permanence
and durability of the Council on Library Resources.

Printed by the Maple-Vail Book
Manufacturing Group

Contents

Preface   vii
Introduction   ix
Explanatory Notes   xvi
List of Abbreviations   xvii
References and Resources   xviii

Okinawan-English Wordbook   1

English-Okinawan Glossary-Index   229

Preface

The *Wordbook* and its Original Manuscript

The original manuscript that led to the *Okinawan-English Wordbook* was produced by the late Dr. Mitsugu Sakihara as a full dictionary, complete with extensive examples of word use in alternate forms, in phrases, and in sentences. That manuscript, compiled over some 20 years, runs to well over 1300 pages, and includes a host of cultural, folkloric, and historical material in addition to the dictionary entries themselves. Mrs. Jean Sakihara, Dr. Sakihara's widow, has kindly given the current editors latitude to bring the manuscript into published form, eventually to comprise two independent volumes, of which this *Wordbook* is the first. There will follow in due course the second book, the dictionary proper, based on Dr. Sakihara's full manuscript.

Acknowledgements

The *Okinawan-English Wordbook* would never have made it to publication without the hard work and generous support in time, effort, and money of numerous individuals and entities.

The editors would like to acknowledge and thank the following:

Mrs. Jean Sakihara, who entrusted the manuscript and Dr. Sakihara's legacy to the current project.

The Center for Japanese Studies at the University of Hawai'i at Mānoa, under the direction of Prof. Robert N. Huey, which has overseen and shepherded this project from its inception. CJS has provided funding to support work on the manuscript derived in part from an endowment to the Sen Soshitsu International Way of Tea Center.

Okinawa Prefecture and Governor Keiichi Inamine, who provided a large commitment to launch the *Wordbook* at the Fourth Worldwide Uchinanchu Festival in Fall 2006.

Pat Crosby at UH Press, who provided the expertise and experience to guide us in transforming a rough manuscript into a book.

Robert Nakasone, of the East-West Center in Honolulu, who acted as the project's direct liaison with the Okinawan prefectural government.

Sally Serafim, who read the pre-publication manuscript and cleaned up inconsistencies, misspellings, and punctuation goofs left by the editors; Dr. Jeffrey J. Hayden, who assisted in preparing the Glossary-Index and proofed all Chinese references; and Keith Leber of UH Press, who painstakingly checked all scientific names for accuracy.

Steve Higa, Judy Higa, Kevin Zane, and Alberta Freidus-Flagg, who assisted in various capacities during the early stages of preparation of the manuscript on which the *Wordbook* is based.

Last, the editors would like to recognize the readers and users of this *Wordbook*, without whose interest, of course, there would be no need for it at all. For the "little" languages of the world to continue to survive and enrich the global cultural milieu, the interest of heritage speakers and new learners in addition to that of native speakers and professional linguists is essential.

Introduction

What "Okinawan" Means

The word "Okinawan" as used here refers to the language, not mutually intelligible with Japanese, traditionally used in the south-central part of the island of Okinawa. One of several Ryukyuan languages, Okinawan is based on the speech encountered in and around Naha and Shuri, that is, the area around the modern capital of present-day Okinawa Prefecture and the old capital of the Kingdom of the Ryukyus. Formerly, it was also the *lingua franca* of the Ryukyuan kingdom that flourished for several centuries before the Ryukyus became part of Japan in 1879.

The Okinawan language recorded in the *Wordbook* is based on the speech of the late Dr. Mitsugu Sakihara, the original author of this dictionary manuscript, who was a native of Naha. He augmented the manuscript by checking it against a number of other sources, noted in the bibliography to the current work. The current editors have also extensively checked *Wordbook* entries against the premier dictionary of Okinawan, the *Okinawa-go jiten*, published in Japanese in 1963, and against the speaker intuitions and unpublished notes of linguists at the University of the Ryukyus.

Sound System and Transcription

Okinawan is a close relative of the Japanese language, and features many of the sound-system characteristics of Japanese, among them a distinction between both long and short consonants and vowels, such as **t** vs. **tt** and **a** vs. **aa**. Okinawan also has a number of features that distinguish it from Japanese, among them a glottal stop that will require special treatment in transcription. For the *Wordbook*, we have chosen a romanization scheme that allows ease of use while maintaining accurate representation of the Okinawan sound system. Here is how the Okinawan system works, and how we write it in romanized transcription.

General comments on the romanization in the Wordbook

For the most part, the romanization in the *Wordbook* can be read as if it were Hepburn-style romanization of Japanese. That is, consonants have more or less the values they have in English, and vowels have roughly the value of Spanish (or, for that matter, Japanese) vowels. As neither English nor the Hepburn system has a consistent orthographic tool for writing the glottal stop sound found in Okinawan, special treatment for that sound is discussed below.

Consonants

In general, consonants and consonant clusters used to write Okinawan items here can be read as if they were English. That is, **b** represents the first sound of 'boy', **ch** the first sound of 'champ', and so on. For the following letters, English does not provide a good model, and a more specific description is required:

- **f**   represents a bilabial fricative, with the two lips as the point of articulation (rather than the upper lip and lower teeth of English f). Rather like intervocalic Spanish v or b, but unvoiced.
- **g**   always represents a hard g, as in English *g*et or *g*um.
- **r**   represents a short flap r, something like the sound in the middle of American English la*dd*er or bi*tt*er. Often interchanged with **d**.

In addition, Okinawan has long consonants that are not normally found in English, except, for example, in certain compounds. These double consonants—**tch, kk, nm, nn, pp, ss, tt**—have the same value as in English, but the sound is held slightly longer. Okinawan **kk**, for example, sounds something like the italicized sequence in this English phrase: bla*ck c*ar. (Note: the **t** used to write the doubled **ch** sound is ignored for alphabetization.)

Vowels

For vowels, the following English examples approximate the sound in question, but the Okinawan vowels are shorter and crisper than the English models given, and do not have the off-glide characteristics of English vowels. (For readers familiar with Japanese, the Okinawan vowels here are the same as the five vowels of Japanese.)

- **a** as in f*a*ther
- **e** as in the name of the letter A
- **i** as in f*ee*t
- **o** as in *o*h
- **u** as in *oo*h, but somewhat less rounded

When doubled, vowels have the same qualities as when single, but are longer in duration. In general, **e** and **o** are found only as long vowels.

The glottal stop

The glottal stop or glottal catch is the sound used in English in the informal words uh-huh 'yes' and uh-uh 'no'. (The former has one of them, and the latter has two.) It is also identical to the Hawaiian sound written with the *'okina*. The sign we use for the glottal is the same as that used for the glottal catch in Hawaiian, namely the inverted apostrophe ('), but since the glottal sound is common in certain positions in words, we have chosen to represent it overtly only when its presence cannot be indicated using more visually friendly conventions.

Wordbook entries starting with the vowel letters **a, e, i, o,** or **u** actually begin with the glottal catch. That is, in word-initial position, **a** represents **'a**, and so forth. To the English speaker this may not be noticeable, since English words with initial vowels also have an automatic (and thus unnoticeable—and unwritten) glottal catch. Unlike English, however, Okinawan words typically maintain their glottal catch when they are pronounced somewhere besides the beginning of an utterance. Thus, **achi·sa-umi·i** 'person sensitive to the heat', a compound word made up of **achi·sa** 'heat' and of **umi·i** 'thinker, feeler' has a glottal catch at the beginning of both **achi·sa** and **umi·i**. In headwords, we use a hyphen (-) to show that the second part of the compound is a separate element, and to indicate the need to treat the **u** there as if it were at the beginning of a word, remembering to pronounce the glottal catch. Non-headword mentions of such items will use the inverted apostrophe in place of the hyphen: **achisa'umii**. (See below for notes on hyphen [-] and raised dot [·] usage.)

Glottal onset vowels contrast with non-glottal, or smooth, vowels in Okinawan for the four pairs listed below. We represent smooth onset vowels with either **y** or **w** preceding the vowel in word-initial position and when words make up the second or later element of a compound (i.e., when they are set off by a hyphen):

- (')**i** ≠ **yi**, as in **in** 'dog' vs. **yin** 'veranda'
- (')**e** ≠ **ye** as in **eema** 'interval' vs. **Yeema** 'Yaeyama [Islands]'
- (')**o** ≠ **wo** as in **ooji** 'fan' vs. **wooji** 'prince'
- (')**u** ≠ **wu** as in **uu** 'Hare (Chinese zodiac)' vs. **wuu** 'cord'

For many speakers, the sound we are writing as **e** (that is, **'e**) at the beginning of words has a subtle on-glide pronunciation that can sound like **'ye**. The **e** spelling has been retained for etymological integrity.

In all other cases (that is, word-internal position) all vowels can be treated as being non-glottal if written as such, or with a raised dot (·) preceding. This includes both similar and dissimilar vowel sequences, such as in the following examples:

> **shi-waashi** 'December' or **aaran-ka·a** 'person who is frank' (long **a** sound)
> **see** 'locust' or **ware·e** 'laughter' (long **e** sound)
> **mii** 'eye' or **umi·i** 'thinker' (long **i** sound)
> **hijai** 'left' or **ficha·i** 'light' (smooth **ai** sequence)

Glottalization in other environments

Okinawan also distinguishes glottalized onset from smooth onset in a few other environments. In these cases as well, the inverted apostrophe is used to indicate glottalization.

The distinction occurs for **y** and **w**, and for the short nasal syllable **n**, which contrast with **'y**, **'w**, and **'n**, as shown by the following pairs:

> **'yaa** 'you' ≠ **yaa** 'house'
> **'waa** 'pig' ≠ **waa** 'circle'
> **'nni** 'rice plant' ≠ **nni** 'chest'
> **'njanaa** 'stammerer' ≠ **njana** 'bitter herb'

For many speakers of Okinawan, especially younger ones, glottalization as a distinctive feature is well on its way to being lost. We retain it in the dictionary for two reasons: first, because it is still found in the speech of older speakers, and second, because it is of etymological significance.

The glottal symbol (') is ignored for purposes of alphabetization.

Symbols—hyphen (-) and raised dot (·)

The *Wordbook* uses two devices to mark boundaries within words, the hyphen (-) and the raised dot (·). Hyphens mark boundaries between independent words joined to form a compound, or between a word and a semantically significant prefix or suffix. Raised dots, on the other hand, mark endings on words that are closely bound to the word and typically represent a grammatical derivative from other forms of the same word. The distinction between the two can be illustrated with a couple of English examples treated as if they were entries in the *Wordbook*. Hyphenation would be used for English 'workman' which as a headword would be **work-man** to show that it is a combination of two items, 'work' and 'man', that together form a single word meaning 'laborer' or 'worker'. Similarly, 'workable' would be **work-able**. On the other hand 'works', 'worked', 'working', and 'worker' would be represented as **work·s**, **work·ed**, **work·ing**, and **work·er** to show that these are all derivations from the base **work** that use dependent suffixes to add the additional meanings.

Hyphens and raised dots are usually deleted for repeated mention of the same entry word in subsequent larger combinations. Thus **aka-chichi** 'dawn' has a hyphen when first listed, but in subsequent entries we find **akachichi-baru** 'farm work before breakfast' and **akachichi-bushi** 'morning star' (among others). The hyphen is used consistently, however, to set off the verb **sun** 'to do' when it is used to make phrasal verbs such as **kufuu-sun** 'to plan, contrive' (from **kufuu** 'a plan, contrivance'), both in headwords and in subsequent mentions. This serves to distinguish it from **·sun** verbs such as **fuu·sun** 'to dry', which conjugate differently despite the apparent similarities in the headword endings.

Okinawan Grammar

The grammar of Okinawan has many features that will seem familiar to those with a knowledge of Japanese, much in the way that, for example, French grammar is fairly accessible to those who know Spanish or Italian. The following outline gives basic information about nouns, adjectives, and verbs in Okinawan. For more detailed information about the syntax, morphology, and other aspects of Okinawan, consult specialized works such as those listed in the **References and Resources**.

Nouns

In Okinawan, as in many languages (though notably not English, for the most part), nouns can have different forms depending on their function, or grammatical role, in a sentence. The forms used for headwords in the *Wordbook* are the most common or basic forms of nouns, used, for example, when the noun is a grammatical object; these are also the forms used for attaching some endings, such as the literary topic marker ·**ya**. The non-basic forms of nouns are always predictable (with one exception) from the form cited as headword, so no special mention of these is made in the body of the *Wordbook*. The chart and discussion below summarize behavior for all nouns.

Nouns in Okinawan change forms and add endings to show the following functions: 1) adding the meaning of 'also' (with ·**n**) or 'to' (with ·**nkai**) to the noun, and 2) making the noun a topic. How the forms change can be determined by looking at what the basic form (the headword form) ends with. For comparison purposes, the literary topic forms are shown as well:

If the headword ends with…	Example	With ·n 'also'	Topic 'speaking of'	Literary topic 'speaking of'
…any long vowel	'yaa 'you'	'yaa·n	'yaa·ya	'yaa·ya
…short a	hisa 'leg'	hisa·n	hisa·a	hisa·ya
…short i	kami 'god'	kami·n	kame·e	kami·ya
…short u	chinu 'horn'	chinu·n	chino·o	chinu·ya
…syllabic n	jin 'money'	jinu·n	jino·o	jin·ya

The system is most transparent for nouns ending in long vowels of any sort; these have no changes to the headword form. Similarly, appending the ·**ya** literary topic marker makes no internal changes in any noun. On the other hand, nouns ending in **n** must "grow" a final vowel, either **u** or **o** depending on the ending, before endings can be attached. Similarly, appending topic markers requires changes in the final vowel of any noun that ends in a short vowel other than **a**.

Behavior of a noun is predictable, though, within the patterns summarized above. Thus, given a headword **kumi** 'rice', for example, the following forms result:

    kumi·n 'rice, too'
    kumi·nkai 'to rice'
    kume·e 'speaking of rice…' (colloquial)
    kumi·ya 'speaking of rice…' (literary)

There is one irregular noun (or pronoun, if you like): **wan** 'I, me' is not topicalized as the expected ***wano·o**, but rather as **wanne·e**. Similarly, 'I, too' is not the expected ***wanu·n**, but rather **wanni·n**. Historically, this irregularity arises from the fossilization of **wan·ni** 'to me' as an alternate form of **wan**, but the details of this change are beyond the scope of this summary. The behavior of **wan** is summarized here:

wan 'I'
wanni·n 'I, too'
wanne·e 'speaking of me…'
wan·ya 'speaking of me…' (This form is regular, of course.)

For other grammatical functions, various grammatical markers append to nouns without requiring any internal changes in the noun (as with the literary topic marker ·**ya**).

Adjectives
Okinawan adjectives, like Japanese, change endings to show tense, negativity, and the like. The regular sentence-ending (nonpast affirmative) form for adjectives is ·**san**, and this form is used for adjective headwords in the *Wordbook*. However, there are two subtypes of adjectives, those for which the adverbial form is ·**ku**, and those with ·**shiku**. Historically, ·**shiku** adjectives did not end in ·**san** but in ·**shan**, as in literary Okinawan and in the obsolete Shuri language of the old male gentry. Based on this model, in *Wordbook* headwords the notation ·**s(h)an** is used to show the ·**shiku** subtype. The table below summarizes the conjugation of adjectives. Note how the adverbial form is used (with topicalization, as if it were a noun ending in **u**) to make the negative form of adjectives.

Headword	Adverbial form	Negative form
·san	·ku	·koo neen
·s(h)an	·shiku	·shikoo neen

Thus, an adjective such as **taka·san** 'tall, high' will occur in the following forms:

taka·san '[it is] tall'
taka·ku (na·in) '[it] (becomes) tall'
taka·koo neen '[it is] not tall'

And **hiruma·s(h)an** 'strange, unusual' will be conjugated as follows:

hiruma·san '[it is] strange'
hiruma·shiku (na·in) '[it] (becomes) strange'
hiruma·shikoo neen '[it is] not strange'

Certain adjectives have adverbial forms that cannot be predicted from their dictionary headword forms. For these, the conjugation information is presented in square brackets as part of the entry for the word. Here are two examples:

Headword	Key	Adverbial form	Negative form
his·san 'thin, weak'	[…shi·ku]	hishi·ku	hishi·koo neen
was·san 'bad, evil'	[…ru·ku]	waru·ku	waru·koo neen

Verbs
Okinawan verbs, like Japanese, conjugate for tense, negativity, politeness, and the like, but with somewhat more complex paradigms, thanks to various sound changes that have affected Okinawan over the centuries. The charts below and on the next

page summarize Okinawan verb paradigms; the discussion below describes the treatment of verbs and their subtyping in the body of the *Wordbook*.

For most verbs, the form of the headword (identical to the Nonpast Affirmative listing in the table on the following page) will give an unambiguous indication of what the rest of the forms of the verb will be. When this information is not predictable, it is given, as it is for irregular adjectives, in square brackets in the body of the entry. Thus, for an example such as **mu·chun**[1] 'to have' the notation [·**tan**, ·**tchi**] shows that the negative nonpast of this verb is **mu·tan** 'doesn't have' and the gerund, **mu·tchi** 'having' (i.e., as in Type IIb2) while for **mu·chun**[2] 'to swell' the lack of such notation indicates a negative in **mu·kan** and gerund in **mu·chi** (i.e., as in Type IIb1).

Information about unpredictable verb endings is given for all verbs of Types Ia2, Ib1, Ib2, Ic1, Ic2, IIa2, IIa3, IIb2, and III, as in the following table, keyed to the Nonpast negative and the Gerund endings. Lines marked "default" refer to the most heavily populated categories of verbs, where simple inspection of the headword form will be assumed to indicate the appropriate category and paradigm, and for which no information is given in *Wordbook* entries. Type IV verbs (irregular; see page xv) also have notation of their respective behaviors in the entries for each item.

	Type	Headword ending	Nonpast negative	Gerund
(default)	Ia1	·in	·ran	·ti
	Ia2	·in	·(r)an	·ti
	Ib1	·in	·ran	·chi
	Ib2	·in	·ran	·tchi
	Ic1	ri·in	·ran	t·ti
	Ic2	ri·in	ri·ran	t·ti
(default)	IIa1	·jun	·gan	·ji
	IIa2	·jun	·dan	·ti
	IIa3	·jun	·dan	·chi
(default)	IIb1	·chun	·kan	·chi
	IIb2	·chun	·tan	·tchi
(default)	IIc	·sun	·san	·chi
(default)	IId	·bun	·ban	·di
(default)	IIe	·mun	·man	·di
(default)	IIf	·nun	·nan	·ji
	III	·n	·ran	·ti

Note that phrasal verbs made by adding **-sun** to a noun or adverb follow the same conjugation pattern as the type IV irregular verb **sun** in isolation. They are distinct from type IIc **·sun** verbs.

The verb forms in the **Okinawan Verbs** chart following are given functional descriptions and glosses in the column headings. The **(y)a**-form is used to attach certain verbal endings, which are identified in the *Wordbook* body as requiring that form.

Okinawan Verbs (based on OGJ)

Type	Nonpast Affirmative ('does')	Clause-ending ('does, and')	(ya)-form (for endings ·bi·in, etc.)	Nonpast Negative ('does not')	Gerund ('doing')	Example	Gloss
Ia1 ...V·in	·in	·i	·ya or ·i	·ran	·ti	tu·in; waka·in	'take'; 'understand'
Ia2 ...a·in	...a·in	...e·e or ...a·i	...a·ya or ...a·i	...a·(r)an	...a·ti	wara·in	'laugh'
Ib1 C·i·in 1	...i·in	...i·i	...i·ya or ...i·i	...i·ran	...i·chi	chi·in	'don (clothes)'
Ib2 (...)(C)i·in 2	...i·in	...i·ri	...i·ya or ...i·i	...i·ran	...i·tchi	chi·in	'cut (it)'
Ic1 ...ri·in 1	...ri·in	...ri·i	...ri·yaor ...i·i	...ran	...t·ti	yumari·in	'can read'
Ic2 ...ri·in 2	...ri·in	...ri·i	...ri·yaor ...i·i	...ri·ran	...t·ti	iri·in	'put in'
IIa1	·jun	·ji	·ja	·gan	·ji	'wii·jun	'swim'
IIa2 ...n·jun 1	·n·jun	...n·ji	...n·ja	...n·dan	...n·ti	kan·jun	'don (hats)'
IIa3 ...n·jun 2	·n·jun	...n·ji	...n·ja	...n·dan	...n·chi	kun·jun	'tie up / down'
IIb1	·chun	·chi	·cha	·kan	·chi	ka·chun	'write'
IIb2	·chun	·chi	·cha	·tan	·tchi	ta·chun	'stand up'
IIc	·sun	·shi	·sa	·san	·chi	na·sun	'give birth to'
IId	·bun	·bi	·ba	·ban	·di	yu·bun	'call'
IIe	·mun	·mi	·ma	·man	·di	yu·mun	'read'
IIf	·nun	·ni	·na	·nan	·ji	shi·nun	'die'
III	·n	·i	·ya or ·i	·ran	·ti	wu·n	'be (animate)'
IV (irregulars)	mensee·n	mensee·i	mensee·ya, mensee·i, or mensee·	mensoo·ran	mensoo·chi	mensoo·chi	'come, go, be [exalting]'
	chuun	chii	chaa	kuun	tchi		'come'
	sun	shii	sa	san	sshi		'do'
	an	ai	aya or ai	nee(ra)n	ati		'be (inanimate)'
	yan	yai	yaya or yai	(ya) aran	yati		'be (copula)'
	'yun	ii	'ya	'yan	ichi		'say'
	umuin	umii, umui	umuya or umui	umaan, umuran	umuti		'think'
	ichun	ichi	icha	ikan	'nji		'go'

Explanatory Notes

The sample below illustrates the content and layout of a typical *Wordbook* entry. For specific information about abbreviations used, see the **List of Abbreviations** and **Bibliographical Abbreviations** following.

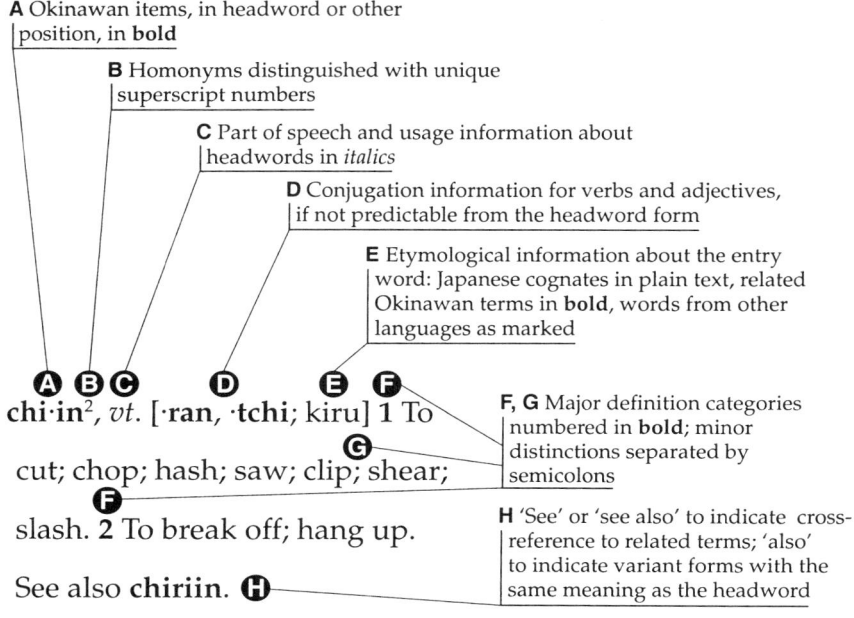

A Okinawan items, in headword or other position, in **bold**

B Homonyms distinguished with unique superscript numbers

C Part of speech and usage information about headwords in *italics*

D Conjugation information for verbs and adjectives, if not predictable from the headword form

E Etymological information about the entry word: Japanese cognates in plain text, related Okinawan terms in **bold**, words from other languages as marked

A B C   **D**   **E F**

chi·in², *vt.* [·ran, ·tchi; kiru] 1 To cut; chop; hash; saw; clip; shear; slash. 2 To break off; hang up.

See also **chiriin**. **H**

F, G Major definition categories numbered in **bold**; minor distinctions separated by semicolons

H 'See' or 'see also' to indicate cross-reference to related terms; 'also' to indicate variant forms with the same meaning as the headword

Additional information in entries

- The following markings give additional information about etymological citations:
  - < indicates the source of a word borrowed from another language, or the base form for a derivation
  - ? indicates an unproven etymological connection
  - * indicates a Japanese term that is no longer in current use or is used only dialectally
- A related term resulting from the addition of a grammatical marker ("particle"), the verb **-sun** 'to do', or certain other items to the headword is given as part of the entry:
  chiidi, *n.* [tsuide] Occasion; chance. ·**ni**, *adv.* By the way; incidentally…
  chiki-bi, *n.* [tsukebi] Arson; incendiarism. **-sun**, *v.* To commit arson…
  shiduu-ga-fuu, *n. humble* Thanks. **-deebiru**, *phr. formal* Thank you. …
- For plants and animals, non-cognate Japanese equivalents and scientific names are provided when possible:
  chiri-bira, *n.* A leek; a scallion [J nira; *Allium ramosum* L.].
- Bibliographical information is presented in square brackets: [UKH]

List of Abbreviations

adj.	adjective	part. adj.	participial adjective
adv.	adverb	part. emph.	particle of emphasis
arch.	archaic	pej.	pejorative
C	Chinese	pers.	person
Cant	Cantonese	phr.	phrase
colloq.	colloquial	pl.	plural
cop.	copula	poet.	poetic
E	English	Port	Portuguese
emph.	emphatic	pref.	prefix
endear.	endearment	pron.	pronoun
hon.	honorific term	sing.	singular
inf.	infantile term	Skt	Sanskrit
interj.	interjection	suff.	suffix
J	Japanese	v.	verb
lit.	literary	vi.	intransitive verb
n.	noun	vt.	transitive verb
onom.	onomatopoeia	...(y)a· + ...	requires (y)a form of verbs
part.	particle		

Bibliographical Abbreviations

Additional information on these and other works of interest is found in the **References and Resources**.

BHEO	*Brief History of Early Okinawa*, Mitsugu Sakihara
FOSR	*Flora of Okinawa and the Southern Ryūkyū Islands*, Egbert H. Walker
GOJ	*Gendai Okinawa jiten*, Ryūkyū Shinpō
GSS	*Gushichan sonshi*, Gushichan-son
IOJ	*Igaku Okinawa-go jiten*, Inafuku Seiki
KCS	*Kadena chōshi, shiryō-hen II*, Kadena-chō
MAK	*Makino's New Illustrated Flora of Japan*, Tomitaro Makino
MO	*Molluscs of Okinawa*, Hirofumi Kubo and Taiji Kurozumi
NJED	*Kenkyusha's New Japanese-English Dictionary*, Koh Masuda
OBJ	*Okinawa bunkashi jiten*, Ryūkyū Seifu Bunkazai Hogo Iinkai
OBS	*Okinawa bunka sōron*, Okinawa Bunka Kyōkai
ODJ	*Okinawa dai-hyakka jiten*, Okinawa Times
OGJ	*Okinawa-go jiten*, Kokuritsu Kokugo Kenkyūjo
OR	*Okinawa rekishi*, Shimabuku Gen'ichirō
RJK	*Ryūkyū jinmeikō*, Higashionna Kanjun
UKH	*Urasoe Kowan hōgen jiten*, Higa Minoru
ZRJ	*Zusetsu Ryūkyūgo jiten*, Nakamoto Masachie

References and Resources

Chamberlain, Basil Hall, 1895. *Essay in Aid of a Grammar and Dictionary of the Luchuan Language*. Transactions of TASJ 23, Special Supplement. Yokohama: Kelley and Walsh.

Funatsu Yoshiaki, 1988. *Utsukushii Okinawa no kotoba* {The beautiful language of Okinawa}. Tokyo: Gikōsha.

Gushichan-son Yakuba Kikaku-ka Gushichan-sonshi Henshū Iinkai, eds., 1963. *Gushichan sonshi* III {History of Gushichan village, vol. 3}. Gushichan, Okinawa: Gushichan-son Yakuba. [GSS]

Gusukuma Chōkyō, 1977. *Okinawa no shizen: shokubutsushi* {Nature in Okinawa: plants}. Tokyo: Shinsei Tosho.

Higa Minoru et al., eds., 1995. *Urasoe Kowan hōgen jiten* {Dictionary of Urasoe-Kowan dialect}. Tokyo: Miyahira Noboru. [UKH]

Higashionna Kanjun, 1977 [1925]. *Ryūkyū jinmeikō* {Treatise on Ryukyuan names}. Tokyo: Meicho Shuppan. [RJK]

Hokama Shuzen, 1971. *Okinawa no gengoshi* {The language history of Okinawa}. Tokyo: Hōsei Daigaku Shuppankyoku.

Ifa Fuyū, comp., 1916. *Ryūkyū-go binran* {Handbook of the Ryukyuan language}. Tokyo: Tōgyō Kenkyūkai.

Inafuku Seiki, comp., 1992. *Igaku Okinawa-go jiten* {Medical dictionary of Okinawan}. Ginowan: Roman Shobō Honten. [IOJ]

Isa Saburō, 1976. *Ryūka kanshō* {Appreciating Ryukyuan poetry}. Privately published.

Iwasaki, Tamihei and Jujiro Tokihiko, eds., 1960. *New English-Japanese Dictionary on Bilingual Principles*, 4th ed. Tokyo: Kenkyūsha.

Kadena-chōshi Henshū Iinkai, eds., 1990. *Kadena chōshi, shiryō-hen* II {Historical materials on Kadena town, vol. 2}. Kadena, Okinawa: Kadena-chō. [KCS]

Kanai Kikuko, 1954. *Ryūkyū no minyo* {Traditional songs of the Ryukyus}. Tokyo: Ongaku no Tomo-sha

Kinjō Chōei, 1974 [1944]. *Naha hōgen gaisetsu* {Outline of Naha dialect}. In Ōfuji Tokihiko and Hokama Shuzen, eds., *Kinjō Chōei zenshū* {The complete works of Kinjō Chōei}, 1:3–150. Naha: Okinawa Taimusu-sha

Kokuritsu Kokugo Kenkyūjo, eds., 1998 [1963]. *Okinawa-go jiten* {Dictionary of the Okinawan language}. Tokyo: Ōkurashō Insatsukyoku. [OGJ]

Kubo, Hirofumi and Taiji Kurozumi, 1995. *Molluscs of Okinawa*. Naha: Okinawa Shuppan. [MO]

Kuwae Chōkō, 1954 [1930]. *Hyōjungo taishō Okinawa-go no kenkyū* {A study of the Okinawan language, with reference to the standard Japanese language}. Naha: Sakima Shoten.

Lebra, W. P., 1966. *Okinawan Religion: Belief, Ritual, and Social Structure.* Honolulu: University of Hawai'i Press.

Lee, S. T., comp., 1961. *A New Complete Chinese-English Dictionary.* Hong Kong: China Publishers.

Makino, Tomitaro, 1980 [1940]. *Makino's New Illustrated Flora of Japan.* Tokyo: Hokuryūkan. [MAK]

Masuda, Koh, ed., 1974. *New Japanese-English Dictionary,* 4th ed. Tokyo: Kenkyūsha. [NJED]

Nakamoto Masachie, 1981. *Zusetsu Ryūkyū-go jiten* {Dictionary of Ryukyu dialects in maps and charts}. Tokyo: Rikitomi Shobō Kinkeisha. [ZRJ]

Nakamoto Masachie and Higa Minoru, eds., 1984. *Okinawa fūbutsushi* {Documents on things Okinawan}. Tokyo: Taishūkan Shoten

Nohara Mitsuyoshi, 1992. *Uchinaaguchi-kō* {Treatise on the Okinawan language}. Naha: Okinawa Taimusu-sha.

Okinawa Bunka Kyōkai, eds., 1970. *Okinawa bunka sōron* {Introduction to Okinawan culture}. Tokyo: Hōsei Daigaku Shuppankyoku. [OBS]

Okinawa Dai-hyakka Jiten Kankō Jimukyoku, eds., 1983. *Okinawa dai-hyakka jiten* {Encyclopedia of Okinawa}. Naha: Okinawa Taimusu-sha. [ODJ]

Okinawa-ken, comp., 1882. *Okinawa taiwa* {Dialogue on Okinawa}. Naha: Okinawa-ken.

Ryūkyū Seifu Bunkazai Hogo Iinkai, eds., 1972. *Okinawa bunkashi jiten* {Dictionary of Okinawan cultural history}. Tokyo: Tōkyōdō Shuppan. [OBJ]

Ryūkyū Shinpōsha Henshūkyoku, eds., 1992. *Gendai Okinawa jiten* {Contemporary Okinawa Encyclopedia}. Naha: Ryūkyū Shinpōsha. [GOJ]

Sakihara, Mitsugu, 1987. *A Brief History of Early Okinawa.* Tokyo: Honpo Shoseki Press. Distributed by University of Hawai'i Press. [BHEO]

Shimabuku Gen'ichirō, 1952. *Okinawa rekishi* {History of Okinawa}.[OR]

Shimabukuro Seibin and Onaga Toshio, eds., 1983. *Hyōon hyōshaku Ryūka zenshū* {Complete collection of Ryukyuan poetry, transcribed and annotated}. Tokyo: Musashino Shoin.

Shimabukuro Zenkō, 1983. *Kotowaza ni miru Okinawa no kokoro* {The Okinawan spirit seen in proverbs}. Privately published.

Shinmura Izuru, ed., 1991. *Kōjien,* 4th ed. {Expansive garden of words}. Tokyo: Iwanami Shoten.

Takihara Yasumori, 1986. *Okinawa-go benrichō* {Handbook of the Okinawan language}. Okinawa Geinō Shuppan.

Walker, Egbert H., 1976. *Flora of Okinawa and the Southern Ryukyu Islands.* Washington: Smithsonian Institution Press. [FOSR]

Okinawan-English Wordbook

A——

aa¹, *n.* [awa] A bubble; foam; froth; scum; suds.
aa², *n. inf.* Opening mouth.
aa-buku, *n.* [abuku] A bubble; suds. Also **aabukuu, abuku.** Same as **aa¹**.
aachu·u, *n. inf.* Heat.
aa·in, *vi.* [au] 1 To fit; suit; be suited to. 2 To agree (with); fit together; correspond to; jibe. 3 To be right; be correct. 4 To pay.
aakee, *n.* A dragonfly. Also **aakeejuu.** [GSS]
aakee-juu, *n.* [akizu*] A dragonfly.
aaki, *n.* [aki] A crevice; a crack; a gap; an aperture.
aakii, *n.* Pathos; a scene of lamentation in drama.
aaki·in, *vi.* 1 To split; cleave; fissure; crack apart. 2 To be inconsistent; contradict.
aa-man, *n.* A hermit crab; a pagurian.
aa-mui, *n.* An indigenous liquor of Okinawa made from millet or rice; awamori.
aaranka·a, *n.* A person who is frank, candid, and artless.
aasa, *n.* [asa] A sea lettuce; a kind of green laver [*Monostroma nitidum* (Wittrock)]. [ODJ]
aasa-irichii, *n.* An Okinawan dish in which dried **moo'aasa** is stir-fried with pork, fish cake, and bean sprouts. [ODJ]
aashi, *n.* [awase] Lined clothes. Same as **aashimun.**
aashi-mun, *n.* [awasemono] A lined kimono.
aa·sun, *vt.* [awasu] 1 To bring together; unite; combine. 2 To set (fit, adjust, adapt, conform) one thing to another; align; synchronize.
aa·sun, *vt.* To mix; compound; knead.
aataabii, *n.* Same as **atabichaa, wattaabii.**
aataabii·nu-kkwa, *n.* A tadpole.
aatcha, *n. inf.* [< atchun] Walking.
aatin-pu·u, *n.* 1 A rough-and-ready guess; a hit-or-miss business. 2 A person who makes haphazard guesses; a blunderbuss. [GSS]
aa-tootu, *interj.* Holy be the god! Amen! May the god be honored! Also **uutootu.**
aa-tu·i, *n.* [awa + tori] Removing the bubbles from the surface of boiling sugar cane juice during the process of making brown sugar. [UKH]
abaa, *n.* An elder sister. Same as **'nmii.** See also **appii.**
aba·chun, *vt.* [abaku] To divulge; disclose; expose. See **abasaa.**
abaichiri·in, *vi.* To suffer terrible hardships. [UKH]
abari·in, *vi.* [abareru] To be violent; riot; run amok; rage (about); be unruly; (of horses) lash out; go wild.
abasa·a, *n. pej.* 1 A prattler; a tattler. [GSS] 2 A hussy; a wanton woman. [UKH] See **abachun.**
abasaa-gii, *n.* Hard, tough hair. [UKH]
abi·in, *vi.* 1 To shout; cry; yell; shriek; scream; howl. 2 (Of dogs, cats) to bark; meow.
abii-suubu, *n.* Shouting match, in which parties insist on speaking without listening to the other party.
abii-takkwa·sun, *vt.* To argue (a person) into silence; talk (a person) down; confute. See **takkwasun.**
abu-gaa, *n.* Same as **kuragaa¹.**
abui, *n.* [abumi] A stirrup; a footstall.
abui-kuu, *n.* [aburi-ko] A grill used to

dry or roast fish or meat; a gridiron.
abu·in, *vt.* [aburu] **1** To roast; broil; toast; grill. **2** To warm; dry. Also **anjun**.
abuna·san, *adj.* [abunai] Dangerous; risky; precarious; perilous. Also **ukaas(h)an**.
abushi, *n.* [abushi] A levee; a ridge between rice paddies.
abushi-bare·e, *n.* [abushi + harai] Rice paddy ridge clearance, a communal rite held in the fourth lunar month to rid rice paddies of vermin. See **abushi**, **mushibaree**.
achaa, *n.* [ashita] Tomorrow. Also **acha**.
achaa-asa, *n.* Tomorrow morning. Also **achaanu'asa**.
achaa·nu-shitimiti, *n.* Early tomorrow morning.
achaa·nu-yusandi, *n.* Tomorrow evening.
achaa·nu-yuuru, *n.* Tomorrow night.
achi, *n. lit.* [aki] Autumn.
achi-bii, *n.* Soft cooked rice prepared over slow heat; gruel.
achibii-mee, *n.* Same as **achibii**.
achi-guni, *n.* A tropical region; a hot region.
achihati-bee·san, *adj.* Fickle; capricious; easily tired of.
achi-hati·in, *vi.* [akihateru*] To grow tired of; become weary of; get sick of; lose interest in; be surfeited with.
achihati-juugwachi, *n.* Lit., boring October, a reference to the lack of holidays in that month. See **wuimi**.
achi-kabi, *n.* [atsugami] Thick paper; cardboard; millboard.
achika·i-guri·s(h)an, *adj.* Difficult to use and handle (of people and tools).
achika·in, *vt.* [·(r)an, ·ti; atsukau] To work (a machine); handle (a tool); manipulate; manage (an affair); deal with (a matter); work (a person) hard; drive (a person) hard; have (a person) at one's beck and call.
achi-ki, *n.* [atsuke] Steam; vapor.

achi-kookoo, *adv.* Piping hot; steaming hot; steaming. See also **hijuruukookoo**.
achima·i, *n.* [atsumari] A meeting; a gathering. Also **surii**.
achima·in, *vi.* [atsumaru] To gather; collect; come together; flock; crowd; swarm; cluster.
achimi·in, *vt.* [atsumeru] To gather; collect; bring together.
achine·e, *n.* [akinai] Trade; business; commerce; a transaction; an occupation.
achinee-anmaa, *n.* A woman merchant; a woman shopkeeper.
achinee-jooji, *n.* [akinaijoozu] Good at business; expert in business.
achinee-mun, *n.* [akinaimono] An article of commerce; merchandise; goods; a commodity.
achinee-nchu, *n.* [akinai-bito] A merchant; a trader; a dealer; a shop owner.
achinee-saa, *n.* A merchant. Same as **achineenchu**.
achineiku, *n. Ficus virgata* [J Hamainubiwa; *Ficus virgata* Reinw. ex Blume]. [FOSR]
achi·nu-iyu, *n.* A tuna.
achiraka, *n.* ·**na**, *adj.* [akiraka] Clear; plain; obvious; evident; manifest; apparent; righteous.
achirashi-keesa·a, *n. colloq.* Reheated food; something used for the second time.
achira·sun, *vt.* To warm (food); heat (food).
achiree, *n.* [atsurae] An order; the article ordered.
achiree·in, *vt.* [atsuraeru] To order; give an order (for an article).
achiree-mun, *n.* Ordered goods. Same as **achiree**.
achisa-kamarasa, *n.* Sensitivity to summer heat.
achisakamarasa·a, *n.* A person who is sensitive to summer heat.

achi·san[1], *adj.* [atsui] Hot; warm; sultry.
achi·san[2], *adj.* [atsui] Thick; heavy; solid.
achisa-oo, *n. colloq.* One who is sensitive to the summer heat.
achisa-umi·i, *n.* A person who is sensitive to the heat, for instance, of summer.
achi-yuu, *n.* Hot water; boiling water.
achoodu, *n.* [akiudo] A broker; a merchant. Also **achooduu**.
achoodu·u, *n. pej.* A merchant; often a woman fish peddler carrying a basket of fish on her head.
a·chun, *vi.* [aku] **1** To open; be opened. **2** To begin; start; open. **3** To be vacated; become vacant. **4** To be not in use; have done with.
ada[1], *n.* [ada] A foe; an enemy; revenge.
ada[2], *n.* [ada] Emptiness; vanity; vain effort; lost labor.
adan, *n.* A pandanus [*Pandanus tectorius* Soland. var. *tectorius*]; a thatch screw pine. Also **adani**.
adan-ashi, *n.* **1** An aerial root of pandanus. **2** A rope made with such aerial roots. [UKH]
adan-baa-mushiru, *n.* A mattress woven of pandanus leaves. See **mushiru**.
adanbaa-saba, *n.* Pandanus leaf sandals. Also **adanbaasaba**.
adani-guchaa, *n.* The fruit of the pandanus.
adu, *n.* [?ato] The heel of the foot; the heel of a shoe.
adu-jiru, *n.* Achilles tendon.
afa-geeri·in, *vi.* **1** (For seasoning) to become weak. **2** To become frivolous; become not serious. See **afasan**.
afageeri-mun, *n.* A frivolous person.
afa-kee, *n.* A bivalve; an animal with a two-valved shell, such as a clam or oyster.
afa-kuu, *n.* Same as **afakee**.
afa-mee, *n.* A meal of rice only, without soup and side dish. [UKH] See **afasan**.
afana·chun, *vi.* To lie on one's back; lie supine.
afa·san, *adj.* [awai] Weak (in taste); watery, not strong; bland; tasteless; insipid; dull.
afii, *n.* An elder brother; buddy. See **appii**.
agaa, *interj.* Ouch!
agaayoo-sun, *v.* To complain of a pain; cry in pain. Same as **yamundoosun**.
agacha·a, *n.* A laborer; a worker; a working man; the laboring population.
aga·chun, *vi.* [agaku] **1** To work; labor; toil; drudge; exert oneself; work hard; hammer at. **2** To make headway; make progress.
aga·i, *n.* [agari] High ground; plateau.
agai-mii, *n.* [agarime] An eye the shape of which goes up toward the outer margin; a person with such eyes.
aga·in, *vi.* [agaru] **1** To rise; ascend; mount; climb up. **2** To progress; improve; advance. **3** To be over; come to an end; be finished. **4** To deep-fry. **5** To be excessive (in a negative sense).
agai-tiida, *n.* The rising sun; the morning sun.
agaitiida-wugama·a, *n.* Lit., one who worships the rising sun; a worshiper of the powerful. See **wugamun**.
agami·in, *vt.* [agameru] To respect; revere; honor; adore; worship; hallow.
agane·e, *n.* [aganai] Economy; saving; husbandry; frugality; thrift.
aganee·in, *vt.* [aganau] **1** To be frugal; be thrifty; economize; save (money, expenses). **2** To purchase; procure; buy.
agari, *n.* [agaru + he*] East. Also **higashi**.
agari-maa·i, *n.* Eastern tour, a religious practice whereby a family or representatives of a clan make a pilgrimage to the ancient sites of their ancestors on the southeastern coast of Okinawa Island. [OBJ, ODJ]
agari·nu-umi, *n.* The eastern ocean; the Pacific Ocean.

agari-nke·e, *adj.* […-mukai] Facing the east.
agata, *n.* That way; over there; way over there.
a·ga-too, *n.* That far; that distant.
agi, *n.* [age] Land (in contrast to sea); the shore (as viewed from sea). See also **tuu**[3], **fukatuu**, **tunaka**.
agi-baarii, *n.* A ritual mock boat race on land. [UKH] See **haarii**.
agi-doofu, *n.* [agedoofu] Fried tofu (bean curd cake).
agi·in, *vt.* [ageru] **1** To raise; lift. **2** To deep-fry. **3** To offer. **4** To vomit.
agijabee, *interj.* An exclamation of failure or mistake. Oops! Dang it! Damn it! Goodness!
agimaa·sun, *vt.* To hurry (up); hasten; press; urge (goad, egg) on; bustle. Also **agimasun**, **namanamaasun**.
agima·sun, *vt.* Same as **agimaasun**.
agi-mun, *n.* [agemono] Fried food; a fried dish.
agi-nchu, *n.* A land person (one who spends his life on land, in contrast to a fisherman or a sailor); a landlubber.
agiya·a, *n.* A method of fishing in which a group of divers with sticks chases fish into a net. [OGJ]
agiyaa-ami, *n.* A kind of fishnet for use in **agiyaa** fishing.
-agu·mun, *v. suff.* [agumu] To become weary of (doing); be at a loss how to (do).
ahaa-ahaa, *n. onom.* A loud laugh.
aha-dan, *n.* Rosary pea [*Abrus precatorius* L.]. [FOSR]
ahii, *n.* Variant of **afii**, **appii**.
ahira·a, *n.* [ahiru] A domestic duck. Also **ahiru**.
ahiru, *n.* [ahiru] Same as **ahiraa**.
ahyaa, *n.* **1** A mother animal. **2** Yeast or other base used to produce such things as vinegar, liquor, salted fish guts, and pickles. **3** A mother pig; a sow.
ahyaa-'waa, *n.* A sow; a mother pig.

ai[1], *n.* [ari] An ant. Also **aikoo**.
ai[2], *interj.* An indication of slight surprise or question. Oh! Oh dear! Gosh!
a·i-ga·mi, *n.* A person who tends to eat all that is available whether needing to or not. See **kamun**.
ai-koo, *n.* An ant. Same as **ai**[1].
ainama-ishi, *n.* Lit., a stone bride. Folkloric reference to an unwilling bride turning to stone rather than marrying. [ODJ]
a·i-nu·i, *n.* [ai-nori] Riding together; sharing a ride.
aiyee-naa, *interj.* An expression of sorrow and surprise. Oh! Dear me! Good heavens!
aja[1], *n.* [aza] A village; a hamlet. The smallest unit of a community, several of which make up a *son* or *choo* municipality.
aja[2], *n.* [aza] A mole; a beauty spot.
ajama, *n.* Thistle. See **njichaa**.
aja-na, *n.* [adana] A nickname; a moniker; a sobriquet.
aja-ware·e, *n.* [azawarai] Ridicule; derision; a sneer. **-sun**, *v.* To ridicule; deride.
aji[1], *n.* [aji] Taste; flavor. See also **maasan**, **niisan**, **amasan**, **njasan**, **karasan**, **suukarasan**, **afasan**, **shiisan**.
aji[2], *n.* A device in the loom which separates the warp top and bottom.
aji[3], *n.* The gills (of a fish); the branchiae.
aji[4], *n.* [? aruji] **1** The rank next highest to prince in the Ryukyu kingdom; lord. **2** A territorial lord of at least one district in premodern Okinawa. Also **anji**.
ajicha·a, *n.* [azuki] Same as **akamaami**.
aji·in, *vt.* To cross; intersect. See also **ajimaa**.
ajika·in, *vi.* [azukaru] **1** To keep; receive (a thing) in trust (custody); receive (money) on deposit; be entrusted with (a thing). **2** To take charge of; be in charge of; assume the care of.

aji-kee, *n*. A giant clam [*Tridacna gigas*]. [ODJ]
ajiki·in, *vt*. [azukeru] 1 To give (a thing) into a person's safekeeping; keep (custody). 2 To commit (a child) to another's care; leave (a child) with (a person).
aji-kuuta·a, *n*. That which is delicious.
aji-maa, *n*. 1 A corner; intersection; crossroads; a crossing. 2 A tofu-making tool, consisting of two pieces of wood in a cross shape. [UKH] See **ajiin**.
ajimaa-musu·bi, *n*. A cross-knot; a cross-tie.
ajin, *n*. A wooden pestle; a pounder.
aji-raa·s(h)an, *adj*. Strong of taste; heavy of taste.
aji-sun, *v*. To taste; try the flavor of.
aka[1], *n*. Same as **akaa**.
aka[2], *n*. [aka] Dirt; filth; grime [particularly of filth on hair or clothes]. See also **hingu**, **irichi**.
aka·a, *n*. [aka] 1 Red. 2 A red thing. 3 Total; complete. Also **aka**[1].
aka-aka·tu, *adv*. [aka-aka to] (Usually pertaining to light or fire) bright; luminous; glistening; sparkling.
aka-bana·a, *n*. A hibiscus; China rose [*Hibiscus rosa-sinensis* L.]. Also **gusoobana**. [ODJ]
akabee, *n. pej*. A person with eczema. [GSS]
aka-bura, *n*. [akaboofura] Bloodworm tree [*Wendlandia formosana* Cowan]. [FOSR]
aka-busa·a, *n*. A redhead.
aka-chichi, *n*. [akatsuki] Dawn; daybreak.
akachichi-baru, *n*. Doing farmwork before breakfast. See **haru**[2].
akachichi-bushi, *n*. A morning star; a star in the dawn. See **fushi**[1].
akachichi-gurashin, *n*. A dark morning; a morning without moon. See **kurashin**.
akachichi-jichuu, *n*. A morning moon. See **chichuu**.
akachichi-mudu·i, *n*. Coming home in the morning after staying away all night for pleasure or working.
aka-chideekuni, *n*. A red carrot. See **chideekuni**.
aka-feisachii, *n*. Convolvulaceae [J Horuto-kazura; *Erycibe henryi* Prain]. [FOSR]
aka-fujoo, *n*. Lit., red impurity; the menses. [ODJ] See also **shirafujoo**.
aka-gaa, *n*. [akage] A redhead. Same as **akagii**, **akabusaa**.
aka-gaara, *n*. [akagawara] A red roof tile.
akagai, *n*. A light; a lamp; light.
aka-gantaa, *n*. 1 A redheaded short bob. 2 A kind of mysterious devil. See **kantaa**.
aka-gi, *n*. [akagi] Autumn maple tree; red tree [*Bischofia javanica* Bl.]. [ODJ]
aka-gi·i, *n*. [akage] Red hair; a redhead. Also **akagaa**.
aka-gumi, *n*. [akagome] A general term for red, brown, or dark brown rice. [ODJ]
aka-gusa, *n*. A spurge; euphorbia [J Shima-nishikisoo; *Euphorbia hirta* L.]. [FOSR] Also **gichafagusa**.
aka-guu, *n*. Food red. [UKH]
aka-hadaka, *n*. [aka-hadaka] Nudity; nakedness.
aka-haji, *n*. [aka-haji] Open disgrace; public insult; crying shame.
akai, *n*. [akari] A *shoji* screen; a paper screen; a paper sliding door. See also **sooji**.
aka-indoo, *n*. [aka-endoo] Field pea [*Pisum arvense* L.]. [FOSR]
aka-iru, *n*. [akairo] The red color. See **akaa**.
aka-iyu, *n*. [aka-uo] A goldfish.
aka-jina·a, *n*. [aka- + zeni] A copper coin; one one-hundredth of a yen. See **jin**[2].
aka·ku na·in, *vi*. [akaku naru] To be-

come red; blush; redden.
aka-maami, *n*. [aka-mame] A red bean; azuki bean [*Vigna angularis* (Wild.) Ohwi & Ohashi]. [FOSR] Also **ajichaa**. See **maami**.
akamai, *n*. Area around the anus. Also **chibinumaai**.
aka-mataa, *n*. A kind of poisonous snake [*Dinodon semicarinatus* (Cope)]. [ODJ]
Akamataa-Kurumataa, *n*. In the Yaeyama Islands, a pair of deities who visit villages periodically in the sixth month of the lunar calendar to bring the harvest.
aka-mii, *n*. [akami] The yolk (of an egg); the yellow; the vitellus.
aka·mun, *vi*. [akamu] To redden; blush.
aka-na, *n*. A beefsteak plant [J shiso; *Perilla frutescens* var. *japonica* (Hassk.) Hara. Erect.]. [FOSR]
akanaa, *n*. An evening glow; sunset colors; an afterglow (of sunset).
akana-baa, *n*. Same as **akana**.
akan-kwaara, *n*. See **akarakwaara**.
aka-'nmaa, *n*. Lit., red horse; A hearse. Same as **gan**[1]. [GSS]
aka-nncha, *n*. A red soil; a red clay.
aka-ngwa, *n*. [akago] A baby; an infant.
akara-hiru, *n*. Broad daylight; the daytime.
akara-kwaara, *adj*. Showy; flashy; gaudy; gorgeous; flowery; florid; dazzling.
akari·in, *vi*. To become separated (as a result of being broken); come off; peel off; (of an animal) get weaned.
aka·san, *adj*. [akai] Red; ruddy; crimson; scarlet; rubicund; reddish.
akase·e, *n*. A riddle; a guessing game. [OBJ]
aka·shi-mun, *n*. A riddle; a puzzle; an enigma; a mystery.
aka·sun[1], *vt*. To guess a riddle; solve a puzzle.
aka·sun[2], *vt*. To pass; spend; spend a night.

aka-tiida, *n*. The red sun; the setting sun.
aka-tu·i, *n*. A bailer. Same as **yuutui**.
aka-ushi, *n*. [akaushi] Red cattle; brown cattle.
aka-yukushi, *n*. A barefaced lie; a pure fabrication; an arrant lie.
akee·in, *vi*. (For the sky) to become red before a typhoon. [UKH]
aki, *interj*. Expression of surprise or sadness. Oh! Why! Goodness!
aki-hana·sun, *vt*. [akehanasu] To fling (open); open wide; leave (a door) open.
aki-hataki·in, *vt*. [ake + hadakeru] To open; bare; open (one's) robe at the front.
aki·in[1], *vt*. [akeru] 1 To open up; unlock (a door); undo (a parcel). 2 To empty (a box, a glass). 3 To stay away (from home). See also **furachun**.
aki·in[2], *vi*. [akeru] To dawn.
aki-mikkwaa, *n*. [akimekura] 1 A person whose eyes are open without vision. 2 An illiterate person.
aki·nu-higan, *n*. [< J akinohigan] Autumnal equinox.
akirami, *n*. [< J akirame] Resignation; abandonment; renunciation.
akirami·in, *vt*. [< J akirameru] To resign oneself; abandon; give up; make the best of one's lot. Same as **yasunjiin**.
akisamiyoo, *interj*. A cry of distress; a cry for help; expression of great surprise or sadness. Heavens! Goodness! See **aki**.
aki-ti, *n*. Next year; following year. [UKH]
aki-yoo, *interj*. Same as **akisamiyoo**.
akkaa, *interj*. Ouch!
ak·ku-kata, *n*. Everywhere one goes.
akku-sun, *v*. To scold; blame.
akku·u, *n*. A perennial fault finder; a person who constantly scolds others; one who is supercritical.
akoo-kuroo, *n*. Break of day; morning

twilight. Same as **akachichi**.
aku, *n*. [aku] Lye; ash. Harshness (in fruits or vegetables). [UKH]
akubi, *n*. [akubi] A yawn; yawning.
aku-gani, *n*. [aka-gane] Copper.
aku-ma, *n*. [aku-ma] A devil; a fiend; an evil spirit. **·nu**, *adj*. Demonic; satanic, fiendish.
aku-nin, *n*. [aku-nin] A bad person; a wicked person; a villain; an evildoer.
aku-nuji, *n*. [aku-nuki] Removal of harshness (from fruits or vegetables).
akuta, *n*. [akuta] Same as **chiri'akuta**.
aku-yin, *n*. [aku-en] Evil destiny; unfortunate relationship. See **yin**[2].
ama, *n*. 1 There; over there; that place; yonder. 2 He; she. See also **amamutii**, **kuma**[2], **'nma**[2].
ama-gahi, *n*. Same as **amagashi**. [GSS]
ama-gasa[1], *n*. [amagasa] An umbrella.
ama-gasa[2], *n*. A moon halo which often appears before rain.
ama-gashi, *n*. A sweet drink made from fermented barley. Also **amagahi**.
ama-gucha·a, *n*. A flatterer; a sycophant.
ama-guchi, *n*. [amakuchi] Sweet words; flattery.
ama-gu·i, *n*. [ama-goi] Supplication for rain; a ritual for rain; a prayer for rain. See also **ami**[1], **kuuin**[2].
ama-guri, *n*. A sudden shower; a squall that tends to come toward the evening; a scud. See also **ami**[1].
ama-ha·i-kuma-ha·i, *n*. **-sun**, *v. colloq*. To move about in confusion; to go hither and thither. See **hain**[1].
ama-haji, *n*. [GSS] Same as **amidai**.
ama·i, *n*. [amari] The remainder; the remnant; the rest; the remaining; the excess.
amai·i-kumai·i, *adv*. (Of speech) faltering; disordered; confused; incoherent.
ama·i-mun[1], *n*. An excess; superfluity; an extra; a surplus; the leftover.
ama·i-mun[2], *n*. An outlaw; a wild fellow; a roughneck; a rowdy.

ama·in[1], *vi*. [amaru] 1 To remain in excess; be left over. 2 Be too many (much); be more than enough; exceed.
ama·in[2], *vi*. To be unruly; be fretful; go wild (applies especially to children or to cats and dogs).
ama-jaki, *n*. [amazake] Vinegar. Also **feei**[2], **shii**[4].
ama-juu, *n*. [amajio] Lightly salted pickles.
a·ma-ku·ma, *n*. Here and there; hither and thither.
ama-maa, *n*. Variant for **aaman**. [GSS]
ama-mi[1], *n*. [amami] Sweetness; a sweet taste; sweet flavor.
Amami[2], *n*. The Amami Islands, northernmost group of the Ryukyu Islands, administratively part of Kagoshima Prefecture.
Amamichuu, *n*. Same as **Amanchuu**.
ama-mii-kuma-mii, *adv*. (Looking) here and there. **-sun**, *v. colloq*. To look around restlessly; stare about; look here and there.
ama-miji, *n*. [amamizu] Sweet water; fresh water.
Amamiku, *n*. Same as **Amanchuu**.
ama-mun, *n*. Sweets; candies; cakes.
ama-mutii, *n*. Over there; thereabouts.
Aman-chuu, *n*. 1 The female creator deity in the Okinawan genesis myth. 2 The mythical first settlers of Okinawa. Also **Amamichuu**, **Amamiku**.
ama·n-kuma·n, *n*. Here and there; everywhere.
amasa·a, *n*. 1 One who is unmanageable or intractable. 2 A slut; a loose woman.
ama-saa·i-kuma-saa·i, *n*. (Touching) here and there. **-sun**, *v. colloq*. To touch here and there blindly trying to begin to do something.
ama·san, *adj*. [amai] Sweet; sugary; sweet-flavored.
amashita-mun, *n*. A daredevil. [UKH]
ama·sun, *vt*. [amasu] To leave (over); let remain; spare.

amayaa

amaya·a, *n.* Same as **amaimun**[2].
ama-yadu·i, *n.* [amayadori] Taking temporary shelter from rain. **-sun**, *v.* To get out of the rain; take shelter from the rain.
amee·in, *vi.* [amaeru] 1 To grow impudent; grow presumptuous; be spoiled; get stuck up. 2 To be elated.
Amerika, *n.* America.
Amerika·a, *n.* An American (person).
Amerika-mun, *n.* American goods; anything made in America.
Amerika-yuu, *n.* The American period in Okinawan history, from 1945 to 1972. See **yuugawai**, **Yamatuyuu**, **Uchinaayuu**.
ami[1], *n.* [ame] Rain; rainfall; shower. See also **amifui**, **uu'ami**, **ku'ami**, **amigwaa**, **arachijaa'ami**, **nagashi**, **nagashi'ami**, **amaguri**, **tiida'ami**, **tiidabui**, **katabui**, **amigumu**, **amigurun**, **uugurun**, **attabui**, **amichibu**, **amidai**, **amikaji**, **amidaimiji**, **amayadui**, **amagui**.
ami[2], *n.* [ami] A net; a casting net; netting.
ami[3], *n.* [ame] Wheat gluten; starch jelly; a candy; sweets.
ami-chibu, *n.* [ametsubu] A raindrop.
ami-dai, *n.* 1 The eaves 2 Under the eaves.
amidai-ishi, *n.* A dripstone.
amidai-miji, *n.* Water collected from the eaves.
ami-fu·i, *n.* [ame-furi] Rainfall; rainy weather.
ami-gumu, *n.* [amagumo] A rain cloud.
ami-gurun, *n.* A rain cloud; darkness due to rain clouds. See also **uugurun**.
ami-gwaa[1], *n.* A little rain; a light rain; drizzle.
ami-gwaa[2], *n.* Candies; cheap candies; taffies.
ami·in, *vi.* [abiru] To bathe; have a bath.
ami-kaji, *n.* [ame-kaze] Rain and wind.
amikoo·in, *vi.* To ferment; undergo fermentation.
a·mi-mun, *n.* [ami-mono] Knitting; crochet; knitted goods. **-sun**, *v.* To do knitting; do crocheting.
amina·a, *n.* A tadpole.
aminboo, *n.* A pond-skater; a water spider.
amishi·in, *vt.* To give someone a bath; bathe someone.
amooi, *n.* Same as **amoori**.
amoori, *n.* [amoru*] Descending to the earth (of a heavenly nymph).
a·mun, *vt.* [amu] To knit (a shirt); crochet (a shawl); braid (one's hair); plait (straw); net (a hammock); entwine (a garland). Also **kumun**[2].
amutu, *n.* A dike; a levee; an embankment.
a·n[1], *vi.* [aru] 1 [Inanimate] To be; exist; occur. 2 To be located; stand. 3 To have; possess; own. 4 To have (something) attached to. 5 To be included. 6 To number; weigh. 7 To find; see. 8 To be had; be got. 9 To experience. 10 To take place; be held.
a·n[2], *adv.* So. See also **anee**.
an[3], *n.* [an] Bean jam.
ana, *n.* [ana] A hole; an aperture; an opening; a slit; a gap; an eyelet.
ana-gaa, *n.* [ana + kawa] Same as **kuragaa**[1].
ana-yaa, *n.* [ana + ya] A shanty; a hovel; a shack. See also **yaa**[1].
anbee, *n.* [anbai] 1 Seasoning; flavoring. 2 A manner; a condition.
an-bin, *n.* A large pottery pitcher with a spout, pottery shaped like a teapot.
anchoo, *n.* Baking soda; saleratus.
a·n-chu, *n.* [< anu-tchu] That person; he; she.
anda, *n.* [abura] Grease; oil; fat; lard.
andaagi·i, *n.* [abur(a-)age] A ball-shaped doughnut made of flour. Also **saataa'andaagii**.
andachaa, *n.* A lizard. Also **oodoo**, **eejaa**. [GSS]

anda-gaaki, *n*. Slightly undernourished. [UKH]
anda-gaami, *n*. [aburagame] A small lard jar, usually of pottery.
anda-gucha·a, *n*. [aburaguchi*] A flatterer; a sycophant.
anda-jira·a, *n*. A lizard. [URH]
anda-jishi, *n*. [abura + shishi] Lard meat. Same as **shirumi**. See **shishi**.
anda-juu·san, *adj*. [abura + tsuyoi] Oily; greasy; fatty.
anda-kashi, *n*. [abura-kasu] 1 A cake of lees remaining after oil is extracted, such as rapeseed cake. 2 That which is left of meat such as pork after the lard is extracted.
anda-musa·a, *n*. [aburamushi] A slug.
anda-nsu(u), *n*. [abura + miso] Miso paste with meat fried in oil.
anda·sun, *vt*. To cause to overflow; make run over (the brim).
andi·in, *vi*. [afureru] To overflow (the bank); run over (the brim); brim over; flood. Also **anriin**.
ane·e, *phr*. So; like that (used in negative sentences). See **an**².
an-gaa, *n*. Same as **anagaa, kuragaa**¹.
an-gutoo·ru, *part. adj*. Like that; such a.
an-gwaa, *n*. [ane + ...] An elder sister; a young girl.
an-gwee, *n. adj*. [an-gai] Contrary to expectation; unexpectedly. **·na**, *adj*. Unexpected; unforeseen.
angwee-yii, *n*. [agura...] Sitting with one's legs crossed; sitting down cross-legged.
aniku, *n*. A fish trap.
anji, *n*. Same as **aji**⁴.
anji-kabi, *n*. Mock paper money to burn in ritual offerings to the ancestors. See **nchabi, unchabi, uchikabi, kabi'anji**.
an·jun, *vt*. [aburu] Same as **abuin**.
ankoo-mayaa, *n*. A monstrous cat.
an-ma, *n*. [an-ma] Massage; a massager; a masseur; a masseuse.
anmaa, *n*. 1 A mother; mama. 2 The madam of a house of courtesans.
anmaa-gooyaku, *n*. [... + kooyaku] A blister plaster.
anmaa-uuya·a, *n*. A boy who constantly clings to his mother; a coward; a mama's boy.
an-maku, *n*. Same as **makuu, uumaku**.
anmasa-mun, *n*. Same as **yakkeemun**.
anma·s(h)an, *adj*. 1 Be sick; have a headache; faint. 2 Find to be a headache; find bothersome.
anmee, *n*. Same as **chii'an**.
an-muchi, *n*. [an-mochi] A rice cake stuffed with bean jam.
annai-kannai, *n*. This way and that. **-sun**, *v*. To do this and that; to be indecisive in action.
an-nee, *n*. [an-nai] 1 Guide; guidance. 2 Invitation.
an-nee·ru, *part. adj*. Like that; such a.
an·nu-mii, *n*. [ami no me] A rough mesh wickerwork of split bamboo that is used instead of wood as ceiling planks; also used for walls. See also **chinibu, shinibu**.
an-raku, *n*. [anraku] Comfort; ease. **·na**, *adj*. Comfortable; easy; cozy.
anri·in, *vi*. Same as **andiin**.
anshe·e, *conj*. And; and then; if that's the case.
anshi, 1 *conj*. Doing this first; then. 2 *adv*. That much; to that extent; how.
anshi·i-kanshi·i, *n*. This way and that way. **-sun**, *v. colloq*. To do this way or that way.
anshi·n-kanshi·n, *adv. colloq*. (Not) in any way; in no way.
an-sun, *vi*. To do so.
ansura·a, *conj*. If that is so; well; then.
a·nu, *adj*. [ano] That.
anu·u-kunu·u, *n*. [ano kono] This and that. **-sun**, *v*. To say this and that; falter; waver; stammer.
appan-garaa, *n*. Despair; disappointment; hopelessness. **-sun**, *v*. To despair, be disappointed.

appii, *n.* An elder brother; a middle (or second) elder brother; a young fellow. [UKH] Same as **afii**. See also **abaa**.
appuri, *n.* Same as **appurigwaa**.
appuri-gwaa, *n.* A toffee; a taffy.
ara, *n.* Hulled rice with impurities.
ara-[1], *pref.* [ara-] New, fresh, first. See **aratabi, aradumeei**.
ara-[2], *pref.* [ara-] Wild, rough, coarse. See **arashigutu, arabaaki, arasan**.
ara-baa, *n.* A saw with rough teeth.
ara-baaki, *n.* A bamboo basket with rough weave.
arachija·a-ami, *n.* A rain in big drops. See also **ami**[1].
ara-dumee·i, *n.* The first marriage for a man. See **araniibichi, tumeein**.
aragaa·in, *vt.* [aragau] 1 To compete. 2 To dispute; argue.
aragee·in, *vi.* 1 (For grains and vegetables) to grow excessively. 2 (For women and children) to become excessively large and strong.
ara·in, *vt.* [·(r)an, ·ti; arau] To wash; clean; purify; cleanse. See also **shinkuchi**.
ara-makai, *n.* Same as **aramakayaa**.
ara-makaya·a, *n.* A common large, rough pottery bowl made in the Tsuboya kilns in Naha.
ara-mooki, *n.* [ara- + mooke] Exorbitant profiting; soft job.
ara-mun, *n.* Coarse food; a poor meal; a plain diet.
a·ran, *cop.* Is not [irregular negative present of **yan**, to be].
ara-niibichi, *n.* [ara- + nebiki*] The first marriage for a woman.
ara-noo·i, *n.* [ara- + nui] A rough sewing; a preliminary sewing; basting.
arappaa, *n.* A rough person; a person who is careless in conduct.
ara·san, *adj.* [arai] Rough; violent; rude. See **ara-**[2].
arashi, *n.* [arashi] A typhoon; a big wind. Same as **ufukaji, teefuu**.

ara-shigutu, *n.* [arashigoto] Heavy work; hard labor.
ara·sun, *vt.* [arasu] To devastate; lay waste; damage; wreak havoc with.
ara-tabi, *n.* [aratabi] The first trip.
aratama·in, *vi.* [aratamaru] 1 To be renewed; be renovated. 2 To change; be altered; be revised; be improved. 3 To be formal; be ceremonious.
aratami, *n.* [aratame] 1 An inspection. 2 A reform; a change.
aratami·in, *vt.* [aratameru] 1 To rectify; reform; correct. 2 To investigate; check.
ara-tushi, *n.* A rough grinding stone.
ara-umi, *n.* A rough sea; a high sea.
arawari·in, *vi.* [arawareru] To appear; come forth; come in sight; show itself.
arawa·sun, *vt.* [arawasu] To show; reveal; indicate.
ari[1], *n.* [are] 1 That; that thing; that person. 2 He; she.
ari[2], *interj.* Look! There!
ari-chi, *n.* [are-chi] Wasteland; barren land.
ari·in, *vi.* [areru] To be wild; rage; rave; go berserk.
ari-kuri, *n.* [are kore] This or that; one thing or another.
ari·n-kuri·n, *n. colloq.* [aremo koremo] This and that randomly; one thing and another haphazardly.
a·ru-bun, *adv.* As much as there is; as much as one has.
aru-mun-neen-mun, *n. colloq.* Any and every thing; the whole lot of.
aru-uppi, *n.* Same as **aru'ussa**.
aru-ussa, *n.* As much as there is; as much as possible. Also **aru'uppi**.
asa[1], *n.* [asa] Ramie; flax; hemp; jute. [*Cannabis sativa* L.]
asa[2], *n.* [asa] Morning. [UKH] See also **shitimiti**.
asa-akee·i, *n.* [asa-ake] Morning glow; dawn; daybreak; break.
asa-ban[1], *n.* [asa-han] Lunch, usually eaten about 3 PM.

asa-ban², *n.* [asa-ban] Morning and evening; day and night; all the time.
asaban-suga·i, *n.* Preparation for lunch.
asa-chiyu, *n.* [asa-tsuyu] Morning dew.
asa-daa, *n.* A shallow rice paddy. [UKH]
asa-da·chi, *n.* [asa-dachi] Departure in the morning.
asa-duri, *n.* Morning lull in the sea breeze.
asa-gau, *n.* [asa-gao] Morning glory.
asagu·in, *vt.* To search for; dig around for (something).
asa·in, *vt.* [asaru] To rake for; hunt for; scrounge for.
asa-jii, *n.* A linen garment worn at funerals. [UKH] See **chiin¹**.
asa-jin, *n.* [asaginu] A linen garment.
asa-kaagi, *n.* [asa-kage] 1 Morning twilight or morning twilight hours. [OGJ] 2 Morning sun rays. [ZRJ] See also **yuukaagi**.
a-sakii, *n.* So many; so much.
asama·s(h)an, *adj.* [asamashii] 1 Wretched; miserable; pitiable. 2 Despicable; mean.
asa-miiguchi, *n.* The morning beginning; the first thing in the morning; the first sale in the morning.
asa-na·a, *n.* A sleepyhead; a late riser.
asan-gani, *n.* A trowel-like agricultural implement.
asa-ni, *n.* [asane] Sleeping late in the morning.
asa-nnaa, *adv.* Early in the morning.
asasaa, *n.* A cicada; a cicala; a locust. Also **jiijaa**, **sansanaa**, **naabikachaa**.
asa·san, *adj.* [asai] Shallow; slight; superficial.
asa-shigutu, *n.* [asashigoto] Any work that is done in the morning.
asati·n-naacha, *n.* The fourth day from today.
asatti, *n.* [asatte] The day after tomorrow.
ashagi, *n.* [ashi + age] 1 Same as **kami'ashagi**. 2 A detached house consisting of one or two rooms often located in the front yard of the main house.
ashi¹, *n.* [ase] Sweat; perspiration.
ashi², *interj. pej.* Yeah; sure.
ashi³, *n.* [ashi] 1 A leg as food (e.g., of a pig). 2 A foot (in idiomatic expressions only). See also **hisa**.
ashiba·a, *n.* A man of pleasure; a libertine; a prodigal son.
ashi·bi, *n.* [asobi] 1 Play. 2 A game; a sport. 3 A pastime; a recreation; pleasure. 4 An excursion; an outing.
ashibi-buri, *n.* Being absorbed in fun.
ashibi-dushi, *n.* A companion in play; a playmate.
ashibi-guni, *n.* A village where entertainment such as dancing and plays thrives; a village where male-female relationships are rather unrestrained.
ashibi-ichuna·sa, *n.* Being busy with having fun.
ashibi-jura·san, *adj.* [<… + chura·san] Being good at performing arts such as singing, dancing, and drama.
ashibi-naa, *n.* Village square where village entertainment is held.
ashibi-ngwe·e, *n.* Playing one's time away; spending one's time in idleness. See **kwain**.
ashibi-shigutu, *n.* Lit., play work; a diversion; easy work.
ashibu, *n.* [asemo] Heat rash.
ashi·bun, *vi.* [asobu] 1 To play; have fun. 2 To make merry; amuse oneself. 3 To be idle; be unemployed.
ashigacha·a, *n.* An impatient person.
ashi-ga·chi, *n.* [?asekaki] Impatience; fretting.
ashi-ga·chun, *vi.* To be impatient; be hasty; fret; become irritated.
ashii, *n.* An afternoon snack; a lunch.
ashija, *n.* [ashida] Footgear; *geta* wooden clogs. See also **tachibaa'ashija**, **gita**, **jita**.
ashijaa-yaa, *n.* A footgear store.

ashi-jiri, *n.* Turf; sod; lawn grass.
ashi-miji, *n.* [ase-mizu] Sweat; profuse perspiration.
ashi-'nma, *n.* A footstool. Same as **kii'nma**.
ashi-tibichi, *n.* Pigs' feet soup.
ashi-tu, *n.* Same as **ashi'utu**.
ashi-utu, *n.* [ashi-oto] The sound of footsteps.
as·san, *adj.* [...sa·ku; asai] Shallow. Same as **asasan**.
ata-bicha·a, *n.* A frog; a toad. Also **wattaabii**.
ata-bichi, *n.* Same as **atabichaa**.
ataga·in, *vt.* To experience; meet; confront. [UKH]
atai[1], *n.* [<atari] A patch of garden within or near one's housing compound, for fruits, vegetables, and flowers, usually for the family's consumption.
ata·i[2], *n.* [atari] About; approximately.
ata·i[3], *n.* Poisoning; toxication.
atai-mee, *adj.* [atari-mae] Proper; natural; usual; of course; necessarily.
ata·in[1], *vi.* [ataru] To be poisoned.
ata·in[2], *vi.* [ataru] 1 To hit; touch. 2 To be exposed to. 3 To win.
ataku-nurii, *n.* Drinking water in a gulp. [UKH] See also **nuriin**.
atara·s(h)an, *adj.* [atarashii] Too good; too dear; precious; valuable.
ataras(h)a-sun, *v.* [atarashisa + ...] To hold as important; cherish; value highly.
atarashi-mun, *n.* A valuable thing.
at·chun, *vi.* [aruku] 1 To walk. 2 To progress; move. 3 To attend. 4 To be healthy. 5 To work.
ati, *n.* [ate] 1 A mark; a sign; a guide. 2 A goal; a purpose; a reason. 3 A clue; an idea. 4 Prudence; discretion. 5 News; tidings; a letter.
ati·in, *vt.* [ateru] To cause (something); hit (the mark). 2 To guess. 3 To succeed. 4 To assign; allot. 5 To meet. 6 To apply (to, for). 6 To expose to.

ati-hanri·in, *vt.* [ate hazureru] 1 To be disappointed. 2 To miss the mark.
ati-munu-i·i, *n.* [ate + mono-ii] Delirious utterances; talking in delirium.
ati-nashi, *n.* [atenashi] Innocence; simplicity; naivete; simplemindedness; innocent persons such as women and children.
ati-soo, *n.* Discretion; thoughtfulness.
atisoo·n-neenu·u, *n. pej.* A person who is indiscreet, thoughtless, injudicious. [GSS]
atta-, *pref.* [? arata] Denotes suddenness; abruptness. See **attabui**, **atta'weeki**, **attabajoo**, **attani**.
at·taa, *n.* Those people; they; their. **·nkai**, to them.
attaa-mun, *n.* Theirs.
atta-bajoo, *n.* A quick glance; something that appears good at first glance.
atta-bu·i, *n.* A sudden rain; a sudden shower. See also **ami**[1].
atta-gutu, *n.* A happenstance; a sudden happening.
atta·ni, *adv.* Suddenly; unexpectedly; without warning.
atta-'weeki, *n.* One who is newly rich; a nouveau riche.
atu, *n.* [ato] 1 Later; behind. 2 Afterwards; future. 3 Consequences; the rest. 4 The next. 5 Descendant; successor.
atu-atu, *n.* [ato-ato] The future; the time to come; a prospect.
atu-bara, *n.* [ato-bara] A child born to the second wife.
atu-chiji, *n.* [ato-tsugi] 1 Succession; inheritance. 2 A successor.
atu-chiri-mun, *n.* A person who has no one to carry on his lineage. [GSS]
atu-dumi, *n.* Same as **atudumeei**.
atu-dumee·i, *n.* A second wife. Also **atudumi**.
atu-kata, *n.* [ato-kata] Traces; marks; vestiges; proofs.

atu-katajiki, *n*. [atò-katazuke] Putting things in order; clearance and rearrangement.
atu-masai-gafuu, *n. phr.* [ato + masari + kahoo] Best luck is reserved for the last one.
atu-mi, *n*. [ato-me] The headship of a family; the family name; the family heir.
atu-mudu·i, *n*. [ato-modori] Regress; backslide; retrogression.
atu-na·i-sachi-na·i, *n*. In front and in back. **-sun**, *v*. To be now in front and now in back.
atu-ninju, *n*. Those who come later.
atu-sachi, *n*. [ato-saki] Order; before and after; the consequences; the circumstances; context.
atu-shijichi, *n*. Retreat; hesitation; flinching. **-sun**, *v*. To retreat; hesitate.
atu-shincha·a, *n*. Backdown; backtracing; retrogression; retreat.
atu-shija·a, *n*. Same as **atushinchaa**. [UKH]
atu-tuji, *n*. A second wife.
awa, *n*. [awa] **1** Millet; foxtail millet [*Setaria italica* (L.) Beauv. var. *italica*]. [FOSR] **2** A millet seed.
awa-mee, *n*. Rice cooked with foxtail millet.
awa-ran, *n*. Whisk fern [*Psilotum nudum* (L.) Beauv.]. [FOSR]
awari, *n*. [aware] Sorrow; grief; pathos. **·na**, *adj*. Sorrowful; doleful; touching.
awata·a, *n*. An impatient person; a hasty person. [UKH]
awati-ba·i, *n*. [awate + hashiri] Hurried steps; quick steps. [UKH]
awati·i-haati·i-sun, *v. colloq*. To greatly fluster oneself; be utterly confused; be flurried; be seized with panic.
awati·in, *vi*. [awateru] **1** To hurry; to hasten. **2** To be surprised; be confused; be flurried.
aya, *n*. [aya] Stripes (of kimono); a hairline (of a textile).

ayaa, *n. formal* A mother.
ayaa·mee, *n*. A married lady of the gentry class. [OGJ]
ayaamee·nu munu kamunee-sshi, *phr. slang* Eating slowly like a lady. [GSS]
aya-gachuu, *n*. A variant of **kachuu**, bonito fish.
ayagu, *n*. A type of ballad sung in the Miyako Islands. See **ayoo**.
ayakaa·in, *vi*. [ayakaru] To be favored by similar good luck; share (another's) good luck.
ayama·chi, *n*. [ayamachi] A misstep; a slip; a mistake.
ayama·i, *n*. [ayamari] An error; a mistake; a slip.
ayama·in, *vi*. [ayamaru] **1** To mistake; err; do wrong; do amiss; slip up. **2** To apologize; beg pardon.
aya-mun, *n*. [aya-mono] A kimono with patterns; textile with designs.
aya-tu·i, *n*. [aya-tori] A cat's cradle; a children's game played with a loop of string which is strung on the fingers to make various patterns.
ayoo, *n*. A general term for the old songs of the Yaeyama Islands. See **ayagu**.

B ———

baa, *n*. [ba] **1** An occasion; a situation. **2** A set; a place. **3** A reason.
baa-baa, *adv*. Descriptive of bursting flames.
baa-chii, *n*. **1** An aunty. **2** A maid.
baa-habaka·i, *n*. Taking up too much space.
baa-kee, *n*. A scramble (for); a struggle (for). **-sun**, *v*. To scramble for; struggle for; compete for.
baaki, *n*. [? hake] A bamboo basket; a crate. [ODJ] See also **tiiru, iidiiru, sooki**[1], **'nmu'areebaaki, miijooki, yunabaaki, hirabaaki, haara, wuubaara**.

-baaki, *suff.* A basketful (usually of produce such as potatoes or oranges).
baaki-ga·mi, *n.* Heavy eating; gluttony; voracity.
baan, *n.* [ban] **1** Watch; vigil; guard; lookout. **2** A keeper; a guard.
baan-yaa, *n.* [ban'ya] A watch-box; a kiosk.
babakwa·sun, *vt.* To cheat; deceive; hoodwink; shortchange.
bachi[1], *n.* A stick with several short pieces of cloth fastened at the end, used to spin a top. See also **kooruu**.
bachi[2], *n.* [bachi] A plectrum; a pick; a drumstick.
bachi[3], *n.* [bachi] Punishment; retribution.
bachi-kanja·a, *n.* The damned.
bachi-kan·jun, *vi.* To suffer God's wrath; be visited with divine punishment.
bajoo, *n.* Appearance; show; look.
·**bakai**, *adv.* [bakari] Only; merely; exclusively. See also ·**bikee**.
baka-raa·s(h)an, *adj.* Foolish; stupid; silly; absurd; ridiculous.
baki·in, *vi.* [bakeru] **1** To transform oneself into something. **2** To disguise oneself as; appear in disguise.
baki-mun, *n.* [bakemono] A monster; an ogre; a goblin; a witch.
bakuchi, *n.* [bakuchi] Gambling; gaming; speculation.
baku-yoo, *n.* [bakuroo] A broker; a horse trader; a middleman; an agent.
ban[1], *n.* [ban] Turn; order.
ban[2], *n. onom.* Bang.
bani, *n.* [bane] A spring; an elastic or steel device that recovers its original shape when released after being distorted.
banin, *n.* Same as **saara**.
banji, *n.* In the midst of; at the height of; prime.
banjoo-gani, *n.* [banjoogane] A carpenter's metal square.

banku, *n.* An outdoor stage. See also **butee**.
banshiruu, *n.* [banjiroo] A guava [*Psidium guajava* L.]. Also **benshiruu**.
bappee, *n.* A mistake; an error; a fault; an accident.
bappee-hippee-sun, *v. emph. colloq.* To keep making mistakes one after another.
bappee·in, *vt.* To make a mistake.
baran, *n.* [J obana] Flowers of **gushichi** grass. See **gushichi**. [OGJ]
baran-boochi, *n.* A broom for indoor use. See also **hoochi**.
bari·in, *vi.* [bareru] To be revealed; be discovered; be found out; be laid bare.
ba-sa, *n.* [basha] A horse carriage; a coach; a cart; a wagon.
ba-saa, *n.* [bashoo] **1** Musa cloth; textile made from Musa banana fiber. **2** A kimono made from Musa cloth. See also **bashuu**.
basaa-jin, *n.* [bashoo + kinu] Okinawan kimono made from Musa cloth.
basaa-nunu, *n.* Musa cloth; Musa textile; Musa fabric.
basa-hicha·a, *n.* A groom; a footman.
basa-na·i, *n.* A banana fruit.
bashuu, *n.* Any of a genus [*Musa*] of treelike tropical plants, with long, broad leaves and large clusters of edible fruits. See also **wuu**[1], **naiwuu**, **basaa**. [FOSR]
bashuu-kabi, *n.* Banana paper. Also **basuushi**.
basuu-shi, *n.* Same as **bashuukabi**.
ba-su, *n.* [basho] **1** A place; a spot. **2** Occasion; time; case. **3** Reason. **4** Emergency. **5** Chance.
batchin, *n.* [bakkin] A fine; a penalty (in terms of money).
bee[1], *interj. pej.* An expression of disdain used mostly by children. No. Never. Also **beeru**.
bee[2], *n.* [bai] Double.

-bee, *suff.* [bai] A suffix meaning a specified number of times; -fold.
bee-bee, *n. inf. onom.* A goat.
beeru, *interj. pej.* Same as **bee**[1].
benshiruu, *n.* Same as **banshiruu**.
bichi, *n.* [betsu] **1** Difference; otherness. **2** Distinction. **3** Discrimination; difference.
bichi-dan, *n.* [betsudan] ·**nu,** *adj.* Special; extraordinary.
-bichii, *suff.* [-beki] Denotes obligation, necessity, duty, or expectation: must.
Bideetin, *n.* [Benzaiten] Sarasvatī; the goddess of fortune, one of the Seven Deities of Good Fortune.
biichaa, *n.* A musk shrew [*Suncus murinus*].
bii-gu, *n.* [Bingo] The upper covering of the *tatami* floor mat, woven with the quality *Bingo* rush.
bii-bii, *n. inf.* Meats; noodles.
Biigu-yii, *n.* [Bingo + i(gusa)] Rush [*Juncus effusus* var. *decipiens* Buchen] produced in Bingo province (present Hiroshima Prefecture). [FOSR]
Biigu-mushiru, *n.* A straw mat made of **Biiguyii**, known for its excellent quality. See also **mushiru**.
·**bi·in,** *suff. formal* [...(y)a· + ...; haberi*] Affixed to verb and adjective stems, denotes respect and formality toward the addressee.
biira·a, *n.* A weakling; a sickly person.
·**bikee,** *part.* [bakari] **1** Only; merely; exclusively. **2** About; approximately. See also ·**bakai,** ·**bikeen,** ·**bikei**.
·**bikeen,** *part.* A variant form of ·**bikee**.
·**bikeen ya aran,** *phr.* Moreover; besides; not only... but also; as well as.
·**bikei,** *part.* A variant form of ·**bikee**.
bin[1], *n.* [beni] Red; crimson; rouge.
bin[2], *n.* [bin] A bottle; a vial; a phial; a decanter; a vase; a jar. See also **yush-ibin, dachibin**.
bin[3], *n.* [bin] Mail; a letter; correspondence.

bin[4], *n.* The area above one's ears. [KCS]
bina·a, *n.* A filthy, dirty, unclean person.
bina·san, *adj.* **1** Dirty, filthy; unclean. **2** Insufficient; inept. **3** Weak; sickly.
bin-choo, *n.* [benkyoo] Study; learning. **-sun,** *v.* **1** To study; learn. **2** To discount (goods).
bin-daree, *n.* A metal basin; a wash basin. Also **mindaree**[2].
bin-gata, *n.* **1** A generic term for stenciled textile designs of various traditional Okinawan motifs. **2** Okinawan fabric with **bingata** designs. See also **eegata, katachiki**.
binjuru, *n.* [Skt Pindola-bhâradvâja] A divining stone. Also **bizuru**.
bin-ri, *n.* [benri] Convenience. ·**na,** *adj.* Convenient; expedient; handy; facile.
bin-roo, *n.* [binroo] A field palm [*Satakentia liukiuensis* (Hatusima) H. E. Moore]. Also **Yeemayashi, noyashi**. See **yaashi**. [FOSR, OGJ]
bin-shii, *n.* A ritual tin decanter for liquor; a portable container for things needed for religious rituals; (by extension also) a wooden container for rice grains, incense, and wine used in clan and communal rites.
binta, *n.* [binta] **1** Sidelocks; tresses in front of one's ears; sideburns. **2** The sides of the face just above the ears.
bin-too, *n.* [bentoo] A box lunch.
bintoo-juu, *n.* [bentoo + juu(bako)] A tiered picnic box.
bira, *n.* Onion; Welsh onion [J negi; *Allium fistulosum* L.]. [FOSR] See also **chiribira, niibiru**.
-biree, *suff.* Denotes association, relationship, or friendship.
biroo, *n.* [biroo] A fan palm [*Livistona chinensis* var. *subglobosa* (Hassk.) Becc.]. [FOSR] Also **kuba**.
bizuru, *n.* Same as **binjuru**.
boo, *n.* [boo] A stick; a club; a cudgel.
boo-boo, *n. inf.* A baby; an infant.
boo-chira·a, *n.* A stubborn person; a

boofuyaa

self-willed person.
boo-fuya·a, *n.* [boohuri] A mosquito larva.
boo-ja·a, *n.* [< boozu] A little boy; an infant. See also **ufuwikiga**, **ufuwinagu**.
boo-ji, *n.* [boozu] A Buddhist priest; a monk.
boo-jishi, *n.* Pork loin.
boo-shi, *n.* [booshi] Headgear; a hat; a cap.
boo-shichina·a, *n.* A day laborer; a casual hire.
boo-suu, *n.* [booshu] One of the twenty-four Chinese seasons, falling in the fifth month of the lunar calendar. See also **suumanboosuu**.
boosuu-bee, *n.* A southerly wind in the **boosuu** rainy season. See **fee**³.
boroboro-juushii, *n. onom.* [boroboro + zoosui] A soft and watery porridge of rice and vegetables.
-bu, *suff.* [bu] Rate; percentage, equivalent to 10 percent.
buchi, *n.* [muchi] A whip; a rod.
buchi-dan, *n.* [butsudan] A family Buddhist altar where ancestral mortuary tablets are enshrined. Also **guriijin**. See also **kwii**³, **shichikigwii**, **tudana**, **ubuchidan**.
buchigee, *n.* Feeling faint; anemia.
buchikun, *n.* A faint; a swoon; a fainting spell.
bu-chirii, *n.* [bukirei*] Dirtiness; uncleanliness; impurity; filthiness.
bu-choohoo, *n.* [buchoohoo] Impoliteness; blunder; clumsiness; rudeness.
bui, *n.* A short stick; a short pole; an exorcism stick. See **mabui'uui**.
bui-mucha·a, *n.* A stick swinger. See **mabui'uui**.
buji, *n.* [buji] Safety; security; peace; tranquility; quietness. ·**na**, *adj.* Safe; secure; peaceful; tranquil; quiet.
bu-kakkoo, *n.* [bukakkoo] ·**na**, *adj.* 1 Unshapeliness; shapelessness. 2 Uncouthness; awkwardness.
bu-kari·i, *n.* Inauspiciousness; a bad omen; bad luck. ·**na**, *adj.* Inauspicious; unlucky. See **karii**.
buku-bukuu-ja, *n.* Foamed tea; Okinawan tea ceremony.
bu-kukuchi, *n.* Unhappiness. ·**na**, *adj.* Unhappy; unpleasant; cheerless.
bun¹, *n.* [bon] A tray; a server; a salver; a platter.
bun², *n.* [bun] 1 Social standing; social status. 2 Grace; dignity.
bun³, *n.* [bun] Share; portion; part; segment; quantity; rate; degree.
bun⁴, *n.* [bon] The *Bon* festival. Also **usooroo**, **sooroo**, **shichigwachi**, **shichigwachijuugunichi**. [ODJ]
buna-gaya, *n.* A tree fairy. Same as **kijimun**, **kijimunaa**.
bunbun, *adv. onom.* Buzzing, like the sound made by mosquitoes or bees.
bun-jiri, *n.* [boogire] A club; a cudgel.
bun-nuu, *n.* [bonnoo] 1 Evil passions; lusts. 2 Worries; cares.
bura, *n.* [hora] A conch shell; a trumpet shell.
bura-gee, *n.* [horagai] A conch shell. Same as **bura**.
buri, *n.* A rock.
buri-, *pref.* Denotes group; crowd.
buri-bushi, *n.* [mure-boshi] A group of stars; numerous stars.
buri-gii-dachi, *n.* That which is gruesome; grisly; frightful.
bu-rii, *n.* [burei] Rudeness; discourtesy; incivility. See also **guburii**.
buri-na·in, *vi.* To crowd together; throng; swarm; herd.
buri-ninju, *n.* A crowd of people; a large number of people.
bu-safuu, *n.* [busahoo] Bad manners; breach of etiquette; disrespect. ·**na**, *adj.* Rude; disrespectful.
-bu·san, *adj.* [-hoshii] The desiderative adjective, generally suffixed to the indefinite form of verbs.

bu-seewee, *n.* Unhappiness; infelicity; misfortune; bad luck. Also **busheewee**.
bu-shi, *n.* [bushi] An expert in martial arts; a man of great physical prowess. See also **samuree**, **yukatchu**.
buta-anda, *n.* [buta + abura] Lard.
butan, *n.* [botan] A peony [*Paeonia suffruticosa* Andr.]. [MAK]
butan-koo, *n.* A peony cake, for ceremonial use. See **chinsukoo**.
bu-tee, *n.* [butai] The stage; the indoor stage. See also **banku**.
butee·in, *vi.* Same as **muteein**.
buu, *n.* [bu] A laborer; a hand; a corvee laborer.
buu-buu[1], *n.* A leeching remedy; a traditional remedy by bloodletting. See also **kankan**[2], **sakuin**, **buubuu**[2].
buu-buu[2], *n. inf.* Water.
buukaa, *n.* A balloon.
buun, *n.* A moth.
buu-saa, *n.* A game for deciding, in which a thumb beats an index finger, an index finger beats a little finger, and a little finger beats a thumb.
bu-eesoo, *n.* [buaisoo] Being unsociable; being unfriendly; unsociability; brusqueness; curtness; bluntness.
byoo-chi, *n.* [byooki] Same as **yanmee**.
byoo-in, *n.* [byooin] Same as **isanuyaa**.
byoo-nin, *n.* [byoonin] A sick person; a patient; an invalid; the sick.

C——

chaa[1], *adv.* How; what.
chaa[2], *adv.* 1 Always, constant. 2 Continual.
chaa[3], *n.* [cha] Tea. See also **ucha**, **katajaa**, **usujaa**, **shanpin**.
-chaa, *suff.* Indicates plural in certain traditional kinship terms, usually as ·**nu-chaa**, ·**n-chaa**.
chaa·biin, *vi. formal* To come; visit. See **chuun**, **chaabira**.
chaa·bira, *vi. hon.* Honorific future of **chuun**, to come.
chaa-chaa, *n. inf.* Daddy; father.
chaa-fiifii, *n.* A medley; a pell-mell; a jumble; being without distinction; equality.
chaa-gana, *adv.* Somehow; at any rate.
chaagi, *n.* [keyaki] A podocarp (type of evergreen) tree; a **chaagi** tree [J inumaki; *Podocarpus macrophyllus* D. Don].
chaa·in, *vi.* [kieru] To be extinguished; (of fire) to go out; die out; blow out; be put out.
chaa-iru, *n.* [chairo] Brown; light brown.
chaa-kashi, *n.* [chakasu] Tea lees; used tea leaves.
chaaki, *adv.* Soon; before long; immediately.
chaan, *n.* [C changji] Fighting cock.
chaa-naabi, *n.* A teapot.
chaa·nu-shin, *n.* [chanoshin] A tea-stalk.
chaaru, *part. adj.* What kind; how. See also **chaayaru**.
chaa-shi, *adv.* How; in what way; by what means.
chaa-shi·n, *adv.* At any cost; at all costs; by all means; in the end; eventually; in every respect; to all appearance.
chaashin-kaashin, *adv.* [emphatic form] Same as **chaashin**.
chaa·sun, *vt.* [kesu] 1 To put out a fire; blow out; extinguish. 2 To turn off; cross out; erase; cancel. See also **fii-chaasaa**.
chaa-yaru, *part. adj.* Same as **chaaru**, but with emphasis.
cha-bun, *n.* [chabon] A tea tray; a tea server.
chabun-jira, *phr. colloq.* Lit., A face round as a tea tray. [GSS] See **chira**.
cha-doogu, *n.* [chadoogu] Tea utensils. See also **chabun**, **chuukaa**, **chawan**, **chataku**. Also **chawandoogu**.
cha-gwashi, *n.* [chagashi] Teacake; light refreshments.
cha-juukaa, *n.* A teapot. See **chuukaa**.

chakku-ya·a, *n.* A hasty person; a bustling fellow; a blunderer. See **chakuchakuu**.

chaku, *n.* [kyaku] A customer; a guest; a visitor. Also **uchaku**.

chaku-basa, *n.* [kyakubasha] A horse-drawn passenger carriage.

chaku-chaku·u, *n. colloq.* A careless person; an absentminded person; a featherbrain. See **chakkuyaa**.

chakushi, *n.* [chakushi] The first son; the heir. Also **choonan, chatchi**.

chakushi-bara, *n.* The eldest-son lineage, the senior lineage of a patrilineal consanguineous group.

chakushi-'nmaga, *n.* The eldest grandson.

chakushi-winagu, *n.* The eldest daughter.

chamishika, *adv.* Serious; grave.

chanpuruu, *n.* A dish in which chopped tofu (bean curd) and vegetables are mixed and cooked with oil.

chan-gutooru, *adj. phr.* What kind of.

changutooru·u, *n.* What kind of thing.

chan-gutu, *adv.* How; in what manner.

chan-kuu-ruu, *n.* A game in which coins placed on the palm of the hand are flipped and caught on the back of the hand.

chan-nagi·in, *vt.* To cast away; throw away; fling away.

chan·tu, *adv.* [chanto] Perfectly; properly; neatly; exactly; right.

chappi, *n.* How much (related to either quantity or size).

charagu, *n.* [?chataku] An eating table for a heap of sweet potatoes. [GSS]

chas·sa, *n.* How much; how many; what; how far.

cha-taku, *n.* [chataku] A teacup holder; a saucer (for a teacup).

chatchaa, *n.* The Japanese nightingale; a bush warbler. [GSS]

chatchi, *n.* Same as **chakushi**.

chatchi-bara, *n.* First-son lineage, the senior lineage of a patrilineal consanguineous group.

chatchi-ushikumi, *n.* Lit., confinement of the first son, referring to a taboo against having a younger son, instead of the first son, succeed to the family headship. [ODJ] See also **shijitadashi**.

cha-uki, *n.* [chauke] Tea cake; between-meal refreshments. Also **chawaki**.

cha-waki, *n.* Same as **cha'uki**.

cha-wan, *n.* [chawan] **1** A teacup. **2** A bowl for rice and soup. See **makai**.

cha-wan-doogu, *n.* [chawan doogu] A tea set; tableware. See also **chadoogu**.

chee, *interj.* An expression of surprise, minor irritation, or admiration. Oh…! Oh, my!

chiba·in, *vi.* [kibaru] To do one's best; endeavor; exert oneself; make efforts; strive; direct one's efforts to. See also **ganbain**.

chibana, *n.* A thistle [*Cirsium brevicaule* A. Gray var. *brevicaule*]. [FOSR] Also **ajama, shima'ajami, njichaa**.

chibi, *n.* [tsubi*] **1** The buttocks; the hips; the nates. **2** One's bottom; end. **3** Conclusion; aftermath. **4** The bottom of a basket or other container.

chibi-garu·u, *n.* A person who is quick and cheerful when asked to do an errand or work. See **gassan, chibigassan**.

chibi-gas·san, *adj.* […-garu·ku] Cheerful and ready for work.

chibi-gussui, *n.* The coccyx. Also **chibinugussui**.

chibi-kuchi, *n.* Coherence; consistency.

chibi-na·in, *vi.* To come in last in a race or competition.

chibi-'nbu·san, *adj.* Lit., heavy-buttocked; unwilling to work.

chibi·nu-gussui, *n.* Same as **chibigussui**.

chibi-nuguya·a, *n.* One who bears the consequences of (another's) failure.

chibi·nu-maa·i, *n.* Same as **akamai**.

chibi·nu-mii, *n.* The anus.

chibi-raa·s(h)an, *adj.* Energetic, brisk, vigorous.
chibi-sagu·in, *vt.* To make a secret investigation, usually in a negative sense.
chibi-sajira·a, *n.* One whose buttocks are lean and bony.
chibi-suncha·a, *n.* One who drags his buttocks or crawls about on his knees; figuratively, one who fails to bring anything to its conclusion or the failure to conclude anything. See **sunchun.**
chibi-tai, *n.* Drooping buttocks. Also **chibitanda.**
chibi-tachuu-yi·i, *n.* A style of sitting in which the person sits with his legs folded, holding his hands in his lap, without the buttocks touching the ground.
chibi-tanda, *n.* Same as **chibitai.**
chibu[1], *n.* [tsubo] 1 A pot; a jar. 2 A wine-cup. See also **mimichibu.** Also **kaami.**
chibu[2], *n.* [tsubo] A unit of land measure six **shaku** square. [Approximately 3.3 m².]
chibu[3], *n.* [tsubo] A moxibustion point.
-chibu[1], *suff.* A counter for wine-cups: cup(s)ful. See **chibu**[1].
-chibu[2], *suff.* [tsubo] A counter for measuring land. See **chibu**[2].
chibu-dukuru, *n.* 1 Effective spots for applying moxa. 2 The vital point.
chibui, *n.* [tsuboori*] Tucking up one's skirt in the back.
chibumi, *n.* [tsubomi] A bud; a flower bud.
chiburu, *n.* [tsuburi*] 1 The head. 2 A bottle gourd; a calabash.
chiburu-kami-ee, *n.* A children's game in which two opponents, either sitting or lying on their stomachs, push their heads against each other.
chiburu-yan, *n.* [tsuburi* + yami] A headache.

Chibuya-machi, *n.* Tsuboya; a pottery market.
Chibuya-yachi, *n.* Pottery made in kilns in Tsuboya in Naha.
chi-byoo, *n.* [kebyoo] Faked illness; feigned illness.
chichara-muuchi·i, *n.* Same as **chikaramuuchii.**
chicharu-kakita, *n.* Having just one kimono to wear on different occasions.
chicha·san, *adj.* [chikai] 1 (In time) close; early; soon. 2 (In distance) near; short; not far off. 3 (In relationship) close; near; akin to. 4 Almost; be close; nearly. Also **chikasan.**
chichi[1], *n.* [tsuki] The moon.
chichi[2], *n.* [tsuki] A month.
chichi[3], *n.* [tsuki] A thrust; a pass; a jab; a stab.
chichi-atai, *n.* [tsukiatari] The end of a road, passage, or corridor.
chichi-ata·in, *vi.* [tsukiataru] To collide; run (knock, bump, hit) against.
chichi-bappee, *n.* Misunderstanding; miscomprehension. Also **chichimachigee.**
chichi-buri, *n.* [kikibore] Listening with rapt attention; being enraptured by (e.g., music).
chichi·chun, *vt.* [·kan, ·chi; tsutsuku] To poke at; peck at; pick at.
chichi-furi·in, *vi.* [kikihoreru] To be enraptured by (e.g., music); be lost in (music).
chichi-guri·s(h)an, *adj.* [kiki-gurushii] Offensive to the ear; disagreeable to hear.
chichi-gutu, *n.* [kikigoto*] An event such as music or a speech worth listening to.
chichi-jooji, *n.* [kikijoozu] A good listener.
chichi-machigee, *n.* [kikimachigae] Same as **chichibappee.**
chichi·mi, *n.* Same as **chichin.**
chichi·mun, *vt.* [tsutsumu] To wrap; do

chichin

up; pack up; bundle.
chichin, *n.* [tsutsumi] A bundle; a package; a packet; a parcel; a bale. Also **chichimi.**
chichi-nagami, *n.* [tsukinagame] Viewing the moon.
chichi-naga·sun, *vt.* [kikinagasu] To take no notice of someone's talk; give no heed to.
chichi·nu-kaaji, *n.* Monthly; every month.
chichi·nu-mun, *n.* [tsukinomono] Menstruation; the menses; period. Also **juugunichii.**
chichi-shii, *n.* End of the month.
chichishi·mi, *n.* [tsutsushimi] 1 Discretion; prudence; modesty; caution. 2 Abstinence; continence.
chichishi·mun, *vt.* 1 To be discreet; to control oneself. 2 To abstain from.
chichi-ukuri, *n.* [tsukiokure] A magazine a month old; a magazine of a previous month.
chichi-utu·sun, *vt.* [kikiotosu] To fail to catch [a word]; miss [a word].
chichi-uushi, *n.* [tsukiusu] A mortar in which grain is pounded with a pestle. See also **uushi, ishi'uushi.**
chichi-waki, *n.* [kikiwake] Reasonableness; listening to reason.
chichi-waki·in, *vt.* To be reasonable; tell the difference by hearing.
chi·chun[1], *vt.* [kiku] 1 To hear; listen. 2 To hear of; learn; understand. 3 To ask; inquire; question. 4 To obey; follow.
chi·chun[2], *vi.* [kiku] 1 To take effect; have effect (on); do (a person) good; be efficacious. 2 To work; act.
chi·chun[3], *vi.* [tsuku] To arrive at; reach; get to.
chi·chun[4], *vi.* [tsuku] To stick (to); adhere (to); be stained (with); touch; reach; engage in.
chi·chun[5], *vt.* [tsuku] To pound (rice); husk. In the sense of husking, also **shiragiin.**

chichuu, *n.* [tsukiyo] A moonlit night. See **chichi**[1].
chi-deekuni, *n.* [ki- + daikon] A carrot [] shima-ninjin; *Daucus carota* L.].
chifafa, *n.* Japanese silverleaf [J tsuwabuki; *Ligularia tussilaginea* Makino (= *Farfugium japonicum* Kitam.)]. [FOSR, MAK, ODJ]
chi-fi-jin, *n.* The highest priestess of the Ryukyu Kingdom, a politico-religious office usually filled by a princess, queen, or queen mother. [ODJ, OR]
chifijin-ganashii, *n.* Term of respect for **chifijin.**
chifijin-udun, *n.* 1 Palace of the **chifijin.** 2 Term of respect for **chifijin.**
chigaa, *n.* Drum with heads of stretched python skin or tanned paper used to accompany **sanshin** playing. See **sanshin.**
chigaa·ruu, *n.* Taking turns; alternation; change; relief; relay; shift.
chiga·in, *vi.* [·(r)an, ·ti; chigau] 1 To differ (from); vary (from); be different (from); be unlike; be dissimilar (to); be varied; be variable. 2 To disagree with; be not agreeable to; be contrary to; run counter to. 3 To be wrong; be mistaken.
chi-gaka·i, *n.* [kigakari] Anxiety; worry; concern; suspense; apprehension; misgivings. Same as **chimugakai.**
chi-gaki, *n.* Intention; aim; effort; attitude.
chigaki·in, *vt.* To work diligently.
chigari, *n.* [kegare] Spiritual pollution.
chigari·in, *vi.* [kegareru] To become impure (in a spiritual sense); become polluted.
chigari-mun, *n.* [kegaremono] A person or thing that is polluted.
chigee, *n.* [tsugai] A joint; an articulation.
chige·e-mi, *n.* Disparity; an error.
chi-goo, *n.* [tsugoo] 1 Circumstances; conditions. 2 Convenience. 3 Occasion;

opportunity.
chi-guchi, *n.* [tsuguchi] An inlet.
chii¹, *n.* [toi] Same as **tii²**.
chii², [kei] Fortune-telling; divination.
chii³, *n.* A well-bucket.
chii⁴, *n.* [tsui] A pair; a couple; a set.
chii⁵, *n.* [ki] A general term denoting spirit, mind, soul.
chii⁶, *n.* [chi] 1 Blood; gore. 2 Consanguinity.
chii⁷, *n.* [chi] 1 Milk. 2 The breast. Also **chiichii**.
chii-an, *n.* A wet nurse. Also **anmee**.
chii-ba, *n.* [kiba] A fang; a tusk; an eyetooth; a canine. Also **chiibaa**.
chii-baku, *n.* A fishing tackle box.
chii-bee·san, *adj.* 1 Quick-tempered. 2 Ambitious; full of desire to work. See **Yamatujiifee**.
chii-bukki, *n.* Swelling with thick clothes. **-sun,** *v.* To become swollen with thick clothes.
chii-bukkwa, *n. colloq.* The breasts.
chii-chii, *n. inf.* [chichi] Same as **chii⁷**.
chiichii-kaakaa-sun, *v. colloq.* To have one's throat choked with food.
chii-chin, *n.* [C duijin] A decoration technique for lacquerware. [OBJ]
chii-dai, *n.* Same as **chirudai**.
chiidaka-mun, *n.* A snob; an impertinent fellow.
chii-daka·san, *adj.* Impertinent; impudent; conceited; audacious.
chii-darakaa, *adv.* Bloodstained; bloody.
chiidi, *n.* [tsuide] Occasion; chance. **·ni,** *adv.* By the way; incidentally; apropos of that; while; when.
chii-fan, *n.* [C jifan] Chicken rice. See **seefan**.
chiiga¹, *n.* One bundle of rice plants.
chiiga², *n.* 1 A square wooden dry-measure box; a pottery liquid-measure jar. 2 Amount of either grain or liquid measured in **chiiga**. Also **mashi²**. See also **chooban**.
chiiga³, *n.* The sounding box of the sanshin musical instrument. See also **sanshin**.
chiiga·a¹, *n. pej.* A mute. See **chiiguu**.
chii-gaa², *n.* A draw well; a well from which water is drawn by hand with a bucket. See **kaa**.
chii-gani, *n.* A fishhook. Also **iyujii**.
chii-gasa-gasa·a, *n.* A person who is impatient and restless.
chii-geeigeei, *n.* An ability to change clothes often to suit different occasions.
chii-gee·in, *vi.* [kigaeru] To change clothes. See **chiin¹, keein²**.
chii-geya·a, *n.* A change of clothes.
chiigu·u, *n.* [tusgu(mu)*] A mute; a deaf-mute. See also **chiigaa¹**.
chii-gwaa, *n.* A fishhook.
chii-hai, *n.* Stiffness (of muscles; sinews, etc.); swelling.
chii-irichi, *n.* Dish of pig blood and meat, fried or stir-fried in oil; stir-fry. [GSS] See **irichii**.
chiiji¹, *n.* [keizu] Genealogy; lineage; pedigree.
Chiiji², *n.* [tsuji] Formerly, the licensed red-light district of Tsuji ward of Naha.
chii-jiru, *n.* [chi + tsuru] A blood vessel; a vein; an artery.
chii-juu·san, *adj.* Stouthearted; strongminded. See **chuusan**.
chii-kaa, *n.* Lineage; pedigree; stock. Also **shiikaa**.
chii-kaki, *n.* New clothes; clothes that have been worn only once or twice.
chii-kana·in, *vi.* [·(r)an, ·ti] To be active; be competitive; be combative.
chiiku, *n.* [keiko] Practice; training; exercise; study; learning. **-sun,** *v.* To practice; exercise.
chii-muchi, *n.* One who has a genealogy; a member of the gentry.
chi·in¹, *vt.* [·ran, ·chi; kiru] To wear; put on (clothes; does not apply to footgear or headgear); get into; be dressed.
chi·in², *vt.* [·ran, ·tchi; kiru] 1 To cut;

chiin

chop; hash; saw; clip; shear; slash. **2** To break off; hang up. See also **chiriin**[1].
chi·in[3], *vt.* [tsuru] To fish; catch fish.
chii·nu-kubi, *n.* [chikubi] The teat(s); the nipple(s). Also **chikubi**.
chii-numi-ngwa, *n.* [chinomigo] A suckling baby; a newborn baby.
chii-ruu, *n.* [kiiro] Yellow; yellowish.
chii-sachi, *n.* [< J keisatsu] Same as **kii-sachi**.
chii-shiji, *n.* [chisuji] Lineage; pedigree; stock; blood.
chii-tachi, *n.* [tsuitachi] The first day of the month.
chii-tatiya·a, *n.* A fortune-teller; a diviner. See **tatiin**.
chijaa-haja·a, *n.* [tsugihagi] **1** A patch; full of patches. **2** Quilting.
chijaa·sun, *vt.* [tsugiawaseru] To join; patch; cement; piece together; splice.
chijaku, *n.* Brass.
chiji[1], *n.* Worse than; inferior to.
chiji[2], *n.* [tsumuji, tsuji] **1** A ridge; a spine (of a mountain chain). **2** A roof. **3** The top; summit.
chiji·chi, *n.* [tsuzuki] Continuance; succession; a sequel.
chiji·chun, *vi.* [tsuzuku] **1** To continue; be succeeded by; follow. **2** To be contiguous; adjoin.
chiji·in, *vt.* To suppress; inhibit; forbid; fence off; ban.
chijimaga·in, *vi.* To shrink up; quail at; flinch.
chijima·in, *vi.* To be shortened; be contracted; be reduced; be abridged; be boiled down; be simplified; be condensed.
chijimi, *n.* [chijimi] Cotton crepe.
chijimi·in, *vt.* [chijimeru] To shorten; contract; reduce; abridge; simplify; condense.
chiji·mun, *vi.* [chijimu] To shrink; wrinkle; crumple; contract; draw.
chijin, *n.* [tsuzumi] A hand-drum; a tabor.
chiji-na·in, *vi.* To worsen; deteriorate; decline. See **chiji**[1].
chijiri, *n.* [chigiri] A promise; a pledge; a vow.
chi-jui, *n.* [chidori] A plover. Also **chijuyaa**.
chi·jun[1], *vt.* [tsugu] **1** To join (one thing to another); repair; patch up; piece together. **2** To succeed.
chi·jun[2], *vt.* [tsugu] To pour (in); fill (a cup; bowl); serve.
chijuu, *n.* **1** Curly hair; frizzy hair. **2** A person with curly or wavy hair.
chijuya·a[1], *n.* Same as **chijui**.
chijuya·a[2], *n.* One whose hair is curly and frizzy.
chika, *n.* [tsuka] **1** A metal fitting which affixes the handle on a sickle. **2** The hilt (of a sword); a (hand) grip (of a knife); **3** A bundle.
chika-guru, *adv.* [< J chikagoro] Lately; recently; nowadays.
chika·in[1], *vt.* [·(r)an, ·ti; tsukau] **1** To use; make use of. **2** To employ. **3** To spend. **4** To send a messenger. **5** To work (a machine).
chika·in[2], *vi.* [tsuku] To be ignited; catch (fire); (of a light) be lighted; be lit.
chika·in[3], *vi.* [tsukaru] To be soaked (in); be steeped (in); be submerged (in); be flooded (with water).
chikaji·chi-guri·s(h)an, *adj.* Difficult to approach; difficult to access.
chikaji·chi-yas·san, *adj.* Approachable; easy to approach; accessible.
chikaji·chun, *vi.* [chikazuku] **1** To approach; get near; come [walk] up to; draw close to. **2** To get acquainted with; associate with; come in contact with.
chikajiki·in, *vt.* [chikazukeru] To bring (a thing or person) close to; allow (a person) to come near; keep company with.
chika-michi, *n.* [chikamichi] **1** A shorter road. **2** A shortcut.

24

chika-mii, *n.* [chikame] Nearsightedness; myopia.
chikana·in, *vt.* [·(r)an, ·ti] To raise (animals); breed; rear; bring up.
chikane·e-mun, *n.* Domesticated animals; cattle; livestock.
chikanee-ngwa, *n.* A foster child. See also **yooshi**[1].
chikara, *n.* [chikara] **1** Strength; force; might; energy. **2** Authority; sway; influence. **3** Assistance; support. See also **chicharamuuchii, tee**[1].
chikara·a, *n.* A strong man; a Hercules.
chikara-muuchii, *n.* [chikaramochi] Rice cake that supplies energy and strength. Also **chicharamuuchii**.
chikari·in, *vi.* [tsukareru] To get tired; become fatigued; be exhausted (mentally). See also **wutain, kutandiin**.
chika·san, *adj.* [chikai] Near; short (road); not far off. Also **chichasan**.
chikashi, *n.* A prop; a stay; a strut; a support; a shore.
chika·sun, *vt.* [kikasu] **1** To tell; inform. **2** To make (a person) agree.
chi-kata, *n.* [jikata] A piece of land; a plot (of ground); an estate.
chika-yu·in, *vi.* [chikayoru] To approach; go (come) near.
chike·e[1], *n.* [tsukai] **1** A messenger; an envoy; a minister. **2** A mission; an errand. **3** An invitation.
chikee[2], *n.* [tsukae] Hindrance; impediment.
chike·e-bina·i, *n.* Wear and tear; loss or pain due to use.
chike·e-michi, *n.* **1** A use. **2** Employment.
chikee-miji, *n.* Miscellaneous-use water; unpotable water that is used for purposes such as laundry or watering the yard.
chike·e-mun, *n.* An employee; a hired hand; a servant.
chikee-tunai, *n.* Neighborhood; a neighbor.

chiki-agii, *n.* [tsukeage] Name of a food, in which fish, carrots, and burdocks are chopped, made into rolls, and deep-fried.
chiki-bi, *n.* [tsukebi] Arson; incendiarism. **-sun**, *v.* To commit arson; set fire to (a house).
chiki-gusui, *n.* [tsuke-gusuri] Medicine for external use; ointment. See **kusui, numigusui**.
chiki·in[1], *vt.* [tsukeru] **1** To attach, affix (one thing to another); set (one thing on another); join (one thing to another); couple (two things together). **2** To fasten; sew on; glue; paste. **3** To enter (in a book); apply (one thing to another). **4** To light; kindle. **5** To mate. **6** To name.
chiki·in[2], *vt.* [tsukeru] **1** To soak. **2** To pickle.
chiki-ji, *n.* [tsukegi] Same as **matchi**.
chikiji-baku, *n.* A matchbox.
chiki-jishi, *n.* Same as **suujikii**. [GSS] See **chikiin**[2], **shishi**.
chiki-mun, *n.* [tsukemono] Pickles; pickled vegetables.
chiki-na, *n.* Pickled greens.
chiki-tuduki, *n.* [tsuketodoke] **1** A gift; a present. **2** Winding-up; clearance; settlement.
chikiya·a-'nma, *n.* A stud; a studhorse; a breeding horse.
chikiya·a-'waa, *n.* A male pig used for breeding.
chikkaa-mukkaa-soon, *phr. colloq.* Untidy; disarrayed and out of order. [GSS]
chiku, *n.* [kiku] A chrysanthemum; a mum.
chi-kubi, *n.* Same as **chiinukubi**.
chikuku, *n.* An owl. See **mayaajikuku**.
chiku-shoo, *n.* [chikushoo] **1** A beast; a brute; a dumb animal. **2** A brute of a person; a person no better than a beast.
chikushoo-mun, *n.* A callous person; a ruthless person; a coldhearted person; a brutal person.

chiku·sun, *vt.* [tsukusu] To exhaust (every means); use up; render (service).
chima-gu, *n.* A hoof; an angula. Also **chimaguu**.
chima·in, *vi.* [tsumaru] **1** To be plugged up; be clogged; be choked. **2** To be jammed. **3** To become shorter; contract. **4** To be cornered; be hard up.
chi-mama, *n.* [kimama] Willfulness; waywardness; egoism; selfishness. ·**na**, *adj.* Willful; self-indulgent; wayward; arbitrary.
chiman·chun, *vt.* To wet and stretch a laundered cloth or kimono so as to prevent wrinkles.
chimi, *n.* [tsume] **1** A fingernail; a claw; a talon; a hoof. **2** A plectrum. **3** A spindle.
chimi-agi·in, *vt.* [tsumiageru] To pile up; stack up.
chimi-dima, *n.* A shipping charge; cargo charge. See **tima**.
chimi·in, *vt.* [tsumeru] To attend (office); be stationed at; cut short.
chimi-juri, *n.* A courtesan who has been monopolized by a customer for a period of time.
chimi-kata, *n.* [tsumekata] A scratch made by a fingernail; a nail mark; a nail scar.
chi·mi-ku·mun, *vt.* [tsumikomu] To load (a car; a cart; a ship, etc.); stow aboard; ship (a cargo).
chimi-kusu, *n.* **1** The dirt under a fingernail. **2** A minuscule amount.
chi·mi-ni, *n.* [tsumini] A load; cargo.
chimu, *n.* [kimo] **1** The liver; liver as a food. **2** The soul; spirit; mentality; thought; heart; feeling; sincerity. **3** Will; intention; **4** Design; fancy; taste. See **kukuru**.
chimu-ama·i, *n.* Mental latitude; mental allowance; composure; complacency.
chimu-asa·san, *adj.* Fickle in love; unchaste; capricious.
chimu-ashigachi-sun, *v.* To feel restless; feel fidgety; feel uneasy.
chimu-bee·san, *adj.* Quick to awake; to be a light sleeper. See also **feesan**.
chimu-biru·san, *adj.* Magnanimous; broad-minded; liberal. See also **firusan**.
chimuchi-geera·sun, *vi.* To be upset; be frightened.
chimu-da·chun, *vi.* [·tan, ·tchi] To be overcome with grief; anguish; lament. See **dachun**.
chimu-daka·san, *adj.* Dignified; refined; graceful. See **takasan**.
chimu-duui-na·in, *vi.* To have things come out as one wishes; to have things one's own way.
chimu-gaashii-sun, *v.* To give moral support; encourage.
chimu-gaka·i, *n.* Anxiety; care; worry. **-sun**, *v.* To weigh on one's mind; feel uneasy about. See also **chigakai**.
chimu-gaki·in, *vt.* To be ready to do something good.
chimu-gana·s(h)an, *adj.* Darling; sweet; charming.
chimu-gawai-mun, *n.* One with an unusual mental attitude; a right-minded person.
chimu-guchi, *n.* The pit of the stomach.
chimu-gukuru, *n.* Mind; spirit.
chimu-guma·a, *n.* **1** A timid person; a coward. **2** A prudent person.
chimu-guma·san, *adj.* **1** Shy; timid; bashful; cowardly. **2** Prudent; circumspect.
chimu-guri·s(h)an, *adj.* Pitiful; pitiable; miserable; wretched.
chimu-guu-mun, *n.* A shy person; a fainthearted person.
chimu-guu·san, *adj.* Shy; timid; bashful. Same as **chimugumasan**.
chimu-hijuru·san, *adj.* Frightened with anticipation of danger.
chimu·i, *n.* Same as **chimuyee**.
chimu-icha·san, *adj.* Sorry; pitiful; pitiable; pathetic; touching.

chimu-ichuna·san, *adj.* Restless; impatient; fidgety.
chimu·in, *vi.* [tsumoru] **1** To accumulate; get accumulated; pile up. **2** To estimate; appreciate.
chimu-iri, *n.* Goodwill; good wishes; regard; kindness; goodness; friendliness.
chimu-jawai, *n.* Affront; offense; pique. See **sawain.**
chimuji, *n.* [tsumugi] Pongee fabric.
chimu-jura·san, *adj.* Kindhearted; compassionate; beautiful in mind. See **churasan.**
chimu-jurii, *n.* Agreement; cooperation.
chimu-juu·san, *adj.* Stout; courageous; strong-willed. See **chuusan.**
chimu-kukuru, *n.* [kimogokoro] Emphatic form of **chimu** and **kukuru**; mind; soul; spirit.
chimu-magi·san, *adj.* Broadminded; tolerant; open-minded.
chimu-mayu·i, *n.* **1** Perplexity; bewilderment; hesitation. **2** Delusion; illusion; infatuation.
chimumayui-sun, *v.* **1** To be bewildered; hesitate. **2** To have illusion; be deluded; hesitate.
chimu-mu·chi, *n.* Composure; mental attitude.
chi·mun^1, *vt.* [tsumu] To load; pile up; heap up; stack.
chi·mun^2, *vt.* [tsumu] To pick (flowers, etc.).
chimu-naga·san, *adj.* Easygoing; leisurely.
chimu-nigee, *n.* Praying in one's inner heart. **-sun,** *v.* To pray in one's heart.
chimu-noo·shi, *n.* Regaining peace of mind; **-sun,** *v.* To restore one's humor; pacify; divert oneself. See **noosun.**
chimu-nubi, *n.* Tolerance; patience; permissiveness. **-sun,** *v.* To be tolerant and forgive.
chimu-sawa·ji, *n.* Nervousness; mental agitation; anxiety.

chimu-shinji, *n.* Hog liver infusion. See **shinjimun.**
chimu-tiichi, *n.* Unity of purpose.
chimu-tu·i-guri·s(h)an, *adj.* Hard to please.
chimu-tu·i-han·sun, *vt.* To offend; incur displeasure.
chimu-tu·in, *vt.* To humor; please; pacify.
chimu-tumee·in, *vi.* To find one's senses; brace oneself; find one's serenity.
chimu-ubii, *n.* Remembrance; keeping a mental note.
chimu-uchi^1, *n.* The pit of the stomach.
chimu-uchi^2, 1 *n.* One's innermost heart. **2** *adv.* At heart; inwardly.
chimu-umi·i, *n.* Imagination; fancy.
chimu-wasamichi, *n.* Uneasiness; fidgetiness; vague apprehension.
chimu-ya·mun, *vt.* To regret; be sorry.
chimu-yee, *n.* [tsumori] An intention; a design; a thought; a purpose.
chimu-yoo·san, *adj.* Timid; fainthearted; pusillanimous; cowardly.
chin^1, *n.* [kin] Gold.
chin^2, *n.* An Okinawa seabream [J minamikurodai; *Acanthopagrus sivicolus* Akazaki].
chin^3, *n.* [kinu] Clothes; (Japanese- or Okinawan-style) dress.
chin^4, [kin] A measurement of weight equivalent to 160 **munmi,** about 0.6 kg.
chin, *n.* Variant for **chinu.** [GSS]
china, *n.* [tsuna] A rope; a hawser.
chi-naa, *n.* Same as **kinaa.**
china-hichi, *n.* [tsunahiki] Tug-of-war; specifically a religious rite performed to the fire deity on the fifteenth of the sixth lunar month to give thanks for and pray for another rich harvest. See also **miinna, wuunna.**
china·jun, *vt.* [tsunagu] **1** To tie; fasten; chain. **2** To connect; link.
china-uubi, *n.* [tsuna-obi] A belt made of straw rope. See also **uubi.**
chin-ba, *n.* [tsumiba] A berth; a pier.

chin-baa, *n.* [kinba] A gold tooth.
chin-bai, *n.* 1 A golden needle used in acupuncture. 2 Acupuncture. See **haai**[2].
chinbee, *n.* One of the thirty-three high priestesses of ancient Ryukyu. [ODJ]
chinbooraa, *n.* Ryukyu-uminina mollusk [*Batillaria multiformis* (Lischke)]. Also **uminna**, **kurubaa**.
chin-buchi, *n.* [kenbutsu] Sightseeing.
chin-buku, *n.* A fishing rod.
chinbuku-daki, *n.* A fishing-rod bamboo [J Hoteichiku; *Phyllostachys aurea* A. & C. Rivière]. Same as **kusandaki**. [FOSR, ODJ]
chin-bun[1], *n.* [kenbun] An inspection; an examination; a survey.
chin-bun[2], *n.* [kenbun] Knowledge; experience; information.
chin-chi·i-jooji, *n.* Expert in wearing kimono.
chinchiki·in, *vt.* To pinch. Also **chinki-in**.
chin-chin, *n.* [C jinjin] A lacquerware decoration technique in which hairline engraving is filled with gold dust.
chin-china·a, *n.* An island warbler [*Cisticola juncidis*]; Japanese fan-tailed warbler.
chin-chi·ru-kaa, *n.* Wardrobe; clothing. See also **'waaji**, **'waajijin**, **churasugaisun**, **issoochiyaa**, **hiijiichiyaa**, **tunjifeejii**, **shigutujin**, **umijin**, **basaajin**. Also **chin**[3], **chirukaa**.
chin-dami, *n.* Tuning.
chi-nee, *n.* 1 A livelihood. 2 A household; a home.
chinee-ninju, *n.* Family members.
chin-gaa, *n.* A well; an artesian well. Same as **kaa**[2].
chin-gushi, *n.* Craftsmen who make articles of precious metal. Same as **kuganijeeku**.
chini, [tsune] 1 *n.* Norm; the normal state of things. 2 *adv.* Always.
chinibu, *n.* 1 A finely meshed wickerwork of split bamboo. Also **shinibu**. 2 Ceilings and walls made of **chinibu** instead of wood planks. See also **annumii**.
chinibu-gachi, *n.* A woven bamboo fence. See also **kachi**[2].
chinju, *n.* [kinjo] The neighborhood; a neighbor.
chinju-bare·e, *n.* Ostracism by the neighborhood.
chinju-bire·e, *n.* Association with the neighbors.
chin-kan, *n.* [kinkan] A kumquat [*Fortunella crassifolia* Swingle]. [FOSR]
chinki·in, *vt.* Same as **chinchikiin**.
chin-kwa, *n.* [kinka] A pumpkin; a squash; a crookneck squash. [*Cucurbita moschata* Duchesne var. *melonaeformis*]. [FOSR] Same as **nankwa**.
chin-maasaa, *n.* A milepost; a distance marker, usually a round pile of stones and earth with a banyan or **akagi** tree planted on top.
chinmaga·in, *vi.* Emphatic form of **magain**; to bend, curve; be crooked; buckle up. See **magain**.
Chin-mamun, *n.* Kinmamon, the highest deity in Ryukyu, who was served by the **chifijin**, the chief priestess in the Ryukyu kingdom. [ODJ]
chin-mi, *n.* Weight; weight by *kin* unit.
chinnama·a, *n.* Same as **chinnan**. [GSS]
chinnan, *n.* A snail. Also **chinnamaa**.
chinnan-oorasee, *n.* A snail fight, in which two snail shells are smashed against each other; the snail whose shell is the first to be cracked loses.
chin-nuku, *n.* [tsuru no ko (imo)] A village taro [*Colocasia esculenta* (L.) Schott]. [FOSR]
chin·nu-kubi, *n.* The neckband (of kimono); a neck (of a shirt).
chin·nu-kuu, *n.* Kimono mending; patching up (of kimono). See **kuu**[2].
chin·nu-wuu, *n.* A cord attached to a (child's) kimono in lieu of a sash.

chin-pin, *n.* [C juanbing] A rolled cake. See also **poopoo**.
chinshi, *n.* A knee; a lap.
chin-su-koo, *n.* [C jin Chu gao] The Golden Cake of Ch'u, dumplings made of rice flour, kneaded with oil, put into molds, and lightly braised. See also **koogwaashi, butankoo**.
chin·tu, *adv.* Exactly; just.
chinu, *n.* [tsuno] A horn; an antler; a tentacle.
chinubi, *n.* Copulation. [GSS] Also **ukayee**. See **chirubun**.
chinu-jeeku, *n.* A horn craftsman.
chinuku, *n.* [kinoko] A mushroom with stalk and top, usually edible.
chinuu, *n.* [kinoo] Yesterday.
chip-pan, *n.* [C jubing] Dried **kunibu** orange comfit. Also **kippan**.
chira, *n.* [tsura] 1 A face; a visage; features. 2 The front and rear sides of a boat.
chira-afa·san, *adj.* Bashful; shy; ashamed.
chira-bu·i, *n.* Turning the other way.
chira-chira, *adv.* [kirakira] Sparklingly; glitteringly; dazzlingly. -**sun**, *v.* To glitter; shine; twinkle; gleam.
chira-chira-bu·i, *n.* [chirachira + furi] A fine rain; a drizzle.
chira-damashi, *n.* Bright looks; intelligent looks. See **tamashi**[1].
chira-fukkwa·a, *n.* A sulky face; a sullen look.
chira-gamachi, *n. pej.* Face. See **kamachi**.
chira-hajika·s(h)an, *adj.* Bashful; coy; demure.
chira·in, *vt.* [·(r)an, ·ti; kirau] To dislike; hate; loathe.
chira-kaagi, *n.* Looks; the face; personal appearance.
chiraka·sun, *vt.* [chirakasu] To scatter about; disarrange.
chirani, *n.* [tsurane] In a drama, a monologue or self-introduction in rhymed long monologue, often in a heightened tone, composed in the classical language with a fixed meter.
chira·nu kusa·a na·ru·ka akku·sun, *phr. slang.* Lit., to scold a person severely until his face turns frontside backward. [GSS]
chira·sun, *vt.* [chirasu] To scatter; strew; disperse; break up. Same as **chiraka-sun**.
chire·e, *n.* [kirai] A taboo; forbidden things.
chiree-mun, *n.* [kirai + mono] A taboo.
chiri[1], *n.* [kiri] Mist; fog.
chiri[2], *n.* [kire] Cloth; a piece of cloth; a slip; a strip.
chiri[3], *n.* [chiri] Dust; rubbish; trash.
chiri[4], *n.* [kiri] Royal paulownia [*Paulownia tomentosa* (Thunb.) Steud.].
chiri[5], *n.* [tsure] A companion; a friend; company.
-chiri, *suff.* [kire] A counter for parcels of farmland. See also **-mashi**.
chiri-akuta, *n.* [chiri-akuta] Rubbish; litter; garbage. Same as **akuta**.
chiri-bira, *n.* A leek; a scallion [J nira; *Allium ramosum* L.]. [FOSR] See also **bira, niibiru**.
chiribira-gwaa, *n.* Same as **niibiru**. [GSS]
chi-rii, *n.* [kirei] Cleanliness; purity; tidiness; neatness.
chiri·in[1], *vi.* [...ri·ran, ...t·ti; kireru] To cut (well); be sharp. See also **chiin**[2].
chiri·in[2], *vi.* [chiru] To fall; scatter; be scattered; be shed.
chiri·in[3], *vt.* [tsureru] To have along; take (with); bring (with).
chirina·san, *adj.* [tsurenai] Heartless; unfeeling; cold; cruel.
chiri-shiti, *n.* [chirisute] A refuse heap; a dump.
chiri-tu·i, *n.* [chiritori] A dustpan.
chiri-tuya·a, *n.* A garbage collector.
chiri-utu·sun, *vt.* To cut down; lop off; strike off; prune off.

chiru

chiru[1], *n.* [tsuru] A string; a cord; a tendon; a vine; a filament.
chiru[2], *n.* [tsuru] Same as **chiruntui**.
chiru·bun, *vi.* [tsurumu] (Of animals) to couple; copulate; pair; cover. See also **ukayee, chinubi**.
chiru-dai, *n.* Disappointment; despair; discouragement. Also **chiidai**. **-sun**, *v.* To be disappointed; be discouraged.
chiruga·in, *vi.* 1 To be connected; be joined; be in succession; range; lie (stand or stretch) in a line. 2 To be submerged; be under (water).
chi·ru-kaa, *n.* Same as **chinchirukaa**.
chiruma·a, *n.* Same as **chirumii**.
chirumii, *n.* Those who are of about the same age. Also **yunuchirumii**.
chiru·n-tui, *n.* [tsuru + no + tori] A crane. Also **chiru**[2].
chiruu-nin, *n.* [kiryuunin] An emigrant or sojourner in a rural area.
chisa-na, *n.* [chisha] Lettuce [*Lactuca sativa* L.]. [FOSR]
chisana-baa, *n.* Same as **chisana**.
chishiri, *n.* [kiseru] A tobacco pipe; a pipe.
chite·e-banashi, *n.* [tsutae-banashi] A legend; a tradition. Also **iichitee**.
chiti, *n.* [tsute] An intermediary; good offices; connections.
chitu, *n.* [tsuto] A souvenir; a gift (from a travel).
chitumi, *n.* [tsutome] Work; duty; service.
chitumi·in, *vt.* [tsutomeru] 1 To serve (in an office); hold (an office); be in the service of; do (or perform) one's duty. 2 To exert oneself; be diligent; be patient.
chiwami·in, *vt.* [kiwameru] To investigate thoroughly; master; go to the end of.
chiyu, *n.* [tsuyu] Dew; dewdrop.
chiyumi·in, *vt.* [kiyomeru] To purify; cleanse; exorcise.
chon-chon, *adv. onom.* Descriptive of liquid dripping: drip; drop.
chon-daraa, *n.* [kyootaroo] 1 A group of begging puppeteers who plied their trade in central and southern Okinawa. 2 The performing arts of this group. [OBJ, ODJ]
chondaraa-gwaa, *n.* Same as **chifafa**. [GSS]
choo-ban, *n.* A square wooden dry-measure box holding one *sho* of grain. See also **chiiga**[2], **munnan, kanabuchi, nakamuigwa, gusaakunakamui, nakamui, ichigoonakamui, gungoonakamui**. [OBJ]
choo-chin, *n.* [choochin] A paper lantern.
choo-dee, *n.* [kyoodai] Siblings; brothers and sisters.
choodee-kasaba·i, *n.* Lit., doubling-up of brothers in the same generation; i.e., replacing the first-born heir with the second son, a taboo practice in family succession. [ODJ, OBJ] See also **shijita-dashi**.
choo-du, *adv.* [choodo] Just; right; precisely; a round number.
choo-gin, *n.* [kyoogen] 1 A form of traditional Okinawan drama, derived from the Edo-period Japanese Noh drama and Kyoogen (the latter a comic interlude during a Noh program). 2 Any drama performance. 3 Anything funny or make-believe. [OBJ, ODJ]
choo-ji, *n.* [chooji] A clove; clove perfume.
chooji-bukuru, *n.* A small perfume bag of cloves.
choo-jika, *n.* [kyoozuka] 1 A mound where Buddhist sutras are buried. 2 A magic formula to recite in case of an earthquake. [OGJ]
choo-mii, *n.* [choomei] Longevity.
choo-min, *n.* [choomen] A notebook; a register; an account.
choo-nan, *n.* [choonan] The eldest son. Also **chakushi**.

choo-roo, *n.* [chooroo] Chief priest of a temple.
Choo-shin, *n.* [Choosen] Korea.
Chooshina·a, *n. pej.* A Korean.
chotchon-gwaa, *n.* A bush warbler; the Japanese nightingale.
tchu, *n.* 1 A person; man; mankind; a man; an individual; a human being. 2 Character; personality; nature. 3 Another; other people; others.
tchu-atu, *n.* Behind others; later than others.
chu-bachi, *n.* [hito + bachi] One strike; one hit; at once.
chu-chibu, *n.* One grain; one drop.
chu-chichi, *n.* [hitotsuki] One month.
chuchichi-gushi, *n.* Every other month.
tchu-chimu-guri·s(h)a, *n.* Benevolence; affection; kindness. **-sun**, *v.* To show benevolence; be kind.
chu-choodee, *n.* One set of siblings; one family.
tchu-damasa·a, *n.* An imposter; a swindler; a crook.
chu-faara, *n.* 1 A full stomach; satiety. 2 Sufficiency; enough.
chu-faashi, *n.* A pair of chopsticks.
chu-fana, *n.* A variant of **chuhana**. [GSS]
tchu-furubasa·a, *n.* One who jumps debts.
tchu-gawa·i-mun, *n.* 1 An eccentric person. 2 An unusual person; a great person.
tchu-hada, *n.* The human skin; the warmth of the skin.
chu-hana, *n.* 1 A short sleep; a nap. 2 One heap. Also **chufana**.
chu-hisa, *n.* A step; short distance.
chui, *n.* [hitori] One person; by oneself; only one person.
chui-chigaaruu, *n.* Taking turns one by one.
chui-dachi, *n.* [hitoridachi] Standing on one's own; self-help; independence.
chui-gurashi, *n.* [hitorigurashi]

chukuigwii

Bachelorhood; spinsterhood; celibacy. Same as **duuchuigurashi**.
chu-iichi, *n.* [hitoiki] 1 One breath. 2 One small effort.
chui-naa, *n.* One by one; individually.
chui-ngwa, *n.* [hitorigo] An only child.
chui-nuya·a, *n.* One-man **sabani** boat used within the reef. [OBJ] See **sabani**, **nuin**^{2}.
chui-shiijii, *adv.* Helping each other.
chui-taree-daree, *adv.* Complementing and cooperating with each other; standing by each other; being interdependent.
chui-usee-usee, *adv.* Looking with contempt upon each other. See **useein**.
chui-uushi-uushi, *adv.* Shifting blame on each other. See **ushiin**.
chui-wikiga-ngwa, *n.* An only son.
chui-winagu-ngwa, *n.* An only daughter.
chujuu·ku, *adv.* Very tightly; very strongly.
chukaa-mii, *n.* A single-fold eyelid.
chu-kaki, *n.* A fragment; a broken piece; a bit.
tchu-kashimas(h)a·a, *n.* A misanthrope; one who hates people. See **kashimas(h)an**.
chu-kata, *n.* 1 One side; one after another. 2 Single-minded devotion.
chukata·a, *n.* A zealot; a single-minded person; a thorough-going person.
chu-keen, *n.* Once; one time.
chu-keetunai, *n.* The neighborhood; the vicinity.
chu-kuchi, *n.* [hitokuchi] One mouthful; one bite; a sip.
chuku·i-bana, *n.* [tsukuribana] An artificial flower.
chuku·i-banashi, *n.* [tsukuribanashi] A fiction; a fable; a made-up story; a fabrication.
chuku·i-gutu, *n.* [tsukurigoto] A fabrication; a fake; a frame-up; a fiction.
chuku·i-gwii, *n.* [tsukurigoe] A feigned

chukuikajai

voice; a forced voice; an affected tone; a falsetto.

chuku·i-kaja·i, *n.* Decoration; ornament; adornment. Same as **kajai**.

chuku·i-kata, *n.* [tsukurikata] How to make (something); a recipe.

chuku·i-kee, *n.* [tsukurikae] 1 Remaking; renovation; reconstruction. 2 An adaptation; a parody. 3 Alteration.

chukuikee·in, *vt.* To renovate; reconstruct; remodel; revamp.

chuku·i-mujukui, *n.* Agricultural products; seasonal products.

chuku·i-mun, *n.* [tsukurimono] 1 Crops; farm produce. 2 Manufactured goods.

chuku·in, *vt.* 1 To make; create; manufacture. 2 To build; erect. 3 To till; cultivate; foster. 4 To make up; prepare.

chuku·i-wakii, *n.* [tsukuriwake] Division of a crop between landowner and tenants.

chuku·i-ware·e, *n.* [tsukuriwarai] A forced, feigned, or strained smile or laughter; a smirk.

chuku·i-yanji, *n.* A defective product; a bungle; a botch.

chukuiyan·jun, *vt.* To botch; bungle; do badly.

chuku·i-yanmee, *n.* Feigned illness.

chukuri·in, *vt.* [tsukurou] 1 To mend; repair; patch up. 2 To put cosmetics on.

chu-kusai, *n.* A set; a suit.

chu-kutuba, *n.* One word; one remark.

chukuya·a, *n.* 1 A maker; a producer; a manufacturer. 2 A farmer; a peasant.

chu-kwii, *n.* [hitokoe] One word.

chu-maa·i, *n.* [hitomawari] One girth, such as of a sash or a tree trunk.

chu-maara·shi, *n.* Difference in age of twelve years.

chu-mama, *n.* Being submissive to others; being obedient to others.

tchu-masa·i, *n.* Being superior to other people.

chu-mi, *n.* [hitome] One glance; one glimpse.

chu-michi, *n.* [hitomichi] One way; one road; cooperation under one policy.

tchu-nami, *n.* [hitonami] Average; common; like anyone else.

tchu·nu kuchi, *phr.* Common talk; a rumor; gossip.

chun-jii, *n.* [C xiangqi] A Chinese-style checker game as played in Okinawa.

tchu·nu-mun, *n.* Things that belong to others; things that are not one's own.

tchunumun-manja·a, *n.* A person who covets things that belong to others. [GSS] See **manjun**.

tchu·nu neebi, *phr.* Mimicry; imitation.

tchu·nu nuchi, *phr.* Human life; life.

chunpee, *n.* Spittle; sputum; saliva.

tchu·nu-mee, *n.* The public; company.

chura·a, *n.* [kiyora] A beauty; a belle; a pretty girl; beautiful things.

churaa·ku, *adv.* 1 Neatly; clearly; tidily. 2 Completely; thoroughly.

chura-gasa, *n.* [kiyora + kasa] Smallpox.

chura-jin, *n.* [kiyora + ginu] Pretty dress; best clothes.

chura-kaagi, *n.* [kiyora + kage] Beauty.

churakaagi·i, *n.* A beauty; a belle; a pretty girl; a good-looking woman.

chura·ku na·sun, *vt.* 1 To cleanse; purify. 2 To wash the bones of the dead. See **shinkuchi**.

chura·san, *adj.* Pretty; beautiful; fine; lovely; clean; clear; tidy.

chura-suga·i, *n.* Gala dress; dress-up.

-sun, *v.* To dress up; be finely dressed.

chura-winagu, *n.* A pretty woman; a beautiful woman.

tchusashi-iibi, *n.* [hitosashiyubi] The index finger. Also **sachi'iibi**.

chu-shikama-shigutu, *n.* Lit., a job for one laborer; a job that can be done before breakfast; an easy job. [ZRJ]

chu-tabai, *n.* One bundle.

chutee·nu hanshi, *n.* A temporary measure; a makeshift; a stopgap. Also **ichuta·nu hanshi**.

chu-tukuma, *n*. Same as **chutukuru**.
chu-tukuru, *n*. One place; one spot.
chu-tuui, *n*. [hitotoori] In a general way; in the main; briefly.
chuu, *n*. [kyoo] Today.
chuu-baa, *n*. A strong person; a person with strength. See also **yoobaa**.
chuu-byoo, *n*. [kyuubyoo] A sudden illness.
chuuchan, *adv*. Immediately; at once; right away.
chuu-chuu, *n*. *inf*. A penis.
chuu-fuu, *n*. [chuufuu] Palsy; paralysis.
chuu-goo, *n*. [choogoo] Consultation; discussion; prearrangement. **-sun**, *v*. To consult; discuss.
chuu·i, *n*. [tsuyori*] Growth; development; recovery.
chuui-bee·san, *adj*. Quick to mature; precocious; premature.
chuu·in, *vi*. [tsuyoru*] To grow strong (vigorous; stout; intense); to recover one's health.
chuui-nii·san, *adj*. Slow to mature.
chuu-jara, *n*. [chuuzara] A medium-size plate. See also **sara**[1].
chuuji[1], *n*. [kyuuji] A waiter; a waitress.
chuuji[2], *n*. [tsuuji] Evacuation of the bowels.
chuu-juu·ku, *adv*. [tsuyotsuyo*] Strong; tight; severe.
chuu-kaa, *n*. A teapot. Same as **chajuu-kaa**.
chuu·ku, *adv*. [tsuyoku] Strongly; powerfully; firmly.
chuuma·in, *vi*. To strengthen itself; intensify itself.
chuumi·in, *vt*. To strengthen; invigorate; intensify.
chuu-mun[1], *n*. [kyoomon] A Buddhist scripture; a sutra; prayers.
chuu-mun[2], *n*. [chuumon] An order; a commission. **-sun**, *v*. To order (an article).
chu·un, *vi. irreg*. [kuun, chan] To come; show up. See also **'njuchun, ichun**,

chichun[3], **tuduchun, menseen**.
chuu·san, *adj*. Strong; powerful; vigorous; serious (illness); violent (words).
chuu-tinshi, *n*. A lark; a skylark.
chu-yaa, *n*. 1 One house. 2 The same house. 3 One family; one household.
chuyaa-ninju, *n*. Members of one household.
chu-yumi, *n*. One yumi, or 80 threads, a term to indicate the fineness or coarseness of a textile. See **yumi**[3].
chu-yuru, *n*. One evening; one night; through the night.
chuu-yuru, *n*. Tonight; this evening.
chu-wakasa·a, *n*. One *sho* liquid measuring jar. See also **nananukuhin, nakajichi, ichinukuhin, mihautuu, ichigoonuu, gushaakuu**.

D———

daa, *interj*. An expression used when making an inquiry or a request. Hey! Say!
daa-gu, *n*. [dango] Dumplings.
daa-guu, *n*. Same as **daagu**. [GSS]
daa-naa, *interj*. Oh, no!
dabi, *n*. [Pali jhâpeta] A funeral. [OBJ, ODJ] See **gan**[1], **tingee, nimbuchaa, shinkuchi**. Also **uukui**. See also **yanajini, shuukaawatai wugami, gusoojitaku**.
dabi-doogu, *n*. Funeral paraphernalia and trappings.
dabi-'waa, *n*. A funeral pig. [OBJ]
dabi-yaa, *n*. A family holding a funeral.
dabu-dabu·u, *n. onom*. Being baggy; puffy; loose.
dachi, *n*. [rachi] 1 Limits; bounds. 2 Progress. Also **rachi**.
da·chi-bin, *n*. Lit., a hugging bottle; an Okinawan-style pottery liquor canteen.
dachi-gachi, *n*. [takegaki] Same as **dakigachi**. See also **kachi**[2].

dachikagu

dachi-kagu, *n.* A bamboo litter used for bedding during summer.
da·chun, *vt.* [daku] To hold in one's arms; embrace; hug.
da·i-mun, *n.* A languid person; a lethargic person; a useless person.
da·in, *vi.* To grow listless; be lethargic; be weary of; flag; drag; languish.
dajaku, *n.* [dajaku] Effeminacy; laziness; indolence. **·na**, *adj.* Effeminate; lazy; indolent.
daki, *n.* [take] Bamboo [Bambusoideae]. [FOSR, ODJ] Also **chinbukudaki, kusandaki, ubidaki, njadaki; karataki, shimaraki, maataku, Yanbarudaki, chinibu**.
daki-boochi, *n.* [take-booki] A broom made of Ryukyu bamboo for outdoor use. See **hoochi**.
daki-buchi, *n.* Roof thatched with small bamboos.
daki-dana·a, *n.* A float of *moosoo* bamboo tied to both sides of a **sabani** boat for additional buoyancy and stability when the boat is in the open sea or carries a heavy load. Also **sagidaki**. See **sabani**.
daki-gaa-saba, *n.* Bamboo-sheath sandals.
daki-gachi, *n.* [take-gaki] A bamboo fence (usually made of **Yanbarudaki** bamboo). Also **dachigachi**. See also **kachi**[2].
daki-jiifaa, *n.* A hairpin made of bamboo used by women during mourning.
daki-kuji, *n.* [take-kugi] A bamboo peg.
daki·n-chibu, *n.* A jar made of bamboo.
daki·nu-kaa, *n.* A bamboo sheath.
daki·nu-kkwa, *n.* [takenoko] A bamboo shoot.
daki·nu-mii-ngwa, *n.* Same as **yamanashingwa**.
daki-uubi, *n.* A bamboo hoop. See also **kani'uubi**.
daki-yuka, *n.* Floor made of bamboo.
daku, *n., adj.* Same as **raku**.

daku-daku, *adv. onom.* Pit-a-pat.
dakumi·chun, *vi.* [dakumeku] To flutter.
dama·in, *vi.* [damaru] To become silent; close one's lips; shut up.
dama·sun, *vt.* [damasu] To deceive; cheat; swindle; trick; hoax; dupe; fool.
dan, *n.* [dan] **1** A step; a stair. **2** A grade; a rank.
dandan, *n.* **·nu**, *adj.* Great; exceeding; awful.
dan-gasa, *n.* (Western-style) umbrella; a parasol. Also **rangasa**.
danju, *adv.* Indeed; really; certainly.
danjuka, *adv.* Indeed; really. Same as **danju**.
dan-pachi, *n.* [danpatsu] A haircut. Also **ranpachi**.
danpachi-yaa, *n.* A barbershop. Also **ranpachiyaa**.
danpu, *n.* [E lamp] A lamp. Also **ranpu**.
danpu-anda, *n.* [ranpu + abura] Same as **shichiyu**. See also **shichitan-yuu**.
dara·a, *n.* A languid person; a lackadaisical person; a slouch. See **Shuidaraa**.
darį-yami, *n.* An evening drink; *sake* drink accompanying dinner; a nightcap.
darumi, *n.* A joint (of the body); an articulation.
daru·san, *adj.* Languid; tired; dull.
daru·u, *n.* A languid person. Same as **daraa, dayaa**.
dashi, *n.* [dashi] Broth; stock; sauce.
dashicha, *n.* A **dashicha** tree [*Randia canthioides* Champ.]. [FOSR] Also **dashika**.
dashi-iyu-gwaa, *n.* Dried small sardines, used to prepare stock.
dashika, *n.* Same as **dashicha**.
datchoo, *n.* [rakkyoo] A scallion [*Allium bakeri* Regel Rakkyo]. [FOSR]; pickled scallions. Also **ratchoo**.
dateen, *adj.* Large; big.
daya·a, *n.* A languid person. Same as **daimun, daraa, daruu**.
dee[1], *n.* [dai] A subject; a theme; a topic;

a title.
dee², *n.* [dai] A stand; a rest; a pedestal; a table; a mount.
dee³, *n.* [dai] A generation; an era.
dee⁴, *n.* [dai] A price; a charge; a rate; a fee.
deebi·ru, *v. cop. formal* [< **du** + **yayabiru**] Copular verb: am, are, is.
dee-chiree, *n.* [daikirai] 1 A strict taboo; a forbidden thing. 2 A poison.
dee-daka·a, *n.* An expensive thing. See **takasan**.
deefaa, *n.* An earthenware mortar. Also **shirihachi**.
dee-ichi, *n.* [daiichi] The first; the foremost thing to do; number one.
dee-ji, *n.* [daiji] A serious matter; a grave matter.
dee-ju, *n.* A kitchen. Also **shimu¹**, **tungwa**.
dee-ku, *n.* [daiku] A master carpenter; a chief carpenter.
dee-kuni, *n.* A radish [J daikon; *Raphamus sativus* L. var. *sativus*].
deekuni-shirii, *n.* A radish grater. Also **shirii**.
dee-myoo, *n.* **Deemyoo** bamboo [*Arundinaria hindsii*]. [FOSR]
dee-ri, *n.* [dairi] A proxy; a deputy; an agency; representation.
dee-yashi·i, *n.* [dai + yasu] A low-priced item; an inexpensive item. See **deedakaa**, **yassan**.
dii¹, *interj.* Come on; come now; well now.
dii², *n.* [ri] Same as **rii²**.
dii-gu, *n.* [deigo] Thorny paulownia [*Erythrina variegata* L. var. *orientalis* Merr.]; India coral bean. [FOSR, ODJ]
dii-jin, *n.* [reizen] Same as **riijin**.
dii sai, *interj. phr.* An expression denoting an urge to collective action used by male speakers. If you please; shall we…?, etc.
dii tai, *interj. phr.* Equivalent of **dii sai**, but used by a female speakers.

du

dika·shi, *n.* [< **dikasun**] Success; achievement.
dika·sun, *vi.* [dekasu] To succeed; work out well; prosper; be successful.
diki·in, *vi.* [dekiru] 1 To do well; be good at; be proficient in; be versed in. 2 To grow well; be produced. 3 To work out well; succeed; finish well
dikiran-nu·u, *n.* An inferior student.
diki·toon, *adj.* Be abundant (harvest); rich (harvest). Also **yukatoon**, **yukatuun**. [GSS]
dikiya·a, *n.* An excellent student; a genius; a prodigy.
dikka, *interj.* Expression denoting an urge to collective action. Let us…. See **dii sai**, **dii tai**.
din, *n.* Same as **rin**.
dincha·a, *n.* Same as **rinchaa**.
dinchi, *n.* [rinki] Same as **rinchi**.
din-gan, *n.* Same as **ringan**.
din-gun, *n.* [dengon] A message; word.
dip-pa, *n.* [rippa] Same as **rippa**.
dip-puku, *n.* [rippuku] Same as **rippuku**.
dis-shin, *n.* [risshin] Same as **risshin**.
-sun, *v.* Same as **risshin-sun**.
don, *n. onom.* Sound of a drum, gun, or one thing bumping against another.
doo¹, *n.* [roo] Same as **roo**.
doo², *part. emph.* As sentence-final particle, indicates a slight emphasis or calls the attention of the listener.
doo-chuu, *n.* [doochuu] A journey; a travel; a tour.
doodin, *adv.* Somehow or other; if you please.
doo-gu, *n.* [doogu] 1 A tool; an instrument. 2 Furniture. 3 Utensils. 4 A means; a tool; a stepping-stone.
doo-ma, *n.* Same as **rooma**.
doo-ri, *n.* [doori] Reason; nature of things.
doo-yi, *part.* Indicates emphasis, especially shouting. See also **doo²**.
du, *part.* Indicates emphasis on word to

duchun

which it attaches. Also **ru**.
du·chun, *vi*. [doku] To get out of the way; move aside; vacate.
du-gee·in, *vi*. [< **duu** + **kee·in**] To fall down; tumble down.
du-gwai, *n*. **1** An aloe. **2** A century plant. See **rugwai**.
du-jin, *n*. [< **duu** + **chin**³] A short undershirt worn over a singlet in formal dress in the premodern period.
duka·sun, *vt*. [dokasu] To remove; move away; get (something) out of the way.
duki·in, *vt*. To remove; move away.
duki-na·in, *vi*. To avoid; step aside.
duki-na·sun, *vt*. To remove; move (something) away; eject.
duku¹, *n*. [doku] **1** Poison; poisonous substance; venom. **2** Harm; injury; virus; malice; spite.
duku², *adv*. Very; excessively, usually in a negative sense.
duku³, *n*. Same as **ruku**.
duku-gee·shi, *n*. [dokugaeshi] An antidote; a counterpoison; an antitoxin.
duku-gusui, *n*. Poison; a poisonous drug.
duku-gwachi, *n*. Same as **rukugwachi**.
du-mangwa·sun, *vt*. Emphatic form of **mangwasun**; to confuse; throw into confusion.
du-mangwi·in, *vi*. [domagureru*] Emphatic form of **mangwiin**; to become confused; be thrown into confusion; be upset; be flurried; lose one's head; be demoralized.
dunbui, *n*. [donburi] A large porcelain bowl. Also **dunburi**.
dunna-mun, *n*. A dull person; a dense person.
dunna·san, *adj*. Dull; dense; obtuse; stolid.
dunsu, *n*. [donsu] Silk damask; satin damask.
dura-gani, *n*. [doragane] A gong.
duru, *n*. [doro] **1** Mud; mire; dirt. **2** Disgrace; dishonor.

duru-bisa, *n*. Muddy feet; muddy shoes. See **fisa**.
duru-buttaa, *n*. Being covered with mud; getting muddy.
duru-duru, *n*. [dorodoro] Muddiness; sloppiness; mushiness.
duru-gwettai, *n*. A muddy place; a quagmire.
duru-michi, *n*. [doromichi] A muddy road.
duru-miji, *n*. [doromizu] Muddy water.
duru-mutaan, *n*. Playing with mud.
dushi, *n*. [dooshi, doshi*] A friend; a companion.
dushi-biree, *n*. Friendly relations; companionship. See **fireein**.
duttu, *adv*. Very; too; by far.
duu, *n*. [doo] The body; self; one's own body. See **chiburu, mimi, kubi, mii**¹, **hana**³, **kuchi**², **kakuji, tii**¹, **udi, kata**³, **nni**⁴, **chii**⁶, **chii**⁷, **wata**³, **fusu, kushi**¹, **mumu**², **karaji, kii**², **chira, mukoo, mayu, mayugi, kumikan, fuu**¹, **fuujira, utugee, fijigee, nniguchi, tani, kuuga, hoo, nagani, kushinagani, chibi, hisa, chinshi, shini, kunda, adu, gufushi, 'waashiba, shichashiba, hashishi, haa**¹, **shiba, nuudii, nuudii'waagwaa, iibi, ufu'iibi, tchusashi'iibi, naka'iibi, narashi, narashi'iibi, iibingwaa, chimi**.
duu-agachi, *n*. Self-support; earning one's own way.
duu-agami, *n*. Self-importance; conceit; snobbery; boast.
duu-bumi·i, *n*. Pride; boast; self-praise; vanity; flattering oneself. See **fumiin**.
duu-buni, *n*. (Human) bones.
duu-chui, *n*. Alone; by oneself; solitude.
duuchui-gurashi, *n*. Same as **chuigurashi**.
duuchui-mun, *n*. An unmarried person; a bachelor; a spinster.
duuchui-munu-i·i, *n*. Talking to oneself; a soliloquy; a monologue.
duuchui-ware·e, *n*. Smiling or laughing

to oneself. See **katti**[1].
duu-gatti, *n.* Arbitrariness; selfishness; egoism; egotism.
duu-guri·s(h)an, *adj.* **1** (When causing trouble to others) painful; regrettable; shameful. **2** Hard; difficult.
duu-jiru, *n.* Lit., own juice; the juice or liquid that comes out of vegetables when cooked (in contrast to liquid that is added). See **shiru**.
duu-kange·e, *n.* Arbitrary decision; dogmatism.
duu-kuru, *adv.* Oneself; in person.
duu-makane·e, *n.* Self-support; providing for oneself.
duu-mu·chi, *n.* One's own.
duu-naa, *n.* Oneself; themselves; ourselves.
duunaa-kuru, *adv.* By oneself; by itself; by yourself; by themselves.
duunii, *n.* Groaning; moaning.
duu-shiru, *n.* **1** Betrothal gift money sent by the bridegroom's family to the bride's family; bride price. **2** The price of a girl sold into prostitution.
duu-tee, *n.* [dootai] The body; the torso; the trunk.
duu-uyame·e, *n.* Self-respect.
duu-u·i, *n.* Selling oneself into bondage.
-sun, *v.* To sell oneself into bondage.
duu-yafara·san, *adj.* Weak in body; sickly.
duu-yas·san, *adj.* [...shi·ku] Easy; facile; plain; comfortable.
duuyashi·i, *n.* Things that are easy to do; simple things.
duuyashi-mun, *n.* An easy thing to do.
duu-yashit·teen, *adv.* Easily; with comfort.

E———

ee[1], *interj.* Hey; say. Used in calling someone of equal or lower status than the speaker. See **ee sai**, **ee tai**.

ee[2], *n.* [ai] **1** Indigo dye. **2** Indigo plant. See also **eechibu**, **ee'iru**, **eenuhana**.
ee-chibu, *n.* [ai-tsubo] Indigo vat. See also **ee**[2], **ee'iru**, **eenuhana**.
ee-choodee, *n.* Same as **eejenda**.
eeda, [aida] **1** *n.* Interval; space. **2** *adv.* During; while; between. See **eeja**.
ee-gasa, *n.* A boil; an eruption; rash. [UKH] See **eein**[2], **kasa**[2].
ee-gata, *n.* [aigata] **1** Indigo-stenciled textile design of Okinawa. **2** Okinawan fabric with indigo stenciled design. See **katachiki**.
ee·in[1], *vt.* [aeru] To dress food with condiments.
ee·in[2], *vi.* To fester; ulcerate.
ee-iru, *n.* [ai-iro] Indigo color; deep blue. See also **ee**[2], **eechibu**, **eenuhana**.
eeja, *n.* [aida] An interval; space; a gap. Same as **eeda**.
ee-jaa, *n.* A lizard. Also **oodoo**, **andachaa**. [GSS]
eeja-gachi, *n.* A linear annotation or note in between lines.
eejenda, *n.* Sisters-in-law whose husbands are brothers. Also **eechoodee**. [UKH]
eeji, *n.* [aizu] A signal; a sign; a call.
eeju, *n.* A colleague; a companion; an associate; a fellow worker. Also **eejuu**.
ee-jumi·i, *n.* [ai-zome] **1** Dying in indigo. **2** Things dyed in indigo.
eejuu, *n.* Same as **eeju**.
eeka, *n.* A relative; a relation; kinfolk; one's family circle. Also **'weeka**.
eeka-harooji, *n.* Relatives; clan.
eeka·nu-chaa, *n.* Plural of **'weeka**.
eeki, *n.* **1** Richness; wealth; a fortune; opulence; affluence. **2** Member of the landed rich in rural areas. Also **'weeki**.
eeki-gumasa, *n.* A rich miser. Also **'weekigumasa**.
eeki·i, *n.* A rich person; a wealthy person. Also **'weekii**. Same as **eekinchu**.
eeki-nchu, *n.* A rich person; a wealthy person. Also **'weekinchu**.

eeku

eeku¹, *n.* An oar; a paddle; a scull. Also **'weeku**.
eeku², *n.* A deformed child with some resemblance to an animal.
eema¹, *n.* A distance; an interval; a space; a period. Also **'weema**.
Eema², *n.* Yaeyama Islands, the southernmost island group in the Ryukyus. Also **Yeema**.
Eema·a, *n. pej.* A person of the Yaeyama Islands. Also **Yeemaa**.
Eema-nchu, *n.* A person of the Yaeyama Islands. Also **Yeemanchu**.
ee·nu-hana, *n.* Bubbles that appear on the surface of indigo dye. See also **ee²**.
ee-nujumi, *n.* Mutual love.
ee-sachi, *n.* [aisatsu] Greeting; civilities; salutations. **-sun**, *v.* To greet; exchange civilities.
ee sai, *interj.* Hey, say. Used by male speakers. See **ee¹**.
ee-soo¹, *n.* [aisoo] Civility; affability; courtesy; sociability; compliments; hospitality.
ee-soo², *n.* [aishoo] Compatibility; congeniality; affinity.
eesoo-mu·chi, *n.* An affable person; a sociable person.
ee-sumi-yaa, *n.* An indigo dye house.
ee·sun¹, *vt.* To give (to a superior); present; offer. [UKH]
ee·sun², *vt.* To press out the pus; extract the milk; let the matter out. [UKH]
ee tai, *interj.* Hey, say. Used by female speakers. See **ee¹**.
ee-ti, *n.* [aite] A mate; a companion; a partner.
eeti-guchi, *n.* For two parties to be unyielding in an argument. **-sun**, *v.* To keep arguing in unyielding spirit. [UKH]
Eigo, *n.* [Eigo] English; the English language. Also **Yeigo**.
eisaa, *n.* A group *Bon* dance performed by the men and women in the villages of Okinawa and the offshore islands.
Also **yeisaa**. See also **bun⁴**.
eetuu, *n.* **1** A partner. **2** An opponent.
eeya·a, *n.* A vegetable salad. [GSS]

F———

faa, *n.* [ha] A leaf, a needle; a blade; a frond; foliage.
faa-fuji, *n.* Grandparents.
faafuu, *n.* [hafu] **1** A house with a gable roof. Also **faafuuyaa**. **2** A tomb with a gable roof.
faafuu-yaa, *n.* Same as **faafuu** (1).
faa-gusari, *n.* Rice that is completely scorched and burned black. See **nanjichi**.
faagusari-mun, *n.* Same as **faagusari**.
faa-ishigwee, *n.* A hoe for pebbly soil. See **ishigwee**.
faa-ukoo, *n.* Same as **hira'ukoo**.
faa-uri, *n.* A coral reef; a cay.
fana-u·i, *n.* [hanauri] Same as **hana'ui¹**. [GSS]
fan-jiri, *n.* Same as **hanjiri**. [GSS]
faru-kai-chiyaa, *n.* Same as **harukaichiyaa**. [GSS]
fa-uta, *n.* [hauta] A popular song; a ballad; a ditty.
fee¹, *n.* [hai] Ashes. Also **hee¹**.
fee², *n.* [hae] A fly. Also **hee²**.
fee³, *n.* [hae*] **1** The south. **2** A southerly wind.
fee-fee-sun, *v.* To pant; gasp (for breath); be out of breath. See also **iichi**.
fee-gasa, *n.* Same as **heegasa**.
fee-gattin, *n.* [hayagatten] A hasty conclusion; a premature judgment. Also **heegattin**.
fee·i¹, *n.* [hayari] Fashion; fad; vogue; popularity. Also **heei**.
feei², *n.* Vinegar. Also **amajaki**, **shii⁴**.
fee·i-juu·san, *adj.* Precocious; premature.
fee·i-kutuba, *n.* [hayari + kotoba] A popular expression; a word in fashion.

Also **heeikutuba**.
fee·in, *vi.* [hayaru] To be in fashion; be in vogue; be popular; come into wide use; spread widely. Also **heein**.
fee-iru, *n.* [hai-iro] The color of ashes; the color gray.
fee·i-uta, *n.* [hayari-uta] A popular song; a ditty.
fee-jara, *n.* [haizara] An ashtray. Also **heejara**.
fee-juri, *n.* A streetwalker; an unlicensed prostitute. See **juri**.
feejuri-ngwa, *n.* Same as **yamanashingwa**. Also **heejuringwa**.
fee-juui, *n.* Precocity; early maturity. See **chuui**.
fee-kaji, *n.* [hae* + kaze] A monsoon wind from the south in summer. See also **kaji**[1].
fee·ku, *adv.* [hayaku] 1 Quick; fast. 2 Early; before; soon. See **heeku**.
fee-maa·i, *n.* [hae* + mawari] A change in the direction of the wind typical of winter in which the wind begins to blow from the south. See also **kaji**[1].
fee-maa·shi, *n.* Premature death; untimely death.
fee-niibichi, *n.* An early marriage; marriage at an early age.
fee-nkee, *n.* [hae* + mukai] A southern exposure; facing the south.
fee-'nmara·a, *n.* One who is born in the early months of the year (i.e., January to March).
fee-'nmari, *n.* Early birth, referring to births in the months of January to March.
fee·nu-kusu, *n.* Freckles; flecks.
fee-ree, *n.* [C beilai] A holdup; a stick-up; highway robbery.
fee·san, *adj.* [hayai] 1 Quick; fast; swift; speedy; rapid. 2 Early; soon. See also **heesan**.
feeshi, *n.* [hayashi] Vocal accompaniment to music.
fee·sun, *vt.* 1 To re-dye; heighten the color. 2 To polish; sharpen. 3 To supply vocal accompaniment to music.
fee-uki, *n.* [hayaoki] Early rising.
fensa, *n.* [hayabusa] A peregrine falcon.
fi-bachi, *n.* [hibachi] A brazier; a firebox. Also **hibachi**.
fi-bana, *n.* [hibana] A spark. Also **hibana**.
fibari, *n.* [hibiware] 1 Chapping (of skin). 2 A crack; a fissure.
fibi·chi, *n.* [hibiki] A sound; a noise; a peal. Also **hibichi**.
fibi·chun, *vi.* [hibiku] 1 To sound; resound; ring. 2 To echo; vibrate; affect. Also **hibichun**.
fi-bu, *n.* [hibu] Daily rate of interest. Also **hibu**.
fi-bu·shi, *n.* [hiboshi] That which is sundried. Also **hibushi**.
fichaa·in, *vi.* [·(r)an, ·ti; hikiau] (For a business) to pay; be profitable; not lose.
fichaa·sun, *vt.* [hikiawasu] 1 To introduce; bring together. 2 To check one against the other; collate. Also **hichaasun**.
ficha·i, *n.* [hikari] 1 Light; rays (of light); a beam; a flash; a glare; a gleam; a twinkle. 2 Gleam; luster; gloss; glaze. Also **hichai**.
ficha·in, *vi.* [hikaru] 1 To shine; be bright; be brilliant; be luminous; glitter; glimmer; flash; twinkle. 2 To luster; be glossy; be lustrous; be shiny. Also **hichain**.
fichee, *n.* [hitai] The forehead; the brow. Also **mukoo**.
fichi[1], *n.* [hiki] 1 A contact; good offices; connections. 2 Broadly, relatives. See also **munchuu**. 3 Help; assistance. See also **hichi**.
fichi[2], *n.* Same as **shichi**[6].
fichi-agi·in, *vt.* [hikiageru] 1 To pull up; raise up. 2 To promote. 3 To withdraw.
fichi-ati, *n.* [hikiate] Check; verification; collation; tally; comparison.

fichichiji

fichi-chi·ji, *n.* [hikitsugi] Taking over (another's duties); handing over (one's duties); succession (to); transfer of control.
fichi-chi·jun, *vt.* [hikitsugu] To take over (another's duties); inherit; succeed to.
fichi-du, *n.* [hikido] A sliding window; a push-up window. Also **hichidu**.
fichi-hana·sun, *vt.* [hikihanasu] **1** To draw apart; pull apart; separate; cut asunder. **2** To outdistance (in a footrace); run ahead (of others). Also **hichihanasun**.
fichi-jashi, *n.* [hikidashi] A drawer.
fichi-mun, *n.* [hikimono] Turnery; a turned article; lathe work. Also **hichimun**.
fichimun-jeeku, *n.* [hikimono + saiku] A turner; a lathe operator. Also **hichimunjeeku**. See **seeku**.
fi·chi-na·in, *vi.* To retire; withdraw; leave; bow out.
fichi-'nmaga, *n.* A great-great-grandchild. Also **hichi'nmaga**.
fi·chi-nuba·sun, *vt.* [hikinobasu] To draw out; prolong; extend; expand.
fi·chi-sa·chun, *vt.* [hikisaku] To tear off; rip up; split; rend.
fi·chi-ta·chun, *vi.* [·tan, ·tchi; hikitatsu] To become animated; set off; look to advantage. Also **hichitachun**.
fi·chi-tati·in, *vt.* [hikitateru] To favor; patronize; support; promote.
fi·chi-uki·in, *vt.* [hikiukeru] **1** To be responsible; answer for; shoulder another's debt. **2** To undertake; take upon oneself; take charge of; consent to. **3** To guarantee; vouch for. Also **hichi'ukiin**.
fi·chi-yushi·in, *vt.* [hikiyoseru] To draw (a thing) near (towards) one; pull nearer; drag in; attract.
fi·chun[1], *vt.* [hiku] Same as **hichun**[1].
fi·chun[2], *vt.* [hiku] Same as **hichun**[2].
fi-dati, *n.* [hedate] Same as **hidati**.
fidati·in, *vt.* Same as **hidatiin**.

fi-dui, *n.* [hidori] Same as **hidui**.
fi-gara, *n.* [higara] Same as **higara**.
fi-gasa, *n.* [higasa] Same as **higasa**.
fi-gataka, *n.* Same as **higataka**.
fi-gwashi, *n.* Same as **higwashi**.
fii[1], *n.* [he] Same as **hii**[1].
fii[2], *n.* [hi] Same as **hii**[2].
fii[3], *n.* [hi] Same as **hii**[3].
fii[4], *n.* [hi] **1** The day; the sun; the sunshine. **2** Daytime. Also **hii**[4], **tiida**.
fii[5], *n.* [he*, hesaki] The stem of a ship; the bow of a boat. See **sabani**.
fii[6], *n.* [hi] The stomach and intestines; the stomach and bowels.
fii-baashi, *n.* [hibashi] Same as **hiibaashi**.
fii-chaasa·a, *n.* A firefighter. See **chaasun**.
fii-chi, *n.* [hiiki] Same as **hiichi**.
fii-chin, *n.* [fuikin*, fukin] Same as **hiichin**.
fii-dama, *n.* Same as **hiidama**.
fii-fira·a, *n.* A person who farts often; a person who is flatulent. See **fiin**.
fii-fu·chi, *n.* [hifuki] A bamboo pipe about 25 cm (10 in.) long used for blowing on a charcoal or wood fire; a bamboo blow pipe. Also **hiifuchi**, **hiifuchaa**, **hiifukaa**.
fii-gachi, *n.* [higaki*] A wooden board fence. See also **kachi**[2].
fiijaa[1], *n.* Same as **hiijaa**[1].
fiijaa[2], *n.* [higawa] Same as **hiijaa**[2].
fiijaa-gaa, *n.* An artesian well. [UKH]
fiijii, *n.* [heizei] (The) usual; habitual; ordinary; everyday. Also **hiijii**.
fiijira, *n.* A cheek. Same as **fuujira**, **fuu**[1].
fii-jiri, *n.* Same as **hiijiri**.
fii-kushi, *n.* Same as **hiikushi**.
fi·in, *vt.* [heru] Same as **hiin**[2]. See also **fii**[1], **hii**[1].
fiira, *n.* [hera] Same as **hiira**.
fiiraa, *n.* Same as **hiiraa**.
fiira·chun, *vi.* [hibiraku] Same as **hiirachun**.
fiisa-magai, *n.* A person who shrinks

from the cold.
fii·san, *adj.* Same as **hiisan**.
fiisa-umi·i, *n.* Same as **hiisa'umii**.
fiitaa, *n.* A winter coat, usually lined or padded with cotton, used by both men and women. Also **hiitaa**.
fii-tati·i, *n.* Same as **hiitatii**.
fii-teechikiya·a, *n.* Kindling; kindling wood; a (fire) lighter.
fiitu, *n.* Same as **hiitu**.
fijai, *n.* [hidari] Same as **hijai**[2].
fijai-migui, *n.* [hidari + meguri] 1 Counterclockwise. 2 Adversity; downward course. Also **hijaimigui**.
fijai-nuudii, *n.* Same as **hijainuudii**.
fijami, *n.* Same as **hijami**.
fijami·in, *vt.* Same as **hijamiin**.
fija-ru·u, *n.* Same as **hijaruu**.
fija·yaa, *n.* Same as **hijayaa, hijaigatti**.
fijichi, *n.* A shuttle (of a loom); a device in a loom for passing the woof thread between the warp threads.
fiji-gee, *n.* [hiji] Same as **hijigee**.
fiji-moo, *n.* Same as **hijimoo**.
fijui, *n.* Same as **hijui**.
fiju·in, *vi.* Same as **hijuin**.
fi·jun, *vt.* [hegu] Same as **hijun**.
fijuru-ashi, *n.* Same as **hijuru'ashi**.
fijuru-kaji, *n.* Same as **hijurukaji**.
fijuru·san, *adj.* Same as **hijurusan**.
fijuru·u, *n.* Same as **hijuruu**.
fijut·teen, *adv.* Same as **hijutteen**.
fi-kaji, *n.* [hikazu] Same as **hikaji**.
fikari, *n.* [hikari] Same as **hikari** (1). See also **fichai, hichai**.
fikasari·in, *vi.* [·ran, ·tti; hikasareru] Same as **hikasariin**.
fikee, *n.* [hikae] Same as **hikee**.
fikee·in, *vt.* [hikaeru] Same **hikeein**.
fikkumi·in, *vt.* [hikkomeru] Same as **hikkumiin**.
fikku·mun, *vi.* [hikkomu] Same as **hikkumun**.
fiku·san, *adj.* [hikui] Same as **hikusan**.
fima-daari, *n.* Same as **himadaari**.
fimicha·a, *n.* An asthmatic.

fimichi, *n.* Asthma. Also **shimichi**.
fimun, *n.* [himon] Same as **himun**.
fin, *n.* [hen] Strange; suspicious-looking; odd; queer. See also **finsun**.
findani-'nma, *n.* Same as **finjani'nma**.
fin-bin, *n.* [henben] Repayment; redemption; refundment. Also **hinbin**.
finjani-'nma, *n.* An untamed horse.
fin-sun, *v.* See also **fin**. Same as **hinsun**.
fin-suu, *n.* Same as **hinsuu**.
finsuu-mun, *n.* Same as **hinsuumun**.
fintoo, *n.* [hentoo] Same as **hintoo**.
fi·nu-kan, *n.* [hinokami] Same as **hinu-·kan**.
fira, *n.* [hira*] Same as **hira**[2].
fira·chun, *vt.* [hiraku] Same as **hirachun**.
firafa-gusa, *n.* Same as **hirafagusa**.
fira·in, *vi.* [·(r)an, ·ti] Same as **hirain**.
firaki·in, *vi.* Same as **hirakiin**[1].
firaku·mun, *vi.* Same as **hirakumun**.
fira·san, *adj.* Same as **hirasan**.
fire·e, *n.* Same as **hiree**. See also **hirain**.
firee-guri·i, *n.* A person who is hard to get along with.
firee-guri·s(h)an, *adj.* Difficult to get along with.
firee·in, *vt.* To go with; get along with; keep company with; associate with.
firee-yashi·i, *n.* A good mixer; a jolly fellow; a person who gets along well with others.
fireeyas·san, *adj.* Same as **hireeyassan**.
firi[1], *n.* [heri] Same as **hiri**.
firi[2], *n.* [heri] Decrease; wear; loss.
firu[1], *n.* [hiru] Same as **hiru**[1].
firu[2], *n.* [hiru*] Same as **hiru**[2].
firu[3], *n.* [hiro] Same as **hiru**[3].
firu-biruu, *adv.* [hirobiro] Extensive; open; wide; spacious; commodious.
firuga·i, *n.* [hirogari] Same as **hirugai**.
firuga·in, *vi.* [hirogaru] Same as **hirugain**.
firugi·in, *vt.* [hirogeru] Same as **hirugiin**.
firuma, *n.* [hiruma] Same as **firu**[1].

firumas(h)an

firuma·s(h)an, *adj.* Same as **hirumas(h)an**.
firu·sa, *n.* [hirosa] Same as **hirusa**.
firu·san, *adj.* [hiroi] Same as **hirusan**.
fi-ruu, *n.* [hiroo] Same as **hiruu**. **-sun**, *v.* Same as **hiruusun**.
fisa, *n.* [hiza] Same as **hisa**.
fisa-kata, *n.* Same as **hisakata**.
fisa-kubi, *n.* Same as **hisakubi**.
fisa-manchi, *n.* Same as **hisamanchi**. **-sun**, *v.* Same as **hisamanchisun**.
fisa-moo, *n.* Same as **hisamoo**.
fisa-naa, *n.* Same as **hisanaa**.
fisa·nu-wata, *n.* Same as **hisanuwata**.
fishi, *n.* Same as **hishi**.
fishi·i, *n.* That which is thin and scanty.
fis·san, *adj.* [...shiku] Same as **hissan**[1].
fita, *n.* [heta] Same as **hita**.
fita·ni, *adv.* Same as **hitani**.
fitchi·in, *vt.* [·ran, ·tchi; hikikiru] To tear off; cut off.
fitchii-baru, *n.* Same as **hitchiibaru**.
fiyoo, *n.* [hiyoo] Same as **hiyoo**.
fu-bashira, *n.* A mast.
fu-bin, *n.* [fuben] Inconvenience; inexpediency. **·na**, *adj.* Inconvenient; unwieldy; unhandy.
fuchaa·in, *vi.* To thrive; grow thick; grow dense; be rampant.
fuchagi, *n.* Rectangular-shaped steamed rice cake with beans on top.
fucha·toon, *adj.* Prosperous; thriving. [UKH]
fuchi, *n.* [fuchi] A cliff; a precipice.
fuchi-banta, *n.* A steep cliff; a precipitous cliff. See **hanta**[1].
fu·chi-chaa·sun, *vt.* [fukikesu] To blow out (a candle or a fire with the mouth).
fu-chigoo, *n.* [futsugoo] Inconvenience; trouble; wrong; impropriety.
fuchi-kee·sun, *vt.* [fukikaesu] **1** (For wind) to blow over. **2** To revive from (a swoon); catch one's breath.
fuchi-ku·mun, *vi.* [fukikomu] Same as **fuchinchun**.
fuchi-n·chun, *vi.* For rain to fall indoors.
Also **fuchikumun, uchi'amisun**.
fuchi-tuba·sun, *vt.* To blow away.
fuchi-yuu, *n.* Boiling water.
fuchukuru, *n.* [futokoro] **1** The bosom. **2** One's pocket; one's purse.
fu·chun[1], *vi.* [fuku] **1** (For wind) to blow. **2** To snore.
fu·chun[2], *vt.* [fuku] **1** To blow (with one's mouth); breathe. **2** To pant for air. **3** To smoke (tobacco). **4** To play (any wind instrument such as a flute, a harmonica, or a bugle).
fu·chun[3], *vi.* [fuku] To boil, come to a boil. See also **fukasun**[1], **wachun**[2], **wakasun**[2].
fu·chun[4], *vt.* [fuku] To cover (a roof); thatch; tile over.
fuda, *n.* [fuda] **1** A tag; a card; a label. **2** A charm. **3** A bid; a ballot.
fudi, *n.* [fude] A writing brush.
fudi-chira·a, *n.* A variant of **sudichiraa**. [GSS]
fudii, *n.* [hoteri] A flash of lightning.
fu-diki, *n.* [fudeki] **1** A poor crop. **2** Failure; bungle; botch.
fudu, *n.* [hodo] Personal height; physique; stature.
fuduchi, *n.* A reed; a device on a loom by means of which the warp is adjusted and the threads of the woof are drawn between the threads of the warp. [OGJ] See also **yumi**[3].
fudu-fudu, *n.* Pubescent age; marriageable age.
fudu-guma·a, *n.* A small person; a shorty. See **gumasan**.
fudu-gu·u, *n.* Same as **fudugumaa**.
fudu-guu·san, *adj.* Small in physique.
fudu-magi·i, *n.* A big (or tall) person.
fuduu·nu-kami, *n.* [< fudoo, Skt Acala, the God of Fire] A toilet deity.
fudu-'waa·sun, *vt.* To raise; make grow.
fudu-'wi·in, *vi.* To grow in stature; grow tall; grow big.
fugan, *n.* [hogami*] The lower belly close to the vagina. [UKH]

fuga·sun, *vt*. [hogasu*] **1** To bore; dig (a hole) through. **2** To embezzle.
fu-gattin, *n*. [fu- + ga(t)ten] Dissent; objection; refusal.
fugi, *n*. [hogeru*] **1** A hole; a gap; an opening. **2** A deficit; a loss; shortage.
fugi·in, *vi*. [hogeru*] To have a hole open (up).
fugu, *n*. [hogo] Wastepaper; old scraps of paper.
fugui, *n*. [fuguri] The scrotum; the testicles.
fui-aga·in, *vi*. (Of weather) to clear up.
fu·i-kee·sun, *vi*. To (suffer a) relapse.
fu·i-mun, *n*. [horimono] Sculpture; carving; engraving.
fu·in[1], *vt*. [horu] To dig; delve; core; excavate; grub up.
fu·in[2], *vi*. [furu] To fall (rain, snow, etc.); come down; descend.
fu·in[3], *vt*. [furu] **1** To wave; shake; swing. **2** To reject; turn down; jilt.
fui-nuchi-baka, *n*. [horinuki + haka] A tunnel-style tomb, often dug into the side of a hill. See also **haka**.
fuji, *n*. [fuji] A wisteria.
fu-jiyuu, *n*. [fujiyuu] Inconvenience; discomfort; poverty; lack of freedom.
fujoo-maki, *n*. [fujoo + make] Defeat due to spiritual pollution. [UKH]
fuka[1], *n*. [fuka] A shark.
fuka[2], *n*. [hoka] Outside; elsewhere.
fuka-akki-sa·a, *n*. Lit., deep-sea walker; a **sabani** boat with a two-man crew used for fishing beyond the reef. [OBJ] See **sabani**, **fuka'atchi**.
fuka-atchi, *n*. **1** Going out; an outing; an airing. **2** Deep-sea fishing. **-sun**, *v*. To gad about; go out.
fuka-iyu, *n*. Deep-sea fish found outside of the coral reefs.
fuka-joo, *n*. The road adjacent to one's gate.
fuka-kajimi, *n*. Deep concealment; hiding deeply. [UKH]
fuka-maa, *n*. The yard inside the gate.

See also **joo**[3]. See **naa**[5].
fuka-maaru·u, *n*. Playing around.
fuka·san, *adj*. [hukai] Deep; dense; profound; intimate.
fuka·sun[1], *vt*. [hukasu] To boil (water). Also **wakasun**[2].
fuka·sun[2], *vt*. To remove the sediment when making tofu bean curd. [UKH]
fuka-tuu, *n*. Deep water in a river or ocean. See also **tuu**[3], **tunaka**.
fuka-umi, *n*. The open sea; the sea beyond the reef.
fuki, *n*. [hoke*] Steam.
fuki·in[1], *vi*. To chirp; sing; twitter.
fuki·in[2], *vt*. To pass through (under) a narrow place by lowering oneself. [UKH]
fukkwi·in, *vi*. [fukureru] **1** To swell (out); fill out; get big; bulge (out); be inflated; expand; dilate. **2** To get sulky; fret; become angry; become sullen.
fukoo, *n*. [hukoo] Being unfilial to one's parents.
fuku[1], *n*. [fukufukushi*] The lungs (usually of animals).
fuku[2], *n*. [huku] Fortune; blessing; luck; bliss.
fukugi, *n*. [fukuge*] Same as **fukuji**.
fuku-gii, *n*. [fukuge] **1** Down, soft, fine hair; peach fuzz. **2** Gooseflesh; goose bumps. **3** Short, uneven hair along the borders of one's hair.
fukui, *n*. [hokori] Dust; a mote.
fukuji, *n*. [fukugi] Lit., happiness tree; **fukuji** tree [*Garcinia subelliptica* Merr.]. [ODJ, FOSR] Also **fukugi**, **sabagwaagii**, **sabakuyooree**, **sabangi**.
fukuji-gachi, *n*. A **fukuji** tree hedge. See also **kachi**[2].
fuku-maami, *n*. The heart (usually of animals).
fukura·s(h)an, *adj*. **1** Proud; haughty. **2** Joyous.
fukura·sun, *vt*. [fukurasu] To expand; bulge; inflate; pump up; blow up; raise; puff.

fukuru

fukuru, *n.* [fukuro] A bag; a sack; a pouch.
fukutaa, *n.* Rags; tatters; tattered clothes.
fukutaa-uudu, *n.* Bedding or quilt made of rags.
fumichi, *n.* [homeki*] Summer heat; heat (of weather).
fumichi-kaja, *n.* A sour smell.
fumichi-maki, *n.* [homeki + make] Succumbing to summer heat; susceptibility to summer heat.
fumi·chun, *vi.* [homeku] **1** To be muggy; be sweltering; (food) become stale and watery. **2** To become animated and lively.
fu-migu·i, *n.* **1** Stagnation in business; inactivity; depression. **2** Indigestion; poor blood circulation.
fumi·in, *vt.* [homeru] To praise; admire; commend; compliment; eulogize.
fumi-kutuba, *n.* [homekotoba] Praise; a compliment; eulogy; laudatory remarks.
funa-bara, *n.* [funabara*] Both broadsides of a boat. See **sabani**.
funa-bin, *n.* [funabin] Shipping service; surface mail service.
funa-chin, *n.* [funachin] Boat fare; ship passage fare.
funa-dama, [funadama] Ship spirit worshiped as a guardian deity of ships, especially among fishermen.
funa-deeku, *n.* [funadaiku] A shipwright; a shipbuilder.
fu-naka, *n.* [funaka] Discord; bad terms.
funa-ku, *n.* [funako*] A sailor; a seaman.
funa-michi, *n.* [funamichi] A sea route; a seaway.
funa-nu·i, *n.* [funanori] A sailor; a seaman; a crew.
funa-tabi, *n.* [funatabi] A sea trip; a sea voyage.
funa-uku·i, *n.* [funaokuri] Giving a person a send-off at a port.

funa-wii, *n.* [funayoi] Seasickness; nausea. Also **funeei**.
fun-baku, *n.* [honbako] A bookcase.
fun-bichi, *n.* [funbetsu] Discretion; prudence; judgment; good sense.
fun-bun, *n.* [honbun] One's duty; one's part.
fundee, *n.* [hoodai] Willfulness; caprice; self-indulgence; whim.
fundee-uumaku, *n.* One who is so overindulged as to be reckless.
fundoo, *n.* A wedge-shaped connector of two pieces of wood.
funeei, *n.* [funayoi] Seasickness; motion sickness. **-sun**, *v.* To get seasick. Also **funawii, funee, fuunee**.
funi[1], *n.* [fune] A ship; a boat. See **sabani, tinma, Yanbaraa, maaran**.
funi[2], *n.* [hone] **1** A bone; a skeleton. **2** A frame. **3** A stalk; a stem; a culm.
funi-gumi, *n.* [honegumi] The frame; physique; build.
fu-ninjoo, *n.* [funinjoo] Unkindness; lack of sympathy; callousness.
funi·nu-kami, *n.* Ship deity, patron of the shipbuilder.
funi-yafara·a, *n.* Lit., a person whose bones are soft; a iithe person; a smooth dancer. [UKH]
funji-ruu, *n.* [funjiro < C wenzilu] A furnace to burn papers containing written letters out of respect for the written letters. [OBJ]
fun-nin, *n.* [honnin] The said person; the person in question; the person himself or herself.
funnu, *n.* [honni] **1** Fact; truth. **2** *adv.* Really; truly.
fu-noo, *n.* [funoo] Nonpayment of taxes and other obligations.
fun-shii, *n.* [C fengshui] Geomancy; *feng shui*.
funtoo, *n.* [hontoo] Truth. **·nu**, *adj.* True; real; actual.
funui, *n.* [funori] A glue plant; funorin.
fura·a, *n.* A madman; a fool; an idiot.

44

Also **furimun**.
fura·chun, *vt*. 1 (For an eye, a mouth) to open. 2 (For a hole) to open up.
furafuraa-sun, *v*. 1 To faint; feel dizzy; feel unsteady. 2 To waver; be shaky.
furari·in, *vi*. [·ran, t·ti] To be rejected; be jilted; be given the cold shoulder.
furii, *n*. [furei] Official notice; notification; proclamation; ordinance; decree; instruction.
furi·in[1], *vi*. [furueru] To shake; tremble; quiver; vibrate.
furi·in[2], *vt*. [fureru] To issue notice; notify; make known.
furi·in[3], *vi*. [fureru] To become insane; go out of one's mind.
furi·in[4], *vi*. [horeru] To fall in love; be attracted to.
furi-makutu(·u), *n*. Foolish honesty; simple honesty; an honest fool.
furi-mun, *n*. A madman; a fool; a crazy. Also **furaa**.
furi-munu-i·i, *n*. Nonsense; silly talk; gibberish.
furi-yuntaku, *n*. Silly talk; idle talk; hokum.
furubasari·in, *vi*. To be destroyed; be ruined.
furuba·sun, *vt*. [horobosu] To destroy; ruin; overthrow; annihilate.
furu·bun, *vi*. [horobiru] To go to ruin; be ruined; cease to exist; die out.
furu-chi, *n*. [furuchi] Old blood; polluted blood, esp. of one who has had syphilis.
furu-doogu, *n*. [furudoogu] Used things; used tools; antiques.
furu-ji, *n*. [furugi] Old clothes; used clothes.
furu-jin, *n*. [furu-ginu] Old clothes; used clothes. See **furuji**.
furuji-yaa, *n*. [furugiya] A secondhand clothes store.
furu-kiji, *n*. [furukizu] An old wound; a scar.
furu-mun, *n*. [furumono] An old article; used items; antiques; curios.
furu-tchu, *n*. A person who has had syphilis.
furu-tuji, *n*. One's former wife; one's old wife (jocular).
fusa, *n*. [fusa] A tassel; a tuft; a fringe.
fusaagi, *n*. The wind in April preceding a sudden deterioration of weather into a typhoon with high waves.
fu-saku, *n*. [fusaku] A poor harvest (crop); a crop failure; crop shortage.
fushi[1], *n*. [hoshi] A star; the stars.
fushi[2], *n*. [fushi] 1 A joint; a knuckle; a knot; a node. 2 A tune; an air.
-fushi[3], **-bushi**, *suff*. Indicates the tune to which a song is to be sung.
fu·shi-ba, *n*. [hoshiba] Dried vegetables such as dried radishes or dried horsebeans. See also **toomaami**.
fu·shi-bii, *n*. Thinly sliced and dried sweet potatoes.
fushiga·ran, *adj*. Unable to suppress one's emotions.
fushi·ji[1], *n*. [fusegi] Defense; safeguard; protection.
fu-shi-ji[2], *n*. [fushigi] Strangeness; wonderfulness; a wonder; a mystery; a miracle; magic. ·**na**, *adj*. Wonderful; strange; marvelous; mysterious; miraculous; magical.
fushi·jun, *vt*. [fusegu] To defend; resist; keep away; prevent; avert; guard against.
fu-shin[1], *n*. [fushin] Doubt; distrust; suspicion; a question. ·**na**, *adj*. Doubtful; suspicious.
fu-shin[2], *n*. [fushin] Building; construction. **-sun**, *v*. To build; construct.
fu·shi-mun, *n*. [hoshimono] Clothes hung up to dry.
fu-shoo, *n*. [hoshoo] Guarantee.
fushoo-nin, *n*. [hoshoonin] A guarantor.
fusoo-woo, *n*. [fusoo-oo] Inappropriateness; unsuitability. ·**na**, *adj*. Unsuitable; unfit; inappropriate; incongruous; unbecoming; improper.

fusu

fusu, *n.* [heso] The navel; the umbilicus. See also **tenbusu**.
fusu-chi·jun, *vt.* To cut the umbilical cord and tie it. [OBJ]
fu-suku, *n.* [fusoku] Insufficiency; shortage; want; deficit; fault; negligence in performing ancestral rites.
fusu-uubi, *n.* [hosobi] In premodern Okinawa, a narrow sash, made of cotton, worn by commoners on official occasions. See **uubi**.
futa, *n.* [futa] A cover; a lid; a cap.
futa-makai, *n.* A bowl with a lid.
fu-tashika, *n.* [futashika] Uncertainty; unreliability; **·na**, *adj.* Precarious; uncertain; unreliable; shaky; hazy.
fu-tassha, *n.* [futassha*] Not skilled; not good at.
futa-uya, *n.* [futaoya] The parents; both parents.
futchaa-mui, *n.* Same as **muimee**[1].
futu, *n.* [futo] Temporary; interim; makeshift; pro tem.
futu·chun, *vt.* [hodoku] To untie; unpack; undo; unravel; loosen.
fu-tuduchi, *n.* [futodoki] Negligence; carelessness.
futu-futu·u-sun, *v.* To shake; tremble with fear; shiver with cold.
futuki, *n.* [hotoke] 1 An ancestral spirit. 2 An image of Buddha. 3 A good-natured person.
futuki-gwaa, *n.* 1 A name given to an infant before it has a formal name. 2 A doll. See **naajikii**.
futuki·i, *n.* A doll. Also **futukigwaa**.
futukii·nu gutoo·n, *phr. slang* As pretty as a doll. [GSS]
fuu[1], *n.* [hoo] A cheek. Same as **fuujira**.
fuu[2], *n.* [hoo*] Good luck; good fortune.
fuu[3], *n.* [ho] A sail.
fuu[4], *n.* [ho] An ear (of grain); head (of wheat).
fuu[5], *n.* [fuu] Manners; customs; morals.
fuu-bashira, *n.* [hobashira] A ship's masts. Also **hashira**.

fuubi, *n.* [hoobi] A reward; a prize.
fuucha·a, *n.* An arrogant person; a swaggerer. [UKH]
fuuchi[1], *n.* [fuuki] 1 A bad cold; influenza. 2 A plague; an epidemic.
fuuchi[2], *n.* [fuigo] A pair of bellows; a forge.
fuuchi[3], *n.* Moxa. See also **yaachuu**.
fuuchi-baa, *n.* Mugwort; wormwood [J yomogi; *Artemisia princeps* Pamp. var. *orientalis* Hara]. [OGJ]
fuuchibaa-juushii, *n.* Rice porridge seasoned with mugwort leaves.
fuuchi·nu-wuuwee, *n.* An annual rite for the god of the bellows, celebrated by carpenters and smiths on the seventh day of the eleventh lunar month. Also **kanjaayaa'ugwan**. [OBJ]
fuudu-gami, *n.* Privy deity. See **fuuru-gami**.
fuu-fuda, *n.* [hoo* + fuda] A talisman; an amulet card with a Sanskrit magical formula inscribed.
fuu-ga, *n.* [fuuga] Being elegant; grace; elegance.
fuu-gawa·i, *n.* [fuugawari] Oddness; strangeness; eccentricity. **·na**, *adj.* Queer, strange; odd; eccentric.
fuu-in, *n.* [fuuin] A stamped seal.
fuu-jira, *n.* [hoho + tsura] A cheek. Also **fuu**[1].
fuujoo, *n.* [hoozoo*] 1 A woman's tobacco pouch made in the shape of a Buddhist sacred jewel. 2 A tobacco pouch.
fuuka·shi, *n.* Exaggeration; bragging.
fuuka·sun, *vt.* To exaggerate; boast.
fuu-kubu, *n.* [hohokubo] A dimple. Also **fuukubugwaa**.
fuunaa, *n.* Imitation; pretense.
fuunee, *n.* Seasickness; nausea. **-sun**, *v.* To get seasick.
fuurin-naa, *n.* Spinach [J hoorensoo; *Spinacia oleracea* L.]. [MAK]
fuuru, *n.* [furo] A privy; a toilet; a lavatory; latrine; a bath (toilet); a pigsty.

fuuru-gami, *n.* Privy deity. [OBJ] Also **fuudugami.**

fuuru-mabui-gumi, *n.* Lit., regaining a soul at the privy. See **fuurugami.**

fuu·s(h)an, *adj.* [hoshii] Be wanting; be desirous; wishing for.

fuu-shin, *n.* [hosen] A sailing ship.

fuushu-gami, *n.* [< J hooshogami] Thick, pure-white paper made of paper mulberry for ceremonial and official use. See also **kabi.**

fuu·sun, *vt.* [hosu] To dry; desiccate; air. See **hiin**[3].

fuuta·i, *n.* [hoo + tare] **1** The wattle; the dangling flesh under the beak of a chicken. **2** Drooping cheeks.

fuya[1], *n.* [hoya] A lamp chimney.

fuya[2], *n. arch.* Shoes; Chinese-style silk shoes worn by the Ryukyu royalty as a part of Chinese attire.

fu-yiiti, *n.* [fuete] Unskillfulness; weakness.

fu-yiti, *n.* [fuete] Same as **fuyiiti.**

fuyu, *n.* [fuyu] Winter.

fuyuu, *n.* [fuyuu] **1** Laziness; idleness; indolence. **2** A lazy person. **-sun,** *v.* To be lazy; be indolent.

fuyuuna·a, *n.* One who is lazy and spoiled.

fuyuu·na-mun, *n.* A lazy person.

G———

ga, *part.* **1** Nominative case marker. **2** Possessive case marker. **3** Question marker (in sentence final position). See also **·nu.**

gaa[1], *n.* [ga] Ego; self; self-will; egoism; egotism.

gaa[2], *n.* [ga] A moth.

gaa-ee, *n.* [< **gaa·in**] Cheering and jostling, in a tug-of-war.

gaa·in, *vi.* To be haughty; be pompous; be arrogant; vaunt.

gaa-juu, *n.* [ga + tsuyoi] A stubborn person; an obstinate person.

gaajuu·san, *adj.* Stubborn; obstinate; headstrong; stiff-necked; pigheaded.

gaa-naa[1], *n.* A lump which is caused by getting hit; a bump; swelling.

gaa-naa[2], *n.* A goose.

gaara-dama, *n.* A comma-shaped jade stone. See also **mitama.**

gaa-tui, *n.* A wild goose. [UKH]

gachi, *n.* [gaki] A glutton; a gourmand.

gachi-chaa, *n.* A sea urchin; an echinoid. Also **gashichaa, maasukwee.**

·gachii, *suff.* [...(y)a· + ...] Denotes action while engaged in another action: while; at the same time (as).

·gachiinaa, *suff.* [...(y)a· + ...] Same as **·giinaa, ·gachii.**

gachi-mayaa, *n.* Lit., a hungry cat; a gluttonous, greedy person.

gachun, *n.* A horse mackerel; a saurel.

gafasaa-warabaa, *n.* A naughty, unruly youngster. [UKH]

gajaa, *n.* A mosquito. Also **gajan.** [GSS]

gajan, *n.* See **gajaa.**

gajimaru, *n.* Small-leaved banyan [*Ficus microcarpa* L. f.]. [FOSR] Also **gajumaru.**

gakayaa, *n.* A mist. [UKH]

gaki-ja·a, *n.* Same as **gakijuu, kakijaa.**

gaki-juu, *n.* A hook; often a hanging hook suspended from the ceiling.

gak-koo, *n.* [gakkoo] A school.

gakkoo-naa, *n.* Same as **Yamatunaa.** See also **naa**[3].

gaku-buri, *n.* A learned fool; a scholar ignorant of the real world. See **furiin**[3].

gaku-mun, *n.* [gakumon] Learning; studies; education. Also **shimi**[1], **tishimigakumun.**

gaku-sha, *n.* [gakusha] A scholar; a man of learning; an academic.

gaku-shii, *n.* [gakusei] A student. Also **shiitu.**

gama, *n.* A grotto; a cavern; a cave.

gamaku, *n.* The waist; the small of the back.

gamaku-buni, *n.* The knucklebone; the hipbone.

gan[1], *n.* [gan] A hearse; a coffin carrier; a palanquin-like collapsible structure, lacquered in vermillion and typically inscribed with Buddhist chants. See also **aka'nmaa, gankoo.**

·ga·n[2], *part.* Even (nominative case).

·gana, *suff.* Attached to an interrogative pronoun, denotes indefiniteness.

·ganaa, *suff.* [...**(y)a·** + ...] Attached to a verb, denotes action while engaged in another action: while.

-ganashii, *suff.* [< kanashii] Attached to a noun, denotes respect.

-ganashii-mee, *suff.* Attached to a noun, denotes the utmost respect.

ganba·in, *vi.* [ganbaru] To make an effort; strain oneself to; hold out firm. Same as **chibain.**

ganba·yaa, *n.* A person who makes persistent efforts; an eager beaver.

gan-choo, *n.* [gankyoo] Same as **mii-ganchoo.**

gani[1], *n.* [kani] A crab.

gani[2], *n. slang* A miser. [UKH]

-gani, *suff.* Attached to male or female gentry class personal names in the premodern period, denotes affection. [RJK]

ganjimi, *n.* A tool to pull out nails or cut wires. [UKH]

gan-juu, *n.* [ganjoo] Being strong; being healthy.

ganjuu-gi·san, *adj.* Appearing to be healthy and strong.

ganjuu-mun, *n.* A healthy and strong person.

gan-koo, *n.* An association for the management and maintenance of a **gan** hearse. See **gan**[1].

ganmara·a, *n.* A practical joker; a prankster.

ganmari, *n.* Mischief; tease; prank.

gan-muchaa, *n.* A funeral palanquin pole bearer. See **gan**[1], **mabui'uui.**

ganshi-naa, *n.* A ring of straw (or other material) rope placed on the head to cushion and balance heavy loads.

gappai, *n.* Beetle-browed; a prominent brow.

gappaya·a[1], *n. pej.* A person with a prominent brow.

gappayaa[2], *n. colloq.* A pestle shaped like a hammer. [UKH]

gara[1], *n.* [kara] A shell; a husk; anything that is empty.

gara[2], *n.* [gara] A pattern, design, or figure of a textile. [UKH]

garasa·a, *n.* [karasu] A crow; a raven. Also **garashi.**

garasaa-gaami, *n.* Hawksbill turtle [*Eretmochelys imbricata* (Linnaeus)]. See also **kaamii.** [ODJ]

garashi, *n.* Same as **garasaa.**

garashi-maga·i, *n.* A cramp in the fingers or toes.

garashi-neei, *n.* Same as **garashimagai.** [UKH]

gasa·a, *n.* **1** A vulgar fellow; a coarse person. **2** An item of inferior quality.

gasami, *n.* A kind of crab.

ga-shi, *n.* [gashi] A famine; a failure of crops. See also **yaasajini.**

gashi-chaa, *n.* Same as **gachichaa.**

gashi-dushi, *n.* A year of famine or other natural disasters.

gas·san, *adj.* [garu·ku; karui] **1** Light in weight; not heavy. **2** Flippant; thoughtless. See **kassan.**

gata, *n.* [gata] A shoal; a shallow; a shallow beach; reclaimed land.

gata-gata, *adv.* [gatagata] **1** With a rattling noise. **2** Shivering; trembling; shaking. **-sun,** *v. onom.* To make a clattering noise. Also **gatagataa-sun.** See also **furiin**[1].

gat-tin, *n.* [gatten] A consent; an agreement.

gee, *n.* [gai] **1** Harm; trouble; hindrance. **2** Defiance; resistance; hostility. **-sun,** *v.* To resist; oppose; defy.

geen, *n.* A grass stick used for exorcism, made of several miscanthus stalks, with a cross tied at one end. See also **san**³.
gen-noo, *n.* A hammer.
geren-geren, *n. colloq.* A mentally deranged person; an insane person. [UKH]
gichafa-gusa, *n.* Same as **akagusa**.
giija·a, *n.* A large brown cicada. See also **sansanaa, naabikachaa**.
·giin, *suff.* Same as **·giinaa**.
·gi·in, *suff.* [...(y)a· + ...] Denotes an action in progress: to be in the process of (doing).
·giinaa, *suff.* [...(y)a· + ...] Denotes action while engaged in another action: while. See also **·gachii**.
giitaa, *n.* A children's game in which children hop around on one leg, holding the toes of the other leg with one hand in the back.
giitaa-mundoo, *n.* A children's game in which each child, holding the right foot with the right hand, and jumping on the left leg, tries to bump his or her opponent off balance.
gijaa, *n.* An evil-tempered woman.
gikicha·a, *n.* Same as **gikichi**. [UKH]
gikichi, *n.* Same as **gikiji**. [UKH]
gikiji, *n.* Orange jessamine [*Murraya paniculata* (L.) Jack]. Also **gikichaa, gikichi**. [FOSR]
gikiji-gachi, *n.* An orange jessamine hedge. See also **kachi**².
gin, *n.* [gin] Silver; argent.
girai-kanai, *n.* Same as **nireekanee**.
giree·in, *vt.* 1 To build and maintain a house or a tomb. 2 To wash bones. See **shinkuchi**. [UKH]
giree-kanee, *n.* Same as **nireekanee**.
-gi·san, *suff.* Denotes likeness or likelihood.
gishi-gishi·i-sun, *v. onom.* [gishigishi] To creak; squeak; grate.
gita, *n.* [geta] Wooden clogs. Also **jita**.

gomu-kan, *n.* A slingshot; a child's toy used for hurling stones or other missiles.
gon-gon, *adv. onom.* Stride in walking; walking briskly.
goo, *n.* [goo] A measure of capacity, equivalent to ten **shaku**, about 0.2 liter or 1.5 gills. [NJED]
goo-gucha·a, *n.* A malcontent; a grumbler.
goo-guchi, *n.* A complaint; a grievance. **-sun,** *v.* To complain; to grumble.
googuchi-haaguchi-sun, *v. emph.* Same as **googuchisun**.
goo-maa-yi·i, *n.* Sitting in a circle. Also **maaruuyii**. [UKH]
goo-micha·a, *n.* A sudden big wave.
gooya·a, *n.* Bitter melon [*Momordica charantia* L. var. *pavel* Crantz]. [FOSR]
gooyaa-chanpuruu, *n.* Stir-fried dish of chopped bitter melon and tofu.
goo-yuku, *n.* [gooyoku] Avarice; greed; rapacity.
gooyuku·u, *n.* An avaricious person; a greedy fellow; a grasping rascal.
gooruu, *n.* Being loose; being lax; being slack.
gu- *pref.* [go-] Denotes honor and respect. Also **u-**.
gu-ban, *n.* [goban] A checkerboard; a *go* board.
guban-aya, *n.* Check pattern; checker-patterned kimono.
gu-bu, *n.* [gobu] A half; fifty percent.
gubu-gubu, *n.* [gobugobu] Fifty-fifty.
gu-burii, *n. polite* [goburei] Rudeness; incivility; a breach of etiquette. See **burii**.
gu-busata, *n. polite* [gobusata] Silence; negligence to write.
guchi¹**,** *n.* [kuki] A stalk; a stem; a pipe; an axis; a caulis of a grass or vegetable. Also **funi**².
guchi²**,** *n.* [guchi] Abusive language; an insult; talking back. **-sun,** *v.* To complain; grumble.

gudun, *n.* [gudon] Stupidity; asininity; silliness.

gufushi, *n.* The round end of bones of hands or feet such as the malleolus or the anklebone.

gu-gwachi, *n.* [gogatsu] May. Also **gungwachi**.

gujira, *n.* [kujira] A whale.

guju-guju-iya·a, *n.* A constant complainer; a persistent grumbler. [UKH]

guku-raku, *n.* [gokuraku] *Sukkavati*; paradise (of Buddhism); the abode of the blessed.

guma·a, *n.* Something small; that which is small.

guma-ami, *n.* A light rain.

guma-ami-gwaa, *n.* A drizzle; a fine rain.

gumaa-gwaa, *n.* Anything small.

guma·a-incha·a, *n.* Mismatches; things that are in pairs but not uniform in size.

guma-bu·i, *n.* A light rain.

guma-gii, *n.* A bush.

guma-gwii, *n.* A low voice; a whisper; a murmur.

guma-ishi, *n.* A pebble; a small stone.

guma-jin, *n.* Small change; loose money.

guma-kee-uchi, *n.* A small plate; a saucer.

guma-machiya, *n.* A small store. Also **machiyagwaa**. See also **magimachiya**.

guma-mun, *n.* Small wares; trinkets; notions; sundries.

gumamun-achine·e, *n.* Sundry goods business.

gumamun-machi, *n.* A sundry goods market.

gumamun-machiya, *n.* A sundry store.

guma-munugatai, *n.* Private talk; whispering.

guma-nusudu, *n.* A petty thief.

guma·san, *adj.* Small; little. Also **gunasan**.

guma-yaa, *n.* A cottage; a hut; a little house; a shack; a pen; a shelter.

gumi, *n.* [gomi] Dust; rubbish; trash.

gumi-uchi, *n.* A duster.

gumu, *n.* [gomu < E gum] Gum; rubber.

gumu-maai, *n.* [gomumari] A rubber ball.

gu-muttun, *n.* [gomuttomo] Being reasonable; being justifiable; being just; being natural; being warrantable.

guna-abii, *n.* A whisper; low voice.

-sun, *v.* To whisper.

gu-nan, *n.* [gonan] A fifth son.

gunan-winagu, *n.* A fifth daughter.

guna·san, *adj.* Same as **gumasan**.

guna-tchu·gwaa, *n.* A little person; a dwarf; a pygmy.

gun-boo, *n.* [go(n)boo] 1 Burdock [*Arctium lappa* L.]. [FOSR] 2 *n. slang* A licentious man; a philanderer.

gunboo-bisa, *phr. slang* Legs as skinny and dark as burdock. [GSS] See **hisa**.

gungoo, *n.* [gogoo] Five **goo** (of grain). See **goo**.

gungoo-chiiga, *n.* A measurement box holding five **goo** of grain. [UKH] See also **chiiga**[2], **goo**.

gungoo-chooban, *n.* Same as **gungoochiiga**. [UKH]

gungoo-nakamui, *n.* Same as **gungoochiiga**.[UKH]

gungoo-rachi, *n.* A cooking pot capable of cooking five **goo** of grain. See **goo**.

gungwacha·a, *n.* Lit., fifth-month thing; sweet potatoes planted in the fifth month. [UKH]

gungwachi, *n.* Same as **gugwachi**.

gungwachi-yukka, *n.* Events held on the fourth day of the fifth lunar month, such as the dragon boat race. [UKH]

gu-niiji, *n.* [go-naigi] An honorific term for someone's wife.

gunmee-naabi, *n.* An iron cooking pot. See **shinmeenaabi**.

guri, *n.* A sediment; a deposit; dregs; lees.

gu-rii, *n.* A bow; a greeting.

gu-riijin, *n.* [go-reizen]·A household

Buddhist altar; a family memorial tablet. Also **buchidan**.

-guri·s(h)an, *suff*. Denotes difficulty: to be difficult to….

guru, *n*. An eggshell. [UKH]

-guru, *suff*. [-goro] Denotes a temporal approximation: approximately; around.

guru-guru, *adv*. *onom*. [gorogoro] Rolling; rumbling; thundering. **-sun**, *v. onom*. [guruguru] To roll one's eyes; goggle; stare.

gurukun, *n*. Generic term for fish belonging to the Caesio family.

guruman-boo, *n*. Same as **kurumaboo**. [GSS]

guru-mun, *n*. A nimble person; a quick person; an agile person.

guru·san, *adj*. Nimble; prompt; astute.

gu-shaaku·u, *n*. A five **shaku** (one-half **goo**) liquid measurement jar. See **chiiga**², **chooban**.

gu-shaaku-nakamui, *n*. A five **shaku** dry measure box. Same as **nakamuigwa**. See **chiiga**², **chooban**, **gushaakuu**.

gushichi, *n*. Miscanthus; Japanese pampas grass [J susuki; *Miscanthus sinensis* Anderss var. *sinensis*]. [FOSR] See also **geen**, **san**³.

gushiku, *n*. A castle; a fort. Also **gusuku**.

gu-soo, *n*. [goshoo] The life to come; the future life. [OBJ]

gusoo-bana, *n*. [goshoo + hana] Lit., a flower of the life to come; a hibiscus. Also **akabanaa**. See also **hana**¹.

gusoo-jitaku, *n*. Death dress. Same as **gusoosugai**. See also **shitaku**. [UKH]

gusoo-michi, *n*. Lit., the road to the future life; the road to a cemetery. See **dabi**.

gusoo-mudu·i, *n*. One who has been revived; one who has returned from the other life.

gusoo-nchu·nu-aajin-gii, *n*. Lit., dead person's pestle tree; Ryukyuan hairpin tree. [J mehirugi; *Kandelia candel* (L.) Druce]. [FOSR, ODJ]

gusoo·nu u-chukui, *n*. Lit., a package for the afterlife; items which are offered at the Buddhist altar on the day of **Shichigwachi juugunichi**, the fifteenth day of the lunar seventh month. [UKH]

gusoo-suga·i, *n*. Dress for one's final journey (i.e., into the afterlife). Same as **gusoojitaku**. [ODJ]

gusuku, *n*. Same as **gushiku**.

gusumichi, *n*. Cartilage; gristle.

gusun-kuji, *n*. A five-**sun** nail (about 15 cm or 6 in.). [UKH]

gu-suuyoo, *n*. [exalting] Audience; group of people; Ladies and gentlemen! See **suuyoo**.

gutee, *n*. [gutai] Hands and feet.

gutoo·n, *part. adj*. [gotoshi*] Like; as; similar. See **kungutooru**.

gutu, *n*. [goto] **·nu gutu**, *adv*. Like; as; as… as; so… as; as if; because.

·gutu, *suff*. [< **kutu**] Same as **·kutu**.

guu¹, *n*. [gu] **1** A coterie; a company; a fellow; a colleague. **2** An accomplice. **2** A pair. **3** A partner in an illicit love affair.

guu², *n*. [go] (The game of) *go*; Japanese checkers.

guufa·a, *n*. A person with a wen (a tumor or a bump).

guufu, *n*. [kobu] A wen; a lump; a swelling; a tumor; a bump.

guui, *n*. A bone at the lower end of the hip. Same as **tumuguu**. [OGJ, UKH]

guuna·a, *n*. A lame person. See **guuni**.

guu-na·in, *vi*. To be intimate with; to make illicit love to; to commit adultery with.

guuna·i-ngwa, *n*. A love child; a child born out of wedlock. See also **yamanashingwa**.

guuna·i-mun, *n*. An adulterer; an adulteress.

guuni, *n*. Lameness; a lame person.

guusan, *n.* A cane; a walking stick.
guushi, *n.* [kushi] A spit; a skewer; an iron stick for digging sweet potatoes.
guutu-miitu, *n.* A pair; a couple; a set.
-guutuu, *suff.* Verbal suffix denoting unwillingness: unwilling to; tries not to.
gu-wun, *n.* Honorable obligation; kindness; favor; a debt of gratitude. See also **wun**².
gu-yuu, *n.* [goyoo] 1 Official business; government service. 2 Honorable (that is, your) business.
·gwaa, ·ngwa, *suff.* Forms a diminutive or a term of endearment.
-gwaa-see, *suff.* Denotes make-believe play: playing (war, house).
gwan, *n.* [gan] A prayer; an invocation; a supplication. See **ugwan**.
gwanku, *n.* [ganko] Obstinacy; obduracy; intransigence.
gwanku·u, *n.* A stubborn person; a headstrong person.
gwan-su, *n.* [ganso] Ancestor; progenitor. Also **ugwansu**. ²
gwan-tan, *n.* [gantan] New Year's Day.
gwasa-gwasa, *adv.* 1 In swarms; crowded with people. 2 Noisily; boisterously; clamorously. 3 In confusion; in disorder.

H———

haa¹, *n.* [ha] A tooth.
haa², *n.* [ha] A blade. See **faa**.
haabeeruu, *n.* [haberu*] A butterfly. Also **haberu**.
haachi, *n.* [hachi] A big plate or bowl. Also **ufujara, uujara**. See **sara**¹, **makai**.
haa-chibura·a, *n.* A toy mask.
haa-daari·i, *n.* 1 Leaving the front of one's kimono open, not properly covering oneself. 2 Being down and out; being down at the heels.
haagaa, *n.* A wheel.
haa-gishi·i, *n.* Grinding (gnashing or grating) one's teeth.
haa-gishi-gishii-sun, *v. emph. colloq.* 1 To grind one's teeth. 2 To grit one's teeth with vexation, pain, or mortification.
haai¹, *n.* [hari] A beam; a girder; a crossbeam.
haai², *n.* [hari] 1 A needle; a pin. 2 An acupuncture needle. 3 A hand (of a clock). 4 Acupuncture.
haai-baku, *n.* [haribako] A needle case.
haai·nu-mii, *n.* A needle's eye.
haa-isa, *n.* [haisha] A dentist.
haa-isa·n-yaa, *n.* A dental clinic.
haai-sashi·i, *n.* A pincushion; a needle pad.
haa-kata, *n.* A tooth-mark.
haa-kusu, *n.* Tartar (on a tooth).
haama, *n.* [hama] The beach; the shore; the strand; the seashore. Also **hama**.
haa-mee, *n.* An old woman; a grandmother.
haamee-kuugi, *n.* Weasel grass [*Pogonatherum crinitum* (Thunb.) Kunth.]. [FOSR] See **kaya**.
haa-moo, *n. pej.* A person who lacks a tooth (teeth).
haara, *n.* A round-shaped bamboo basket for holding ramie fiber. Also **wuubaara**. See also **baaki**.
haa-rii, *n.* [C palong] The traditional boat race (Chinese dragon boat race), a communal rite on the fourth day of the fifth lunar month. See also **jiibaarii**.
haashi, *n.* [hashi] A pair of chopsticks. Also **umeeshi**.
haatuya·a, *n.* 1 A hen that has stopped laying eggs. 2 A variety of chicken. [ODJ]
haa-uchagee, *n.* Protruding teeth; buckteeth. See also **uchagain, uchagiin**.
haaya, *n.* A pillar; a column; a post. See also **nakabaaya, muyabaaya, hajibaaya, fuubashira, hashira**.
haa-yami, *n.* Toothache. See **yamun**.
haa·yee, *n.* Running; race.

haayee-gongon-sun, *v. colloq.* To run as fast as one can.
haayee-suubu, *n.* A footrace.
haba, *n.* [haba] **1** Breadth; width. **2** Influence.
haba·chun, *vi.* To make good progress; make headway; eat a lot.
habaka·in, *vi.* [habakaru] To spread out and take too much space.
haberu, *n.* A butterfly. [GSS] Same as **haabeeruu.**
habu¹, *n.* A habu poisonous snake; a pit viper [*Trimeresurus flavoviridis* Hallowell]. [OGJ]
habu², *n.* A stock; the part of the axe to which the blade is attached. See also **wuunu.**
habu-kakuja·a, *n.* A person with snake-like square and prominent jaws. See **kakuji.**
habutan, *n.* [habotan] Same as **tamanaa.**
habutan-irichaa, *n.* Cabbage stir-fry. See also **irichii.**
hacha·a, *n.* [hachi] A bee; a wasp; a hornet.
hachaa·nu-shii, *n.* A beehive.
hacha-gumi, *n.* A sugared, puffed rice candy ball.
hachi, *n.* [hachi] Eight. See **yaachi.**
hachi-, *pref.* [hatsu-] Indicates the first time or occasion of an event or action.
hachi-at·chi, *n.* Lit., first walk; the first time a woman who has given birth to a child leaves the house.
hachi-baru, *n.* First field.
hachi·chuun, *vi.* To come on the spur of the moment.
hachi-gwachi, *n.* [hachigatsu] August.
hachigwachi juugu-ya, *phr.* The fifteenth night of the eighth lunar month, time of a domestic rite for the moon god.
hachi-ka soo-gwachi, *phr.* The twentieth day of the new year, time of a domestic rite marking the formal end of the New Year season. Also **juugunichi soogwachi.**
hachikoo·san, *adj.* **1** Itchy; creepy. **2** Ticklish.
hachi-mujukui, *n.* **1** First fruits; first produce. **2** A rite celebrating the first produce. See **mujukui.**
hachi-nanka, *n.* The first of the **nanka** Buddhist memorial services held every seventh day for forty-nine days after a death. See **nanka.**
hachi-nin, *n.* Eight people. Also **yattai.**
hachi-ubii-nadi·i, *n.* First holy-water drawing, a domestic rite performed with the first water drawn from the well on New Year's Day.
hachi-ugwan, *phr.* First prayers of the new year.
hachi-unchi, *phr.* [hatsu + unki] First fortune, the first fortune-telling rite of the new year for an individual or family.
ha·chun¹, *vt.* [haku] To vomit; spit; throw up.
ha·chun², *vt.* [haku] **1** To put on; wear; have on. **2** To indemnify (a person for a loss) largely in terms of money; compensate (a person for loss); make up for a loss. See also **hakiin, wancha-meein.**
hada, *n.* [hada] The skin; the body.
hada-fuu·sa, *n.* Love of the body; a euphemism for lust. See **fuus(h)an.**
hada·ka, *n.* [hadaka] A nude; a naked body; bald; uncovered.
hadaka-muji, *n.* [hadakamugi] Rye; naked barley [*Hordeum vulgare* var. *coeleste* L.]. [FOSR] Also **ufumujaa.** See **muji².**
hadaka-muuchi·i, *n.* One who is naked (often of a child).
hadoobi, *n.* [hadaobi] Loincloth. Same as **sanaji.**
haga·a, *n. pej.* Baldness; a baldhead.
ha-gachi, *n.* [hagaki] A letter; correspondence; a postcard.
hagama, *n.* [hagama] A broad-brimmed

haganaa

iron pot for cooking rice. See also **shaakuu, kama**[2].
haga-na·a, *n*. A woman as strong as steel. See **hagani**.
hagana·san, *adj*. Insufficient; short; deficient.
ha-gani, *n*. [hagane] Steel.
haga·sun, *vt*. [hagasu] To strip off; tear off; rip off; peel off.
hagi, *n*. [hage] Barren (sterile; infertile) soil.
hagi-chiburu, *n*. [hage + tsuburi] A bald head.
hagi-jooki, *n*. Same as **sagijooki**. [GSS]
hagi·i, *n*. A bald-headed person; a baldpate.
hagi·in, *vi*. [hageru] **1** To grow bald; peel off; come off; exfoliate. **2** To become sore; be inflamed.
hagi-moo, *n*. Wasteland; barren land; a wasteland; a wilderness where no trees grow.
hagoo-gi·san, *adj*. Filthy looking; dirty looking.
hagoo-mun, *n*. **1** A dirty thing. **2** A vulgar fellow.
hagoo-rii, *adj*. Terrible; exaggerated; bombastic; hyperbolical.
hagoo·san, *adj*. **1** Filthy; dirty. **2** Tickling; ticklish. **3** Uncanny; weird; creepy. **4** Vulgar; indecent; obscene.
hagoo-umi·i, *n*. A ticklish person.
haha-minna, *n*. Same as **sasaminna**. [GSS]
ha·i-funi, *n*. [hashiri + fune] A speedy ship; a speedy boat.
ha·i-gami, *n*. [harigami] A patched paper; a poster; a placard; a sticker.
ha·i-kaa, *n*. A river; a flowing river.
hai-karaa, [E high + collar] **1** *n*. A stylish person; a smart person; a dandy. **2** *adj*. Chic; stylish: smart; chichi; fashionable; up-to-date; foreign-style.
ha·in[1], *vi*. [hashiru] To run.
ha·in[2], *vt*. [haru] **1** To spread out. **2** To expose (what should not be seen). See

marubai.
haja·a, *n*. Wax tree poisoning. [GSS] See also **hajigi**.
hajaa-gii, *n*. Same as **hajigi**. [GSS]
haji[1], *n*. [haji] **1** Shame; disgrace; dishonor; discredit. **2** Private parts.
haji[2], *n*. [hazu] **1** Ought to; should; be expected to. **2** Will; shall.
haji-baaya, *n*. The pillars around a house, outside the rain doors, and supporting the eaves.
ha-jichi, *n*. [hari + tsuki] Tattooing, especially on the back of women's hands. [ODJ]
haji-chira·a, *n*. A shameless person.
haji-gi, *n*. [hajinoki] A wax tree [J haze; *Rhus succedanea* L.] [FOSR] Also **hajiki, hajaagii**.
haji·in, *vt*. To take (clothes) off; disrobe.
hajika·s(h)an, *adj*. [hazukashii] Be ashamed; be shy; be bashful.
haji-ki, *n*. Same as **hajigi**.
haji-ma·i, *n*. [hajimari] The beginning; the start. Same as **hajimi**.
hajima·in, *vi*. [hajimaru] To begin; commence; start; open; originate in.
hajimi, *n*. [hajime] The beginning; commencement; inception; the opening; the start; the threshold. Also **hajimai**.
hajimi·in, *vt*. [hajimeru] To begin; start; commence.
ha·jun[1], *vt*. [hagu] To peel off.
ha·jun[2], *vt*. To distribute; divide; apportion.
haka, *n*. [haka] A grave; a tomb. See also **uhaka, shinju, faafuu, kaaminakuubaka, fuinuchibaka, niibibaka, munchuubaka, shiruhirashi, jiishigaami, sudigachi, yushiri, kariyadu, warabibaka, haru**[2], **haruyaa**. [ODJ] See also **dabi, yanajini**.
haka-bushin, *n*. Building a tomb.
hakadu·in, *vi*. [hakadoru] To advance; progress; make good progress; make headway.
haka-guchi, *n*. **1** The start; the begin-

ning; a clue. **2** The actual spot; the scene; a job site.

hakaguchi-aki·in, *vt*. To start (doing work); originate.

hakai, *n*. [hakari] A balance; a weighing beam; a scale; a measure.

hakai·nu-mii, *n*. [hakari no me] Notches of a balance.

haka·in, *vt*. [hakaru] To measure; gauge; weigh; survey.

haka-ji, *n*. [hakaji] A cemetery; a graveyard. See **jii**[1].

hakama, *n*. [hakama] A traditional undergarment worn by both sexes of the gentry class in the premodern period.

haka-mee, *n*. [hakamairi] A visit to the tomb. Also **uhakamee**.

haka·nu-gu-suuji, *n*. [haka no goshuugi] Celebration with prayer rites and festivities upon completion of the construction of a tomb.

haka·nu-joo, *n*. Entrance to a tomb.

hakaraa·s(h)an, *adj*. [hakabakashii] Rapid; expeditious; speedy.

hakare·e, *n*. [hakarai] Management; arrangement; disposal; discretion.

hakari-gutu, *n*. [< J hakarigoto] A stratagem; a trick; a plot; scheme; maneuver.

haka·sun, *vt*. To make (a person) pay for damage; make (a person) compensate; make indemnify.

hakaya·a-mushi, *n*. Lit., a measuring worm; an inchworm. See **hakain**.

haki, *n*. [hake] A brush.

haki·in, *vt*. [haku] **1** To wear (something around neck). **2** To compensate; make up; reimburse. See **hachun**[2]. See **wanchameein**.

hakka, *n*. [hakka] Japanese mint; mint; peppermint [*Mentha arvensis* var. *piperascens* Malinv.].

haku, *n*. [hako] A box; a case; a casket; a chest; a coffer; a package.

hakujoo[1], *n*. [hakujoo] Coldheartedness.

hakujoo[2], *n*. [hakujoo] Confession;

avowal. **-sun**, *v*. To confess; avow.

-shimi·in, *vt*. To make (a person) confess.

hama, *n*. [hama] Same as **haama**.

hama·in, *vi*. **1** To strive (for, to do); labor (for, to do); devote oneself to (work). **2** To get into; be caught in; be stuck in.

hama-urii, *phr*. Same as **sangwachi sannichi**. [OBJ]

ha-mun[1], *n*. Cutlery; edged tools; knife.

ha-mun[2], *n*. [hamono] An odd piece; a remnant; a fragment; incomplete odds and ends; an incomplete set.

hamun-jin, *n*. Small change (of money).

han, *n*. [han] A stamp; a seal. Also **in**[2].

han-, *pref*. [han-] Half-.

hana[1], *n*. [hana] A flower; a blossom.

hana[2], *n*. [hana] A promontory; a cape; a headland.

hana[3], *n*. [hana] The nose; a snout; a muzzle.

-hana[4], *suff*. [hana] Denotes beginning; incipience.

hana-atai, *n*. A flower garden.

hana-bachi, *n*. [hana-bachi] A flower pot.

hana-bi, *n*. [hanabi] Fireworks; a firecracker.

hana-bira·a, *n. pej*. A flat-nose.

hana-bukkwa, *n. pej*. A raised portion of the nose; the nose.

hana-da·i, *n*. Snivel; watery discharge from the nose.

hanadaya·a, *n. pej*. One who snivels.

hana-fu·chun, *vi*. To snore.

hana-fura·chun, *vi*. To be proud of; be haughty.

hana-gami, *n*. [< J hanagami] A paper handkerchief; tissue.

hana-gasa, *n*. A flowery hat used in Okinawan dance. See **kasa**[1].

hana-gi, *n*. A tree or a shrub grown and cultivated primarily for its flowers.

hana-gii, *n*. Nose hair.

hana-gumi, *n*. Rice washed and sanctified as an offering to the deities.

hana-guni, *n.* A village where music, dancing, and singing are popular.
hana-guusan, *n.* A flowery cane, a stick about three or four feet in length used in dances.
hana-gwii, *n.* Nasal voice; a twang.
hana-hichi, *n.* A head cold.
hana-hiji, *n.* A mustache.
hana-ichi, *n.* [hanaike] A flower vase to hold floral offerings on the family Buddhist altar.
hana-jaka·i, *n.* [hanasakari] Flowers at their best; be at one's best.
hana-jaki, *n.* [hanazake] Consecrated liquor offered to a deity or family Buddhist altar.
hana-ji[1], *n.* [hanaji] Nasal hemorrhage; nosebleed.
hanaji[2], *n.* Variant of **sanaji**. [GSS]
hana-kaji, *n.* [hanakaze] A (head) cold.
hana-katamaya·a, *n.* A stuffed nose.
hana-kusu, *n.* [hanakuso] Nasal mucus; snot.
hana-mi, *n.* [hanami] Flower viewing.
hana-moo, *n.* **1** A person with flattened bridge of the nose (such as of congenital syphilis patients). **2** A person with a flat nose.
hana-munu-i·i, *n.* Nasal tone; nasal voice. **-sun**, *v.* To speak in a nasal voice; twang.
hana-mushiru, *n.* [hanamushiro] A straw mat with a flower design.
hana·nu-ana, *n.* The nostrils.
hana·nu-sachi, *n.* [hananosaki] **1** Tip of one's nose. **2** A short distance.
hana·nu-shima, *n.* Licensed gay quarters; a red-light district.
hana-piipii, *n.* Blocked nose due to a cold.
hanari, *n.* [hanare] **1** An offshore island; an isolated island; (on Okinawa specifically) islands other than Okinawa, i.e., Kume, Iheya, Izena, Ie, Ike, Kudaka, etc. **2** A detached house.
hana·shi, *n.* [hanashi] A talk; a conversation; a story. **-sun**, *v.* [hanashisuru] To talk; tell a story; speak; converse; chat.
hanashi-buku, *n.* Recitation.
hanashi-kwatchii, *n.* A useful as well as interesting talk.
hana-shiru, *n.* [hanashiru] Watery discharge from the nose; snivel.
hana·sun[1], *vt.* [hanasu] To talk; speak; chat.
hana·sun[2], *vt.* [hanasu] To release; let go.
hana-uchi, *n.* Fluffing; cotton bedding. Same as **wata'uchi**[1].
hana-u·i[1], *n.* [hanaori] Lit., flowery weaving; a type of Okinawan textile in which every other warp and woof are raised. Also **fana'ui**. [GSS]
hana-u·i[2], *n.* [hanauri] A flower seller; a flower girl.
hana-ware·e, *n.* A sardonic laugh; an ironical smile. See also **warain**.
hana-wuu, *n.* [hanao] The front strap of *geta* wooden clogs or sandals.
han-bun, *n.* [hanbun] A half.
hanbun-jini, *n.* Half-dead; all but dead.
hanbun-michi, *n.* Same as **hanmichi**.
hanbun-waakii, *n.* [hanbun + wake] Halving.
han·chi-gee·in, *vi.* [hajiku + kaeru] To flip back; spring back; recoil.
han·chun, *vt.* [hajiku] **1** To flip; snap. **2** To repel; reject.
hanchu·u-yaama, *n.* A rattrap worked by means of a spring. Also **'wenchu-yaama**. See **hanchun**.
handama, *n.* Temple potherb [J suizenjina, harutama; *Gynura bicolor* (Wild.) DC]. [FOSR, MAK]
handi, *n.* [hazure] Excess warp in weaving.
handi·in, *vi.* [hazureru] **1** To come off; be dislocated. **2** To miss; be beside the point. **3** To be contrary to.
handuu, *n.* A pottery jar with wide mouth used to store water for cooking

and drinking. See **kaami**.
handuu-gaami, *n*. Same as **handuu**.
haneechi, *n*. Bustle and stir; prosperity.
hanee·chun, *vi*. 1 To become lustrous; become glossy. 2 To become cheerful, merry, and animated.
haneeka·sun, *vt*. [hanayaka] To enliven; cheer up; beautify.
haneeki·in, *vt*. Same as **haneekasun**.
han-guru·shi, *n*. [hangoroshi] Lit., half-killing; beating a person nearly to death.
hani, *n*. [hane] 1 A feather; a wing. 2 A fin; a pinna; plumage.
hani·in, *vt*. [haneru] To leap; spring up; jump; hop; prance; buck up; (of a ball) bounce; recoil; spatter; splash; snap; crack; spark.
hanji, *n*. [hanji] Divination by **yuta** shaman or other fortune-teller.
han-jiri, *n*. [han + chi·in] A washbasin. Same as **taaree**. Also **fanjiri**.
hanjoo, *n*. [hanjoo] Prosperity; success; thriving. -**sun**, *v*. To prosper; thrive.
hanki, *n*. Glans penis.
hanki·in, *vi*. [hajikeru] For the penis skin to peel back so that the inside becomes revealed.
hanki·nu ugwan, *phr*. Sacred grove of phallicism. See also **hoohai utaki**.
hankwa, *n*. [hanka] Luxury; extravagance; gorgeousness.
han-mee, *n*. [hanmai] Food; rice as food.
han-michi, *n*. [hanmichi] Halfway; midway; a distance of one-half **ri**.
han-shii, *n*. An old woman; a grandmother.
han·sun, *vt*. [hazusu] 1 To untie; take off. 2 To avoid; miss.
-**han·sun**, *v. suff*. [hazusu] Denotes failure: to fail to….
hanta[1], *n*. 1 An end; an edge; a tip. 2 A cliff.
hanta[2], *n*. [hanta] Being busy.
hanti-gutu, *n*. [< **hanta**[1]] Risky work; dangerous work; perilous project.

harubi

hanti-waja, *n*. An adventure; a venture; a risky attempt; a hazard.
-**hara**, -**bara**, *suff*. Indicates lineage.
harabi, *n*. [haraobi] Same as **hara'uubi**.
hara-gaagii, *n*. A section of a boat, a board for the side. See **sabani**.
hara-gee, *n*. Same as **saragee**, **nabigee**. [GSS]
hara·in, *vt*. [·(r)an, ·ti; harau] 1 To pay. 2 To dust off.
harama·a, *n*. [< **haramun**] Pregnancy.
harami, *n*. Fish eggs.
hara·mun, *vi*. [haramu] To become pregnant.
hara-tiichi, *n*. 1 Siblings with the same mother. 2 Those with the same idea; co-conspirators.
hara-uubi, *n*. [haraobi] A horse's saddle girth; a breast band. Also **harabi**, **harubi**.
hara-waka·i, *n*. Siblings with the same father but different mothers. See **wakain**[2].
hare·e[1], *n*. [harai] Purification; exorcism.
hare·e[2], *n*. [harai] Payment; bill.
hari, *n*. Weathering; aeration.
hari·in, *vi*. [hareru] To clear up; cease to rain.
hari-yaku, *n*. Clearance of misfortune or bad luck, traditionally associated with the years following one's birth year in the Chinese zodiac cycle, namely, years 13, 25, 37, 49, 61, and 73.
haru[1], *n*. [haru] The spring season.
haru[2], *n*. [hara] A farm; a tract of open country, mainly cultivated farmland. 2 [euphemism] A tomb. See also **taa**[1], **taahataki**, **taabukkwa**, **ufubaru**, **harugwaa**, **haru tageesun**, **haru nu mujukui**, **harudunai**, **harumigui**, **haru atchun**, **harusaa**, **harushigutu**, **harumuchi**, **harumutchaa**, **akachichibaru**, **fitchiibaru**, **haruyaa**.
haru-atcha·a, *n*. A farmer; a peasant.
haru at·chun, *vt*. To practice agriculture.
harubi, *n*. [harobi] Same as **hara'uubi**.

haru-doogu, *n.* Farm implements. See **kwee**[1], **irara, irana, kama**[1], **hiira, fiira, iifuyaa, maaga, oodaa**.

haru-dunai, *n.* Field neighbors; people whose fields are located next to each other.

haru-gwaa, *n.* A small agricultural field.

haru-juukoo, *n.* A memorial service at the tomb, referring to all masses after the **shinkuchi**. See **suukoo, shinkuchi**.

haru·kai-chiya·a, *n.* Work clothes on the farm. Also **farukaichiyaa**. [GSS]

haru-michi, *n.* A road going through fields.

haru-migu·i, *n.* 1 Patrol of one's fields. 2 Patrol of tombs.

harumi·in, *vt.* To explain oneself; vindicate oneself; exculpate oneself (from a charge).

haru-mu·chi, *n.* One who has many fields. Also **harumutchaa**.

harumutcha·a, *n.* Same as **harumuchi**.

haru·nu arabi, *phr.* Curse or retribution of the tomb often caused by trouble or damage at the tomb.

haru·nu higan, *n.* Spring equinox.

haru·nu mujuku·i, *n.* Crops from the fields.

haru-sa·a, *n.* Same as **haru'atchaa**.

haru-shigutu, *n.* Agriculture, particularly, work in the fields. See also **shigutu**.

haru-shikuchi, *n.* Agriculture; farmwork. Same as **harushigutu**.

haru-suubu, *n.* [haru + shoobu] Agricultural-yield contest. See also **haruyamasuubu**.

haru tagee·sun, *vt.* Same as **haru atchun**.

haru-yaa, *n.* 1 A hut near agricultural fields for temporary stay during the busy season. 2 A funeral urn in a farm hut style. See **jiishigaami**.

haru-yama-suubu, *n.* Agriculture and forestry contest. See also **harusuubu**.

hasa, *n.* A gusset for the inner thighs of skirts or underarm of a coat; a gore.

hasamari·in, *vt.* [·ran, t·ti; hasamareru] To become sandwiched (between two things); be pinned under; be between two things or persons.

hasa·mun, *vt.* [hasamu] To insert; interpose (between two things).

hasan, *n.* [hasami] A pair of scissors

hashi, *n.* [hashi] 1 A bridge. 2 A ladder; stairs.

hashi-bashi, *n.* [hashibashi] Every nook and cranny; all the corners.

hashidu, *n.* Same as **hashiru**.

hashira, *n.* [hashira] A ship's mast.

hashi-raa·s(h)an, *adj.* Sagacious; intelligent; wise; clever; bright; smart.

hashiru, *n.* A sliding door; a door; a shutter. See also **nakabashiru**. Also **hashidu**.

hashiru-guchi, *n.* The doorway; the doorstep.

hashiru·nu mii, *n.* A knothole in a sliding door.

hashiru·nu-san, *n.* A bolt lock system for sliding doors.

ha-shishi, *n.* The gums; the tooth-ridge; the gingiva.

hashittu, *adv.* Firmly; tightly; in good health, especially after an illness.

hashoo-fuu, *n.* [hashoofuu] Tetanus; lockjaw.

hata[1], *n. suff.* [hata] Side; near; by.

hata[2], *n.* [hata] A flag; a banner; a standard; a pennant.

hata[3], *n.* [hata] Same as **nunubata**.

hatachi, *n.* [hatachi] Twenty years old.

hata-gashira, *n.* [hatagashira] A banner with bamboo staff, 5–6 m high, at the top of which is attached a decorated lantern with streamers inscribed with slogans.

hata-hataa-sun, *vi. emph. colloq.* To suffer a sharp and extreme pain.

hataki, *n.* [hatake] A dry cultivated field; a farm; a garden; a plantation. See also **haru**[2], **moo, atai**[1].

hata-mun, *n.* A loom used to make

coarse straw mattresses such as **niku-buku**.
hataracha·a, *n*. A worker; a good worker; an eager beaver.
hatara·chi, *n*. [hataraki] **1** Work; labor; efforts. **2** Ability; resources. **3** Earnings; income; pay.
hatarachi-kwaa, *n*. Overwork; overexertion; strain.
hatara·chun, *vi*. [hataraku] To work; labor; toil; exert oneself; serve (at).
hata-suga·shi, *n*. Banner waving, a ritual purging evil spirits performed immediately after the *Bon* festival on the sixteenth of the lunar seventh month. [ODJ]
hata-u·i, *n*. [hataori] Weaving.
hata-uya·a, *n*. A weaver.
hatchaka·in, *vi*. To happen to meet; come across.
hatchiri·in, *vi*. To burst; break open.
hati, *n*. [hate] An end; a close; a termination; a conclusion; the result; the outcome.
hati·i, *n*. [< **hati·in**] A reckless person; a daredevil.
hati·in, *vt*. [hateru] **1** To end; terminate; be finished. **2** To go beyond the limit.
hat-tachi, *n*. [hattatsu] Development; growth; progress; advance.
hat-tu, *n*. [hatto] Law; prohibition; a ban; taboo.
ha-ui, *n*. [haori] A Japanese short-coat; a *haori* coat.
hayama·i-gutu, *n*. Rashness; prematurity.
hayami·in, *vt*. [hayameru] To hasten; speed up.
hee[1], *n*. Same as **fee**[1].
hee[2], *n*. Same as **fee**[2].
hee-fuki, *n*. The southerly wind in the fifth lunar month. [OBJ]
hee-gasa, *n*. Scabies, a kind of eczema found on the head. Also **sami, feegasa**.
hee-gattin, *n*. [hayagatten] Same as **feegattin**.

hee·i, *n*. [hayari] Same as **feei**.
hee·i-kutuba, *n*. [hayari-kotoba] Same as **feeikutuba**.
hee·in, *vi*. [hayaru] Same as **feein**.
hee-jara, *n*. [haizara] Same as **feejara**.
hee-juri-ngwa, *n*. Same as **yamana-shingwa, feejuringwa**.
hee-kacha·a, *n*. [haikaki] An ash rake; a (stove) poker.
hee·ku, *adv*. [hayaku] Early (in time); before; in the old times. Also **feeku**.
hee-kurusa·a, *n*. A flyswatter.
heerin·chun, *vi*. To enter: fall in one's way.
hee·san, *adj*. [hayai] Same as **feesan**.
hibachi, *n*. [hibachi] Same as **fibachi**.
hibana, *n*. [hibana] Same as **fibana**.
hibichi, *n*. [hibiki] Same as **fibichi**.
hibi·chun, *vi*. [hibiku] Same as **fibi-chun**.
hi-bu, *n*. [hibu] Same as **fibu**.
hi-bu·shi, *n*. [hiboshi] Same as **hibushi**.
hicha, *n*. [shita] Same as **shicha**[2].
hichaa·sun, *vt*. Same as **fichaasun**.
hicha·i, *n*. [hikari] Same as **fichai**.
hicha·in, *vi*. [hikaru] Same as **fichain**.
hichi, *n*. [hiki] A lever. See also **fichi**[1].
hichi-du, *n*. [hikido] Same as **fichidu**.
hichi-gwachi, *n*. [shichigatsu] Same as **shichigwachi**.
hichigwachi-eisaa, *n*. Same as **shichigwachi'eisaa**.
hichi-hana·sun, *vt*. [hikihanasu] Same as **fichihanasun**.
hichiji, *n*. [hitsuji] The Ram as the eighth of the twelve calendrical animal signs. See also **hiijaa**[1], **meenaahiijaa**.
hichiki·in, *vt*. Same as **shichikiin**.
hichi-mun, *n*. [hikimono] Same as **fichi-mun**.
hichi-mun-jeeku, *n*. [hikimono + saiku] Same as **fichimunjeeku**.
hichi-'nmaga, *n*. Same as **fichi'nmaga**.
hichi-nu·jun, *vt*. [hikinuku] **1** To pull out; extract; uproot. **2** To choose; pick out.

hi·chi-suu, *n*. [hikishio] An ebb tide; low water.
hi·chi-ta·chun, *vi*. [·tan, ·tchi; hikitatsu] Same as fichitachun.
hi·chi-tu·in, *vt*. [hikitoru] 1 To take over; take charge of; look after. 2 To claim (a lost article).
hi·chi-uki·in, *vt*. [hikiukeru] Same as fichi'ukiin.
hichi-uushi, *n*. [hiki-usu] A stone handmill; a quern.
hichi-wata·sun, *vt*. [hikiwatasu] To deliver; transfer; hand over; turn over; surrender; extradite.
hi·chun[1], *vt*. [hiku] 1 To draw; pull; tug; haul. 2 To deduct; subtract; decrease. 3 To solicit; tout. 4 To lead. 5 To install. Also fichun[1]. See also hippain.
hi·chun[2], *vt*. To play (an instrument). Also fichun[2].
hidati, *n*. [hedate] 1 A barrier; a partition; reserve; estrangement; alienation. 2 Distinction; discrimination. Also fidati.
hidati·in, *vt*. To alienate; estrange; part; set apart; screen; shield. Also fidatiin.
hidiri, *n*. [< J hideri] Same as hyaai.
hi-du·i, *n*. [hidori] Fixing a date; selecting a date (for moving, a wedding, building a house, etc.). Also fidui. See also tuin.
hi-gan, *n*. [higan] 1 The equinoctial week. 2 Buddhist services performed during the equinoctial week in the second and eighth lunar months. 3 Nirvana. [OBJ, ODJ]
hi-gara, *n*. [higara] Auspiciousness of the day; the kind of day. Also figara.
hi-gasa, *n*. [higasa] A parasol. Also figasa. See kasa[1].
higashi, *n*. [higashi] East; eastern; easterly. Also figashi, agari.
hi-gataka, *n*. A sunshade; an awning; a sun blind. Also figataka. See also kataka.
hi-gwashi, *n*. [higashi] Dry confections.

Also figwashi. See also kwaashi.
hii[1], *n*. [he] A fart; flatulence; breaking wind. Also fii[1].
hii[2], *n*. [hi] Fire; flame; blaze; light. Also fii[2].
hii[3], *n*. [hi] A fault; a misdeed; a mistake; unjustness. Also fii[3]. Same as hiikushi.
hii[4], *n*. [hi] Same as fii[4]. Also tiida.
hii-baashi, *n*. [hibashi] A pair of tongs; a set of fire irons. Also fiibaashi.
hii-batara·chi, *n*. Lit., fire work; extremely busy work, such as at a fire. [GSS]
hiichi, *n*. [hiiki] Favor; patronage; partiality; favoritism. Also fiichi. -sun, *v*. To be partial; show favoritism.
hiichin, *n*. Same as fiichin. Also fiichi.
hii-chin, *n*. [fuikin*, fukin] A dishcloth; a dishtowel; a table napkin. Also fiichin.
hii-dama, *n*. [hidama] A fireball as a premonition of disaster; a spirit of the deceased burning as a ball of fire. Also fiidama, tamagai.
hiidama-gee·shi, *n*. A magic formula, invoked by making a commotion such as ringing a bell or beating a drum, performed at the village entrance to keep a hiidama fireball away from the village. Same as hiigeeshi (1).
hii-fucha·a, *n*. Same as fiifuchi.
hii-fu·chi, *n*. Same as fuufuchi.
hii-fuka·a, *n*. Same as hiifuchaa.
hii-gee·shi, *n*. Lit., driving a fire back. 1 Same as hiidamageeshi. 2 A communal firefighting pond. 3 A stone lion regarded as a protector from fire, evil spirits, or epidemics. See keesun.
hii-gucha·a-sun, *v*. To drink directly from a pot without using a cup. See hiijaa[2], kuchi[2].
hii-gukuchi, *n*. See kukuchi[2].
hii-guni, *n*. A cold country.
hii-hii-tuu, *n*. 1 Complete equality. 2 A draw in a game or fight. 3 Dying out.

hiija, *n.* [hida] Wrinkles; lines; furrows; pleats.

hiijaa[1], *n.* [hitsuji] A goat. Also **fiijaa**. See also **hichiji**.

hii-jaa[2], *n.* [hi + kawa] A well or spring from which water is made available by means of a conduit.

hiijaa-shishi, *n.* Goat meat.

hii-jii, *n.* [heizei] Same as **fiijii**.

hiijii-chiya·a, *n.* Same as **issoochiyaa**.

hii-jimi, *n.* [hizeme] A fire attack.

hii-jiri, *n.* Embers. Also **fiijiri**.

hii-kushi, *n.* [hikuse] A fault; a defect; a flaw; a blemish; a foible. Also **fiikushi**, **hii**[3], **fii**[3].

hi·in[1], *vi.* [·ran, ·tchi; heru] To recede; run low; ebb.

hi·in[2], *vt.* [·ran, ·tchi; hiru] To void; evacuate; fart; sneeze.

hi·in[3], *vi.* [·ran, ·tchi; hiru] To dry; lose moisture; dessicate. See **fuusun**.

hii-mutu, *n.* [himoto] The origin of a fire. Also **hiimuutu**.

hii-naa, *n.* [hinawa] A match-cord; a fuse, generally made of hemp palm hair. [UKH]

hiira, *n.* [hera] A spatula; a trowel. Also **fiira**.

hiiraa, *n.* A cockroach. Also **fiiraa**, **toobiiraa**.

hiiraa moo·i, *phr.* Lit., a cockroach's dance; moving about busily under work pressure. [GSS]

hiira·chun, *vi.* [hiiragu* < hibiraku*] To smart with pain. Also **fiirachun**.

hii·san, *adj.* [hie-] Cold (of weather or climate). Also **fiisan**. See also **hijuru-san**.

hii·sa-oo, *n. colloq.* One who is sensitive to cold.

hiisa-umi·i, *n.* One who is sensitive to cold. Also **fiisa'umii**.

hii-su, *n.* Ebb tide; low tide.

hiitaa, *n.* Same as **fiitaa**.

hii-tai, *n.* [< J heitai] A soldier.

hii-tati·i, *n.* 1 Chimney. 2 A lighthouse in the premodern period, consisting of a stone lantern on top of a pile of rocks on a high hill. 3 A beacon; a signal fire (flare); a rocket. Also **fiitatii**.

hiitu, *n.* A porpoise; a dolphin. Also **fiitu**.

hija, *n.* [< J hiza] A knee; a lap. See **hisa**.

hija·a, *n.* A person with a luxurious beard. See **hiji**.

hijai[1], 1 *n.* Lit., left; the guardian deity of the tomb; the deity who oversees the other world. [ODJ]. 2 *pref.* Abnormal; unclean. See **hijeetiinagaa**, **hijainuudii**, **hijai'uchaashi**, **hijeegun**, **hijaimigui**, **hijaruu**. [OGJ, ZRJ]

hijai[2], *n.* [hidari] Left; the left side. Also **fijai**.

hijai-gatti, *n.* Left-handed.

hijai-kutuba, *n.* Lit., left-handed language; abnormal language; accented speech. [UKH]

hijai-migu·i, *n.* (Business) taking a turn for the worse. See **migui**.

hijai-naa, *n.* A taboo rope; a rope twisted to the left, used to ward off evil or to indicate a purged area. Also **shoojinnaa**, **subinaa**, **shirunna**[1]. See also **shimakusarashi**, **naa**[4].

hijai-nushi, *n.* A wrestling technique, in which the opponent is thrown down left to right. See **shima**[3], **nushi**[1].

hijai-nuudii, *n.* Tone deafness. Also **fijianuudii**.

hijai-uchaashi, *n.* Wearing a kimono with the left front on top of the right front. See **uchaasun**.

hijami, *n.* A barrier; a distinction; a partition; an interval; that which separates. Also **fijami**.

hijami·in, *vt.* To separate; distance; set apart; interpose; shield; leave behind.

hija·mun, *vi.* [higamu] To be jaundiced; be biased; be soured. [UKH]

hijana, *n.* [hidana] Shelf for firewood at the back of ovens in the kitchen. [UKH]

hijaru·u, *n.* **1** Awkwardness; clumsiness; gawkiness. **2** An awkward person; a clumsy person. Also **fijaruu**.
hijaruu-gi·san, *adj.* Looking clumsy; looking foolish; maladroit; bungling.
hijaya·a, *n.* Left-handedness; a southpaw; a left-handed person. Also **fijayaa**. See **hijai**[2].
hijee-gun, *n.* Placing soup and rice the reverse (wrong) positions on a tray. See **kumun**[2].
hijee-tii-naga·a, *n.* A thief. See **hijai**[1].
hiji, *n.* [hige] **1** A beard; whiskers. **2** An aerial root. See also **shichahiji, hanahiji, yamahijaa**.
hiji-gee, *n.* [hiji] An elbow. Also **fijigee**.
hiji-moo, *n.* A beardless man; beardlessness; a natural lack of facial hair. Also **fijimoo**.
hiju·i, *n.* Cold; chill; chilly air. Also **fijui**.
hiju·in, *vi.* To grow cold; grow chilly. Also **fijuin**. See also **hijurasun**.
hi·jun, *vt.* [hegu] To shave off; slice off thin. Also **fijun**.
hijura·sun, *vt.* To make something cold; cool; refrigerate.
hijuru-ashi, *n.* A cold sweat due to illness. Also **fijuru'ashi**.
hijuru-gucha·a, *n.* A person sensitive to hot food. [UKH] See **kuchi**[2].
hijuru-kaji, *n.* A cold wind. Also **fijurukaji**.
hijuru·san, *adj.* (Of things and persons) cold; chilly; icy; freezing. Also **fijurusan**. See also **hiisan**.
hijuru-miji, *n.* Cold water.
hijuru·u, *n.* **1** Coldness (things and persons). **2** A coldhearted person; a dispassionate person. Also **fijuruu**.
hijuruu-kookoo, *n.* Extreme cold; stonecoldness. See also **achikookoo**.
hijut·teen, *adv.* Feeling chilly. Also **fijutteen**.
hi-juu, *adv.* Constantly; incessantly; always.
hi-kaji, *n.* [hikazu] The number of days.
Also **fikaji**.
hikari, *n.* [hikari] **1** Light. Same as **hichai**. **2** Authority; power; influence. **3** Honor; prestige.
hikasari·in, *vt.* [·ran, t·ti; hikasareru] To be drawn by; to be touched with; to be seduced by. Also **fikasariin**.
hikee, *n.* [hikae] **1** A copy; a memo. **2** An assistant. Also **fikee**.
hikee·in, *vt.* [hikaeru] **1** To make a copy; write down. **2** To be in waiting. **3** To hold back. Also **fikeein**.
hikee-ju, *n.* [hikaejo] A waiting room; a lobby.
hik-kaki·in, *vt.* [hikkakeru] To hook; hang; hitch; catch.
hikkumi·in, *vt.* [hikkomeru] To make (a person or thing) withdraw or pull back. Also **fikkumiin**.
hikku·mun, *vi.* [hikkomu] To withdraw; retire; stand back. Also **fikkumun**.
hiku·san, *adj.* [hikui] (of space) low; (of social status) low. Also **fikusan**.
hima, *n.* [hima] **1** Time. **2** Leisure; spare time. **3** Dull; slack. **4** Leave; furlough; a vacation. **5** Dismissal; discharge.
hima-daari, *n.* **1** Time-consuming. **2** Wasting time without earning. Also **fimadaari**. See **taari**.
hi-mudu·i, *n.* [himodori] Returning in one day.
hi-mun, *n.* [himon*, hibun] An epitaph. Also **fimun**.
hina-gata, *n.* [hinagata] An example; standard. Also **finagata**.
hina·in, *vi.* To decrease; diminish; dwindle; subside.
hinara·sun, *vt.* To reduce; decrease; diminish; lessen; abate.
hin-bin, *n.* [henben] Same as **finbin**.
hinga·a, *n.* A dirty fellow. See **hingu**.
hinga·sun, *vt.* To let one escape; allow one to flee.
hingi·in, *vi.* To escape; flee; run away.
hingi-maa·i, *n.* Lit., fleeing and going around. **-sun**, *vi. colloq.* To flee (dodge,

run) from place to place.
hingi-'nma, *n.* A runaway horse.
hingu, *n.* Filth; grime; dirt.
hinji-mun, *n.* A contrary person; a delinquent; a scoundrel. See **hingiin.**
hin-pun, *n.* [C pingfeng] A screening wall located between a house front and the gate.
hin-sun, *vi.* To become sulky; be peevish; pout; sulk. Also **fin-sun.**
hinsuu, *n.* [< J hinsoo] Poverty; indigency; need. Also **finsuu.**
hinsuu-mun, *n.* A poor person; the poor. Also **finsuumun.** See also **kuushiimun.**
hinsuumun·nu taka yiitan·nee·sshi, *phr. slang.* Lit., being as happy as a poor person given a falcon. [GSS]
hinta, *n.* Same as **shinta.** [GSS]
hin-too, *n.* [hentoo] A reply; an answer; a response. Also **fintoo.**
hi·nu-kan, *n.* Fire deity; hearth deity. [OBJ] Also **finukan.**
hip-pa·in, *vt.* [hipparu] 1 To pull; draw; jerk. 2 To stretch. 3 To arrest; to bring. See also **hichun**[1].
hira[1], *n.* [hire] A fin.
hira[2], *n.* [hira*] A slope; an incline; a hill; uphill. See **sakabira, saka**[2]. Also **fira.**
hira-baaki, *n.* A flat basket also used as a tray.
hira·chun, *vt.* [hiraku] To open; unfold. Also **firachun.**
hira-fa-gusa, *n.* A (broad-leafed) plantain; whiteman's foot [J oobako; *Plantago asiatica* L.]. [FOSR, ODJ]
hira-gwee, *n.* A flat hoe which is widely used to till wet paddies and dry fields. See **kwee**[1].
hira·in, *vi.* [·(r)an, ·ti] To keep company with; associate with; serve. Also **firain.** See **hiree.**
hiraka·sun, *vt.* To flatten; level.
hiraki·in[1], *vi.* 1 To become flat. 2 To sit down; get tired and sit down. Also **firakiin.**

hiraki·in[2], *vi.* [hirakeru] To become open; become civilized; be enlightened.
hiraku·mun, *vi.* To become numb; be paralyzed. Also **firakumun.**
hira·ku na·in, *vi.* To sit cross-legged; sit comfortably.
hira-mushiru, *n.* A fine mattress made of fiber or cotton threads. Also **shichimushiru.** See also **mushiru.**
hira-pettaa, *n. colloq.* Anything that is flat.
hira·san, *adj.* [hirai*] Flat; level. Also **firasan.**
hira-ukoo, *n.* Flat incense. Also **faa'ukoo, shima'ukoo, kuru'ukoo.**
hire·e, *n.* Friendship; fellowship; association; company. Also **firee.** See **hirain.**
hireeyas·san, *adj.* [...-yashi·ku] Friendly; amicable; easy to get along with. Also **fireeyassan.**
hiri, *n.* [heri] The edge; the verge; the brink; the hem; the border; the edging (of tatami mats); a fringe (of curtain). Also **firi**[1].
hiru[1], *n.* [hiru] Midday; day (as opposed to night). Also **firu**[1].
hiru[2], *n.* [hiru*] Giant garlic [J ninniku; *Allium scorodoprasum* var. *viviparum* Regel]. [FOSR] Also **firu**[2].
hiru[3], *n.* [hiro] A fathom; a unit of length and depth traditionally equivalent to two arms outstretched. Also **firu**[3].
hiruga·i, *n.* [hirogari] Extent; expanse; prosperity of descendants. Also **firugai.**
hiruga·in, *vi.* [hirogaru] To spread (out); cover over; widen; stretch; multiply. Also **firugain.**
hirugi·in, *vt.* [hirogeru] To spread; enlarge; extend; expand; widen. Also **firugiin.**
hiru-ma, *n.* [hiruma] Afternoon; day; daytime; late lunch. See **hiru**[1], **firu**[1]. Also **firuma.**
hiruma-nin·ji, *n.* An afternoon nap.

hiruma·s(h)an, *adj.* Unusual; wonderful; strange; extraordinary; weird; bizarre; incredible; mysterious. Also **firumas(h)an.**

hiru·sa, *n.* [hirosa] Width; breadth; extent; area; dimension. Also **firusa.**

hiru·san, *adj.* [hiroi] Wide; broad; large; spacious; roomy; vast. Also **firusan.**

hi-ruu, *n.* [hiroo] A lawsuit; litigation; legal proceedings. Also **firuu. -sun,** *vt.* To sue (a person for damages); file suit (for); take legal proceedings (against). Also **firuusun.**

hisa, *n.* [hiza] A foot; a leg; a paw; a limb. Also **fisa.**

hisa-daakaa-sun, *v.* To stand on one's toes.

hisa-kata, *n.* A footprint; a track. Also **fisakata.**

hisa-kubi, *n.* An ankle. Also **fisakubi.**

hisa-manchi, *n.* [hizamazuku] Sitting straight; sitting square with one's legs folded underneath. **-sun,** *v.* To sit in a formal position with one's legs folded underneath.

hisa-manchu·u, *n.* Same as **hisamanchi.**

hisa-moo, *n.* A person without one leg. Also **fisamoo.**

hisa-naa, *n.* The instep of the foot. Also **fisanaa.**

hisa·nu-wata, *n.* The sole of the foot. Also **fisanuwata.**

hishi, *n.* [hise] An atoll; a lagoon island; a shore reef. Also **fishi.**

his·san[1], *adj.* Thin; light; weak. Also **fissan.**

his-san[2], *n.* [hissan] Reading, writing, and arithmetic.

hita, *n.* [heta] Unskillfulness. **·na,** *adj.* Unskillful; inexpert; unskilled. Also **fita.**

hita·ni, *adv.* [hitasura] Earnestly; intently; fervently; solely. Also **fitani.**

hitchii, *adv.* All day long; incessantly; constantly.

hitchii-baru, *n.* To work all day without returning home for lunch. Also **fitchiibaru.**

hitchii-gushi·i, *n.* Every other day.

hitchii-shikuchi, *n.* A day's work; amount of work that takes from morning till evening.

hitchiki·in, *vt.* [hittsukeru] To join; stick; paste; attach.

hitchiri·in, *vi.* [...ri·ran, ...t·ti] To get torn off; get pulled off; get wrenched off. See also **fitchiin.**

hiti·in, *vt.* Same as **shitiin.** See also **kachihitiin.**

hitimiti, *n.* Same as **sutumiti, shitimiti.**

hitimiti-mun, *n.* Same as **shitimitimun.**

hiya, *interj.* Yo! yo-ho!

hi-yaki, *n.* [hiyake] Sunburn; suntan.

hiya-mika·sun, *vi.* To let out a yell of **hiya.** See **hiya.**

hiyat·teen, *adj.* Coolly; in a chilly way.

hi-yoo, *n.* [hiyoo] A day laborer; a laborer paid by the day. Also **fiyoo.**

hiyoo-saa, *n.* A day laborer. Same as **hiyoo.**

hoo, *n.* [poto*] The female genitals; vagina. See also **hoosun, hoomisun.** Also **hoomi.**

hoochaa, *n.* [hoochoo] A kitchen knife; a cleaver.

hoo-chaku, *n.* A firecracker.

hoochi, *n.* [hooki] A broom. See also **waraboochi, baranboochi, dakiboochi, suutiichibaaboochi.**

hoochi-bushi, *n.* [hookiboshi] A comet.

hoochi-kachi, *n.* Sweeping and cleaning. Same as **hoochi.** See **-kachi.**

hoo·chun, *vt.* **1** To sweep; sweep with a broom. **2** To box; hit on the side of the face.

hoo-gaku, *n.* [hoogaku] A direction.

hoogen-fuda, *n.* Lit., a dialect tag; a demerit marker used in Okinawan schools ca. 1910–1945 for students caught speaking Okinawan instead of standard Japanese. [ODJ]

hoo-hai, *n.* A magic formula to drive

away evils or fires. See **hoo, hain**².
hoohai muuchii, *n*. Lit., vagina exposure rice cake; rice cakes associated with the rite of **hoohai**. Also **muuchii**. See also **hoohai, hoohai utaki**.
hoohai utaki, *n*. Sacred Grove of Vagina Exposure, a popular name for Uchikanagusuku Sacred Grove in Kanagusuku, Shuri. [ODJ]
hoo·i-kakan, *n*. A pleated skirt with a long train reserved for upper class ladies in the premodern period. See also **kakan, dujin**.
hoo·in¹, *vi*. [hau] To crawl; creep; grovel; trail.
hoo·in², *vt*. [hooru] 1 To scatter about; strew. 2 To sprinkle.
hooji, *n*. [hooji] A general term for Buddhist functions such as funerals, anniversaries, and memorial services.
hooka, *n*. [hooka] Tricks; stunts; magic; acrobatics.
hooka-saa, *n*. A magician; a juggler; a sleight-of-hand performer.
hoo-mi, *n*. Same as **hoo**.
hoomi-sun, *v*. Same as **hoosun**.
hoo-sun, *v*. To have sexual intercourse; have coitus. See **hoo**.
hoota·nu-kui, *n*. [hotaru] A firefly. [GSS] Also **jiinaa**.
hoo-too, *n*. [hootoo] Dissipation; profligacy; debauchery.
hootoo-mun, *n*. A prodigal; a debauchee; a libertine.
hootu, *n*. [hato] A pigeon; a dove.
hootu-nni·i, *n*. [hatomune] A woman with a bulging chest like a pigeon.
hoo-wiigoo, *n. pej*. A lewd woman. See **wiigoosan**.
hyaa, *n. interj*. Indicates insult and insolence.
hyaai, *n*. A drought; dry weather.
hyaai-ami, *n*. Rain in a drought; welcome rain.
hyaai-dushi, *n*. A year of drought.
hyaai-gannai, *n*. Thunder without rain during a drought.
hyaakuu-gwaa, *n*. A name given to an infant before it has a formal name. See **naajikii**.
hyaku, *n*. [hyaku] One hundred. Also **hyaaku**.
hyaku-ichi·i, *n*. [hyakuichi] A liar; one who tells one truth out of a hundred.
hyaku-soo, *n*. [hyakushoo] A commoner.
hyoo-ban, *n*. [hyooban] 1 Criticism. 2 Reputation; fame; popularity; popular opinion. 3 Notoriety. **-sun**, *vt*. To talk about; gossip; criticize.
hyoo-shi, *n*. [hyooshi] 1 A rhythm; measure; (musical) time. 2 A chance; the moment; timing.
hyooshi·na-mun, *n*. Happenstance; chance; fortuity.
hyoo-tan, *n*. [hyootan] A bottle gourd. Same as **chiburu**.

I———

-i, *interrog. suff*. Appended to sentences to form yes/no questions.
ibai, *n*. Edge of a fight or exhibition ring such as in prizefights, wrestling, or bullfights; ringside.
iba·in, *vi*. [< J ibaru] To be proud; be haughty; be inflated with pride.
iba-michi, *n*. A narrow road.
ibami·i, *n*. A small and narrow place.
ibami·in, *vt*. [sebameru] To narrow; reduce; contract.
iba·san, *adj*. [semai] Narrow; small; limited (in area). See also **shibasan**.
ibaya·a, *n*. A braggart; a vain person; a boastful person.
ibi¹, *n*. [ebi] 1 A shrimp. 2 A lobster.
ibi², *n*. 1 The inner sanctuary of a holy grove; a holy grove where a god resides; a god itself. 2 A divine stone. 3 Spirit of the ancestral founder of a village.

ibinagii

ibi-nagii, *n.* Same as **iibinagii**. [GSS]
ibi·nu-mee, *n.* 1 An entrance to an **ibi** holy sanctuary. [ODJ]
ibira[1], *n.* A tool used to fasten the thatch on a roof. [UKH]
ibira[2], *n.* A large rice ladle used on festive occasions. [UKH]
ibira·a, *n.* A miser; a niggard; a stingy fellow. Also **irasaa**. [GSS]
ibira-gwaa, *n.* Same as **mishigee**. [GSS]
ibiri·in, *vi.* To be stingy; be niggardly.
icha[1], *n.* [ita] A board; a plank. Also **ita**.
icha[2], *n.* [ika] A cuttlefish; a squid. Also **ika**.
ichaa·sun, *vt.* To bring together; cause to meet.
icha·gachii, *adv.* Same as **ichigachii**.
icha·ganaa, *adv.* Same as **ichigachii**.
icha-garasu, *n.* Salted cuttlefish shreds. See **karasu**[1].
icha-gwaa, *n.* A small cuttlefish; a dried cuttlefish.
ichai, *n.* [ikari] An anchor. Also **ikai**.
ichai-hanchai, *n. colloq.* A dialogue. **-sun**, *v.* To ask and answer questions.
icha·in, *vi.* [·(r)an, ·ti; ikiau] 1 To meet by chance; come across; see (only of persons). 2 To meet; interview. 3 (For a cord, etc.) to reach; (for financial balance sheet) to meet. 4 To have sexual intercourse.
ichanda, *n.* Free; without charge. See **tada**[1].
ichanda-jin, *n.* Wasted money; unearned money.
ichanda-mun, *n.* A thing free of charge; gratis.
ichanda-nanji, *n.* Working hard without recompense.
icha·san, *adj.* 1 Pitiful; be sorry. 2 Precious; ill-spared.
iche·e, *n.* [ikiai] A meeting; an interview; an audience.
ichi[1,] *n.* [ichi] One. See also **tiichi**.
ichi[2], *n.* [ike] A man-made pond; a pool; a cistern; a basin. See also **kumui**[2].

ichi[3], *n.* [itsu] When; what time.
i·chi[4], *n.* [iki] An outbound trip.
ichi[5], *n.* [eki] Gain; profit; benefit; advantage.
ichi[6], *n.* [eki*] Divination based on the I-ching [Book of Changes].
i·chi-ata·i, *n.* The end of a road.
ichi-ban, *n.* [ichiban] The most; the best; the number one. Also **itchin**[3].
ichi-bana, *n.* [ikebana] The art of flower arranging.
ichiban-ja, *n.* [ichibanza] The best room in a house; the drawing room; parlor where visitors are received. Also **ufu-jaa**. [GSS]
ichi·chi, *n.* [itsutsu] Five; five years old.
ichichi-mii, *n.* [itsutsume] The fifth.
ichi·chun, *vi.* [ikiru] To live; subsist; exist.
ichi-dee, *n.* [ichidai] One's lifetime; one generation.
ichi-deeji, *n.* [ichidaiji] An emergency; a serious happenstance; a matter of great importance.
ichi·gachii, *adv.* In passing; on one's way.
ichi-gee·in, *vi.* [ikigaeru] To become restored to life; be revived.
ichigeera·sun, *vt.* [ikigaerasu] To restore to life; revive.
ichi-goo-nakamui, *n.* A one-**goo** dry measure box. Same as **nakamui**. See **chiiga**[2].
ichigoonu·u, *n.* A one-**goo** liquid measurement jar. See also **chuwakasaa**.
ichi-gwachi, *n.* [ichigatsu] January.
ichi-hati, *n.* [ikihate] The end; the extremity.
ichi-ichi, *n.* [ichiichi] One by one; singly; individually; separately.
ichi-jama, *n.* 1 An apparition of a live person. 2 A sorcerer; sorcery. **-sun**, *vt.* To curse, anathematize; imprecate evil upon (a person); wish a person ill.
ichijama·a, *n.* A sorcerer.
ichi-jimu, *n.* One's feelings; true senti-

ments as a human being. See **chimu**.
ichika, *n*. [itsuka] Someday; once; in due time; sooner or later.
ichiku, *n*. A cousin. Same as **ichuku**.
ichi·karan-ichi·chi, *n. colloq.* Life that cannot be lived; life which is so poor that it is not worth living. [GSS]
ichi-mabui, *n*. The spirit of a living person. See **mabui**.
ichi-mi, *n*. [ikimi] The fact of being alive in this world; this life; the world of the living.
ichimi-tutuuma, *n*. Same as **ichimitutuumi**.
ichimi-tutuumi, *n*. Throughout one's life; for life; as long as one is alive. Also **ichimitutuuma**.
i·chi-mudu·i, *n*. [ikimodori] Going and returning; a round-trip.
ichi-mun[1], *n*. [ikimono] A living being; a living creature.
ichi-mun[2], *n*. A clan; the relatives.
ichimun-jurii, *n*. A clan meeting.
ichi-mushi, *n*. A beast; an animal; a brute.
ichi-nanka, *n*. The Buddhist memorial service on the thirty-fifth day after death. See also **nanka**.
ichinichi sookwan, *phr.* Dying suddenly in one day; a person who dies a sudden death. [UKH]
ichi-nin, *n*. [ichinen] One year.
ichi-ninchi, *n*. [inchineki] The first annual memorial service. See **ninchi**[1].
ichi-ninmee[1], *n*. [ichininmae] One portion; a person's share; one helping.
ichinin-mee[2], *n*. [ichinenmae] One year ago.
ichi-nuku-hin, *n*. A five-**goo** liquid measuring jar. See also **chuwakasaa**.
ichi-nuku·in, *vi.* [ikinokoru] To survive; outlive.
ichiri-jika, *n*. [ichirizuka] A stone or pillar showing the distance in **ri** (approximately 4 km or 2.5 mi.).
i·chi-shiji, *n*. [ikisugi] Going too far; going to extremes.
ichi-shi·ni, *n*. [ikishini] Between life and death.
ichi-ta·in, *vi.* To be attentive to details; be most considerate. (Used only in negative forms.) See **ichitaran**.
ichita·ran *vi. neg.* To be careless; be inattentive; be thoughtless.
ichi-tchu, *n*. A live person (as opposed to a dead one). See **shinitchu**.
ichi-wakari, *n*. A lifelong separation; a long parting.
ichu, *n*. [ito] Silk. Also **iichu, itu**.
ichubi, *n*. [ichigo] 1 A Ryukyu berry [*Rubus grayanus* Maxim.] Also **munjuru'ichubi, taka'ichubi**. 2 A Ryukyu rose berry [*Rubus croceacanthus* Lév.]. [FOSR]
ichui, *n*. [ikioi] 1 Force; vigor; power. 2 Energy; vigor; spirit; dash; vivacity. 3 Influence; power; might; sway. See also **shii**[1].
ichu-jin, *n*. Same as **itujin**. [GSS]
ichuku, *n*. [itoko] A cousin. Also **ichiku**.
ichuku-kasabai, *n*. The taboo doubling up of cousins' mortuary tablets on one family altar. See **choodeekasabai, shijitadashi**.
ichuku-mii-kkwa, *n*. The daughter of one's cousin.
ichuku-mii-'nmaga, *n*. The female grandchild of one's cousin. [UKH]
ichuku-wii-kkwa, *n*. The son of one's cousin.
ichuku-wubamaa, *n*. [itokooba] A female cousin of one's parents. Also **ichikuwubamaa**.
ichuku-wujasaa, *n*. [itokooji] A male cousin of one's parents. Also **ichikuwujasaa**.
Ichumana·a, *n*. 1 A person of the town of Itoman. 2 A fisherman [of Itoman].
Ichuman-u·i, *n*. Lit., selling to Itoman; apprenticeship of children, typically boys about ten years of age, to the fishermen's town of Itoman in exchange

ichun

for an advance. See also **yatuingwa, suutaa.**
i·chun, *vi. irreg.* [iku] To go; proceed; visit; leave.
ichuna·s(h)an, *adj.* Busy; occupied; engaged.
ichuta, *n.* A little while.
ichuta·nu-hanshi, *n.* A temporary measure; a shift; an expedient measure. Also **chuteenuhanshi.**
ichu·u, *n.* Variant of **iichuu.** [GSS]
i-fee, *n.* [ihai] Same as **iifee.**
i-fuu·na, *adj.* [ihuu-na] Strange; odd; singular; suspicious-looking.
ifuu·na-kaja, *n.* Odor; bad smell.
i-gu, *n.* [igo] After this; from now on; hereafter; in the future.
iguma·sun, *vt.* **1** To plan with ardor; be enthusiastic in undertaking. [OGJ] **2** To forewarn; foretell. [UKH]
i-gun, *n.* [yuigon] Will; one's last injunctions; one's dying wish.
ihii-ahaa, *adv.* Cheerfully; with laughter. **-sun,** *vi. colloq.* To talk cheerfully with laughter.
ii[1]**,** *interj.* Yes; affirmative response (to an equal or inferior). See also **uu**[2]**, oo.**
ii[2]**,** *n.* [i] Same as **yii**[1]**.**
ii[3]**,** *n.* [i] Same as **yii**[2]**.**
ii[4]**,** *n.* [yui] Same as **yuimaaruu, yiimaaru, yii**[3]**.**
ii[5]**,** *n.* [e] Same as. See **yii**[4]**.**
ii[6]**,** *n.* [i] The stomach; the paunch (of an animal).
i·i-aa·sun, *vt.* [iiawasu] To talk over and decide; consult with.
i·i-ati·in, *vt.* [iiateru] To guess right; make a good guess.
iibi, *n.* [yubi] A finger; a toe. See also **ufu'iibi, tchusashi'iibi, naka'iibi, narashi**[3]**, narashi'iibi, iibingwaa.**
iibi-ban, *n.* [yubiban] A thumb impression; a thumbprint.
iibi-banchi, *n.* Plucking strings of (musical instrument) with one's fingers (instead of with a plectrum).

iibi-kakiyee, *n.* A game in which two players interlock the middle fingers of their right hands and each tries to twist the opponent's fist down. [OBJ]
iibi-nagii, *n.* [yubigane] A ring; a finger ring. Also **ibinagii.** [GSS]
iibi-ngwaa, *n.* **1** A little finger. **2** (As a gesture) one's woman, one's sweetheart.
iibi·nu-sachi, *n.* A fingertip.
iibi-uusee, *n.* A game of thumb wrestling played by two people. [OBJ]
i·i-bun, *n.* [iibun] **1** One's say; one's claim; **2** An objection; a grievance.
iichi, *n.* [iki] A breath; breathing. See also **feefee-sun.**
i·i-chiki, *n.* [iitsuke] An order; a command; instruction.
iichiki·in, *vt.* [iitsukeru] **1** To tell; command; instruct. **2** To tell (on a person); tell tales.
iichi-madii, *n.* Suffocation; asphyxiation. See **-madii.**
iichi-mii, *n.* A breathing hole.
iichiri, *n.* Same as **yiichiri.**
i·i-chite·e, *n.* [iitsutae] An oral tradition; a legend; a folktale. Also **chiteebanashi.**
iichu, *n.* [ito] Silk. Also **itu.**
iichu-jin, *n.* A silk kimono.
iichuu, *n.* [ito] A thread; a cotton thread. Also **ichuu.**
ii-diiru, *n.* A lunch basket with lid made of bamboo peculiar to Yonaguni Island. [ODJ] See also **tiiru.**
ii-fee, *n.* [ihai] A mortuary tablet; a memorial tablet. See also **ifee, tootoomee, shiru'iifee.** [ODJ]
iifu, *n.* Gravel or mud washed down the bed of a stream; sediment.
ii-fuya·a, *n.* A pointed spatula.
ii-gaai, *n.* An argument; a dispute; a quarrel; a fracas. Also **iigaaee.**
ii-gaaee, *n.* Same as **iigaai.**
i·i-ha·i, *n.* [iiharu] Assertion; insistence; persistence.

i·i-ha·in, *vt.* [iiharu] To persıst; insist; assert.
ii-hicha, *n.* Top and bottom; upper and lower; high and low; all classes of people. [UKH] See **'wiishicha.**
ii-i-ii, *interj.* Same as yiiyiyii.
ii·in, *vt.* [ueru] Same as **'wiiin.**
ii-jee, *n.* Same as **mishigee.** [GSS]
ii-kaa, *n.* [ekoo] A clothes rack; a clotheshorse.
ii-kakuji, *n.* The upper jaw. [UKH] See **'wii, kakuji.**
ii-ke·e, *n.* [uekae] Transplanting. [UKH] -sun, *vt.* To transplant. See **'wiiin.**
i·i-kkwa, *n.* An overstatement; a misstatement.
i·i-kkwa·in, *vi. pej.* To say; speak; make a statement.
i·i-machige·e, *n.* [iimachigai] Misspeaking; misstatement.
i·i-magi·in, *vt.* To distort; misrepresent; quibble.
i·i-maka·sun, *vt.* [iimakasu] To confute; talk (a person) down; refute.
i·i-maki·in, *vi.* [iimakeru] To be defeated in argument.
i·i-mama, *n.* As one says.
i·i-mi, *n.* [irime] An increase in volume. -sun, *vt.* To increase in volume or quantity.
i·i-mudu·sun, *vt.* [iimodosu] To cancel (a negotiation); take back what was said.
i·in[1], *vt. irreg.* [iu, yuu] See **'yun.** [UKH]
i·in[2], *vt.* [·ran, ·tchi; iru] To shoot; let fly (an arrow); fire a shot.
i·in[3], *vi.* [·ran, ·tchi; iru] To need; require; want.
i·in[4], *vi.* [·ran, ·tchi; iru] To enter; go in.
iina, *adv.* Already. Also [poetic] ina.
i·i-najiki, *n.* [iinazuke] A fiancé; a fiancée.
i·i-naraa·shi, *n.* Upbringing; everyday training; discipline; breeding.
i·i-naraa·sun, *vt.* To discipline; to instruct at home.

ijuumun

ii-ngwa, *n.* Same as **'wiingwa.**
i·i-'nja·sun, *vt.* [iidasu] To start speaking; broach (a matter); bring up; propose; suggest.
i·i-noo·sun, *vt.* [iinaosu] To rephrase; restate; correct oneself.
i·i-nuku·sun, *vt.* [iinokosu] To leave a message; leave word.
iiraa, *n.* A jellyfish.
iiriki·san, *adj.* Same as **'wiirikisan.**
i·i-shiji, *n.* [iisugi] An overstatement; an exaggeration.
i·i-shiji·in, *vt.* [iisugiru] To overstate; exaggerate; go too far in saying.
i·i-shitara·sun, *vt.* To speak ill of; abuse; disparage.
ii-su, *n.* [< J isu] A chair; a sofa; a chaise longue; a couch; a divan.
i·i-tati·in, *vt.* [iitateru] 1 To exaggerate. 2 To declare; make an assertion.
i·i-u·chi, *n.* [iioki] A message for one who is away.
i·i-waki, *n.* [iiwake] An excuse; an apology; explanation.
ii-wata, *n.* The intestines; the entrails; the gut.
i·i-wata·shi, *n.* An order; an instruction.
ii-wee, *n.* [iwai] A festival; a ritual; a celebration. See **uuwee, yuuwee.**
i·i-yan·jun, *vt.* [·dan, ·ti] To make a slip of the tongue; make a mistake in the use of words.
ija·a, *n.* A brave man; the brave; a courageous person. See **iji.**
ijai, *n.* [izari*] Fishing by torchlight at night.
ijai-bii, *n.* [izaribi*] A fishing fire; a fishing torch.
ijasa·a, *n.* A miser; a stingy fellow. [UKH]
iji, *n.* [iji] 1 Courage; pride; willpower; backbone. 2 Anger; temper. See **ijiri.**
iji-juu, *n.* A person of firm (strong) character. See **chuusan.**
ijijuu-mun, *n.* A person of firm (strong) character. Same as **ijijuu, ijirumun.**

ijimi·in, *vt.* [ijimeru] To bully; be cruel; persecute; oppress; abuse; harass. See **mimijun**.
ijimirari·in, *vt.* [ijimerareru] To be bullied; be harassed; be abused.
ijiri, *n.* Courage; valor; prowess; bravery; boldness. See **iji**.
ijiri-mun, *n.* A person of steady (strong) character. Same as **ijijuu**.
iju, *n.* Small camellia [J himetsubaki; *Schima superba* Gard. & Champ.].
ijun, *n.* [izumi] An artesian well; a spring; a fountain.
ijun-gaa, *n.* A spring; an artesian well. [UKH]
ika, *n.* [ika] A cuttlefish. Also **icha**².
ikai, *n.* [ikari] Same as **ichai**.
i-kata, *n.* [igata] A mold; a cast; a matrix.
ikira-ninju, *n.* A small number of people.
ikira·san, *adj.* Scarce; few. See also **kuuteen**, **uhi**, **ufusan**, **mandoon**.
ikirasa-ufusa, *n.* Quantity; amount; smallness or largeness.
i·ki-yoo-ha·ri-yoo, *n. colloq.* Go away and stay away. [GSS]
ik·ka, *n.* What day of the month. See also **nannichi**.
ikkeera·sun, *vt.* To upset and spill (or empty) the contents. See **keerasun**.
ikkeeri·in, *vi.* To upset and spill; overflow; run over. See **keeriin**.
iku-, *pref.* [iku-] How (much, many).
iku·chi, *n.* [ikutsu] How many.
iku·keen, *n.* How many times.
ikusa, *n.* [ikusa] A war; a battle.
ikusa-atu, *n.* Lit., after the war; postwar; after World War II; after 1945.
ikusa-buni, *n.* [ikusabune] A warship; a man-of-war.
i·ku-sachi, *n.* [ikusaki] A destination.
ikusa-gwaasee, *n.* Playing at war. **-sun**, *v.* To play at war; have a mock fight.
ikusa-mee, *n.* Lit., before the war; before World War II.

ikusa-yuu, *n.* [ikusayo] A war period; time of war.
iku·tai, *n. formal* How many persons.
iku-tatii, *n.* Many ways; various kinds.
i-kutuba, *n.* A proverb; a saying.
imashimi, *n.* [imashime] Admonition; warning; caution.
imashimi·in, *vt.* To admonish; warn; caution.
imense·en, *v. hon.* To be. See also **menseen**.
imi¹, *n.* [yume] A dream; a vision; an illusion. [OBJ]
i·mi², *n.* [imi] Mourning.
i-mi³, *n.* [imi] Meaning; sense; significance.
imi-aki, *n.* [imiake] The end of mourning.
imi-gaka·i, *n.* [imigakari] One whose relationship to the deceased requires him to be in mourning.
imi·in, *vt.* To press for; demand; request. See also **seejuku**.
imi-se·en, *vt. hon.* See **'yun**, **unnukiin**.
i-mun, *n.* [imono] Cast metal; casting; molding.
imun-naabi, *n.* [imono + nabe] A cast-iron pot; a cast-iron pan.
imun-yakkwan, *n.* A cast-iron teakettle.
in¹, *n.* [inu] 1 A dog. 2 The Dog as the eleventh of the twelve calendrical animal signs.
in², *n.* [in] A seal; a stamp. Also **han**.
inaka, *n.* [inaka] The country; the countryside; a rural area.
inaka·a, *n. pej.* A country bumpkin; countrified person; rustic; a hick; a provincial.
inaka-fuuji, *n.* [inaka + fuugi] Rustic customs and appearance; country ways.
inaka-nchu, *n.* A countrified person; a provincial, particularly one from rural areas of central and southern Okinawa.
inaka-suda·chi, *n.* [inakasodachi] One

raised in a rural area.
ina-muduchi, *n.* A soup in which pork is cooked with white miso paste. Also **inamuruchi.**
incha·a, *n.* That which is short; a short one.
incha·a-mancha·a, *n. colloq.* Being irregular in length. Also **inkaamankaa.** [GSS]
incha·a-naga·a, *n. colloq.* That which is uneven in length.
incha·ku-na·sun, *vt.* To shorten.
incha·san, *adj.* Short; brief.
inchoo, *n.* A short person; a shorty.
indaagii, *n.* A swing.
indii, *n.* A turnip [J kabura; *Brassica rapa* L. var. *rapa*]. [FOSR] Also **kabu, 'nndii.**
indoo, *n.* Same as **induumaami.**
induu, *n.* [endoo] Same as **induumaami.**
induu-maami, *n.* [endoomame] A pea; green pea; garden pea [*Pisum sativum* L.]. [FOSR] Also **induu, indoo.** See also **maami.**
in-gwa, *n.* [inga] 1 Karma; fate; destiny. 2 Misfortune. **·na,** *adj.* Unfortunate.
in-gwaa, *n.* A puppy; a small dog.
ingwaa-booi, *n.* On all fours; on one's hands and knees. See **hooin.**
inin-bii, *n.* The spirit, appearing as a ball of fire, of a person having died an unfortunate death.
inin-dui, *n.* A cuckoo. See **tui.**
inin-jaa-yama, *n.* A thresher; a threshing machine. See **yaama.**
injin-maami, *n.* [ingen mame] A kidney bean [*Phaseolus vulgaris* L.]. [FOSR] See also **maami.**
inkaa-mankaa, *n.* Same as **inchaamanchaa.** [GSS]
in-mayaa, *n.* Dogs and cats; an animal; a beast.
in·nee-sun·nee, *n. colloq.* Things turning out as one says or thinks.
in-niku, *n.* An inking pad.
in-numi, *n.* A flea. Also **numi**^{2}.

inoo, *n.* A shoal; shallows; shallow sea inside a reef.
inoo-ak·ki-saa, *n.* A **sabani** boat with four- or five-man crew, used mainly for **agiyaa** fishing within the reef. [OBJ] See **sabani, agiyaa.**
inoo-iyu, *n.* Fish that inhabit the shallow coral waters. See **inoo.**
in-tuku, *n.* [intoku] A secret act of charity; good done anonymously.
inu-gan, *n.* A dog-god. [ODJ]
ip-pai, *n.* [ippai] 1 A cupful; a glassful. 2 A drink. 3 Being full of.
ip-pee, *adv.* Very; extremely.
ip-poo-nke·e, *n.* Bias; partiality to one side.
ippun-ukoo, *n.* A big and thick incense stick. [UKH]
ira·a, *n.* 1 A lewd fellow; a lecher. 2 Sexual desire; sexual appetite. See **iru.**
iraa-mii, *n.* An amorous glance; an ogle.
iraa·sun, *vt.* To make an advance (usually a small amount); pay for another (a small amount temporarily). See **karasun**^{1}, **irain.**
irabu-chaa, *n.* Generic term for fish belonging to the Scaridae family. [ODJ]
ira·bun, *vt.* [erabu] To choose; select.
ira-bu·u, *n.* A kind of sea snake [*Laticauda semifasciata*]. [ODJ]
irabuu-shinji, *n.* An **irabuu** sea snake infusion, used as a tonic. See **shinjimun.**
ira·in, *vt.* [·(r)an, ·ti; irau*] To borrow (something to be returned in equivalent amount later). See **kain**^{1}, **iraasun.**
irana, *n.* A sickle. Also **kama**^{1}, **irara.**
irana·nu-yii, *n.* The handle of a sickle.
iranpaa-sun, *v.* To hesitate to say; be reluctant to say; falter.
irara, *n.* A sickle. Same as **irana, kama**^{1}.
ira-saa, *n.* Same as **ibiraa.** [GSS]
iree, *n.* [irae*] Response; answer.
iree·in, *vi.* [iraeru*] 1 To answer; reply; respond to. 2 To solve; do; answer. 3 To repay; reward.

iri

iri[1], *n.* West.
iri[2], *n.* A gimlet; a drill; an auger.
iri-baa, *n.* [ireba] A false tooth.
iricha, *n.* [iraka*] **1** The roof ridge. **2** Roof.
iricha·a, *n.* Gooseflesh; goose skin.
irichi, *n.* **1** A scale (of fish). **2** Dandruff. **3** The roof ridge. See **iricha**.
irichi-gumu, *n.* A fractocumulus cloud; scale cloud.
irichi·i, *n.* Dish fried in oil; a stir-fry. See also **chii'irichi, habutan'irichaa, kuubu'irichaa, maamina'irichaa, soomin'irichaa, toonakashii'irichaa**. [GSS]
irichi-jina, *n.* A rope used to fasten the ridge of a thatch roof. [UKH]
iri-chiri·i, *n.* **1** Same as **shikama(a)**. [ODJ] **2** A live-in employee; a resident worker.
irichi-ukusa·a, *n.* A fish scale remover.
iri·chun, *vt.* To fry an **irichii** dish.
iri-daka, *n.* Revenue; earnings; an income. Also **iriraka**.
iri-e·e, *n.* [iriai] Dusk; evening.
iri-fa, *n.* Income; revenue. [UKH]
iri-fuda, *n.* A tender; a bid; a ballot.
iri-gaaee, *n.* Same as **iigaai**.
iri-gan, *n.* [iregami] A tress of false hair; a switch; a rat.
iri-gasa, *n.* The measles; rubella.
iri-guchi, *n.* [iriguchi] Entry; entrance; gate.
iri-hana, *n.* **1** The first brew of tea. **2** Place closest to the entrance of a house.
iri-hi, *n.* [irihi] The setting sun.
iri·in, *vt.* [ireru] **1** To put (take, bring) in; admit; include. **2** serve (food).
iri-kee·in, *vt.* [irekaeru] To replace (A with B); substitute (B for A); transpose; switch.
iri-makkwa, *n.* Lit., western pillow; placing a pillow in such a way that the person's head faces west.
iri-mee, *n.* [irimae*] Income; revenue.
iri-mun, *n.* [iremono] A vessel; a container; a receptacle.
iri-musa·a, *n.* Sweet potatoes eaten by worms. See **mushi**[1].
iri-muuku, *n.* [irimuko] A man who marries into his wife's family; a son-in-law who joins his wife's family.
iri-muuku·u, *n. pej.* Same as **irimuuku**.
iri-raka, *n.* Same as **iridaka**. [UKH]
iri-yuu, *n.* [iriyoo] Need; want; demand; necessity.
iru, *n.* [iro] **1** A color; a hue; a tint. **2** Complexion; color; a look. **3** Love; lust. **4** A kind; a sort.
iru-iru, *n.* [iroiro] Variety; many kinds. ·**nu**, *adj.* Various; many kinds of.
iru-jura·sa, *n.* Beauty of colors and designs. See **churasan**.
iru-jura·san, *adj.* Beautiful, in colors and complexion; blooming; florid. See **churasan**.
iru-ka, *n.* [iroka] Feminine charms; beauty.
iru-kuru·u, *n.* A person with a dark complexion. See also **irushiruu**.
iru-nuga·a, *n.* A pale person.
iru-nugi·in, *vi.* To lose color; turn pale.
iru-shiru·u, *n.* A person with a light complexion. See also **irukuruu**.
iru-yuku, *n.* [iroyoku] Lust; carnal desire; sexual passion; sensual pleasure.
isa, *n.* [isha] A medical doctor; a medical practitioner; a physician; a surgeon.
isami·in, *vt.* [isameru] To encourage; urge; stimulate.
isa·nu-yaa, *n.* Same as **isan-yaa**.
isa·n-yaa, *n.* A medical clinic; a hospital. Also **byooin**.
isatuu, *n.* A praying mantis.
i-see, *n.* [isai] Details; particulars.
ishi, *n.* [ishi] **1** A stone; a rock; a pebble. **2** A jewel; a precious stone. **3** A stone (playing piece) for the game of *go*.
ishi-ban, *n.* A slate. [UKH]
ishi-ban-furi-gwaa, *n.* A slate pencil. [UKH]
ishi-bashi, *n.* [ishibashi] A stone bridge.

ishi-bee, *n.* [ishibai] Lime (calcium oxide).
ishi-chijin, *n.* [ishi + tsuzumi] A stone that sounds like a drum when beaten.
ishi-duuru, *n.* [ishidooroo] A stone lantern. See also **tuuru**.
ishi-gachi, *n.* [ishigaki] A stone wall.
ishigachi-chima·a, *n.* A workman who builds a stone fence. See **chimun**[1].
ishigachi-gakui, *n.* Same as **ishigakui**. [UKH]
ishi-ga-karaa, *n.* Same as **ishigangaraamichi**. [UKH]
ishi-gakui, *n.* That which is surrounded by a stone fence, such as a house. Also **ishigachigakui**.
ishi-gangaraa-michi, *n.* A rocky, pebbly road. Also **ishigakaraa, ishikakaraamichi**.
ishi-gan-too, *n.* [C Shi Gangtang] A rectangular stone, about one or two feet high; inscribed with the three characters **ishi-gan-too**, allegedly the name of the ancient Chinese general Shi Gangtang. [ODJ]
ishi-guruu, *n.* Gravel; small pebbles; shingle.
ishi-guu, *n.* Fine gravel of crushed coral. Often used to pave roads.
ishiguu-michi, *n.* A road paved with crushed coral gravel.
ishi-gwee, *n.* A hoe with a triangular or rectangular blade. Also **faa'ishigwee**. [OBJ]
ishi-jeeku, *n.* [ishizaiku] A stone mason.
ishi-ji, *n.* [ishizue] **1** A foundation stone; a cornerstone. **2** A flat stone, in an entryway, on which to leave one's shoes when entering the house.
ishi-jiishi, *n.* A funeral urn made of coral stone in the shape of a shrine. See **jiishigaami**.
ishi-kakaraa-michi, *n.* Same as **ishigakaraa**.
ishi-kijai, *n.* [kiza*] Stone steps; a stone stairway.

ishi-kubiri, *n.* A pebbly small slope.
ishi-naagu·u, *n.* A girls' pebble-tossing game. See **nagiin**.
ishi-uushi, *n.* A stone mortar for grinding grain. See also **chichiuushi, uushi**.
ishi-yuuchi, *n.* A stone hatchet.
i-shoo, *n.* [ishoo] Clothes; clothing; dress; garments; apparel; costume; a wardrobe. See also **chin**[3].
iso-baare, *n.* One of the annual rites in the eleventh lunar month on Hatoma Island. [ODJ]
isoo·s(h)a, *n. lit.* Delight; gladness; joy.
isoo·s(h)an, *adj.* Joyful; delightful; glad; pleased.
is-san, *n.* [issan] At full speed; as fast as one's legs can go.
issan-baayee, *n.* Running at full speed.
issoo-chiya·a, *n.* Clothes for everyday wear; at-home wear; homewear; a housedress; housecoat. Also **hiijiichiyaa**. See also **chiin**[1].
issoo-naadii, *n.* One after another; one and all. Also **issoonaarii**.
isu·ji, *n. adv.* [isogi] Haste; hurry; dispatch; in a hurry; in haste; hastily; quickly; without delay.
isu·jun, *vi.* [isogu] To hasten; hurry.
ita, *n.* [ita] A board; a plank; a plate; a sheet. Also **icha**[1].
ita-bishi, *n.* A flat reef; a board-like reef.
itabu, *n.* A heavy wooden board, about 39 by 81 cm, used to press folded kimonos. Also **ichabu**. [KCS, OGJ]
itajira, *n.* [itazura] **1** Waste; in vain. **2** Mischief.
itajira-gutu, *n.* [itazuragoto] Futility; uselessness; wastage.
ita·mun, *vi.* [itamu] To be damaged; be spoiled; be injured; be rotten; be worn out.
itashiki-bara, *n.* An annual rite on the seventeenth of the seventh lunar month, after the *Bon* festivities. [ODJ]
itcha·i-'njita·i, *n.* Going in and out.
-sun, *v.* To go in and out.

it-chii, *n*. [ittsui] A pair.
it-chin[1], *n*. [ikken] A case; an affair.
it-chin[2], *n*. [ikkin] Unit of weight, equal to one **chin**[4] or 160 **munmi** (approximately 0.6 kg or 1.3 lbs.).
it-chin[3], *adv*. The most.
it·taa, *n*. You (*pl*.); your house; your (*sing*. and *pl*.). See also **'yaa**[1].
it-tucha, *n*. Same as **ittuchi**.
it-tuchi, *n*. [ittoki] For a while; a short time.
ittugayoo, *n*. A girls' game of marbles. [OBJ].
itu, *n*. [ito] Silk. Same as **iichu**, **ichu**.
itu-jin, *n*. A silk kimono. [GSS] Also **ichujin**.
ituma, *n*. [itoma] A leave (of absence); vacation; furlough.
itu-mun, *n*. [itomono] Silk goods.
itu-mushi, *n*. A silkworm.
iwa, *n*. [iwa] A rock; a crag. Also **ufu'ishi**.
iwari, *n*. [iware] An origin; a history; a reason; a cause.
iya, *n*. [ena] The placenta; the afterbirth. Also **iyaa**. See **kkwabukuru**, **atu**.
iyai, *n*. A message. Also **iyee**. **-sun**, *v*. To give a message.
iyai-mun, *n*. A thing left in one's charge to be delivered to somebody else.
iya-ware·e, *n*. Lit., placenta-laughing, a ceremony held following the burial of the placenta from a recent birth in order to ensure that the newborn will be a cheerful child. See **iya**.
iyee, *n*. Same as **iyai**.
iyu, *n*. [uo] A fish; a fish as a living thing and as food. See also **inoo'iyu**, **fuka'iyu**, **sakana**.
iyu-jii, *n*. Same as **chiigani**.
iyu-kwaasa·a, *n*. A fisherman; a person who catches fish.
iyu-machi, *n*. A fish market. See also **machi**[1].
iyu·nu-mii, *n*. A fish eye; fish meat.
iyu-tuya·a, *n*. A (professional) fisherman.
iyu-uya·a, *n*. A fishmonger.
izai-hoo, *n*. A ritual test of qualification for priestesses on Kudaka Island, held every twelve years in the year of the Horse, for three days starting from moonrise on the fifteenth day of the eleventh month. [OBJ, ODJ]

J————

jaa[1], *n*. [ja] A (large) snake; a serpent. See also **habu**[1].
jaa[2], *n*. [za] **1** A seat. **2** A position; a post. **3** A room. Also **zaa**.
jaafee, *n*. Confusion; mess; being unmanageable.
jaafee-gutu, *n*. Difficulty; trouble; distress.
jaafee-mun, *n*. A rascal; a rowdy.
jaa-garu, *n*. Black clay soil. See **kucha**[2], **maaji**.
jaama, *n*. [?zama] A plight; a predicament; being lost; puzzlement.
jaama-keeri·in, *vi*. To be thrown into utter confusion; be seized with panic.
jaama-tiima, *n*. Being lost completely; complete bewilderment.
jaa-mucha·a, *n*. One who enlivens a party; the life of a party. See **muchun**[1].
jaashi, *n*. [zashu] A chief priest.
jaga-'nmu, *n*. Irish or white potato [jagaimo < Jagatara imo < Jakarta potato; *Solanum tuberosum* L.].
jahi-bai, *n*. A **sanshin** the sounding box of which is covered with Indian python skin. See also **sanshin**.
jahichi, *n*. Same as **jashichi**. [GSS]
jama, *n*. [jama] A hindrance; an obstruction; a barrier; an inconvenience.
jan-nin, *n*. [zannen] Regret; repentance; disappointment; vexation; chagrin.
jap-pi, *n*. [zappi] Miscellaneous expenses; incidentals.
ja-shichi, *n*. [zashiki] **1** A room; an

apartment; a parlor. 2 A bed. Also **jaa**[2], **jahichi, jashiki, tuku**[4]. See also **ichibanja, nibanja, nakamee, sanbanja, uraja, kucha**[1], **ashagi, meenuyaa.** [ODJ, GSS]

jashichi-doogu, *n.* Bedding.

jashiki, *n.* [zashiki] Same as **jashichi.** [GSS]

jee-muku, *n.* [zaimoku] Wood; lumber. Also **zeemuku.**

jeemuku-yaa, *n.* [zaimokuya] A lumberyard; lumber supplier.

jee-san, *n.* [zaisan] An estate; a fortune; property; means. Also **zeesan.**

jiban, *n.* [jiban*, juban] An undershirt; underwear.

ji-bata, *n.* [jibata] A low traditional loom without legs. See **hata**[3].

ji-bita, *adj.* Vulgar; crude; mean; base; gross.

jibita-mun, *n.* A vulgar fellow.

ji-bun, *n.* [jibun] Time; hour; season; proper time; opportunity.

jichashi, *n.* A louse egg; a nit. Also **jisashi.**

jichi·nu-uya, *n.* [jitsunooya] A real parent; a true parent.

jifaa, *n.* A variant of **jiifaa.** [GSS]

ji-fi, *adv.* [zehi] 1 Certainly; surely; without fail; by all means. 2 Right or wrong; propriety; justice. Also **jihi.**

ji-ganee, *n.* Land rental. Also **kanee.**

ji-guku, *n.* [jigoku] Hell; Hades; the inferno.

ji-hi, *adv.* Same as **jifi.**

jii[1], *n.* [ji] Ground; land; earth; soil.

jii[2], *n.* [ji] A Chinese character; a letter; an ideograph (*kanji*); a word.

jii[3], *n.* [ji] Piles; hemorrhoids. See **jiiyanmee.**

jii[4], *n.* [zui] 1 The marrow; the hollow inside a bone. 2 The hollow inside a stem such as a bamboo.

jii[5], *n.* [gi] Justice; righteousness.

jii-anda, *n.* Brains; gray matter.

jii-baarii, *n.* A mock boat race on land. See **jii**[1], **haarii.**

jiibu, *n.* 1 A muzzle covering a horse's mouth to keep it from eating farm products. 2 A net bag made of straw.

jii-buku, *n.* 1 In construction, packing the earth by pounding with either a heavy weight or a log lifted by a group of laborers with a pulley and let drop. 2 A laborer, usually female, who does such work.

jii-faa, *n.* 1 A traditional women's hairpin. 2 A **sanshin** tuning peg. Also **jifaa.** [GSS] See also **karakui, mudi.**

jii-gui, *n.* Discontent; displeasure; grievance.

jiigui-haagui, *adv.* Fretfully; peevishly; grumbling.

jii-guru·u, *n.* A dark complexion.

jiiguya·a, *n.* A grumbler; a malcontent.

jiija·a, *n.* A cicada [cicadidae]; a cicala. Also **asasaa, sansanaa, naabikachaa, giijaa.**

jii-jiki·i, *n.* Daikon radishes pickled in brown sugar and awamori liquor.

jii-ka·chi, *n.* A calligrapher.

jii-maami, *n.* A peanut.

jii-maami-doofu, *n.* A tofu cake made with sweet potato starch and strained lees of peanuts.

jii-mee, *n.* 1 Upland rice [*Oryza sativa* L. var. *terrestris* Makino]; rice grown in a dry field. [FOSR] 2 Local rice (in contrast to imported rice). See also **shimagumi.**

jiina·a, *n.* A firefly. Also **jinjin, hootanukui.**

jiinaa-bii, *n.* Glow of fireflies. See **hii**[2].

jii-nchu, *n.* Natives of a village; a village's original settlers and their descendants. See also **chiruunin.**

jii·nu-kami, *n.* Earth deity; deity of the locality. See **tuutiikun.**

jii-nuu, *n.* [geinoo] Performing arts such as music and dance.

jiinuu-mu·chi, *n.* 1 A person talented in the performing arts. 2 A person with

jiinuushi

many talents.
jii-nuushi, *n.* [jinushi] A landowner; a landlord; a landholder.
jii-ru, *n.* **1** A sunken hearth; a hearth made in the floor. **2** A ritual hearth for a woman to warm herself in the week after giving birth. [ODJ]
jiiru-shiji·chi, *n.* Same as **jiirushinchi**.
jiiru-shin·chi, *n.* The ceremony of sunken hearth clearance, when the sunken hearth for the nursing mother is cleared and visitors are allowed in her room, usually on the seventh day after childbirth.
jiishi-gaami, *n.* [zushigame] A pottery funeral urn containing the bones of the deceased. See also **ishijiishi, tirajiishi, udunjiishi, yaajiishi, haruyaa**. See **haka, shinkuchi**.
jii-shiru, *n.* Underground water oozing out of the ground. [UKH]
jii-ute·e, *n.* [jiutai] Choral singing and music in the **kumi'udui** dance dramas or traditional dances.
jii-yanmee, *n.* [ji-yamai] Piles; hemorrhoids. See **jii**[3].
ji-jaku, *n.* [jishaku] A magnet; a compass.
ji-joo, *n.* [jijoo] Circumstances; reasons; the situation.
ji-kan, *n.* [jikan] Time; an hour. See also **tushi**[1].
jikoo, *adv.* Exceedingly; excessively; terribly; highly.
jiku, *n.* [jiku] An axis; an arbor; a spindle; a shaft.
ji-mama, *n.* [jimama] Selfishness; egoism; egotism; willfulness; self-indulgence; caprice; whim. See **wagamama**.
ji-man, *n.* [jiman] Pride; boastfulness; vanity; self-conceit; egotism.
jin[1], *n.* [zen] A small dining table (often for individual use); a tray; a footed tray. Also **ujin**.
jin[2], *n.* [zeni] Money; cash; coin; funds; currency.

jin-baku, *n.* [zenibako] A money box.
ji-nan, *n.* [jinan] A second son.
jin-boo, *n.* A coin stick used in dancing.
jin-bukuru, *n.* A purse; a wallet.
jin-bun, *n.* [zonbun] Talent; ability; wisdom; resourcefulness.
jinbuna·a, *n.* A man of wisdom; a wise man; a man of resources.
jinbun-kusara·a, *n.* A fool; a simpleton; a dunce.
jinbun-mu·chi, *n.* A man of resources; a wise man.
jin-daka, *n.* [zenidaka] A sum of money; an amount of money.
jin-gunju·u, *n.* A miser; a niggard.
ji-nin, *n.* [genin] A manservant.
jin-iri·i, *n.* [zeni-ire] A wallet; a purse.
jin-irimi, *n.* High cost; a lot of expenditures.
jin-jin, *n. inf.* Same as **jiinaa**.
jin-karasa·a, *n.* A moneylender; a usurer. See also **koorigashii**.
jinkoo, *n.* [ginkoo] A bank.
jin-kwan, *n.* [genkwan] The entrance; the porch; the front door; the vestibule.
jin-mi, *n.* [ginmi] Inquiry; investigation; scrutiny.
jin-mooki-juku, *n.* Exclusively money-making work; mammonism.
jin-naa, *n.* [zeninawa] A cord of copper coins.
jin-tii, *n.* [jintei*] Personality; personal appearance; personal character; the person himself.
jin-too, *n.* Truth; reality; actuality.
jinu, *pron. interj.* Used in questions concerning two or more things or persons; which; what. See **jiru**.
jiraba, *n.* [? shirabe] A type of ballad in the Yaeyama Islands. [ODJ]
ji-ri, *n.* [giri] A sense of duty; obligation; a sense of honor, decency; courtesy.
jiru, *pron.* Which one.
jisashi, *n.* Same as **jichashi**.
ji-shichi, *n.* [jisetsu] The season; the time of the year; an opportunity.

ji-shii, *n.* [jisei] The trend of the times; the spirit of the age; the conditions of life; the times.
jita, *n.* Same as **gita**.
jitchin, *n.* [zukin] A hood; a kerchief; a skullcap.
jit-chuu, *n.* [gekkyuu] A (monthly) salary; (monthly) pay.
jitoo, *n.* [shutoo] Vaccination; inoculation. **-sun**, *v.* To vaccinate; be inoculated with vaccine.
ji-yuu, *n.* [jiyuu] Freedom; liberty; as desired.
joo[1], *n.* A stopper; a cork; a plug.
joo[2], *n.* [joo] Feeling; sentiment; emotion; passion; love; sympathy. See also **nasaki, jooyee, chimu**.
joo[3], *n.* [to] **1** A gate; a gateway. **2** An entrance and the nearby road. See also **uchijoo, fukajoo, fukamaa, joofuka, mun**[1].
-joo, *suff.* [-joo] Counter for **tatan** mats, which are used as a measure of room size. See also **tatan**.
joo-bata, *n.* A fertile field; fertile farm.
joo-batara·chi, *n.* Hard work; diligence.
joo-chibai, *n.* Fine work; work well done.
joo-chiji·ri, *n.* Closing the gate to shut out undesirables, such as the spirits of the deceased. See **shinimabui, chijiin**.
joo-diki, *n.* [joodeki] A good performance; a master stroke; a fine success.
joo-fu, *n.* [joohu] A high quality ramie cloth.
joo-fuka, *n.* Outdoors. See **joo**[3], **fuka-joo**.
joo-gu, *n.* [joogo] A funnel.
-joogu, *suff.* [joogo] Denotes a person who loves a particular food.
joo-guchi, *n.* The doorway; the entranceway.
joohicha·a, *n.* Same as **jooshichaa**.
joohichi, *n.* Same as **jooshichi**.
joohita, *adv.* Constantly; without end; always; all the time.

jooi, *adv.* By far; a great deal; out and away.
joojoo-kamii-gwaa, *n.* A jack-in-the-box; a toy made of either a box or a pot from which an animal figure jumps when the lid is lifted.
joo-noo, *n.* [joonoo] Payment to the authorities; a tax; a duty (on goods); an imposition; dues; rates. Also **zaikin**.
joo-shicha·a, *n.* [zooshiki*] A household maid; a scullery maid. Also **joohichaa**.
joo-shichi, *n.* [zooshiki*] Cooking work; domestic work; housekeeping duties. Also **joohichi**.
joo-too, *n.* [jootoo] Superiority; something of excellent quality.
joo-yee, *n.* [jooai] Affection; love; tenderness. See also **nasaki, joo**[2], **chimu**.
jooyee-mu·chi, *n.* An affectionate person.
juku, *n.* [zoku] Manners; customs of the period; local customs.
-juku, *suff.* Denotes persistence in one thing. See **jinmookijuku**.
jun, *n.* [jun] Normalcy; naturalness.
jun-puu, *n.* [junpuu] A favorable wind; a tailwind.
jun-taku, *n.* [juntaku] Abundance; superfluity.
juri, *n.* [ryoori] A courtesan; a prostitute; a female entertainer. See also **juri-nukuuga, chimijuri, feejuri**.
juri-aga·i, *n.* A former courtesan.
juri-anmaa, *n.* A mistress of a house of courtesans; a madam.
juri-ashi·bi, *n.* Patronage of courtesans.
juri-bakuyoo, *n.* A broker of courtesans.
juri-ganee, *n.* The price of a courtesan, which the customer pays to the courtesan house. See **kanee**.
juri-gunboo, *n.* One who goes from one house of courtesans to the next.
juri-'nma, *n.* Festival of the Courtesans, held on the twentieth of the first month of the lunar calendar. Also **juri'uma**.

juri·nu-kuuga, *n.* Lit., courtesan's egg; 1 Peanuts candied in white sugar. 2 Young girls sold into prostitution, usually less than ten years of age.
juri·nu-kkwa, *n.* A child born to a courtesan.
juri·nu-yaa, *n.* A courtesan house; a brothel.
juri-u·i, *n.* Being sold as a courtesan.
juri-uma, *n.* See **juri'nma**.
juri-yuba·a, *n.* A patron of **juri**; one who hires a courtesan.
juu[1], *n.* The tail; the end.
juu[2], *n.* [juu] Ten. See also **tuu**[2].
juu-baku, *n.* [juubako] 1 A tier of square boxes (esp. of lacquerware) fitting one over the other; a picnic lunch box. 2 A set of such boxes containing incense, rice grain, and wine for ritual purposes.
juu-bun, *n.* [juubun] Enough; sufficient; satisfactory.
juu-fu·i, *n.* 1 Wagging the tail (of a dog) in joy. 2 Flattery.
juu-gu, *n.* [juugo] Fifteen.
juugu-nichi, *n.* [juugonichi] 1 The fifteenth day. 2 Menstruation.
juugunichi·i, *n.* Menstruation. Also **juugunichi**. See also **chichinumun**.
juugunichi-soogwachi, *n.* Same as **hachikasoogwachi**.
juugu-ya, *n.* A full moon night (specifically on the fifteenth of the eighth month of the lunar calendar).
juu-gwachi, *n.* [juugatsu] October.
juu-hachi, *n.* [juuhachi] Eighteen.
juu-hichi, *n.* [juushichi] Same as **juushichi**.
juu-ichi, *n.* [juuichi] Eleven.
juu-juu, *adv.* [juujuu] Repeatedly; over and over; sincerely.
juu-ku, *n.* [juuku] Nineteen.
juu-mukkoo, *n.* A bird or animal that does not have a tail.
juu-ni, *n.* [juuni] Twelve.
juuni-shi, *n.* [juunishi] The twelve calendar animal signs (terrestrial branches). See **nii**[5], **ushi**[1], **tura**, **uu**[1], **tachi**[2], **mii**[2], **'nma**[1], **hichiji**, **saru**, **tui**, **in**[1], **yii**[1].
juu-san, *n.* [juusan] Thirteen.
juu-shi, *n.* [juushi] Fourteen.
juu-shichi, *n.* [juushichi] Seventeen. Also **juuhichi**.
juu-shichi-hachi, *n.* [juushichihachi] 1 Seventeen or eighteen. 2 Puberty; adolescence; marriageable age.
juu-shii, *n.* [zoosui] Rice gruel with miso paste and vegetables.

K———

kaa[1], *n.* [kawa] The skin; a hide; a fur; leather; bark.
kaa[2], *n.* [kawa] 1 A well; an artesian well; a fountain. 2 A river (in compound words). Same as **yiigaa**. See also **kaara**[2], **ijun**, **kurumagaa**, **chiigaa**[2], **chingaa**, **hiijaa**[2].
-kaa[3], *suff.* Indicates an extreme degree of a situation.
kaa-bishi·i, *n.* A thing or person with thin skin. Also **kaabisuu**.
kaa-bisu·u, *n.* Same as **kaabishii**.
kaa-bucha·a, *n.* Same as **kaabuchii**.
kaabuchi·i, *n.* The **kaabuchii** orange [*Citrus keraji* Hort. ex Tanaka var. *kabuchii*]. Also **kaabuchaa**. [ODJ]
kaabui, *n.* [? kabu] White mold which grows on such things as miso bean paste. [UKH]
kaabuya·a[1], *n.* [kawahori*, koomori] A bat; an aerial mammal.
kaabuya·a[2], *n.* An infant's motion of shaking its head sideways.
kaa-chii, *n.* [kashi; C xiazhi] The summer solstice.
kaachii-bee, *n.* A strong and stable south-southwesterly wind that blows about the time of the summer solstice in June. See **fee**[3].
kaaga·a, *n.* 1 A shadow; a silhouette; a

shadow figure. 2 A reflection; an image. See **kaagi**.
kaagaa·nu-shiru, *n.* Lit., reflection soup; a clear soup with no solid ingredients.
kaa-gani, *n.* A freshwater crab. See also **umigani**.
kaagi, *n.* [kage] 1 Looks; appearance. 2 Shade. See **kaagaa**.
kaagi-bu·shi, *n.* Drying in the shade.
kaagi-gawa·i, *n.* A change in one's appearance due to old age or illness.
kaa-gufa·a, *n.* Lit., one with hard skin; an obstinate person; a stubborn person. [UKH]
kaa-gutsu, *n.* [kawagutsu] A leather shoe.
kaa-ha·in, *vi.* 1 To grow a skin, hide, film, etc.; become shriveled and grow film on top. 2 To become greedy; be reluctant to give up.
kaa-jeeku, *n.* [kawa-zaiku] 1 Leatherwork. 2 A leather-worker. See **seeku**.
kaaji, *adv.* Every time; whenever.
kaakaa, *n. inf.* Bitter; astringent.
kaa-kanja·a, *n.* 1 A person with blurred vision. 2 Blurred vision.
kaa-kasa·a, *n.* Smoked crucian carp.
kaaka·sun, *vt.* [kawakasu] Same as **kaarakasun**.
kaakasu·u, *n.* Smoked fish.
kaaki·i, *n.* [kake] 1 A bet; a wager; a gamble. 2 A pledge made between children by hooking each other's little finger. **-sun**, *v.* To bet; wager; back (a horse).
kaaki·in, *vi.* [kawaku] To become dry (throat); to dry up (water); feel thirsty.
kaa-ma, *n.* A distant place.
kaa-mee, *n.* Worshiping wells and springs as an annual village rite, or as a clan-level rite once every few years. See also **agarimaai**. [ODJ]
kaami, *n.* [kame] An earthenware pot; jar. See also **mijigaami, handuu, karasugaami, chibu**[1]**, nanbangaami, nanban**.
kaamii, *n.* [kame] A turtle; a tortoise.
kaamii kee·sun, *v. phr. slang.* Lit., to forcibly turn a turtle over; rape. [GSS]
kaamii-kuu, *n.* [kame + koo] Same as **kaaminakuu**.
kaami·na-kuu, *n.* Tortoise shell.
kaaminakuu-baka, *n.* A turtleback tomb. See **haka**.
kaami·nu-chibi-tiichi, *n.* For the ashes of a husband and wife to be deposited in the same funeral urn after death.
kaami·nu-hoogai, *n.* An annual ritual invoking a rich harvest, good fishing, and a safe journey, held on the 25th to 26th of the sixth lunar month in villages in Nago. [ODJ]
kaa·nu-funshii, *n.* The geomantic evaluation of a well. See **funshii**.
kaa·nu-kami, *n.* Deity of the well or spring.
kaara[1], *n.* [kawara] A roof tile.
kaara[2], *n.* [kawara, riverbed] A river; a stream; a brook.
kaara[3], *n.* The keel. See also **funi**[1].
kaara-banta, *n.* A bank; a riverside.
kaara-buchi, *n.* [kawarabuki] A house with a tile roof. Also **kaarayaa**.
kaara-buubuu, *n.* A children's game in which shards of tile are tossed, the winning toss being the shard landing closest to the first toss. [ODJ]
kaara·chun, *vi.* [kawaku] To dry (up); to be parched. See also **kaakiin**.
kaara-ishi-gachi, *n.* Wall made of tiles and stones. See also **kachi**[2].
kaaraka·sun, *vt.* To make (something) dry; dessicate; weather. Also **kaaka-sun**.
kaara-yaa, *n.* [kawaraya] Same as **kaara-buchi**.
kaara-yacha·a, *n.* [kawarayaki] A tile maker; a tile manufacturer.
kaasa, *n.* [kashiwa] A general term for broad leaves used to wrap food. See **yuuna, wuu**[1]**, kuba**. [ODJ]

kaaramuuchi

kaasa-muuchi, *n*. A rice cake wrapped in **kaasa** leaves.
kaa-saree, *n*. [kawa-sarae] Cleaning a well.
kaa-shii, *n*. [kasei] 1 Help; assistance; aid; support; backing. 2 A helper; an assistant. Also **kashii**. **-sun**, *vt*. To assist; help; aid; give support to. Also **kashiisun**.
kaa-taa, *n*. Joint ownership; co-ownership. **-sun**, *v*. To own (something) jointly; hold (something) in common.
kaa-uri·i, *n*. Lit., descent to a spring; a rite observed for the birth of a child. See **ubumiji, ubukaa, ubiinadii, ubuyu**. [OBJ, ODJ, OGJ]
kaa-uubi, *n*. [kawaobi] A leather belt.
kaba, *n*. Smell; scent; odor. See **kaja**.
kaba-anda, *n*. Clove hair oil; perfume.
kaba-kaja, *n*. A fragrance; an aroma.
kaba·s(h)an, *adj*. [kaba·ku; kanbashii] Fragrant; aromatic.
kabi, *n*. [kami] Paper. See also **waradooshi, basuushi, bashuukabi, mumudakabi, sugiwara, fuushugami, minugami**.
kabi-anji, *n*. The rite of burning mock paper money, the currency of the afterlife. See **uchikabi, nchabi, anjikabi**.
kabi-an·jun, *vt*. To burn **uchikabi** (mock paper money). See also **uchikabi, ubun**.
kabi-dippu·u, *n*. Same as **kabitippuu**.
kabi-gi, *n*. Paper mulberry tree [J kajinoki; *Broussonetia papyrifera* (L.) l'Hérit.]. [FOSR]
kabi-jin, *n*. Paper money; paper currency; a bill.
kabi-shicha·a, *n*. A paper maker.
kabi-tippu·u, *n*. [kami-deppoo] A toy popgun that shoots paper wads. Also **kabidippuu**.
kabi-uchi, *n*. A round iron stamp about 10 cm long and 3.75 cm in diameter, molded at one end with a ring shape, used to impress symbols on **uchikabi**.

See **uchikabi**.
kabu, *n*. [kabu] Same as **indii**.
kabu·i-mun, *n*. Headgear; a hat; a cap. [UKH]
kabu·in, *vi*. To lose money in business. Same as **kanjun**.
kabutu, *n*. [< J kabuto] A warrior's helmet; a headpiece. See also **kantu**.
kacha, *n*. [kachoo] A mosquito net.
kachaashi·i, *n*. A type of **sanshin** music and dance characterized by a very quick tempo and discord.
kachaa·sun, *vt*. [kakiawaseru] To stir up; churn; disturb; mix up; throw into confusion.
kacha·mun, *vt*. To scratch; claw; maul.
ka·chi[1], *n*. [kachi] A victory; a win; a conquest; a success.
kachi[2], *n*. [kaki] A hedge; a fence. See also **ishigachi, kaaraishigachi, fiigachi, dakigachi, gikijigachi, fukugigachi, chinibugachi**.
kachi[3], *n*. [kaki] A stone fishing weir about three feet high, extending in a crescent shape from the seashore into the offing.
kachi[4], *n*. [kachi] Going on foot; walking.
-kachi, *suff*. Following a word denoting work or movement, indicates the idea of repetition. See **susuikachi, hoochikachi**.
kachi-chiki, *n*. [kaki-tsuke] A note; a memo; a document.
kachi-hiti·in, *vt*. Emphatic form of **hitiin**. [GSS]
kachi-hoo·in, *vt*. To scatter about; disarrange.
kachi-hooya·a, *n*. One who cannot keep his or her room tidy and in order; a slob. Also **shigeerasaa**.
kachi-ikusa, *n*. [kachi-ikusa] A victorious war.
kachi-iri·in, *vt*. To make an entry; make a note; make a notation; make a side note.

ka·chi-keera·sun, *vt.* To capsize; overturn.
kachi-maki, *n.* [kachimake] Victory or defeat.
kachimi·i-han·sun, *vt.* To miss catching; let (a person) escape; fail to catch; miss.
kachimi·in, *vt.* To grasp; seize; catch; take hold of.
kachi-mingwa·sun, *v.* To disturb; upset; disarrange.
kachi·mi-nsooree, *n.* Children's game of hide-and-seek.
ka·chi-mun, *n.* [kakimono] A writing; a document.
kachi·nu-mii-ngwa, *n.* Same as yamanashingwa.
ka·chi-shiga·in, *vt.* Emphatic form of shigain.
ka·chun¹, *vt.* [kaku] 1 To write. 2 To draw; to paint.
ka·chun², *vt.* [kaku] 1 To scratch. 2 To be disgraced; be put to shame.
ka·chun³, *vt.* [kaku] To construct; fabricate; make.
ka·chun⁴, *vi.* [·tan, ·tchi; katsu] To win; to conquer; to be superior.
kachuu, *n.* [katsuo] A bonito fish; tuna fish; skipjack; butterfish. See also shimagachuu, maagachuu, ayagachuu.
kachuu-bushi, *n.* [katsuo-bushi] A dried bonito.
kachuu-gwaa, *n.* Dried small fish.
kadu¹, *n.* [kado] 1 A corner; a turn. 2 An edge. 3 Being unsociable; being stiff.
kadu², *n.* Faithfulness; honesty; integrity.
ka-fuu, *n.* [kafuu] A family tradition; a family custom.
kafuu-mu·chi, *n.* A person who is blessed with good fortune.
kafuu-shi, *n.* (To an inferior) thanks.
kagama·in, *vi.* [kagamu] To stoop; lean over; crouch; bend forward.
kagan, *n.* [kagami] A mirror; a looking glass.

kage·e, *n.* 1 Territory; fief; sphere of control; sphere of influence. 2 One who is under such authority.
kagee·in, *vt.* [kakaeru] To control; rule; govern; manage; protect.
kagi-bu·shi, *n.* [kageboshi] Drying (a thing) in the shade, often of plants, leaves, etc.
kagi·in, *vi.* [kakeru] To be absent; lack.
ka-gin, *n.* [kagen] Degree; condition; seasoning.
ka-gu, *n.* [kago] A palanquin; a litter.
kagu-ka·chi, *n.* [kagokaki] A palanquin bearer.
kagusami·in, *vt.* 1 To supervise; to supervise someone at study. 2 To protect; protect with divine power.
kai, *n.* [kari], Expedience. ·nu, *adj.* [karino] 1 Temporary; provisional; interim. 2 Expedient; makeshift; improvised. ·ni, *adv.* Temporarily; provisionally.
·kai, ·nkai, *part.* [kai] Indicates direction or destination; to; for, toward.
kaidaa-jii, *n.* Non-Chinese character hieroglyphs used in the Yaeyama Islands in the premodern period. See also warajan, suuchuumaa.
kaigu, *n.* [kaiko] Silkworm.
kai-kun, *n.* [kaikon] Reclamation of waste land. -sun, *v.* To reclaim waste land; bring land under cultivation.
ka·i-mun, *n.* [karimono] A borrowed thing; a rented item.
ka·in¹, *vt.* [kariru] To borrow; get a loan; rent.
ka·in², *vt.* [karu] To cut; clip; crop.
ka·i-ya, *n.* [kariya] A temporary hut; a scaffold; a stand.
kaja, *n.* Smell; fragrance; scent. See kaba.
kaja·a, *n.* A thing with a lot of sinew; a person whose personality is sinewy and tough. [UKH] See kaji⁴.
kaja·i, *n.* [kazari] An ornament; a decoration.
kajai-mun, *n.* Same as kajai.

kajain

kaja·in, *vt.* [kazaru] **1** To decorate; ornament. **2** To embellish; garnish. **3** To exhibit; display. **4** To affect; be affected.
kaji[1], *n.* [kaze] A wind; a typhoon; a breeze. See also **iichi, ufukaji, kajoosan, sujoosan, turi**[1]**, turiin, turumun, kuchi**[1]**, kuchikaji**[1]**, nishikaji, feekaji, kajimaai, keeshi.** [OBJ]
kaji[2], *n.* [kaze] A cold.
kaji[3], *n.* [kaji] A rudder; a helm; a steering wheel.
kaji[4], *n.* [kaji] **1** A fiber; textiles. **2** A muscle; a sinew.
kaji[5], *n.* [kazu] A number; a figure.
kaji[6], *n.* The nape; the scruff (of the neck).
-kaji, *suff.* Denotes every; each; with.
kaji-bu·shi, *n.* [kageboshi] Same as **kagibushi**.
kajichiri-abii, *n.* To scream at the top of one's voice; shriek; screech.
kaji-fu·chi, *n.* [kazehuki] A typhoon. Also **teefuu**.
kaji-gaa, *n. pej.* Slang term for **kaji**[6].
kaji-guruma, *n.* [kaze guruma] A toy windmill; a pinwheel. See **kajimayaa**.
kaji-gwee, *n.* Barnyard manure; compost.
kaji·i, *n.* **1** A tenacious fellow; one who will not give up easily. **2** A vulgar fellow.
kaji-kaji, *adv.* [kazukazu] Numerous; many.
kaji-kaki·in, *vt.* To make sure; promise; emphasize.
kaji-kataka, *n.* A windbreak; protection from wind.
kaji-maa·i, *n.* A change in the wind's direction.
kaji-ma·chi, *n.* A whirlwind (on the land); a tornado; a twister. See also **ruu, ruusagai**.
kaji-maya·a, *n.* **1** A windmill; a pinwheel. **2** The ninety-seventh birthday celebration. **3** A crossroads; four corners. **4** A gardenia. [OBJ, OGJ, ODJ]

kajimayaa-gi, *n.* A cape jasmine [J Kuchinashi; *Gardenia jasminoides* Ellis var. *jasminoides*]; a gardenia. [FOSR] Also **kuchinashi**.
kajimi-fuka·sun, *vt.* To store (lay) away; tuck away; lock away. [UKH]
kajimi·in, *vt.* To hide (a thing) as precious; store away. Same as **kwakkwasun**.
kaji-na·ran-mun, *n.* An insignificant person; worthless being (term of humility referring to oneself).
kaji·nu-nii, *n.* Origin of the wind; where the wind comes from. [UKH]
kajira, *n.* Under the eaves; scarcement. [UKH] See also **kajiramaai**.
kajira-ishi, *n.* Stones bordering a pillar foundation in home construction. [UKH]
kajira-maa·i, *n.* Scarcement under the eaves to drain rainwater. See **kajira**.
kajiri, *n.* [kagiri] **1** A limit; limits; bounds. **2** A deadline; a time limit.
-kajiri, *suff.* [kagiri] As much as...; as hard as...; to the utmost....
kaji-tu·i, *n.* [kajitori] Steering; a steersman; a helmsman.
kajoora, *n.* Eruption of the skin; a poisonous plant rash. [UKH]
kajoori-mun, *n.* Hives; nettle rash.
kajoo·san, *adj.* Windy; of strong wind.
kajura, *n.* [< J kazura] A wig; a periwig.
kajuu·in, *vt.* [kazoeru] To count; reckon; calculate; number; enumerate. Also **yumun**.
kaka·i-machibu·i, *n.* Pestering; harassment. **-sun**, *v. colloq.* To pester; harass; annoy.
kaka·i-mun, *n.* Demon possession.
kaka·in, *vi.* [kakaru] **1** To hang (on, from); be suspended (on, from). **2** To catch (on something). **3** To be caught; be trapped. **4** To be built; be laid. **5** To call (on a phone). **6** To begin; start; commence. **7** To take; be needed; be required; cost. **8** To splash (on); be

exposed to. **9** To be imposed on; be levied; fall on. **10** To catch; work. **11** To attack; turn on. **12** To be on; be showing. **13** To consult; see. **14** To depend on; hang on.

kaka·i-sawa·i, *n*. An obstacle; a hindrance; an impediment.

kaka·i-shiga·in, *vi*. To cling to; hang on; hold on to; take hold of. [UKH]

kakaji·in, *vt*. To gnaw; nibble (at); bite (at); crunch.

kakan, *n*. A pleated skirt for women in the premodern period. See also **dujin, hooikakan.**

kakashi, *n*. [kakashi] A scarecrow.

kakawa·i, *n*. [kakawari] Relation; relationship.

kaki, *n*. [kake] An overcharge; a fancy price.

-kaki, *suff*. Counter for chops of meat or anything else representing a part of a whole; a bit; a slip; a scrap; a slice; a chop. [GSS]

kaki·in[1], *vt*. [kakeru] **1** To hang; suspend; hook. **2** To put (a thing) over; cover (a thing) with. **3** To build; construct; install. **4** To make (a telephone call); turn on (a radio, phonograph). **5** To sprinkle (on); pour (on). **6** To put on (glasses, etc.) **7** To multiply. **8** To levy (tax).

kaki·in[2], *vi*. [kakeru] **1** To lack; be short of; be missing; be devoid of. **2** To break off; chip.

kaki-jaa, *n*. A hook; a gaff; a fluke; a barb. [UKH] See **gakijuu, gakijaa.**

kaki-jiku, *n*. [kakejiku] A hanging scroll.

kaki-kutuba, *n*. A play upon words; a pun; a paronomasia.

kaki-mu·chi, *n*. [kakemochi] Holding two jobs concurrently.

kaki-mun, *n*. [kakemono] A hanging scroll (picture or calligraphy).

kaki-ye·e, *n*. [kakeai] Negotiations; a bargain.

kak-koo[1], *n*. **1** Tattered clothes; rags. **2** A diaper. **3** A wick made of rags.

kak-koo[2], *n*. [kakkoo] **1** A shape; a form; a figure; appearance; dress. **2** A posture; a pose.

kaku[1], *n*. [kako] A sailor; a boatman.

kaku[2], *n*. [kaku] A square. See **shikaku.**

kaku-baai, *n*. A square pillar or post.

kaku-gu[1], *n*. [kakugo] Readiness; preparedness; resolution.

kakugu[2], *n*. Treasuring; cherishing; keeping under lock and key; careful protection. **-sun**, *vt*. To treasure; to cherish; to keep under lock and key.

kaku·i, *n*. [kakoi] An enclosure; a paling; a fence.

kaku·in, *vt*. [kakou] **1** To enclose; to fence. **2** To preserve; to keep. **3** To keep a mistress.

kakuji, *n*. Jaw; lower jaw. See also **utugee, habukakujaa, iikakuji.**

kaku·mun, *vt*. [kokumu] To encircle.

kakure-yaa, *n*. [< J kakureya] A confinement house; a house of shelter. [OBJ]

kakuri-bushi, *n*. Lit., a hidden warrior; an expert in martial arts (usually *karate*) who is not publicly known as such. Same as **kumaibushi.**

kaku·shi-gutu, *n*. [kakushigoto] A secret; a thing kept secret.

kaku·sun, *vt*. [kakusu] To conceal (an object); ensconce (oneself); hide (an object); cover (a thing); keep confidential. Same as **kwakkusun, kwakkwasun.**

kama[1], *n*. [kama] A sickle. Also **irana.**

kama[2], *n*. [kama] A cooking oven.

kama-buku, *n*. [kamaboko] A fish cake.

kamachi, *n*. [kamachi] **1** A frame bar on top of the entrance in a farmhouse. **2** The head (slang).

kama-du, *n*. [kamado] An oven.

kama·in, *vt*. [kamau] To mind; care about; interfere with; meddle in.

kama-jee, *n*. A cricket. See **see.**

kama-jii, *n*. [kamasu] A straw bale; a straw bag.

kamajisa·a, *n.* Unsociable person; blunt person.
kamajishi, *n.* [? kamashii*] Bluntness; unsociability.
kama-nta, *n.* **1** A lid for large pots and cauldrons, often of straw. **2** An angler; a frogfish. **3** A secret lover (male). See also **naabinufuta**.
kamasaa, *n.* [kamasu] A barracuda.
kamaras(h)a·a, *n.* A person who is difficult to please; a constant complainer.
kamara·s(h)an, *adj.* Difficult to please.
kamasu, *n.* [kamasu] Same as **kamajii**.
kamee, *n.* [kamae] **1** Structure. **2** A style; an appearance. **3** A posture; a position; an attitude.
kamee·i-mun, *n.* A find; anything found on the road. Also **tumeeimun**.
kamee·in, *vt.* **1** To find (something lost); look for. **2** To seek and obtain. **3** To marry a woman.
kami, *n.* [kami] A god; goddess; deity.
kami-achine·e, *n.* A woman peddler who carries her wares on her head. Also **kami'ui**.
kami-arabi, *n.* Divine curse afflicting a group.
kami-ashagi, *n.* A divine hut; a village shrine. Also **ashagi, tunu**.
kami-ashibi, *n.* [kami + asobi] Divine play, a period of feasting, drinking, and dancing following a major community rite.
kami-daari[1], *n.* Divine retribution (often in the form of an undefined malady) inflicted upon an individual for failure to perform duties in service to the deities. See **taariin**[1].
kami-daari[2], *n.* Spirit possession in a shamanic trance. See **taariin**[2].
kami-futuki, *n.* [kami-hotoke] Gods and Buddhas; Shinto and Buddhist deities.
kami-gudee, *n.* Prehistoric period.
kami·in, *vt.* **1** To place (a thing) on one's head (for the purpose of transporting it). **2** To receive (a thing) from superior [polite expression]. **3** (For a cow) to thrust up with its horns. **4** To place (a thing) on top.
kami-ku, *n.* The first half of a **Ruuka** (Ryukyuan short poem). See **Ruuka**.
kami-naa, *n.* A divine name for a deity or a high-ranking priestess.
kami-nchu, *n.* One who serves a god; a priestess. See also **yuta, nuru**.
kami-nige·e, *n.* [kami + negai] A prayer to a god.
kami-ninji, *n.* Faith in a god; dependence on a god.
kami-nuku·shi, *n.* Leftover food.
kami·nu-yuu, *n.* [kaminoyo] The age of the gods, the beginning of the world.
kamirari·in, *vi.* To suffer pain from cramps, spasms of the stomach. See **kamiin** (3).
kamirariya·a, *n.* One who suffers chronic cramps of the stomach; one who suffers from gastralgia.
kami-u·i, *n.* Same as **kami'achinee**.
ka·mun, *vt.* [kamu] **1** To eat; take; consume. **2** To live (on); subsist (on).
kan[1], *n.* [kan] Intuition; perception; the sixth sense; instinct.
kan[2], *n.* [kan] The midwinter; cold; coldness.
ka·n[3], *adv.* Thus; so; in this manner.
kan[4], *n.* [kan] A unit of weight, equivalent to 1,000 **munmi** (approximately 3.8 kg or 8.3 lbs.). [NJED]
kana[1], *n.* [kana] A bundle of undyed threads not yet put on a reel (for spinning).
kana[2], *n.* [kana] The Japanese syllabary.
kana-ami, *n.* [kanaami] Wire netting; a tool with wire net for toasting a rice cake or fish. [UKH]
kanaa·sun, *vt.* To chew; masticate; digest.
kana-bai, *n.* A hoe the entire blade of which is iron. See **kanikiibai**.
kana-buchi, *n.* A three-**goo** grain mea-

surement box. See **chiiga**².

kana-bui, *n*. The inborn capacity of certain people to see ghosts.

kana-ganaa·tu, *adv*. Friendly; kindly; affectionately; affably.

kanagee·in, *vt*. 1 To enclose; build an enclosure. 2 To stop skidding. [UKH]

kanagi·in, *vt*. To tuck (gather) up one's skirt; tuck up one's hem.

kana-gu, *n*. [kanagu] A metal fitting.

kana·in, *vi*. [·(r)an, ·ti; kanau] 1 To be strong and healthy; be able to work. 2 To be fulfilled; be realized. 3 To be equal in a fight. 4 To become favorite.

kana-jicha·a, *n*. A hammer. Also **kana-jichi**. [UKH] See **seejichaa**.

kana-jichi, *n*. [kanazuchi] Same as **kanajichaa**.

kana-kudii, *n*. [kanna-kuzu] Wood shavings. Also **karakurii**. See **kanna**.

kanami, *n*. [kaname] An important point in social intercourse; greeting.

kanami-jooji, *n*. [kaname + joozu] One who is tactful (diplomatic).

kana-mun, *n*. [kanamono] Ironware; hardware; metal mountings; metal fittings.

kanamunu-ya·a, *n*. [kanamonoya] A hardware dealer; a hardware store; an ironmonger.

kana·s(h)an, *adj*. [kana·ku; kanashii] Lovely; affectionate.

kanasa-sun, *vt*. To love; be fond of; have an affection for; hold someone or something dear. See also **shikan**.

kanashi·i, *n*. A lover; a sweetheart.

kanashi-ngwa, *n*. A darling child; one's beloved child.

kan-byoo, *n*. [kanbyoo] Nursing; tending a sick person. **-sun**, *vt*. To nurse; tend; care for; attend.

kan-chige·e, *n*. [kanchigai] Misunderstanding; misapprehension. **-sun**, *v*. To misjudge; guess wrong; misunderstand.

kanchi·in, *vt*. [kamikiru] To bite off;

kangeein

gnaw off; cut off with the teeth.

kanda, *n*. [kazura] 1 Vines. 2 Sweet potato as a plant; sweet potato vines. See also '**nmu**.

kanda-baa, *n*. Sweet potato leaves.

kandabaa-juushii, *n*. A porridge of rice and sweet potato leaves.

kanda-buni, *n*. [… + hone] Sweet potato stems, dried and used as fuel.

kanee, *n*. 1 Land rent; tenant fee; land tax. 2 Tax in general. **-sun**, *v*. To tenant a farm; sharecrop. [UKH]

kanee-gaka·i, *n*. Tenant farming; farming soil owned by another, paying rent either in cash or in shares of produce.

kanee-gaki, *n*. Having one's soil tilled by tenants.

kane·e-gufa·a, *n*. A person who is difficult to feed (on account of fastidious food habits); a fussy eater. [UKH] See **kanain, kufasan**.

kane·e-guri·s(h)an, *adj*. Hard to feed; having difficult eating habits. [UKH]

kanee-jin, *n*. A tenant fee.

kane·e-mun, *n*. A good worker; a hard worker.

kanee-yas·san, *adj*. […shi·ku] Easy to feed; being not fastidious. [UKH]

kangee, *n*. [kangae] Thought; ideas; thinking; a notion; a conception; a plan; an opinion; a belief; an intention; a resolution; hope; wish; desire; imagination.

kangee-gutu, *n*. [kangaegoto] 1 Something to think about. 2 Concern; preoccupation; worry.

kangee·in, *vt*. [kangaeru] 1 To think (of, on, about, that…); believe; suspect. 2 To view (a thing); be of the opinion that…. 3 To intend to (do); mean to (do); plan to (do). 4 To expect; hope; fear. 5 To guess; imagine; suppose; fancy. 6 To regard (a thing) as; consider (a person to be); take (a thing, person) for. 7 To be discreet; be prudent. 8 To consider; take (a matter) into consideration; care for. **9** To consider; think over (a matter); deliberate on. **10** To reflect; reconsider; recall. **11** To be ready; be prepared for.

kangee-kata, *n.* One's way of thinking; one's point of view; how to think.

kani[1], *n.* [kane] **1** A T-shaped metal carpenter's rule; a measure; a yardstick. **2** Common sense; rationality.

kani[2], *n.* [kane] Metal.

kani[3], *n.* [kane] A bell; a temple bell; a hand bell.

kani-butuki, *n.* An image of Buddha cast in metal. [UKH]

kani-buubuu, *n.* [kanabunbun] A gold bug; a May beetle.

kanichi, *n.* [kannuki] A locking bar or pole used in a tug-of-war. See **chinahichi**.

kani-gaa, *n.* A mine. See **kaa**[2].

kani-gara, *n.* A crowbar.

kani-handi·in, *vi.* **1** To become senile; be in one's dotage. **2** To lose rationality. See **kani**[1], **handiin**.

kani·in, *vt.* To block; bar.

kani-kiibai, *n.* A hoe in which only the tip of the blade is iron. See **kanabai**.

kaniku, *n.* Sandy ground near a beach; horse racing ground.

kani-kuji, *n.* An iron nail. See also **kiikuji**.

kaniku-jii, *n.* Sandy area near a beach. [UKH]

kani-kusu, *n.* [kanakuso] Slag; dross.

kani-maa·sun, *vt.* To spread one's arms in order to enclose (a thing or a person). [UKH]

kani-ucha·a, *n.* A bell striker.

kani-u·chi, *n.* A bell striker; a euphemism for **ninbuchaa**.

kani-uubi, *n.* Metal hoop, usually of iron or brass. See also **daki'uubi**.

kanja·a, *n.* [kajiya] A smith; a blacksmith. Same as **kanjeeku**. See also **mee'uchi**.

kanjaa-doogu, *n.* A smith's tools. See also **fuuchi**[2], **hiibaashi, shin**[1], **taaree, toonii**.

kanjaa-yaa, *n.* A blacksmith's shop.

kanjaa-yaa-ugwan, *n.* See **fuuchinuwuuwee**.

kan-jeeku, *n.* A blacksmith. [UKH] Same as **kanjaa**.

kanji[1], *n.* [kanji] A Chinese character.

kanji[2], *n.* [kaburi] **1** A mane. **2** A crest (of a fowl).

kanji·in, *vt.* [kanjiru] To feel; be conscious of; experience.

kanji-mun, *n.* [kaburimono] **1** Headgear; headdress. **2** A coverlet; a quilt to cover oneself at night.

kan-joo, *n.* [kanjoo] Counting; calculation; accounts; tab.

kan-jumi, *n.* [< J kanzume] Canned food.

kan·jun, [kaburu] **1** *vt.* To put on (a cap). **2** *vi.* To become indebted; incur loss.

-kan·jun, *suff.* [kaburu] Indicates the state of being overflowing with something.

kanjuya·a, *n.* A kingfisher.

kan-kan[1], *adv.* Thus; so and so; such and such.

kan-kan[2], *n.* Bloodletting; remedy by letting blood. [UKH] Also **buubuu**[1].

kan-kara·a, *n.* An empty tin can.

ka·n-kuuye·e, *n.* Biting each other, as in fighting. [UKH]

ka·n-kuu·in, *vt.* To bite at; snap at; fasten one's teeth upon.

kan-michi, *n.* A consecrated path leading to and from a sacred grove. See **dabi, kami**.

kan-mu·chi, *n.* A necessity; a necessary article. [UKH]

kanmui, *n.* [< J kanmuri] A crown.

kanna, *n.* [kanna] A (carpenter's) plane.

kannaaji, *adv.* [kanarazu] Surely; for sure.

kan-na·i, *n.* [kaminari] Thunder; a thunderbolt.

kan-neeru, *adj*. This sort of.
kanpacha·a, *n*. A person with a bald scar.
kanpachi, *n*. A patch of baldness, usually due to scarring.
kanpuu, *n*. A traditional women's hairknot style, in which the hair is rounded on top of the head and pinned. Also **Uchinaakanpuu**.
kanraa-gani, *n*. A land crab. [UKH]
kan-sachi, *n*. [kansatsu] A license.
kan·shi, *adv*. Thus; in such a way.
kanshi·in, *vt*. [kabuseru] To put (something) on; to cover with.
kan-sui, *n*. [kamisori] A razor.
kan-suka, *adv*. This much; this hard.
kanta·a, *n*. 1 Short bob hairstyle. 2 A girl with a short bob. See **kantu**.
-kantii, *suff*. Indicates difficulty or hesitation in action.
kantu, *n. pej*. [kabuto] The hair; a head of hair.
kantu·u, *n. formal* A girl with a short bob. See **kantaa**.
kappa, *n*. [kappa] A raincoat.
kara[1], *adv*. [kara] From (a starting point in time or space); via, by way of (a route); by means of a mode of transportation; (made) from (a material).
kara[2], *n*. [kara] Emptiness; vacancy; vacuum.
kara[3], *n*. [kara] A pod; a hull; a shell; a boll (of cotton).
-kara, *suff*. Head [of cattle]; a counter word used for domesticated animals such as cattle and pigs.
kara-bisa·a, *n*. A person who goes barefoot. See **hisa**, **karahisa**.
kara-chiburu, *n*. Lit., empty head; a skull; the cranium.
kara-funi, *n*. A skeleton.
kara-haai, *n*. A compass.
kara-hisa, *n*. Barefoot. See also **kara-bisaa**.
kara·in, *vt*. [·(r)an, ·ti] To raise (an animal).

kara-jaki, *n*. Alcoholic drink which is not diluted. [UKH] See **saki**.
karaji, *n*. [kashira] 1 Hair of the head; tresses; locks. 2 Traditional hairstyle of women.
karaji-gii, *n*. Hair of the head.
karaji-kwe·e, *n*. Lit., hair-eater; a long-horned beetle.
karakara·a, *n*. A kind of sake vessel, usually round with a flat bottom.
kara-ku·i, *n*. [karakuri] Pegs for the **sanshin**. Also **jiifaa**, **mudi**. See **sanshin**.
kara-kurii, *n*. Same as **kanakudii**.
kara-mun, *n*. Bitter, spicy food.
kara-naa, *n*. A Chinese-type name, added to Okinawan names by the upper gentry in premodern Okinawa. See also **naa**[3].
kara-rii, *n*. An empty hand. [UKH] Same as **nnadii**. See also **tii**[1].
kara·san, *adj*. [karai] (Spicy) hot; pungent (flavor); sharp.
karashi, *n*. [karuishi] A pumice (stone). Also **karuishi**.
kara-shini, *n. colloq*. [karazune] The shin. [UKH]
kara·shi-yaa, *n*. [kashiya] A house for rent; a rental house.
kara-su[1], *n*. [kara-shio*] Salted fish; salted fish guts. See also **karasugwaa**.
kara-su[2], *n*. [kara-shio*] Low tide; a little low tide. [UKH]
karasu-gaami, *n*. A salt-pickled fish jar. See also **kaami**.
karasu-gwaa, *n*. Same as **karasu**.
kara·sun[1], *vt*. [kasu] To lend; loan; advance; give credit. See **iraasun**.
kara·sun[2], *vt*. [karasu] To let wither; blight; let dry; season (wood).
karata, *n*. [karada] The body; physique; build; constitution; frame.
kara-taki, *n*. [kara-take*] Giant timber bamboo [J madake; *Phyllostachys bambusoides* Sieb. & Zucc.]. [FOSR]
kara-ti, *n*. An art of self-defense of Okinawa characterized chiefly by

the use of no weapons but one's own hands and feet. Also **tii**. See also **pin'an, naihanchi, passai, kuusankuu**.

kara-tootoomee, *n*. Lit., empty Buddhist altar; a person who maintains a family Buddhist altar unattached to rights of inheritance. [UKH]

kara-wata, *n*. An empty stomach; hunger. [UKH]

kara-yuka, *n*. A bare floor; floor without mattress.

kari-baa, *n*. [kareha] A dead leaf; a withered leaf.

kari-gii, *n*. [kareki] A withered (dead) tree. [UKH] Also **kariki**.

kari-gusa, *n*. Withered grass. [UKH] Also **karikusa**.

kari-gwii, *n*. A hoarse voice. [UKH]

ka-rii, *n*. [karei] Happiness; propitiousness; joyous event; luck. See **bukarii**.

kari-icha, *n*. A dried cuttlefish. [UKH]

kari·in[1], *vt*. To raise (an animal). Same as **karain**. See **chikanain**.

kari·in[2], *vi*. [kareru] To wither; die; perish.

karii·na-mun, *n*. An item of lucky omen. [UKH]

kari-ki, *n*. [kareki] Same as **karigii**.

kari-kusa, *n*. [karekusa] Same as **karigusa**.

kari-suu, *n*. [kare-shio*] A small tide; a tide without a great change in sea level.

kari-yadu, *n*. Lit., temporary lodging; a temporary tomb. Also **yushiri**. See also **haka**.

kari-yushi, *n*. Happiness; auspiciousness. See **karii, yushi'ashi**.

karu, *n*. [kado] Same as **kadu**[1].

karu-garuu-tu, *adv*. [karugaruto] Lightly; easily.

karu-ishi, *n*. [karuishi] Same as **karashi**.

karu·ku-na·sun, *vt*. 1 To lighten; reduce; alleviate. 2 To ceremonially wash and remove the flesh from the bones of a dead person, usually done seven years after death. See **shinkuchi**.

karu·mun, *vi*. [karumu*] To give birth to; be delivered of.

karunji·in, *vt*. [koronjiru] To slight; make light of; belittle; underrate; despise.

karu-waja[1], *n*. [karuwaza] Acrobatics; acrobatic performance. Same as **hooka**.

karu-waja[2], *n*. Light work; easy work. [UKH]

kasa[1], *n*. [kasa] A hat; an umbrella.

kasa[2], *n*. [kasa] A scab; a slough; syphilis; pox; a blotch.

kasaba·in, *vi*. [kasabaru] 1 To be piled up; lie one upon another. 2 To be bulky; become voluminous.

-kasabi, *suff*. Layer; a counter suffix used for sets or layers of things. See also **-mashi, -chiri**.

kasabi·in, *vt*. To pile up; lay one upon another.

kasa-buta, *n*. [kasabuta] A dried scab; an encrustation. Also **kasanta**.

kasagi·in[1], *vi*. To become pregnant.

kasagi·in[2], *vt*. To carry things on one's back or in a **tiiru** basket on one's back, tied with a loop of strap, the other end of which goes around the forehead of the carrier.

kasagi-nchu, *n*. A pregnant woman.

kasagira·sun, *vt*. To make (a woman) pregnant.

kashi[1], *n*. [kasu] Dregs; lees; grounds; sediment. Also **guri**.

kashi[2], *n*. [kase] 1 A skein of threads of the warp; a reel; a hank. 2 A reeling tool for the warp, shaped like the letter H.

kashi-aya, *n*. Vertical stripes; vertically striped cloth.

kashichi, *n*. The beginning end of a bolt of fabric.

kashichi-i, *n*. [kashiki- + ii*] Steamed glutinous rice.

kashigaa, *n*. A straw bag.

kashigaa-bukuru, *n*. Same as **kashigaa**.

kashigui, *n.* Phlegm; sputum. [GSS]
ka-shii, *n.* [kasei] Same as **kaashii.** **-sun,** *vt.* Same as **kaashii-sun.**
kashi·in[1], *vi.* [kasureru] (For the voice) to become hoarse; become husky.
kashi·in[2], *vi.* To drink hard; carouse; revel; swig. [UKH]
kashi-jee, *n.* Sake lees; draff; brewers' grain.
kashi-kashi, *adv. onom. colloq.* Quickly; fast.
kashima·s(h)an, *adj.* Annoying; bothersome.
kashi-nuchi, *n.* Threads of the warp and woof.
kashira, *n.* [kashira] A leader; a chief; a head; a captain; a foreman; a boss.
kashitira·a, *n.* [kasutera < Port castella < pão de Castella] Sponge cake.
kas·san, *adj.* [...ru·kku; karui] Light (childbirth, illness). See **karukunasun, gassan.**
kas-shin, *n.* [kassen] An intervillage bullfight meet. [UKH]
kata[1], *n.* [kata] A side; a party; a direction.
kata[2], *n.* [kata] **1** A model; a pattern; a mold; a matrix. **2** A style; kind. **3** A pattern; cut. **4** A picture. **5** A pawn.
kata[3], *n.* [kata] The shoulder.
kata-, *pref.* Indicates one of a pair.
-kata, *suff.* Denotes the direction, side; region.
kata-baru, *n.* A tideland; a dry beach; a beach at ebb tide; a mudflat. See **gata.**
kata-biichi, *n.* Favoritism; partiality.
kata-bu·i, *n.* A localized rain shower, typically in summer. See also **ami**[1].
kata-buni, *n.* [katabone] The shoulder bone; the shoulder blade.
katachi[1], *n.* [kataki] **1** An enemy; a foe; an adversary. **2** One who is incompatible.
katachi[2], *n.* [katachi] **1** A form; a shape. **2** Appearance; figure.
kata-chiburu-yami, *n.* A migraine headache. Also **katachiburuyan.**
kata-chiki, *n.* [katatsuke] Print-stenciled cloth. See **bingata, eegata.**
kata-chimu, *n.* Halfhearted.
katachi·nu-mee, *n.* A bowl of heaped rice with chopsticks stuck erect at the center offered to the spirits of the dead. [OBJ] Same as **muimee**[2].
kata-fa, *n.* [katawa] Deformity; malformity.
katafa·a, *n.* A deformed person; a crippled person; a disabled person.
kata-ficha·a, *n. pej.* Same as **katafichimun.** [GSS]
kata-fi·chi, *n.* Deformity; malformation. Also **katahichi.**
katafichi-mun, *n.* A deformed person; a malformed person. Also **katahichimun.**
kata-guu, *n.* One of a pair (of things such as shoes).
kata-ha, *n.* [kataha] A single edge.
kata-haba, *n.* The breadth of one's shoulders.
kataha-shiigu, *n.* A single-edged knife.
kata-hichi, *n.* Same as **katafichi.**
katahichi-mun, *n.* Same as **katafichimun.**
kata-hisa, *n.* One leg; one foot.
kata·in, *vt.* [kataru] To talk; tell; relate; narrate.
kata-jaa, *n.* Strong tea. See **chaa**[3].
katajiki·in, *vt.* [katazukeru] **1** To put (things) in order; tidy up (a room); clean up. **2** To clear away; put away; stow away; put back. **3** To dispose of; deal with; bring (a matter) to a conclusion; solve (a problem). **4** To give one's daughter in marriage.
kataka, *n.* **1** Cover; shelter; shade. **2** Protection.
kata-kashira, *n.* Men's topknot worn in the days of the Ryukyu kingdom.
katakuchi-ware·e, *n.* A half smile; a slight smile.
kata-kushihaji, *n.* Slipping out of one

arm of a kimono (so that it will be easier to work). [UKH]
kata-kushinuji, *n.* Same as **katakushihaji.**
katama·a, *n. pej.* Same as **katamii.** [GSS]
katama·i, *n.* [katamari] A lump; a mass; a clod (of soil); a gobbet (of meat); a group; a crowd; pejorative reference to a person.
katama·in, *vi.* 1 To harden; become solid; stiffen; set; settle; solidify. 2 To congeal; coagulate; clot; curdle. 3 To gather together; assemble; bunch up; clutter.
katami, *n.* [katami] A keepsake.
-katami, *suff.* Indicates a load carried on the shoulder.
kata-michi, *n.* [katamichi] One way; each way.
kata-mii, *n.* [katame] 1 One eye. 2 A person with one eye.
katami·in[1], *vt.* [katameru] To make (a thing) stiff, solid.
katami·in[2], *vt.* To carry on the shoulder.
katamiya·a, *n.* A bearer.
katana, *n.* [katana] 1 A big knife; a mountain knife. 2 A sword.
katan·chi, *n.* [katamuki] Inclination; gradient; slant; slope; tilt.
kata-n·chun, *vi.* To incline; lean to; be tipped over; lurch; tilt.
kata-ni·i, *n.* Half-cooked; Half-boiled.
kata-nki·in, *vt.* To tip; tilt; slant; incline; list.
kata-ruugeei, *n.* A kimono the horizontal half of which is made of a different color or pattern from the top half. [UKH]
kata·san, *adj.* [katai] 1 Hard; solid; stiff; tough; tight. 2 Thick; strong; heavy.
kata-shimi, *n.* [katasumi] A corner; a nook. See **shimi**[2].
kata-sudi, *n.* [katasode] A sleeve; an arm (of clothes).
kata-tii, *n.* [katate] One hand; single hand.

kata-tima, *n.* [katadema] Spare time.
katatima-shigutu, *n.* A side job; a part-time job; a job which does not require full time.
kata-udi, *n.* [kataude] 1 One arm. 2 A right-hand man; one's lieutenant.
kata-umu·i, *n.* [kataomoi] One-sided love; unrequited love.
kata-uya, *n.* [kataoya] One parent; a single parent.
kata-waki, *n.* A partial and unfair distribution.
kata-wari, *n.* 1 A fragment; a bit. 2 One of the same party.
kati·in, *vt.* To make a side dish of.
kati-mun, *n.* A side dish.
katti[1], *n.* [katte] Selfishness; willfulness; one's own way.
katti[2], *n.* One who has experience in work or in a technical field. [UKH]
kawa, *n. lit.* [kawa] A river. See **kaara**[2].
kawa·i, *n.* [kawari] A substitute; in lieu of; instead of; replacement.
kawa·i-mun, *n.* [kawarimono] 1 A strange thing; an unusual thing. 2 An eccentric person. 3 A commendable person.
kawa·in, *vi.* [kawaru] 1 To change; undergo a change; alter. 2 To replace; take the place of; be substituted. 3 To be different from; vary from.
kawatta kutu, *n.* [< J kawatta koto] An unusual happening; a strange happenstance.
kaya, *n.* [kaya] Hay; thatch; straw; a general term referring to **magaya, haa-meekuugi.** [ODJ, FOSR]
kayaa·sun, *vt.* To carry over repeatedly.
kaya-buchi, *n.* [kayabuki] Thatching, mostly with miscanthus.
kayabuchi-yaa, *n.* [kayabukiya] A house with a thatched roof. Also **ka-yayaa.**
ka-yaku, *n.* [kayaku] Gunpowder; powder; explosives. [UKH]
kaya-yaa, *n.* Same as **kayabuchiyaa.**

kayu·i, *n*. [kayoi] Going back and forth; frequenting; living out. [UKH]
kayu·in, *vi*. [kayou] To commute; go to and from; frequent. [UKH]
kee[1], *n*. [kai] **1** A spoon. See also **shimudoogu**. **2** A clam. **3** A shellfish.
kee[2], *n*. [kayu] A soft rice gruel. Also **ukee**.
kee[3], *n*. [ke*] A chest for clothes.
kee[4], *n*. [kai] Scull; oar; paddle. Also **eeku**[1].
-kee, *suff*. [kai] A counter for floors or stories in buildings.
kee·i[1], *n*. [kaeri] A return route; a return trip; the way back home. Also **keeimichi**.
kee·i[2], *n*. Change; money returned as the difference between the price and the money given. Also **keeshimudushi**.
keei-jibun, *n*. Time to go home; time to return.
keei-michi, *n*. Same as **keei**[1].
kee·in[1], *vi*. [kaeru] **1** To return; come back; go back; leave. **2** To go back; leave; be off. **3** To turn back; return to. **4** To come again.
kee·in[2], *vt*. [kaeru] **1** To change; alter; shift; vary; reverse. **2** To reform; revise; remodel; renovate. **3** To change; turn; convert; exchange; barter. **4** To renew; substitute.
kee-jin, *n*. [kaeginu] Spare clothing; a change of clothes.
keejoo, *n*. A **sanshin** of the highest quality.
kee-kuru·bun, *vi. emph*. To fall; tumble. Same as **kurubun**.
-keen, *suff*. [-kai] Indicates the number of times or frequency.
keera·sun, *vt*. **1** To turn upside down; turn over. **2** To make (someone) return; send back.
keeri·in, *vi*. To tumble; fall; roll down.
keerin-kurubin, *adv*. **1** Tumbling about; rolling about. **2** Lolling about; being idle. **-sun**, *v. colloq*. To tumble about; roll about.
keeru·u, *n*. [< kaeru] Exchange; reciprocity; give and take. **-sun**, *v. colloq*. To exchange. Same as **keein**[2].
-keesaa, *suff*. Added to verbs, indicates repeated action: to do repeatedly; something done repeatedly.
kee·shi, *n*. [kaeshi] **1** A return gift. **2** A return call. **3** An aftershock (of an earthquake); the trailing half of a typhoon (follow after the eye has passed). **4** Any object such as **ishigantoo** that has the power to repel malevolent spirits.
keeshi-ma·a, *n*. Wearing clothes inside out.
kee·shi-mudu·shi, *n*. Same as **keei**[2].
kee·sun, *vt*. [kaesu] **1** To return; give back. **2** To put (a thing) back. **3** To repay; return (a favor). **4** To plow a field.
keete·e, *adv*. [kaette] Rather (than); better (than).
kee-tu·i-baakuu, *n*. Being in great demand; being at a premium.
kee-tu·in, *vt*. To swipe; pilfer; purloin; walk away with.
kee-tunai, *n*. The neighborhood; the neighbors. Also **chukeetunai**.
kee-uchi, *n*. A small plate. See also **kujara**, **sara**[1].
kee-ushi, *n*. Same as **keeuchi**. Regional slang in Gushichan. [GSS]
kek-kwa, *n*. [kekka] Result; consequence; effect; outcome. [UKH]
kibui, *n*. [keburi*] Same as **kibushi**.
kibu·in, *vi*. [kebui*] To smoke; smolder; be smoky.
kibu·san, *adj*. Smoky; smoldering.
kibushi, *n*. Smoke; fumes. Also **kibui**.
kibushi-kaja, *n*. Smoking odor; odor of smoke.
kichi, *n*. A rafter.
kiga, *n*. [kega] **1** A wound. **2** Damage.
kiga-nin, *n*. A wounded (injured) person; the wounded.

kii[1], *n.* [ki] A tree; wood; timber.
kii[2], *n.* [ke] Hair on the body of humans or animals; hair on vegetation; feathers; down. See also **karaji, karajigii, kantaa, kantuu, kantu, binta, machigi, sakamachigi, mayu, mayugi, hanagii, nnigii, kiibisaa, wachigi, wachikuugi, kuugi, shinigi, 'nbugi, fukugii, kiimoo, hijimoo, kiihagaa, kiimaa, kiimiiguchi**.
kii-bai, *n.* A wooden hoe.
kii-bisa, *n.* Stilts. See **hisa**.
kii-bisa·a, *n.* A person with thin hair. See **kii**[2], **hissan**[1].
kii-buri-dacha·a, *n. emph.* Gooseflesh; goose bumps.
kii-butuki, *n.* A wooden image of the Buddha.
kii-chichicha·a, *n.* A woodpecker [*Dendrocopos kizuki*]. Also **kiichitchaa**.
kii-fukuga·a, *n.* Goose bumps; gooseflesh. [UKH]
kii-fukuga·a-rachi, *n.* Same as **kiifukugaa**. See **tachun**[1].
kii-fuujoo, *n.* A fisherman's wooden pillow, doubling as a waterproof container for tobacco and matches, etc.
kii-gata·a, *n.* A person who is hairy; a person with dense body hair. [UKH] Also **kiimaa**.
kii-haga·a, *n.* One whose hair has fallen out.
kii-jeeku, *n.* A carpenter. See **seeku**.
kii-ji, *n.* A wooden stake; a post; a pile; a picket.
kii-jiran, *n.* [kejirami] A crab-louse. See **shiran**.
kii-jiri, *n.* A wood chip; a block; a splinter. See **chiriin**[1].
kii-jukuri·i, *n.* Preparation of lumber for building a house. See **chukuin**.
kii-kashi, *n.* Sawdust.
kii-kuji, *n.* [kikugi] A wood peg.
kii-kusu, *n.* Planing refuse; wood shavings.
kii-maa, *n.* Same as **kiigataa**.

kii-makkwa, *n.* [kimakura] A wooden pillow.
kii-mii-guchi, *n.* The hairline along the forehead or on the nape.
kii-moo, *n.* One who has no hair where there ought to be hair.
kii-mumu, *n.* [kemomo*] Peach [*Prunus persica* (L.) Batsch]. [FOSR]
kii-musa·a, *n. colloq.* Same as **kiimushi**.
kiimushi, *n.* [kemushi] A caterpillar.
ki·in, *vt.* [·ran, ·tchi; keru] To kick; give a kick.
kii-'nma, *n.* A footstool; a step; a stool. Also **ashi'nma**.
kii-'nmu, *n.* Tapioca plant; cassava [J tapioka; *Manihot esculenta* Crantz].
kii-nubu·i, *n.* [kinobori] Tree climbing.
kii·nu-faa, *n.* [kinoha] A tree leaf.
kii·nu-kaa, *n.* Tree bark.
kii·nu-kaagi, *n.* Shade of a tree.
kii·nu-mata, *n.* A fork of a tree.
kii·nu-nai, *n.* A fruit of a tree; fruit.
kii·nu-nii, *n.* A tree root.
kii·nu-shin, *n.* A treetop; branch tips.
kii-racha·a, *n.* For the hair to stand on end. [UKH] See **tachun**[1].
kii-ramun, *n.* Firewood. Same as **tamun**. [UKH]
kii-roogu, *n.* Lumber; a log. [UKH]
kii-sachi, *n.* [< J keisatsu] The police; the police force; a police station. Also **chiisachi**.
kiishi, *n.* A tool for putting salted sands into **oodaa** baskets. See **oodaa, maasudoogu**.
kii-ui, *n.* [kyuuri] A cucumber.
kii-ushi, *n.* A wooden mortar. See **uushi**.
kii-yama, *n.* A wooden plow. See **yaama**.
kijai, *n.* A stairwell. [UKH]
kija·mi-kuubu, *n.* Shredded kelp. [UKH]
kija·mun, *vt.* [kizamu] To chop up; mince; hash; shred.
kijari, *n.* Same as **wuimi**.

kiji, *n.* [kizu] **1** A wound; an injury; a hurt; a cut. **2** A fault; a flaw; a defect; a crack; a bruise (on fruit).

kiji-chi·chun, *vi.* [kizutsuku] To become wounded; be injured.

kiji-hoo·in, *vt.* To pick and eat a bit of everything at random.

kiji-mun, *n.* A tree fairy; a tree spirit. Also **kijimunaa.** See also **seema, bunagaya.**

kijimuna·a, *n.* Same as **kijimun.**

ki·jun, *vt.* **1** To mix; stir. **2** To make cynical remarks; slander; libel.

ki-naa, *n.* **1** Land reclaimed by means of burning. **2** Reclaimed land. Same as **chinaa.**

kinchaku, *n.* [< J kinchaku*] A money pouch; a purse. Also **jinbukuru.** [UKH]

kin-sa, *n.* [kensa] An inspection; an examination. [UKH]

kip-pan, *n.* Same as **chippan.**

kiri-chi, *n.* Ability to harm another person. [UKH]

ki·ri-kuruba·sun, *vt.* To kick (a person) down. [UKH] See **kiin.**

ki·ri-'nma, *n.* A kicking horse; a boys' game.

kisa, *n.* Same as **kissa.**

ki·ri-shiti·in, *vt.* To throw (a person) away. [UKH]

ki·ri-too·sun, *vt.* [ketaosu] To kick (something or a person) down. [UKH]

ki·ri-tuba·sun, *vt.* [kitobasu] To kick (something or a person) away. [UKH]

ki-ryuu, *n.* [kiryuu] A sojourner; a temporary resident. [UKH]

kissa, *n.* [? sakki] Earlier; a little while ago.

kita, *n.* [keta] A beam; a crossbeam; a girder.

ki·tchai-kuru·chai, *n.* Kicking and beating. **-sun,** *v. colloq.* To kick and beat; give (a person) a sound thrashing. [GSS]

kitchaki, *n.* A stumble; a false step; a failure; a setback. **-sun,** *v.* To stumble; lose one's footing.

kooba, *n.* [kooba] A factory.

koo-gaakii, *n.* Covering one's face with a towel.

koogu maga·in, *vi.* To get a bent back due to old age. Same as **kushi magain.**

koogu·u, *n.* **1** An old person with a bowed back. **2** A crookback; a hunchback.

koo-gwaashi, *n.* Rice-flour cake, made especially for New Year's Day. Also **kuugwaashi.** See also **chinsukoo.**

koo·i-mun, *n.* Purchase; shopping; marketing.

koo·in, *vt.* [kau] To buy; purchase.

koo·i-ngwee, *n.* Buying and eating of snacks between meals (often by children). See **kwain.**

kooji, *n.* [kooji] **1** Yeast; leaven; malted rice; malt. **2** Mold; mildew; must.

koo-jin, *n.* [koojin] **1** Hearth deity who reports the wrongdoings of the family to the Heavenly Emperor. **2** Telling on a person; squealing on a person. **-sun,** *v.* To tell on someone; to tattle; to inform on someone.

kooji-maa, *n.* A kimono with square pattern. [UKH]

koojinaa, *n.* A tattletale; a squealer; an informer. See **koojin.**

kooree-gusu, *n.* [koorai + koshoo] A red chili pepper [J toogarashi; *Capsicum annuum* L. var. *annuum*.].

koori[1], *n.* A wicker trunk.

koori[2], *n.* [< J koori] Ice. See **kuuri.**

koori-gashi·i, *n.* [< J koorigashi] Usury; a usurer; a loan shark. See also **jinkarasaa.**

koori-jaataa, *n.* [koori + satoo] Rock candy.

koo-ru, *n.* [kooro] An incense burner; a funeral incense burner. Also **ukooru, kuuru.**

koorumaa, *n.* Same as **kooruu.** [UKH]

kooruu, *n.* A top (children's toy). Also

mukkuu². See also **bachi**¹.
koosa·a¹, *n.* Hitting with the middle finger joints of a fist.
koosa·a², *n.* One who has scabies.
kooshi¹, *n.* An itch; scabies; psora.
kooshi², *n.* [kooshi] A lattice; latticework; bars; a grille; fretwork.
kootu, *n.* **1** Tip of nail, talon, claw; hoof. **2** Derogatory term for human hands.
kooya·a, *n.* A buyer.
koo-yaku, *n.* [kooyaku] A plaster; a salve. [UKH]
ku-ami, *n.* [koame] A light rain; a drizzle; a fine rain.
kuba, *n.* A fan palm [J biroo; *Livistona chinensis* R. Br. var. *subglobosa* (Hassk.) Becc.]. [ODJ] See also **biroo**, **maani**.
kuba-gasa, *n.* A hat made from the fronds of the **kuba** tree.
kuba·in, *vt.* [kubaru] To distribute; assign; deliver.
kuba-jii, *n.* A well bucket made from a fan palm leaf.
kuba-niibu, *n.* A ladle made from a fan palm leaf. Same as **uburu**.
kuba·nu-faa-yuu, *n.* Lit., age of the fan palm leaves; the primitive age in Okinawa.
kubi¹, *n.* [kubi] **1** Neck (of body) **2** Neck of a kimono or a coat; the collar. **-na·in**, *vi.* To be dismissed; be fired. See also **yaanukubi**, **kubichiridushi**, **kubidaki**, **kubigaa**, **kubikaji**, **kubiriin**, **kubiraa**, **kubiwuuriin**.
kubi², *n.* A wall (in a house).
kubi-chiri-dushi, *n.* A sworn friend; a friend in need; a devoted friend.
kubi-daki, *n.* The height or depth up to one's neck.
kubi-gaa, *n.* [kubi + kawa] The nape; the scruff (of the neck).
kubi-kaji, *n.* The back of the neck.
kubira·a, *n.* One who dies by hanging.
kubiri·in, *vi.* To hang by the neck.
kubiri-ji·ni, *n.* Death by hanging.
kubi-wuuri·in, *vi.* **1** To have one's neck broken. **2** To bow one's head in submission; submit; surrender.
kubumi·in, *vi.* [kubomeru] To make a dent; make hollow; make a depression. Same as **hikkumiin**.
kubu·mun, *vt.* [kubomu] To dent; become hollow; become depressed. Same as **hikkumun**.
kubun, *n.* [kubomi] A hollow; a cavity; a dent; a pit; a pothole.
kubu-shimi, *n.* A cuttlefish.
kucha¹, *n.* A room in a house typically located in the back (normally on the northern side) reserved as extra room for napping, childbirth, children, or for a young married couple. Also called **uraja**.
kucha², *n.* A kind of stone, usually marlstone from the tertiary period, found in the central and southern regions of Okinawa Island. See also **jaagaru**.
kucha³, *n.* Alkaline soil that is dissolved in water and used to wash hair.
kuchi¹, *n.* [kochi] An easterly wind, especially in the early spring. Also **kuchikaji**¹. See **kaji**¹.
kuchi², *n.* [kuchi] A mouth.
kuchi³, *n.* [kotsu] A human bone (after death).
-kuchi¹, **-guchi**, *suff.* Denotes a language or a dialect.
-kuchi², **-guchi**, *suff.* Denotes a beginning.
kuchi-bee·san, *adj.* Facile with words; quick in speech. See **heesan**.
kuchibi, *n.* Same as **kuchubi**. [UKH]
kuchi-binsa·a, *n.* A good talker. [UKH]
kuchi-biru, *n.* [kuchibiru] A lip. [UKH]
kuchi-bita, *n.* [kuchibeta] A poor speaker.
kuchi-bushi, *n.* A mouth warrior; one who talks big but has no ability.
kuchi-buucha·a, *n.* A haughty person; a proud person. [UKH]
kuchi-dati, *n.* A play without a definite scenario, only a rough outline; an

improvisational play. See also **kumi-wudui**.
kuchi-dumi, *n.* [kuchidome] Forbidding a person to speak.
kuchi-feejuraa, *n.* A glib talker; a glibber. [GSS]
kuchi-gaayee, *n.* Verbal fight; quarrel. [UKH]
kuchi-gansui, *n.* [kuchi + kamisori] A sharp-tongued person.
kuchi-gas·san, *adj.* [...ru·ku; kuchigaru] Indiscreet; glib; talkative.
kuchi-gufa·a, *n.* A person with a blistering (stinging or sharp) tongue; an acrimonious person.
kuchi-gufa·san, *adj.* Having a vicious tongue; acrimonious. See **kufasan**.
kuchi-guruma, *n.* [kuchiguruma] Cajolery; wheedling.
kuchi-gushi, *n.* [kuchiguse] A habit of saying; one's favorite saying.
kuchi-gutu, *n.* A dispute.
kuchi-hagoo·san, *adj.* Foul-mouthed; abusive.
kuchi-janshin, *n.* [kuchijamisen] Humming a **sanshin** tune.
kuchi-kaji[1], [kochikaze] Same as **kuchi**[1].
kuchi-kaji[2], *n.* [kuchikazu] 1 (Number of) words; speech. 2 The number of mouths to feed; the number of dependents.
ku·chi-ki, *n.* [kuchiki] A dead tree.
ku·chi-kuuya·a, *n.* Fish or animal meat about to spoil that has a biting taste.
kuchi-maa·i, *n.* An excuse; a pretext. **-sun**, To prevaricate; equivocate.
kuchi-mu·chun, *vi.* [·tan, ·tchi] To earn one's living.
kuchi-nashi, *n.* A gardenia. Also **kajimayaagi**.
kuchi-'nbu·san, *adj.* Taciturn; slow of speech.
kuchi-'nbu·u, *n.* A man of few words.
kuchi-nii·san, *adj.* Lacking an appetite.
kuchi-noo·shi, *n.* A savory; something to remove an unpleasant aftertaste.

kuchi·nu-mee, *n.* Working just enough to feed oneself. **-sun**, *v.* To work just enough to feed oneself.
kuchiru·jun, *vi.* [kutsurogu] To relax; unbend; feel at ease.
kuchisa, *n.* [? < J kutsuu] 1 Pain; agony; anguish; torture. 2 Distress; trouble; suffering; hardship. See **kuchisan**. **-sun**, *v.* To suffer; feel pain; be afflicted with.
kuchi-sabi·san, *adj.* [kuchisabishii] Not really hungry, but wanting to eat something.
kuchi-sachi, *n.* [kuchisaki] Lip service; insincerity.
kuchi·san, *adj.* Painful; tormenting; distressing; harassing.
kuchi-sanshin, *n.* Same as **kuchijanshin**.
kuchi-shiba, *n.* 1 Lips. 2 Reputation; rumor.
kuchi-shiru, *n.* Saliva; slaver; drool.
kuchi-suu·in, *vt.* To kiss.
kuchi-yagama·s(h)an, *adj.* [kuchi-yakamashii] Sharp-tongued; fault-finding; carping; critical.
kuchu, *n.* [kutsu] A shoe; shoes.
kuchubi, *n.* A wart. Also **kuchibi**.
kuchugu·in, *vt.* [kusuguru] To tickle; titillate. See also **wachakuin**.
ku·chun, *vi.* [·tan, ·tchi;] To rot; decay; crumble into decay.
kuda, *n.* A stripping tool; a primitive thresher.
kuda·chun, *vt.* [kudaku] To smash; crush; shatter.
kudaki·in, *vi.* [kudakeru] To break; be broken; be smashed; be crushed; be shattered.
kudami, *n.* A step; a stool; a footstool.
kudami·in, *vt.* To trample down; tread on; stamp down.
kuda·shi, *n.* [kudashi] Diarrhea; purgation. See also **kusuhiri**.
kuda·sun[1], *vt.* [kudasu] To have loose bowels; purge (the bowels).

kudasun

kuda·sun[2], *vt.* [kudasu] Lit., to dispatch downwards; to send (someone) from mainland Japan to Okinawa, or from Shuri (the capital) to an outlying area of Okinawa.
kudee, *n.* Shelves in the Buddhist altar.
kudi, *n.* A sib priestess; a clan priestess. Also **ukudi**.
kudu·chi, *n.* A popular, often instructive, epic poem.
kufa·a, *n.* That which is hard.
kufa-chiburu, *n.* Anyone who is hardheaded; one who is inflexible.
kufa-diishi, *n.* See **kuba**.
kufa·in, *vi.* [kowaru*] **1** To grow hard; become solid. **2** To become wakeful, wide-awake. **3** To be on unfriendly terms.
kufa-mee, *n.* Hard-cooked rice.
kufami·in, *vt.* To solidify; harden.
kufa-mushiru, *n.* A coarse straw mattress such as **nikubuku**. See **mushiru**.
kufa·san, *adj.* Hard; solid; tough.
kufuu, *n.* [kufuu] A device; a contrivance; an invention; a scheme; a plan; an expedient; a measure. **-sun**, *v.* [kufuusuru] To devise; contrive; invent; plan.
kugani, *n.* [kogane] Gold.
kugani·i, *n.* A mandarin orange. Also **kuganiikunibu**.
kugani-ngwa, *n.* A child as precious as gold.
kugani-jeeku, *n.* [kogane + saiku] A metal worker; a silversmith; a goldsmith.
kuga·sun, *vt.* [kogasu] Same as **kugarasun**.
kugara·sun, *vt.* [kogasu] To scorch with strong heat; singe; char. Also **kugasun**.
kugari·in, *vi.* [kogareru] **1** To burn; char; scorch. **2** To pine; yearn; long; be deeply in love with; be dying for.
kugari-ji·ni, *n.* [kogarejini] To be in burning love with; long for.
kugashi, *n.* A liquid food made of rice, a ground-rice gruel. See **niikugashi**, **namakugashi**.
ku-gata, *n.* This side; over here.
ku·ga-too, *n.* This far; this distant.
kugee·in, *vi.* **1** To move about; rock; quake; pitch. **2** To toss and turn over in bed.
kuguni·in, *vt.* To be careful; be prudent; be discreet.
kugwachi, *n.* [kugatsu] September. Also **kungwachi**.
kui, *n. poet.* [koi] Love; tender passion.
ku·i-buni, *n.* [kuribune] A dugout canoe.
kuichaa, *n.* A group dance performed during rituals for rain or rich harvest in the Miyako Islands.
kui-ka, *n.* [koika] A love poem.
ku·i-kee·in, *vt.* [kurikaeru] **1** To change one for another; swap. **2** To appropriate (money) for other use; divert (money) for another purpose.
ku·i-keesa·a, *n.* A repeater; one who repeats things. [UKH]
kui-keeshi-geeshi, *adv.* [kurikaeshigaeshi] Repeatedly.
ku·i-kee·sun, *vt.* [kurikaesu] To repeat; reiterate; do (something) over again.
ku·i-maa·sun, *vt.* [kurimawasu] To shift and contrive; make do; manage.
ku·in, *vt.* [kuru] To reel in; wind.
ku-jara, *n.* A small plate. Also **kee'uchi**. See **sara**[1].
kuji[1], *n.* [kuji] A lot; lottery; a raffle.
kuji[2], *n.* [kugi] A nail.
kuji[3], *n.* [kuzu] Starch; sweet potato starch. See also **kuju**[1], **'nmukuji**.
kuji-bichi, *n.* [kujibiki] Drawing lots. **-sun**, *v.* To draw lots. See **kuji**[1], **hichun**[1].
kuji-gufa·a, *n.* One who is unlucky in a lottery. See also **kujiyafaraa**.
kuji·in, *vt.* [kujiru] **1** To dig up; grub; pick (one's nose or teeth). **2** To pry into; examine closely; be cynical.
ku-jike·e, *n.* [kozukai] A janitor.

kuji-muchi, *n.* A starch cake made with sweet potato starch.
ku-jin, *n.* [kozeni] Small change; loose change.
kuji-nuja·a, *n.* A nail puller; pincers.
kujiri-gooshi, *n.* Cloth with a splashed pattern.
kujiri·in, *vi.* [kuzureru] Same as **kundiin.**
kuji-yafara·a, *n.* One who is lucky in a lottery. See also **kujigufaa.**
kuju¹, *n.* Sweet potato starch. [UKH] Same as **kuji³.**
kuju², *n.* [kozo*] Last year.
kuju·sun, *vt.* [kuzusu] To destroy; demolish.
ku-juu, *n.* [kujuu] Ninety.
kukucha·a, *n.* A person with epilepsy. See **kukuchi².**
kukuchi¹, *n.* [kokochi] Feelings; sentiments. See also **bukukuchi.**
kukuchi², *n.* Epilepsy; an epileptic fit. See also **mijigukuchi, hiigukuchi.** [UKH]
kuku·i, *n.* [kukuri] A conclusion.
kuku·i-baai, *n.* A needle for blind stitching.
kuku·in, *vt.* 1 To tie; bind; bundle; strap. 2 To make a separated couple reconcile. 3 To blindstitch; whip (a seam). 4 To conclude.
kuku-mui, *n.* A bud (of flower).
kuku·mun, *vt.* [kukumu*] To keep (something) in the mouth; suckle; suck; lap.
kukunu-chi, *n.* [kokonotsu] Nine.
kukunu-tai, *n.* Nine people.
kukuraki, *n.* Heartburn. Also **kukureeki.**
kukureeki, *n.* Same as **kukuraki.**
kukurii, *n.* [kokoroe] 1 Knowledge; information; readiness; understanding. 2 Directions; instructions; orders.
kukuri·in, *vt.* [kokoroeru] 1 To know; understand; be aware of; be posted on. 2 To give consent. 3 To be careful; pay attention.
kukuru, *n.* [kokoro] Mind; spirit; mentality; intention; thought. See **chimu.**
kukuru-gaki·in, *vt.* [kokorogakeru] To try; endeavor; set one's heart on.
kukuru-gawa·i, *n.* [kokorogawari] A change of mind; backsliding; fickleness; lack of faith.
kukuru-iri, *n.* Kindness; goodness; goodwill; a favor.
kukurumi, *n.* [kokoromi] A tryout; a trial; a test; an attempt.
kukuru-mu·chi, *n.* [kokoromochi] Feeling; sensation; mood; a frame of mind; personality. [UKH]
kukuru-yas·san, *adj.* [...shi·ku; kokoroyasui] Friendly; intimate; familiar.
kukuwoo, *n.* [kokuoo] A king.
kuma¹, *n.* [kuma] A bear.
ku·ma², *n.* Here; this place; this person.
kuma-ba, *n.* A fine-toothed saw for use in cabinetwork. [UKH]
kuma-guma, *n.* [komagoma] In pieces; in detail.
kuma·i-bushi, *n.* Same as **kakuribushi.** [UKH]
kuma·in¹, *vi.* [komoru] To seclude oneself; shut oneself up; be confined.
kuma·in², *vi.* [komaru] 1 To be distressed; be in trouble; suffer from. 2 To be destitute of; be in need.
kuma-jina, *n.* Fine sand [UKH]
kuma-kaa, *n.* Hereabouts.
kuma-kii, *n.* Small fragments; broken pieces.
kuma-noo·i, *n.* Fine sewing. [UKH]
kuma·san, *adj.* Modest; reserved; frugal; thrifty. See also **arasan.**
kumashiraa, *n.* A miser; a niggard; a stingy person. [UKH]
kuma-tu, *n.* A fine grinding stone. [UKH] See also **tushi².**
kumeeki, *n.* 1 Simplicity; modesty; frugality. 2 Details; particulars.
kumeeki·in, *vt.* 1 To practice economy; be frugal. 2 To pay minute attention.

kumeekiya·a, *n*. A thrifty (frugal) person.
kumi[1], *n*. [kome] Rice. See also **'nni**[1], **noogumi, jiimee, mumi, 'nnishiyaa'uushi, mumigara, uushi, ajin, nuka, ara, kumichiji, miimee**[2], **kumidaara, muchigumi, sakugumi, majin, 'nnimajin, kumigura**.
kumi[2], *n*. A filter tank used in a salt field. See **maasudoogu**.
kumi[3], *n*. [kumi] **1** A class. **2** A company; a party; a batch; a group. **3** A set (of cups, etc.).
kumi-are·e-jiru, *n*. Whitish water from washing rice before cooking.
kumi-chiji, *n*. A grain of rice.
kumi-daara, *n*. [komedawara] A sack of rice. Also **kumiraara**.
kumi-gura, *n*. [komegura] Rice granary; rice storehouse.
kumi·in, *vt*. [komeru] **1** To put into; include. **2** To load; charge. See also **kumirariin**.
kumi-kan, *n*. [komekami] The temples.
kumi-machi-ya, *n*. **1** A rice store. **2** A rice dealer.
kumira·a, *n*. Water hen of the rail family; gallinule; moorhen [*Gallinula chloropus* (Linnaeus)]. [ODJ]
kumi-raara, *n*. Same as **kumidaara**.
kumirari·in, *vi*. To be confined; be jailed.
kumi-tu·in, *vt*. To dip up; draw up.
kumi-wudui, *n*. Okinawan classical drama, usually in operetta form, combining music, dance, and drama.
kumi-wuuki, *n*. [kome-oke] A rice chest; a rice bin. See **wuuki, shiiwuuki**.
kumu, *n*. [kumo] A cloud; the clouds.
kumu·i[1], *n*. [kumori] Cloudiness; cloudy weather.
kumui[2], *n*. A pond; a marsh; a pool; a lake.
kumu·in, *vi*. [kumoru] To become cloudy; become overcast.

kumuja·a, *n*. **1** A pockmark; a pit. **2** A person with a pitted face.
kumuji, *n*. A pockmark; a pit.
ku·mun[1], *vt*. [kumu] To draw water; ladle; scoop.
ku·mun[2], *vt*. [kumu] **1** To braid; plait. **2** To construct; assemble. **3** To unite with; conspire with. **4** To act in concert with. See also **amun**.
ku·mun[3], *vt*. To put on (footwear); to wear (shoes).
ku·mun[4], *vi*. [komu] To be crowded; be packed; be jammed; be full up.
kumuu, *n*. **1** Joint surety. **2** Joint liability on guarantee. [UKH]
kumuya·a-'waachichi, *n*. Cloudy weather. [UKH]
kun-, *pref*. Attached to a verb, indicates strong emphasis. See also **kunchikain, kunchiin**.
kunaa·sun, *vt*. Same as **kunasun** (1).
kuna·sun, *vt*. [konasu] **1** To trample; tread on. **2** To slight; ride roughshod over (a person). **3** To digest; reduce to powder. **4** To till; plow.
kuncha·a, *n*. **1** A leper. **2** A beggar; a mendicant. See **kunchi**[1].
kunchaki·in, *vt*. To splash water on (somebody); throw water on.
kunchee·ru gani, *phr. slang*. Lit., A tied-up crab; used figuratively of a person who is in a fix. [GSS]
kunchi[1], *n*. Leprosy.
kun-chi[2], *n*. [konki] Stamina; patience; perseverance; energy.
kunchi-busuku, *n*. [konki + fusoku] Lack of stamina; lack of perseverance.
kun-chichi, *n*. [kon- + tsuki] This month.
kunchi-gusui, *n*. A tonic; an invigorant; a restorative. See **kunchi**[2].
kun-chi·in, *vt*. [·ran, ·tchi] To take a shortcut; cut across; jaywalk.
kun-chika·in, *vt*. To work (a person) hard; keep another's nose to the grindstone; sweat (one's employees); abuse.

kunchiri-michi, *n.* A shortcut; a shorter way.
kunchi-suubu, *n.* Competitiveness relying on patience and perseverance (rather than ability).
kunchi-ujinii, *n.* [konki + oginai] Nourishing food; food that gives stamina.
kunda, *n.* [komura] The calf of the leg. Also **kunra**.
kundi·in, *vi.* [kuzureru] To crumble; go to pieces; collapse; give way; cave in. Also **kujiriin**.
kundu, *n.* [kondo] This year; this time.
kuneeda, *n.* [konaida] The other day; some time ago; recently.
kunee·in, *vi.* [koraeru] **1** To be patient; endure; forgive. **2** To make peace with; become reconciled with.
kun-gutoo·ru, *part. adj.* Such; such as this; of this kind. See **gutoon**.
kun-gwachi, *n.* [kugatsu] Same as **kugwachi**.
kuni, *n.* [kuni] A country; a domain; a land; a state.
kunibu, *n.* A generic term for citrus; a **kunibu** orange [*Citrus nobilis* Lour]. [ODJ]
Kuninda, *n.* A community of Chinese descendants located in what is now Kume-cho, Naha.
kun-ji, *n.* [konji] Bluish background (of a fabric).
kun-joo, *n.* [konjoo] An evil intention; a cross temper; cantankerousness.
kunjoo-mun, *n.* [konjoomono] A cantankerous person.
kun·jun, *vt.* [·dan, ·chi; kubiru] To tie; bind; fasten; truss; lash; brace.
kun-koo, *n.* [kunkoo] Distinguished service; merit; exploits (of war).
kunkoo-mu·chi, *n.* [kunkoomochi] A person with distinguished service.
kun-kun-shii, *n.* The music notation system used for Ryukyuan music. Also **kururunshii**.

kun-kurubaasee, *n.* Jostling. -**sun,** *v. colloq.* To hustle and jostle.
kunpa·in, *vi.* [? funbaru] **1** To stretch one's legs; straddle. **2** To hold out; persist in. **3** To exert oneself.
kunra, *n.* Same as **kunda**. [UKH]
kun-shimi·in, *vt. emph.* To tie; fasten. See **shimiin**[3].
kun-taba·in, *vt. emph.* To tie up firmly.
kunteen, *n.* A little. [UKH] Same as **kuuteen**.
kun-tu·in, *vt. emph.* To take by force; plunder; snatch.
kunu-guru, *adv.* [konogoro] Nowadays; at present.
kunu-hyaa, *n. pej.* This damned fellow; a wretch like this; you damned wretch.
kunu-uchi, *n.* [konouchi] Before long; in a few days.
kunu-yuu, *n.* [konoyo] This world; the land of the living; this life.
kun-yaku, *n.* [konnyaku] **1** Konnyaku; devil's tongue [*Amorphophallus konjac* K. Koch]. [FOSR] **2** A paste made from konnyaku starch.
kuppi, *n.* This much; this big.
kura[1]**,** *n.* [kura] Storehouse; warehouse; storage. See also **mijigura**.
kura[2]**,** *n.* [kura] A saddle (fastened on the back of a horse or other animal).
kuraa, *n.* Sparrow. Also **kuraagwaa**.
kuraa-gwaa, *n.* Same as **kuraa**.
kurabi·in, *vt.* [kuraberu] To compare to; compare with; contrast.
kura-gaa[1]**,** *n.* A spring in a subterranean cavern. Also **abugaa, anagaa, angaa, kuragoo**.
kura-gaa[2]**,** *n.* A variety of sweet potato. [ODJ]
kuraga·i, *n.* Darkness; the dark.
kura-goo, *n.* See **kuragaa**.
kurai, *n.* [< J kurai] Same as **kuree**.
kuraji, *n.* [kurage] A jellyfish.
kurami, *n.* A footstool; a step. [UKH]
kura·shi, *n.* [kurashi] Life; livelihood; subsistence; circumstance.

kura·shi·guri·s(h)an, *adj.* Hard to make a living.

kura·shi-kata, *n.* [kurashikata] How to make a living; a way of life; a style of living.

kura-shin, *n.* [kurasumi] Darkness; the dark.

kurashi-yas·san, *adj.* [...shi·ku] Easy to make a living.

kura·sun, *vt.* [kurasu] To live; make a living; support oneself; earn one's livelihood.

kuree, *n.* [kurai] Rank; grade; court rank. Also **kurai.**

kuri[1]**,** *n.* [kure] A stave; thin, curved strips of wood forming the sides of a barrel or bucket.

kuri[2]**,** *n.* [kuri*] Black ink (of a cuttlefish).

kuri[3]**,** *pron.* [kore] This; this thing; this matter; this person.

kurii, *n.* [? kurui] The period of sexual excitement in animals; heat (for females); rut (for male deer, goat, sheep, etc.)

kurii-maya·a, *n.* A cat in heat.

kuri·in, *vi.* [kuruu] To be in heat. [UKH]

kuri-kaa, *n.* Hereabouts; this neighborhood.

kuri-kara, *n.* [kore kara] From now on; hereafter; in the future.

ku-roo, *n.* [kuroo] Hardship; trouble; suffering.

kuru, *n.* [koro] About; approximately (of time).

-kuru, *suff.* Indicates the self.

kuruba·a, *n.* Same as **chinbooraa.**

kurubasha·a, *n.* A rice paddy roller-leveler. Also **kurubashii.** See also **kweeminkaa.**

kuru-ba·shi, *n.* [korobashi] A tool used to make small ruts in salt-bearing sand in order to accelerate evaporation. See **maasudoogu.**

kurubashi·i, *n.* A tool for smashing clods in rice paddies. [GSS]

kuruba·sun, *vt.* [korobasu] To roll (something) over; tumble (a person) over; throw (a person) down.

kuru·bun, *vi.* [korobu] To tumble down; fall down; roll over; trip over.

kuru-chi, *n.* [kuroki] Ryukyu ebony [J Ryuukyuu kokutan; *Diospyros ferrea* var. *buxifolia* (Rottb.) Bakh.].

kuru-gaa, *n.* A highly water-resistant black fiber growing on the top of the **maani** (Formosan sugar palm). See **maani.**

kurugaa-jina, *n.* A highly water-resistant rope made of **kurugaa** fiber from **maani** (Formosan sugar palm). See **china.**

kuru-guma, *n.* [kurogoma] Same as **kuru'uguma.**

kuru-jaataa, *n.* [kurozatoo] Brown sugar. See also **saataa, shirujaataa.**

kuruma, *n.* [kuruma] 1 A wheel. 2 A wheeled vehicle; a carriage; a wagon; a cart. 3 A car; a taxi. 4 A rickshaw; a cart pulled by man.

kuruma·a, *n.* Same as **kurumahichaa.**

kuruma-boo, *n.* A pole for threshing beans or wheat. Also **gurumanboo.** [GSS]

kuruma-gaa, *n.* A well from which water is drawn by means of a bucket and pulley. See **kaa**[2]**.**

kuruma-hicha·a, *n.* [kurumahiki] A rickshaw puller. Also **kurumaa.**

kuruma-naa, *n.* The yard of a sugar mill. [UKH]

kuru-maya·a, *n.* A black cat.

kuru·mun, *vi.* To blacken; turn black; darken.

kurun, *n.* [koromo] A priest's habit; a costume.

kuru-naa, *n.* A black rope.

kuru-nboo, *n.* [kuronboo] A black person; a Negro. [UKH]

kurun-gee·i, *n.* [koromogae] Change of dress; a seasonal change of clothing.

kuru-run-shii, *n.* Same as **kunkunshii.**

kuru·san, *adj.* [kuroi] Black; dark; dusky; swarthy.
kuru-shibiri·in, *vi.* To become dark and shriveled.
kurushimi·in, *vt.* [kurushimeru] To torment; torture; goad; harass; harry; plague.
kurushimirari·in, *vi.* To be tormented; be tortured; be harassed.
kuru-shuu, *n.* [kuroshio] The Black Current.
kuru·sun, *vt.* [korosu] 1 To kill (mainly animals). 2 To beat up; strike; hit.
kuru·u, *n.* [kuro] 1 Black; something black. 2 The (political) opposition. 3 One who is ostracized from communal activities.
kuru-uguma, *n.* Black sesame. Also **kuruguma**.
kuru-ukoo, *n.* Black incense. Same as **hira'ukoo**.
kusa[1], *n.* A filaria; filariasis, a tropical disease characterized by sudden high fevers, leading to elephantiasis.
kusa[2], *n.* [kusa] Grass; a weed.
kusa·a, *n. colloq.* The back. Same as **kushi**[1].
kusaa-na·in, *vi.* Same as **kushinain**.
kusaa-na·sun, *vt.* Same as **kushinasun**.
kusa-bana, *n.* [kusabana] A flowering plant; a flower.
kusabi, *n.* [kusabi] Same as **shikkwa**.
kusa-bukkwa·a, *n.* A precocious person; a pedantic person.
kusa-furi·in, *vi.* [... + furueru] To suffer from filaria.
kusa-furiya·a, *n.* A patient with filaria.
kusa-gucha·a, *n.* Speaking angrily. [UKH] See **kuchi**[2].
kusa·i[1], *n.* [kusari] A chain; a tether. Also **kusari**.
kusa·i[2], *n.* [kusari] Control; controlling power.
kusa·in[1], *vt.* [kusaru*] 1 To control; manage; govern. 2 To unite; join together.
kusa·in[2], *vi.* [kusaru] Same as **kusariin**.

See also **shiin**[1].
kusa·i-yas·san, *adj.* [...shi·ku; kusariyasui] Perishable; easy to spoil.
kusa·jun, *vt.* To shave off.
kusa-ka·i, *n.* [kusakari] Mowing.
kusa-kaya·a, *n.* A mower.
kusa-ki, *n.* Vegetation; greenery; trees and grasses.
kusa-kusaa-sun, *v.* [kusakusa] To have the blues; feel depressed.
kusami·chun, *vi.* To be indignant; be enraged.
kusa-muna·a, *n.* A sassy talker; an impertinent talker.
kusa-munu-i·i, *n.* Precocious way of talking, especially by the young; saucy talk.
kusan, *n.* Same as **kusandaki**.
kusan-daki, *n.* Same as **chinbukudaki**.
kusa·nu-mii, *n.* In the grassy area; in the grassland.
kusa·nu-nii, *n.* [kusanone] Grass roots.
kusara·a, *n.* Same as **kusarimun**.
kusa·ri, *n.* Same as **kusai**[1]. [UKH]
kusari·in, *vi.* [kusareru*] To rot; decompose; decay; putrefy; addle; corrupt. Also **kusain**[2], **shiiin**[1].
kusari-mun, *n.* [kusaremono] A spoiled thing; a rotten thing.
kusa·san, *adj.* [kusai] Stinking; ill-smelling.
kusati, *n.* [koshiate] Backing; protection; support.
kusa-tu·i, *n.* [kusatori] Weeding.
kushi[1], *n.* [koshi] 1 The back part (of body); the back including the waist; back. 2 The back; the rear. See also **nagani, kushinagani, gamaku, kusaa, yaanukushi, kushinain, kushinasun, kushikaki, kushigakisun, kushihajii, kushi magain, koogu magain**.
kushi[2], *n.* [kuse] A habit; a custom; a foible.
kushi[3], *n.* [kuse] A fault; a defect.
kushi[4], *n.* Avoidance; evasion; shirking.
-sun, *v.* To avoid; evade; shirk; dislike.

kushi⁵, *n.* [kushi] A fine-toothed comb. See also **sabachi**.

kushichi¹, *n.* [koshiki*] A food steamer box with a wooden frame and a bamboo drainer at the bottom. Also **kushichii**.

ku-shichi², *n.* [koseki] A family register.

kushichi·i, *n.* [koshiki] Same as **kushichi¹**. Also **sheeroo**. [UKH]

kushi-gaki-sun, *v.* To depend on.

kushi-hajii, *n.* Stripping to one's waist.

kushi·in, *vt.* 1 To clothe (a person); dress (a person). 2 To supply clothing. See also **chiin¹**.

kushi-kaki, *n.* [koshikake] A chair; a stool.

kushi maga·in, *vi.* Same as **koogu magain**.

kushi-nagani, *n.* The back (of the body). See also **kushi**.

kushi-na·in, *vi.* To be in the back of.

kushi-na·sun, *vt.* To have another person in the back of one; show one's back to another.

kushi-yukkwii, *n.* A day of rest after the planting of rice is completed. [ODJ]

kusu, *n.* [kuso] Feces; excrement; dung.

kusu-hiri, *n.* Diarrhea; loose bowels. See also **kudashi**.

kusui, *n.* [kusuri] 1 A medicine; a remedy. 2 Nourishment; nutrition. 3 Glaze; enamel. See **chikigusui**, **numigusui**.

kusui-dee, *n.* [kusuri-dai] A charge for medicine; a doctor's bill.

kusui-mun, *n.* Nutritious food.

kusui-uushi-gwaa, *n.* A druggist's mortar; a muller.

kusui-yaa, *n.* [kusuriya] A drugstore; a pharmacy; a druggist.

kusui-yuu, *n.* Lit., (something) for medicinal use; a year's portion of brown sugar set aside for one family. [UKH]

kusu kwe·e, *n.* Lit., eat shit; a ritual expression to banish the evil associated with sneezing.

kusu-maya·a, *n.* A shit dropper; shitter.

See **main**.

kusu-takkwe·e, *n.* Same as **kusu kwee**. See **kusu**.

kuta-chichi, *n.* Last month. Also **kwita-chichi**.

kutandi, *n.* Fatigue; exhaustion; tiredness. See **chikariin**. Also **kutanri**.

kutandi·in, *vi.* [kutabireru; kutabureru*] To become tired; tire; grow weary. See also **wutain**, **chikariin**.

kutandi-noo·shi, *n.* An evening drink. Also **kutanrinooshi**, **wutainooshi**.

kutanri, *n.* Same as **kutandi**.

kutanri-noo·shi, *n.* Same as **kutandi-nooshi**.

ku-tin, *n.* [koten] Classical music and dance of Okinawa, usually referring to **ufubushi** dance and music. See also **fa'uta**.

kutu¹, *n.* [koto] 1 A thing; a matter. 2 An event; an incident; an accident. 3 An experience.

kutu², *n.* [koto] Same as **kutuu**.

·**kutu**, *suff.* [koto] Denotes reason or cause: because. Also ·**gutu**.

kutuba, *n.* [kotoba] A dialect; local accent; language; expression.

kutuba-jike·e, *n.* [kotobazukai] One's manner of speaking; diction; expression. See **chikain¹**.

ku-tushi, *n.* [kotoshi] This year; the current year. Also **kundu**.

kutuu, *n.* [koto] A koto, a Japanese harp-like musical instrument with twelve strings. Also **kutu²**.

kutuwa·i, *n.* [kotowari] Refusal; declining.

kutuwa·in, *vt.* [kotowaru] To decline; refuse; reject.

kuu¹, *n.* [ko] Powder; meal; dust.

kuu², *n.* Repair; mending; tinkering.

kuubaa, *n.* A spider.

kuubu, *n.* [konbu] Sea tangle; kelp; seaweed.

kuubu-iricha·a, *n.* Same as **kuu-buirichii**.

kuubu-irichii, *n.* A stir-fried food with chopped kelp and pork as the main ingredients. See also **irichii.**
kuubu-'nbushi·i, *n.* Seaweed pottage.
kuuchoo, *n.* [C hukong] A three-stringed Chinese fiddle, which is a part of a traditional Okinawan music ensemble.
kuu-fu·chun, *vi.* To produce powder; become powdery.
kuuga, *n.* 1 A (chicken) egg. 2 With a name of an animal, its eggs. 3 A testicle. See also **tamagu.**
kuuga·nu-akamii, *n.* The yolk of an egg.
kuu-gi, *n.* Pubic hair. See also **wachikuugi, haameekuugi.**
kuu-gusui, *n.* Powdered medicine.
kuu-gwaa-gwee, *n.* Same as **kuugwee.** [UKH]
kuu-gwaashi, *n.* Same as **koogwaashi.**
kuu-gwee, *n.* Chemical fertilizer.
kuu·i-muuku, *n.* [koimuko] Same as **kwiimuuku.**
kuu·in¹, *vt.* [kuu] To bite at; snap at; fasten one's teeth on. Also **kankuuin.**
kuu·in², *vt.* [kou] To ask a girl to marry.
kuu·in³, *vt.* To close; shut.
kuu-iyu, *n.* A carp.
kuu-iyu-shinji, *n.* A carp infusion, used as a fever reducer. See **shinjimun, taa'iyu.**
kuuja·a, *n.* An oarsman; a rower; an oar. See **kuujun.**
kuu-ji¹, *n.* [kuji] A lawsuit; a litigation. Also **hiruu.**
kuu-ji², *n.* [koogi] The government; the authorities.
kuuji-gutu, *n.* Government business; official duty.
kuuji-mu·chi, *n.* Public expenses; government account.
kuu·jun, *vt.* [kogu] To row (a boat); pull an oar; scull.
kuukuu-mee, *n.* Brown rice.
kuu-kwa, *n.* [kooka] A safflower [J benibana; *Carthamus tinctorius* L.]; a dyer's saffron. [FOSR]
kuu-kwee, *n.* [kookai] A regret; repentance; compunction. **-sun,** *v.* To regret; repent of; be sorry for; be penitent for; suffer remorse.
kuu-mya, *n.* A ramie bag for carrying a baby on one's back. [ODJ]
kuuri, *n.* [koori] Rock candy. Also **kuurijaataa.** See **koori².**
kuuri-buutu, *n.* Gelidium jelly (made from agar-agar).
kuuri·in, *vi.* [kooreru*] To collapse; break down.
kuuri-jaataa, *n.* Same as **kuuri.**
kuuri-yas·san, *adj.* [...shi·ku] Fragile; delicate; frail; breakable.
kuu-ru, *n.* Same as **ukooru.**
kuu·san, *adj.* [koi] (Of drinks such as coffee or tea) strong; thick; heavy.
kuu-san-kuu, *n.* One of the traditional forms of karate.
kuushii-kaashii, *n.* Patching and darning; patchy; full of patches.
kuushii-mun, *n.* A poor person; an indigent person. Same as **hinsuumun.** See also **yuchikunamun.**
kuu-su, *n.* [koshu] Old wine; aged sake.
kuusu-jaki, *n.* Same as **kuusu.** See **saki.**
kuu·sun¹, *vt.* [kowasu; kobosu*] To destroy; demolish; break.
kuu·sun², *vt.* To stop up (a hole); cover (a cleavage).
kuuteen, *n.* A little (relating to amount). Also **kuuten, kunteen.**
kuuten, *n.* Same as **kuuteen.**
kuuten-gwaa, *n.* A little; a tiny bit.
kuuwee-kutu, *n.* [? kowai koto] A matter of grave concern; a serious affair; an emergency.
kuuya·a, *n.* A suitor for a woman's hand; a wooer.
kuyaku, *n.* One's share in expenses; a share in expenses; an allotment in expenses. [UKH]
kuya·mi, *n.* [kuyami] Regrets; mourning; condolences.

kuya·mun, *vt.* [kuyamu] To regret; be sorry; lament; mourn.
ku-yoo, *n.* [kuyoo] A memorial service; a requiem.
kuyumi, *n.* [koyomi] A calendar; a lunar calendar; a solar calendar.
kkwa, *n.* [ko] A child; a boy; a girl; offspring.
kkwa-biicha·a, *n.* One who is partial to his or her own child. See **hiichi**.
kwaadeesaa, *n.* Indian almond [J momotamana; *Terminalia catappa* L.]. [FOSR, ODJ]
kwaa-gi, *n.* [kuwaki] A mulberry tree [J shimaguwa; *Morus australis* var. *glabra* Koidz.]. Also **nandeeshii**. [FOSR, ODJ]
kwaagi·nu-mii, *n.* See **kwaagi**. Also **nandeeshii**.
kwaa-gwaa, *n.* A portion of a boat which forms the bottom joint running from stem to stern; a keel. See **sabani**.
kwaari·in, *vi. vulgar* [kurawareru] **1** To be eaten up. **2** To lose in gambling.
kwaasa·riin, *vi.* [·riran, ·tti] To be run over.
kwaashi, *n.* [kwashi*, kashi] Confection; cake; sweet.
kwaashi-guu, *n.* Confectioners' flour. [UKH]
kwaashi-yaa, *n.* [kashiya] A sweet shop; a confectionery.
kwaa·sun, *vt.* [kurawasu] **1** *pej.* To feed. **2** To run over (a person or an animal).
kwabi, *n.* [kabi] Luxury; extravagance. **·na**, *adj.* Luxurious; extravagant.
kwabi·in, *vi.* To be luxurious, be extravagant.
kwabii·ti, *adv.* Being extravagant.
kkwa-bukuru, *n.* The placenta; the afterbirth. See also **iya**. [UKH]
kwachi-doo, *n.* [katsudoo (-shashin)] A movie; a motion picture.
kwachi-kwachii-sun, *v.* To be enraged; bristle. See **wajiwajii-sun**.
kwa-fuu, *n.* [kahoo] Good fortune; luck. Also **fuu**[2].

kwa-gun, *n.* [kagon] Saying too much; going too far in speech.
kwa·in, *vt. vulgar* [kurau] **1** To eat. **2** To gain (for instance, in gambling). **3** Vulgar emphatic suffix.
kwaji, *n.* [kwaji*, kaji] A fire; a conflagration.
kwakki·in, *vi.* To hide; hide oneself; take cover. Also **kwakkwiin**.
kwakkushi-gutu, *n.* [kakushigoto] A thing kept secret; a secret.
kwakku·sun, *vt.* [kakusu] To hide (something); conceal (something); cover (a fact). See **kakusun**. Also **kwakkwasun**. See also **ushiikuganiin**.
kwakkwa·sun, *vt.* To hide; conceal. See **kajimiin**. Also **kwakkusun, kakusun**.
kwakkwi·in, *vi.* See **kwakkiin**.
kkwa-muchi, *n.* Motherhood; status of having a child.
kkwa-muya·a, *n.* [komori] A babysitter.
kkwamuyaa-uta, *n.* A lullaby.
kwan[1], *n.* [kwan*, kan] The government; the authorities.
kwan[2], *n.* A volume; a book; a reel (of movie film).
kkwa-nasa·a, *n.* A pregnant woman; a woman who is good at having babies. [UKH] See **kkwanashijooji**.
kkwa-na·shi, *n.* Childbirth; parturition; delivery.
kkwanashi-jooji, *n.* A woman who is good at having a baby. See **kkwanasaa**.
kkwa-nashimiya·a, *n.* A midwife. See **sanba**[2].
kkwa-nashi-yaa, *n.* The family that has a childbirth. [OBJ]
kkwa-na·sun, *vt.* To give birth to (a baby); be delivered of (a baby).
kwanbaku, *n.* A coffin.
kwanchee-baku, *n. pej.* A coffin. Same as **kwanbaku**.
kwan-kwan, *adv.* (Of a person) refined; dignified; commanding; respectable; grand.
kwan-muchi, *n.* Government

expense[s].
kwan·nin, *n.* [kannin] An official.
kwan·nu·jin, *n.* Public funds; government funds.
kwan-nun, *n.* [kannon] Avalokiteśvara; the Goddess of Mercy.
kwa-shi·i, *n.* Uterus; womb.
kwa-soo-ba, *n.* [< J kasooba] A crematorium; a crematory.
kwatai-nintai, *n.* Eating and sleeping. **-sun**, *v. colloq.* To eat and sleep; to do nothing but eat and sleep. Same as **ukiteekweekwee**.
kwat-chii, *n.* [kwakkei*] A treat; a dinner; a feast.
kwatchii-gwaashii, *n.* Playing at housekeeping. See **-gwaasee**.
kkwa-umi·i, *n.* A doting parent; a parent who is very fond of his or her child.
kwee[1], *n.* [kuwa] A hoe; a spade. See also **hiragwee, tamatagwee, mimatagwee, ishigwee, faa'ishigwee, taa'uchaagwee**.
kwee[2], *n.* [koe] Fertilizer; manure; night soil.
kwee-buta·a, *n.* Same as **kweetaa**.
kwe·e-buu, *n.* Luck in food. See **fuu**[2].
kwee-doogu, *n.* Same as **kweefiira**.
kwe·e-doori, *n.* [kuidaore] Ruining oneself by extravagance in food. See **kweetoosun**. [UKH]
kwee-fiira, *n.* Hoe and trowel; agricultural implements. Same as **kweedoogu**.
kwee·in, *vi.* [koeru] To put on weight; grow plump; grow fertile.
kwe·e-kuchi, *n.* Food expenses; food prices.
kwee-minkaa, *n.* A green manure mixer with broad blade wheels. See also **kurubashaa**. [ODJ]
kwee-mun, *n.* [kurai- + mono] 1 Food; provisions; edibles. 2 A victim; prey.
kweena, *n.* Travel songs, songs which pray for the safety of the travelers.

kwee-niibu, *n.* A ladle for night soil.
kweeta·a, *n.* A fat or plump person. Also **kweebutaa**.
kwe·e-too·sun, *vt.* [kurai- + taosu] To eat (a person) out of house and home; eat (a person) up; sponge upon (a person); live at another's expense. See **kweedoori**.
kwee-wuuki, *n.* [koeoke] A fertilizer bucket; a manure bucket. See **wuuki**.
kwii[1], *n.* [koe] A voice; news (of a person).
kwii[2], *n.* [kui] A stake; a post; a pile; a picket.
kwii[3], *n.* A closet; a wardrobe. See **kuuin**[3].
kwii-chi·in, *vt.* [·ran, ·tchi; kuikiru] To bite off.
kwii-daka·san, *adj.* Of the voice, high-pitched. [UKH]
kwii-gaa·i, *n.* [koegawari] The change of voice.
kwii·in, *vt.* [koeru] 1 To cross over; go across; pass; go over; go beyond. 2 To exceed; be in excess of; be more than; surpass; excel.
kwii-muuku, *n.* A man who is solicited to marry into a woman's family. Also **kuuimuuku**.
kwi·in, *vt.* [kureru] 1 To give (other to subject, or subject to other); present; let (a person) have; supply. 2 To do something for a person; bestow; confer. See **kwimisooree, utabimisheen**.
kwi·i-saga·in, *vt.* [kuisagaru] To hang on to; hold on to. [UKH] See **kuuin**[1].
kwi-misoo·ree, *phr. formal* Please; formal form of **kwiin**. Also **kwimisoori**.
kwi·ta-chichi, *n.* Last month. [UKH] Also **kutachichi**. See **kwiiin**.

ma(a)-

M———

ma(a)-, *pref.* **1** Beautifying prefix for childhood names of members of the old gentry class. **2** True-; pure-. See **warabinaa**.
maa, *n.* Where; what place; whereabouts.
-maa, *suff.* Indicates dense growth (of hair or vegetation).
maa-anda, *n.* Rapeseed oil.
maachi, *n.* [matsu] A Ryukyu pine tree [*Pinus luchuensis* Mayr.]. [FOSR] Also **machi**³.
maachi-baa, *n.* [matsuba] A pine needle.
maachi-kasa·a, *n.* [matsu-kasa] A pinecone. Also **machinkasaa**. [GSS]
maachi-naba, *n.* A hatsutake mushroom. [J hatsutake; *Lactarius hatsudake* Tanaka]. [ODJ, MAK] See **naba**.
maachi·n-kasa·a, *n.* Same as **maachikasaa**. [GSS]
maachi·nu-anda, *n.* Pine resin; rosin.
maachu·u, *n.* A pine forest.
maada, *adv.* [mada] (Not) yet; still; as yet; so far. Also **naada**.
maa-fanacha·a, *adv.* Flat on one's back.
maaga, *n.* A harrow; a rake.
maa-gachuu, *n.* Same as **kachuu**.
maa·gana, *n.* Somewhere, anywhere.
maagu, *n.* A basket made of miscanthus.
maagu·u, *n.* A thing that is crumpled and wrinkled. See **maguin**.
maaguu-hiigu·u, *adv.* Full of wrinkles and creases. See **maguihiigui**.
maa-gwee, *n.* A hoe with an iron-tipped blade.
maai¹, *n.* [mari]. A ball; a handball.
maa·i², *n.* [mawari] **1** The environs; the surroundings. **2** Circumference; the border; the girth. **3** The twelve-year cycle of calendrical animal symbols (Chinese zodiac).
maa·in, *vi.* [mawaru] To turn; go round; revolve; rotate; spin. **2** To spread all over.

maai-nagi-yee, *n.* [mari + nageai] Playing ball. **-sun**, *v.* To play ball.
maai-uuchee, *n.* [mari + uchiai] A ball-striking game.
maa-ji, *n.* [< **ma(a)-** + **jii**¹] The dark acidic soil, with relatively little humus, of Ryukyu limestone. See also **kucha**², **jaagaru**.
maajin, *n.* Millet [J kibi; *Panicum miliaceum* L.]. [FOSR, ODJ]
maaka, *n.* A rice paddy leveler pulled by farmers.
maa·ku-maa·ku, *adv.* Having the appearance of enjoying one's food. See **maasan**.
maa·madi·n, *adv.* Anywhere; to the end of the world; through thick and thin; to the utmost. See **·madii**, **·n**.
maami, *n.* [mame] **1** Beans; soybeans. **2** The kidney. See also **akamaami**, **induumaami**, **injinmaami**, **toofumaami**, **toomaami**.
maami-gaa, *n.* Bean pod; bean shell.
maami-garaa, *n.* Beanstalk.
maami-naa, *n.* Bean sprouts.
maamina-iricha·a, *n.* Bean sprouts and pork stir-fry. See also **irichii**. [GSS]
maami·na-kuu, *n.* Soybean flour.
maa-mutii, *n.* Which direction.
maani, *n.* A Formosan sugar palm [J kurotsugu; *Arenga engleri* Becc.].
maa·n-kwi·n, *n.* Everywhere; all over.
maanna, *n.* Same as **mannagwaa**, **sajee**.
maa-ran, *n.* [Cant ma-laahm] A southern Chinese-style sailing ship with two masts. Also **Yanbaraa**, **Yanbarushin**.
maaru, *n.* [mawaru] **1** Turn; succession. **2** Order; the sequence of things or events; series.
maaru·u-yi·i, *n.* Sitting in a circle. Also **goomaayii**. [UKH]
maa·san, *adj.* Delicious; tasty.
maa-soo·ru tchu, *phr.* A person who has died (a natural death). See **shinin**, **maasun**.
maa-su, *n.* [mashio*] Salt.

maasu-doogu, *n.* Salt-making tools. See also **suuhama, maasuyadui, sashi, sara**², **kurubashi, oodaa, kiishi, tamagwaa, kumi**². [ODJ]
maasu-kwee, *n.* Same as **gachichaa**.
maa·sun, *vi.* To die; pass away; perish; expire.
maasu-nii, *n.* Cooking with salt only.
maasu-tacha·a, *n.* A salt maker.
maasu-uya·a, *n.* A salt dealer; a salt peddler. See **uin**.
maasu-yadu·i, *n.* A salt-making hut at a salt field.
maataku, *n.* The common bamboo [*Bambusa oldhamii* Munro].
maa-uuu, *n. inf. onom.* A cat; a kitten.
maa-wuu, *n.* Ramie [J karamushi; *Boehmeria nivea* Gaudich.]. [FOSR, ODJ]
maa-yuu·i, *n.* A hairstyle, usually for children, in which a round knot is made on top of the head. [KCS, OBJ]
mabui, *n.* [maburi*] The vital, life-sustaining human spirit; a soul; a spirit (usually, of a living person). Also **mabuyaa**. See also **shinimabui**.
mabui-gumi, *n.* Enticing the lost soul back into the body.
mabui-nugi, *n.* Withdrawal of **mabui** from the body in response to action of an external supernatural agency.
mabui-uti·i, *n.* Loss of the soul, usually from shock or fright.
mabui-uu·i, *n.* An exorcism to chase away the spirit of a recently deceased person. Also **munu'uui, yaazaree, yaabarai**. [OBJ] See **mabuiwakashi** (2).
mabui-waka·shi, *n.* **1** An incantation to separate the soul of a living person from that of a dead person. **2** A rite performed the night of the forty-ninth day after a death, in which the spirit of the deceased is ritually entombed and made unable to return to its earthly home. See also **mabui'uui**. [OBJ]
mabuya·a, *n.* Soul. Same as **mabui**.
machi¹, *n.* [machi] **1** A market; a fair. **2** A town; a city. Also **machigwaa**.
ma·chi², *n.* [maki] An eddy; a whirlpool; a vortex; a spiral; a maelstrom.
machi³, *n.* [matsu] Same as **maachi**.
machibui-kaabui-sun, *v. colloq.* To become twisted and tangled; become entangled; become complicated.
machi-bu·in, *vi.* [matsuwaru] To entwine; clasp itself around; get tangled up.
machi-gata, *n.* Same as **machikata**.
machige·e, *n.* [machigai] A mistake; a fault.
machi-gi, *n.* [matsuge] Eyelashes.
machi-gwaa¹, *n.* A market. See also **machi**¹.
machi-gwaa², *n.* A wrestling technique in which the opponent is collared and tripped. See **shima**³.
ma·chi-kabi, *n.* [makigami] A roll of paper.
machi-kaji, *n.* [maki + kaze] A whirlwind; an eddywind; a vertiginous wind.
machi-kantii, *n.* Waiting in vain; waiting eagerly.
machi-kata, *n.* Urban area; a city; a town. Also **machigata**.
machi-wara, *n.* [makiwara] A wooden pole about four feet tall, used in martial arts training.
machi-ya, *n.* [machiya] A store; a shop.
machiya-gwaa, *n.* A small store; a sundry goods store. Also **gumamachiya**.
ma·chun¹, *vt.* [maku] To roll (paper); wind; coil.
ma·chun², *vt.* [·tan, ·tchi; matsu] To wait; abide; watch for.
ma·chun³, *vt.* [maku] **1** To sow (seed); plant (seed). **2** To sprinkle (water); scatter.
madi, *part.* [made] Till; until; to; up (down) to.
-madii, *suff.* Loss.
madu, *n.* [mado] A gap: an opening space; spare time.

mafana, *n.* High noon; midday; noontide. [UKH]

ma-fee, *n.* Due south.

ma-fu, *n.* A main sail; a spread-out sail. See **fuu**³.

ma-fukkwa, *n.* A hot summer day.

mafu-ya·a, *n.* A person with frizzy hair. [GSS]

maga·i, *n.* [magari] 1 Anything curved or bent. 2 A bay. See also **wan**¹.

maga·in, *vi.* [magaru] 1 To bend; curve; swerve; be bent; buckle; give in. 2 To turn; round; make a turn. 3 To warp. 4 To be crooked; be perverse. 5 To lean; incline. 6 To be against reason.

ma-gara, *n.* Those who are of the same male lineage.

ma-gaya, *n.* Miscanthus [*Imperata cylindrica* var. *major* C. E. Hubb.]. [FOSR] Usually referred to as **kaya**.

magaya·a-higaya·a, *n.* Winding; curving. **-sun**, *v.* To wind; meander; curve.

magi-abii·sun, *vt.* To cry aloud; shout; talk aloud; scream.

magi-gwii, *n.* A loud voice; a stentorian voice.

magi·i, *n.* Something or somebody big.

magi·in, *vt.* [mageru] To bend (a thing or a person); distort (a thing or a person); pervert (a person or thing).

magi-machiya, *n.* A large store. Also **ufumachiya**. See also **gumamachiya**.

magi·san, *adj.* Large; big. See **ufusan**.

magu¹, *n.* A cylindrical basket with lid, made of pampas grass and **maani** sugar palm bark.

magu², *n.* [magu(wai)*] Marriage.

magu·i, *n.* 1 Wrinkles; lines; furrows. 2 Creases; rumples; folds.

magui-hiigui, *adv.* (Becoming) wrinkly. **-sun**, *v. emph. colloq.* (Of skin, kimono, or paper) to become full of wrinkles and crumples. See **maaguuhiiguu**.

magu·in, *vi.* To become wrinkled; become furrowed.

magura·a, *n.* A person who does not pay back money or return borrowed items. [GSS]

ma·in, *vt.* [maru] To excrete; defecate; evacuate bowels.

ma·i-nuga·sun, *vt.* (Of the rectum or uterus) to let fall or slip out of place.

maji, *adv.* [mazu] 1 First; first of all; in the first place; to begin with. 2 Well; now; anyway; anyhow.

maji·in, *vt.* [mazeru] To mix; admix; mingle; blend.

maji-mun¹, *n.* A goblin; a monster; an apparition. See **manjun**, **mabui**.

maji·mun², *vt.* To pile up; stack up; heap up; lay.

maji·n, *n.* [< majimun²] A pile of harvested rice. Same as **'nnimajin**.

-majin, *suff.* Counter for piles of harvested rice.

ma-jiri, *n.* [magiri] A district encompassing a dozen or more villages. See also **mura**, **aja**¹.

majun, *n.* Being together; being with. Also **majuun**.

majuun, *n.* Same as **majun**.

Makaa, *n.* The female divinity, the gatekeeper of Buddhist temples. See **Niwoobutuki**.

makai, *n.* [?magari, ?makari*] A bowl (for rice or soup). See also **wan**³, **mee-makai**, **ubunwan**, **shirumakai**, **aramakai**, **haachi**, **wanbuu**, **sunkan**.

-makai, *suff.* Counter for bowlfuls (of food).

makai-doogu, *n.* Tableware; a dinner set; eating utensils. See also **makai**, **mishigee**, **umeeshi**, **ujin**, **sara**¹.

maki, *n.* [make] A defeat; a loss.

-maki, *suff.* [make] Denotes getting a rash or being poisoned by lacquer.

maki·in, *vi.* [makeru] 1 To lose (a game, etc.); be beaten; be defeated. 2 To get a discount.

mak-kaara·a, *n.* [makka] Deep red; crimson.

mak-kuuru·u, *n.* [makkuro] Deep black;

deep blackness.
makkwa, *n.* [makura] A pillow.
makutu, *n.* [makoto] Sincerity; faithfulness; honesty.
maku·u, *n.* A naughty person; a daring person; a brave person. Also **uumaku, anmaku**.
mama, *n.* [mama] 1 Intact; as it is; as it stands. 2 As; according to.
mama-, *pref.* [mama] Denotes relationship due to a remarriage: step-.
mama-choodee, *n.* A stepbrother; a stepsister.
mama-kkwa, *n.* A stepchild.
mama-uya, *n.* A stepparent.
mami-kashi·i, *n.* [mamekasu] Beancake; soybean meal.
mami-wanda·i, *n.* Process of beating dried beans to remove the husks.
mamu·i, *n.* [mamori] Protection; defense; adherence (to a rule).
mamu·in, *vt.* [mamoru] To abide by; adhere to; protect; defend.
ma-mukoo, *n.* Straight across; face-to-face; just opposite.
ma-mun, *n.* A god; a great man who has divine power.
man, *n.* [man] Ten thousand; a myriad.
man-, *pref.* Same as **maru-**.
manacha, *n.* [manaita] A chopping board. Also **marucha**.
man-buri, *n.* Falling headlong in love. **-sun**, *vi.* To be head over heels in love with; be gone with.
manchaa-hinchaa, *n.* A medley; a pell-mell; a melange; a jumble.
manda·chun, *vt.* To hug tightly; clasp a person in a tight embrace.
man-damashi, *n.* [... + tamashii] Entire soul.
mandoo·n, *vi.* [·ti] To exist in large quantity; be ample. See also **ufusan, uhooku, dateen**.
man-gatami·i, *n.* Being wholly responsible; bearing the entire burden. See **katamiin**[2].

man-gura, *n.* The vicinity; the neighborhood.
man-guru, *n.* (In time) about; approximate.
manguusuu, *n.* A mongoose.
mangwa·sun, *vt.* [magure] To confuse; puzzle; misguide; bewitch. Also **dumangwasun**.
mangwi·in, *vi.* [magureru] To be confused; become lost; be bewildered.
mani, *n.* [mane] Copying as a model.
man-ichi, [man-ichi] 1 *n.* An emergency; an unlikely event. 2 *adv.* By any chance.
mani-gutu, *n.* [manegoto] A form of atavism with a negative, disvalued connotation; simulating the action of an ancestor.
ma-nishi, *n.* True north; due north. See **nishi**.
manja·a-bushi, *n.* Venus; the day star. Also **yuubanmanjaa**. See **manjun**.
man·jun, *vt.* [maburu*] 1 To look with envy at. 2 To keep watch over. See also **miimanjun**.
manki·in, *vt.* To admix; mix; blend; mingle.
man-man, *n. inf.* Food; meal; cooked rice.
man-maru, *n.* [manmaru] A perfect circle.
man-maru·u, *n.* Something which is a perfect circle.
manna-gwaa, *n.* Same as **maanna, sajee**.
man-naka, *n.* [mannaka] 1 The middle; the center. 2 Halfway; midway.
man-nin, *n.* [mannin] Populace; masses of people.
man-numi-sun, *vt.* [marunomisuru] Same as **mannun-sun**.
man-nun, *n.* [marunomi] Swallowing up (whole). **-sun**, *vt.* To swallow (something) whole.
man-richi, *n.* [manriki] A vise; a jack.
man-san, *n.* [mansan] Full birth, a rite of passage held for a child on the seventh

manzai

day after birth.
man-zai, *n.* [manzai] **1** A comic stage dialogue. **2** A **manzai** performer.
map-paa, *n.* Turf; sod; a patch of grass. [GSS]
mara, *n.* [Skt mâra] The penis.
mari, *n.* [mare] Rarity. **·na**, *adj.* Rare; unusual; unique; far between. **·ni**, *adv.* Rarely; seldom; uncommonly.
maru, *n.* [maru] **1** A circle. **2** Entirety; wholeness.
maru-, *pref.* [maru] **1** Denotes circle-shaped; roundness. **2** Entirely; wholly; completely. Also **man-**.
maru-baai, *n.* A round pillar. [UKH]
maru-ba·i, *n.* Being completely exposed (especially of private parts). See **hain**².
maru-booji, *n.* [maruboozu] Close-clipping of the hair.
maru-bun, *n.* [marubon] A round tray.
maru-cha, *n.* A chopping board. Also **manacha**.
marucha·nu gutoo·ru chira, *n. slang* A face square as a chopping board. [GSS]
maru·chi-jin, *n.* A big sum of money in whole numbers. Also **ufujin**.
maru·chun, *vt.* [?marogeru*] To assume control of; rule (over); govern; reign.
maru-hadaka, *n.* [maruhadaka] Complete nudity; complete nakedness.
maru-keeti, *n.* Occasional; rare; few and far between.
maru-maruu·tu, *adv.* [marumaruto] completely; thoroughly.
marumi·in, *vt.* [marumeru] **1** To round; make round (into a ball). **2** To make (a person) obey; get (a person) to trust.
maru-mooki, *n.* [marumooke] A clear gain; a clear profit.
maru·mun¹, *vi.* [maromu*] **1** To become round. **2** To be settled; be united.
maru-mun², *n.* A thing which is complete.
maru-mun³, *n.* **1** A play; a comic interlude or supplementary play in a **kumi-wudui** performance. **2** A jokester. See

kumiwudui.
maru-ndi·i, *n.* Completely wet; soaked. See **ndiin**.
maru·san, *adj.* [marui] **1** Round; rotund. **2** Circular. **3** Globular; spherical.
maru·u, *n.* [maru] That which is round; a circle.
maru-washi·i, *n.* Forgetting completely.
maru-yaki·i, *n.* [maruyake] Total destruction by fire.
masa·i, *n.* [masari] Superiority; excellence.
masa·in, *vi.* [masaru] To surpass; excel; be better than; be superior to.
ma-saka·i, *n.* [masakari] Being at its best; being at the peak.
mashi¹, *n.* [mashi] Being better; being good; being fine; being nice.
mashi², *n.* [masu] A wooden measure box. See **chiiga**².
-mashi, *suff.* [< ? masu] A counter for parcels of rice paddy land. See also **-chiri**.
ma-shikaku, *n.* [mashikaku] A true square; a regular square.
ma-shisa·a, *n.* Same as **mashishi**.
ma-shishi, *n.* Lean meat. Also **mashisaa**, **masshishi**.
mas-saaraa, *n.* Deep blue; very pale; pallid.
mas-sachi, *n.* [massaki] The very first; the head; the foremost; the very beginning.
mas-shiru·u, *n.* [masshiro] Pure white; snowy white; immaculate whiteness.
mas-shishi, *n.* Same as **mashishi**.
mata¹, *adv.* [mata] **1** Again; once more; for the second time; repeatedly. **2** Too; also; as well; likewise.
mata², *n.* [mata] The thigh; the crotch; the groin; a fork of a tree.
mata-bashi, *n.* The groin; between the thighs.
matabashi-gooyaku, *n.* Lit., a plaster between the thighs; a double dealer; an opportunist.

mata-bee, *n.* A second growth from the cut stub of a rice plant.
mata-dumee·i, *n.* A second marriage for a man. See **tumeein**.
mata-gashi, *n.* [< J matagashi] Underlease; sublease; borrowing secondhand.
mata-ichuku, *n.* [mata-itoko] A second cousin; persons whose parents are cousins.
ma-taku·u, *n.* Same as **mattakuu**.
mata-mu·chi, *n.* A second marriage for a woman.
mata-mun, *n.* A perfect, flawless thing.
mata-niibichi, *n.* A second marriage, referring mostly to women.
mata-'nmaga, *n.* A great-grandchild.
mata-nu·i, *n.* Riding (a horse) astride. See also **subanui**.
mata·san, *adj.* [matai*] Perfect; complete; whole.
mata·shii-mun, *n.* 1 A complete thing. 2 A dependable person.
matchi, [< E match] *n.* A match. See also **chikiji**.
matta·chi, [mattaku] 1 *adv.* All; altogether; entirely; completely. 2 *adj.* Just like; being the exact image of....
mattaku·u, *n.* A (toy) kite. [OGJ] Also **matakuu, mattaraa**.
mattara·a, *n.* 1 A swallow. 2 Same as **mattakuu**.
mat-teen, *adv.* Round; in a circle: like a full circle. See **maru-**.
mat-tooba, *adv.* Straight; correct.
mattooba·a, *n.* 1 That which is straight. 2 One who is simple and honest.
matu, *n.* [mato] A target; a mark; an object; a focus.
ma-tumu, *n.* [matomo*] 1 Stern; aft; astern. 2 Wind from the stern; a tailwind.
ma-'wii, *n.* [maue] Directly above; directly on.
maya·a, *n.* A cat.
mayaa-guchi, *n.* Lit., a cat's mouth; a person who cannot eat hot food.
mayaa-jikuku, *n.* A horned owl; a long-eared owl. See **chikuku**.
mayaa·nu chira ara·in-nee, *phr. slang* Washing the face haphazardly, in the manner of a cat grooming itself. [GSS]
mayaasari·in, *vi.* [mayowaseru] To be seduced; be bewitched.
mayaa·sun, *vt.* [mayowasu] To seduce; bewitch (by magical power).
mayu, *n.* [mayu] Eyebrow. Also **miimayu**.
mayu-gi, *n.* [mayuge] Eyebrow. Same as **mayu**.
mayu·i, *n.* [mayoi] 1 Bewilderment; skepticism. 2 Delusion; illusion. 3 Infatuation.
ma-yunaka, *n.* [mayonaka] Midnight.
mee[1], *n.* [mai] Cooked rice. See also **kufamee, achibii, achibiimee, ukkeemee, 'waayuu, awamee, mun**[2], **munu**.
mee[2], *n.* [mae] 1 The front; the fore (part). 2 Presence. 3 Before; ago. 4 Nearby; side; neighborhood.
-mee[1], *suff.* [mae] Denotes one portion, one's own share.
-mee[2], *suff.* [mai] A counter for thin items such as paper or clothes.
mee-[3], *pref.* [mai-] Every.
-mee-[4], *suff., pref.* [mae] Indicates respect.
mee-asa, *n.* [maiasa] Every morning.
mee-ba, *n.* [maeba] A front tooth.
mee-baa, *n.* Buckteeth; projecting teeth. [UKH]
mee-bare·e, *n.* [maebarai] Advance payment; prepayment.
mee-bisa, *n.* A front leg. See **shiribisa**.
mee-chaa, *n.* A woman's loincloth.
mee-chintaa-sun, *vi.* To fall forward.
mee-dani, *n.* Rice seedling.
mee-dumu, *n.* The bow; the prow; the stem; the head. Also **meerumu**. See **tumu**[1].
mee-gai, *n.* [maegari] An advance; an advance in pay.

mee-gaki, *n.* A wrestling technique in which the wrestler hooks the opponent's foot from inside and pushes him over. See **shima**³.

mee-gantu·u, *n.* A traditional men's hairstyle. See **kantu**.

mee-guchi, *n.* [maeguchi] The front; the front door.

mee·in, *vi.* [moeru] To burn; blaze; be in flames.

mee-iwa·i, *n.* [maeiwai] Celebration in advance. **-sun,** *v.* To celebrate in anticipation. Same as **meesuuji**.

mee-jikee, *n.* Same as **jooshichaa**. See **chikain**¹.

mee-jiku, *n.* Lit., front desk; a small stand for mortuary tablets, incense burners, and artificial flowers. See **dabidoogu**.

mee-jin, *n.* [maesen*] Money paid in deposit before receipt of goods.

mee-kaniti, *n.* [mae + kanete] Beforehand; in advance; previously; in anticipation.

mee-makai, *n.* A rice bowl. See **makai**.

meenaa, *n.* A sheep. Also **meenaahiijaa**. See **hiijaa**¹.

meenaa-hiijaa, *n.* Same as **meenaa**.

mee-nachi, *n.* [mainichi] Every day; each day. Also **meenichi**.

mee-na·i-na·i, *n.* Pushing oneself forward; asserting oneself; being obtrusive.

mee-nin-yi·i, *n.* Lit., sitting every year; repeated cultivation of the same crop on the same ground.

mee-nu·i, *n.* [mae + nori] Pasting threads before weaving to yield a smooth hand in finished cloth.

mee·nu-yaa, *n.* 1 A detached room. Also **ashagi**. 2 A storeroom for firewood or agricultural implements.

mee-sa·a, *n.* A flatterer; a sycophant.

meeshi¹**,** *n.* A pair of chopsticks. Usually **umeeshi**.

meeshi²**,** *n.* Flattery; adulation; a compliment; coquetry; flirtation. **-sun,** *v.* To flatter; curry favor; adulate. See **meesaa**.

mee-suuji, *n.* Celebration in advance. Same as **mee'iwai**.

mee-u·chi, *n.* A striker; an assistant blacksmith. See **kanjaa**.

mee-uubi, *n.* Tying one's sash in front.

mee-wikiga, *n.* A gentleman; a man of honor.

mee-winagu, *n.* A lady; a gentlewoman.

mee-yu·i-yu·i, *n.* Same as **meenainai**.

mee-yuru, *n.* [maiyoru] Every night.

me-nseebi·in, *v. formal* To come; go; visit; be [exalting]. See **chuun, ichun, wun**¹.

me-nsee·n, *v.* [exalting] To come; call; go; be. See **chuun, ichun, wun**¹.

mi-bun, *n.* [mibun] 1 One's social position, standing, status; one's station in life; one's walk of life. 2 Circumstances; means. 3 A rank; one's identity; origin; birth.

michi¹**,** *n.* [michi] 1 A road; a way; a thoroughfare; a highway; a path; a lane. 2 Journey; distance. 3 A course; a way; a channel; a means; a step. 4 A duty; morality; teachings; doctrines; truth; reason; justice. 5 A line; a career.

michi²**,** *n.* [mitsu] Honey; nectar.

-michi, *suff.* [michi] Indicating method or road. See also **-kata**.

michi-bappee, *n.* Taking the wrong way.

michi-bata, *n.* The roadside; the wayside.

michi-bushin, *n.* Road construction; a community project of road construction. [UKH] See **fushin**².

michi-fijami, *n.* Placing of houses or other buildings on the opposite side of the street. See **hijami, fijami**.

michi-guyaa, *n.* A junction of three roads; a trifurcated road.

michi-gwaa, *n.* A path; an alley.

michi·in¹**,** *vt.* To close; shut.

michi·in[2], *vt*. [michiru] To fill up; pack.

michi-junee, *n*. A procession through the streets such as in conjunction with a tug-of-war or festival event. See **chinahichi**.

mi-chiki, *n*. [mitsuke] 1 Judgment; an expert opinion; appraisal; estimation. 2 Diagnosis. 3 Prospect; an outlook.

michi-kumaa·sun, *vi*. To respect the taboo on returning from a funeral by the same route taken to the funeral. [UKH]

michi-kumi·in, *vt*. To shut up; lock up; cage in; confine.

mi-chimu·i, *n*. [mitsumori] 1 An estimate; assessment; a quotation. 2 Hopes; expectations; trust.

michi-naka, *n*. [michinaka] En route; on the way; in transit; halfway.

michi-su, *n*. [michishio] High tide.

michi-yurari, *n*. [michi + yurari] Loitering on the way; dawdling along the way.

mi·chun, *vi*. [·tan, ·tchi; mitsu*] 1 To be filled; be supplied; be satisfied. 2 To wax.

midari, *n*. [midare] Unrest; disorder; disturbance; turbulence; agitation.

midari·in, *vi*. [< J midareru] 1 To go out of order; be in disorder; be confused. 2 To be disturbed; be agitated; be chaotic; be in a troubled state. See **njariin**.

midari-yuu, *n*. [midare + yo] Turbulent times; troubled times.

miduri, *n*. [midori] A sprout; a spear; a germ; a bud. Also **miruri**.

mi-fun, *n*. [mihon] A sample; a swatch; a specimen.

migachi, *n*. [meigaki] An inscription or signature on ritual objects such as a sword hilt, bell, or mortuary tablet.

miga·chun, *vt*. [migaku] To polish.

mi-gawa·i, *n*. [migawari] A substitute; a scapegoat; a vicarious victim; a sacrifice.

migu·i, *n*. [meguri] 1 Circumference; girth. 2 Revolution; circulation; flow. 3 Food digestion. 4 Management.

-migui, *suff*. Indicates a girth or a circle.

migui-duuru, *n*. A revolving lantern usually displayed on the night of the *Bon* festival. See also **tuuru**.

migui-mun, *n*. An activist; a hard worker.

migu·in, *vi*. 1 To go round; revolve; rotate; spin; gyrate. 2 To stop by; stop at; go around the corner.

migura·sun, *vt*. 1 To turn (a thing); revolve (a wheel); spin (a top). 2 To pass (a thing) around; send around; 3 To forward; transmit. 4 To lend one's money out at interest.

mi-gutu, *n*. [migoto] Splendid; fine; excellent.

mi-hau-tuu, *n*. A three-**goo** liquid measurement jar. See also **chuwakasaa**.

mii[1], *n*. [me] 1 An eye. 2 A hole. 3 A fault; a loss. 4 Graduation on a scale; scale notches; a cross on a chess board. 5 A standpoint; situation. 6 Infantile term for a scolding look.

mii[2], *n*. [mi] The Serpent, the sixth of the twelve calendrical animal signs.

mii[3], *n*. [mi] 1 A seed; a nutlet; a fruit. 2 Substance; contents. 3 Ingredients. See also **nai**[2].

mii[4], *n*. Being full.

mii[5], *n*. In; within; inside; within something that is dense.

mii[6], *n*. Fish meat.

mii-[1], *pref*. [me] Denotes female.

mii-[2], *pref*. [nii-] Denotes new.

-mii, *suff*. [-me] Ordinal suffix for numbers.

mii-ba, *n*. [miba] Appearance; show; look.

mii-ba·i, *n*. [mebaru] Generic term for fish belonging to the Epinephelidae family.

mii-bana, *n*. [mebana] Female flower.

mii-buu, *n*. [mebo*]A sty (in the eye). Also **miindai**[2].

mii-chi, *n*. [mittsu] Three. Also **san**[1].

miichi-bushi, *n.* [mitsuboshi] Three stars; Orion's belt.
miichi·in, *vt.* [·ran, ·tchi; mikiru] To abandon; forsake; give up.
miichiki·in[1], *vt.* To stare at; gaze at.
miichiki·in[2], *vt.* [mitsukeru] To find; discover; spot; detect.
mii-chira·a, *n. pej.* One who has a scar near the eyes. See **chiin**[2].
mii-data·s(h)an, *adj.* Outstanding; conspicuous; notable; important.
mii-daya·a, *n.* A person with sluggish, sleepy eyes; Heavy eyelids. See **tain**.
mii-dui, *n.* [mendori] A hen.
mii-dushi, *n.* A new year; the New Year. Also **soogwachi**.
mii-duu·san, *adj.* Long time no see.
mii-faafaa, *n.* Being dazed because of disappointment, shyness. **-na·in**, *vi.* To become dazed because of bashfulness, shame, disappointment.
mii-ficha·in, *vi.* [me ga hikaru] To glare at; scowl at; stare fiercely at; look angrily at.
mii-fuga·a, *n.* Same as **miifugaajin**.
mii-fugaa-jin, *n.* A coin with a hole in the center. See **fugiin**.
mii-fukkwa·a, *n.* A sweet oleander [J todaigusa; *Euphorbia helioscopia* L.].
mii-gaa, *n.* An eyelid.
mii-gaara, *n.* A concave tile. See also **wuugaara**.
mii-ganchoo, *n.* Eyeglasses. Also **ganchoo**.
mii-guchi, *n.* The first customer (of the day); the first sale (of the day).
mii-gufa·i, *n.* Same as **miikufai**.
mii-guru-guru·u, *adv.* With goggle eyes. **-sun**, *v.* To stare; goggle; roll one's eyes.
mii-gusoo, *n.* **1** New Year rite for those who died during the past year, held on the sixteenth day of the first month of the lunar calendar. **2** The newly dead.
mii-gusui, *n.* [megusuri] Eye drops; eyewash; eye ointment.

mii-gwaa, *n.* Small eyes; a person with small eyes.
mii-haga·a, *n. pej.* A person with sore eyes.
mii-hagi, *n.* An eye inflammation; a person with such an inflammation.
mii-hichara·san, *adj.* Dazzling; flaring; blinding; radiant. See **hichain**.
mii·in[1], *vi.* [mieru] **1** To be able to see; be in sight. **2** To see; catch sight of; be seen; be visible; show; meet the eye. **3** To look (like); show. **4** To seem; appear.
mii·in[2], *vi.* [moeru] To come out; spring up; grow up.
mii-indee, *n.* A sty (in one's eye). Also **miindai**.
miijaa-koojaa, *adv.* Grumbling; complaining. **-sun**, *v. emph. colloq.* To complain incessantly; keep grumbling. [GSS]
mii-jin, *n.* New clothes. See **chin**[3].
mii-jiru, *n.* [mezuru] Lit., female string; the third string (the lowest one when held horizontally) of the **sanshin**, producing the highest note.
mii-jooki, *n.* A round, shallow winnow, made of bamboo. See also **baaki**.
mii-kagan, *n.* Diver's glasses.
mii-koogaa, *n.* Having hollows under one's eyes due to fatigue.
mii-kufa·i, *n.* Waking. Also **miigufai**.
mii-kufa·in, *vi.* To wake up; awake.
mii-kufaya·a, *n.* **1** Sweets given to a child when it wakes up in the morning. **2** A light sleeper. **3** An insomniac.
miiku·ni, *adv.* Newly; anew; afresh.
mii-kuragan, *n.* Fainting; dizziness; loss of consciousness.
mii-kusa·a, *n. pej.* One who constantly has an eye discharge.
mii-kusu, *n.* Eye secretions; eye discharge; mucus from the eyes.
miikusu·nu uppi, *phr.* Lit., as little as eye mucus; just a little. [GSS]
mii-kuu, *n.* A blind person. Also **mikkwaa**.

miikkwa, *n.* A niece. See also **wiikkwa**.
mii-maa·sun, *vi.* To become dizzy; lose consciousness; faint.
mii-man·jun, *vt.* [·**dan**, ·**ti**; mimamoru] To watch and protect; keep watch over. Also **manjun**.
mii-mayu, *n.* Lit., eye and eyebrows; looks; (personal) appearance. See **mayu**.
mii-me·e[1], *n.* [mimai] An inquiry after an illness or a disaster; expression of sympathy. Also **mimee**.
mii-mee[2], *n.* The first rice crop of the year.
mii-mii-kuji·i, *n. colloq.* Faultfinding; picking faults. -**sun**, *v. colloq.* To go into the minutest details; be excessively fastidious. See **kujiin**.
miimii-kumaguma·a, *n.* The minutest particulars.
mii-mii-mii, *n.* [me-me-me] Lit., eye-eye-eye; an instructive game for young children.
miimuku-juri, *n.* Same as **miimuuku-juri**. See **niibichi**.
mii-mun[1], *n.* A new thing; a new article.
mii-mun[2], *n.* The female (of animals). See also **wuumun**[2].
mii-muna·a, *n.* Same as **miimun**[2]. See also **wuumunaa**.
mii-muuku, *n.* A new bridegroom.
mii-muuku-juri, *n.* A courtesan for a bridegroom. [OBJ]
mii-nada, *n.* Tears. Also **nada**[1].
miinada-soosoo, *adv.* Sobbing; with tears running down in torrents.
mii-nara·in, *vt.* [·(r)an, ·ti; minarau] To learn by observation; follow another's example.
mii-nari·in, *vi.* [minareru] To get used to seeing; be familiar to.
mii·n-dai, *n.* Same as **mii'indee**.
mii-nichi, *n.* [meinichi] The anniversary of a death.
mii-nishi, *n.* The first northerly wind of the fall.

mii-'nji·in, *vi.* [moederu] To bud; sprout; to put forth buds.
mii-nna, *n.* The female portion of a tug-of-war rope set, opposite to the male portion of rope. See **chinahichi**.
mii·nu-chibi, *n.* The corner of the eye. See **miinukuchi**.
mii·nu-fuchi, *n.* The edge of the eyelid.
mii-nugara·sun, *vt.* [minogasu] To overlook; miss intentionally; pass over; let go unchallenged.
mii·nu-kuchi, *n.* The inner corner of the eye. See **miinuchibi**.
mii·nu-mee, *n.* [menomae] Before one's eyes; under one's very eyes; in full view of.
mii·nu-shin, *n.* The pupil (of the eye); one's eyes.
mii·nu-wuu, *n.* (For an image) to flicker and linger; flit; flitter; swim in one's head. See **wuu**[2].
mii-pachi-pachi·i, *adv.* Winking. -**sun**, *v. onom.* To wink one's eyes.
mi·i-sagi·in, *vt.* [misageru] To look down; hold in contempt; scorn; disdain; slight.
mii·san, *adj.* [nii-*] New; fresh.
mi·i-shi·in, *vt.* [·**ran**, ·**tchi**; mishiru] To recognize; know by sight; become acquainted (with).
mii-shiru, *n.* Eye discharge; non-teary secretion of the eye.
mi·i-shiti·in, *vt.* [misuteru] To abandon; forsake; discard; cast off; give away.
mii-shu, *n.* [meisho] A famous spot.
miitoo·n neen, *phr.* [mittomo nai] Unsightly; ungainly; unseemly; indecent.
mii-tu, *n.* [meoto] A couple; a husband and wife.
mi·i-tuduki·in, *vt.* [mitodokeru] To ascertain; verify; make sure (of); assure oneself (of); witness.
mii-tuji, *n.* A new wife; a bride; a newly married wife.
miitunda, *n.* Husband and wife; a (married) couple.

miitunda-munu-gata·i, *n.* Pillow talk; talk in bed between a husband and wife.

miitunda-nami, *n.* Two waves that come close together.

miitunda-ooye·e, *n.* A quarrel between husband and wife; a marital spat.

mii-u·chi, *n.* A wink; a blink.

mii-uti·i, *n.* Death; one's last moments. **-sun**, *vi.* To die.

mii-waki, *n.* Same as **miwaki**.

mii-waki·in, *vt.* Same as **miwakiin**.

mii-waku, *n.* [meiwaku] **1** Shame; dishonor; disgrace; discredit. **2** Trouble; inconvenience; annoyance.

mii-ware·e, *n.* [mewarai] A smile with the eyes. Also **miware**.

mii-yaa, *n.* **1** A new house; a new building. **2** A house that has newly established itself.

mii-ya·mi, *n.* An eye disease.

mi·i-yan·jun, *vt.* To mistake (fail to recognize); misjudge; fail to see.

mii-yas·san, *adj.* [...**shi·ku**] **1** Easy to see; obvious. **2** Presentable; good enough to be seen.

mii-yoo-sun, *vi.* To wink to signal.

mii-yumi, *n.* A new bride.

mii-zooroo, *n.* Eye measure; by rule of thumb; by guess. [GSS]

miji, *n.* [mizu] Water. See also **numimiji**, **buubuu**[2], **miji'amii**, **miji'aree**, **mijigaami**, **mijikumi**, **tinshii**, **amidaimiji**, **miji maayaa**, **miji maain**, **mijikaja**, **miji kajasun**, **ubii**, **ubiinadii**.

miji-ami, *n.* [mizuame] Starch syrup; glucose.

miji-ami·i, *n.* [mizuabi] Bathing in cold water.

miji-are·e, *n.* [mizuarai] Laundering in water only, without soap.

miji-bukuru·u, *n.* [mizubukuro] A blister; a vesicle; a bladder.

miji-daki, *n.* The depth of water; the volume of water.

miji-gaami, *n.* [mizugame] A water jug. See **kaami**.

miji-gami, *n.* [mizugami] Water god.

miji-gani, *n.* [mizugane*] Mercury.

miji-gasa, *n.* The chickenpox; varicella.

miji-gasa·a, *n.* Same as **mijigasa**.

miji-guchi, *n.* [mizuguchi*] A floodgate; a sluice; the gate of a lock.

miji-gukuchi, *n.* Same as **kukuchi**[2].

miji-gura, *n.* Water storage; water tank.

miji-guruma, *n.* [mizuguruma] A waterwheel.

miji-gusui, *n.* [mizugusuri] A liquid medicine.

miji-gwee, *n.* [mizugoe] Liquid manure.

miji-hani·in, *vt.* To splash water.

miji-haniye·e, *n.* Splashing water play.

miji-iru, *n.* [mizuiro] Blue; light indigo color.

miji-kaagaa, *n.* Water mirror; reflection in the water.

miji-kagin, *n.* [mizukagen] The proper temperature of water for a particular task.

miji-kaja, *n.* Smell of water in decaying food. **-sun**, *v.* To smell of water (of decaying food).

miji-kani, *n.* Lead.

miji-kubusa·a, *n.* [mizukoboshi] **1** A vessel, often of pottery, used to wash underwear. [UKH] **2** A chamber pot. [UKH] **3** *arch.* Traditionally, a vessel to hold water used by women to wash themselves after using the toilet. [OGJ]

miji-kumi, *n.* [mizu-kumi] Drawing water from a well and filling jugs for domestic use.

miji-maa·in, *vi.* (Of food) to rot and become watery.

mijimaaya·a, *n.* Food that has gone rotten and become watery.

miji-maki, *n.* [mizu + make] Being sensitive to a change of water, such as in another locality.

miji-mu·i, *n.* [mizumori] Rite of drinking water as a sign of consummation of marriage on the day of a wedding.

See also **ubiinadii**. [ODJ]
miji-mutaan, *n*. Playing in the water; dabbling in water. **-sun**, *v*. To play in the water.
miji-'nmu, *n*. [mizuimo] Village taro [*Colocasia esculenta* Schott var. *aquatilis* Kitamura]. [ODJ] See **taa'nmu**.
miji·nu-mii, *n*. Under water; in the water.
miji·nu shidigafuu, *phr*. Thanksgiving for water, a communal rite held in the tenth lunar month. Also **miji·nu shi-rigafuu**.
miji-shigutu, *n*. Scrubbing and washing; kitchen work.
miji-ushi, *n*. A water buffalo.
mijun, *n*. A sardine.
mika-jichi, *n*. [mikazuki] A new moon; a crescent moon; the sickle moon.
mi-kan, *n*. [mikan] A mandarin orange; a tangerine.
-mika·sun, *suff*. To make the sound of….
mi-kata, *n*. [mikata] A friend; an ally; a supporter.
miki, *n*. [miki] Ceremonial liquor; consecrated liquor. See also **yunooshi**, **uns(h)aku**. [ODJ]
mikii, *n*. Same as **mikiimayaa**.
mikii-maya·a, *n*. [mike] A tortoiseshell cat.
mikkwa·a, *n*. [mekura] Same as **miikuu**.
mikkwa·sa-mun, *n*. A hateful fellow; an abominable person.
mikkwa·san, *adj*. [nikurashii] Hateful; detestable; provocative.
mi-kuchi, *n*. A term of respect for another's mouth. See **kuchi**[2].
mi-ku·mi, *n*. [mikomi] Hope; promise; prospects.
miku·mun, *vt*. [mikomu] 1 To expect; anticipate; rely upon; figure on. 2 To estimate; allow (for loss); take (something) into account. 3 To put trust in; place confidence in.
mima·a, *n*. [< **mimi**] A person with hearing difficulty. See also **minkaa**, **minkujiraa**.
mimata-gwee, *n*. [mimata kuwa] A three-forked hoe.
mi-mee, *n*. [mimai] Same as **miimee**[1].
mimi, *n*. [mimi] 1 An ear. 2 An earlike handle.
mimi-chibu, *n*. [mimitsubo] A small jar with ears on three sides.
mimi-da·i, *n*. A person with large earlobes. See **tain**.
mimi-gaa, *n*. [mimigawa] An earlobe; an earlap.
mimigaa-sashimi, *n*. A traditional dish of pigs' ears and jaws in vinegar.
mimi-gani, *n*. Hearing ability.
mimi-gui, *n*. Judas' ear (mushroom) [J kikurage: *Auricularia auricula-judae* (Fr.) Quél]. [ODJ]
mimija·a, *n*. An earthworm.
mimiji, *n*. [mimizu] Same as **mimijaa**.
mimi·jun, *vt*. 1 To rub; crumple; massage. 2 To abuse; bully; torment; illtreat. See also **ijimiin**.
mimi-kujiri·in, *vi*. [… + kojireru] To lose the auditory function.
mimi-kusu, *n*. [mimikuso] Earwax.
mimi·nu-kkwa, *n*. The eardrum; the drum membrane.
mimi·nu-mii, *n*. An ear cavity.
mi-nanka, *n*. A Buddhist memorial service held on the twenty-first day after death. See **nanka**.
mi-nare·e, *n*. [minarai] An apprentice; a learner; a student (of a trade).
minbui, *n*. The satiated condition after one has eaten his fill of pork.
min-buku, *n*. [menboku] Face; countenance; honor; dignity.
min-chaabui, *n*. A crown of vines and grasses, worn by the **nuru** priestess at religious rites.
min-chanba, *n. pej*. Same as **mintanba**.
mincha·san, *adj*. Noisy; boisterous; uproarious.
min-daree, *n*. Same as **bindaree**.
min-dee, *n*. A sty (on the eyelid).

mindoo

min-doo, *n*. [mendoo] Trouble; difficulty.
mingwa·sun, *vt*. [nigorasu] To make (water) muddy and turbid; make cloudy; stir up.
mingwi, *n*. Muddiness; turbidity; impurity.
mingwi·in, *vi*. [nigoru] To become muddy and turbid.
min-jai, *n*. Ear discharge. See **tain**.
min-jichi, *n*. A title; an appellation; a name.
min-ka·a, *n*. Same as **minkujiraa**.
min-kujira·a, *n. pej*. A deaf person; a person hard of hearing. Also **minkaa**.
minna, *n*. Starwort [*Stellaria aquatica* (L.) Scopoli]. [FOSR]
min-na·i, *n*. [miminari] Ringing, buzzing in the ears; tinnitus. **-sun**, *v*. To have a ringing in one's ears.
min·nu-ku, *n*. [mizunoko] An inedible food offering used to lure malevolent spirits away from stealing edible food offered to ancestral spirits.
min-saa, *n*. [? < J mensaaji] A fabric with a thick woof used as material for sashes; a sash made of **minsaa** cloth.
minsaa-uubi, *n*. A sash of **minsaa** cloth worn by commoners in premodern Okinawa.
mi·n-tama, *n*. [medama] An eyeball.
min-tama·a, *n*. A person with big eyes.
mi·n-tami, *n*. [medama] An eyeball. Same as **mintama**.
min-tana, *n*. [mizutana*] A (kitchen) sink.
min-tanba, *n. pej*. [mimitabu] A derogatory term for ears. Also **minchanba**.
minta-uchi-gwee, *n*. A wooden hoe.
minu-gami, *n*. [< J minogami] Handmade paper made of paper mulberry bark. See also **kabi**.
mirikin-kuu, *n*. [< J merikenko] Same as **mujinakuu**.
miruku, *n*. [Miroku] The Maitreya bodhisattva, a Buddhist saint. See also

niraikanai, mirukuyuu. [OBJ]
miruku-yuu, *n*. A year or an age of abundance; a year of good harvest.
miruri, *n*. [midori] A sprout; a bud; a shoot. [UKH] Same as **miduri**.
misachi, *n*. [misaki] Same as **sachi**[2].
mishi-gee, *n*. A ladle for rice; a rice paddle. Also **iijee, ibiragwaa**. [GSS]
mishi·in, *vt*. [miseru] To show; let (a person) see; exhibit; display.
mi-shiji·ri, *n*. A divine oracle; divine message; a revelation (from a god).
mishi-kuuga, *n*. [mise- + …] 1 An egg placed in a hen's nest to induce the hen to lay eggs. 2 A child adopted temporarily in hope of inducing the adoptive mother to have her own natural child.
mishi-mun, *n*. [misemono] A show; an exhibition.
mishi-uki, *n*. Providing board; meals.
mi-tama, *n*. A large, comma-shaped, semi-precious jade stone jewel worn by the **kaminchu** priestess. See also **gaaradama**.
mita·sun, *vt*. [mitasu] To fill up; make full.
mit-chai, *n*. [mitari*] Three people.
mitchakaan, *n., adv*. Being full; being filled up; brimming.
mitchiri, *n*. [mikiri] A bargain; sacrifice goods; cut-rate goods.
mitumi·in, *vt*. [mitomeru] 1 To recognize; perceive; observe. 2 To appreciate. 3 To approve; admit.
mi-uku·i, *n*. [miokuri] Seeing (a person) off; a send-off.
mi-unchi, *n*. Term of respect for the face of a noble person such as a king.
mi-waki, *n*. [miwake] 1 Distinction; discrimination. 2 Judgment; identification. Also **miiwaki**.
mi-waki·in, *vt*. [miwakeru] 1 To distinguish (from, between); be able to tell (one from another); discriminate (between). 2 To judge (of a person);

identify (things); recognize. Also **mii-wakiin**.
mi-ware, *n. poet.* Same as **miiwaree**.
miya, *n.* [miya] A shrine. Often **umiya**.
miyaku, *n.* [miyako] A capital; a city; a town.
mi-yarabi, *n.* [me + warabe] A maiden; an unmarried country girl.
mi-yati, *n.* [meate] A guide; an aim. Also **mi'ati**.
moo, *n.* [no] A field (not under cultivation or planted in trees); the wilds; wilderness.
-moo, *suff.* Denotes lack of a (particular) body part.
moo-aasa, *n.* A type of terrestrial alga [*Nostoc commune* Vaucher]. [ODJ]
moo-ashibi, *n.* Outdoor get-together with music and dancing traditionally held at night after work in rural areas.
moo·i[1], *n.* [mai] Dance. See also **wudui**.
mooi[2], *n.* An unkempt head of hair; disheveled hair.
mooi·i, *n.* A person with unkempt hair such as a child.
moo·in, *vi.* [mau] **1** To dance (on the spur of the moment). **2** To come to one's feet in glee.
mooki, *n.* [mooke] Profits; gains; earnings.
mooki·in, *vt.* [mookeru] To make a profit; earn; cash in.
mooki-juku, *n.* Pursuing profit only.
moo-moo[1], *n. onom, inf.* Cattle; a cow; an ox.
moo-moo[2], *n.* A cowrie shell [*Cypraea moneta*]. [MO] Also **moomoogwaa**, **subi**[2], **shibi**.
moomoo-gwaa, *n.* Same as **moomoo**[2].
moo-nayaa, *n.* A field where nothing is planted; a wasted field. [GSS]
moosagi, *n.* Tale-telling; backbiting; informing on a person. **-sun**, *v.* To tell on; squeal; inform.
mooya·a, *n.* A dancer.
muchaga·in, *vi.* [mochiagaru] To be lifted; be raised; be heightened.
muchagi·in, *vt.* [mochiageru] To raise; lift; heave; hold up.
mucha-mucha-sun, *v. onom. colloq.* To be sticky; be adhesive.
muchi[1], *n.* [mochi] Same as **muuchii**.
muchi[2], *n.* [mochi] Plaster; mortar; stucco.
muchi[3], *n.* [mochi] Bird-lime; a sticky substance spread on twigs to catch birds. Also **yanmuchi**.
mu·chi-banmee, *n.* Bringing one's own lunch (or paying for lunch out of one's pocket) as a laborer. See **hanmee**.
mu·chi-chi·ri, *n.* [mochikiri] Monopoly; sole ownership.
muchichiri-shigutu, *n.* Work that one does all by oneself; monopoly.
muchichiri-yaa, *n.* A detached dwelling (not a unit in multiple housing).
mu·chi-dee, *n.* Endurance; stamina; tenacity. See **tee**[1].
muchi-gumi, *n.* Glutinous rice [*Oryza sativa* L. var. *glutinosa* Blanco]. [FOSR]
mu-chii, *n.* [mukei] One who has no genealogy; a commoner.
muchi-jeeku, *n.* A plasterer. See **seeku**.
muchika·s(h)an, *adj.* [mutsukashii] **1** Hard; difficult. **2** Hard to understand. **3** Troublesome; delicate. **4** Doubtful; hopeless. **5** Glum; sullen.
mu·chi-ku·mun, *vt.* [mochikomu] **1** To carry [bring, turn] in. **2** To propose; approach (a person) with.
mu·chi-mee, *n.* [mochimae] **1** One's share; one's duty. **2** Ancestors who are one's duty to look after.
mu·chi-na·shi, *n.* [motenashi] **1** Care; repair; mending. **2** Help; aid; assistance.
mu·chi-nii, *n.* Carry-on baggage.
mu·chi-noo·sun, *vt.* [mochinaosu] **1** To improve; rally; pick up; recover; revive. **2** To change the method of carrying (something).
muchi·san, *adj.* Sticky, tacky, adhesive.
mu·chiye·e, *n.* An old disease; a chronic

complaint or affliction. [UKH]

mu·chun[1], *vt.* [·**tan**, ·**tchi**; motsu] **1** To have; take; hold. **2** To carry; have (on one's person) **3** To own; possess, keep; be endowed with. **4** To have; hold (an opinion); cherish. **5** To be in charge of. **6** To hold out; keep; maintain. **7** To wear; last long; hold. **8** (for women) To marry; (for women) to have a child.

mu·chun[2], *vi.* To swell; become swollen; bloat. See also **mukumun**.

mudi, *n.* [moji*] A peg to tighten or loosen the string of a **sanshin**. Also **jiifaa, karakui, mudi**. See also **sanshin**.

mudi·in, *vt., vi.* [mojiru] To bend; twist; wring.

mudu·i, *n.* [modori] Return; coming (going) back; a return trip.

mudu·in, *vi.* [modoru] To return; go back; (of women) divorce and return to one's parental home.

mudu·sun, *vt.* [modoru] To return (something); make (one) return.

mu-fun, *n.* [muhon] **1** Rebellion; revolt; treason. **2** Resistance; defiance; insubordination.

mu-gaku, *n.* [mugaku] Illiteracy; ignorance. ·**na**, *adj.* Illiterate; ignorant.

mugee, *n.* [omogai] (Of horse) a headstall; headgear; the part of the bridle that goes around the head. Also **muugee**.

mugee·in, *vi.* To boil; bubble; seethe.

mu-gun, *n.* [mugon] Silence; muteness.

mu-hoo, *n.* [muhoo] Injustice; unlawfulness; outlaw.

mui, *n.* [mori] A hill; a mountain. See **yama**.

mu·i-aga·in, *vi.* [moriagaru] To swell; rise.

mu·i-agi·in, *vt.* [moriageru] To heap up; pile up.

mui-gwaa, *n.* A little hill.

mu·i-mee[1], *n.* A person in charge of an event or festival. See **juri'nma**. Also **futchaamui**.

mu·i-mee[2], *n.* A heaped rice offering to the dead. [OBJ] Also **katachinumee, futchaamui, nuchaashi'ubun**.

mu·in[1], *vi.* [moru] To leak; be leaky; escape. Also **muriin**.

mu·in[2], *vt.* [moru] To pile (heap) up.

mu·in[3], *vt.* [mogu] To pick (fruit) off a tree; pluck off; wrest (from).

mu·i-ubai, *n.* Same as **muimee**[2].

mu-ji[1], *n.* [moji] A letter; a character.

muji[2], *n.* [mugi] A generic term that covers **ufumuji, 'nnamuji, hadakamuji, ufumujaa**.

muji[3], *n.* A **taa'nmu** stalk.

muji·na-kuu, *n.* [muginoko] Flour. Also **mirikinkuu**.

mu-joo, *n.* [mujoo] Being cruel; being coldhearted.

mu-juku·i, *n.* Agriculture; engaging in agriculture.

muju-muju-sun, *vi. onom.* To feel itchy; be impatient; be anxious; be irritable.

mukaja·a, *n.* A centipede. Same as **nkaji**.

mu-kiji, *n.* [mukizu] Uninjured; unwounded; flawless; perfect.

-mukkoo, *suff.* Denotes a person who has a part of his body missing. Same as **-moo**.

mukkuu[1], *n.* **1** A bud. **2** A small fruit. See also **nai**[2].

mukkuu[2], *n.* Same as **kooruu**.

mukoo, *n.* The forehead. Also **fichee**.

mukoo-bare·e, *n.* A shipping (transmission) service in which the receiver pays the charges.

mukui, *n.* [mukui] Retribution; punishment.

mukuirari·in, *vi.* [mukuirareru] To be rewarded; be compensated.

muku·mun, *vi.* [mukumu] To become swollen in a limited area; bloat in a localized area. See also **muchun**[2].

muku-ruku, *n.* [mokuroku] A catalogue; a list of articles; an inventory.

muku-ru·mi, *n.* [mokuromi] A plan; a

mumi, *n*. [momi] Unhulled rice; rice in the husk.
mumi-gara, *n*. [momigara] Rice chaff.
mu-min, *n*. [momen] Cotton; cotton cloth.
mumu[1], *n*. [momo] African rubra; bayberry [*Myrica rubra* Sieb. et Zucc.].
mumu[2], *n*. [momo] A thigh; a ham; the femur.
mumuda-kabi, *n*. Paper made of paper mulberry bark. See also **kabi**.
mumu-iru, *n*. [momoiro] Rose; pink.
mu·mun, *vt*. [momu] 1 To rub; crumple; massage. 2 To dispute hotly.
mun[1], *n*. [mon] A gate. See also **joo**[3].
mun[2], *n*. [mono] Food; a meal. See **munu**.
-mun, *suff*. Food; person; thing(s).
mu-nanka, *n*. A Buddhist memorial service held on the forty-second day after death. See also **nanka**.
mun-ban, *n*. [monban] A gatekeeper; a doorkeeper.
mun-chuu, *n*. [monchuu] A clan; patrilineal consanguineous group descended from a common ancestor. [ODJ] See also **fichi**[1].
munchuu-baka, *n*. A common tomb for the members of a clan. See also **haka**.
munchuu-gashira, *n*. A clan chief; hereditary leader of a clan; the eldest male in the founding house.
munchuu-jurii, *n*. [monchuu + soroi] A clan meeting.
mun-dani, *n*. Bait; feed.
mun-doo, *n*. [mondoo] A dispute; a quarrel.
mun-gun, *n*. [mongon] A composition; a writing; an article; an essay.
muni-agi, *n*. [muneage] Ridgepole raising, a house construction rite.
mun-jire·e, *n*. [... + kirai] Food to be avoided when sick; taboo food.
mun-juru, *n*. Barley straw.
munjuru-ichubi, *n*. A barley berry [*Rubus parvifolius* L. var. *parvifolius*]. [FOSR] See **ichubi**.
munjuru·u, *n*. A conical hat made of barley straw.
mun-mi, *n*. [monme] A unit of weight equivalent to 1/1000 of a **kan**[4] (approximately 3.8 g). [NJED] See **chin**[4], **kan**[4].
mun-nan, *n*. A four-*go* grain measurement box. See **chiiga**.
mun-naraa·shi, *n*. [mononarawashi*] Home training; home education; discipline.
mun·nu-ati, *n*. Prudence; consideration; discretion; judiciousness.
mun-tacha·a, *n*. A cook; a kitchen maid.
munu, *n*. 1 Food; meal. See also **mun**[2]. 2 A person. 3 A matter; substance; affairs. See also **kweemun**, **hanmee**, **shitimitimun**, **asaban**[1], **yuuban**, **ashii**, **miikufayaa**. [ZRJ]
munu-akase·e, *n*. A riddle; a puzzle.
munu-gata·i, *n*. [monogatari] A story; tale; talk; a narrative; an account; a legend. **-sun**, *vt*. To recite; narrate; recount; give an account of.
munu-gushi[1], *n*. Being hard to please with respect to food; fussy eater. See **kushi**[4].
munu-gushi[2], *n*. Demeanor; (a person's) movements; a manner.
munu-ii-jooji, *n*. Good at greeting and handling people; a good speaker.
munu-i·i-kata, *n*. How to speak; how to use words; the art of conversation.
munu-jibun, *n*. Mealtime.
munu-ji·chi, *n*. [monozuki] Idle curiosity; fancifulness; a whim; eccentricity.
munu-kangee, *n*. Thought; consideration; meditation. **-sun**, *vt*. To consider; think; meditate.
munu-kuuya·a, *n*. A beggar; a mendicant.
munu·nu-yuku, *n*. Appetite.
munu-shi·chi, *n*. [monozuki] Same as **munujichi**.

munushiri

munu-shi·ri, *n.* A knowledgeable person; a fortune-teller; a diviner.
munu-soodan, *n.* Consultation.
munu-ubi·i, *n.* Memory; remembrance. Also **ubi**[1].
munu-uji, *n.* [monooji] Timidity. **-sun**, *v.* To feel timid.
munu-umi·i, *n.* [monoomoi] Pensiveness; anxiety.
munu-uu·i, *n.* Chasing away the devil. See **mabui'uui**.
munu-ware·e, *n.* [monowarai] A laughingstock; standing joke.
munu-washiri, *n.* [monowasure] Forgetfulness; failure of memory.
munu-yuma·a, *n.* A prattler; a person who talks about others excessively.
munu-yu·mun, *vi.* To prattle; chatter; talk.
muppara, *adv.* [moppara] Entirely; solely; exclusively.
mura, *n.* [mura] A village; a hamlet; a rural community. Also **shima**[1].
mura-ashi·bi, *n.* A village drama, usually held on the night of the fifteenth day of the eighth lunar month. [OGJ]
mura-bare·e, *n.* [mura + harai] Banishment; expulsion from the village as punishment for a crime.
mura-gaa, *n.* A village's common well.
mura-gani, *n.* A village gong.
mura-gashira, *n.* A village headman.
mura-hajishi, *n.* Outskirts of a village.
mura-jakee, *n.* A village boundary. Also **sakee**.
mura·nu-kee·shi, *n.* A magical formula or a structure to bar evil or calamity from entering a village. See **shimakusarashi**. [ODJ]
murasachi, *n.* [murasaki] Purple; amethyst; violet.
mura-wugan-ju, *n.* A sacred site of the village; the ritual site of a community.
mura-yaa, *n.* A village office.
muri, *n.* [< J muri] Unreasonableness; unnaturalness.

muri·in, *vi.* [moreru] Same as **muin**[1].
muru, *adv.* All; every one; completely; wholly; in all.
muru-haku, *n.* [morohaku*] The best grade of **aamui** Okinawan liquor.
murun, *n.* [moromi] Unrefined sake; sake that has been brewed but not refined.
muru-noo·i, *n.* Complete recovery.
murushi, *n.* A lump; a mass; a clod (of soil).
musat·tu, *adv.* Not in the least; not at all.
mushi[1], *n.* [mushi] An insect; a bug; a worm; vermin.
mushi[2], *adv.* [moshi] If; in case of; provided that. Same as **mushika**.
mushi-ba, *n.* [mushiba] Same as **mushikweebaa**.
mushi-bare·e, *n.* [mushibarai] Insect eradication, a communal rite held during the fourth lunar month. Also **abushibaree**.
mushi·in, *vt.* [mushiru] To pluck off; pull off, tear off; pick off.
mushika, *adv.* [< J moshika] If. Same as **mushi**[2].
mushi-kwe·e-baa, *n.* [mushi(kui)ba*] A decayed tooth.
mushiru, *n.* [mushiro] A straw mat; straw matting. See also **kufamushiru, hiramushiru, shichimushiru, Biigumushiru, sachiyii, shichitoo, yiimushiru, adanbaamushiru**.
mushiru-yaama, *n.* A mat loom.
mushi-uturu·u, *n.* Dislike of insects.
mu-shoo, *adv.* [mushoo] Same as **mushooni**.
mushoo·ni, *adv.* [mushooni] Very much; to excess; excessively.
musubi·i, *n.* [musubi] A contract; an agreement.
musu·bun, *vt.* [musubu] To tie, knot; fasten (together); bind; conclude; contract; join in marriage.
-mutaan, *suff.* [< **mutabun**] Denotes playing, tampering, trifling with.

muta·bun, *vt.* To play with; tamper with; trifle with.

mutari·in, *vt.* To possess; hold; carry.

mutchaka·in, *vi.* To stick to; adhere to. See also **takkwain**.

mu·tchi chuun, *vt.* [motte-kuru] To bring over; fetch; get.

mu·tchi-i·chun, *vt.* [motte-iku] To take (something) along.

mutchoo-hitchoo, *adv.* Wavering. **-sun,** *v. emph. colloq.* To be indecisive and tardy; hesitate and hold off; waver. [GSS]

mutee·in, *vi.* To grow big; fatten; prosper; grow thick and wild; luxuriate; flourish. Also **buteein**.

mutee·i-sakee·i, *adv.* Prosperous; flourishing; opulent; affluent; thriving.

muti[1], *n.* Direction; side.

-muti[2], *suff.* Denotes a group of; a clan of.

muti·in, *vi.* [moteru] To be made much of; be welcomed; be popular with; be a favorite (with).

muttumu, *n.* [mottomo] Of course. **·na,** *adj.* Reasonable; logical; sensible.

mutu, *n.* [moto] **1** The beginning; the genesis; the origin. **2** One's origin; one's ancestors. **3** The foundation; the basis; the source. **4** The cause; the origin. **5** A base; raw materials. **6** Capital; the principal; the cost. **7** Once; before; formerly. Also **muutu**.

mutu-biree, *n.* An old friend; an old sweetheart; an old flame. See **hiree**.

mutu-michi, *n.* The main road.

mutu-shin, *n.* Capital. Same as **muutu**.

muu, *n.* [mo] An alga; seaweed; duckweed.

muuchi, *n.* [muttsu] Six; six years old.

muuchii, *n.* [mochii*] **1** A rice cake. **2** Abbreviation for the **hoohai-muuchii** rite. Also **muchi**[1]. See also **hoohaimuuchii, muuchiiwuimi, hoohai'utaki**.

muuchii-wuimi, *n.* [... + orime] Rite of Rice Cakes, observed on the eighth day of the twelfth month of the lunar calendar. See also **hoohai'utaki**. [ODJ]

muugee, *n.* Same as **mugee**.

muuku, *n.* [muko] A son-in-law; husband of one's daughter; bridegroom.

muuku-choodee, *n.* [muko-kyoodai] Brothers-in-law whose wives are sisters.

muutu, *n.* Same as **mutu**.

muutu-dukuru, *n.* Same as **muutuyaa**.

muutu-yaa, *n.* The main household within a clan; any parent house within the patrilineal consanguineous group. Also **muutu, muutudukuru, ufuyaa**.

muuya-baaya, *n.* [moya* + hashira] A pillar located inside a house.

mu-yee, *n.* [moai] A mutual finance system. Also **yuuree**.

muyee-baka, *n.* A tomb built with funds made by means of **muyee**. Also **yuureebaka**. [ODJ]

mu-yoo, *n.* [moyoo] **1** Appearance. **2** The state of affairs. **3** Design or pattern of textiles.

mu-yuku, *n.* [muyoku] Unselfishness; freedom from avarice.

mu-yuu, *n.* [muyoo] **1** Uselessness. **2** Without business. **3** Being forbidden. **4** *adj.* **·na** Needless; unnecessary.

muyuu·shi, *n.* [moyooshi] **1** A gathering; a meeting; an entertainment; a sideshow. **2** An urge; a sign.

muyuu·sun, *n.* [moyoosu] **1** *vt.* To hold (a meeting). **2** *vi.* (For an urge) to come upon one. **3** *vi.* To show signs of.

Myaaku, *n.* The Miyako Islands; Miyako Island, the largest island of the Miyako Islands in the Ryukyus. Also **Naaku**[1].

Myaaku-nchu, *n.* A person from Miyako Island. Also **Naakunchu**.

Myaaku·u, *n. pej.* A person from Miyako Island. Also **Naakuu**[1].

myaku, *n.* [myaku] Pulse; pulsation. Also **naaku**[2].

myoo-ga, *n.* [myooga] Honor; glory;

myooji

pride. Also **nooga**.
myoo-ji, *n*. [myooji] A family name; a surname. Also **nooji**. See also **yaannaa**.

N———

·**n**, *part*. And; as well as; both… and; too; also; even; not… either; as many as; even if; either… or.
·**na**[1], *suff*. Verb ending expressing a hope or wish.
·**na**[2], *suff*. *lit*. Verb ending expressing prohibition.
·**na**[3], *suff*. Denotes attributive form of adjectives and certain nouns. See also ·**nu**.
naa[1], *n*. **nat·taa**, *n. pl. formal* You. See also **'yaa**, **unju**.
naa[2], *interj*. Expresses hesitation, vacillation; seeking understanding.
naa[3], *n*. [na] A name (of a person or a thing); an appellation. See also **yaannaa**, **yagoo**, **myooji**, **nooji**, **karanaa**, **warabinaa**, **Yamatunaa**, **gakkoonaa**. [OBJ, RJK]
naa[4], *n*. [nawa] **1** A rope; a cord. **2** A fishing line.
naa[5], *n*. The front yard of a rural household compound, often used as a work area.
naa[6], *adv*. Ending or being completed.
naa[7], *adv*. Too; also; already.
naa[8], *part*. A mild interrogative.
naa[9], **1** A mustard plant. **2** Leafy vegetable. See also **oofa**, **shimanaa**[2].
naa-, *pref*. Followed by a reduplicated noun, denotes the concept of each, individual, or respective.
-naa[1], *suff*. Denotes an open space or ground. See **naa**[5].
-naa[2], *suff*. Denotes a fixed number of portions or a fixed degree of action for each.
naa-asatti, *n*. The day after tomorrow.
naa-baru, *n*. Syphilis. Also **nanbangasa**.

naabeeraa, *n*. A sponge gourd; vegetable sponge [J hechima; *Luffa cylindrica* (L.) M. Roem]. Also **nanbeeraa**.
naabi, *n*. [nabe] A pan; a saucepan; a pot.
naabi-doogu, *n*. Pots and pans and ladles. See also **shimudoogu**.
naabi-kacha·a, *n*. A kind of cicada [J Ryukyu aburazemi; *Graptopsaltria bimaculata* Kato]. Also **jiijaa**, **asasaa**, **sansanaa**.
naabi-kachi-kachi·i, *n*. Same as **naabi-kachaa**.
naabi·na-ku·u, *n*. A tinner; a person who repairs tinware.
naabi·nu-futa, *n*. A pot lid made of wood. See also **kamanta**.
naacha, *n*. The next day; the following day.
naacha-asa, *n*. The next morning; the following morning.
naacha-mii, *n*. Tomb visitation by the bereaved the day after a funeral. See also **hachinanka**, **mabuiwakashi**. [OBJ]
naachamii-jira, *n. slang*. A very sad face like that of a bereaved person. [GSS]
naa-chiri-jiri, *adv*. Scatteringly; broken up; severally.
naada, *adv*. Same as **maada**.
Naafa, *n*. Naha; important port and urban center in premodern Okinawa; prefectural capital in the modern period.
Naafa·a, *n. pej*. A Naha person.
Naafa-guchi, *n*. Naha dialect.
Naafa-nchu, *n*. A Naha person.
naagi, *n*. [miyage] A gift; a souvenir. Also **naagimun**, **chitu**.
naagi-mun, *n*. [miyagemono] A gift; a souvenir. Same as **naagi**.
naagu, *n*. [nago] A lifelong servant; a tenant peasant.
naa-ha·iba·i, *n*. Scattering. **-sun**, *v. emph. colloq*. To scatter; break up.
naa-hi·n, *adv*. More, further; even more.

naa-iru·u, *n.* An infamous fellow; a lecher; a lewd man.

naa-jiki·i, *n.* [nazuke] Naming of a newborn infant, usually held on the seventh day after birth. See also **kaa'urii, mansan, soojibari, jiirushinchi, jiirushijichi, hyaakuugwaa, futukigwaa, warabinaa, naajiki'uya.** [ODJ, OBJ]

naajiki-ubagii, *n.* Naming of a newborn baby; the food to celebrate the birth of the baby. See also **ubagii.**

naajiki-uya, *n.* Lit., a naming parent; a godparent. See **naajikii.**

naaka[1]**,** *n.* [naka] The interior; the inside; the center; the middle.

naaka[2]**,** *n.* Relationship. See **naka**[2].

naaka·a-fuuka·a, *n.* A thing that is hollow and empty.

Naaku[1]**,** *n.* Same as **Myaaku.**

naaku[2]**,** *n.* [myaku] Pulse; pulsation. See **myaku.**

Naaku-nchu, *n.* Same as **Myaakunchu.**

Naaku·u, *n. pej.* Same as **Myaakuu.**

naa-mee-mee, *n.* Each one; individually.

naa-nchu, *n.* [naa[7] + nchu < mitu] The year after next. Also **naayaan.**

naasati, *n.* The day after tomorrow.

naashibi, *n.* [nasubi] A garden eggplant [*Solanum melongena* L.].

naa-shiru, *n.* [nawashiro] A rice nursery; a bed for rice plants.

naashiru-mabu·i, *n.* A rice nursery protector; a scarecrow.

naa-waka·i-waka·i, *n.* Each one departing on his/her own way.

naa-yaan, *n.* The year after next. Also **naanchu.**

naa-yuru, *adj.* Famous; renowned; well-known.

naba, *n.* A mushroom; a fungus. See also **maachinaba.** [MAK]

nabaku·in, *vt.* To tease; make fun of; ridicule. [GSS]

naban-gasa, *n.* [nanbangasa] Syphilis. Also **nabaru.**

nabara·a, *n.* A syphilis patient; a patient with venereal disease. [GSS]

nabaru, *n.* Same as **nabangasa.**

nabi·chun, *vi.* [nabiku] **1** To flutter; wave; stream. **2** To bend to; bow to; obey; be swayed by.

nabi-gee, *n.* A soup ladle. Also **saragee, haragee.**

nabigee-jira, *phr. colloq.* Lit., A face as flat as a rice paddle. [GSS]

nabika·sun, *vt.* [nabikasu] **1** To conquer; subdue; win (a person) over (to one's side). **2** To flutter; wave.

nacha·i-warata·i, *n.* Crying and laughing. **-sun,** *v. emph. colloq.* Now crying, now laughing; to change attitude suddenly.

nachi, *n.* [natsu] Summer; summertime; the summer season.

na·chi-aka·sun, *vt.* To cry all night; weep the night away.

na·chi-busa·a, *n.* A crybaby; a weakling.

na·chi-gee-gee, *adv.* With violent crying; with convulsive sobbing.

nachi-guchi, *n.* Early summer. Also **wakanachi.**

na·chi-gutu, *n.* [nakigoto] A complaint; a grievance; a whimper.

na·chi-gwii[1]**,** *n.* [nakigoe] A tearful voice; a cry; a scream; a whine.

na·chi-gwii[2]**,** *n.* [nakigoe] (Of birds and animals) a cry; a song; a call; a note; chirping; cawing; clucking; crackling; quacking; neighing; mooing; bleating; barking; mewing; etc.

na·chi-jira, *n.* [nakizura] A tearful face.

nachika·s(h)an, *adj.* [natsukashii] Sad; sorrowful.

nachi-maki, *n.* [natsumake] Susceptibility to summer heat. **-sun,** *v.* To suffer from the summer heat. Also **fumichimaki.**

nachi-mun, *n.* [natsumono] Summer clothes.

na·chi-neebi, *n.* [naki + manebu] False tears; crocodile tears. **-sun,** *v.* To cry

false tears; feign weeping; shed crocodile tears.
na·chi-ware·e, *n.* [nakiwarai] A tearful smile.
nachoora, *n.* Corsican weed [*Digenea simplex* (Wulfen) Agardh]. [ODJ]
nachoora-shinji, *n.* Corsican weed infusion, used as a vermifuge. See **shinjimun**.
na·chun[1], *vi. lit.* [naku] To cry; call; howl; roar; bay; growl; bark; whine; yelp; meow; moo; neigh; whinny; bray; trumpet; chatter; grunt; bleat; crow; cluck; cackle; peep; gobble; coo; quack; caw; croak; sing; chirp; twitter; warble; chirrup. See also **utain** (3), **abiin, fukiin**[1]. (OGJ)
na·chun[2], *vi.* [naku] To cry; weep; shed tears; sob; whimper; wail; lament; bewail; moan; bemoan.
nada[1], *n.* [namida] Tears. Also **miinada**.
nada[2], *n.* [nada] The open sea.
nada-guru-guru·u-sun, *v.* To be moved to tears; to have one's eyes glisten with tears.
nadami·in, *vt.* [nadameru] To soothe; calm (down); pacify; mollify; appease; placate; humor.
nada-yashiku, *adv.* Calmly; moderately; conciliatorily.
nada-yas·san, *adj.* Calm; quiet; mild; gentle.
nada-yoo·san, *adj.* Easily moved to tears; maudlin; given to weeping; sentimental.
na-fuda, *n.* [nafuda] A nameplate; a doorplate; an identification tag.
naga·a, *n.* [< **naga-**] That which is long. See also **inchaa**.
naga-ami, *n.* [naga-ame] A long rain. Also **nagabui**.
naga-at·chi, *n.* [naga-aruki] A long walk; a long trip.
naga-bi·chun, *vi.* [nagabiku] To be prolonged; be delayed.
naga-boo·i, *n.* Posture of lying sprawled; sprawl.
naga-bu·i, *n.* [nagaburi] A long rain; a long spell of rainy weather. Also **naga'ami**.
naga-chiba·a, *n.* One who overstays one's welcome. See also **nagachibi**.
naga-chibi, *n.* [nagashiri] Same as **nagachibaa**.
naga-chiji·chi, *n.* [nagatsuzuki] Permanency; perpetuity; continuance.
naga-dee, *adv.* A long time.
naga-ichi, *n.* [nagaiki] Longevity; long life.
naga-jaa, *n.* [nagaza] A long stay; a long visit. See **nagachibi**.
nagami, *n.* [nagame] A view; a sight.
nagami·in, *vt.* To view; see; look at; watch; gaze at; stare at.
naga-muchi, *n.* [nagamochi] Durability; endurance.
naga-mun, *n.* Lit., long thing; taboo substitution for **habu** snake.
nagani, *n.* The back (of human and animals).
naga-nin, *n.* [naganen] A long time; many years.
nagari, *n.* [nagare] 1 A flow; a stream; a current. 2 A forfeiture; foreclosure.
nagari·in, *vi.* [nagareru] 1 To flow; stream; run; course; trickle; ooze; drain. 2 To be forfeited; be foreclosed.
nagari-kaa, *n.* [nagaregawa] A river; a running river. Also **haikaa**. See also **kaa**[2], **kaara**[2].
naga·san, *adj.* [nagai] Long.
naga·shi, *n.* [nagashi] Same as **nagashi'ami**.
nagashi-ami, *n.* [nagashiame] A sudden rain or shower; a squall. Also **nagashi**. See also **ami**[1].
naga·sun, *vt.* [nagasu] 1 To pour; dash; drain; flush; let (water) flow; spill (blood). 2 To float; set adrift; let (a ship) drift. 3 To wash away; scrub. 4 To forfeit (a pawn); foreclose (a pawn). 5 To exile; banish; deport; maroon. 6 (Of

a taxi) to cruise for fares; (of a performer) to sing from door to door.
naga-uui, *n.* [nagaoi] A long pursuit; a losing chase.
naga-yami, *n.* [nagayami] Same as **nagayanmee**.
naga-yanmee, *n.* [nagayamai] A chronic illness.
naga-yii, *n.* Same as **nagachibi**.
nagee, *n.* [nagai] A long time; a long while.
nagee·san, *adj.* Long (in time); (for) a long time to have elapsed.
nagi, *n.* Length.
nagi-duushi, *n.* All the way; all the time; without break; continuously.
nagi-hoori, *n.* [nage + hoori] Leaving things scattered about; being untidy; disarrangement. **-sun**, *v.* To leave things scattered about.
-nagii, *suff.* (In regard to time) about; ...or thereabouts.
nagi·in, *vt.* [nageru] To throw; cast; hurl; fling; pitch.
-nagiina, *suff.* In spite of; although.
nagu·ri, *n.* [nagori] Parting; leave-taking; farewell; a memory; keepsake; remains; traces.
naguri-naguri·i-tu, *adv.* Wistful; reluctant of parting.
nagusami, *n.* [nagusame] Comfort; consolation; solace; balm; diversion.
nagusami·in, *vt.* [nagusameru] To comfort; console; (give) solace; soothe; alleviate; divert.
nagusami-mun, *n.* Object of pleasure; a plaything; a toy.
nai[1], *n.* [nari] Personal appearance; dress; costume.
na·i[2], *n.* [nari] A fruit; a berry; a seed; a nutlet.
nai-cha·a, *n.* [< naichi] A person from the main islands of Japan; a Japanese.
naichaa-wutu, *n.* The Japanese husband of an Okinawan woman.
naichaa-yumi, *n.* [naichi + yome]

A Japanese woman married to an Okinawan; an Okinawan woman married to a Japanese.
nai-chi, *n.* [naichi] The main islands of Japan (as opposed to the Ryukyus); Honshu, Kyushu, Shikoku, and Hokkaido; Japan proper; Japan. See also **Yamatu**.
na·i-chi·in, *vi.* [narikiru] To become (something) completely.
-nai-gaataa, *suff.* Denotes the condition of becoming or being on the verge of (something).
na·i-han·chi, *n.* [nari + haijiki] One of the traditional forms of karate.
na·i-han·sun, *vi.* To fail to become; end in failure.
na·i-mun[1], *n.* [narimono] That which makes sound; musical instruments. See **nain**[3].
na·i-mun[2], *n.* [narimono] Fruit; crops; farm products.
naimun-gii, *n.* A fruit tree.
na·in[1], *vi.* **1** To become; turn into. **2** To be able to. **3** To go; stop by.
na·in[2], *vi.* [naru] To bear (fruit); be in fruit.
na·in[3], *vi.* [naru] To sound; ring; peal; jangle.
na·i-wuu, *n.* A banana (fruit) tree.
najiki, *n.* [nazuke] Pretense; make believe; affectation; simulation.
-najiki·i, *suff.* Denotes pretending, feigning, faking.
najiki·in, *vi.* [nazukeru] To pretend; affect; feign; fake; make as if.
naka[1], *n.* [naka] The midsection of a boat. See **sabani**, **naaka**[1].
naka[2], *n.* [naka] Relations; relationship; terms. See **naaka**[2].
nakaba, *n.* [nakaba] **1** Half; semi-. **2** The middle; the center; halfway point. **3** Partly; in part; partially.
naka-baaya, *n.* The principal pillar of a house.
naka-bashiru, *n.* [naka + hashiru]

Partition doors between rooms in a house.
naka·da·chi, *n.* [nakadachi] A go-between; a matchmaker in marriage; an intermediary.
naka-dana, *n.* The section of a boat where the **haragaagii** boards are located. See **sabani**.
naka-fuu, *n.* A style of Ryukyuan short poem that consists of twenty-eight syllables in four lines (7-7-8-6).
naka-guu, *n.* [nakago] A nucleus; kernel; core.
naka-iibi, *n.* [nakayubi] The middle finger.
naka-iri, *n.* [nakairi] Intermediation; mediation; medium.
naka-jichi, *n.* A seven-**goo** liquid measurement jar. Same as **nananukuhin**. See also **chuwakasaa**.
naka-jin, *n.* **1** The center; the middle; the heart; the focus. **2** The nucleus; the core (of a body or fruit). **·nu**, *adj.* Central; middle; leading.
naka-jiru, *n.* [nakazuru] The middle string of the three strings of the **sanshin**. See **sanshin**.
naka-mee, *n.* A living room.
naka-mi, *n.* **1** Intestines of animals such as pigs as food. **2** Contents; substance.
nakami·nu-shiimun, *n.* Soup of pig's intestines. See **shiimun**[2].
naka-mu·i, *n.* A one-**goo** dry measure box. Also **ichigoonakamui**.
nakamui-gwaa, *n.* A half-**goo** dry measure box; Same as **gusaakunakamui**. See **chiiga**[2], **nakamui**.
naka-mukashi, *n.* The medieval age; historical age. See also **ufunkashi**.
naka-noo·i, *n.* [nakanaori] Reconciliation; peacemaking. **-sun**, *v.* [nakanaorisuru] To reconcile (with); make peace (with); be friends again (with).
nakara, *n.* A half; halfway; a half the amount.

naka-tagee, *n.* [nakatagai] **1** Incompleteness; condition of being either too short or too long, or too much or too little. **2** A woman who has passed marriageable age. **3** Discord; dissension.
naka-tii, *n.* [nakate] Medium size.
naka-yashi·mi, *n.* [nakayasumi] A recess; a break.
naka-yuku·i, *n.* A recess; a break. See also **nakayasumi**.
nama[1], *n.* [nama] Uncooked; raw; rare (of meat).
nama[2], *n.* [ima] The present; the present day; this time; now; soon; shortly.
nama-cha·a, *n.* A reckless person; an impudent person.
nama-chi, *n.* Recklessness; rashness; temerity; impudence. **·na**, *adj.* Foolhardy; rash; headlong; daredevil.
nama-chiburu-yan, *n.* A slight headache.
nama-gata, *adv.* Just now; a moment ago. See **namasachi**.
nama-guru, *n.* About this time; at this time of (day, night, the year).
nama-guru·shi, *n.* Same as **hangurushi**.
namahi, *n.* Same as **namashi**. [GSS]
namai, *n.* [namari] Lead.
namaja·a, *n.* An insensitive person; an audacious person.
nama-jibun, *adv.* [imajibun] About this time.
nama-jira, *n.* Audacity, impudence, shamelessness.
namajira·a, *n.* A brazen fellow; an unscrupulous person.
namajira-ware·e, *n.* An impudent smile; a cheeky, shameless smile.
nama-kugashi, *n.* See **kugashi**.
nama-miji, *n.* [namamizu] Unboiled water.
nama-mun, *n.* [namamono] Raw food; undercooked food; uncooked food.
nama-nama·a-sun, *vt. emph. colloq.* To hurry; hasten; urge on. [GSS] See also

agimaasun.

nama·nu-yuu, *n.* The present age; modern times.

namari·in, *vi.* [namaru] To grow dull; become blunt; be weakened.

nama-sachi, *adv.* Just now; a moment ago; a few minutes ago; a little while ago. Same as **namagata.**

namashi, *n.* [namasu] A dish of raw fish and vegetables seasoned in vinegar. Also **namahi.**

nama-shiibai, *n.* Leakage of urine due to nervousness. See **shiibai.** [UKH]

namate·e, *n.* A joker; a buffoon; a humorist.

nama-ware·e, *n.* [namawarai] A derisive smile; a scornful laugh; sneer; derision. Same as **usuwaree.**

nami[1], *n.* [nami] A wave; a surge; a billow; a ripple; a surf.

nami[2], *n.* [nami] Ordinary; common; standard.

nami·in, *vt.* [nameru] To lick; nibble; taste.

nami-kaji, *n.* [namikaze] 1 Wind and waves; rough seas. 2 Strife; a quarrel; dissension.

nami-keeri, *n.* The beach; the line where the waves touch the shore. [GSS]

nami-musa·a, *n.* A slug; a dew snail.

nami-mushi, *n.* Same as **namimusaa.**

namiti, *n.* [< nami] On average; in general; on the whole.

namujaa, *n.* An incorrigible person; an obstinate person; a blockhead.

nan, *n.* [nan] 1 Trouble; disaster. 2 A fault; a blemish.

nan-, *pref.* [nan-] Indicates what or how [many].

nana-chi, *n.* [nanatsu] Seven; seven years of age.

nanachi-bushi, *n.* [nanatsuboshi] Ursa Major; the Big Dipper.

nana-iru-muutii, *n.* Lit., seven-colored cord (for tying the hair); a folkloric expression warning against meddling in the affairs of others. [ODJ]

nana-nan-ka, *n.* The Buddhist memorial service on the forty-ninth day after death. Same as **shijuukunichi.** See also **nanka.**

nana-nukuhin, *n.* A seven-goo liquid measurement jar. Same as **nakajichi.** See **chuwakasaa.**

nan-ban, *n.* [nanban] 1 *arch.* The Southern area, roughly Southeast Asia today; Southern barbarians; Europeans arriving in the Ryukyus and Japan via the south. 2 Same as **nanbangaami.**

nanban-gaami, *n.* [nanbangame] Southern style unglazed jar. See **kaami.**

nanban-gasa, *n. arch.* Syphilis. Also **naabaru.**

nanbeeraa, *n.* Same as **naabeeraa.** [GSS]

nan-bun, *n. formal* [< J nanibuɴ] Anyway; anyhow; at any rate.

nan-dee, *n.* Same as **kwaagi.**

nandee-shii, *n.* Same as **kwaagi.**

nan-du, *n.* [< J nando] How many times.

nan-duchi, *n.* [< J nandoki] What time.

nanduru-mun, *n.* A slippery thing.

nanduru·san, *adj.* Slippery; smooth; glassy.

nanduru·u, *n.* That which is slippery.

nani-gashi, *n.* [< J nanigashi] A certain person; Mr. So-and-so.

nanja, *n. arch.* [nanryoo*] Silver. See also **gin.**

nan-ji, *n.* [nangi] Hardships; difficulties; sufferings. See also **nanjikunji.**

nanjichi, *n.* Scorched food; scorched rice. Also **faagusari.**

nanji-kunji, *n.* Hardship; trouble; suffering. **-sun,** *v. emph. colloq.* To suffer extreme hardship; undergo troubles. See also **nanji.**

nanji-sa·a, *n.* One who toils.

nan-ka, *n.* [nanoka] Memorial rites held every seventh day during the forty-nine-day mourning period after death.

See **hachinanka, tananka, minanka, yunanka, ichinanka, munanka, nanananka, shijuukunichi**. See also **suukoo**.
nankuru, *adv.* By itself; naturally.
nankuru-mii, *n.* Wild growth; autogenesis.
nan-kwa, *n.* [nanka] Same as **chinkwa**.
nan-nichi, *n.* How many days. See also **ikka**.
nan-san, *n.* [nanzan] Difficult delivery; complicated birth.
nan-tuu, *n.* [nattoo] A cake made from 'nmukashi (sweet potato residue, after the starch is removed).
nanu·i-gashira, *n.* [nanorigashira] The initial character in a personal name, traditionally shared by all male members of the same patrilineal gentry group.
naraa·shi, *n.* [narawashi] **1** A habit; a custom; a usage; a convention; a practice. **2** Education; instruction; upbringing; discipline.
naraa·sun, *vt.* [narawasu] To teach; instruct (in); give lessons (in); show; tell; educate.
narabi·in, *vt.* [naraberu] To arrange things in rows; put (things, people) side by side; juxtapose; place things in order.
nara·in, *vt.* [·(r)an, ·ti; narau] To learn; study; be taught (in); take lessons in; practice; be trained.
narashi[1], *n.* A bamboo dress hanger; a kimono hanger.
nara·shi[2], *n.* Average. Also **tunami**. See **narasun**.
narashi[3], *n.* Same as **narashi'iibi**.
narashi-iibi, *n.* The third finger.
nara·sun[1], *vt.* [narasu] **1** To level; flatten. **2** To average.
nara·sun[2], *vt.* To grind (wheat) into flour.
nara·sun[3], *vt.* [narasu] To play (a musical instrument).

nare·e, *n.* [narai] A habit; a custom; the usual way. See also **nari**.
nari, *n.* [nare] A habit; a custom; a usage; a practice; a convention.
nari·in, *vi.* [nareru] To get used to; grow familiar with; get accustomed; become experienced.
nari-mun, *n.* Fragile articles such as pottery. [OGJ]
narimun-doogu, *n.* Earthenware; porcelain; china; crockery; pottery.
nari-yuchi, *n.* [< J nariyuki] The course of events; the development (of an affair).
naru-bichi, *adv.* [narubeku] If possible. Same as **nari, naree**.
nasaga·sun, *vt.* To speak ill of one absent; backbite.
nasaki, *n.* [nasake] **1** Sympathy; compassion. **2** Affection; love.
nashi-chira·a, *n.* The last-born child.
nashi-hanjoo, *n.* Delivery; parturition; a childbirth; a birth. Also **hanjoo**. -**sun**, *v.* To give birth to (a baby); be delivered of (a baby).
nashi-hirugi, *n.* Propagation of offspring.
nashi·in, *vt.* [nasuru] To rub (on); spread; smear; daub.
na·shi-jichi, *n.* The month of parturition.
nashi-mee, *n.* Before childbirth.
nashi-mun·nu-kkwa, *n.* One's true child; one's child by blood.
nashi-ngwa, *n.* A child that one gave birth to; a beloved child.
nashi-uya, *n.* A natural parent; one's birth parent.
na·sun[1], *vt.* [nasu] **1** To make; make (something) of (a person); change (one thing into another) **2** To move; move aside.
na·sun[2], *vt.* [nasu] To bear; give birth to; be delivered of; bring forth; (of animal) breed; drop; calve; pup.
nat·taa, *pron. plur.* You. See **naa**[1].

nba, *interj. colloq.* An expression of rejection: No; nay. Also **npa**; **nnpa**.
'nbashi, *n.* Giant taro [*Alocasia odora* (Lodd.) Spach]. [FOSR, ODJ]
'nbu-gi, *n.* [ubuge] Downy hair or lanugo. Also **fukugii**.
'nbukkwi·in, *vi.* [oboreru] To drown; be drowned.
'nburaa·san, *adj.* **1** Dignified; grave; solemn; serious. **2** Courtly; courteous; gentlemanly; graceful; elegant.
'nburi·in, *vi.* [mureru] To become steamed; be steaming hot; be sultry.
'nbu-sa·a, *n.* A steaming basket.
'nbu·san, *adj.* [omoi] Heavy.
'nbushi, *n.* [omoshi] A weight; a sinker; burden (on one's mind).
'nbushi·i, *n.* A pottage with pork, tofu, vegetables, and miso bean paste. See **toofu'nbushii, oofa'nbushii, kuubu'nbushii**. [OBJ, ODJ]
'nbu·sun, *vt.* [musu] To steam; heat (warm) with steam.
n-chabi, *n.* Mock paper money that is burnt in offering to ancestral spirits on the evening of the last day of the *Bon* festival. See also **kabi'anji, unchabi, waradooshi**. [OGJ, OBJ]
-nchoon, *adv.* Even.
nchu, *n.* The year before last. Also **mituu, nntchu**.
n·chun, *vt.* [muku] To peel (an orange); pare (an apple).
nda, *interj.* Let me see; hey.
nda·sun, *vt.* [nurasu] To wet; moisten; dampen. Also **nrasun**.
·ndi, *conj.* Marks a quotation or citation; [say, ask] that…; …[so] that….
ndi-gara, *n.* A cast-off skin or shell.
ndi·in, *vi.* [nureru] To become wet; become damp. See **marundii**.
nee[1], *n. arch.* [nawi*] Earthquake.
nee[2], *n.* [nae] A sapling; a seedling.
neebi, *n.* [manebi] Mimicry; imitation.
neega·a, *n.* A lame person. Same as **neeguu**.
neegu, *n.* Lameness.
neegu·u, *n.* A lame person. Also **neegaa, neejaa, guunaa**.
nee·in[1], *vi.* [naeru] To wither; droop; weaken.
nee·in[2], *vt.* To hold out; stretch out; reach out; extend.
neeja·a, *n.* A lame person. Same as **neeguu**.
nee·jun, *vi.* [naegu*] To become lame.
nee·n, *vi.* [nai] (Irregular) negative of **an**[1]: there is no…; …do not exist; be gone; be missing; want; lack; be devoid of; finish; get through (as suffix on **·ti** forms).
nee-nee[1], *n.* [nainai] Privately; confidentially; secretly.
nee-nee[2], *n. endear.* [< J ane] Big sister; term of address of a sibling for an older girl.
neeri·in, *vi.* To droop; wither; wilt; be limp.
nen-nen, *n.* Sleep. Same as **ninnin**[2].
'ngaa-'ngaa, *adv. onom.* Sound of a baby crying.
·ni, *interrog. adv.* Marks a negative question phrase.
ni-ban, *n.* The second.
niban-ja, *n.* The second room (in a house). See also **ichibanja**. [ODJ] Also **nakamee**. [GSS]
nichi, *n.* [netsu] **1** Fever; temperature. **2** Heat; warmth.
ni-fee, *n.* Gratitude; thankfulness; appreciation. **-deebiru,** *interj.* Thank you. See also **kafuushi, shiduugafuu**.
niga·in, *vt.* [·(r)an, ·ti; negau] To desire; wish; hope; pray for.
nige·e, *n.* [negai] A wish; a desire; petition; request.
ni-gutu, *n.* [negoto] Talking in one's sleep.
ni-gwachi, *n.* [nigatsu] February. Also **ningwachi**.
nii[1], *n.* [ne] **1** A root; **2** The cause of a disease. **3** Muscle stiffness. **4**

Hardening one's heart.
nii², *n.* [ni] A load; a burden; a cargo.
nii³, *n.* [ne] A price.
nii⁴, *n.* [ne] A sound; a tone; (musical) note; (a bell's) ring; a voice. See also **utu**.
nii⁵, *n.* [ne] The Rat, the first of the twelve calendrical animal signs.
niibi, *n.* A kind of sandstone, red, gritty, and hard.
niibi-baka, *n.* A cave tomb dug into a **niibi** sandstone hill. See **haka**.
nii-bi·chi, *n.* A wedding; a wedding ceremony; marriage.
niibichi-jaa, *n.* A wedding hall.
niibichi-suuji, *n.* A wedding party; a wedding celebration.
nii-biru, *n.* A wild onion [*Allium grayi* Regel]. [FOSR] Also **chiribiragwaa**.
niibu, *n.* A ladle; a dipper; a scoop.
niibu-gwaa-bushi, *n.* The Big Dipper.
niibu·i, *n.* Sleepiness. **-sun**, *vi.* To be sleepy; be drowsy; slumberous.
niibui-kaabui, *n.* Sleepiness. **-sun**, *vi. emph. colloq.* To be sleepy; feel drowsy.
niibui-mii, *n.* Heavy eyelids.
nii-buta·a, *n.* A boil; a furuncle. Also **niibutu**.
niibutu, *n.* [nebuto] Same as **niibutaa**.
niibuya·a, *n.* A sleepyhead; a heavy sleeper.
niichi, *n.* [neiki] The breathing of a sleeping person.
nii-dukuru, *n.* The founding family of a village. See also **niitchu, niigan, kami'ashagi, niiya**. [ODJ, OR]
nii-fuda, *n.* [nifuda] A label; a tag; a docket; a baggage tag.
nii-gan, *n.* Lit., root deity; a sister of the **niitchu**, the male head of the founding family of a village. See also **wunai, wikii, niidukuru, niiya, niitchu**. [ODJ, OR]
nii-gui, *n.* The root of a tree.
nii-guruma, *n.* A cargo cart.
nii-ishi, *n.* [neishi] A foundation stone;
a cornerstone; a footstall.
nii-ji·chun, *vi.* [nezuku] To take root; strike root.
nii-kee, *n.* [nikai] A second floor; a second story.
nii·ku, *adv.* Slowly; tardily.
ni·i-kuga·shi, *n.* See **kugashi**.
ni·i-kuga·sun, *vt.* To scorch food and have it stick to the pot.
ni·i-kugeera·sun, *vt.* To have food boil over with high heat.
ni·i-kuta na·in, *vi. phr.* (Of food) to be cooked until it becomes shapeless.
nii-muchi, *n.* [nimotsu] A cargo; luggage; load. Also **nimuchi**.
ni·in¹, *vt.* [·ran, ·chi; niru] To boil; cook; do (meat, etc.).
ni·in², *vt.* [neru] To knead; mash.
ni·in³, *vi.* [·ran, ·chi; niru] To look like (something; somebody); be alike; resemble.
nii-nai, *n.* A fruit grown near the root of a vine. See also **shimunai**.
nii-nii, *n. endear.* [nii < ani] A big brother; an older sibling; familiar term for an older male.
nii·nu-fa-bushi, *n.* The North Star.
nii·san, *adj.* [? nibi-*] **1** Slow; late. **2** Unsavory; unpalatable.
nii-s(h)ee, *n.* [nisai] A young man; youth.
niisee-taa, *n.* Plural for **niis(h)ee**.
niita·sa-sun, *vt.* [netasa*] To bear (a person) a grudge; feel resentful about (something); feel bitter toward (somebody).
nii-tchu, *n.* The root person, the patrilineally descended head of the founding household of a village. See also **niidukuru, niigan, niiya**. [ODJ]
nii-ya, *n.* The root house, the founding house of a consanguineous village community. See also **niidukuru**.
nii-yakkee, *n.* [niyakkai] A burden; a drag; an encumbrance.
ni-jama, *n.* [nezama] One's sleeping

posture. Also **ninjijama**.
niji, *n*. [neji] A screw; a cock. See **nijiri**.
niji·i-juu·san, *adj*. Patient; forbearing; persevering; enduring; stoic.
niji·in[1], *vt*. To endure; tolerate; suffer; put up with.
niji·in[2], *vt*. [nigiru] To clasp; grasp; grip; clutch.
niji·in[3], *vt*. [?tsuneru] To pinch; nip; give a pinch.
nijiri, *n*. [nigiri] A screw; a faucet.
nijiri-mee, *n*. [nigiri + mai] A rice-ball. [GSS]
ni-juku·i, *n*. [nizukuri] Packing; baling; crating.
nikaa, *n*. [nikawa] Glue; animal glue.
nikka, *adv*. Late; tardy.
niku, *n*. [niku] **1** Meat; fish; game. **2** Flesh. See also **shishi**.
niku-buku, *n*. [nekobuki] A large, coarse straw mattress.
niku·mun, *vt*. [nikumu] To hate; dislike; detest; abhor.
nikun, *n*. A pimple; acne.
ni-muchi, *n*. Same as **niimuchi**.
nin, *n*. [nen] Attention; care; caution.
-nin[1], *suff*. A counter for persons.
-nin[2], *suff*. A counter for years.
ninbucha·a, *n*. Beggar saints of the Nembutsu sect (Jodo Pure Land sect) of Buddhism; Nembutsu-chanting mendicants.
ninbuchaa-shiidu, *n*. Chief of the **ninbuchaa**.
nin-buchi, *n*. [nembutsu] A Buddhist invocation; repetitive recitation of the sacred name of Amitabha.
nin-chi[1], *n*. [nenki] An annual memorial service for the dead. See also **ichininchi, yunui, wakajuukoo, ufujuukoo, uwaijuukoo, shinkuchi, harujuukoo**. [ODJ]
nin-chi[2], *n*. [nenki] **1** A worker's term of service; a term of apprenticeship. **2** Experience; training.
ninchi-jiri, *n*. [nenkigire] The completion of one's term of service.
nindari·in, *vi*. To be able to sleep. Also **ninrariin**.
nin-dee, *n*. [nendai] An age; an epoch; a period; a (historical) date.
nin-gaki, *n*. A desire; an ambition; an aspiration.
ningaki·in, *vt*. To plan, aspire to; aim at; make efforts.
nin-guru, *n*. [nengoro] A lover (either male or female); sweetheart.
nin-gwachi, *n*. [nigatsu] The second lunar month. Also **nigwachi**.
ningwachi-kajimaa·i, *n*. Volatile wind condition occurring around the second month of the lunar calendar.
ningwachi-umachii, *n*. Ritual offering of the first wheat crop on the fifteenth day of the second lunar month. [ODJ]
nin-gwan, *n*. [nengan] One's prayer; one's dearest wish.
nin-i·ri, *n*. [nen-iri] Care; caution; enthusiasm. **·ni**, *adv*. Carefully; scrupulously; attentively; deliberately.
ninja·a-gwaa, *n*. A wrestling technique in which the wrestler holds his opponent with one arm on his back and pulls his opponent down as he himself goes down on his back. See **shima**[3], **ninjun**.
ninji, *n*. Faith; belief; creed.
ninji-busuku, *n*. Lack of sleep; insufficient sleep.
ninji-chigee, *n*. Straining (one's neck, etc.) during sleep. **-sun**, *v*. To strain one's neck in sleep.
ninji-gukuchi, *n*. One's feeling in bed.
ninji·in, *vt*. [nenjiru] To believe; have faith; pray.
ninji-jama, *n*. One's sleeping posture. Same as **nijama**.
ninji-munugatai, *n*. Pillow talk; sweet nothings.
nin-jin, *n*. [ningen] A person; a human being.
nin-jiri, *n*. [nenkiri*] Term employment

ninjoo

(for a fixed number of years); payment for a fixed number of years.
nin-joo[1], *n.* [ningyoo] A doll; a person as cute as a doll.
nin-joo[2], *n.* [ninjoo] Human feelings; human nature.
nin-ju, *n.* [ninzu] A number of people; members of a group.
ninju·nu-sunawa·i, *n.* Sufficient number of people.
nin·jun, *vi.* [·**dan**, ·**ti**; nemuru] To sleep; go to sleep; fall asleep; retire; share the bed with; be confined to bed.
nin-juu, *n.* [nenjuu] All year round; throughout the year.
ninmee-naabi, *n.* An iron pot of the **ninmee** (roughly, medium) size. See **shinmeenaabi**.
nin-nin[1], *n.* [nen-nen] Every year; from year to year; year after year; year in and year out; annually.
nin-nin[2], *n. inf.* [< **ninjun**] Sleeping. Also **nennen**.
ninrari·in, *vi.* To be able to sleep. Also **nindariin**.
nin-richi, *n.* [nenriki] Willpower; will; faith.
ninshi·in, *vt.* To send (someone) to sleep; let sleep; lay down (on the side).
ninshi-too·chun, *vt.* To let (a person) stay in bed; let someone sleep.
nin-soo, *n.* [ninsoo] Physiognomy; looks; facial features.
nin-suku, *n.* [ninsoku] A laborer; a hand; a longshoreman; stevedore.
nirai-kanai, *n.* Same as **nireekanee**.
niree-kanee, *n.* In Okinawan cosmology, the other world, whence the gods visit, apart from the human world, variously believed to be an island beyond the seas or at the bottom of the ocean. Also **niraikanai**, **gireekanee**, **giraikanai**.
niri[1], *n.* The handle of an instrument such as an axe. See **wuunu**.
niri[2], *n.* Sand or grit which is mixed in rice.
niri·in, *vi.* To become bored (with); get tired of; get sick of; develop a dislike for.
nishi, *n.* [nishi] North (in the traditional meaning); west. See also **iri**.
nishichi, *n.* [nishiki] **1** Brocade. **2** Fine dress.
nishi·i, *n.* [nise] A sham; an imitation; a fake; a counterfeit.
nishi·in, *vt.* [niseru] To imitate; copy; model on.
nishi-kaji, *n.* The northerly wind.
nishi-mun, *n.* [nisemono] A counterfeit; a fake; a bogus; imitation. Also **nishii**, **yukushimun**.
nishi-nke·e, *n.* Facing northward; northern exposure.
Nishi·nu-umi, *n.* [nishinoumi] The East China Sea.
nita-kamanta, *n. emph. colloq.* Persons who are alike.
ni-uchi, *n.* [neuchi] Value; worth; merit; estimation.
niwa, *n.* [< J niwa] A garden; a courtyard; a yard. [OGJ] See also **naa**[5].
niwa-gi, *n.* [niwaki] A garden tree; shrubbery.
Ni-woo, *n.* [nioo] A deva (male divinity). See **Niwoobutuki**.
Niwoo-butuki, *n.* [nioo + hotoke] A pair of divinities who are gatekeepers of Buddhist temples. See **Niwoo**, **Makaa**.
niwu·i, *n.* [nioi] A smell; an odor; a scent.
nja, *n. pej.* A serf-like laborer such as **irichirii**, **shikama(a)**.
nja-daki, *n.* Hedge bamboo [*Bambusa multiplex* (Lour.) Raeusch.]. [FOSR] See also **ubidaki**.
njai-chai, *n.* Coming and going; traffic. **-sun**, *v.* To go back and forth.
nja-mi, *n.* [nigami] A bitter taste; bitterness; gall.
nja-na, *n.* [nigana] Bitter herb [*Crepidiastrum lanceolatum* (Houtt.)

Nakai var. *lanceolatum*]. Also **nnjana**.
'**njana·a**, *n*. A stammerer; a stutterer.
njana-fuuchibaa, *n*. Bitter herb and mugwort (shoots), medicinal tonics.
'**njani**, *n*. Stammering; stuttering.
njara·a, *n*. A difficult man to deal with; a hard man to please.
njari, *n*. [midare] Disorder and entanglement of hair, thread, etc.
njari·in, *vi*. [midareru] 1 To be disturbed; be disheveled. 2 To be chaotic; be in disorder. See **midariin**.
njari-mun, *n*. A rascal; a rowdy; a roughneck.
'**njaru**, *adj*. Last; preceding.
nja·san, *adj*. [nigai] Bitter.
'**nja·sun**, *vt*. [dasu] 1 To put out; take out; bring out. 2 To extend; hold out; reach out. 3 To stick out; thrust out. 4 To send; post. 5 To publish; issue. 6 To present; send in. 7 To serve; offer. 8 To turn out; produce; yield. 9 To pay; give; chip in; contribute. 10 To achieve (a speed of).
nja-ware·e, *n*. [nigawarai] A forced smile; a bitter smile. -**sun**, *vi*. To force a smile; smile grimly.
'**nji**, *interj*. Used to confirm the veracity of something or someone. Is that so? Really?
nji, *n*. [nogi] A thorn; a splinter; a spine; a prickle; an awn.
nji-cha·a, *n*. Thistle [*Cirsium brevicaule* A. Gray var. *brevicaule*]. Also **chibana, shima'ajami**.
'**nji-fa**, *n*. Expenditure; expenses.
'**nji-guchi**, *n*. [deguchi] An exit; a way out; a gateway.
'**nji-hangwi**, *n*. Absconding; an elopement. -**sun**, *v*. To run away, elope; abscond.
'**nji·in**, *vi*. [deru, izu*] 1 To come out; appear; emerge; come forth. 2 To be found. 3 To step out; go out; leave. 4 To attend; be present. 5 To be published; come out (in print). 6 To start from; come from. 7 To stick out; protrude.
'**nji-i·ri**, *n*. [deiri] Incoming and outgoing; revenue and expenditure.
'**njiri-mee**, *n*. Expenditure; expense; cost; outlay.
njiri·n-tii, *n*. The right hand.
'**nji-ta·chi**, *n*. [idetachi] Departure; starting.
nju, *n*. [mizo] A ditch; a gutter; a gully; a channel. See also **shiiri**. Also **nnju**.
'**nju·chun**, *vi*. [ugoku] 1 To move; stir; budge; shift. 2 To shake; swing; sway. 3 To work; operate; run; go. 4 To move. 5 To be influenced; be swayed. 6 To be moved; be touched; be affected. 7 To vary; change.
nju-miti, *adv*. Very; exceedingly; very much. [GSS]
·**nkai**, ·**kai**, *part*. Indicates direction or place; to; at; by; for; on.
nka·in, *vi*. [·(r)an, ·ti; mukau] 1 To face; front; look out; be opposite (to). 2 To meet; confront; oppose; defy. 3 To proceed (to); go (to); head (toward). 4 To grow; tend toward.
nkaja·a, *n*. *colloq*. Same as **nkaji**.
nkaji, *n*. [mukade] A centipede. Also **nkajaa, mukajaa**. [GSS]
nkashi, *n*. [mukashi] Antiquity; ancient times; former years; old days; long time ago.
nkashi-banashi, *n*. [mukashibanashi] An old tale; a legend; folklore; reminiscences.
nkashi-nchu, *n*. [mukashibito] 1 People in the old days; our forefathers. 2 A deceased person.
nke·e, *n*. [mukai] The opposite side; on the opposite side (of street, etc.).
nkee·in, *vt*. [mukaeru] 1 To go out to meet; receive; play host to; welcome; greet. 2 To invite; call; send for.
nke·e-kaji, *n*. [mukaikaze] A headwind; an adverse wind.
nki·in[1], *vi*. [mukeru] To peel off; come off.

nki·in², *vt.* [mukeru] To turn (on, toward); face; direct (to, toward); train (a weapon) on (something).

'nma¹, *n.* [uma] **1** A horse; a nag; a mount; a pony; a steed; a mare; a stallion. **2** A bridge (for either shamisens or kotos). **3** The Horse as the seventh of the twelve calendrical animal signs. Also **uma**.

'n-ma², *pron.* **1** There; over there. **2** *pron. formal* He; she.

'nma-dima, *n.* Horse fee, in money, wine, or rice, in exogamous marriage by the bride, paid by the bridegroom to the young men of the bride's village. Also **'nmajaki**. See **'nma**¹, **tima**. [OBJ]

'nmaga, *n.* [mago < umago*] A grandchild.

'nma-jaki, *n.* **1** Same as **'nmadima**. **2** Same as **sakijaku**.

'nma-jurii, *n.* [umazoroe] A horse race; horse racing. Also **'nmasuubu**.

'nma-meesaa, *n.* A horse dancer, referring to courtesans who dance astride a wooden horse during the **juri'nma** festival. See **juri'nma**.

'nma·n-chimi, *n.* [umanotsume] A horseshoe.

'nma-'nmaa, *n. inf.* A horse. Same as **onma**.

'nma·nu-shishi, *n.* Horse meat.

'nma·nu-yaa, *n.* [umaya] A horse stable. Also **'nma·n-yaa**.

'nmari, *n.* [umare] **1** Birth; origin. **2** Lineage. **3** One's birthplace.

'nmari-bii, *n.* [umarebi] Birthday.

'nmari-dushi, *n.* [umaredoshi] Birth year, one's year of birth reckoned according to the twelve animal signs of the calendar. See also **kajimayaa**, **tushibii**, **hariyaku**, **tookachi'uuwee**. [OBJ]

'nmari·in, *vi.* [umareru] To be born; come into being.

'nmari-jichi, *n.* [umaretsuki] One's inborn qualities; inborn temperament; character.

'nmari-jima, *n.* [umarejima] One's birthplace; one's home village.

'nmari-jimu, *n.* [umare + kimo] Purity of mind like an infant. [UKH]

'nmari-jishi, *n.* One's natural disposition.

'nma-rikaa, *n.* Hereabout; around here; this neighborhood.

'nmari-kaa·in, *vi.* [umarekawaru] To be born again; reincarnate.

'nma-tai, *n.* A groom; a horse-keeper; a stableman.

'nma-'wii, *n.* [umaoi] A horse racecourse; a racetrack; the turf.

'nmeeshi, *n.* A pair of chopsticks. Also **meeshi**¹, **umeeshi**.

'nmi¹, *n.* [umi] The sea; the ocean. Also **umi**¹.

'nmi², *n.* [umi] Pus; purulent matter.

'nmi³, *n.* [ume] Plum; Japanese apricot; an *ume*. [*Prunus mume* Sieb et Zucc.]. Also **umi**². [FOSR]

'nmi-⁴, *pref.* Same as **umi-**.

'nmi-bushi, *n.* [umeboshi] A salt-pickled plum.

'n-mii, *n.* An elder sister; an unmarried woman.

n-moo, *n. inf.* Squatting.

'nmu, *n.* [imo] A sweet potato [*Ipomoea batatas* Lam.]. Also **umu**.

'nmu-aree-baaki, *n.* A bamboo basket for holding and washing sweet potatoes. See also **baaki**.

'nmu-gaa, *n.* Sweet potato skins used as feed for pigs.

'nmu-kashi, *n.* [imokasu] Sweet potato residium after starch has been removed.

'nmu-kuji, *n.* [imokuzu] Sweet potato starch, used for food and for starching linen.

'nmukuji-andagii, *n.* A sweet potato starch cake. [ODJ]

'nmukuji-putturuu, *n.* A soft sweet po-

tato starch cake. [ODJ]
'**nmukuji-shirii**, *n*. A sweet potato grater. [ODJ]
'**nmu-machi**, *n*. A sweet potato market.
'**n·mun**, *vi*. [umu] **1** To ripen; become ripe (fruit). **2** To fester; form pus.
'**nmu-ni·i**, *n*. Mashed sweet potato.
'**nmu-nu-kuchi**, *n*. Lit., mouth of sweet potato; a taciturn person; a person of few words. [GSS]
'**nmu-wakashii**, *n*. Miso soup with sweet potatoes. [GSS]
'**nn**, *interj. colloq.* Affirmative response (to intimates or inferiors): Yes; yeah; all right. See **uu**², **oo**, **ii**¹.
nna¹, *n*. [muna] Emptiness; void; hollowness.
'**n-na**², *n. inf*. Doody; doodoo; poop; poopoo.
'**nna-bi**, *n*. Broken rice.
nna-dii, *n*. Empty-handed. Also **kararii**.
nna-duu, *n*. Same as **nnadii**.
'**nnagee**, *n*. Chaff; rice hulls; rice husks.
nna-guruma, *n*. An empty cart; an unoccupied car (cab).
'**nnaji**, *n*. [unagi] An eel.
'**nna-muji**, *n*. Wheat [J komugi; *Triticum aestivum* L.]. [FOSR] See **muji**².
nna-shiru, *n*. A clear soup. Same as **kaagaanushiru**.
nna-tarugaki, *n*. False hopes; hoping against hope. **-sun**, *vt*. To entertain vain hopes; hope against hope.
nna-tootoomee, *n*. Lit., empty mortuary tablets; having ancestral mortuary tablets without the benefits of inheritance.
nnatu, *n*. [minato] A port; a harbor.
nna-yaa, *n*. A vacant house; an unoccupied house.
nna-yashichi, *n*. Vacant premises; vacant housing compound.
nncha¹, *adv*. Indeed; really; I see; to be sure
nncha², *n*. Soil; clay; earth.
nncha-buku, *n*. A clump of soil.
nncha-mutaan, *n*. Playing with mud.

'**nndii**, *n*. Same as **indii**.
'**nni**¹, *n*. [ine] A rice plant [*Oryza sativa* L. var. *sativa*]. [FOSR]
nni², *n*. [mine] A mountain peak; a summit; a ridge of hills or mountains.
nni³, *n*. [mune] The ridge of a roof.
nni⁴, *n*. [mune] The chest; the heart.
nni-agi, *n*. [mune + age] A house framework raising ceremony. [OBJ]
nni-gii, *n*. [munage] Chest hair.
nni-guchi, *n*. The pit of the stomach; the breast.
'**nni-kai**, *n*. [inekari] Rice reaping; rice harvesting.
'**nni-majin**, *n*. A pile of harvested rice. Same as **majin**.
'**nni-shiri-shiri·i**, *n*. Same as '**nnishiri'uushi**.
'**nni-shiri-uushi**, *n*. A grinding mortar. Also **shiri'uushi**.
'**nni-shiya·a-uushi**, *n*. [shiya·a < shiri] A wooden rice chafing mortar.
nnjana, *n*. Same as **njana**.
nn-ju, *n*. Same as **nju**.
nn·jun, *vt*. [·**dan**, ·**chi**; **miru**] **1** To see; look (at); take a look (at); lay eyes on; stare; witness; watch. **2** To observe; look (at); inspect; visit. **3** To see (the sights); visit (a town). **4** To read; see; look through; look over. **5** To examine; consult (a dictionary). **6** To judge; read; tell. **7** To regard (as); take (for); look upon (as). **8** To estimate (at); calculate; value (at). **9** To look after; take care (of); attend. **10** To try; attempt.
'**nn-maagii**, *n*. A fan palm. See **kuba**.
'**nn-mee**, *n*. A grandmother; an old lady.
'**nnmii**, *n*. A sister. See '**nmii**.
nnna, *n*. [minna] All; each; everybody; everything.
nnnnn, *interj. colloq.* No (to inferior or intimate). See **wuuwuwuu**.
nnpa, *interj. colloq.* Same as **nba**.
nnsu, *n*. [miso] Fermented bean paste; miso. Also **yinsu**, **nsu**.

nnsuna-baa, *n.* Red beet; Swiss chard [J *fudanso*; *Beta vulgaris* L. var. *crispa* L.]. [ODJ]
nnsu·nu-shiru, *n.* [misoshiru] Miso (bean paste) soup.
nnu, *n.* [mino] A raincoat made of straw or field palm leaves.
nonka·a, *n.* [< nonki] An easygoing person; a happy-go-lucky person.
noobu, *n.* [byoobu] A folding paper screen.
noo-ga, *n.* [myooga] Same as **myooga**. [GSS]
noo-gumi, *n.* Upland rice cultivated without irrigation (*Oryza sativa* L. var. *terrestris* Makino) [FOSR] Also **jiimee**. See **kumi**[1].
noo·i-mii, *n.* [nuime] A seam; a stitch; a suture (of wounds).
noo·i-mun, *n.* [nuimono] Sewing.
noo·in[1], *vt.* [nuu] To sew; stitch.
noo·in[2], *vt.* [nau] To twist (straws) to make (a rope).
noo·in[3], *vi.* **1** To be mended; be repaired; be fixed; be all right again. **2** To get well; get better; recover (from illness); be restored (to health); be cured (of a disease); (wound) heal. **3** To be corrected; be rectified; be reformed. **4** To be restored; return to normal.
noo-ji, *n.* [myooji] Same as **myooji**. See also **yaannaa**.
noo-noo, *n. inf.* A flower.
noo·sun, *vt.* **1** To mend; repair; refit. **2** To reform; correct; remedy; redress; rectify. **3** To alter; change; shift. **4** To cure; remedy; make whole; heal. **5** To restore; recover. **6** To adjust; set right.
no-yashi, *n.* A field palm. See **binroo**.
npa, *interj. colloq.* Same as **nba**.
-npaa, *suff.* Following certain verb forms, denotes unwillingness or reluctance.
nsu, *n.* Same as **nnsu**.
·nu, *part.* **1** Possessive case marker; of. **2** Nominative case marker.
nubaga·in, *vi.* [nobiagaru] To stop by;

drop in for a short visit.
nuba·sun, *vt.* [nobasu] To extend; lengthen; postpone; defer.
nubi, *n.* [nobi] **1** Elasticity; ductility. **2** Postponement; deferment. **3** Tolerance; leniency.
nubi-nubi, *adv.* [nobinobi] Being put off from day to day; being delayed for a long time.
nubu·i, *n.* [nobori] Ascent; rise; an uphill road.
nubui-bira, *n.* An uphill climb; an ascent; an upward slope; a climb; upgrade. See also **uribira**.
nubu·in, *vi.* [noboru] **1** To go up; climb up; ascend. **2** To go up (to town).
nubu·n, *vi.* [nobiru] To become extended; become longer; become stretched; become delayed.
nubushi, *n.* [nobose] A rush of blood to the head; vertigo; dizziness.
nubushi·in, *vi.* [noboseru] To be dizzy; be feverish.
nuchaashi·i, *n.* A potluck-style party when everyone brings some food or pays for his own share.
nuchaashi-ubun, *n.* Same as **muimee**[2].
nuchaa·sun, *vt.* For a group of people to chip in money or food for a common objective; chip in.
nu·chi[1], *n.* [nuki] A beam; a principal horizontal timber of a building. Also **nuchigi**.
nu·chi[2], *n.* [nuki] The woof; the weft; the threads that run crosswise.
nuchi[3], *n.* [inochi] Life.
nuchi-aya, *n.* A horizontal-striped cloth.
nuchi-gafuu, *n.* Fortunate escape from death.
nuchi-gi, *n.* A beam. Same as **nuchi**[1].
nuchigi-yaa, *n.* Same as **nuchijiyaa**.
nuchi-gusui, *n.* [inochi + kusuri] **1** Life's elixir. **2** Food rich in nourishment; very tasty food.
nuchiji-yaa, *n.* A house with beams. Also **nuchigiyaa**.

nuchi-kajiri, *n.* [inochikagiri] For one's dear life; as if one's life depended on it.

nu·chi-kuru·sun, *vt.* To stab (a person) to death.

nu·chi-mun, *n.* Embroidery. **-sun,** *vt.* To embroider.

nuchi·nu-uya, *n.* [inochinooya] A savior of one's life.

nuchi-shin, *n.* Fund-raising; collection of donations. See **nuchun**².

nuchi-shita·a, *n.* A daredevil; a reckless person.

nuchi-shiti-mun, *n.* [inochi + sute + mono] Same as **nuchishitaa**.

nuchi-shiti-waja, *n.* [inochi + sute + waza] A life-risking work.

nu·chun¹, *vt.* [nuku] **1** To go through; pierce; penetrate. **2** To thrust; poke.

nu·chun², *vt.* [nuku] To raise (money; contributions); collect (money, etc.).

nu·chun³, *vi.* [noku] To divorce; break up; part.

nu·chun⁴, *vi.* [noku] To leave; step aside; vacate. Same as **duchun**.

nudai-kwatai·sun, *v. emph. colloq.* To drink and to eat; have a spree.

nugaa·in, *vi.* [nogareru] **1** To be released from; be exempted from; be excused from; escape from; dodge (a blow). **2** To evade; shirk; elude. Also **nugain**.

nugaa·sun, *vt.* [nogasu] To let (one) get away; allow (one) to escape.

nugi-bai, *n.* Gaining admission to an event or theatre without paying.

nugi·in, *vi.* To come out (off); fall out (off); slip out.

nugi-mun, *n.* [nokemono] An outcast; one who is left out; one who is excluded.

nugu·in, *vt.* [nogou*, nuguu] To wipe; mop. Also **susuin**.

nui, *n.* [nori] Paste; starch; glue.

nui-bichi, *n.* [nuri-biki] Freehand application of resist paste to cloth.

nu·i-gusui, *n.* [nurigusuri] External medicine.

nu·i-mun¹, *n.* [norimono] A vehicle; a [public] conveyance; transportation.

nu·i-mun², *n.* [nurimono] Lacquerware.

nuimun-machi, *n.* A lacquerware market.

nuimun-yaa, *n.* A lacquerware store.

nu·in¹, *vt.* [nuru] To paint; spread; plaster.

nu·in², *vi.* [noru] To ride (a horse; bicycle); take (a train; car); get on; board (a ship; an airplane).

nu·i-'nma, *n.* A riding horse.

nuji-fa, *n.* A rite of exorcism for leading a lost spirit to the tomb. See also **nuru**. [ODJ]

nuji-gachi, *n.* [nukigaki] **1** Extraction; excerption; selection. **2** An excerpt; an abstract; a summary.

nuji-sachi, *n.* A prefabricated device.

nuju·mi, *n.* [nozomi] A hope; a wish.

nuju·mun, *vt.* [nozomu] To hope; wish; desire; propose in marriage.

nu-jun¹, *vt.* To deceive; cheat; swindle; trick. Same as **damasun**.

nu·jun², *vt.* To draw; extract; take off.

nuka, *n.* [nuka] Rice bran.

nuku·i, *n.* [nokori] The remainder; the residue; the leftovers; the remnant; the rest; the surplus.

nuku·in, *vi.* [nokoru] **1** To stay (behind); be left; be left over (-behind). **2** remain; linger; be remembered.

nuku-jiri, *n.* [nokogiri] A (hand) saw.

nukumi·in, *vt.* [< J nukumeru] To warm; heat; heat up.

nuku·mun, *vi.* [nukumu] To warm (oneself); take warmth.

nuku-nuku·u·tu, *adv.* Comfortably warm.

nuku·san, *adj.* [nukui] Warm; mild.

nuku·shi, *n.* [nokoshi] Leftovers (usually of food).

nukutama·in, *vi.* To warm oneself.

nukutami·in, *vt.* To warm; heat.

numi¹, *n.* [nomi] A chisel.

numi

numi[2], *n.* [nomi] A flea. Also **innumi**.
nu·mi-dushi, *n.* A drinking companion.
nu·mi-gusui, *n.* [nomigusuri] Medicine taken orally. See **chikigusui**, **kusui**.
nu·mi-ku·mun, *vt.* [nomikomu] **1** To swallow; choke down; drink in. **2** To understand; grasp; take in.
nu·mi-miji, *n.* [nomimizu] Drinking water. Also **nunmiji**. See **chikeemiji**.
nu·mi-mun, *n.* [nomimono] A drink; liquor; a beverage.
nu·mun, *vt.* [nomu] **1** To drink; taste; get a drink; swallow. **2** To smoke. **3** To drink alcoholic beverages.
nun-chaku, *n.* A nunchaku weapon consisting of two truncheons connected with strong cords at one end.
nun-dunchi, *n.* [nu(u)ru + tunchi] The shrine-residence of the **nuru**, the chief village priestess. See also **nurudunchi**.
·nu 'njitooti, *phr.* [< **'nji·in**] In spite of; when; though; and yet.
nu-nu, *n.* [nuno] Cloth; textile. See **maawuu**, **basaa**, **mumin**, **iichuu**.
nunu-bata, *n.* [nunobata] A loom. Also **hata**[3].
nunu-daki, *n.* [nuno-take] Length of a roll of textiles.
nunu-machi, *n.* [nunomachi] Cloth market.
nuraari·in, *vi.* To be scolded; be rebuked; be reprimanded.
nura·in, *vt.* To scold; chide; rebuke; reprove; reprimand.
nura·i-takkwa·sun, *vt.* To scold away; rebuke (a person) strongly; take (a person) to task.
nuri·in, *vi.* To feel inclined (to do); feel enthusiastic (about doing).
nuru, *n.* Semi-divine priestesses of Okinawa's indigenous religion. [OBJ, ODJ] Also **nuuru**.
nuru-dunchi, *n.* A term of respect for a **nuru** priestess' house which has a shrine for sacred fire. Also **nundunchi**. [ODJ]

nuru-gami, *n.* Personal guardian spirit of the **nuru** chief village priestess.
nurumi·in, *vt.* To warm (the water); make lukewarm.
nuru·mun, *vi.* To become tepid; (water) become less cold; (hot water) become less hot; cool off.
nurun-turun-sun, *vi. emph. colloq.* To be absentminded; be blank; be stupefied.
nuru·san, *adj.* Tepid; lukewarm; not hot enough.
nuru-yuu, *n.* Lukewarm water.
nu·shi[1], *n.* [noseru] A wrestling technique in which the opponent is thrown right to left. See **shima**[3].
nushi[2], *n.* [noshi] Adornment for a gift. Traditionally a long, thin strip of dried abalone, now usually made of paper.
nushi-gwaa, *n.* Same as **nushi**[1].
nushi·in, *vt.* [noseru] **1** To place or put (a thing) on (something). **2** To carry; take in; take (a person) aboard; load; accommodate. **3** To record; put on record; mention; put (a name in a book).
nushiki·in, *vt.* To hold out; extend; reach out.
nusuda·a, *n. slang* Same as **nusudu**. [GSS]
nusudu, *n.* [nusutto] A thief; a robber; a burglar.
nusudu-ngwe·e, *n.* Eating by stealth.
nusu·mun, *vt.* [nusumu] To steal; commit theft; pilfer; filch; purloin; make free with; rob.
nuu, *adv.* What; which; whichever; whatever.
nuudii, *n.* [nodo] The throat.
nuudii-guufu, *n.* The Adam's apple. Also **nuudiikookoo**.
nuudii-jiru, *n.* The vocal cords.
nuudii-kookoo, *n.* Same as **nuudi-iguufu**.
nuudii-'waagwaa, *n.* The uvula.
nuuji, *n.* [niji] A rainbow.
nuu-mee, *n.* Brown rice.
nuunchi, *adv.* Why; how come.

nuu-n-kwii, *adv.* Anything and everything; every and all.
nuu-nuu, *n.* What and what.
nuuri, *n.* [nori] Moss.
nuuru, *n.* Same as **nuru**.
nuushi, *n.* [nushi] 1 The owner; the proprietor. 2 One's master. See also **shujin**.
nzo, *n. lit.* A female sweetheart.
nzoo·san, *adj.* Lovely; cute; charming.

O———

okkaa, *n.* [okkaa] Mom; mommy; mother.
omoro, *n.* Japanized rendition of **umuru** or **umui**.
Omoro Sooshi, *n.* Japanized rendition of **Umuru Usooshi**.
onma, *n. inf.* [< uma] A horse; a horsy.
oo, *interj.* Yes (to one senior in age but inferior in social status).
oo-ban, *n.* The last; the bottom; the tail (end).
oo-bee, *n.* [aobae] A blowfly.
oo-daa, *n.* A basket made of pandanus roots. See **maasudoogu**.
oo-daki, *n.* [aodake] A green bamboo.
oodoo, *n.* A lizard. See **andachaa, eejaa**. [GSS]
oo-fa, *n.* [aoba] Leafy vegetables; greens. See also **oosa, naa⁹, shimanaa², yaasee**.
oofa-'nbushii, *n.* Vegetable pottage.
oo-fijuru·u, *n. onom. emph.* That which is awfully cold or chilly.
oo-fijut·teen, *adj. onom. emph.* Extremely cold; very chilly.
oo-guru·san, *adj.* [aoguroi] Dark blue.
oo-gusu, *n.* The last one; the bottom; the tail end. See **ooban**.
oo·in, *vi.* To fight; wrangle; brawl.
oojaa-niisee, *n.* A green (raw) youth; a greenhorn; a fledgling; a novice.
ooji, *n.* [oogi] A fan; a folding fan.

ooji-me·e, *n.* [oogi-mai] A fan dance.
ooji·nu-funi, *n.* Frames of a fan.
oo·jun, *vt.* [aogu] To fan; use a fan.
oo-kusa, *n.* Green grass.
oo-kwan, *n.* [ookan] A highway; a thoroughfare; a main road.
oo-mun, *n.* [aomono] Green, unripe fruits.
oo-najaa, *n.* A blue-green snake.
oo-nami, *n.* [aonami] The blue waves.
oorasaa-ushii, *n.* A fighting bull. [UKH]
oo-ruu, *n.* [aoiro] Blue; greenish blue; green. See also **miji'iru**.
ooruu-bii, *n.* A Jack-o'-lantern; a will-o'-the-wisp; *ignis fatuus*.
oo-sa, *n.* Same as **oofa**. [GSS]
oosaaraa, *n.* 1 A beanbag. 2 Girls' play with beanbags, which are thrown up in the air and caught as they fall down.
oosaarii, *adv. arch.* [? oo sa-are] Yea; yes, sir; let it be so. [UKH]
oo-sabi, *n.* [aosabi] Green oxidation; patina.
oo·san, *adj.* 1 Blue; azure; green. 2 Unripe. 3 Inexperienced.
oo-suu, *n.* A sudden depth a little off the shore. [UKH]
oo-too, *n.* [ao- + Too (+kunenbo)] The **ootoo** orange [*Citrus oto* Hort. ex Y. Tanaka.]. [FOSR]
oot-teen, *adv.* Freshly green; vividly green; verdant.
oo-ya·a, *n.* A fighter; one who loves to fight; one who is quick to fight.
oo-yee, *n.* A quarrel; an altercation; a brawl; a fight. **-sun**, *vi.* To have a quarrel; altercate; wrangle; fight; scuffle.
ooyee-tiiyee, *n.* A fierce fight. **-sun**, *vi. colloq.* To quarrel vigorously.
otoo, *n.* [< J otoo] Dad; daddy; father.

P

paakuu, *n. onom. inf.* [pakupaku] Smoking tobacco; puffing.
paa-paa, *n.* 1 An old woman. 2 A grandmother; a granny.
paarankuu, *n.* A small drum with leather head on one side only.
pa-chin, *adv. onom.* [pachin] Sound of a small explosion or shattering.
paku-paku, *adv. onom.* [pakupaku] Sound of opening and closing the mouth incessantly as in smoking, talking, or eating.
pan, *adv. onom.* Sound of something popping or exploding.
papaya, *n.* A papaya [*Carica papaya* L.].
pas-sai, *n.* One of the traditional forms of karate.
patchi, *n. onom. inf.* Hitting; knocking.
patchi·i, *n.* A boys' game in which pasteboard cards with pictures of popular heroes are laid on the ground and players take turns hitting at them with their own cards.
pattaru-geeya·a-sun, *vi. onom. colloq.* To kick and struggle; sway and fling one's arms and legs in struggle.
pee, *n. onom. inf.* Infantile term for spitting something out.
peepee, *n. onom. inf.* Something dirty; filth.
penki, *n.* [penki] Paint.
penki-yaa, *n.* [penkiya] 1 A painter (of buildings, etc.). 2 A paint store.
pii-pii, *adv. onom. colloq.* Poverty. **-soon,** *adj. colloq.* Being poor.
piipii-kaakaa, *n. onom. emph. colloq.* Abject poverty; indigence; penury. **-soon,** *adj. colloq.* Suffering from dire poverty.
pin-an, *n.* One of the traditional forms in karate.
pirin-paran, *adv. onom. colloq.* Fluency in speaking, especially of a European language.
piyo-piyo·o, *n. onom. colloq.* A chick.
pon, *adv. onom. colloq.* [pon] Sound of an object falling into water.
poo-poo, *n.* [C bobo] A cake of dough filled with minced pork or miso, introduced from China. See also **chinpin.**
puu, *adv. onom. colloq.* [puu] Sound of blowing, such as in breaking wind.

R

-raa·s(h)an, *suff.* [-rashii] Indicates resemblance or having a characteristic of; appear; look like; seem.
rachi, *n.* Same as **dachi.**
rafutee, *n.* A traditional Okinawan dish in which chopped pork is slow cooked with soy sauce, sugar, and awamori liquor.
raku, *n.* [raku] 1 Comfort; ease. 2 Relief. **·na,** *adj.* Easy; comfortable; light; simple; soft. Also **daku.**
raku-chaku, *n.* [rakuchaku] A settlement; an end; a conclusion.
raku-raku·tu, *adv.* In comfort; comfortably.
ran-gasa, *n.* Same as **dangasa.**
ran-pachi, *n.* [danpatsu] Same as **danpachi.**
ranpachi-yaa, *n.* Same as **danpachiyaa.**
ranpu, *n.* [ranpu < lamp] Same as **danpu.**
ratchoo, *n.* Same as **datchoo.**
ri, *n.* [ri] A unit of distance roughly equivalent to 4 km (2.5 miles). [NJED]
ri-bichi, *n.* [ribetsu] A divorce. **-sun,** *v.* To divorce. Also **nuchun**[3].
rii[1], *n.* [rei] Etiquette; decorum; courtesy; a salutation. See also **riiji**[2].
rii[2], *n.* [ri] Interest (on a loan or deposit). Also **dii**[2], **riifii.**
rii-chi, *n.* [C lizhi] Lychee [*Litchi chinensis* Sonn]. [FOSR]
rii-fii, *n.* [rihei*] Interest rate.
rii-ji[1], *n.* Same as **shirikuji.**

rii-ji², *n.* [reigi] Courtesy; propriety; decorum; a gift to express gratitude or a wedding gift.

rii-jin, *n.* [reizen] **1** A Buddhist altar in which ancestral spirits are enshrined in the home; **2** a Buddhist mortuary tablet. Also **diijin**. See also **buchidan**.

-rikaa, *suff.* Indicates approximate place or whereabouts.

rikka, *interj.* Same as **dikka**.

ri-kucha·a, *n.* [rikutsu] A cunning fellow; an argumentative person.

ri-kuchi, *n.* [rikutsu] **1** Cunning; craftiness. **2** Opposition. **3** Reason; logic.

rin, *n.* [ren] A lotus [*Nelumbo nucifera* Gaertn.]. [FOSR] Also **din**.

rin-cha·a, *n.* [rinki] A jealous person. Also **dinchaa**.

rin-chi, *n.* [rinki] Jealousy, especially between a man and a woman. See also **dinchi, 'waanai**.

rin-gan, *n.* [C longyan] A longan; a dragon's eye [*Euphoria longana* Lamarck]. Also **dingan**.

rin-gwa, *n.* [renga] Brick.

rin-su, *n.* [rinzu] Figured satin: a patterned silk fabric with smooth finish, glossy on the face and dull on the back.

rip-pa, *n.* [rippa] Quality of being fine, handsome, honorable, superb, magnificent; excellent; splendid. Also **dippa**.

rip-puku, *n.* [rippuku] Anger; offense; rage; wrath. **-sun**, *vi.* To be angry; take offense; be offended. Also **dippuku**. See also **wajiin**.

ris-shin, *n.* [risshin] **1** Advancement in life; success in life; a rise in the world. **2** Marriage (for women). Also **disshin**. **-sun**, *vi.* To marry (for women).

ri-tuku, *n.* [ritoku] Profits; benefit; gains; returns.

ri-yuku, *n.* [riyoku] Greed; avarice; covetousness.

roo, *n.* [roo] A candle; wax.

roo-hoo, *n.* [ryoohoo] Both sides; both parties.

roo-ma, *n.* [C laomao] Dotage; senility. Also **dooma**.

roo-shin, *n.* A wick.

roo-tati·i, *n.* [rootate] A candlestick.

·ru, *part.* Same as **·du**.

rugwai, *n.* **1** An agave; a pita; a century plant [J Ryuzetsuran; *Agave americana* L.]. **2** Aloe [*Aloe arborescens* Mill.]. [ODJ] Also **dugwai**.

ruk-kaku, *n.* [rokkaku] A hexagon.

ruku, *n.* [roku] Six. Also **duku³, muuchi**.

ruku-gwachi, *n.* [rokugatsu] June. Also **dukugwachi**.

ruku-juu¹, *n.* [rokujuu] Sixty; sixty years old.

ruku-juu², *n.* [Rokujoo] Thin-sliced tofu marinated in salt water and broiled.

ruu, *n.* [ryuu] **1** Dragon. **2** Waterspout. Also **duu**.

Ruu-chuu, *n.* Ryukyu. Also **Duuchuu**.

ruu-guri·s(h)an, *adj.* Same as **duuguris(h)an**.

Ruu-ka, *n.* [Ryuuka] A general term for Ryukyuan lyric poetry. See also **uta**.

ruu-sagai, *n.* Waterspout; tornado on the sea. Also **ruu**.

ruu-ya, *n.* A jail; prison.

S———

·sa, *part.* Attached to apocopated form of verbs denotes a slight emphasis.

saa, *n.* [? saga] One's spiritual energy; one's spiritual power; the measure or extent of one's spiritual power.

saa-, *pref.* Denotes a small amount; a little.

saa-bee-mun, *n.* [< saa + fee(·san) + -mun] A bold person; a person of courage. [UKH]

saa-daka-'nmari, *n.* A person born with strong spiritual power.

saa-daka·san, *adj.* Of great spiritual power. See **takasan**.

saa-daka-tchu, *n.* A person with strong spiritual power; a high priestess.
saa-fuu-fuu, *adv.* Slightly drunk; slightly inebriated.
saa·i, *n.* [sawari] Morning sickness.
saai-maki, *n.* Infirmity due to morning sickness.
saa·in, *vt.* [sawaru] To touch; feel.
saaja·a, *n.* [sagi] A white heron; a snowy egret.
saa-jaa·tu-na·in, *vi.* To feel refreshed; feel relieved; feel all right.
saaji[1], *n.* [sagi] Same as **saajaa**.
saaji[2], *n.* A headband.
Saakaganashii, *n.* Same as **Shaakaganashii**.
saa-kuu, *n.* [C shaguo] An earthenware pot, usually for making soft rice gruel. Also **shaakuu**.
saa-maki, *n.* A case of one's spiritual energy overpowering physical prowess.
·saani, *part.* Indicating means, tool, or material used; with; of. Same as **·sshi**.
saara, *n.* [sawara*] A swab; a scrubbing brush. Also **banin**.
saa·ree san-gwan, *phr.* Lit., if (you) touch (it), (it'll cost you) three **kan** (of coppers); a cautionary saying.
saaru·u, *n.* [saru] **1** A monkey; **2** The Monkey, the ninth of the twelve calendrical animal signs. **3** A person who looks like a monkey. **4** A person who imitates others. Same as **saru**.
saa·shi, *n.* A lock.
saashi·nu-kwa, *n.* A key.
saa-taa, *n.* [satoo] Sugar; brown sugar. See also **shirujaataa, kurujaataa**.
saataa-baan, *n.* The turn for a family to use a communal sugar cane pressing machine. [UKH]
saataa-bakuyoo, *n.* A brown sugar broker. [UKH]
saataa-bee, *n.* Lime which is used to make brown sugar. See **fee**[1].
saataa-damun, *n.* Fuel, usually tree leaves, sugar cane bagasse, or cycad leaves, used to heat the cauldrons in sugar production. [UKH] Also **saataaramun**.
saataa-daru, *n.* [satoo + taru] Brown sugar barrel, made of wooden staves with bamboo belting. [UKH] Also **saataararu**.
saataa-gama, *n.* A cauldron for boiling sugar juice into syrup in the process of making brown sugar. [UKH]
saataa-gii, *n.* Sugar tree [J nezumimochi; *Ligustrum japonicum* Thunb]. [FOSR]
saataa-guruma, *n.* A sugar cane press.
saataa-jiki, *n.* [satoozuke*] Food preserved in sugar.
saataa-juku·i, *n.* [satoozukuri] Sugar manufacture.
saataa-kija·a, *n.* In sugar processing, a worker who stirs boiling sugar juice. [UKH] See **kijun**.
saataa-maaru·u, *n.* The turn for a family to make sugar at a communal mill. [UKH]
saataa-naabi, *n.* A sugar cauldron. [UKH]
saataa-nanjicha·a, *n.* Scorched brown sugar.[UKH] See **nanjichi**.
saataa-niibu, *n.* A large ladle for use in ladling the sugar juice. [UKH]
saataa-poopoo, *n.* A fried roll of flour mixed with sugar. [UKH]
saataa-ramun, *n.* Same as **saataadamun**. [UKH]
saataa-raru, *n.* [satoo + taru] Same as **saataadaru**. [UKH]
saataa-shii, *n.* Squeezing the sugary juice out of sugar cane. [UKH]
saataa-shii-suubi, *n.* A party to celebrate the completion of sugar making. [UKH]
saataa-tacha·a, *n.* The person who tends to the furnace in the process of making brown sugar. [UKH] See **tachun**[2].
saataa-wuuji, *n.* Sugar cane. Also **wuuji**.

saataa-wuuki, *n.* A wooden barrel for brown sugar. [UKH]
saataa-yaa, *n.* A sugar mill. See **saataa-maaruu.**
saataa-yuu, *n.* Sugar syrup condensed by boiling. [UKH]
saa-ware·e, *n.* A sneer; a derisive smile; a scornful laugh.
saa-yuu, *n.* [sayu] Plain hot water.
saba[1], *n.* A general term for any kind of light sandal, made of leather, straw, reed, bamboo bark, etc. See **adanbaasaba, dakigaasaba, warasaba.**
saba[2], *n.* A shark. Also **fuka**[1].
saba-anda, *n.* Shark's liver oil.
saba·chi, *n.* A comb; a rough-toothed comb. See also **sabachun**[1], **kushi**[5].
sabachi-baku, *n.* Lit., comb box; a black lacquered box for women's toiletries like combs. [UKH]
sabachi·nu-faa, *n.* The teeth of a comb.
sabachi·nu-mii, *n.* [kushi no me] The fineness of a comb.
saba·chun[1], *vt.* [sabaku] To comb out (hair); sort out a messy situation
saba·chun[2], *vt.* [sabaku] To judge; decide (on a case); settle (a matter).
saba·chun[3], *vt.* [sabaku] To sell; find a market for; dispose of; handle.
sabagwaa-gi, *n.* Same as **fukuji.** [UKH]
sabaku-yooree, *n.* Same as **fukuji.** [GSS]
saba·n-gi, *n.* Lit., slipper tree; same as **fukuji.** [UKH]
sabani, *n.* A small fishing boat; a canoe-type narrow, light boat with sides meeting in a sharp edge at each end. See **chuinuyaa, inoo'akkisaa, agiyaa, fuka'akkisaa.** [OBJ] See also **fii**[3], **naka**[1], **tumu**[1], **chira, funabara, sukujin, tana**[2], **kwaagwaa, haragaagii, nakadana, uchikiyaagii, dakidanaa, sagidana.**
sabi, *n.* [sabi] Rust.
sabi-jiru, *n.* A clear, tasteless, unseasoned soup.
sabi-kuu·in, *vi.* To rust; become rusty.

sachimaai

sabi-mun, *n.* A poor quality food.
sabiri·in, *vi.* [sabireru] To decline in prosperity; become desolate.
sabi-sabii·tu, *adv.* Frugally.
sabi·san, *adj.* [sabishii] Desolate; deserted; solitary; cheerless. Also **sabissan.**
saboori·in, *vi.* 1 For wood to become decayed and brittle. 2 To become desolate.
saboori-kaa, *adv.* In desolation; in ruins; out of repair.
sachi[1], *n.* [saki] 1 The point (of a pole); the tip (of the tongue); the nozzle (of a hose). 2 The first; priority. 3 Earlier than; in advance of. 4 Ahead; away. 5 The future. 6 The past; former.
sachi[2], *n.* [saki] A cape; a promontory; a headland. Also **misachi.**
sachi[3], *n.* [satsu] Paper money.
sachi-bai, *n.* [sakibashiri] A vanguard; a pioneer; the lead; the initiative.
sachi-chi·in, *vi.* [·ran, ·tchi; sakikiru] To be in full bloom; be all out; be at (its) best.
sachi-chiri·in, *vi.* Same as **sachichiin.**
sachi-da·chi, *n.* A leader; a precursor; a pioneer; a guide; a forerunner. **-sun,** *vi.* To lead; be a leader; be a guide.
sachi-da·chun, *vi.* [sakidatsu] 1 To precede; head; go in advance of. 2 To leave behind; die first; precede (someone) in death. See **tachun**[1].
sachi-dumi, *n.* A former wife. Also **sachirumi.** [UKH] See **tumeein.**
sachi-dushi, *n.* [saki + toshi] Former times; past years.
sachi-guchi, *n.* 1 An early turn. 2 A prior commitment; previous appointment.
sachi-iibi, *n.* Same as **tchusashiiibi.**
sachi-kan·jun, *vi.* [·dan, ·ti] To be in luxuriant bloom; bloom in profusion; be in its glory.
sachi-maa·i, *n.* [sakimawari] Arrival before another; getting ahead of an-

sachinain

other; anticipating another (in doing something).
sachi·na·in, *vi*. To get ahead; to precede.
sachi-ninju, *n*. Those people who have preceded (arrived or gone earlier).
sachi·nu-yuu, *n*. [sakinoyo*] A (historical) period before today; old times; ancient times. [UKH]
sachi-rumi, *n*. Same as **sachidumi**. [UKH]
sachi-tugayaa, *n*. Anything with a pointed tip. See **tugain**.
sachi-tuji, *n*. [saki + toji*] A former wife; the first wife.
sachi-wutu, *n*. [saki + otto] A former husband; the first husband.
sachi-yii, *n*. [sakii] Rush; shichito rush, used for matting [*Cyperus malaccensis* var. *brevifolius* Böckeler]. [FOSR] See also **mushiru, yiimushiru**.
sa·chun[1], *vi*. [saku] To bloom; blossom; open.
sa·chun[2], *vt*. [saku] To rend; rip; tear; split.
sadama·in, *vi*. [sadamaru] To be decided; be determined; be fixed.
sadami, *n*. [sadame] A rule; regulation; law; fate.
sadami·in, *vt*. [sadameru] To decide; regulate; determine.
safun, *n*. [< sabon < Port sabão] Soap. [UKH]
saga·i[1], *n*. [sagari] Lowlands; low-lying ground; bottomland.
saga·i[2], *n*. Purchase on credit.
sagai-goo·i, *n*. Purchase on credit.
sagai-mii, *n*. An downward slanting eye; a person with such eyes.
saga·in[1], *vi*. To buy and sell on credit.
saga·in[2], *vi*. [sagaru] 1 To come down; lower. 2 To hang down; fall; dangle from. 3 To lose a degree of freshness (for instance, of fish).
sagai-tiida, *n*. A setting sun.
sagai-unbu·in, *vi. emph. colloq*. 1 To dangle; hang down (from); be pendant. 2 To depend on; to sponge on. [GSS]
sagee·sun, *vt*. [sagasu] To search for; look for. See also **kameein, tumeein**.
sagi-daki, *n*. Lowered bamboo. Same as **sagidana**.
sagi-dana, *n*. Lit., hanging-down shelf; bamboo poles attached to both sides of a boat for buoyancy and stability; outriggers. Also **dakidanaa**. See **sabani**.
sagi-gusui, *n*. A purgative. See **kusui**.
sagi·in, *vt*. [sageru] To lower; hand down; dangle from; clear; remove.
sagi-jooki, *n*. A hanging basket; a bamboo basket hung from the ceiling for storing food. See also **sagisooki, sooki**[1]. [GSS, UKH]
sagi-sooki, *n*. Same as **sagijooki**.
sagu, *n*. In sanshin music, an interlude; a strain; an accompaniment. [UKH]
sagu·i, *n*. [saguri] 1 Exploratory proposal; sounding. 2 Stealing into a house (room) to see a woman.
sagu·in, *vt*. [saguru] 1 To feel for; to look for; to grope about with hands and feet. 2 To spy upon. 3 To explore; probe.
sai[1], *interj. adv*. [? < sa-are) Vocative interjection, used by a male to draw attention, or to show respect; (by a male visitor) to call those within. See also **tai**[1], **sari, tari, oosaarii**.
sai[2], *n*. A short metal truncheon shaped like the letter E.
sai-ban, *n*. [saiban] 1 Trial; justice. 2 Court of justice.
sai-nan, *n*. [sainan] A disaster; an accident; a misfortune; a mishap. [UKH]
saita, *adj*. Strange; queer; weird.
sajee, *n*. [sazae] A top shell [*Marmarostoma argyrostoma* (Linnê)]. [ODJ] Also **maanna, mannagwaa**.
sa-ji[1], *n*. 1 A caretaker in a village office. 2 A receiver; a collector; a priest charged with collecting ritual offerings or fees in the village; a female elected to this duty in the patrisib group.

saji², *n.* A scoop net; a dip net.
saka¹, *n.* [sakasa] Being opposite; reverse(d).
saka², *n.* [saka] A slope; an incline; a hill; downhill. See also **hira²**.
saka-bira, *n.* [saka + hira] A steep incline. See also **hira²**.
saka-imi, *n.* [sakayume] A dream which is contrary to the actual event. See also **soo'imi**.
saka-jichi, *n.* [sakazuki] A small wine cup.
saka-ju·i, *n.* [sakazori] Shaving against the grain; shaving upward. [UKH] See **suin**.
saka-machigi, *n.* [sakamatsuge] Ingrown eyelashes.
saka-miji, *n.* [sakamizu*] 1 Counterflowing water. 2 Reverse water, that is, lukewarm water made by adding the hot water to the cold water (in reverse of the normal order), used to bathe the deceased. See **shinkuchi**.
sakana, *n.* [sakana] A side dish served with drinks. See also **iyu**.
saka-na·in, *vi.* To become inverted; become upside down or inside out. [UKH]
sakana-yaa, *n.* [sakanaya] An Okinawan-style restaurant.
sakana-yaa-winagu, *n.* A waitress; a barmaid.
saka-ngwa, *n.* [sakago] A breech birth.
saka-ya, *n.* [sakaya] A brewery. See **sakimachiya**.
sakee, *n.* [sakai] A boundary; a border; the frontier.
sakee·in, *vi.* [sakaeru] To prosper; thrive.
sakee-mii, *n.* [sakaime] Border; boundary; dividing point.
saki, *n.* [sake] 1 An alcoholic drink, averaging from 20 to 40 percent alcohol, usually referred to as **aamui**. 2 Any alcoholic drink such as Japanese *sake*.
saki-bin, *n.* [sakebin] A *sake* bottle.

saki-gaami, *n.* [sakegame] A large *sake* jar.
saki-gura, *n.* [sakegura] A liquor warehouse.
saki-gushi, *n.* [sakeguse] A drinking habit.
saki-gwee·i, *n.* Getting fat from drinking alcoholic drinks. [UKH] See **kweein**.
saki·in, *vi.* [sakeru] To tear; rend; burst; rip; crack. [UKH]
saki-jaa, *n.* A party where alcoholic drinks are served. [UKH]
saki-jaku, *n.* A person who tends to become short-tempered when drunk. See also **'nmajaki**. [UKH]
saki-jooguu, *n.* [sakejoogo] A drinker; a tippler.
saki-kwe·e, *n.* A drinker; a drunkard; a souse; a guzzler; an alcoholic.
saki-machiya, *n.* [sakemachiya] A *sake* shop. See also **sakaya**.
saki-mu·i, *n.* [sakamori] A betrothal; a marriage engagement.
saki-nu·mi-dushi, *n.* A boon companion; a drinking friend. [UKH]
sak-koobi, *n.* A hiccup.
sak-kwii, *n.* [shakkuri; sakuri*] A cough.
saki-taru, *n.* [sakadaru] Liquor barrel. [UKH]
saku¹, *n.* [sako*] A ravine; a gorge; a dell.
saku², *n.* [shaku] Temper; irritability.
saku³, *n.* Same as **shaku¹**.
saku⁴, *n.* Same as **shaku²**. Also **-sa(a)ku**.
saku-gumi, *n.* Non-glutinous rice. Also **sakumee**.
saku·in, *vt.* [s(h)akuru*] 1 To perform a bloodletting remedy with a razor. [UKH] 2 To scratch or prick oneself (accidentally). [OGJ] See **buubuu¹**.
saku-mee, *n.* Same as **sakugumi**.
saku-mu·chi, *n.* [shakumochi] A temperamental person. Also **sakuu**. See **saku²**.

sakura

sakura, *n.* [sakura] **1** A cherry tree; cherry blossoms [*Prunus* L.]. **2** (In Okinawa) cold season cherry [*Prunus campanulata* Maxim.]. [ODJ, FOSR]
saku·san, *adj.* [sakui*] Fragile; brittle; easy to break; being not sticky. See **shipusan**.
saku·u, *n.* Same as **sakumuchi**.
sama·a, *n.* **1** An itch caused by flea bite. [UKH] **2** A person with gooseflesh. [OGJ]
sama·in, *vi.* [sameru] Same as **samiin**¹.
sama-jama, *n.* [samazama] A variety; a diversity. ·**nu**, *adj.* Various; many kinds of.
sama·sun¹, *vt.* [samasu] **1** To cool; let (a thing) cool. **2** To get (a person) sober.
sama·sun², *vt.* [samasu] To awake; wake up.
samatagi, *n.* [samatage] Hindrance; obstacle.
samatagi·in, *vt.* [samatageru] To prevent; hamper; hinder.
sami, *n.* [same] Same as **heegasa**. [UKH]
sami·in¹, *vi.* [sameru] **1** To cool (down); get cold. **2** To abate; subside. **3** To become sober. Also **samain**.
sami·in², *vi.* [sameru] To wake up; awaken.
sami·in³, *vi.* [sameru] To come off (color); fade away; lose color.
samure·e, *n.* [samurai] The gentry class; a member of the gentry class. See also **bushi**, **yukatchu**.
san¹, *n.* [san] Three, especially in compound words. See **miichi**.
san², *n.* A crosspiece; a bolt (for a door).
san³, *n.* A taboo sign; an exorciser that consists of a loop made of grass leaf, miscanthus, straw, or banana leaf, placed especially upon ritual food offerings or unattended box lunches to chase away evil spirits. [OBJ] See also **geen**, **gushichi**.
san⁴, *n.* [san] Childbirth; childbearing; a delivery.

sanagi, *n.* Same as **sanaji**. [GSS]
sanaji, *n.* A loincloth; a waistcloth; a breechcloth. Also **hanaji**², **sanagi**. [GSS]
san-ba¹, *n.* [sanba] A midwife.
san-ba², *n.* [C sanpa] A simple musical instrument consisting of three wood or bamboo pieces strung together. [OBJ, OGJ]
san-ban, *n.* [sanban] Third place.
san-ban-dui, *n.* [sanbandori] The third rooster; a rooster which crows about four to five AM. [UKH]
san-ban-ja(a), *n.* [sanbanza] Third room (in a house). [ODJ].
san-bashi, *n.* [< J sanbashi] A wharf; a pier; a quay.
san-du, *n.* [sando] Three times.
sangu, *n.* [sango] Coral.
san-gwachi, *n.* [sangatsu] March.
sangwachi-sannichi, *n.* A festival for children and youths, involving various food traditions, held on the third day of the third month of the lunar calendar. [OGJ]
sangwachi-sannichi·i, *n.* Purification rite for women held on the third day of the third month of the lunar calendar. See also **hama'urii**. [ODJ]
sangwachi-ujuu, *n.* Same as **sangwachisannichii**. [UKH]
sangwachi-umachii, *n.* Rite of wheat harvest, held on the thirteenth day of the third lunar month.
san-gwana·a, *n. pej.* Lit., three-copper (coin) person; a two-bit whore; a streetwalker.
sani, *n.* [sane] **1** A seed; a kernel. **2** Sperm.
sani-mun-tiiru, *n.* A small basket for seeds. [UKH]
sani-neenu·u, *n.* An infertile male.
sani-'nmu, *n.* Seed sweet potatoes. [UKH]
san-jan, *adv.* [sanzan] Severity. ·**nu**, *adj.* Severe; harsh; wretched; miserable;

thorough.

sanji·n-soo, *n.* [sanzesoo] A fortune-teller; a diviner.

san-jun-kuji, *n.* A three-sun (approximately 9 cm or 3.5 in.) nail.

san-ju-rachi, *n.* A rice cooker large enough to cook three *sho* of rice. [UKH] See **tachun**².

san-juu, *n.* [sanjuu] Thirty; thirty years of age.

san-juu-san-ninchi, *n.* [sanjuu-sannenki] Thirty-third anniversary of a death. [OBJ]

san-kaku, *n.* [sankaku] A triangle; triangularity.

san-mee-naabi, *n.* An iron cooking pot. See **shinmeenaabi**.

san-min, *n.* Calculation; reckoning; account.

san-muyuu·shi, *n.* The inception of labor pains.

san-nan, *n.* [sannan] A third son.

san-nin, *n.* A shell ginger plant [*Alpinia speciosa* (Wendl.) K. Schum. var. *speciosa*]. [FOSR] Also **gettoo**.

sannin-jina, *n.* A rope made of **sannin** fiber. [UKH]

san-pin, *n.* Same as **shanpin**.

san-sagi, *n.* Bass tuning in **sanshin** music.

san-san, *adv. onom.* Restlessly; uneasily; nervously.

sansana·a, *n.* **1** A cicada [*Cryptotympana facialis facialis* Walker]. **2** A tomboy; a romping girl. [ODJ] See also **jiijaa**, **naabikachaa**.

san-shii, *n.* [sansei] Agreement; approval. **-sun**, *vi.* [sansei suru] To approve; agree (with).

san-shin, *n.* [C sanxian] A three-stringed musical instrument with a roughly square sound box and a long neck. See **jahibai**, **shibubai**, **wuujiru**, **nakajiru**, **miijiru**, **chiigaa**³, **soo**², **karakui**, **jiifaa**, **mudi**, **kunkunshii**.

sanshin-chukuya·a, *n. colloq.* Same as **sanshinjeeku**. [UKH]

sanshin-haya·a, *n.* Same as **sanshinjeeku**.

sanshin-hicha·a, *n.* A gifted **sanshin** player. [UKH]

sanshin-jeeku, *n.* A **sanshin** maker. [UKH] See **seeku**.

sanshin-jooji, *n.* An expert **sanshin** player. [UKH]

san-ya, *n.* [san-ya] Wasteland; a wilderness; a field; a plain.

sara¹, *n.* [sara] A plate; a dish; a platter; a saucer. See **haachi**, **ufujara**, **uujara**, **chuujara**, **kujara**, **surii**². [GSS]

sara², *n.* A wooden bowl used to pour brine on a salt field. See also **maasudoogu**.

sara-, *pref.* Indicating new or afresh.

sara-banji, *n.* The golden age; the height of prosperity.

sara-gee, *n.* A soup ladle. Same as **nabi-gee**. [GSS]

sara-makutu·u, *n.* A person who is foolishly honest; being honest to a fault.

sara-mii-mun, *n.* Brand new item.

sara-saraa-nami, *n.* [sarasara + nami] Rippling waves; wavelets.

sarashi, *n.* [sarashi] Bleached cotton cloth.

sara·sun, *vt.* [sarasu] **1** To bleach; fade. **2** To expose.

sara-utii, *n.* A prostitute who has not yet sold her first sexual favors. [UKH]

saree·in, *vt.* [saraeru] To dredge (a ditch); clean out (a well).

sari, *interj. adv.* Vocative interjection used by males; same as **sai**¹, but more formal. See also **sai**¹, **tai**¹, **tari**.

saru, *n.* The Monkey, the ninth of the twelve calendrical animal signs. See also **saaruu**.

sarumata, *n.* [sarumata] Men's undershorts.

sasa-minna, *n.* Red pimpernel [J rurihakobe; *Anagallis arvensis* L. var. *arvensis*]. Also **hahaminna**. [GSS, FOSR] *sasariin*

sasari·in, *vi.* [sasareru] To be stabbed; be stung.
sashi, *n.* A leveler used to level the sand in a salt field. See **maasudoogu**.
sashiba, *n.* [sashiba] A falcon; a hawk [*Butastur indicus* (Gmelin)].
sa·shi-chikee, *n.* [sashitsukae] Inconvenience; impediment; objection; trouble; interference.
sa·shi-chima·in, *vi.* [sashitsumaru] **1** To be cornered; be in a fix; be embarrassed for. **2** To come to a deadlock; be stuck.
sa·shi-gusui, *n.* Eyedrops; eyewash.
sa·shi-hanka·a, *n.* An intruder; a presumptuous fellow; a forward person.
sashihanki-gutu, *n.* Intrusion; intervention; meddling.
sashi-hanki·in, *vi.* To intrude; be forward; be officious.
sashi-ishi, *n.* A stone for testing one's lifting strength.
sashika, *n.* An extended sloping roof.
sa·shi-kasa, *n.* A parasol.
sa·shi-ki, *n.* [sashiki] A cutting; a set; cuttage.
sa·shi-ku·mun, *vt.* [sashikomu] Same as **sashinchun**.
sa·shi-kuru·sun, *vt.* [sashikorosu] To stab to death.
sa·shi-mi, *n.* [sashimi] Sliced raw fish.
sa·shi-mun, *n.* [sashimono] Joinery; cabinet work.
sashimun-jeeku, *n.* A cabinetmaker.
sashimun-saa, *n.* Same as **sashimun-jeeku**.
sa-shin, *n.* [shashin] Photograph.
sashi-n·chun, *vt.* To insert; thrust in; put in. Also **sashikumun**.
sa·shi-tumi·in, *vt.* [sashitomeru] To prohibit; forbid; suspend; suppress. [UKH]
sa·sun, *vt.* [sasu] **1** To pierce; thrust; stab; prick. **2** To wear (a sword on one's side). **3** To lift up high.
sata, *n.* [sata] **1** Information. **2** Rumor; reputation. **3** Regards.
sattimu-sattimu, *interj.* [satemo satemo] Indeed; truly; verily (used mostly by women).
satu, *n. poet.* A beau; a lover (term used by female for male). Also **satume(e)**.
satu·in, *vi.* [satoru] To realize; sense; discern; perceive; understand.
satu-me(e), *n. poet.* Beau; lover. Also **satu**.
sawai[1], *n.* Muslin delaine, a lightweight woolen cloth, often printed, used as dress fabric.
sawa·i[2], *n.* [sawari] Illness; abnormality in health.
sawa·in, *vi.* [sawaru] **1** To hinder. **2** To adversely affect. **3** To hurt.
sawa·jun, *vi.* [sawagu] To make a disturbance; be uproarious; be excited.
saya, *n.* [saya] Same as **shii**[2].
sayaka, *n. adv.* [sayaka] Clearly. ·**na**, *adj.* Clear; bright.
sayumi, *n.* A newly woven textile. Also **sayun**.
sa-yuu, *n.* [sayuu] **1** Left and right. **2** Equal in value.
see, *n.* A locust; a grasshopper. See **kamajee**. Also **shee**.
seechi, *n.* Same as **sheechi**.
see-fan, *n.* [C caifan] Rice with chopped vegetables. See also **yuuchiji**, **tunfan**, **chiifan**. [ODJ]
see-gwaa, *n.* A freshwater shrimp. See **see**.
see-jicha·a, *n.* [saizuchi] A mallet. Also **kanajichaa**, **sheejichaa**.
seejuku, *n.* [saisoku] Pressing; urging; a demand. -**sun**, *v.* To press; demand. See **imiin**.
seeki, *n.* [< **sun** + **akiin**[2]] Land reclamation. Also **sheeki**.
seeki·in[1], *vt.* To reclaim (land). Also **sheekiin**[1].
seeki·in[2], *vt.* To dispose of (matters) quickly one by one; finish one by one; bring things to a conclusion. Also

sheekiin[2].
seeki-jii, *n*. Reclaimed land. Also **sheekijii**.
seeku, *n*. [saiku] A carpenter; a craftsman; a technician. Also **sheeku**.
seeku-doogu, *n*. [saikudoogu] Carpenter's tools. See **nukujiri, numi**[1], **kanna, gennoo, banjoogani, hichi**. Also **sheekudoogu**.
seeku-shigutu, *n*. Carpenter's work. Also **sheekushigutu**.
seema, *n*. A tree fairy. See **kijimun**.
see-wee, *n*. [saiwai] Happiness; fortune. Also **sheewee**.
sen-ba, *n*. [senba*] A threshing tool, consisting of a comb-like section through which rice plants are pulled and the grains stripped off. [GSS]
sensuruu, *n*. A mayfly (order Ephemeroptera); a drake-fly. Also **shensuruu**.
Shaaka-ganashii, *n*. The Lord Buddha; Shakyamuni Buddha. Also **Saakaganashii**.
shaakuu, *n*. Same as **saakuu**. See also **hagama**.
shaku[1], *n*. [shaku] 1 A unit of length equivalent to ten **sun**, approximately 0.303 m (0.995 ft.) [NJED]; 2 A measure; a rule; a scale; length. Also **saku**[3].
shaku[2], *n*. [shaku] A unit of capacity equivalent to 0.02 l (0.15 gills); one-tenth of a **goo**. [NJED] Also **saku**[4], **-sa(a)ku**.
shanpin, *n*. [? C xiangpian] A Chinese tea. Also **sanpin**. See **chaa**[3].
shee, *n*. Same as **see**.
shee-chi, *n*. [saichi] 1 Intelligence. 2 An intelligent person; an intelligent and selfish person. [UKH] Also **seechi**.
sheejichaa, *n*. Same as **seejichaa**.
sheeki, *n*. Same as **seeki**.
sheeki·in[1], *vt*. Same as **seekiin**[1].
sheeki·in[2], *vt*. Same as **seekiin**[2].
sheeki-jii, *n*. Same as **seekijii**.
shee-ku, *n*. Same as **seeku**.
sheeku-doogu, *n*. Same as **seekudoogu**.
sheeku-shigutu, *n*. Same as **seeku-shigutu**.
shensuruu, *n*. Same as **sensuruu**.
shee-roo, *n*. [seiroo] A steamer; a steaming basket. [UKH] Same as **kushichii**.
shee-tuuba·a, *n*. Lit., one with flying talent. 1 A greedy person; an avaricious person; a selfish person. [UKH] 2 A clever person; a crafty person.
shee-wee, *n*. Happiness. [UKH] Same as **seewee**.
·shi, *suff*. Verb nominalizer, attached to the apocopated form of a verb; that which...; what...; the one that....
shiba, *n*. A tongue. See also **shicha**[1].
shibai, *n*. [shibai] A drama; a play. See also **wudui**.
shibai-shii, *n*. An actor; an actress.
shibaki, *n*. Wild cinnamon [J yabunikkei; *Cinnamomum japonicum* Sieb. ex nees.]. [UKH]
shiba·san, *adj*. Same as **ibasan**.
shiba-sashi, *n*. Rite to ward away evil, held in the eighth lunar month. [ODJ] See also **yookabii**.
shiba-ya, *n*. A theater.
shibee, *n*. [< **shiba**] A harelip.
shibee·in, *vi*. [sobaeru*] To frolic; be unruly. [UKH]
shibi, *n*. Same as **moomoo**[2]. Also **subi**[2].
shibi-moomoo, *n*. Arabian cowrie [J yakushimadakara; *Cypraea arabica*]; a variety of cowrie that inhabits the shallow shore areas near the low tide line. [MO]
shibi-ranka, *n*. [shibiranga; < C chiwei luanhua] A Taoist magic formula written on a beam in order to invite happiness and drive away misfortune from the household. [ODJ, OBJ]
shibiri, *n*. A small amount of stool; the constipation that is its cause. [UKH]
shibiri·in, *vi*. [shibireru] To become numb; be paralyzed. [UKH]
shibu, *n*. [shibu] Astringent juice (of

shibubai

unripe persimmon or banana); persimmon tannin.
shibu-bai, *n*. [shibuhari] 1 That which is painted with a tanning agent. 2 A **sanshin** with a sounding box covered with Musa banana-fiber paper and tanned with the astringent juice of the banana. See **sanshin**.
shibu-gaki, *n*. [shibugaki] An astringent persimmon. [UKH]
shibui, *n*. A winter melon; wax gourd; Chinese preserving melon [J toogan; *Benincasa hispida* (Thunb) Cogn.].
shi-bu-ichi, *n*. [shibuichi] One-fourth; one quarter.
shibu·i-gara(a), *n*. Bagasse, the residue left after the juice has been extracted from sugar cane. [UKH, OGJ]
shibu·in, *vt*. [shiboru] To wring; squeeze; press; extract.
shibui-wata, *n*. Dysentery; loose bowels with a gripping pain.
shibun-gani, *n*. (A) wire; wiring.
shibu·san, *adj*. [shibui] 1 Astringent; puckery. 2 Rough; obstinate. 3 Sober; chaste; quiet and simple.
shibu·u, *n*. [shibu] That which is astringent and bitter.
shicha[1], *n*. [used only in compounds and set phrases] A tongue. See **shiba**.
shicha[2], *n*. [shita] The lower part; the bottom; the base. Also **hicha**.
shichaara, *n*. The lower area; suburb.
shicha-ba, *n*. A lower tooth.
shicha-bakama, *n*. An underskirt.
shicha-batara·chi, *n*. Lit., low work; a kitchen maid.
shicha-dan, *n*. The lower step (tier); the lower rank; the lower berth. See also 'wiidan.
shicha-dii, *n*. A bribe. See **tii**[1].
shicha-ga·chi, *n*. [shitagaki] A rough copy; a draft.
shicha-gi, *n*. [shitagi] Same as **shichaji**.
shicha-gukuru, *n*. [shitagokoro] A hidden intention; a hidden agenda; an ulterior motive; an underlying motive.
shicha-hiji, *n*. A goatee.
shicha-ji, *n*. Underwear; an undergarment; an undershirt; underclothes; lingerie. Also **shichagi**.
shicha-kata, *n*. The lower classes; the masses.
shicha-nu·i, *n*. [shitanuri] An undercoating.
shicha-shiba, *n*. Lower lip.
shicha-wata, *n*. The lower abdomen.
shicha-yaku, *n*. [shitayaku] A minor employee; an underling; a subordinate official.
shicha-yakunin, *n*. A subordinate government official; an underling.
shichi[1], *n*. [shichi] Pawning; a pledge; hock.
shichi[2], *n*. [shichi] Seven. See **nanachi**.
shi·chi[3], *n*. [suki] ·**na**, *adj*. Liked; fond of; loved.
shichi[4], *n*. [shiki] A ceremony; rituals; rites.
shi-chi[5], *n*. [shiki] The four seasons.
shichi[6], *n*. [shikii] The threshold; the doorsill. Also **fichi**[2].
shichi-bi, *n*. [setsu + hi] Same as **wuimi**.
shichi-bushichi, *n*. Likes and dislikes; taste(s).
shichi-gwachi, *n*. [shichigatsu] 1 July. 2 A popular name for the *Bon* festival, an annual rite held for three days from the thirteenth to the fifteenth of the seventh month of the lunar calendar. See also **bun**[4], **usooroo**. [OBJ] See also **uukui**. Also **hichigwachi**.
shichigwachi-juugunichi, *n*. Lit., the fifteenth day of the seventh lunar month. Same as **bun**[4].
shichigwachi-eisaa, *n*. The *Bon* dance on the night of the fifteenth (or sixteenth) day of the seventh lunar month. Also **hichigwachi'eisaa**.
shichiki[1], *n*. [suetsuke] Furniture that is built into the house.
shichiki[2], *n*. [shitsuke] Discipline;

breeding; upbringing; training children in etiquette and manners at home.
shichiki-gwii, *n.* **1** A built-in closet. **2** A kind of Buddhist altar. See **kwii**[3].
shichiki·in, *vt.* [shitsukeru] **1** To punch; hit; beat; thrash; bully. **2** To scold. **3** To teach manners. Also **hichikiin.**
shi·chi-mun, *n.* [shikimono] A carpet; a rug; a floorcloth; a mattress. See **shichun**[1].
shichi-mushiru, *n.* Matting. Same as **hiramushiru.** See also **mushiru.**
shichiraa, *n.* A sea cucumber; a sea slug; a trepang. [UKH]
shichitan-yuu, *n.* [sekitan + yu] Petroleum; lamp oil; kerosene. Also **danpu'anda.** See also **shichiyu.**
shichi-ya, *n.* [shichiya] A pawnshop.
shichi-yu, *n.* [sekiyu] Petroleum; kerosene; gasoline.
shi·chun[1], *vt.* [shiku] To spread.
shi·chun[2], *vt.* [suku] To like; be fond of.
shi-da·i, *n.* [sudare] A bamboo blind.
shida-kaji, *n.* A cool breeze.
shida·mun, *vi.* [suzumu] To cool oneself; enjoy the cool air.
shida·san, *adj.* [suzushii] Cool; refreshing.
shi-dee[1], *n.* [shidai] **1** Circumstance; reason. **2** Order; precedence.
-shi-dee[2], *suff.* [shidai] As soon as...; at the instant....
shidee·ni, *adv.* Gradually; by and by. Also **shideeshideeni, shireeni.**
shidi-ga-fuu, *n.* Same as **shiduugafuu.**
shidi-gara, *n.* A cast-off skin; a slough; an empty shell. See **shidiin.**
shidi·i, *n.* Emergence (of a bug); growing wings.
shidi·in, *vi.* **1** To be hatched; hatch. **2** To be born (of noble lineage). **3** *vt.* To receive (from a very high-ranking personage).
shiduu, *n.* Same as **shiidu.**
shiduu-ga-fuu, *n. humble* [... + kwahoo*, kahoo] Thanks. **-deebiru,** *phr.*

formal Thank you. Also **shidigafuu.** See also **nifee.**
·shi·ga, *part.* However; but; and yet. See **·shi.**
shiga·in, *vt.* [sugaru] To cling to; hang on; depend on.
shigara-nami, *n.* A tsunami; a tidal wave; a seismic wave. Also **shiga-rinami.**
shigari-nami, *n.* Obsolete form of **shigaranami.**
shiga-ta, *n.* [sugata] Appearance; figure.
shigee-rasa·a, *n.* Same as **kachihooyaa.** [UKH]
shigi·in, *vt.* [suguru] To tie (a thong to a clog); fit (a clog with cords). [GSS]
shigu, *adv.* [sugu] Immediately; right away; as soon as.
shigu-jini, *n.* Same as **shigumaashi.** **-sun,** *v.* To die instantly; die on the spot.
shigu-maashi, *n.* Instantaneous death; instant death. Also **shigujini.**
shigu·sun, *vt.* [sugosu] To pass; exceed; be more than.
shi-gutu, *n.* [shigoto] Work; labor; business; employment; occupation; a task. See **asashigutu, yuushigutu, chushikamashigutu, umishigutu, harushigutu, taashigutu, yamashigutu, seekushigutu, achinee, umisaa, umi'atchaa, harusaa, haru'atchaa, yamasaa, yama'atchaa, shikuchi, waja.**
shigutu-ba, *n.* [shigotoba] The place of one's employment; one's office.
shigutu-jaku·u, *n.* A person who gets irritable and short-tempered under work pressure. [UKH] See **saku**[2].
shigutu-jin, *n.* Work clothes; workaday clothes; coveralls. See **chin**[3].
shigutu-wata, *n.* Warming up after one starts working. [UKH]
shii[1], *n.* [sei] Energy; spirit; vitality; inner power; strength. See also **ichui, shiji**[1].

shii

shii², *n*. [saya] A sheath; a scabbard. Also **saya**.
shii³, *n*. [su] A nest.
shii⁴, *n*. [su] Vinegar. Also **amajaki, suu¹**.
shii⁵, *n*. A rock; a crag.
shii⁶, *interj*. A call to chase away birds and other small animals.
shii⁷, *n*. [sue] The end; the close; the future.
shii⁸, *n*. [se] Rapids (in a river); a torrent; shallows; a shoal. [UKH]
shiibai, *n*. Urine; piss. See also **nama-shiibai**. **-sun**, *v*. To urinate; relieve oneself; piss; pee.
shiibai-bukuru, *n*. The urinary bladder. Also **shiibaijichin**.
shiibai-jaara, *n*. A urinary pot, buried in the ground, from which urine was taken for use as fertilizer. [UKH]
shiibai-jichin, *n*. Same as **shiibaibukuru**. [UKH]
shiibai-kaja, *n*. Urine odor. [UKH]
shiibaya·a, *n*. *pej*. A pisser.
shiibai-yandi, *n*. Gonorrhea; urethritis.
shii-ban, *n*. The last one in an order of anything. [UKH]
shii-bii·san, *adj*. Chilly; rather cold; slightly cold.
shiibu, *n*. A sledge. [ODJ]
shii-bun, *n*. [soebun] An addition; a premium; an extra; a throw-in.
shiichi, *n*. A rectangular stone, serving as an incense burner, placed in front of the door into a tomb. [UKH]
shii·chun, *vi*. To retreat; step back; move over; make room. [UKH] See **shii-kasun, shiikiin**. Also **shijichun**.
shii-daka·san, *adj*. Awe-inspiring; lofty (in a spiritual sense); exalted; spiritual; of high divine power. See also **shijidakasan**.
shii-du, *n*. [? shizu*, ? sendoo] 1 A leader; a boss; the chief; the head; a priest. 2 A beggar saint; same as **ninbuchaa**. Also **shiduu, shiiru**. See **ninbuchaa**.

shiidu-yaa, *n*. A leader of the beggar saints. [UKH]
shiigu, *n*. A pocket knife.
shiigu-doogu, *n*. Knives; cutlery.
shii-gumu·i, *n*. [sugomori] Nesting. **-sun**, *v*. To nest.
shii·in¹, *vi*. [sueru] To spoil; turn sour; go bad; become stale; go rotten. See also **kusariin, kusain²**.
shii·in², *vt*. [soeru] To add; increase; throw an extra in.
shii-ippee, *adv*. [sei-ippai] With all one's might; to the best of one's ability; as hard as possible. [UKH]
shiija, *n*. [? sujoo*] A senior; an elder; the elder siblings, either brother or sister. See **uttu, afii, yatchii**.
shiija-kata, *n*. The elders; the seniors.
shiijakata-shidee, *n*. Arrangement in the order of age or seniority
shiija-wikii, *n*. An elder brother (from his younger sister's viewpoint).
shiija-wunai, *n*. An elder sister (from her younger brother's viewpoint).
shiiji, *n*. [seiji] Governing; politics.
shii-jima, *n*. The last match in sumo wrestling. See **shima³**.
shii-joo, *n*. [? seizo] A person who inspects the quality of brown sugar. [UKH]
shiijoo-nin, *n*. 1 A sugar inspector. 2 A sugar maker. [UKH]
shiijoo-saa, *n*. A stoker; one who tends to the sugar furnace. [UKH]
shii-kaa, *n*. Same as **chiikaa**.
shii-kaja, *n*. Smell of food turned sour. [UKH]
shiika·sun, *vt*. To remove; take away; put out of the way; get rid of. [UKH] See **shiichun**.
shiiki·in, *vt*. To shift; slide; move. [UKH] See **shiichun**.
shii-kwa, *n*. [suika] A watermelon [*Citrullus lanatus* (Thunb.) Matsum. & Nakai].
shii-kwaasa·a, *n*. A **shiikwaasaa** lime

[*Citrus depressa* Hayata]. [ODJ] See also **yunaji**. See **shii**⁴, **kwaasun** (1).
shiikwa-ui, *n*. Same as **shiikwa**. [GSS]
shii-mi, *n*. Diving underwater. **-sun**, *v*. To dive; submerge; swim underwater.
shii-mii, *n*. [seimei] The spring season when the celestial longitude is at 15°, one of the twenty-four seasons of the lunar calendar; the most pleasant season. See also **ushiimii**.
shiimii-chaa, *n*. A general term for the fresh tea produced around the **shiimii** season. See **shiimii**, **chaa**³.
shiimii-nishi, *n*. A chilly northern wind that blows around the time of the **shiimii** season. [UKH]
shiimi-jooji, *n*. A good diver. [UKH]
shii-mun¹, *n*. [sue- + mono] **1** Sour or stale food. **2** Vinegared dish; pickled dish.
shii-mun², *n*. [suimono] Soup. Often **ushiimun**. Also **ushiru**¹.
shiimun-wan, *n*. A soup bowl.
shi·in¹, *vt*. [·ran, ·tchi; shiru] **1** To know; be aware of; learn. **2** To become acquainted with. See also **shitchoon**.
shi·in², *vt*. [suru] To rub; chafe; file.
shii-nari·in, *vi*. [shinareru] To become accustomed to do.
shii-na·sun, *vt*. To finish well; perfect.
shiinoo, *n*. [suinoo*] A fine filter used for liquid or powder; a percolator.
shii-noo·sun, *vt*. [shinaosu] To do over again; try again; begin afresh.
shiira, *n*. Suffering; trouble; disease.
shiiri, *n*. **1** A gutter; a sewer. **2** A night-soil reservoir.
shiiru, *n*. Same as **shiidu**.
shii·sa, *n*. Acidity; sourness.
shiisa·a, *n*. [shishi] A gargoyle in the form of a lion-dog, usually placed on top of the house roof to drive away evil. See **shiishi**¹.
shiisa-amasa·a, *n*. That which is sweet and sour.
shiisaa-moo·i, *n*. Same as **shiishimooi**.

shiisaa-waawuu, *n*. *slang* An ugly-looking person like a pottery **shiisaa** dog. See **shiisaa**, **waawuu**. [GSS]
shii·san, *adj*. Sour; acid; tart.
shii-shi¹, *n*. [shishi] **1** A lion; a lion-dog, specifically the mystical lion in the traditional Chinese image. **2** A lion dance such as that held on the fifteenth night of the eighth lunar month in most villages and towns. See **shiisaa**.
shiishi², *n*. [susu] Soot.
shii-shichi, *n*. [seishitsu] Nature; disposition; temperament; character.
shii-shii, *n*. *inf. onom*. Urine; pee-pee.
shiishii-dama, *n*. Same as **shishidama**. [FOSR]
shiishi-moo·i, *n*. A lion dance, usually held on the night of August 15.
shiishi·nu-shiru, *n*. Soup with meat.
shii·ti, *adv*. [shiite] Forcibly; against one's will.
-shiiti, *suff*. Including; inclusive of; together with. See **shiin**².
shii-tu, *n*. [seito] A student; a pupil; a schoolboy; a schoolgirl. See also **gakushii**.
shii-tujuma·in, *vi*. To have it finished; have it completed. [UKH] Same as **tujimain**.
shii-tujumi·in, *vt*. To finish; complete; perfect; get through with. [UKH] Same as **tujimiin**.
shii-ushi, *n*. The last match in a bullfight. [UKH]
shii-uwa·in, *vt. emph*. [< J shiowaru] To complete; finish; conclude. See **sun**¹.
shii-wuuki, *n*. A rice bin. Also **kumi-wuuki**. See **shimudoogu**.
shii-yan·ji, *n*. Failure; blunder; mistake.
shii-yan·jun, *vt*. [·dan, ·ti] To fail to accomplish; be unsuccessful in doing; make a mistake; commit a blunder.
shii-yas·san, *adj*. [...**shiku**; shiyasui] **1** Easy to do. **2** Easy to live.
shii-yoo, *n*. [shiyoo] A method; a way; a remedy; a course.

shi-jama, *n.* [shizama] A bad attitude; a plight; a predicament.

shiji[1], *n.* Deity; divine power; divine spirit. See also **shii**[1].

shiji[2], *n.* [suji] **1** Line; lineage; paternal relation. **2** Logic; reason. **3** Line; plot. **4** Fiber.

shiji[3], *n.* [sugi] A Japanese cedar; a cryptomeria.

shiji[4], *n.* [suzu] Tin.

-shiji, *suff.* [suji] A counter for slender things.

shijichi, *n.* A small lighting device made of zinc or tin-plate, fueled by rapeseed oil or petroleum.

shiji·chun, *vi.* Same as **shiichun**.

shiji-daka-dukuru, *n.* A place that harbors great spiritual power, often a sacred grove. See **utaki**.

shiji-daka·san, *adj.* Possessing great spiritual power.

shinji-gusui, *n.* [senjigusuri] Medical decoction.

shiji·in[1], *vt.* [senjiru] To decoct; make a decoction; infuse. Also **shinjiin**.

shiji·in[2], *vi.* **1** To pass (by); go past; pass through. **2** To elapse; go on; go by; expire; be out. **3** To exceed; pass; be above; be over; be more than.

shijika, *n.* [shizuka] Quiet; stillness.

shiji-kami·in, *vi.* To place spiritual power on the head, the act of receiving spiritual power, performed by a priestess on taking office. See **kamiin**.

shijimi·in, *vt.* [shizumeru] To arrange in order; put to rights; tidy up (a room).

shiji·mun, *vi.* [shizumu] **1** To sink; be submerged; go down. **2** To feel subdued.

shi-jin, *n.* [shizen] **1** Nature. **2** Natural phenomena.

shi-jin·ni, *adv.* [shizen] Naturally.

shijiri, *n.* [suzuri] An ink slab.

shiji-tada·shi, *n.* **1** Lineage clarification. **2** Insistence on abiding by family succession taboos. See **tachiimajikui**, **winagugwansu, choodeekasabai, ichukukasabai, chatchi'ushikumi**. [OBJ, ODJ]

shi-juu, *n.* [shijuu] Forty; forty years old.

shijuu-kunichi, *n.* The Buddhist memorial service on the forty-ninth day after a death. See **nanka, suukoo**.

shika, *n.* [< J shika] A deer.

shika·a, *n.* A coward; a poltroon; a recreant.

shika-boo, *n.* Same as **shikaa**.

shi-kaki, *n.* [shikake] **1** A device; a contrivance; a mechanism; a trick. **2** A beginning; a sign of beginning.

shikaki·in, *vt.* [shikakeru] **1** To begin to do; set about; start; commence. **2** To challenge; bid defiance to; strive.

shi-kaku, *n.* [shikaku] A square; a quadrilateral. (Also **shikkaku**.)

shikaku·u, *n.* Something square. (Also **shikkakuu**.)

shikama(·a), *n.* A serf-like laborer òr such a laborer in the employ of the landed rich. [ODJ] See also **irichiri**.

shika·mun[1], *vi.* To fear; be afraid; be frightened; be scared.

shika-mun[2], *n.* A coward. See **shikaa**.

shika·n, *vt.* [sukanu] To dislike; hate; abhor.

shika-raa·s(h)an, *adj.* Lonely; lonesome; deserted.

shikara·shi, *n.* Experience.

shikara·sun, *vt.* To experience; go through; undergo; have a personal knowledge of; master.

shika·san, *adj.* Cowardly; timid; fainthearted. See **shikaa, shikama(a)**.

shikashi·i-maashi·i, *n.* Coaxing, humoring. **-sun**, *v. emph.* To coax; humor; cajole. See **shikasun**.

shika·sun, *vt.* [sukasu] **1** To coax; humor. **2** To cajole. **3** To dupe; delude.

shi-kata, *n.* [shikata] **1** A way; a method. **2** (In negative sense) state of affairs; things.

shikata·a neen, *phr.* [shikata ga nai] Cannot help (it); (it) cannot be helped; it is no use (doing); there is no use in (doing).
shika·tu, *adv.* [shikato] For sure; for certain; surely; positively; clearly.
shika-ware·e, *n.* A diffident smile; a timid laugh. See **shikaa**.
shi-kee, *n.* [sekai] The world.
shiki·in, *vt.* 1 To set; place; stabilize. 2 To get food ready to cook; get a cooking pot ready.
shi-kin, *n.* [seken] The world; society; life.
shikin-banashi, *n.* [seken-banashi] Small talk; gossip; chat.
shikin-nami, *n.* [sekennami] Average; ordinary; common.
shikin-uman'chu, *n.* Masses of people; the masses; the people; the populace.
shik-kan, *n.* [sekkan] Corporal punishment (to discipline a child).
shikkwa, *n.* A wedge; a chock; an object put under a thing so that it will not move. Also **kusabi**.
shikoo·i, *n.* Preparation; readiness.
shikoo·i-mukoo·i, *n. emph.* (Various) preparations. **-sun**, *v.* To make all sorts of preparations; get ready in various ways. [GSS, UKH]
shikoo·in, *vt.* To ready; prepare; arrange; provide.
shikubuu, *n.* An unfloored part of a kitchen. Also **sukubuu**.
shi-kuchi, *n.* Work; labor; business; toil; employment; a task; an occupation; a mission. Also **shigutu, waja**.
shikuchi-saa, *n.* A worker; a laborer; a wage earner.
shi-ku·mi, *n.* [shikumi] 1 Contrivance; device. 2 Plan; plot.
shi-ku·mun, *vt.* [shikomu] To plan; contrive; train.
shima[1], *n.* [shima] 1 A village; a community. 2 One's home village. 3 One's fief. 4 An island.

shima[2], *n.* [shima] A textile design.
shima[3], *n.* [sumoo] Wrestling, particularly of Okinawan style. See also **nushi**[1], **nushigwaa, hijainushi, machigwaa, tiinujaa, meegaki, tin-meegaki, ninjaagwaa, Uchinaajima, shimanaa**[1]. [OBJ]
shima·a, *n.* 1 A villager. 2 A local product; a local person. See **shima**[1].
shima-ajami, *n.* A thistle [*Cirsium brevicaule* A. Gray var. *brevicaule*]. See **ajama, chibana**.
shima-bare·e, *n.* An exile to an island. [UKH]
shima-chabi, *n.* Unavoidable pains and sorrows of living on an isolated island such as Okinawa.
shi-machi, *n.* [shimatsu] 1 Circumstances; facts of a case; the particulars. 2 Management; dealing; disposal; settlement. [UKH]
shima-chideekuni, *n.* Carrots grown in Okinawa; local carrots.
shima-chinnan, *n.* Indigenous snails. [UKH]
shima-gachuu, *n.* Local bonito. See **kachuu**.
shima-gumi, *n.* Native rice grown in Okinawa, in contrast to imported rice. See **jiimee**.
shima-guni, *n.* [shimaguni] An island country.
shima-guni-kunjoo, *n.* Insularism; provincialism.
shima-gusarasa-naa, *n.* Same as **shimakusarashi**.
shima-ijai, *n.* A plow of which only the blade is iron, used for plowing with cattle. [GSS]
shima-in, *n.* A native dog.
shima-kankaa, *n.* Same as **shimakusarashi**.
shima-kii-ui, *n.* Native cucumber.
shima-kusarashi, *n.* An annual rite to keep epidemics away from a village, usually carried out in the second lunar

shimakutuba

month. Also **shimagusarasanaa**. See also **muranukeeshi**. [ODJ]

shima-kutuba, *n*. Language of one's native locality.

shima-maa·i, *n*. A ritual round of the village by the village priestess accompanied by the **niitchu** and other male functionaries.

shima-migu·i, *n*. Same as **shimamaai**. [UKH]

shima-naa[1], *n*. A sumo wrestling arena.

shima-naa[2], *n*. Local greens [J takana; *Brassica juncea* Czern. et Crosson var. *integrifolia* Sinsk.]. [FOSR, ODJ] Also **naa**[9].

shima-naga·shi, *n*. [shimanagashi] Exile; banishment.

shima-nchu, *n*. A person from one's own village; a fellow villager.

shima-raki, *n*. Indigenous bamboo used for making barrel hoops. [UKH] See **daki**.

shima-rui, *n*. Indigenous chickens. [UKH] See **tui**.

shima-runai, *n*. The next village; the next island. [UKH] See **tunai**.

shima·sun, *vt*. [sumasu] **1** To finish; get through with; go through; conclude. **2** To make do with; manage with.

shima-tu·in, *vi*. To wrestle, particularly in the Okinawan style. See **shima**[3].

shimatuya·a, *n*. A wrestler.

shima-u-koo, *n*. Local incense. Same as **hira'ukoo**.

shima-uta, *n*. A song of one's own village; one's own home songs.

shima-yama, *n*. A plow only the blade of which is iron. See **yaama**.

shi-me·e, *n*. [sumai] Address; home.

shimee-ka, *n*. A dwelling; a residence; a home.

shimi[1], *n*. [sumi] **1** Chinese ink; an ink stick. **2** Learning; study. Also **gakumun**, **tishimigakumun**.

shimi[2], *n*. [sumi] A corner. Also **katashimi**.

shimi[3], *n*. [sumi] Charcoal. Also **tan**[2].

shimi[4], *n*. [shimi] A stain; a blot; a spot; a smut; a smear; a smudge.

shimichi, *n*. Same as **fimichi**. [GSS]

shimi-chibu, *n*. [sumitsubo] A carpenter's ink pad.

shimi·in[1], *vt*. [semeru] **1** To attack; assault. **2** To condemn; censure; criticize.

shimi·in[2], *vt*. [(se)shimeru] To make (someone) do (something); cause (a person) to do; force (a person) to do.

shimi·in[3], *vt*. [shimeru] **1** To tie up; tighten; strangle; wring. **2** To shut; close.

shimiji, *n*. [shimeji] A champignon; an edible mushroom, esp. the meadow mushroom. [UKH].

shimikee·in, *vi*. To moisten; become damp.

shimiki, *n*. [shimerike] Moisture; humidity.

shimi-kuru·sun, *vt*. To strangle (a person) to death.

shimi-naa[1], *n*. A carpenter's inking line.

shimi-naa[2], *n*. A line used to fasten roofing thatch. See **shimiin**[3].

shimi-nchu, *n*. In premodern Okinawa, a commoner who could read and write. See **shimi**[1], **tchu**.

shimi-raara, A sack of charcoal. See **taara**.

shimi-san, *n*. Learning. [UKH]

shimi-shimi-sun, *v*. To become moist; become humid. [UKH]

shimiya·a, *n*. A person who fastens roofing thatch. See **shimiin**[3].

shimi-yee, *n*. [semeai] Attacking each other. [UKH]

shimu[1], *n*. [shimo] **1** A lower place; a distant place (from the capital). **2** A kitchen. Also **deeju**, **tungwa**.

shimu[2], *n*. [shimo] Cold shower in early winter.

shimu-batara·chi, *n*. A servant hired to do kitchen work. See **hatarachun**.

shi-muchi[1], *n*. [shomotsu] Same as

sumuchi.
shimuchi[2], *n.* Personality; character; disposition; temper.
shimu-chichi, *n.* November.
shimuchi-waru·u, *n.* A mean person; a mean personality.
shimu-doogu, *n.* Kitchen tools and utensils. See also **kamanta, naabinufuta, chaanaabi, imunyakkwan, yakkwan, yakwan, hagama, shaakuu, deefaa, shirikuji, riiji, niibu, mishigee, nabigee, hoochaa, marucha, wanbuu, sunkan, sara**[1]**, makai, shirumakai, anbin, umeeshi, meeshi**[1]**, kee**[1]**, ujin, kumiwuuki, shiiwuuki, banin, fiichin, naabidoogu**.
shimu-jimu, *n.* [shimojimo] The lower class. Same as **shichakata, shimukata**.
shimu-kakiya·a, *n.* A shower in late autumn or early winter. [GSS]
shimu-kata, *n.* 1 The lower region; the Shimajiri area; area distant from the capital. 2 The lower class.
shimu-ku, *n.* The second half of a **Ruuka** poem; the lower two hemistichs of a **Ruuka**. See **Ruuka**.
shi·mun[1], *vi.* [sumu] 1 To end; terminate; be concluded. 2 To be sufficient; have no need.
shi·mun[2], *vi.* [sumu] To become clear; clear; clarify; become lucid.
shimu-nai, *n.* Fruit grown near the top end of a vine, usually smaller and less healthy. Also **suuranai**. See also **niinai**.
shimuru, *n.* An egg that does not hatch. [UKH]
shin[1], *n.* 1 [san] A locking device on a sliding door. 2 [sen] A stopper; a stopcock; a plug; a tap.
shin[2], *n.* [sen] 1 Effect; result. 2 Worth. 3 Use.
shin[3], *n.* [shin] 1 The core; the nucleus. 2 Mind; one's right mind; one's senses. 3 One's conscience; real motive. 4 A lamp wick. 5 A tip (of a twig or a leaf).
shin[4], *n.* [sen] One thousand.

shin[5], *n.* [shin] The new calendar; the solar calendar.
shin[5], *n.* [sen] A line.
shina[1], *n.* [suna] Sand; grit. Also **uru, yuni**.
shina[2], *n.* [shina] A thing; an article.
shina[3], *n.* [shina] 1 Elegance; grace. 2 Fine character; quality.
shina-ba, *n.* [sunaba] A sandbox; a sand pit.
shina-ganiku, *n.* Sandy soil; the sands. Also **shinaji**. [UKH] See **kaniku**.
shina-hama, *n.* [sunahama] A sandy beach. [UKH]
shina·in, *vi.* [·ran, ·ti; shinau] Same as **uchain**.
shina-ji, *n.* [sunaji] Same as **shinaganiku**.
shina-jiri, *n.* [shinagire] Being out of stock; being sold out.
shina-mun, *n.* [shinamono] A thing; an article; merchandise.
shi-nasaki, *n.* [shinasake] 1 Sympathy; compassion. 2 Affection; love.
shina-shina·a, *n. emph.* Imminent death, moribundity. **-sun**, *vi.* To be about to die.
shin-baai, *n.* A pillar or post in the four corners of a house. [UKH]
shin-ba·i, *n.* [shinbari] A bolt or a bar used to lock a door.
shin-bichi, *n.* [senbetsu] A farewell gift; a farewell present.
shin-bii, *n.* [senbei] A flat rice cracker.
shinboo, *n.* [shinboo] An axle; a shaft; an arbor; a piston rod; a stem (of a top).
shi·n-chiri·in, *vi.* To become perfectly clear; be crystal clear.
shindaka·sun, *vt.* [suberakasu*] Let slip; slide; glide.
shindan, *n.* [sendan] Chinaberry; Persian lilac; Pride-of-India [*Melia azedarach* L.]. [FOSR]
-shindee, *n.* [shidai] As soon as; in order. See also **-shidee**[2].

shindi·in, *vt.* [suberu] **1** To slide; glide; skate. **2** To slip.
shin-doo[1], *n.* Same as **shinroo**.
shin-doo[2], *n.* A memorial service; a mass for the dead. [UKH] **-sun**, *v.* To hold a memorial service.
shin-duu, *n.* [sendoo] A captain (of a ship); a mariner.
shinduu-suu, *n.* Honorable captain (of a ship).
shin-gwachi, *n.* [shigatsu] April.
shingwee-wuuki, *n.* A large bucket for night soil. [UKH]
shini, *n.* [sune] The shank.
shinibu, *n.* Same as **chinubi**.
shi·ni-gaataa, *n.* Being about to die. [UKH]
shi·ni-gau, *n.* [shinigao] A dead face; a death mask.
shini-gi, *n.* [sunege] The hair on the shank.
shi·ni-mabui, *n.* Dead spirit; dead soul; the spirit of the recently deceased. See also **mabui'uui, geen, joochijiri, suugeeshi**. [OBJ]
shi-nin, *n.* [shinin] A dead person; a corpse (when the death has resulted from accident or violence).
Shiniri-chuu, *n.* The male creator deity in the Okinawan creation myth recorded in the *Omoro sōshi*. Also **Shirunichuu**. See also **umuru**.
Shiniri-ku, *n.* Same as **Shinirichuu**.
shi·ni-tchu, *n.* A dead person (as opposed to a living one). See also **shinin, ichitchu**. [UKH]
shi·ni-yanja·a, *n.* One who has failed at suicide. See **-yanjun**.
shin-ji, *n.* [senji] Decoction; decocted soup. See also **shinjimun**.
shin-jichi, *n.* [shinjitsu] **1** Truth; reality; fact. **2** Sincerity; honesty; kindness.
shinji-gusui, *n.* [senjigusuri] A medical decoction; an infusion.
shin-ji·in[1], *vt.* [shinjiru] To trust; believe; accept as true.

shin-ji·in[2], *vt.* [senjiru] To boil; decoct; infuse; make a decoction of.
shinji-mun, *n.* [senjimono] A decoction; an infusion; nutritious food; a nourishing meal. Also **shinji**. See also **taa'iyushinji, kuu'iyushinji, irabuushinji, chimushinji, nachoorashinji, njanafuuchibaa**. [ODJ]
shin-ju, *n.* [senzo] **1** Ancestor; ancestry. **2** An ancestral tomb.
shin-ka, *n.* [shinka] **1** A vassal; a retainer; a subject. **2** One's family member; one's colleague; one's friend.
shin-kee, *n.* [shinkei] **1** A mentally ill person; a deranged person; an insane person. **2** Insanity; madness.
shin-kuchi, *n.* [senkotsu] The washing of the bones of a deceased person, performed by the females of the family assisted by the males. **-sun**, *v.* To perform the bone-washing ritual. See **sakamiji, jiishigaami, tanabata, arain, gireein, churakunasun, karukunasun, chukuriin, harujuukoo**. [ODJ, OBJ]
shinmeehan-naabi, *n.* An iron cooking pot. See **shinmeenaabi**.
shinmee-naabi, *n.* A large conical iron pot, chiefly used for boiling sweet potatoes; a cauldron. See also **ninmeenaabi, sanmeenaabi, shinmeehannaabi, gunmeenaabi**. [ODJ]
shin-mi, *n.* **1** The pivot. **2** A vital point; a pivot; a linchpin.
shin-nin, *n.* [sennin] A hermit; one who through meditation and ascetic practices has acquired supernatural powers.
shin·nu, *adj.* [shinno] Proper; correct; orthodox.
shinri-goosaa, *n.* Pushing a fist hard and sliding it off instead of hitting with a fist. See **shindiin, koosaa**[1].
shin-roo, *n.* [shinroo] Anxiety; concern; care; apprehension. Also **shindoo**[1]. **-sun**, *vi.* To be anxious; worry; be concerned.

shin-shii, *n*. [sensei] A teacher; a master.
shin-soogwachi, *n*. New Year's Day according to the solar calendar.
shinta, *n*. A lid for a cauldron. [GSS] Also **hinta, kamanta**.
shin-taku, *n*. [sentaku] Washing; laundry; cleaning. **-sun**, *vt*. To do laundry; to wash.
shin-taku-mun, *n*. [sentakumono] The wash; the washing; the laundry.
shintaku-yaa, *n*. [sentakuya] 1 A laundry; a washing-house. 2 A laundryman; a laundrywoman; a cleaner.
shin-tii, *n*. [shintei] The bottom of one's heart; one's inner thoughts; one's motive.
shinubi, *n. lit*. [shinobi] 1 Incognito travel; a private visit. 2 A rendezvous; an assignation. 3 A secret agent; a spy.
shinu·bun, *vi*. [shinobu] 1 To bear; stand; endure. 2 To conceal oneself; hide oneself; meet clandestinely.
shinugu, *n*. A rite, usually in the seventh lunar month, of passing from the harvest to the start of a new cycle of planting or for purification and to invoke a rich harvest. [ODJ, OBJ]
shinu·jun, *vt*. [shinogu] 1 To endure; bear; stand; keep out. 2 To pull through; tide over.
shi·nun, *vi*. [·nan, ·ji; shinu] (Traditionally, of animals or due to unnatural circumstances) to die; be gone; be killed. See also **maasun**. [OGJ, UKH].
shipita·i-mun, *n*. A weakling; a coward.
shipita·in, *vi*. To be disheartened; be discouraged; be ruined; sink in fortune.
shipitaya·a, *n*. Same as **shipitaimun**.
shippee, *adv*. With all one's might; to the best of one's ability; to the utmost.
shippira·a, *n. pej*. 1 That which is flat. 2 A person short in height; a shorty.
shippiraka·sun, *vt*. To flatten; collapse; deflate.

shiragiin

shippiraki·in, *vi. emph*. (Of a balloon) to deflate; (of a box or bag) to flatten. Same as **shippiriin**.
shippiri·in, *vi*. To collapse flat; be crushed flat. [UKH] Also **shippirakiin**.
shippu·in, *vt*. [? suu] To suck; suckle; chew.
shipu-gufaa, *n*. Same as **hirafagusa**. [GSS]
shipu-gusa, *n*. Same as **hirafagusa**. [GSS]
shipukara·san, *adj*. [shiokarai] Same as **suujuusan**.
shipu·san, *adj*. Sinewy and tough. See also **shipuu, sakusan**. [UKH]
shiputa·in, *vi*. To become damp, especially damp and salty. See **shittain**.
shiputa·i-na·chi, *n*. Prolonged weeping; crying on and on.
shiputaya·a, *n*. A stubborn person; a resolute, tenacious person.
shipu·u, *n*. A thing or person that is sinewy and tough. See also **shipusan**. [UKH]
shira-akaga·i, *n*. Dawn; daybreak; morning twilight.
shira-aki, *n*. Dawn; break of day. [UKH]
shiraa-kusaa, *n*. All directions. [UKH]
shira-bee, *n*. Tinea, or ringworm, of the face, a disease which causes loss of pigment resulting in white patches of skin. [IOJ]
shirabi, *n*. [shirabe] An examination; an inspection; an inquiry.
shirabi·in, *vt*. [shiraberu] To investigate; examine; survey; study.
shirabi-mun, *n*. [shirabemono] A matter for study; a matter for enquiry.
shira-fujoo, *n*. Lit., white impurity, a reference to a taboo about childbirth in Miyako and Yaeyama. [ODJ].
shira-ga, *n*. Same as **shiragi**.
shiraga·a, *n. pej*. A gray-haired person.
shira-gi, *n*. Gray hair. Also **shiraga**.
shiragi-gumi, *n*. Polished (cleaned) rice.
shiragi·in, *vt*. [shirageru] To clean rice;

shiraginami

polish rice. Also **chichun**[5].
shiragi-nami, *n*. White-crested waves on the reefs. [UKH]
shiragi-nuja·a, *n*. Tweezers for removing gray hairs. See **nujun**[2].
shira-hama, *n*. [shirahama] White sandy beach.
shirai[1], *n*. [shiroari] A termite.
shirai[2], *n*. A rattan blind. [UKH]
shirakaji, *n*. A cool breeze. [UKH]
shirama·a, *n*. One who has lice.
shiran, *n*. [shirami] A louse; lice.
shira-nami, *n*. [shiranami] White-crested waves; whitecaps; breakers.
shira·n-chu, *n*. [shiranu hito] A stranger.
shiran-fuuna·a, *n*. Feigned ignorance.
shirashi, *n*. [shirase] **1** Information; a report. **2** News. **3** An omen.
shira·sun, *vt*. [shirasu*] To report; notify; inform.
shiree·ni, *adv*. Same as **shideeni**.
shiree-shiree·ni, *adv*. See **shideeni**.
shiri-bisa, *n*. A rear leg (of a four-legged animal). See **meebisa**, **hisa**.
shiri-chi·in, *vt*. To cut by rubbing. See **shiin**[2].
shiri-gafuu, *interj*. Same as **shidigafuu**.
shiri-gara, *n*. A cast-off skin; exuviae; a slough. See **shidiin**.
shiri-guru, *n*. Same as **shirigara**.
shiri-hachi, *n*. Same as **deefaa**.
shiri-ha·jun, *vt*. To graze; abrade; chafe.
shiri·i, *n*. Same as **deekunishirii**.
shiri·in, *vi*. Same as **shidiin**.
shi·ri-kiji, *n*. [surikizu] A scratch; a bruise; a graze; an abrasion.
shi·ri-kuji, *n*. [surikogi] A wooden pestle. Also **riiji**[1].
shi·ri-ku·mun, *vt*. To rub in; grind and mix.
shi·ri-uushi, *n*. [suriusu] A huller; a grinding mortar. Also **'nnishiri'uushi**, **'nnishirishirii**. [GSS]
shi·riyee, *n*. [shiriai] An acquaintance.
shiru, *n*. [shiru] **1** Soup; sap; juice. **2** Broth. **3** Liquid. See also **nnsunushiru**, **suushiru**, **shiishinushiru**, **ushiru**, **duujiru**.
shiru-guma, *n*. White sesame.
shiru-ha·in, *vi*. For food such as vegetables to exude water as a part of the process of decay. Also **ashihain**.
shiru-hira·shi, *n*. Desiccation of a corpse. See also **shinkuchi**. [ODJ]
shiru-iifee, *n*. The custom of wrapping the mortuary tablet with white paper, on which is written the posthumous name of the deceased. [ODJ] See also **iifee**.
shiru-indoo, *n*. Green pea [*Pisum sativum* L.]. [FOSR] See **induumaami**.
shiru-jaataa, *n*. [shirozatoo] White sugar; refined sugar. See also **saataa**.
shiru-ji, *n*. [shiroji] **1** A white (back)ground. **2** A white fabric; white clothes.
shiru-kabi, *n*. [shirokami] White paper.
shiru-kani, *n*. [shirokane*] Tin.
shirukuchi-maakuchi, *n*. On all four sides; everywhere.
shiru-makai, *n*. A soup bowl.
shiru-mi, *n*. [shiromi] **1** The white of an egg; albumen. **2** The fat of pork, chicken, etc. Also **shirumii**.
shiru-mii, *n*. [shirome] The white of the eye.
shiru-naabi, *n*. A soup pot.
shiru-na·in, *vi*. To liquefy; to melt.
Shiruni-chuu, *n*. Same as **Shinirichuu**.
shiru-nna[1], *n*. Same as **hijainaa**.
shiru-nna[2], *n*. A clam. See also **taanna**.
shiru-nunu, *n*. [shironuno] White cloth.
shiru·san, *adj*. White; fair (of skin complexion).
shirushi, *n*. [shirushi] A sign; a mark; a badge; a memento; an emblem; an omen; foreboding.
shiru-shina, *n*. White sand.
shiru-shita, *n*. [shiroshita] Molasses.
shiru-tchu, *n*. [shirohito*] An albino.
shiru·u, *n*. [shiro] White (color). **·nu**, *adj*. White.

shiru·u-kuru·u, *n.* [shirokuro] **1** White and black. **2** Good and bad; innocent or guilty. **3** (In politics) the orthodox faction and the opposition faction; progressive faction and the conservative faction.

shishi, *n.* [shishi] Dietary meat, such as pork, beef, goat, chicken, and rabbit, etc. See also **mashishi, masshi, mashisaa, andajishi, shirumi, murushi, andakashi, minbui, suujikii, andansu(u), nakaminushiimun, ashitibichi, mii³, 'waanushishi, ushinushishi, 'nmanushishi, hiijaashishi**.

shishi-burii, *n.* Shivering; trembling; shuddering. **-sun**, *v.* To shiver (with cold); tremble (with fear); shudder (with horror). See **furiin¹**.

shishi-dama, *n.* Rosary bead; Job's tears [J juzudama; *Coix lachryma-jobi* L. var. *lachryma-jobi*]. [ODJ, OGJ] Also **shiishiidama**.

shishi·i-kutuba, *n.* Polite language; an honorific term. See **shishiin¹**.

shishi·in¹, *vt.* To take extra care; be polite; be attentive.

shishi·in², *vt.* [susuru] To sip; sup; suck up.

shishi-kwe·e-gasa, *n.* A variety of scab on one's back. [UKH]

shishi-machi, *n.* Meat market (for animal meat such as pork and beef).

shishimi·in, *vt.* [susumeru] **1** To recommend. **2** To persuade.

shishi·mun, *vi.* [susumu] To advance; go forward; move on.

shi-shoo, *n.* [shishoo] A teacher; an instructor, especially of traditional and performing arts.

shitaga·in, *vi.* [·(r)an, ·ti; shitagau] To obey; submit oneself to; yield to.

shitai, *interj.* [? shitari] Well done! Good work!

shi-taku, *n.* [shitaku] Readiness; preparation; dressing up; outfitting. **-sun**, *v.* To get ready; prepare.

shita-kwee-munu-i·i, *n.* Indistinct and unclear speech as if the speaker were eating his tongue. [UKH]

shitari·in, *vi.* [sutareru] To fall into disuse; go out of use; become obsolete; become outmoded.

shita-taka, *n. adv.* [shitataka] Terrible; terribly.

shitataka-mun, *n.* A rowdy person; a roughneck.

shi-tati·in, *vt.* [shitateru] **1** To prepare; make a custom order; make especially for. **2** To raise (an animal). **3** To grow (a plant).

shit-chi, *n.* [shikke] Humidity; moisture.

shitchoo·n, *vt.* [< **shiin¹**] To know. See **shiin¹**.

shiti-gara, *n.* Things abandoned; things thrown away as useless; junk.

shitigara-mun, *n.* A person who is as unwanted as useless junk.

shiti·in, *vt.* [suteru] To discard; cast aside; throw away; abandon. Also **hitiin**.

shiti-maku, *n.* A very naughty child; a daring person; a daredevil.

shitimiti, *n.* Morning. Also **sutumiti, hitimiti**.

shitimiti-mun, *n.* Breakfast. Also **hitimitimun**. See also **asaban¹, yuuban**.

shiti-u·i, *n.* [suteuri] A sacrifice sale. **-sun**, *v.* To sell at a sacrifice; sell cheaply. Also **yashi'ui**.

shitta·in, *n.* **1** To become wet. **2** To become damp. See **shiputain**.

shitta-ka·a, *n.* [shittaka(buri)] A person who talks big without really knowing the subject; a braggart with a haughty demeanor; a know-it-all.

shitu, *n.* [shuuto] Parents-in-law. See also **wikigashitu, winagushitu**.

shitu-uya, *n.* [shuutooya] Parents-in-law. See **shitu**.

shi-uwa·in, *vt.* [shiowaru] To accomplish; finish.

shiwa

shiwa[1], *n.* [sewa] Care; anxiety. **-sun**, *vi.* To worry; be nervous.
shiwa[2], *n.* [shiwa] Wrinkles; lines; furrows; crow's feet.
shi-waashi, *n.* [shiwasu] December.
shiwa-gutu, *n.* A sorrow; a worry.
shiwa-sa·a, *n.* A person with a habit of worrying; nervous personality.
shiyawashi, *n.* [shiawase] Happiness.
shi-yoo, *n.* [shiyoo] A method; a way; how to do.
shiyoo-muyoo, *adv.* Being ready; preparedly. [UKH]
shi-zama, *n.* [shizama] **1** An act. **2** An attitude. **3** A deed.
shonga-nee, *n.* [?< J shoo ga nai] A type of Okinawan folk song characterized by the theme of sadness of parting.
shoo-boo, *n.* [shooboo] Firefighting.
shoo-jichi, *n.* [shoojiki] Honesty. **·na**, *adj.* Honest.
shoojin-naa, *n.* [shoojin + nawa] Same as **hijainaa**.
Shui, *n.* Shuri, former capital of the Ryukyu Kingdom, presently a part of Naha City. Also **Sui**.
Shui-dara·a, *n. pej.* The easy and indulgent manner of Shuri people.
Shui-kutuba, *n.* Shuri speech. Also **Suikutuba**.
Shui-nchu, *n.* A person of Shuri. Also **Suinchu**.
Shui-tin-ganashi, *n.* His Majesty who reigns in Shuri (referring to the Ryukyuan king). Also **Suitinjanashi**. See **-ganashii**.
shu-jin, *n.* [shujin] **1** Husband. **2** Master or proprietor. **3** The host; the hostess. See also **nuushi**.
shuku, *n. arch.* Same as **suku**[1].
shu-muchi, *n.* [shomotsu] Same as **sumuchi**.
shu-nin, *n.* [shonin] Various people; a crowd. [UKH]
shuu-bata, *n.* Beach; seaside.
shuu-kaa-wata·i·nu wugami, *n.* A funerary rite for one who has died overseas; a ritual homecoming for the soul of such a deceased person. See **yanajini**. [ODJ]
shuu-nii, *n.* [shio + ni] Cooked with salt seasoning only, particularly of fish.
shuu·nu-hana, *n.* [shionohana] Salt sprinkled for ritual purification.
shuuraa·s(h)an, *adj.* [shiorashii] Sweet; tender; gentle.
shuu-shin, *n.* [shuushin] Devotion; love; setting one's heart on.
shuu-tee, *n.* [shotai] A household.
shuutee-doogu, *n.* [shotaidoogu] Household goods. See also **tanshi, yoofukudanshi, suku**[1]**, ujin, umeeshi, danpu, naabi, kama**[2]**, hoochaa, manacha, kumibaku, taaree, bindaree**.
shuwa, *n.* Same as **shiwa**[1]. [UKH]
soo[1], *n.* [shoo] **1** Disposition; wisdom. **2** Temper; mind.
soo[2], *n.* [sao] **1** A pole; a rod. **2** A neck (of a musical instrument). **3** *n. slang* The penis.
soo-ba, *n.* [sooba] **1** The current market (price). **2** A quotation.
soo-bee, *adj.* [shoobai] Poorly made; of poor quality.
soo-dan, *n.* [soodan] **1** A consultation; a conference. **2** Talk; advice. **-sun**, *v.* To consult; confer; talk over.
soo-doo *n.* [soodoo] **1** Disturbance; agitation; uproar. **2** A quarrel; a brawl; a fracas.
soo-dukuru, *n.* A vital part; a vital point; a sore spot; a vulnerable spot.
soo-gaa, *n.* [shooga] Common ginger [*Zingiber officinale* Roscoe].
soo-gara, *n.* Physique; frame; physical make. [UKH]
sooga·san, *adj.* [? sawagashii] Noisy; boisterous.
soo-gwachi, *n.* [shoogatsu] January; the first month. See also **hachika soogwachi**.
soogwachi-jin, *n.* A New Year's Day

dress.

soogwachi-machi, *n.* A New Year's market, which opens in the first month of the year.

soogwachi-mucha·a, *n.* Lit., New Year's bearer; a fairy-like, imaginary person, often an old man, who brings plenty of treats for New Year's Day festivities.

soogwachi-'waa, *n.* A pig slaughtered for New Year's Day festivities.

soo-hoo, *n.* [soohoo] Both parties; both sides.

soo-i, *n.* [sooi] **1** Difference; disagreement. **2** Disparity; a gap; discrepancy.

soo-imi, *n.* A true dream; a dream that comes true. See also **saka'imi, imi**[1].

soo·in, *vt.* [sowaru] To take along; bring with; be accompanied by.

soo·i-ngwa, *n.* A child brought by a second wife (or husband).

soo-ira·a, *n.* A clever child; a smart child; a bright child.

soo-iya·a, *n.* Same as **sooiraa**.

soo-ji[1], *n.* [sooji] **1** Cleaning; dusting. **2** Sweeping.

soo-ji[2], *n.* [shooji] **1** Wickerwork of bamboo. **2** A sliding paper door or screen. Also **akai**.

sooji-bari, *n.* Abstinence clearance, when the parturition period officially comes to an end, usually on the seventh day after childbirth. See **naajikii**.

soo-jimu, *n.* Genuine mind; true heart. See **chimu**.

soo-jiraa, *n.* Dried fish meat.

sooki[1], *n.* A bamboo basket; a crate.

sooki[2], *n.* The ribs. Also **sookibuni**.

sooki-baaki, *n.* Lit., bamboo baskets (with an open mesh, incapable of holding water), a metaphor for being a spendthrift. [GSS]

sooki-buni, *n.* Same as **sooki**[2].

sooma·a, *n.* A squint-eyed person; a cross-eyed person.

soo-mi, *n.* **1** A side glance; ogling. **2** Squint eyes. **-sun,** *vt.* To look askance; ogle at; squint at. See **subami , suumi**.

soo-min, *n.* [soomen] Vermicelli; fine noodles.

soominaa, *n.* A white-eye; a silver-eye [*Zosterops japonicus*].

soominaa·nu munu kamun-nee·sshi, *phr.* Lit., eating like a white-eye; eating very little. [GSS]

soomin-iricha·a, *n.* Noodle stir-fry. See also **irichii**.

soo-mun, *n.* [shoomono] The genuine article; authentic stuff.

soo-naa, *n.* One's real name; one's autonym (in contrast to one's pseudonym).

soo-nuga·a, *n.* An absentminded person; a careless person; a scatterbrain; a fool. See **soo**[1].

soo-nugi·in, *vi.* To be confused; be flurried; lose one's head; panic.

soo-raa·s(h)an, *adj.* Wise; trustworthy; intelligent. See **soo**[1].

soo-roo, *n.* Same as **usooroo, hichigwa-chi**.

sooroo-miji, *n.* The *Bon* festival water. See **ubukaa, bun**[4].

soo-shichi, *n.* [sooshiki] A funeral. See **dabi**.

soo-soo, *adv.* [soosoo] Early; immediately; promptly; without delay.

soosoo-baabaa, *n.* A blunderer; a careless man.

soo-uya, *n.* True parent; natural parent.

soo-wuu, *adj.* [soo-oo] Appropriate; suitable.

soo-yuu, *n.* [shooyu] Soy sauce.

sooyuu·nu-shiru, *n.* [shooyunoshiru] Soy sauce soup; soup seasoned with soy sauce.

·sshi, *part.* By; through; by means of; with. See also **·saani**.

-su, *suff.* [shoo] A unit of capacity, equivalent to 1.8 l or 3.8 pints. See also **goo**.

suba[1], *n.* [soba] **1** Buckwheat [*Fagopyrum esculentum* (L.) Moench. FOSR]. **2**

suba

Buckwheat noodles. **3** Okinawan **suba** noodles.
suba², *n*. [soba] **1** A side; by (the side of); at one's side; beside. **2** Vicinity; neighborhood. **3** A concubine.
suba-mi, *n*. A side glance. **-sun**, *v*. To look askance (at). See **soomi**.
suba-nu·i, *n*. [sobanori*] Riding sidesaddle. See also **matanui**.
subi¹, *n*. Sperm. [GSS]
subi², *n*. Same as **moomoo**². Also **shibi**.
subi·chun, *vt*. [sobiku*, shoppiku] **1** To arrest; take (a person) into custody. **2** To drag; trail. Also **sunchun**.
subi-naa, *n*. Same as **hijainaa**. See **naa**⁴.
suda·chi, *n*. [sodachi] **1** Breeding; upbringing. **2** Growth.
suda·chun, *vi*. [·tan, ·tchi; sodatsu] To grow (up); be brought up.
sudati·in, *vt*. [sodateru] **1** To bring up; raise. **2** To foster; nurse. **3** To cultivate; breed.
sudati-kata, *n*. [sodatekata] How to bring up a child; a method of raising.
sudati-michi, *n*. How to raise infants; the art of rearing children.
sudati-uya, *n*. A foster parent. Also **sudatinu'uya**.
sudi, *n*. [sode] A sleeve; an arm (of a garment).
sudi-chira·a, *n*. A coarse, sleeveless Musa fiber kimono worn by farmers. Also **fudichiraa**, **sudikiraa**. [GSS]
sudi-gachi, *n*. [sodegaki] A small, temporary tomb attached to one of the wings of the regular tomb, used in the event of an unusual death such as that of a child. See also **haka**.
sudi-kira·a, *n*. Same as **sudichiraa**. [GSS]
sudi-miji, *n*. Water of rejuvenation. Same as **wakamiji**.
suga·i, *n*. **1** Dress; attire. **2** Personal appearance. **3** Preparation; readiness.
suga·in, *vt*. **1** To dress (attire, clothe, array); wear (a dress). **2** To get ready;

prepare.
sugari·in, *vi*. To cool oneself; enjoy the cool breeze.
suga·sun, *vt*. To cool; let in fresh air; admit cool air; ventilate.
sugi·in, *vi*. [sogeru] To splinter down to a smaller size; waste away.
sugi-wara, *n*. Paper made of paper mulberry tree bark. See also **kabi**.
sugu·in, *vt*. **1** To beat; strike; hit. **2** To pull (cloth, beard, branches) through one's fingers.
sugura·a, *n*. A genius; a talented person; an able student.
sugurari·in, *vi*. To get beaten up; be hit.
suguri·in, *vi*. [sugureru] To excel; surpass.
suguri-mun, *n*. Same as **suguraa**.
suguri-nchu, *n*. A superior person; a man of virtue; a man of talent.
suguri-ngwa, *n*. A talented child.
Sui, *n*. Same as **Shui**.
Sui-kutuba, *n*. Same as **Shuikutuba**.
su·in, *vt*. [soru] To shave.
Sui-nchu, *n*. Same as **Shuinchu**.
Sui-tin-ganashi, *n*. Same as **Shuitinjanashi**.
su-joo¹, *n*. [sujoo] **1** Birth; parentage. **2** Lineage; stock; origin. **3** Identity.
sujoo², *n*. **1** Experience. **2** Original nature; upbringing. **3** Mirth; pleasure; merriment. **-sun**, *vi*. To be happy; be gratified.
sujoo-nin, *n*. A man of refined culture or taste; a man about town.
sujoo·san, *adj*. Breezy; cool.
suk-kwii, *n*. [sokui*] A paste made by kneading cooked rice.
suku¹, *n*. A desk. Also **shuku**.
suku², *n*. [soko] **1** Bottom. **2** A valley; a ravine. **3** A marsh; a swamp.
suku-bara·a, *n*. Storage for firewood, usually located near the entrance to the kitchen hut.
suku-bun, *n*. [shokubun] Duty; what one is supposed to do.

sukubuu, *n.* Same as **shikubuu**.
su-kucha·a, *n.* [sokotsu] A careless person.
su-kuchi, *n.* [sokotsu] 1 Carelessness; absentmindedness. 2 Comicality; joke.
suku-hi, *n.* [sokohi] Glaucoma, cataracts.
suku·i, *n.* [sukui] 1 Relief; help. 2 Rescue; salvation.
suku·in[1,] *vt.* [sukuu] To rescue; save.
suku·in[2], *vt.* [sukuu] To scoop; ladle.
suku-jin, *n.* The thickest board of a boat, constituting the bottom. See **sabani**.
suku·mun, *vt.* [sukumu] 1 To crouch. 2 To cower; flinch.
sukuna·in, *vt.* [·(r)an, ·ti; sokonau] To harm; hurt; damage; spoil.
sukwee·sun, *vi.* To be distressed; be troubled; be in a difficulty; feel awkward.
sumi, *n.* [some] 1 A birthmark. 2 A bruise.
sumi·in, *vt.* [someru] To dye; color.
sumi-kata, *n.* [somekata] A method of dyeing.
sumi-mun, *n.* [somemono] 1 Dyeing. 2 Dyed goods.
sumimun-yaa, *n.* [somemonoya] 1 A dye shop. 2 A dyer (a person). Also **sumiyaa**.
sumiyaa, *n.* Same as **sumimun-yaa**.
su-muchi, *n.* [shomotsu] A book. Also **shumuchi, shimuchi**[1].
sumuchi-kwe·e-mushi, *n.* 1 A bookworm. 2 A bibliophile; a bibliomaniac.
sumuchi-machi-ya, *n.* A bookstore. Also **hon-yaa**.
sumu·chun, *vi.* [somuku] 1 To disobey; defy; turn one's back to. 2 To rebel against.
su-mumu, *n.* [sumomo] A sour peach; Japanese plum [*Prunus salicina* Lindl]. [FOSR]
s·un[1], *vt.* [san, sshi; suru] 1 To do; try; play; attempt; act; practice. 2 To cost; be worth; be valued. 3 To serve as; act as.
sun[2], *n.* [son] 1 Loss. 2 Disadvantage.
-sun, *vt.* To suffer a loss; make a loss; be out of pocket.
sun[3], *n.* [sun] A unit of length, equivalent to approximately 3 cm or 1.2 in. [NJED]
·sun, *causative suff.* Following a verb, indicates the causing or allowing of an action for another person. See **shimiin**[2].
sunawa·i, *n.* [sonawari] 1 Preparation. 2 Provisions. 3 Facilities; equipment.
sunawa·in, *vi.* [sonawaru] 1 To be equipped (with); be installed. 2 To be provided (with); be endowed with.
sun·chun, *vt.* Same as **subichun** (2).
sunee, *n.* [suae] Same as **suunee**.
sun-kabu·i, *n.* A business loss.
sun-kan, *n.* [? C zhenggeng] A Chinese-style medium-size bowl. See **makai**.
sun-shii, *n.* [? C xunzi] A dried bamboo shoot.
sun-tuku, *n.* [sontoku] Loss and gain.
su-nui, *n.* [sunori] A variety of edible seaweed [J mozuku; *Cladosiphon okamuranus* Tokida]. [ODJ]
sura, *n.* Same as **suraba**.
suraa·sun, *vt.* [< **suriin**] 1 To gather; call together. 2 To collect; complete.
sura-ba, *n.* A shipyard; a dockyard. Also **sura**.
sura-urushi, *n.* The launching of a ship. [OBJ]
su-rii[1], *n.* [soroi] A meeting; a gathering; an assembly.
surii[2], *n.* Same as **kee'uchi**. [GSS] See **sara**[1].
surii-jurii, *n.* Being together in harmony (of a group of people). [GSS]
suri·in, *vi.* [sorou] 1 To gather together. 2 To become complete.
suru-ban, *n.* [soroban] An abacus.
suru-gaa, *n.* [shuro + ...] Hemp palm fiber.

surugaa-china, *n*. Hemp palm rope.
surugaa-jina, *n*. A net made of hemp palm fiber. [UKH]
surugaa-nnuu, *n*. A hemp palm raincoat. [UKH]
suru-ita, *n*. Same as **taanoosaa**.
sushi·in, *vt*. [soshiru] **1** To slander; libel; defame. **2** To rebuke; blame; criticize.
sushi·ri, *n*. [soshiri] Slander; libel; censure; blame.
su-soo, *n*. [so-soo] Carelessness; heedlessness; a fault; an oversight.
susu, *n*. [suso] **1** The skirt (of a dress); the train (of a dress); the bottom (of the trousers, etc.). **2** The base (of a hill).
susu·i, *n*. A scrub-cloth; a dust cloth; a dishtowel; a mop.
susu·i-ka·chi, *n*. Mopping; wiping with a damp cloth.
susu·in, *vt*. **1** To wipe; mop; swab. **2** To scrub. Also **nuguin**.
sutichi, *n*. [sotetsu] Same as **suutiichaa**.
sutu, *n*. [soto] **1** The external part. **2** The outer side; on the outside; on or to the outside; in the open.
sutumiti, *n*. [tsutomete*] Morning. Also **shitimiti**, **hitimiti**.
suu[1], *n*. Vinegar. Also **shii**[4].
suu[2], *n*. [shu] Father; dad. Also **shuu**.
suu[3], *n*. [shio] **1** Saltwater; brine. **2** The tide. Also **suumiji**, **usumiji**, **usu**.
suu- *pref*. [soo] Denotes all, complete, in the gross.
suu-bana, *n*. Spindrift. See **suu**[3].
suu-banji, *n*. State of strong running tide.
suu-bata, *n*. [shio-hata] A shoal; shallows; beaches.
suubata-kuji·i *n*. Taking cowries, octopi, and small fish in the shallows.
suu-bi, *n*. A current (in the ocean).
suu-bu, *n*. [shoobu] A match; a contest.
suu-buta, *n*. [shiobuta] Same as **suujikii**.
suu-chiki, *n*. [shiozuke] Same as **suujikii**.

suuchiki-gaami, *n*. A jar for salted pork.
suu-chuu-maa, *n*. [C shuchouma] A limited writing system in premodern rural Miyako and Yaeyama, comprised of pictographs, symbolic numbers, and simplified Chinese characters. See also **kaidaajii**, **warajan**.
suu-daka, *n*. [soodaka] The total amount; the grand total. See **takasan**.
suu-dee, *n*. [soodai] A male whose duty is to collect ritual fees or offerings from the villagers.
suu-gee·shi, *n*. Brine antidote, a purification rite for those who have attended a funeral. See also **shinimabui**.
suu-guchi, *n*. A beach; a strand; a shore.
suu-hama, *n*. A salt field; a salt farm. See **maasudoogu**.
suu·in, *vt*. [suu] Breathe in; inhale; sup; suck.
suu·i-'nja·sun, *vt*. To suck out; draw out.
suu-ji[1], *n*. A path; an alley; a lane; an alleyway.
suu-ji[2], *n*. [shuugi] **1** A celebration; a congratulation. **2** A congratulatory gift. **-sun**, *v*. To celebrate; congratulate; felicitate.
suuji-jaa, *n*. A celebration party.
suu-jika·a, *n*. Same as **suujikii**. [GSS]
suu-jiki·i, *n*. Salted pork. Also **suubuta**, **chikijishi**, **suujikaa**, **suuchiki**.
suu-juu·san, *adj*. Salty; briny; saline; too salty. Also **suukarasan**, **shipukarasan**.
suu-kaa, *n*. A river or a spring with salty water, though without direct contact with the ocean.
suu-kangee, *n*. Public opinion; a consensus of opinion; basic idea.
suu-kara·san, *adj*. [shiokarai] Same as **suujuusan**.
suu-koo, *n*. [shookoo] A Buddhist mass; a memorial service. See also **nanka**, **ninchi**[1], **uwaijuukoo**. [ODJ]
suu-ku, *n*. [shooko] Evidence; proof; testimony.

suu-kukui, *n.* [sookukuri] Conclusion; general conclusion.

suu-man, *n.* [shooman] One of the two parts of the rainy season; one of the twenty-four seasons of the lunar calendar, generally falling in May in the solar calendar.

suuman-boosuu, *n.* [shooman-booshu] Rainy season, generally late May and early June in the solar calendar. See **suuman, boosuu.**

suumi, *n.* Peeping; peeking; a peep; a peek. **-sun,** *v.* To peep; peek. See **soomi.**

suu-mii, *n.* [soomei] Intelligence; sagacity; wisdom.

suu-miji, *n.* Same as **suu³, usumiji.**

suu-mun, *n.* [shoomon] A deed; a bond; a paper; a certificate.

suu-nee, *n.* [suae] Vinegared dish. Also **sunee.**

suu-nii, *n.* [shioni] **1** Boiling (fish) with salt. **2** A dish of boiled fish seasoned with salt.

suu·nu-hana, *n.* Purification salt that is sprinkled on one's body and around the doorway upon returning from a funeral.

suura, *n.* A treetop; twigs.

suura-nai, *n.* Same as **shimunai.**

suu-shiru, *n.* Salt soup.

suu-taa, *n.* Lit., father; an employer of apprentices in the town of Itoman. See **Ichuman'ui.**

suu-tee, *n.* [shotai] A household; a home; economy.

suutee-ara·san, *adj.* Bad at housewifery; bad at housekeeping.

suutee-doogu, *n.* [shotaidoogu] Household articles; domestic utensils; furniture. See also **tanshi, kee³, koori¹, uudu, fukutaa'uudu, makkwa, kacha, tabakubun, naabi, kama², hoochaa, manacha, makaidoogu, ujin.**

suutee-kuma·san, *adj.* Thrifty at household management; good at housewifery.

suutee-mu·chi, *n.* [shotaimochi] A family man; a married person.

suutee-wata·shi, *n.* Transfer of household management from parents to children, or from mother-in-law to the daughter-in-law.

suutiicha·a, *n.* [sotetsu] A sago cycad [*Cycas revoluta* Thunb.]; a sago palm. [FOSR] Also **sutichi, suutiichi.**

suutiichi-baa-boochi, *n.* A broom made of cycad leaves for outside use. See also **hoochi.**

suu-tuku, *n.* Benefit.

suuyoo, *n.* [sooyoo*] A term of address to a group of people socially inferior to the speaker; everyone; each one of you; all of you. See also **gusuuyoo.**

suu-yudun, *n.* A state of calm; windless conditions. See **yudumun.**

T———

ta-, *pref.* Two.

taa¹, *n.* [ta] Rice field; rice paddy. See also **haru².**

taa², *pron.* [ta*] **1** Who, whom; whose. **2** Somebody; someone; anybody; anyone.

·taa, *suff.* Plural suffix for personal nouns, pronouns, and households.

taaba-jeeku, *n.* An unskilled carpenter; an amateur carpenter.

taabi, *n.* [tabi] Japanese-style socks; digitated socks.

taa-bukkwa, *n.* Rice paddies; a plain or valley with a large area of rice paddies.

taa-chi, *n.* Two.

taachi-macha·a, *n.* A person with two whorls of hair on the head.

taachi-mishi·i, *n.* Giving birth every other year.

taachi-wa·i, *n.* Dividing in two; halving in two.

taachu·u, *n.* Twins.

taa·doo·shi, *n*. Conversion of wet rice paddies into dry fields. See **toosun**.
taa-faa-kuu, *n*. [C dahuagu] A Chinese-style musical drama introduced from China toward the end of the fourteenth century. [OBJ]
taa·gana, *n*. Somebody; someone. See **·gana**.
taagu, *n*. [tago] A bucket. See also **wuuki**.
taa-gusa, *n*. [tagusa] Weeds in the rice fields. See **kusa**².
taa-gushiree, *n*. Preparation of rice paddies for planting rice.
taa-gutu, *n*. [tawagoto] 1 Talking deliriously. 2 Silly talk; nonsense.
taa-hataki, *n*. [ta-hatake] Cultivated fields, both dry fields and wet paddies.
taa-iifee, *n*. A Japanese water beetle.
taa-iyu, *n*. A crucian (carp); a roach (fish); a gibel.
taa-iyu-gashira, *n*. Lit., boss of the crucian carps; the king of the hill.
taa-iyu-shinji, *n*. An infusion of roach fish, used as a fever reducer. See **shinjimun**.
taa-maa, *n*. A (large) dragonfly.
taa-'nmu, *n*. [taimo] Village taro [*Colocasia esculenta* Schott var. *aquatilis* Kitamura]. [FOSR, ODJ] Also **miji'nmu**, **chinnuku**.
taa-nna, *n*. A mud-snail; a pond-snail. See also **shirunna**².
taa-'nnaji, *n*. A rice-paddy eel.
taa-noosa·a, *n*. A rice-paddy leveler, consisting of a long pole with a flat board attached crosswise at the end. Also **suru'ita**. See **noosun**.
taara, *n*. [tawara] A straw sack; a straw bale (for rice, etc.).
-taara, *suff*. Counter for sacks or bags (of rice, wheat, etc.).
taaree, *n*. [tarai] A tub; a washbasin. Also **hanjiri**, **fanjiri**. [GSS]
taari, *n*. Possession; obsession; haunting.
taarii, *n*. [C daren] Father; also as a term of address, father.
taari·in¹, *vi*. [dareru] To be wasted; be prolonged (illness).
taari·in², *vi*. To be possessed by a spirit. See **kamidaari**.
taa-shigutu, *n*. [tashigoto] Agricultural work in the rice paddy. See also **shigutu**.
taa-suki, *n*. [ta + suki] A wooden plow.
taa·tcha, *n*. *inf*. Standing up. See **ta-chun**¹.
taa-ucha·a-gwee, *n*. A rice-paddy tilling hoe whose entire blade is made of iron. See **uchun**², **kwee**¹.
tabai, *n*. [taba] A bundle.
-taba·i, *suff*. Counter for bundles (of firewood, etc.).
taba·in, *vt*. To bind; tie; make a bundle.
tabaku, *n*. [tabako] Tobacco.
tabaku-bun, *n*. [tabakobon*] A tobacco tray.
tabaku·nu-fee-kusu, *n*. A cigarette butt; stub. See **fee**¹.
tabaku-yaa, *n*. [tabakoya] A tobacco shop.
tabasa, *n*. A gap; crevice; a crack; a chink; an aperture.
tabi, *n*. [tabi] Traveling; travels; a journey; a tour.
tabi-da·chi, *n*. [tabidachi] Departure; setting out on a journey.
tabi-gukuru, *n*. [tabi + kokoro] Sentiments of travel.
tabi-ninju, *n*. [tabininzu] A group of travelers.
tabi·nu-tchu, *n*. A traveler; a stranger.
tabi-su, *n*. A family one of whose members is away on a journey. See **tabisunugusuuji**, **wuduyee**.
tabi-suga·i, *n*. Traveling outfit; traveling attire.
tabisu·nu-gusuuji, *n*. A rite to pray for the safety of a traveler. See also **kweena**. [ODJ]
tabu, *n*. [tabunoki] A **tabu** tree [*Persea*

thungu Kosterm]. [ODJ]
tabu·in, *vt.* [tabau*] 1 To accumulate; amass. 2 To collect; gather. 3 To keep; preserve.
tabun, *adv.* [tabun] Maybe; probably; perhaps.
tachi¹, *n.* [tachi] A sword; a large sword.
tachi², *n.* [tatsu] The Dragon, the fifth of the twelve calendrical animal signs.
tachi³, *n.* [taki] A waterfall; a cascade.
tachibaa-ashija, *n.* [futatsu + ha + ashida] High wooden clogs for rainy weather; rain clogs. See also **ashija**.
ta-chichi¹, *n.* Next month.
ta-chichi², *n.* Two months.
ta·chi-fa, *n.* [tachiba] 1 A standpoint; a footing. 2 Livelihood; circumstances.
ta·chi-gari, *n.* [tachigare] Blight; standing decayed.
ta·chi-guri·s(h)an, *adj.* Difficult (to make a living).
ta-chii, *n.* Another lineage; not the same lineage.
tachii-majiku·i, *n.* [… + mazekuru] 1 Succession to the household headship by one who is not related by blood. 2 A taboo against inheritance of the mortuary tablets by one who is not paternally related to the family. [ODJ] See also **shijitadashi**. See **mankiin**.
ta·chi-juku, *n.* Livelihood. See **-juku**.
ta·chi-kantii, *n.* Hard living; difficulty in earning a livelihood; economic distress. See **-kantii**.
tachi-machi, *adv.* [tachimachi] Suddenly; at once; immediately.
ta·chi-masa·in, *vi.* [tachimasaru] To be superior; be excellent.
ta·chi-mee, *n.* Being before marriage (only in reference to a female).
ta·chi-mudu·i, *n.* [tachimodoru] A divorced woman.
ta·chi-na·chi, *n.* Howling; a howl.
ta·chi-nka·in, *vi.* [tachimukau] To confront; come face to face; fight against.
ta·chi-nu·chun, *vi.* [tachinoku] To vacate; leave.
ta·chi-shikuchi, *n.* Work that requires standing up.
ta·chi-toori, *n.* The vicissitudes of fortune; rise and fall. See **tooriin**.
ta·chi-'wii·ji, *n.* Treading water; swimming in the form of standing up.
ta·chi-yas·san, *adj.* […shi·ku; tachiyasui] Easy to make a living; comfortable in livelihood.
ta·chi-ye·e, *n.* [tachiai] Presence; attendance; witnessing.
ta·chun¹, *vi.* [·tan, ·tchi; tatsu] 1 (For a person) to stand up; rise; get on one's feet; (a thing) stand erect; (a building) stand; be built; be set up; be accomplished. 2 To pass; elapse; pass by. 3 To leave; start; depart. 4 To be sharp. 5 To have an erection; be erect.
ta·chun², *vt.* [taku] To make a fire and cook.
tada¹, *n.* [tada] 1 Gratis; free. 2 Mere; sole. 3 Nothing. 4 Usual; common; simple. See also **ichanda**.
tada², *adv.* [tada] Merely; simply; solely; only; idly.
tada·sun, *vt.* [tadasu] 1 To correct; rectify. 2 To examine; investigate; inquire into.
tadeema, *adv.* [tadaima] Now; right now; soon; directly; immediately. Also **tareema**.
tagee, *n.* [tagai] Same as **utagee²**.
tagee·in, *vt.* [tagaeru] To break one's promise; fail to keep a promise.
tagee·sun, *vt.* [tagaesu*, tagayasu] To till; plow; cultivate; put under cultivation. See also **keesun**, **uchun²**, **haru'atchun**.
tagu·in, *vt.* [taguru] To haul in (a rope); pull in (a line) hand over hand; reel in.
tai¹, *interj. adv.* Vocative interjection, used by female speakers to show respect or to draw attention. See **tari**, **sai¹**, **sari**.
tai², *n.* Two persons; both persons.

-tai¹, *suff*. Counter denoting a number of people. See **-nin¹**.

-tai², *suff*. One in charge of (an area of resource). See also **atai¹**.

ta·in, *vi*. [taru*, tareru] 1 To hang (of a curtain); droop (of the tail); drop; lower (of one's head); hang down; dangle; trail; sag. 2 To drip; drop; fall in drops; ooze; run down; trickle. See also **tarasun**.

ta·i-saga·in, *vi*. [taresagaru] To dangle; hang down.

taji·in, *vi*. [tagiru] To boil; seethe; be on the boil.

tajini·in, *vt*. [tazuneru] 1 To look for; search for; make inquiry for; seek for; look for. 2 To ask a question; inquire. Also **tanniin, tajuniin**.

tajira·shi-keesa·a, *n*. Food that has been kept heated.

tajira·sun, *vt*. To heat (food); reheat (food). Also **tajirashikeesun**.

tajuniin, *vt*. Same as **tajiniin**.

taka, *n*. [taka] A hawk; a falcon. See also **wuutaka**.

taka·a, *n*. A tall person. [UKH]

ta-kaa-mii, *n*. A double eyelid.

taka-bira, *n*. A high slope. [UKH] See **hira²**.

takabu·in, *vi*. [takaburu] To be proud; be haughty; be arrogant.

taka-dima, *n*. [takai + tema] A high wage.

taka-hana, *n*. [takai + hana] High ground; a high, projecting, and windy place like a cliff.

taka-hata, *n*. [takahata] Lit., a tall loom; a later, improved loom, operated by pedal and with chair for the weaver.

taka-ichubi, *n*. A roasting pan berry [*Rubus sieboldii* Blume]. See **ichubi**. [FOSR]

taka-maa, *n*. [medaka] A killifish. Also **takamaamii, takamami**.

taka-maa-mii, *n*. Same as **takamaa**.

taka-ma-mi, *n*. Same as **takamaa**.

takara, *n*. [takara] A treasure; a precious thing.

takara-ngwa, *n*. [kodakara] A child; treasure of a child.

taka-riifii, *n*. High interest rate; usury.

taka·san, *adj*. [takai] 1 High; tall; raised; lofty (in spatial relationship or social position). 2 High (price); expensive. 3 High, loud (voice).

taka-soo, *n*. A tall, lanky person; gangling fellow.

taka-uchaaga·a, *n*. A self-important person; a snob.

taka-uchaga·i, *n*. Holding one's head high; haughtiness; arrogance. See **uchagain**.

taka-u·i, *n*. Selling at a high price.

taka-ujin, *n*. A small, individual dining table about 1 ft. high. See also **ujin**.

taka-ware·e, *n*. A loud laugh; a boisterous laugh; a guffaw. See **warain**.

ta-keen, *n*. Twice.

takeen-mii, *n*. The second time. **·ni**, *adv*. For or on the second time. **·nu**, *adj*. The second. **·ya**, *adv*. On the second time.

taki¹, *n*. [take] 1 A hill. 2 A sacred grove. See also **utaki**.

taki², *n*. [take] Personal height; physical stature (of a person).

taki-bun, *n*. 1 Status; station. 2 One's natural talents.

takichiki·in, *vi*. To reach the worst condition (in sickness); be in terminal condition.

taki-fudu, *n*. Physique; body build; physical constitution; body structure; frame.

taki-mui, *n*. Hills and woods. See also **mui**.

takkuru·sun, *vt*. To beat up; knock; strike; hit; thrash; lick.

takkwaa·sun, *vt*. To join (together); stick; paste; attach.

takkwai-mukkwai-sun, *vi. emph*. 1 To be soft and sticky. 2 To flirt (between man and woman). See **takkwain**.

takkwa·in, *vi.* [·(r)an, ·ti] **1** To stick to; cling to; cleave to. **2** (For a child) to keep close to its mother. **3** To flirt (between man and woman). See **mutchakain, tatchikain.**

tak-kwii, *n.* Lineage; pedigree; stock; family line.

taku, *n.* [tako] An octopus.

taku·bun, *vt.* To fold (clothes, paper, etc.); furl (a sail, a flag).

ta-kuku, *n.* [takoku] A foreign country; a strange country; another province.

takuma, *n.* [takumi] Cleverness; wisdom; sagacity.

takuma·a, *n.* A clever person; a smart fellow; a shrewd man; a wise man.

taku·mun, *vt.* [takumu*, takuramu] To scheme; plan; play a trick.

tama[1]**,** *n.* [tama] **1** A ball; a bead; a sphere; a globe; a bulb. **2** A lens; glass. **3** An electric bulb. **4** Jewelry; a precious stone; a gem. **5** A bullet; a shot; a shell; a slug. **6** Euphemism for testicle.

tama[2]**,** *n.* [tama] Chance; fortuity; accident; rarity.

tama-ba·i, *n.* A glass pane such as glass window; a glass door. See **hain**[2].

tama-ga·i, *n.* [tamagaru*] A bad omen; an omen of death such as a fireball in the sky. Also **hiidama.**

tamagu, *n.* [tamago] The egg of a chicken or other bird. See also **kuuga.**

tama-gwaa, *n.* A hydrometer to measure saline content. See **maasudoogu.**

tama·i, *n.* [tamari] A puddle; a pool; a water hole. Also **mijitamai.**

tama·in[1]**,** *vi.* [tamaru] **1** To collect; gather; accumulate; heap. **2** (For an amount of money saved) to grow. **3** To be in arrears; be overdue.

tama·in[2]**,** *vi.* To bend; be bent; yield; be pliant; be supple. See also **tamiin**[2].

tama-kugani, *n.* [tama-kogane] Gems and gold; things that are as precious as gems and gold.

taman, *n.* A **taman** fish [J hamafuefuki;

Lethrinus nebulosus (Forsskål)]; generic term for the fish *Lethrinus nebulosus.* [ODJ]

tama-naa, *n.* [tamana] A cabbage [*Brassica oleracea* L. var. *oleracea*]. [FOSR] Also **habutan.**

tamashi[1]**,** *n.* [tamashii] **1** Spiritual strength; spiritual motivation. **2** Discretion; common sense.

tamashi[2]**,** *n.* Each person's share; portion.

tamashii, *n.* [tamashii] Spirit of the dead; soul of the dead. See also **mabui, shinimabui, mabuiwakashi, gusoo, kami, mabui'uui.**

tamata-gwee, *n.* A forked hoe used to dig sweet potatoes or carrots. See **kwee**[1].

tamatoo, *n.* [tomato] A tomato [*Lycopersicon esculentum* Mill.]. [FOSR]

tama-wuuki, *n.* Same as **wuukikagan.**

tama-yubai, *n.* [tamayobai*] A rite to call back the departed soul of the deceased. [ODJ]

tami, *n.* [tame] **1** Good; advantage; benefit; profit; welfare; sake. **2** To; in order to; so as to; for; for the sake of. **3** Because (of); on account of; since; thanks to. **4** As a result (of); in consequence (of).

tami·in[1]**,** *vt.* [tameru] To save; accumulate; amass; heap; pile up.

tami·in[2]**,** *vt.* [tameru] To bend; train (a twig).

tami·shi, *n.* [tameshi] **1** A trial; an attempt; a test; an experiment. **2** A precedent; an example; an instance; a case.

tami·sun, *vt.* [tamesu] To try; attempt; test; sample.

tamu·chun, *vi.* [·tan, ·tchi; tamotsu] **1** To preserve; keep. **2** To support; sustain. **3** To last; hold; (food) keep; (clothes) wear well.

tamun, *n.* Firewood; wood for fuel.

tamun-uya·a, *n.* A firewood seller. See **uin.**

tan

tan¹, *n.* [tan] A roll of cloth, about twelve yards.
tan², *n.* [tan] Same as **shimi**³.
tana¹, *n.* [tana] **1** A shelf; a rack. **2** trellis(work); lattice(work).
tana², *n.* [tana] A gunwale; the sideboards that join the bottom of a boat. See **sabani**.
tana-bata, *n.* [tanabata] The Festival of the Weaver, a rite held on the seventh day of the seventh lunar month. [OBJ, OGJ, ODJ]
tana-bi·chun, *n.* [tanabiku] To trail; hang over; lie over.
tana-gaa, *n.* A crayfish.
tana-gee, *n.* A freshwater shrimp.
ta-naka, *n.* The middle; midway; in-between.
ta-nan-ka, *n.* The Buddhist memorial service on the fourteenth day after death. See **nanka**.
tanashi, *n.* Formal summer robe for both men and women in the premodern era.
tancha·a, *n.* A quick-tempered person; an impatient person; a person of impetuous temper.
tan-chi, *n.* [tanki] A quick temper; a short temper; irritability; touchiness; irascibility; petulance; testiness.
tandi, *adv.* Please; kindly; pray; I beg; by all means.
tani, *n.* [tane] A penis; a male organ; a phallus. See also **fugui**, **soo**², **chuuchuu**, **kuugi**, **hoo**, **mara**, **main**.
tani-gaa·i-mun, *n.* A novelty; a hybrid; a mutation; an eccentric person.
ta-nin, *n.* [tanin] **1** Another person; others. **2** An unrelated person. **3** An outsider. **4** A stranger.
tankaa¹, *n.* Same as **tankaa'uuwee**.
tankaa², *n.* The house across the street. See also **tankaamankaa**.
tankaa-gee·i, *n.* Exchange of items of equal value.
tankaa-mankaa, *n.* One's nearest neighbors; houses in one's neighborhood. See also **tankaa**².
tankaa-naa, *n.* Equality; evenness. See **-naa**².
tankaa-uuwee, *n.* The birthday party for the first full one year. [OBJ]
tankaa-yi·i, *n.* Sitting face to face.
tanki·in, *vt.* **1** To be careful of one's health. **2** To use discretion; make allowances; be tactful.
tan-mee, *n.* A grandfather; an old man. See **taarii**.
tan-mii, *n.* [tanmei] A short life; a brief span of life.
ta-nna, *n.* [tazura] A bridle; reins.
tanni·in, *vt.* [tazuneru] Same as **tajiniin**.
tan-shi, *n.* [tansu] A chest of drawers; a cabinet; a bureau.
tan-tui, *n.* [tanetori] The sowing of rice seeds in a nursery and rites associated therewith. See also **yaheegami**. [ODJ]
tanu·mi, *n.* [tanomi] A request; a favor.
tanu·mun¹, *vt.* [tanomu] **1** To request; ask; beg. **2** To entrust (something to a person; a person with something); trust (a person with something); charge (a person to do something). **3** To engage; hire; employ. Also **tanunun**, **tarumun**.
ta·nu-mun², *n. pej.* Who. See also **taa**².
tanu·nun, *vt.* Same as **tanumun**.
tanushimi, *n.* [tanoshimi] Pleasure; enjoyment; delight; happiness.
tanushi·mun, *vt.* [tanoshimu] To take pleasure in; enjoy; enjoy oneself.
taraa·in, *vi.* [·(ra)n, ·tti] To be quite enough; be supplied in plenty. See also **tareein**.
tara(a)·n, *adj.* Be short; be insufficient; be not enough; be lacking.
tara·sun, *vt.* [tarasu] **1** To hang down; suspend; slouch. **2** To drop; drip; spill; let fall. See also **tain**, **tariin**¹.
taree·in, *vt.* To supply (wants); supplement; make up for; fill up (a gap).
tareema, *adv.* Same as **tadeema**.

tari, *interj. adv.* Same as **tai**[1], but showing a higher degree of respect.
tari·in[1], *vi.* [tareru] To drip; trickle; ooze. See also **tain**, **tarasun**.
tari·in[2], *vt.* To brew; distill.
tari·in[3], *vi.* [< J tariru] To be enough; be sufficient; suffice.
taru, *n.* [taru] A cask; a barrel; a keg.
tarugaki·in, *vt.* To count on; bank on; look forward to; hope for; depend on.
taru·mi-nchu, *n.* One whose help has been requested; a helper.
taru·mun, *vt.* [tanomu] Same as **tanumun**.
tashi, *n.* [tashi] Complement; supplement; help; a spare.
tashi·in, *vt.* To fry (in a hot pan); stir-fry; fry in oil.
tashika, *adv.* [tashika] Certainly; surely; for certain.
tashikami·in, *vt.* [tashikameru] To make sure; verify; ascertain; confirm; authenticate.
tashiki, *n.* [tasuke] Help; aid; assistance.
tashiki·in, *vt.* [tasukeru] **1** To help; aid; assist; stand by; second. **2** To save; rescue; succor. **3** To relieve; give relief to. **4** To spare. **5** To reinforce; support; back up. **6** To promote; be conducive to.
ta-shima, *n.* Some other village; another community; a foreign place.
tashi-mee, *n.* [tashimae] Advance; supplement; complement; help; compensation.
tashimee·in, *vt.* To supplement; help; aid; conpensate; reimburse.
tashinami, *n.* [tashinami] **1** Taste; relish. **2** Prudence; discretion; modesty. **3** Accomplishment.
tas-sha, *n.* [tassha] Being healthy; strong; expert; skilled.
tas-shi, *n.* [tasshi] A public (government) notice; an order; notification.
tatacha·a, *n.* Lit., hitting-fishing; a type of fishing where divers drive the fish into nets by striking rocks and corals.
tata·chun, *vt.* [tataku] To strike; beat; knock; slap; rap; thrash; clap (hands).
tatai, *n.* [tatari] A curse; an evil spell; a retribution (often by an evil spirit or a supernatural being).
tata·mun, *vt.* [tatamu] To fold; furl.
tata·n, *n.* [tatami] A *tatami* mat, rectangular six feet by three feet; matting (Japanese-style thick mat made of straw). See also **yiidatan**, **mushiru**, **nikubuku**, **-joo**.
tatan-yaa, *n.* [tatamiya] A *tatami* maker; a *tatami* dealer.
tatchika·in, *vi.* To join; cling to; stick to. See also **takkwain**, **mutchakain**.
tatchiki·in, *vt.* To make (something) stick to; make (something) cling to; make (something) adhere to. See also **takkwaasun**.
tat-chuu, *n.* [tatchuu] Anything that is pointed and standing, such as a pillar or a tall building.
tati, *n.* [tate] Length (in contrast to width); height; a vertical.
tati-fuda, *n.* [tatefuda] A notice board.
tati-gee·in, *vt.* [tatekaeru] **1** To advance; pay in advance. **2** To pay for another. **3** To loan.
tati·in, *vt.* [tateru] To stand; build; establish; set up; make (a daughter) marry; note; write in.
tati-yuku, *n.* [tateyoko] Length and breadth; lengthwise and breadthwise.
tatta, *adv.* [tatta] Soon; gradually; often.
tat·taa, *n. pl.* of **taa**[2], who: who-all.
tatui[1], *n.* [tatoe] **1** A precedent; a former example. **2** A metaphor; a simile; allegory; a fable.
tatui[2], *conj.* [tatoe] If; even if; though; admitting that…; supposing that….
tatui-bana·shi, *n.* [tatoebanashi] A fable; an allegory; a parable.
tatui·in, *vt.* [tatoeru] To compare (to); use a metaphor; speak figuratively.
tau-chii, *n.* [C douji] A fighting cock.

tayu·i, *n.* [tayori] **1** News; tidings; correspondence; mail. **2** Reliance; dependence. **3** A friend; a relative.

tayu·in, *vt.* [tayoru] To depend on; rely on.

tee^1, *n.* Strength to endure; endurance; resiliency. See also **chikara**.

tee^2, *n.* [tai(matsu)] A torch made of bamboo, pampas grass, sugar cane bagasse, and the like. Also **tubushi**.

tee^3, *n.* [tai] An embryo.

tee-buku, *n.* [taiboku] A large tree.

tee-bun, *n.* [? daibu] A lot; plenty; much; many.

tee-byoo, *n.* [taibyoo] A serious illness.

tee-chi·chun, *vi.* [takitsuku] To become ignited; become kindled.

tee-chiki·in, *vt.* [takitsukeru] **1** To light; kindle; ignite. **2** To instigate; excite.

teefa, *n.* A joke; a jest; fun.

teefa·a, *n.* A joker; a buffoon; a humorist; a wag; a clown.

tee-fuu, *n.* [taifuu] A typhoon. See also **ufukaji, arashi**.

tee-gee, *adv.* [taigai] **1** Generally; mostly; reasonably. **2** Loose; not exact; not strict; fuzzy.

teegee-janmin, *n.* A rough estimate or computation; an approximate figure. See **sanmin**.

tee-haku, *n.* [taihaku] Refined white sugar.

tee·in, *vi.* [taeru] To be wasted; become scanty; become scarce; become short of; become extinct; perish.

tee-ku, *n.* [taiko] A drum; a tambourine.

-teeman, *part.* Even if; though.

-teen, *part.* Same as **-teeman**.

tee-shichi, *n.* [taisetsu] Importance; significance.

tee-soo, *n.* [taishoo] A chief; a head; a leader. See also **shiidu, kashira**.

teetee-munu-i·i, *n. onom.* Speaking thickly and inarticulately.

ten-busa·a, *n.* A person with a protruding navel.

ten-busu, *n.* A protruding navel. See **fusu**.

ti-baku, *n.* [tebako] A case; a box; a casket.

ti-bana·sun, *vt.* [tebanasu] To dispose of; let go one's hold (of); release one's hold (on); do away with.

tichi^1, *n.* [teki] An enemy; a foe; an opponent; a rival.

tichi^2, *n.* [tetsu] Iron.

tidan, *n.* [< shudan] A means; a measure; a way; a step.

ti-dashiki, *n.* [tedasuke] Help; assistance

tidee, *n.* A treat; an entertainment; a repast.

tidee·i, *n.* **1** Same as **tidee**. **2** Hospitality; a warm reception.

tidee·in, *vi.* To entertain (a person at dinner, etc.); treat a person to something; give something.

ti-fun, *n.* [tehon] A model; an example; a copy; a pattern; a paragon.

ti-gaka·i, *n.* [tegakari] **1** A handhold. **2** A clue; a lead.

ti-gami, *n.* [< J tegami] A letter; mail; communication.

ti-ganee, *n.* Help; assistance.

tiganee-sa·a, *n.* A helper; an assistant.

ti-gara, *n.* [tegara] A merit; a feat; an exploit.

ti-gukuru, *n.* [tegokoro] Allowance; discretion; consideration.

ti-guma, *n.* Skillfulness; dexterity.

ti-gu·mi, *n.* [tegumi] Arrangement; preparation.

tigusu, *n.* [tegusu] Silkworm gut; natural worm gut; fishing gut. Also **tigusui**.

tigusui, *n.* [tegusuito] Same as **tigusu**.

tii^1, *n.* [te] **1** The hand; the arm; the paw. **2** A hand; help. **3** Hand; handwriting; per.manship. **4** Being busy. **5** A handle. **6** A means; a skill; a method. **7** The karate martial art.

tii^2, *n.* [toi] A conduit; an eaves trough; a

drainpipe; a gutter. Also **chii**[1].
tii-aka, *n*. [te-aka] Dirt from the hands.
tii-anda, *n*. Extra effort and care in preparation of food.
tii-anda-'nja·sun, *v*. To pay extra care and effort in preparing food.
tii-ara·san, *adj*. [tearai] (In handling) rough; rude; harsh.
tii-bee·san, *adj*. [tebayai] Quick; nimble; agile; quick to anger. See **heesan**.
tii-biku, *n*. A hand harpoon (agricultural tool), a hardwood stick about 30–50 cm in length with a sharp end or with an iron tip blade, used in planting sweet potato vines or removing weeds.
tii-buchukuru, *n*. [te + futokuro] **1** Having one's hands in one's pockets. **2** Doing no work.
tii-busuku, *n*. [tebusoku] Shortage of hands.
tii-chi, *n*. [hitotsu] One; a unit; oneness; likeness.
tiichi-gachi, *n*. [hitotsugaki*] Itemization; writing one by one.
tiichi-mun, *n*. [hitotsumono*] Sameness; oneness; identity.
tiichi·n, *adv*. Not at all; not in the least.
tiida, *n*. [? tentoo] The sun.
tiida-ami, *n*. A sudden rainfall while the sun is shining. See also **ami**[1].
tiida-bu·i, *n*. Same as **tiida'ami**. See also **ami**[1].
tiida-buui, *n*. Basking in the sun.
tiida·n-mii, *n*. A place in the sun.
tiida·n-nukuu, *n*. Same as **tiidabuui**.
tii-daru·san, *adj*. Fatigued in one's hands and arms.
tii-gushi, *n*. [teguse] Light-fingeredness; a pilfering habit; kleptomania.
tii-guusan, *n*. Sitting on floor leaning backward with two hands on the floor supporting oneself. See **guusan**.
tii-haaji, *n*. Same as **tiisaaji**. [GSS]
tii-hagoo·san, *adj*. Impatient with.
tii-hisa-machibu·i, *n*. Coiling around the hands and feet; drag; encumbrance.
tiihisa-nra·sun, *vi*. Lit., to get one's hands and feet wet; to engage in physical labor and hardships. See **ndasun**.
tii-iri, *n*. [teire] Repair; maintenance.
tii-jikaan, *n*. [tezukami] Grabbing with the hand(s). **-sun**, *vt*. **1** To grab with the hands; take in one's hand. **2** To eat with one's fingers.
tii-jiki·in, *vt*. [? tenazukeru] **1** To win over. **2** To look after.
tii-kachi, *n*. Indian hawthorn; Yedo hawthorn [J sharinbai, *Rhaphiolepis umbellata* (Thunb.) Makino var. *umbellata*], a plant the roots of which were used for a textile dye. [ODJ] Also **tikachi**.
tii-kagin, *n*. **1** Allowance; discretion. **2** Knack; tact; skill.
tii-maamaa-sun, *v. colloq*. To be confused; be thrown into confusion; be upset; be flurried; be demoralized.
tii-maami, *n*. A blister on the hand.
tii-makkwa, *n*. [temakura] Use of one's arm as a pillow. **-sun**, *v*. To make a pillow of one's arm.
tii-manichi, *n*. [temaneki] Beckoning.
tii-moo, *n*. A person without an arm.
tii-mukkaa, *n. pej*. Same as **tiimoo**.
tii-mukkoo, *n. pej*. Same as **tiimoo**.
tii-mutaan, *n*. Playing using the hands; making mischief with one's hands.
ti·in[1], *vi*. [teru] (For the sun or the moon) to shine.
tiin[2], *n*. [< tii + wuun; teono] A hack; a chopper; a small carpenter's hatchet whose blade is at an angle like a hoe. See also **wuunu**.
tii-naa, *n*. The back of the hand.
tii-naga·a, *n*. Lit., one whose hands are long; a sneak thief; a pilferer. [GSS]
tii-naga·san, *adj*. Be light-fingered; be a kleptomaniac.
tii-nare·e, *n*. [tenarai] Same as **tinaree**.
tiin-dati·i, *n*. The ceremony of inaugurating the construction of a house. See **tatiin**.

tii nee·in, *phr.* **1** To turn one's hand to; attempt; meddle with. **2** To start a fight. See **neein**².

tii-nii, *n.* [teinei] **1** Politeness; civility; courtesy. **2** Care; scrupulousness; thoroughness.

tii-nii·san, *adj.* Slow with one's hands; slow in work.

tii-njari, *n.* **1** Getting one's hands dirty. **2** Getting oneself into an annoying situation. See **njari**.

tii 'nja·sun, *phr.* **1** To pick a fight. **2** To make advances to (a woman).

tii-nkee, *n.* [temukai] Resistance; opposition; defiance; struggle. Also **tinkee**. **-sun,** *v.* To resist; oppose; defy; struggle.

tii·nna, *n.* (In tug-of-war) a hand rope, referring to numerous small ropes attached to the main tug. See **chinahichi**.

tii·nu-aya, *n.* A fingerprint; a handprint; the lines of the palm.

tii·nu-hira, *n.* [tenohira] See **tiinuwata**.

tii-nujaa, *n.* A wrestling technique, in which the wrestler puts his arm on the opponent's back and twists him down. See **shima**³, **nujun**².

tii·nu-kubi, *n.* Wrist.

tii·nu-uchi, *n.* [tenouchi] **1** One's intention; a secret plan. **2** Skill; capacity.

tii·nu-ura, *n.* [tenoura] Same as **tiinuwata**.

tii·nu-wata, *n.* The palm of the hand. Also **tiinuhira**.

tiiru, *n.* **1** A hand basket woven with bamboo; a bamboo basket with a handle. **2** A deep bamboo basket with a strap. **3** A bamboo basket to hold caught fish; a creel. See also **baaki**.

tii-saaji, *n.* A hand towel; a handkerchief. Also **tihaaji**. See **wunaigami**, **shiji**¹. [OBJ, BHEO, GSS]

tii-sagu·i, *n.* [tesaguri] Groping; feeling one's way.

tii-shicha, *n.* [teshita] One whose status, rank, or wealth is below that of the speaker.

tii-shigutu, *n.* [teshigoto] Manual work; working with one's hands.

tii-shu, *n.* [teishu] Master of the household; a host (at a party); husband.

tii-too, *n.* [teitoo] Mortgage; collateral; security.

tii-toodaachii, *n.* Hands folded. **-sun,** *vi.* To look on with hands folded; stand idly by; remain indifferent.

tii-ukuri, *n.* [teokure] **1** Being past remedy. **2** Missing a chance.

tii-wachare·e, *n.* Being troubled with; being annoyed by; suffering from involvement with.

tii-wata·shi, *n.* [tewatashi] Delivery; personal delivery; handing over directly. Also **tiwatashi**.

tiiwoo-sawoo, *adv.* Being upset; being in confusion; right and left; this way and that; every which way. **-sun,** *v.* To be upset; to be confused.

tii-yoo, *n.* A gesture with the hands; a gesticulation.

tiiyoo-hisayoo, *n. colloq.* Gesture with hands and feet; gesture with all of one's body.

tii-yurusa·a, *n.* Riding with one's hands free, such as in tightrope walking or riding a bicycle without one's hands on the handlebars.

tii-yuru·sun, *v.* To let go of one's hands.

ti-jikun, *n.* A clenched fist; the knuckles.

ti-juku·i, *n.* [tezukuri] Homemade; handmade; homegrown. See **chukuin**.

ti-kachi, *n.* Same as **tiikachi**.

ti-kaji, *n.* [tekazu] Trouble; pains; care.

tiku, *n.* [teko] A lever; a jack.

ti-kuba·i, *n.* [tekubari] Arrangements; preparations

tima, *n.* [tema] **1** Time; labor; trouble. **2** Wages. See also **chimidima**.

tima-chin, *n.* [temachin] Daily wages.

tima-daari, *n.* Being time-consuming; being troublesome.

ti-mani, *n.* [temane] A gesture; gesticu-

lation; signs; a hand signal.
tima-tuya·a, *n.* A wage earner; a day laborer.
ti-miji, *n.* [temizu] Water scooped up with the hands.
tin[1], *n.* [ten] 1 The heaven; the sky; the air; the firmament; the celestial sphere. 2 Heaven. 3 Heaven's will; Providence; God. 4 Nature; laws of nature; fate; destiny.
tin[2], *n.* [ten] A dot; a speck; a speckle; a blot; a stain.
ti-nami, *n.* [tenami] Skill; ability; performance.
ti-nare·e, *n.* [tenarai] 1 Practice; exercise. 2 Calligraphy practice. Also **tiinaree**.
tin-bachi, *n.* [tenbatsu] Heaven's vengeance or judgment; divine retribution.
tinchama, *n.* Mischief; roguery; wanton mischief.
tinchama·a, *n.* A mischievous child; a naughty kid.
tin-chi, *n.* [tenki] The weather. Also **'waachichi**.
tin-ga, *n.* [tenka] 1 The whole country; the land; the realm; the public; the world. 2 Having one's own way.
tin-gaara, *n.* The Milky Way; the galaxy.
tin-gachuu, *n.* [tengajuu*] Velvet material.
tin-gee, *n.* [tengai] A funeral canopy or a funeral baldachin held over an image of a Buddha, a priest, or a coffin. Also **tingeebakama**.
tingee-bakama, *n.* Same as **tingee**.
tin-gu, *n.* [tengu] A braggart; a boaster; a conceited person.
tin-joo, *n.* [tenjoo] 1 The ceiling. 2 In the ceiling. See **annumii**.
tinjoo-gita, *n.* Crossbeams in the ceiling.
tinma, *n.* [tenma] A barge; a sampan; a cargo boat; a lighter.
tin-maku, *n.* [tenmaku] A tent; a pavilion; a shelter tent.
tin-meegaki, *n.* A wrestling technique, similar to **meegaki**, in which the wrestler hooks his foot over his opponent's foot from the outside and throws him down. See **shima**[3].
tin-mii, *n.* [tenmei] God's will; Heaven's decree; destiny; fate; karma; one's life.
tin-mun, *n.* [tenmon] 1 Astronomy; heavenly phenomena. 2 Astrology.
tin-nin, *n.* [tennin] A celestial nymph; a heavenly maiden. [BHEO, OR]
tin·nu-kami, *n.* [tennokami] Heavenly deity, vaguely assumed to be the supreme deity.
tin·nu-tchu, *n.* Same as **tinnin**.
tinpura, *n.* [< J tenpura] Tempura; Japanese fry; fritter.
tinsagu, *n.* A balsam [*Impatiens balsamina* L.]; a garden balsam; a touch-me-not; a jewelweed. Also **tinsaaguu**.
tinsagu·nu-hana, *n.* A balsam flower. See **tinsaguu**.
tin-shii, *n.* [tensui] Rainwater.
tinshii-gaami, *n.* A large jug usually placed under the eaves to collect and store rainwater for drinking and for making tea.
tinshiikan, *n.* [tengusa] Agar.
tinuja, *n.* A handcraft; manual arts, such as embroidery.
tip-puu, *n.* [teppoo] A gun; a rifle; a firearm.
tira, *n.* [tera] A temple; a church; a chapel.
tira-jiishi, *n.* A funeral urn in a temple style. See **jiishigaami**.
ti-shimi-gakumun, *n.* Calligraphy and reading; learning; study; knowledge. Also **gakumun**, **shimi**[1].
ti-soo, *n.* [tesoo] The lines of the palm; palmistry.
ti-waki, *n.* [tewake] Division of work; dividing work among several persons.
ti-wata·shi, *n.* [tewatashi] Same as **ti-iwatashi**.
ton-ton-mii[1], *n.* Ducks and drakes; a

children's play of throwing flat stones across water so that they skip.
ton-ton-mii[2], *n.* A goby fish; a mudskipper [*Periophthalmus vulgaris* Eggert].
too[1], *adv.* Ready; already; enough.
too[2], *interj.* Come now; come.
too[3], *n.* Flatness; evenness; flat land.
Too[4], *n.* [C Tang] China.
Too-achine·e, *n.* Trade with China.
too-baru, *n.* A plain; a prairie. See **haru**[2].
too-biira·a, *n.* A cockroach. Same as **hiiraa, fiiraa**.
too-bira·a, *n.* A Taiwanese fighting fish.
too-bun, *adv.* [toobun] For the present; for the time being; for some time to come.
too-chan, *n. colloq.* [toochan] Dad; daddy.
too-fu, *n.* [toofu] Bean curd; tofu. See also **yushidoofu**.
toofu-maami, *n.* Soybeans [*Glycine max* (L.) Merr.]. See also **maami, ufuchijaa**.
toofu-machi, *n.* A tofu market.
toofu·na-kashi·i, *n.* Same as **toofunukashii**.
toofu·na-kashi·i-iricha·a, *n.* Bean curd lees and pork stir-fry.
toofu-'nbushi·i, *n.* Bean-curd pottage.
toofu·nu-kashi·i, *n.* A dish of bean curd lees. Also **toofunakashii (toofunukahi** [GSS]). See **kashi**[1].
toofu-uushi, *n.* A mortar to grind soybeans to make tofu.
Too-guchi, *n.* The Chinese language.
too-kachi, *n.* [tokaki] A rice measure leveler, made of a bamboo stick with one end cut diagonally.
too-kachi-uuwee, *n.* A celebration of one's eighty-eighth birthday. [OBJ, ODJ]
too-maami, *n.* A broad bean; a horse bean [J soramame; *Vicia faba* L.]. [FOSR] See also **maami**.
too-makkwa, *n.* [toomakura] A rattan pillow.
toomi·in, *vt.* To level; flatten.

toonachin, *n.* Common sorghum [*Sorghum bicolor* (L.) Moench]; corn; Indian corn; maize. [FOSR]
toonachin-muuchii, *n.* Common sorghum rice cake; rice cake with common sorghum mixed in.
-too naran, *phr.* Following negative verb forms, must….
Too-nchu·u, *n.* A Chinese.
tooni, *n.* A pig trough. Also **toonii**.
tooni-kacha·a, *n.* A tool to clean out a trough. See **kachun**[2].
toori·in, *vi.* [taoreru] **1** To fall; come down; topple. **2** To break down; fall in a faint. **3** To be ruined; go to ruin; collapse. **4** To drop; go bankrupt.
tooshinbai, *n.* Mumps; parotitis.
too·sun, *vt.* [taosu] **1** To bring down; throw down; get (a person) down; fell (a tree); floor (a person). **2** To defeat; beat; overthrow; ruin. **3** To bilk; leave unpaid. See also **ushitoosun**.
tootoo-mee, *n.* **1** The moon (children's term). **2** A mortuary tablet. See **iifee**.
Too-yaa-maa, *n.* **1** A pupa; a chrysalis. **2** Lit., where is China, a children's game.
·**tu**[1], *part.* [to] **1** And. **2** With; along with; accompanied by. **3** Against.
-tu[2], *suff.* [to] A unit of capacity, approximately 18 liters or 19 quarts. [NJED]
tu·bi-icha·a, *n.* Japanese common (or flying) squid [J surumeika; *Todarodes pacificus* Steenstrup].
tu·bi-nami, *n.* Choppy waves in the tenth month.
tu·bi-ta·chun, *vi.* [·tan, ·tchi; tobitatsu] To take wing; take off; rise in the air.
tu·bi-winagu, *n.* A wanton woman; a woman of easy virtue. [GSS]
tu·bun, *vi.* [tobu] To fly; take wing; sail through the air; soar.
tubushi, *n.* [toboshi*] A pine torch. Also **tee**[2].
tubuu, *n.* [tobiuo] A flying fish; fish that belong to the Exocoetidae family.
tuchi, *n.* [toki] **1** Time; hour; moment.

2 Case; occasion; season; time. **3** Opportunity; chance. **4** The times; the time; the day. See also **jikan**.

tuchi, *adv.* [toki] When; at the time.

tuchi-duchi, [tokidoki] **1** *n.* Each occasion; each season. **2** *adv.* Sometimes; at times; every now and then; at intervals.

tuchii, *n.* [tokei] A watch; a clock; a timepiece.

tu-dana, *n.* [todana] **1** A closet; a shelf with door; (for food and utensils) a cupboard; a sideboard; a closet; (with lock) a locker; (for clothing) a wardrobe; (for documents) a file cabinet. **2** A built-in Buddhist altar. See **kwii**³.

tudu·chun, *vi.* [todoku] **1** For (a hand) to reach; get to (at); attain to. **2** (For an article) to arrive; reach. **3** To be attained; be realized; be gratified.

tuduki, *n.* [todoke] **1** A report; a notice; a notification. **2** Delivery; forwarding.

tuduki·in, *vt.* [todokeru] **1** To report; notify; register. **2** To deliver; send; hand over.

tudukuu·in, *vi.* [todokooru] **1** To stagnate; be left undone. **2** To fall into arrears; be overdue; be delayed. **3** To have indigestion.

tuduma·in, *vi.* Same as **tumain**.

tuga, *n.* [toga] **1** A fault; blame. **2** A charge; an offense; a penalty.

tuga·i, *n.* [togari] A pointed top.

tugai-figai, *n.* Unevenness of surface; roughness of surface.

tugai·i, *n.* A skinny person with pouty lips.

tuga·in, *vi.* [togaru] (For the tip of a thing) to become sharp; become pointed; taper off to a point.

tugami, *n.* [togame] Blame; censure; carping.

tugami·in, *vt.* [togameru] To find fault with; blame; censure; reprove; reprimand.

tuga-nin, *n.* [toganin] A criminal; a convict; a culprit; an offender.

tu-guchi, *n.* A ferry (crossing). Also **watanji**, **watai**.

tui, *n.* [tori] **1** A bird; a chicken; a hen; a cock; a rooster; fowl. **2** The Cock, tenth of the twelve calendrical animal signs.

tu·i-chi·ji, *n.* [toritsugi] **1** Intermediation; an agent; a middleman; agency. **2** Answering the door; attention to a call.

tuichi·jun, *vt.* [toritsugu] **1** To act as an agent; intermediate. **2** To answer the door; usher in; announce. **3** To transmit; convey.

tui-chikanaya·a, *n.* A poultryman; a chicken farmer. See **chikanain**.

tu·i-chimi·in, *vt.* [toitsumeru] To cross-examine; cross-question; examine closely; press for an answer; press a question home.

tu·i-chiraka·sun, *vt.* [torichirakasu] To scatter about; put in disorder; clutter.

tuichira·sun, *vt.* Same as **tuichirakasun**.

tu·i-dukuru, *n.* [toridokoro] Worth; a merit; a redeeming point; a good point; an attraction.

tui-gwaa, *n.* A little bird.

tu·i-hakara·in, *vt.* [·(r)an, ·ti; torihakarau] To manage; arrange; dispose of; settle; deal with.

tu·i-kee·sun, *vt.* [torikaesu] To recover; regain; take back.

tu·i-mee, *n.* [torimae] One's share; one's portion.

tui-mii, *n.* [torime] Nightblindness.

tu·i-mu·chun, *vt.* [·tan, ·tchi; torimotsu] To do the honors; welcome.

tu·i-mudu·sun, *vt.* [torimodosu] To recover; regain; take back.

tu·in, *vt.* [toru] **1** To take (in hand); hold; seize; catch; grab; get hold of. **2** To receive; procure; obtain; gain. **3** To adopt; take; engage. **4** To prefer; choose; pick; take. **5** To buy; get; earn; have. **6** To get; obtain; gather; pick; pluck. **7** To eat; take; have. **8** To charge;

ask. **9** To manage; transact; take. **10** To make out; interpret. **11** To remove; take off; take away. **12** To catch; seize. **13** To deprive; rob a person of. **14** To capture; seize; annex. **15** To need; pay; require. **16** To subscribe to.

tu·i-na·shi, *n*. [torinashi] **1** Intercession; intervention; mediation. **2** Good offices; recommendation.

tu·i-noo·sun, *vt*. [torinasu] To rectify; intercede (for a person); plead for.

tui·nu-kuuga, *n*. A chicken egg.

tui·nu-yaa, *n*. A henhouse; a chicken coop.

tu·i-shiga·in, *vt*. [torisugaru] **1** To cling to. **2** To entreat.

tu·i-shima·in, *vt*. [torishimaru] To control; manage; oversee; superintend; supervise.

tu·i-shima·ri, *n*. [< J torishimari] Control; discipline; regulation; oversight; supervision.

tui-shirabi, *n*. [torishirabe] An investigation; an examination; an inquiry; a questioning.

tu·i-tati, *n*. [toritate] Appointment; assignment; elevation; promotion; advancement.

tu·i-tati·in, *vt*. [toritateru] To appoint; assign; promote; advance.

tu·i-utu·sun, *vt*. [toriotosu] To let fall; to let slip; drop; miss one's hold.

tu·i-ye·e, *n*. [toriai] Association; company; friendship; acquaintance.

tuja, *n*. A harpoon; a gaff; an iron. See **tujun**.

tuji, *n*. [toji*] A wife.

tuji-kata, *n*. One's wife's family or relatives.

tujiki, *n*. **1** Admonition; a lecture; order. **2** A message.

tujiki·in, *vt*. To admonish; order; command; send a message to.

tuji-kkwa, *n*. One's wife and children; one's family

tujima·in, *vi*. **1** To be settled; be realized; be concluded. **2** To be well arranged; become consolidated. **3** To reach an agreement. Also **shiitujumain**.

tujimi·in, *vt*. To bring (a matter) to a conclusion; complete (work); realize (a project). Also **shiitujumiin**.

tuji-miitu, *n*. A married couple; husband and wife.

tuji·nu-kookoo, *n*. A man filial to his wife; a henpecked husband.

tu·jun, *vt*. [togu] **1** To whet; sharpen (a knife, a sword); grind (an axe); hone (a razor). **2** To wash (rice).

tu-ka[1], *n*. [tooka] **1** Ten days; ten days' time. **2** The tenth day of the month. Also **tuuka**.

·**tuka**[2], *part*. **1** Conjunction for joining items in a non-exhaustive list; and… etc. **2** Indicates uncertainty; some such…, …or something.

tuka·sun, *vt*. [tokasu] To melt; dissolve; fuse; smelt. **2** To mix (flour).

tu-kee, *n*. [tokai] **1** Crossing the ocean; a voyage. **2** Ocean.

tuki·in, *vi*. [tokeru] **1** To melt; thaw; run. **2** To dissolve.

tukkachimi·in, *vt*. [tottsukamaru] To catch; arrest.

tukkui, *n*. [tokkuri] A liquor bottle of the traditional style.

tuku[1], *n*. [toku] Goodness; moral excellence; virtue; a good quality; grace.

tuku[2], *n*. [toku] **1** A profit; a gain. ·**na**, *adj*. Profitable; gainful; economical; paying. **2** Advantage. ·**na**, *adj*. Favorable; advantageous.

tuku[3], *n*. [toko] Alcove (in a room).

tuku[4], *n*. [toko] A bed; quilts.

tuku-mu·chi, *n*. [tokumochi] A man of virtue.

tuku·nu-ma, *n*. An alcove. Same as **tuku**[3].

tukuru, *n*. [tokoro] **1** A place; a spot; a scene; a locality; a region; a district. **2** A point; a feature. **3** A part; an excerpt; a passage (from a book or speech). **4** A thing; what. **5** Time; moment. **6** Extent. **7** A case; an occasion. **8** A counter for people.

tukuru-bare·e, *n*. [tokorobarai] Banishment from one's place of residence.

tukuru-dukuru, *n*. [tokorodokoro] Here and there; at places; sporadically.

tukutu, *adv*. [tokuto] **1** Deliberately; seriously; carefully. **2** Feeling refreshed; feeling fine.

tuma·i[1], *n*. [tomari] A lodging; a stay; a sojourn.

tuma·i[2], *n*. [tomari] A port; a wharf; a pier; anchorage.

tuma·i-kuruu, *n*. A variety of sweet potato that is sweet and light purple in color.

tuma·in, *vi*. [tomaru] **1** To lodge; stay; stop. **2** To halt; stop; come to a stop; cease.

tumee·i-dumee·i, *n*. Searching repeatedly. **-sun**, *v. emph. colloq*. To search for again and again all over. [GSS]

tumee·i-mun, *n*. A find; a thing found and picked up.

tumee·in, *vt*. **1** To search; seek; look for; locate. **2** To find (a thing that is lost); pick up. **3** (For a man) to marry. See also **muchun**[1].

tumi·in, *vt*. [tomeru] **1** To stop; bring to a halt. **2** To forbid; prohibit. **3** To fasten; fix. **4** To let (someone) stay overnight.

tumu[1], *n*. [tomo] The stern; the rear end of a ship.

tumu[2], *n*. [tomo] Same as **utumu**.

tumu-guu, *n*. Same as **guui**. [OGJ, UKH]

tumu-kaji, *n*. [tomo-kaze] A tailwind; favorable wind.

tunai, *n*. [tonari] **1** A next-door neighbor; a neighboring house. **2** Next; adjacent; adjoining; **·nu**, *adj*. Next; neighboring; adjacent.

tunai-bire·e, *n*. Neighborliness; neighborhood relations. See **hiree**.

tu-naka, *n*. [tonaka] The offing; the open sea. Also **tuu**[3], **fukatuu**. See also **agi**.

tunami, *n*. Same as **narashi**[2]. See **tuunamiin**.

tunchi, *n*. **1** Status of steward or assistant steward of a district in premodern Okinawa; **2** A mansion.

tundaa-bun, *n*. [C dongdaopen] A round or multiple-sided legged tray comprised of nine sections with either lacquered or ceramic trays.

tundoo, *n*. Wharf; pier.

tun-fan, *n*. [C tunfan] Pork rice. See **seefan**.

tun-gwa, *n*. A kitchen hut; a kitchen detached from the main dwelling. See **shimu**[1].

tunja·a-mooya·a-sun, *vi*. Same as **tunjaimootaisun**.

tun·jai-moo·tai, *n*. Jumping and dancing. **-sun**, *vi. colloq*. To dance and jump in happiness. Also **tunjaamooyaasun**. [GSS]

tunjaku, *n*. [tonjaku] **1** Treatment; handling; service. **2** Nursing; tending (a patient).

tunji-feejii, *n*. Attire that is in between everyday wear and holiday dress; something slightly dressy but not quite holiday dress. See also **chinchirukaa**.

tun-jii, *n*. [tooji] The winter solstice.

tunjii-biisa, *n*. Cold weather that comes about the time of the winter solstice. See **hiisan**.

tunji·in, *vi*. [tobideru] **1** To jump out. **2** To protrude; project.

tun(u)·jun, *vi*. To leap; spring (up); jump; hop; prance; splash; snap.

tun-kee·in, *vi*. [tobikoeru] To turn around; look back; turn one's head; look over one's shoulder.

tun-kwi·in, *vt*. [tobu + mau] To jump (vault); leap over; fly over.

tun-moo·in, *vi*. To jump up out of surprise; leap (dance) for joy.

tun·ta·chi-yi·i, *n*. Squatting down; sitting on one's heels; crouching. **-sun**, *vi*. To squat; sit down on one's heels; crouch; hunker down.

tunturu-mooyaa-sun, *vi*. To dance with joy; jump with joy.

tunu, *n*. [tono] A holy structure and/or its site. See also **kami'ashagi**. [OBJ]

tunuu-manuu, *n*. Wavering; vacillation; looking to left and right.

tura, *n*. [tora] **1** A tiger; **2** The Tiger; third of the twelve calendrical animal signs.

tura·sun, *vt*. [torasu] **1** To give; present (a thing to a person); let (a person) have. **2** To do (a thing) for (a person); have the kindness to do.

turi[1], *n*. A calm; a calmness; a lull; subsidence.

turi[2], *n*. [torii] A Shinto shrine archway; a castle archway or gate.

turi·in, *vi*. To become calm; lull; be softened; subside.

turubai-kaabai, *n*. Absentmindedness. **-sun**, *v. emph. colloq*. To be absentminded.

turubai-mun, *n*. An absentminded person; an idler; a fool; a half-wit; a goof. Also **turubayaa**.

turubaya·a, *n*. Same as **turubaimun**.

turu-mika·sun, *vi*. To doze (off); take a nap; sleep for a spell.

turu·mun, *vi*. **1** To stagnate; be stagnant; settle. **2** To hesitate. **3** To stammer; falter.

turu·san, *adj*. [toroi*] Dull (of people); slow-witted.

tushi[1], *n*. [toshi] **1** A year; a calendar year. **2** Age; years; time of life. Also **tuushi**.

tushi[2], *n*. [toishi] A whetstone; a rubstone; a grindstone; a hone. See also **kumatu**.

tushi-bi, *n*. The traditional birthday, which falls on the first day of the first month in years with the same calendrical animal sign as the birth year; the traditional birthday party held once every twelve years; the birthday celebration.

tushi-guru, *n*. [toshigoro] Puberty; a marriageable age.

tushi·nu-yuuru, *n*. New Year's Eve. [ODJ]

tushi-shicha, *n*. [toshishita] Junior in age.

tushi-shiija, *n*. Senior in age. Also **tushi'wii**.

tushi-washiri, *n*. [toshiwasure] A year-end party.

tushi-'wii, *n*. [toshiue] Same as **tushishiija**.

tushui, *n*. Same as **tusui**.

tusui, *n*. [toshiyori] An old person; an aged person; an elder; the aged; old people. Also **tushui, utusui, utusui-kata**.

tusui-mii, *n*. Presbyopia; hyperopia; hypermetropia; farsightedness due to old age.

tusui-yoo·i, *n*. Senility; infirmity of old age.

tutan, *n*. [totan] Zinc.

tutchiri, *n*. The **kasuri** design; a splashed pattern; cloth with splashed patterns. Also **yiichiri**.

tutin, *adv*. [totemo] Rather (than); better (than); sooner (than); preferably.

tutun-ba, *n*. A slaughterhouse; an abattoir; a shambles. Same as **'waasaayaa**.

tuu[1], *n*. [too] Rattan.

tuu[2], *n*. [too] Ten; ten years of age. See also **juu**[2].

tuu[3], *n*. [? tooi, ? tsu] **1** The offing; the open sea. **2** A strait. See also **tunaka, fukatuu, agi**.

tuu-asa, *n*. [tooasa] A shoaling beach; a shallow beach.

tuu-chii-ku, *n*. See **tuutiikun**.

-tuu·i, *n*. [toori] Like; the same.

tuu·i-michi, *n*. [toorimichi] A pathway; a passageway; route.

tuu·in¹, *vi.* [tooru] 1 To go along (through, past); pass (by, along, through). 2 To pass (an exam). 3 To pass (for, as). 4 To pass; prevail; be admissible. 5 To pervade; penetrate; go around.

tuu·in², *vt.* [tou] To ask (a person something); put a question to; make an inquiry.

tuu-jin, *n.* [tooshin] A lamp wick.

tuu-maa·i, *n.* [toomawari] A roundabout way (route, course); a circuitous route; a circuit; a detour. Also **tuumigui**.

tuu-michi, *n.* [toomichi] A long way; a long journey. See also **tuumaai**.

tuu-migu·i, *n.* Same as **tuumaai**.

tuu-nami·in, *vt.* To average; level; flatten. See **tunami**.

tuu-nu·chun, *vi.* [toonoku] To become far off and distant; recede (from view); get away; (sound) die away in the distance; keep at a distance; keep away from.

tuuru, *n.* [tooroo] A lantern; a paper lantern, usually of traditional style, made of wood, bamboo, and paper. See also **ishiduuru, utuuru, miguiduuru**.

tuu·san, *adj.* [tooi] Distant; far; remote.

tuushi, *n.* [toishi] Same as **tushi¹**.

tuu·sun, *vt.* [toosu] To let (a person) pass; pass (a thing) through; let go by; run (a thread) through; carry through; keep to one's principles; persist; continue

tuu-tai, *n.* Ten people. Also **juunin**.

tuu-tii-kun, *n.* [? C Tudishen] Originally a Chinese Taoist deity of earth and agriculture, localized in Okinawa after 1698 as a deity of business, health and longevity, safety, etc. Also **tuuchiiku**. [OBJ]

U———

u-, *pref.* [o-, on-] Denotes respect and politeness. Also **gu-**.

ubagii, *n.* [< **ubii** + **agi·i** (< **agiin**)] Food to celebrate the birth of a baby, to be partaken of by the parents, offered to the ancestors, and shared by visitors and relatives on the day of the infant's naming. [OBJ] Also **naajiki'ubagii**.

ubi¹, *n.* [oboe] 1 Memory; learning; understanding. 2 Recollection; remembrance; experience. Also **ubii**.

ubi², *n.* [obi] A hoop.

ubi-daki, *n.* Lit., hoop bamboo [*Bambusa glaucescens* Sieb. ex Merr.; *Bambusa multiplex* (Lour.) Raeusch]. Also **njadaki**. See **njadaki**. [ODJ, FOSR]

ubi-dee, *n.* Ability to memorize; memory; memorization.

u-bii, *n.* Lustral water; the holy water to be offered to the deities.

ubii-gachi, *n.* [oboegaki] A memorandum; a memo; a note; minutes; proceedings.

ubii-guri·s(h)an, *adj.* [...guri·ku] Hard to remember.

ubi·in, *vt.* [oboeru] 1 To commit to memory; fix in one's mind; remember; memorize. 2 To learn; acquire; master; understand. 3 To feel; know; experience.

ubii-nadi·i, *n.* 1 Stroking with holy water, by placing a few drops of water on the forehead in homage to the well deity or water deity. 2 Stroking with holy water, a part of marriage confirmation rites. 3 A magic formula of rejuvenation in which holy water is drawn from the birth spring of a village and stroked three times on the forehead with the middle finger. 4 A clan rite held in the first, third, and eighth lunar months, in which the clan priestess and a group of women retrieve holy water. [ODJ, OGJ] *ubijini*

ubiji·ni, *adv.* [oboezuni] Unintentionally; involuntarily; unconsciously; unawares; spontaneously; instinctively.

ubi-'nja·sun, *vt.* [oboedasu] To recollect; remember; think back; call to mind.

ubiraji, *adv.* Unawares; unintentionally. Same as **ubijini**.

ubiraji-gutu, *n.* An unexpected event.

u-buchi-dan, *n.* [obutsudan] A Buddhist altar. Also **buchidan**.

ubu-gaa, *n.* Same as **ubukaa**.

ubu-gami, *n.* Deity of birth, who controls and decides the fate of newborn infants.

ubugami-mundoo, *n.* A Ryukyu-wide legend about the fate of newborn infants and ritual practices to ensure good fates. [ODJ]

ubu-jin, *n.* [ubu-ginu] Baby clothes; swaddling clothes. [ODJ]

ubu-kaa, *n.* A birth well or spring; a well or spring the water from which is used for the first bath or for ritual application of water to the forehead of an infant. See also **ubumiji, sooroomiji**. [ODJ]

u-buku, *n.* [obuku] A bowl of cooked rice offered to the deities and the ancestral spirits. [UKH] See also **usandee**.

ubu-miji, *n.* The birth water. See **ubukaa**.

u-bun[1], *n. formal* The meal; (cooked) rice. See **munu**.

u-bun[2], *n.* [obon] A small tray. [GSS]

ubun-chiji, *n.* The boiled rice grain.

ubun-nijirii, *n.* A rice ball.

ubun-wan, *n. formal* A rice bowl. Also **meemakai**.

uburu, *n.* Ladle made of a fan palm leaf. Same as **kuba niibu**.

uburu-jichi, *n.* [oborozuki] A hazy, misty moon. [UKH]

uburu-jichuu, *n.* [oborozukiyo] A misty moonlit night; a night with hazy moon.

ubu-yu, *n.* A newborn infant's first bath; the first cleaning bath. See also **ubumiji, ubukaa**. [ODJ]

u-cha, *n. formal* [ocha] Tea. See **chaa**[3].

uchaa·sun, *vt.* [uchiawaseru] 1 To prearrange; arrange (a matter with a person). 2 To cooperate with; combine; unite effort with. 3 To neatly arrange the collars of kimono.

uchaga·in, *vi.* [ukiagaru] 1 To float; surface. 2 To become clear and vivid (of designs); become flashy.

uchagi·in, *vt.* [uchi + ageru] To push up; make (a person, a thing) look up.

ucha·in, *vi.* [·(r)an, ·ti; uchiau] 1 To become; befit; suit; be suitable; match well; suit with; be in keeping with; be harmonious. 2 To combine two talents. 3 To combine (one thing with another); have two things. Also **shinain**.

ucha·i-shina·i, *n.* Being perfectly matched; being very well suited for each other; a perfect harmony.

uchakki, *n.* [uchikake] A casual gown, worn by both male and female.

u-chaku, *n.* Same as **chaku**.

u-cha-too, *n.* [ochatoo] Tea offered to the deities and ancestral spirits.

u-cha-uki, *n.* [chauke] Teacake; between-meal refreshments.

uche·e-kane·e, *n.* Combination of one thing with another; proficiency in two things.

uchi, *n.* [uchi] 1 The inside; the interior; indoors. 2 A house; one's home. 3 Within; while; during. 4 Between; among; out of.

uchi-aki·in, *vt.* [uchiakeru] To disclose; reveal; confide (a secret) to another. [UKH]

uchi-ami, *n.* Rain which comes inside a house (mostly due to a wind.) **-sun**, *v.* For rain to come indoors due to wind. See also **uchikumun**.

uchi-atai, *n.* **-sun**, *v.* To feel criticized by apparently innocent remarks.

uchi-ba, *n.* [uchiwa] **1** Being moderate; being conservative; moderation. **2** Partial payment; deposit; bargain money.
uchi-chi, *n.* A bruise; a contusion; internal bleeding.
u-chichu·u, *n. inf.* Mr. Moon.
uchidu, *n.* [ochido] A fault.
uchi-fuka, *n.* **1** Inside and outside. **2** In and out of the house. **3** Relatives and strangers.
uchi-furi·in, *vi.* To fall in love completely. See also **manburi**.
uchi-gani, *n.* A gong. [UKH]
uchi-gumi·i, *n.* Making an association for business or other projects. **-sun**, *v.* To make a union.
uchi-gusa, *n.* [ukigusa] A floating weed; a duckweed.
uchi-gutu, *n.* Domestic chores; household work. Same as **jooshichi**. [UKH]
uchi·in[1], *vi.* [utsuru] **1** To move (to another place); transfer. **2** To become empty; become vacant. **3** To be infected with; catch (a cold); contract (an illness).
uchi·in[2], *vi.* [utsuru] **1** To be reflected; be imaged; be mirrored; be on the screen. **2** (Colors or designs) to match; go well with. **3** (Of photos) to be taken; to come out.
uchi-kabi, *n.* Brown paper on which mock copper coins are struck with a metal mold, burned during the *Bon* festival as an offering of the money for use in the afterlife to one's ancestral spirits. Also **anjikabi**. See also **nchabi, kabi'anjii, waradooshi**.
uchikabi-ucha·a, *n.* A metal stamp about 10 cm long and about 2 cm in diameter, used to strike coin patterns on **uchikabi**. See **uchikabi**.
uchi-kaki, *n.* [uchikake] A lady's long gown in the premodern period. [OBJ]
uchi-kawa·in, *vi.* [uchikawaru] To undergo a complete change; change drastically.
u-chike·e, *n.* [otsukai] An errand; a messenger.
uchi-kee·sun, *vt.* [uchikaesu] To hit back; bounce back. [UKH]
uchiki·in, *vt.* To put firmly down; place at a proper place; lay down.
uchikiya·a-gii, *n.* Thin wood and bamboo boards protecting the sides of a boat against the constant friction of rowing. See **sabani**.
uchiku·mun, *vi.* [uchikomu*] For rain to fall indoors. Same as **uchi'amisun**.
uchi-kwa·in, *vt.* To devour; eat up voraciously; swallow up.
uchi-mumu, *n.* The inner part of the thigh.
Uchinaa, *n.* The native term for Okinawa, variously used in the strict sense of Okinawa Island only, Okinawa and its outlying islands, the entire area of Okinawa prefecture (Okinawa, Miyako, and Yaeyama island groups), or a synonym for the Ryukyus (Amami-Ōshima, Okinawa, Miyako, and Yaeyama groups).
Uchinaa-guchi, *n.* The Okinawan language; the Okinawan dialect.
Uchinaa-jima, *n.* Okinawan wrestling. See also **shima**[3]. [ODJ]
Uchinaa-kanpuu, *n.* A traditional Okinawan women's hairstyle. Also **kanpuu**.
Uchinaa-mun, *n.* A product, often fresh produce, made or grown in Okinawa.
Uchinaa-nchu, *n.* An Okinawan.
Uchinaa-soogwachi, *n.* The New Year's Day according to the lunar calendar; the Okinawan New Year's. See also **Yamatusoogwachi**.
Uchinaa-yuu, *n.* Okinawan period, the period in Okinawan history when Okinawa was a sovereign nation, namely before 1879; roughly, the days of the Ryukyu kingdom. See also **yuugawai, Yamatuyuu, Amerikayuu**.

uchi-nagani, *n.* Roast beef or pork.
uchi-na·sun, *vt.* To end; terminate; conclude.
uchiri, *n.* [oki] Embers; live charcoal.
uchi-soodan, *n.* [uchisoodan] An informal consultation; an informal talk; a private discussion.
uchi-ta·chun, *vi.* [·tan, ·tchi; ukitatsu] To be conspicuous; be prominent; stand out; contrast with.
uchiti, *n.* [okite] A law; a regulation; legislation.
uchi-umi, *n.* [uchiumi] An inland sea; an arm of the sea.
uchiwa[1], *n.* [uchiwa] A round-shaped fan.
uchi-wa[2], *n.* [uchiwa] A family circle; the inside; close relatives; being among close friends.
uchi-yu, *n.* [ukiyo] The transitory world; the floating world (of the Edo period of Japan).
uchukwi·i, *n.* A *furoshiki* (cloth wrapper); a wrapping cloth.
uchukwii-jichin, *n.* A *furoshiki* package.
u·chun[1], *vt.* [oku] 1 To put; place; position. 2 To leave (a thing) behind. 3 To leave; allow; let. 4 To hold; store (up). 5 To engage; keep; employ.
u·chun[2], *vt.* [·tan, ·tchi; utsu] 1 To hit; beat; knock; clap (one's hands). 2 To fire; shoot; discharge. 3 To drive in; hammer. 4 To water; sprinkle (with water). 5 To play (the game of *go* or to gamble). 6 To take revenge. 7 To till (a field).
u·chun[3], *vi.* [uku] To float; rise to the surface; be buoyed up.
uchu·shi, *n.* [utsushi] A copy; a counterpart; a transcript; a duplicate; an imitation; a facsimile.
uchu·sun[1], *vt.* [utsusu] 1 To copy; transcribe. 2 To imitate; copy; trace; reproduce. 3 To describe; depict; express. 4 To reflect (in a mirror); project.
uchu·sun[2], *vt.* [utsusu] 1 To move; remove; shift. 2 To pour; empty (a vessel). 3 To infect; transmit a disease.
uchu-u, *n.* [uchi] Internal conditions; inside affairs.
uchuubi, *n.* [choomi] Appreciation of food; relish; sampling of food. **-sun**, *v.* To appreciate food; sample food.
uchuuji, *n.* Reception; welcome; service. **-sun**, *v.* To welcome; receive (company); do the honors. [UKH]
udaa·sun, *vt.* [odosu] To scare; frighten; scold in a loud voice.
udi, *n.* [ude] An arm; the upper and lower arms; the lower arm. See also **keena**.
udi-jikara, *n.* [ude + chikara] Muscle; brawn; physical strength.
udi-kaki·i, *n.* Arm wrestling.
udi-kaki·in, *vi.* To arm wrestle.
udi-makkwa, *n.* [udemakura] Making a pillow of someone's arm. See also **tiimakkwa**.
uduki·in, *vi.* [odokeru] To incur a loss; suffer a loss. Also **urukiin**.
u-dun, *n.* A mansion; the residence as well as the status of an **aji** lord in the premodern days.
udun-jiishi, *n.* A funeral urn in a mansion style. See **jiishigaami**.
uduru·chun, *vi.* [odoroku] To be surprised; be astonished; be amazed; be startled.
uduruka·sun, *vt.* To surprise (a person); startle (a person); amaze; astound; shock.
ufee, *adv.* Same as **uhee**.
ufii, *n.* Same as **uushi**. [GSS]
ufu-, *pref.* [oo-] Denotes largeness.
ufu-afii, *n.* The eldest brother.
ufu-ami, *n.* [ooame] A heavy (pelting, torrential) rain; a big rainfall; a downpour.
ufu-anmaa, *n.* The elder or eldest sister of one's parent.
ufu-aya, *n.* [ooaya] Large patterns (of a kimono).

ufu-ayaa, *n*. The eldest sister of either parent; the eldest maternal aunt.
ufu-baa, *n*. An aunt who is an immediate younger sibling of one's parent.
ufu-baru, *n*. A large farm.
ufu-basan, *n*. 1 Pruning shears. 2 A pair of shears used to make thatched roofs.
ufu-bisa·a, *n. pej.* A person whose legs are enlarged on account of elephantiasis. [GSS]
ufu-buni, *n*. [oobune] A large ship.
ufu-bushi, *n*. Classical music and songs of Okinawa.
ufu-chijaa, *n*. Soy beans, used for tofu bean curd cake. Also **toofumaami**.
ufu-chinee, *n*. A large household; a large family; a rich family.
ufu-dunchi, *n*. Lit., a big mansion. 1 Polite term for a house belonging to someone else other than the speaker. 2 Main family of a gentry-class clan. See also **ufuyaa**.
ufu-dun-moo·i, *n*. [... + **tun-moo·in**] Astonishment; great surprise.
ufu-gee, *n*. [As food] Stomach (of animals such as pig, etc.); intestines.
ufu-gii, *n*. A big tree.
ufu-guchi, *n*. Tall talk; boasting; bragging; exaggeration; grandiloquence; highfalutin palaver.
ufu-gwii, *n*. A loud voice.
ufu-ii, *n*. The best room in a house; a drawing room. Also **ichibanjaa**. [UKH]
ufu-iibi, *n*. The thumb; the big toe. See **iibi**.
ufu-iichi, *n*. A deep breath; a sigh; a sigh of relief; a sigh of grief.
ufu-ji, *n*. Lit., big land; Okinawa Island proper, as distinct from smaller offshore islands. Also **ufuji**.
ufu-jimu, *n*. [... + **chimu**] A big heart; generosity; liberality.
ufu-jimu·u, *n*. A generous person; a liberal, lavish giver.
ufu-jin, *n*. A large sum of money; a pile of money. Also **maruchijin**.
ufu-jinee, *n*. A large household.
ufu-jiru, *n*. A vein. [UKH]
ufu-juukoo, *n*. The big mass, referring to the twenty-fifth and thirty-third year masses for the souls of the dead. See **suukoo, ninchi**[1].
ufu-kaji, *n*. A typhoon; a storm. Also **arashi, teefuu**.
ufuku na·in, *vi*. To increase; multiply.
ufu-kuuga·a, *n. pej.* A person whose testicles are enlarged on account of elephantiasis. [GSS]
ufu-makutu·u, *n*. A person who is simple and honest.
ufu-machiya, *n*. A large store. Also **magimachiya**. See also **gumamachiya, machiyagwaa**.
ufu-maru, *n*. A large open space without any structures. [UKH]
ufu-michi, *n*. A main (broad, principal) road or street; a leading thoroughfare; an avenue; an arterial highway.
ufu-mujaa, *n*. Rye; naked barley. [UKH] Also **hadakamuji**. See **muji**[2].
ufu-muji, *n*. [oomugi] Barley.
ufu-munu-i·i, *n*. Boasting; bragging; exaggeration; grandiloquence; highfalutin speech. See also **ufuguchi**.
ufu-muutu, *n*. The head family; the grand head family; the origin; the founding house of a patrilineal consanguineous group.
ufu-ninju, *n*. [oo + ninzu] A great many people; a multitude; a mass of people.
ufu-nkashi, *n*. [oomukashi] Antiquity; long, long ago; the prehistoric age in contrast to a middle antiquity or historical age.
ufu-'nmee, *n*. A great grandmother; the elder sister of one's grandparent.
ufu-'nmii, *n*. The eldest sister; a big sister.
ufu-nusudu, *n*. A great thief.
ufu-ruma·a, *n*. A big person either in height or weight. [UKH]

ufusan

ufu·san, *adj.* Abundant; plentiful; many; much; a lot of.

ufusa·ni-katajikiruu, *n.* Decision by majority.

ufu-soo, *n.* A careless person; a rash person; a fool; a half-wit. Also **ufusoomun**.

ufu-suu, *n.* A spring tide.

ufu-tchu, *n.* An adult; a grown-up.

ufu-tchu-fuunaa, *n.* Behavior like an adult; assumption of a grown-up air.

ufu-tchu-shigutu, *n.* Work for an adult; difficult work.

ufu-turubai, *n.* Absentmindedness; an absentminded person. [UKH]

ufu-ufuu·tu, *adv.* Full; fully; ample; amply; copiously; abundantly.

ufu-umi, *n.* [ooumi] A great ocean; a great sea. Also **uutu**.

ufuu-suu, *n.* The eldest paternal uncle.

ufuu-taarii, *n.* [C daren] An uncle; an elder brother of either parent.

ufuu-tanmee, *n.* A great-grandfather.

ufu-uubi, *n.* A broad sash of satin and cotton worn by men of the upper classes in premodern Okinawa as part of the official attire indicating the wearer's rank. See **uubi**.

ufuu-yatchii, *n.* The eldest brother; a big brother.

ufu-'waaji, *n.* One's best clothes; one's holiday suit. [UKH]

ufu-ware·e, *n.* [oowarai] Great laughter; loud, uproarious laughter; a burst of laughter. See also **warain**.

ufu-wata, *n.* 1 A big belly; a big belly such as that of a pregnant woman. 2 The colon; the large intestine. -**sun**, *v.* To have a big belly; become pregnant.

ufu-wata·a, *n. pej.* Big-bellied person; woman heavy with child.

ufuwata-mun, *n.* A pregnant woman. [UKH, OGJ]

ufu-wikiga, *n.* Lit., a big man; ritual protective euphemism for a girl baby.

ufu-winagu, *n.* Lit., a big woman; ritual protective euphemism for a boy baby.

ufu-yaa, *n.* Same as **muutuyaa**. See also **muutu**.

ufuyaa-ninju, *n.* A large family; an extended family.

ufu-yashi·i, *n.* A quiet, gentle person; a good-natured person; a credulous person.

ufu-yas·san, *adj.* [...-**yashi·ku**] Gentle; mild; meek; quiet; good-natured; docile; kind.

ugachi, *n.* Positiveness; being enterprising.

u·ga-chika·sa, *n.* So near; so close.

ugan[1], *n.* A small shrine.

ugan[2], *n.* Same as **ugwan**.

u-gan-juu, *n. formal* [ganjoo] Healthy and strong.

u·ga-too, *n.* Very far; being very distant.

uguchi-yoo·san, *adj.* Mentally feeble. [UKH]

ugu·i, *n.* [ogori] 1 A treat; luxury; extravagance. 2 Pride; arrogance; insolence.

ugui-mun, *n.* A proud person; an arrogant person; a haughty person.

ugu·in, *vi.* [ogoru] To be proud; be haughty.

uguishi, *n.* [uguisu] A (Japanese) bush warbler.

u-guma, *n.* [goma] Sesame [*Sesamum orientale* L.]; a sesame seed; gingili plant.

uguma-anda, *n.* Sesame oil; gingili.

u-gwan, *n.* [ogan] A prayer; devotions; supplication. Also **ugan**[2].

ugwan-doogu, *n.* Paraphernalia of supplication. See **binshii, juubaku, ukkoo, hanagumi, saki**.

ugwan-gutu, *n.* Matters that require prayers and supplication such as a series of misfortunes and illnesses.

u-gwan-ju, *n.* A sacred place; a holy grove where a god is enshrined. Also **wuganju**.

u-gwan-su, *n.* Same as **gwansu**[2].

u-haka, *n.* [ohaka] A tomb; a grave; cemetery.

u-haka-me·e, *n.* [ohakamairi] A visit to one's family tomb.

uhee, *adv.* A little while; a little. [UKH]

uhi, *n.* That much; so much; to that extent; in that degree; only that; that alone; so little. Also **ufi, uppi**.

uhooku, *n.* [ooku] A large quantity; a lot; much; a lot; plenty; an abundance; a great many.

ui, *n.* [uri] A melon.

ui-daka, *n.* [uridaka] The amount of sales; sale; proceeds.

ui-mun[1], *n.* [urimono] An article for sale; merchandise.

ui-mun[2], *n.* [orimono] Textile; cloth; fabric; woven stuff.

u·in, *vt.* [uru] 1 To sell; make a sale; offer for sale. 2 To gain fame. 3 To betray; deceive; squeal on.

ui-nuku·i, *n.* [urenokori] Remainders; remnants; goods left unsold.

ui-nuku·shi, *n.* [urenokoshi] Remnants; leftover goods; goods left unsold.

ui-saba·chun, *vt.* [urisabaku] To sell; deal in; dispose of; work off.

ui-tuba·sun, *vt.* [uritobasu] To sell off; dispose of.

uji[1], *n.* [uji] A maggot; a grub; a larva.

uji[2], *n.* [uji] A clan name; lineage; birth; blood; stock.

uji·in, *vi.* [ojiru] To fear; dread; be afraid of; be frightened; be scared.

u-jin, *n.* [ozen] A small, low, individual dining table; an individual table; a tray. See also **taka'ujin**.

ujina·in, *vt.* [·(r)an, ·ti; oginau] To take in nourishment to build up stamina; eat nourishing food; supplement one's food.

ujine·e, *n.* [oginai] Nutriment; nourishing food to build up stamina.

ujini·i, *n.* Same as **ujinee**. [UKH]

ujiraa·s(h)an, *adj.* (Of women and children) beautiful; lovely; cute; sagacious; intelligent; clever; bright.

ujuma·sun, *vt.* To wake (someone) up. [UKH, OGJ]

ujumi, *n.* A chance; an opportunity.

ujumi·in, *vt.* [uzumeru] 1 To bury; inter; inhume; cover up. 2 To fill in; plug up; inlay (with). 3 To fill up; make up; cover (a loss).

uju·mun, *vi.* To awaken; wake up.

ujun-biira, *n.* A wooden trowel for use in the rice paddy.

ukaa·s(h)an, *adj.* 1 Dangerous; perilous; risky. 2 (Of a patient) critical; serious.

ukaasa-shigutu, *n.* Risky work.

ukaba·sun, *vt.* To let float; set (a ship) afloat; launch (a new ship).

ukabi·in, *vt.* [ukaberu] To let float; launch. Also **ukabasun**.

uka·bun, *vi.* [ukabu] 1 To float; keep afloat; rise to the surface. 2 (For soul) rest in peace; enter Nirvana.

ukaga·in, *vt.* [·(r)an, ·ti; ukagau] To spy on; peek into (through); secretly investigate.

uka·in, *vi. pej.* (For a man) to have sexual intercourse. See also **hoosun, ichain**.

u-kaja·i, *n.* [okazari] Ornaments; decorations; offerings (often on an alcove in a room or on the Buddhist altar).

u-kaji, *n.* [okage] 1 Patronage; (nonmonetary) indebtedness; favor; grace; help; support; backing. 2 A perquisite; an emolument; a privilege.

u-kaki-busee, *n.* Government (honorific); reign.

u-kama·nu-mee, *n.* A dirt floor space in front of ovens.

u-kami-gutu, *n.* Divine matter; rites; spiritual matters that require attention.

ukasari·in, *vi.* [ukasareru] 1 To be carried away; be exhilarated; be captivated. 2 To be delirious with a fever; be in a delirium.

ukat·tu, *adv.* [ukatto] Carelessly; thoughtlessly; inadvertently. Also **ukkattu**.

ukattu·u, *n.* An absent-minded person; a careless person. Also **ukkattuu**.
ukayee, *n.* Copulation. See **chirubun**. [GSS]
u-kee, *n.* [okayu] Same as **kee**².
ukee·in, *vi.* To hesitate; waver; hold back; vacillate; be reserved; be diffident.
ukee-mee, *n.* Same as **ukee**. [GSS]
ukee-umii, *n.* Reserve; restraint; diffidence; hesitation.
uki, *n.* [uke*] A float; a cork; a buoy.
uki-chiki, *n.* [uketsuke] A reception desk; an usher.
uki-dui, *n.* [uketori] A receipt; a voucher; an acknowledgment. Also **ukitui**.
uki-gusa, *n.* [ukikusa] A floating weed.
uki-hanshi, *n.* Response; negotiation; a reply; reception; dealing (with people).
ukihan·sun, *vt.* To fail to catch.
uki-hintoo, *n.* A reply; an answer; a response. Also **ukifintoo**.
uki·in¹, *vt.* [ukeru] 1 To receive; accept; be given; have; take; get; obtain; contract. 2 To catch (a ball). 3 To take (a test). 4 To receive; suffer.
uki·in², *vi.* [okiru] 1 To get up; get out of bed; leave one's (sick) bed. 2 To wake up; awake. 3 To get up; rise; pick oneself up.
uki·in³, *vt.* [ukeru] To float; set (a ship) afloat; waft; launch. Also **ukabiin**.
uki-mu·chi, *n.* [ukemochi] Charge; matter in one's charge; one's stint.
ukimu·chun, *vt.* To take charge of; take (something) in one's charge.
uki-nin, *n.* [ukenin*] (Personal) guarantor; a guaranty; reference.
uki-shigutu, *n.* Contract work; a contract job; piecework Also **ukishikuchi**.
uki-shikuchi, *n.* Same as **ukishigutu**.
ukitee-kwe·e-kwe·e, *n.* Lit., waking up and eating. **-sun**, *v. colloq.* To go to bed after eating, and after eating go back to bed; to do nothing but eating and sleeping. Also **kwatainintai**.

uki-tu·i, *n.* [uketori] A receipt; a voucher; an acknowledgment. Also **ukidui**.
ukitu·in, *vt.* 1 To receive; get; accept. 2 To understand; learn.
uki-waja, *n.* A contract; a contracted job.
ukka, *n.* A debt; arrears; arrearage; liability; dues.
ukka-bare·e, *n.* Repayment; discharge (a debt); liquidation.
ukka·tu, *adv.* [ukatto] See **ukattu**.
ukkattu·u, *n.* See **ukattuu**.
ukkee, *n.* See **ukkeemee**.
ukkee-mee, *n.* Rice cooked so soft that it cannot be picked up with chopsticks.
uk-koo, *n.* [okoo] Incense. Also **ukoo**.
uk-kuru·bun, *vi.* To tumble down; fall (down to the ground); have a fall.
ukoo, *n.* Same as **ukkoo**.
u-kooru, *n.* An incense burner; a funeral incense burner. Also **kooru**.
u-kudi, *n.* A kin group priestess whose duty is to serve the ancestral deities. Also **kudii**, **ukudii**. See also **wunai'ukudi**, **wikii'ukudi**. [OBJ]
ukufi, *n.* Cataract.
ukui-kee·sun, *vt.* To send back; return.
uku·i-mun, *n.* [okurimono] A present; a gift.
uku·in¹, *vt.* [okuru] 1 To send (an item); forward; transmit; ship (a thing). 2 To send (a person) away. 3 To escort; see (a person) home; attend a funeral.
uku·in², *vi.* [okoru] 1 To happen; come to pass; occur; take place; develop. 2 To originate in; arise from; grow out of.
ukune·e, *n.* [okonai] 1 An act; one's doing; a deed. 2 Conduct; deportment; behavior.
ukuri·in, *vi.* [okureru] 1 To be late; be tardy; be behind schedule. 2 To fall behind; fall back; lag behind; be outstripped; be retarded. 3 To lag behind; be out of touch with; be behind the times. 4 (Of a watch) to lose time; to run slowly.
uku·sun, *vt.* [okosu] 1 To raise up (what

has fallen); set up; set upright; pick (a person) up. 2 To wake up; awake; arouse. 3 To help (a person) to become prosperous.

ukuta·in, *vi.* [okotaru] To neglect (one's duties); be negligent (of duty); be remiss (in the discharge of one's duties); be off one's guard.

uku-yama, *n.* [okuyama] Same as **yama'uku**.

uma, *n.* Horse. See **'nma**[1].

umaari·in, *vi.* [omowareru] 1 To seem; appear; look. 2 To be thought of; be considered.

u-machi·i, *n.* [omatsuri] Festivals related to agriculture.

umaga, *n.* See **'nmaga**.

u-ma-nchu, *n.* The people; the citizens; the public; the populace.

umari·in, *vi.* See **'nmariin**.

u-meeshi, *n.* (A pair of) chopsticks. See also **chufaashi, meeshi**[1].

u-meeshi-baku, *n.* A chopstick case.

umi[1], *n.* [umi] The sea; the ocean. Also **'nmi**. See also **tuu**[3], **fukatuu, agi, tunaka, inoo, umi'atchaa**.

umi[2], *n.* See **'nmi**[3].

umi-, *pref.* Denoting love and affection, used with a personal name or a term of personal relationship. Also **'nmi-**.

umi-atcha·a, *n.* A sailor; a seaman; a fisherman. Same as **uminchu**.

umi-baku, *n.* A small, waterproof wooden box for matches and clothing carried aboard a fishing boat.

umi-bata, *n.* [umibata] The beach; the seashore; the seaside.

umi-boochaa, *n.* [umi + hoochoo] A fisherman's knife.

umi-bushi, *n.* See **'nmibushi**.

umi-chi·chun, *vt.* [omoitsuku] To hit upon (an idea), think up; devise.

umi-chi·in, *vt.* [omoikiru] To resign oneself to; get over (a loss); give no further thought; resolve; determine.

u-michi-mun, *n.* See **hinukan**.

umi-chi·ri, *n.* [omoikiri] 1 Resignation; abandonment. 2 Decision; resolution.

umi-chit·chi, *adv.* [omoikitte] Decisively; resolutely; boldly; daringly; once and for all; firmly.

umi-chitu, *adv.* [omoikitte] Radically; decisively; resolutely; firmly.

umi-doogu, *n.* [umi + doogu] Fishing tools. See also **chii**[2], **naa**[4], **uminaa, chinbuku, ami**[2], **eeku**[1], **fuu**[3], **yuutui, tiiru, kee**[4].

umi-gaami, *n.* [umigame] The sea turtle. Also **'nmigaami**.

umi-gani, *n.* A sea crab; a crab which lives in the sea. See also **kaagani**.

umi·i, *n.* [omoi] Thought; idea; mind; sense; feeling; emotion; sentiment. See **umui**[1].

umii-duui, *n.* [omoidoori] Being after one's own heart; being satisfactory; being desired.

umii-hama·in, *vi.* To strive; labor; be diligent; apply oneself to.

umii-kugari·in, *vi.* Same as **umuikugariin**.

umi·in, *vt.* [umeru] To bury; inter. Also **ujumiin**.

umii-noo·sun, *vt.* [omoinaosu] To reconsider; think better of; think twice.

umii·nu-fuka, *n.* [omoinohoka] Unexpected event. **·nu**, *adj.* Unexpected; unanticipated; surprising; accidental.

umii-shiji, *n.* [omoisugi] Overanxiousness; excessive worry.

umii-yamii-sun, *vi. colloq.* To be depressed; worry; hesitate.

umi-jin, *n.* Fisherman's clothes; clothing worn at sea.

umijitu-ganawa·i, *n.* That one's wishes become fulfilled; things turning out as one desires. **-soon**, Be according to one's wishes.

umijitu-gufa·sa, *n.* That one's wishes fail to be fulfilled.

umijitu-gufa·san, *adj.* Not according to one's wishes.

umijitu-kanawa·in, *vi*. To come out as one desires; to have wishes fulfilled.

umi-kai-chiya·a, *n*. A fisherman's work clothes. [GSS]

umi-kaji, *n*. [umikaze] A sea breeze; the sea wind.

u-mi-kaki·in, *vt*. [polite] To show (something) to (someone). Polite form of **mishiin**.

umi-kii, *n*. 1 A term of address for a male by his female sibling. 2 A term of address by a female to a male member of higher social class but junior in age.

umi-kijaa·sun, *vt*. To stir up a lagoon or thereabouts to fish. [UKH]

umi-maachi, *n*. [umimatsu] Black coral.

umi-mayaa, *n*. A sponge.

umi-naa, *n*. A fishing line. Also **naa**[4].

umi-naa·ku, *adv*. At peace; without worries.

umi-nai, *n*. A sister from the standpoint of her brother.

uminai-bi, *n*. A princess; a royal daughter.

uminchaki·ran, *adj*. Unexpected; unanticipated; unforeseen; casual; unsuspected; never dreamed of; accidental.

umi-nchu, *n*. A fisherman. Also **umi'atchaa**.

umi-ngwa, *n*. A term of respect for someone else's child; a beloved child; a darling child.

umi-nna, *n*. Same as **chinbooraa**.

umi-'nma-gwaa, *n*. A seahorse.

umi·n yuran, *phr*. [omoimo yoranai] Unexpected; unforeseen; beyond one's expectation; unlooked-for; unsuspected; unanticipated; inconceivable.

umi-nzo, *n. poet*. A (female) sweetheart.

umi-saa, *n*. Same as **umi'atchaa**.

umi-satu, *n. poet*. A (male) sweetheart.

umi-shigutu, *n*. [umishigoto] Any work related to the sea, such as fishing or sailing.

umi-shiija, *n*. A darling elder brother or sister.

umi-ta·chun, *vi*. [·**tan**, ·**tchi**; omoitatsu] To think of doing; make up one's mind to.

umitati·in, *vt*. [umetateru] To reclaim the land.

umi-uttu, *n*. A darling younger brother or sister.

umu, *n*. A sweet potato. See **'nmu**.

umu-da·chun, *vi*. [·**tan**, ·**tchi**; omodatsu] To be outstanding; be chief; be important.

umu-datchoo·ru, *adj*. Principal; leading; chief.

umu·i[1], *n*. [omoi] Thought; sentiment; mind; sense; heart; feeling; love; wish; affection; pleasure; care; worry; experience. See also **umii**.

umu·i[2], *n*. [omoi] Songs and poems that are sung on ritual and festive occasions. See also **omoro**, **Omoro Sooshi**, **umuru**, **Umuru Usooshi**.

umu·i-ata·in, *vt*. [omoiataru] To call to mind; recall; think of; suspect; have an inkling of.

umu·i-chi·chun, *vt*. [omoitsuku] To hit upon (an idea); think up.

umu·i-chi·in, *vt*. [·**ran**, ·**tchi**; omoikiru] To give no further thought; abandon; relinquish; resign oneself to.

umu·i-duui, *n*. [omoi-doori] As one wishes.

umu·i-kee·sun, *vt*. [omoikaesu] To think over; think better of; reflect on oneself.

umu·i-kugari·in, *vi*. [omoikogareru] To pine (yearn, sigh) for; be deeply in love with; be dying for (a woman). Also **umiikugariin**.

umu·in, *vt*. [**umaan~umuran**, ·**ti**; omou] 1 To think (of; about; over). 2 To believe; hold; be convinced. 3 To feel; feel like; be inclined. 4 To look upon (as); regard (as). 5 To hope; expect; anticipate. 6 To imagine; picture (to oneself); suppose; guess. 7 To take for; mistake for. 8 To recall; remember; recollect. 9 To will (do); intend (to do); be going

to (do). **10** To wish; desire; want. **11** To think of; love; care for; sigh for; yearn for. **12** To wonder (if). **13** To suspect.
umu·i-nuku·sun, *vt.* [omoinokosu] To regret leaving; leave with regret.
umu·i-sugu·sun, *vt.* [omoisugosu] To be overanxious; make too much of; worry too much.
umu·i-ta·chun, *vt.* [·tan, ·tchi; omoitatsu] To plan; project; resolve; make up one's mind.
umu·i-umurari·in, *vi.* To love and be loved; mutually love.
umu·i-umu·ti, *adv.* Being consumed with love.
umu·i-yamii, *n.* Gloom; sadness; depression; dejection. **-sun,** *v.* To worry; be depressed.
umu-kaji, *n.* [omokage] Visage; (one's) face (image, figure); traces; vestiges; shadow; memory.
umu-kutu, *n.* [omoukoto] Thought; the usual thought.
umu-muchi, *n.* [< J omomuki] A purpose; an aim; business.
umunji·in, *vt.* [omonjiru] To honor; respect; have regard for.
umuru, *n.* [omoi] Same as **umui**².
Umuru Usooshi, *n.* Book of Sentiments, the earliest poetic anthology of the Ryukyus, compiled 1531–1623. [BHEO]
umus·san, *adj.* Interesting; entertaining; enjoyable; amusing. See also **'wiiriki-san**.
umu·tai-kangee·tai, *n.* Thinking and contemplating. **-sun,** *v. colloq.* To deliberate; turn (a matter) over and over in one's mind.
umuti, *n.* [omote] **1** The surface; the face; the right side. **2** The obverse; the head. **3** The exterior; the outside. **4** The front; bow of ship. **5** Outdoors; in the open air. **6** Matting.
umuti-muchi, *n.* [< J omotemuki] (Something) in the open; (something conducted) in public (ostensibly, officially, formally).
umuya·a, *n.* A sweetheart; a lover.
umuyaa-gwaa, *n.* A sweetheart; a lover.
umuyoo, *adv.* Vaguely; indistinctly; hazily.
un¹, *n.* [un] Destiny; fate; one's lot; fortune; luck. Also **wun**¹.
un², *n.* [on] Same as **wun**². See also **unji, wunji**.
unaji, *n.* [unaji] The nape; the scruff (of the neck).
unbu·in, *vi.* To be affected; assume airs; put on airs.
unbu-yaa, *n.* A snob; an affected person; a dude.
un-chabi, *n.* Mock paper money to burn at the equinoctial Buddhist service.
un-chee, *n.* [C wengcai] Water spinach [*Ipomoea aquatica* Forsk.].
un-chi, *n.* [unki] Destiny; fate; one's lot; fortune.
un-chikee, *n.* [ontsukai] Honorable invitation; honorable reception; honorable company. **-sun,** *v.* To invite; go to welcome (a person).
un-chu, *pron.* He; she; the person.
un-dumi, *n.* [< umi + tumi·in] A taboo on fishing or entering the sea, usually about the time of harvest in the fourth or fifth lunar month. [ODJ].
une, *interj.* An interjection expressing surprise, dismay, relief, etc.; Oh my! Oh dear!
un-geeshi, *n.* [ongaeshi] Requital of a favor; repayment of a kindness.
un-gutooru, *part. adj.* Such; like that; that sort of.
uni¹, *n.* [oni] An ogre; a fiend; a demon; a devil.
uni², *n.* [une] A ridge (in a field); a furrow; a groove.
u-nige·e, *n.* [onegai] A request.
uniki·in, *vt.* Same as **unnukiin**.
unjaagii, *n.* Playing on a swing. [GSS]
un-jami, *n.* A sea god festival held in various villages in northern Okinawa

unjani

in the seventh month of the lunar calendar. See also **niraikanai, ashagi, ushideeku.** [ODJ]
unjani, *n.* Watermelon seeds. [UKH]
unji, *n.* [ongi] Same as **wunji.** See also **wun**².
unju, *pron. sing. formal* You. See also **'yaa.**
unju-naa, *pron.* **1** *pl.* You. **2** *sing.* You [polite] **3** Your house; your family. See also **unju, 'yaa.**
u-nkee, *n.* [omukae] **1** *formal* Welcome. **2** Rite of welcome to the ancestral spirits on the night of the thirteenth day of the lunar seventh month. Also **usooroo'unkee.** See also **bun**⁴.
unmii, *n.* See **'nmii.**
un-nagee, *n.* Such a long time.
unna-kunna, *n. colloq.* Like this and like that; such as this and such as that.
unnuki·in, *vi.* To respectfully state, say mention. Also **unikiin.**
unsaku, *n.* Unrefined sake liquor that is offered to the gods. Also **unshaku.** See also **miki.**
unshaku, *n.* Same as **unsaku.**
u·nu, *part. adj.* [sono] That; those.
unu-baa, *n.* [sonoba] **1** The place; the spot. **2** The occasion; the situation.
unu-hyaa, *n. pej.* That rascal.
unu-mama, *n.* [sono-mama] As it is; as you find it; in that condition; intact.
uppi, *n.* That much; that big; the more… the more. See also **uhi, ufi.**
uppi-gwaa, *n.* Only that much; only that big; a trifle.
uppi-naa, *n.* That big; that much.
ura¹**,** *n.* [ura] **1** Bay; inlet; a gulf; a creek. **2** The seacoast; the beach.
ura²**,** *n.* [ura] **1** The reverse side; the wrong side; the undersurface. **2** The opposite; the reverse; the contrary. **3** The back; the rear. **4** The lining.
uraaki·in, *vt.* To soak (in); steep (in).
uraa·sun, *vt.* To threaten without words. [UKH]

ura-gee·in, *vi.* [uragaeru] To be turned upside down or inside out.
ura-geeshi, *n.* [uragaeshi] Inside out; upside down.
ura-gee·sun, *vt.* [uragaesu] To turn inside out; turn upside down; turn over.
ura-goosa, *n.* Jealousy; being green with envy. **-sun,** *v.* To be jealous of; envy.
ura-hara, *n.* [urahara] The contrary; the reverse; the opposite.
ura-ja, *n.* **1** The back room; the women's room (in a traditional Okinawan house). **2** A room where a courtesan receives customers in the red-light quarters.
ura-ji, *n.* [uraji] Lining (cloth); cloth for lining.
uramari·in, *vi.* [uramareru] To be resented; be reproached. See **uramun.**
uramasa·sun, *vt.* [urayamu] To envy; be envious of; be jealous of.
urami, *n.* [urami] A grudge; spite; hatred; rancor; enmity; hostility; malice; ill will.
ura·mun, *vi.* [uramu] To bear (a person) a grudge; feel resentment at (something); be bitter against (a person). See **uramariin.**
Uranda, *n.* [? < J Oranda < Port Olanda] Europe; the West; the Occident.
Uranda·a, *n.* A Westerner; a European; an American.
Uranda-guchi, *n.* A European language, particularly English.
ura-nee, *n.* [uranai] Fortune-telling; divination; a fortune-teller.
ura-nuchi-munu-i·i, *n.* A satire; sarcasm; irony; innuendo.
ura-uchi, *n.* [urauchi] Lining; backing.
ura-umuti, *n.* **1** Both sides, the surface and back. **2** The wrong side out.
uri¹**,** *pron.* That; it; he; she.
uri²**,** *interj.* There! Look!
uri-bira, *n.* A downhill; a descent; a declivity; a downward slope. See also **nubuibira.**

urii[1], *n.* [uruoi] Moisture; moistening the earth with rain.
urii[2], *n.* [urei] Sorrow; grief; distress; trouble; affliction.
urii-gutu, *n.* [ureigoto] Unhappiness; sorrow; infelicity; grief.
uri·in[1], *vi.* [oriru] 1 To come down; step down; descend. 2 (From a car) to alight from; get off; leave. 3 (A bird) to alight; settle (on the ground); swoop; (an airplane) land. 4 (Frost) to fall.
uri·in[2], *vi.* [ureru] 1 To be in demand; be salable. 2 To be well known; become popular.
uri-jin, *n.* The second and third lunar months when the wheat starts sprouting; early summer.
urijin-bee, *n.* Southerly wind that blows in the second and third lunar months.
uri·kara, *adv.* Since then; after that; and then; from that time on.
uritai-nubutai, *n.* Getting down and going up. **-sun**, *v. colloq.* To go down and up.
uri·tu·n-kuri·tu·n, *adv. colloq.* With this person and with that person.
uriyoo, *n.* Urging to hurry up; pressing to speed up. [UKH]
uroo·san, *adj.* Thin; fine; slender.
uru, *n.* 1 Sand; fine sand; grit. 2 A coral tree. [UKH] Also **shina**[1].
urun, *n.* Same as **udun**.
ururu·chun, *vi.* Same as **uduruchun**.
uruka, *n.* [oroka] Stupid; stupidity.
uruki·in, *vt.* Same as **udukiin**. [UKH]
Uruma, *n. poet.* Ryukyu; Okinawa. [ODJ]
uruma·a, *n.* A noisy cricket; *Mecopoda elongata*. Same as **urumajee**.
uruma-jee, *n.* Same as **urumaa**.
Uruma-jima, *n. poet.* Land of Uruma; Ryukyu Islands or Okinawa Islands.
urushi, *n.* [urushi] 1 A lacquer tree [*Rhus javanica* L.]. [FOSR] 2 Lacquer; varnish. See also **hajiki**.
urushi-maki, *n.* [urushimake*] Lacquer poisoning.
uru·sun, *vt.* [orosu] 1 To take down; bring down; lower; let down. 2 To launch; lower. 3 To drop; let fall; let down. 4 To set (a passenger) down; drop; discharge; off-load. 5 To relieve (a person) of his role; demote. 6 To use (for the first time). 7 To have an abortion. 8 To weigh (anchor). 9 To sow (seeds).
uru-ubii, *n.* [uro-oboe] A faint memory; a hazy recollection.
uruu-dushi, *n.* [< J uruu-doshi] A leap year; an intercalary year.
uruu-jichi, *n.* [< J uruuzuki] A leap month. Also **yunjichi**.
usaa·riin, *vi.* [·riran, ·tti; osowareru] 1 To be attacked. 2 To be pressed; be suppressed. 3 To be overcome (by a disease).
usaa·sun, *vt.* To press (something) with; push something over something else.
u-sadami, *n.* [o- + sadame] Heaven's mandate; Heaven's will; destiny.
usagi·in, *vt.* [oshiageru] To offer; present; give; consecrate; sacrifice. See also **kwiin**.
usagi-muchi, *n.* A round, mirror-shaped, flat rice cake offered to a deity on New Year's Day, usually in a set of two, one small and another large.
usagi-mun, *n.* [oshiagemono] 1 An offering. 2 (To one socially superior) a gift; a present. 3 A bribe.
usaji, *n.* [usagi] A rabbit; a hare.
u-sakati, *n.* A family's share of the expense needed for clan rituals.
usakii, *n.* So much; so many.
usakii-naa, *n.* An excessive quantity.
usama·in, *vi.* Same as **wusamain**.
usami, *n.* [osame] Same as **wusami**.
usan-dee, *n.* 1 Food offering (to the deities) that is brought down from the altar to be consumed by the family. 2 A hand-me-down. See also **ubuku**, **jiiguyaa**. [UKH]

useein

usee·in, *vt.* [osaeru] To despise; scorn; disdain; think little of; look down upon.

useera·riin, *vi.* To be looked down on; be laughed at; be derided; be made light of. [UKH]

u-shaku, *n.* [oshaku] Serving liquor.

ushi[1], *n.* [ushi] **1** Cattle; a cow; a bull; an ox. **2** The Ox as the second of the twelve calendrical animal signs.

ushi[2], *n.* A variant of **uushi**. [GSS]

ushi-aasee, *n.* A bullfight. Same as **ushi'oorasee**, **ushi'aashi**.

ushi-aashi, *n.* A bullfight. Also **ushi'oorasee**.

ushi-bakuyoo, *n.* [ushi-bakuroo] A cattle broker.

ushichi·in, *vt.* [·ran, ·tchi; oshikiru] **1** To cut by force; chop. **2** To have one's own way; push one's way through; face it out.

ushi-chikanaya·a, *n.* A cattle raiser; one who raises cattle. [UKH] Also **ushi-kanayaa**. [UKH]

ushi-chiki·in, *vt.* [oshitsukeru] **1** To press against; thrust (something on a person); pin against; hold against. **2** To force on; compel. **3** To force on; foist upon; impose upon.

ushi-deeku, *n.* A women's group dance, with hand drums and singing, to express gratitude for a rich harvest, usually held on the fifteenth day of the eighth lunar month. [OBJ, ODJ]

ushii, *n.* [usui] One of the twenty-four lunar-cycle seasons. [UKH]

ushii-gachi, *n.* [< usuin + kachun] Tracing. **-sun**, *v.* To trace. [UKH]

ushii-kugani, *n.* A secret. [UKH]

ushii-kugani·in, *v.* To keep (something) secret. Also **kwakkusun**.

u-shii-mii, *n.* [seimei] The **ushiimii** rite, honoring ancestors with a ritual visit to the family tomb and offerings of food, observed on a day between the twenty-second day of the second lunar month and the third day of the third lunar month. See **shiimii**.

u-shi·i-mun, *n.* Same as **shiimun**[2].

ushi·in, *vt.* To cover; overlay; overspread; drape. See also **usuin**.

ushi-jaki, *n.* A person who becomes aggressive when drunk. [UKH]

ushi-kaki·in, *vt.* [oshikakeru] To force oneself into; intrude on; go uninvited.

ushi-kanaya·a, *n.* Same as **ushichi-kanayaa**.

ushi-keera·sun, *vt.* To bring down; throw down.

ushi-ki·in, *vt.* [·ran, ·tchi] To push; thrust; shove; bunt; bob.

ushi-kumi·in, *vt.* To push (press; thrust; force; squeeze; stuff, jam) in; herd in. Also **ushinchun**.

ushi-magi·in, *vt.* [oshimageru] **1** To forcibly bend. **2** To defeat.

ushi-moo, *n.* Same as **ushinaa**. [UKH]

ushi-naa, *n.* A bullring.

ushi-na·in, *vt.* [·(r)an; ·ti; ushinau] **1** To lose (something); be deprived of (one's loved one); **2** To miss (a chance).

ushi-nchi·i, *n.* [< ushinchun] Tucked-in style of fastening women's clothes. Also **ushinkii**. See also **uubi**. [GSS]

ushin·chun, *vt.* Same as **ushikumiin**. See also **ushinchii**.

ushi-nki·i, *n.* Same as **ushinchii**. [GSS]

ushi·nu-chii, *n.* [ushi no chichi] Cow's milk.

ushi-nuki·in, *vt.* [oshinokeru] To push away (aside); shove aside; force aside.

ushi·nu-shishi, *n.* [ushinoshishi*] Beef.

ushi·nu-yaa, *n.* A cattle stable.

ushi-oorasee, *n.* A bullfight in which two bulls are made to fight each other. Also **ushi'aasee**. See also **ushinaa**. [OBJ]

u-shirashi, *n.* [oshirase] An oracle; an inspiration; a revelation; a divine message.

u-shiru[1], *n.* [shiru] Soup; broth. Also **shiru**.

ushiru[2], *n.* [ushiro] The nape (esp. of a woman); the scruff of the neck.
ushiru-kubu, *n.* The hollow of the nape; the scruff.
u-shiru-wan, *n.* A soup bowl.
ushi·san, *adj.* [usui] **1** Thin; **2** Light (color); weak (coffee); watery (milk); pale. **3** Stupid. Also **ususan**. See **hissan**.
ushi-too·sun, *vt.* [oshitaosu] To push over; push down. See also **toosun**.
ushi-ushi, *n.* Compulsion. ·**ni**, *adv.* Forcibly; by compulsion.
ushi-'waasaa, *n.* A cattle butcher.
ushi-waki·in, *vt.* [oshiwakeru] To push apart; push (elbow or force) one's way through.
ushu, *n.* [ushio] Same as **usu**.
usooroo, *n.* [shooryoo] **1** The ancestral spirits; the spirits of the dead who are being honored in the *Bon* Festival. **2** The *Bon* rite, held for three days from the thirteenth to fifteenth of the seventh lunar month. Also **unkee**, **bun**[4], **shichigwachi**.
usooroo-u-nke·e, *n.* Rite performed to welcome the ancestral spirits on the night of the thirteenth day of the seventh lunar month. Also **unkee**, **bun**[4], **shichigwachi**.
u-sooroo-uukui, *n.* [...u- + ukui] Sending off of the ancestral spirits, a rite of sending off the ancestral spirits before midnight of the last day of the *Bon* festival. Also **uukui**. See also **bun**[4]. [OBJ]
us-sa[1], *n.* That much; so much; to that extent; only that; that alone.
us·sa[2], *n.* [ureshisa] Joy; delight; gladness. **-sun**, *v.* To be glad; be pleased; rejoice.
ussa-gi·san, *adj.* Seem delighted; seem joyful; seem happy. See **-gisan**.
ussa-kwaataa, *n.* Rapture; jubilance. **-sun**, *v.* To jubilate; be extremely delighted. See also **uss(h)an**.
us·s(h)an, *adj.* Joyful; delightful; happy; pleasant; gratifying; glad; pleased.
ussanaa, *adv.* This much; this many.
ussa-ussa·a, *adv.* Merrily; joyfully; gleefully; cheerfully.
usu, *n.* [ushio] The tide; seawater; brine. See also **suu**[3], **maasu**, **suubi**, **michisu**, **suubana**, **goomichaa**, **usukumun**. Also **ushu**.
usu-akagai, *n.* Twilight before sunrise or after sunset.
usuba·sun, *vt.* To put (something) upside-down.
usu-buri-mun, *n. pej.* A fool; a simpleton; a half-witted fellow. [GSS]
u-sudee, *n.* [oshudai] A condolence gift; a congratulatory gift.
usu-gura·san, *adj.* [usugurai] Dim; dimly lit; dusky; in semidarkness.
usu·in, *vt.* **1** To cover; veil; hang over; push down. **2** To hide; conceal; sheathe; lap. **3** To brood on (eggs). See also **ushiin**.
usu-jaa, *n.* [usucha] Weak tea. See **chaa**[3].
usuku, *n.* Large-leaved banyan [J akoo; *Ficus superba* var. *japonica* Miquel]. [FOSR]
usu-kuma·a, *n.* A person who draws brine, needed for making tofu bean curd. [UKH]
usu-ku·mun, *vt.* To draw brine for making bean curd.
usuma·s(h)an, *adj.* Dreadful; horrible; horrific.
u-su-mee, *n.* Grandfather.
usu-miji, *n.* Also **ushumiji**. Same as **usu**.
usumutuu, *n.* A farm kitchen, usually with a dirt floor. Also **shimu**[1], **tungwa**. [UKH]
usuri, *n.* [osore] Respect; reverence; awe.
usuri·in, *vt.* [osoreru] **1** To respect; revere. **2** To fear; dread; be afraid.
usu·u, *n.* A fool; a simpleton; mentally retarded person; learning disabled person.

usu-waree, *n.* [usuwarai] A faint smile; a half-smile. Also **namawaree**.

uta, *n.* [uta] A poem; an ode; a verse; poetry; the traditional Okinawan poem consisting of four stanzas totaling thirty syllables (in lines of 8-8-8-6); a song; a ballad. Also **Ruuka**.

utabi-mishe·en, *vt.* [exalting] To give; grant; do; favor with. See **kwiin**.

utaga·in, *vt.* [·**ran**, ·**ti**; utagau] To doubt; be doubtful; suspect; be suspicious of; distrust; mistrust.

utagee[1], *n.* [utagai] Doubt; a question; skepticism; uncertainty.

u-tagee[2], *n. formal* [otagai] Each other's; mutuality; reciprocity. See also **tagee**[1].

uta·i-koota·i, *n.* Buying and selling. **-sun**, *v. colloq.* To buy and sell.

uta·in, *vt.* [·**(r)an**; ·**ti**; utau] **1** To sing; chant. **2** To recite. **3** *vi.* (Of roosters) to crow.

u-takabi, *n.* A ritual to apotheosize; enshrining of a deity; a sacred ritual to offer prayers; a prayer; an incantation.

u-taki, *n.* [otake] [exalting] A sacred grove in a hill or woods. See also **taki**[1].

utama-biikuu, *n.* Hesitation. [GSS]

uta-muchi, *n.* A prelude in music; an introduction in music. [UKH]

utari·in, *vi.* [...**ri·ran**, ...**t·ti**; utareru] To be bitten by a **habu** snake.

uta-sa·a, *n.* A singer.

uta-sanshin, *n.* Music.

uta-utaya·a, *n.* A singer.

utaya·a, *n.* A singer.

ut-chaki·i, *n.* [uchikake] A long outer kimono.

ut-chaki·in, *vt.* [uchikakeru] To slip a kimono on one's shoulders.

utchaki-mun, *n.* A curse; retribution.

utchan-giirii, *n.* Desertion; leaving (a thing or a person) behind.

utchan-nagi·in, *vt.* [utchari, nageru] To neglect; lay aside; leave (a thing) alone.

utcharaka·sun, *vt.* [< J utcharakasu] To neglect; lay aside; abandon.

utchee-hitchee, *adv. colloq.* **1** Repeatedly; many times. **2** Turning and twisting one's body. **-sun**, *v.* **1** To repeat. **2** To turn and twist. [UKH]

utchee·in, *vi.* **1** To turn inside out; toss about in bed. **2** To be thrown backward; be astounded; **3** To become converse; reverse. **4** To betray; turn one's coat. **5** To retrogress; degenerate; backslide.

utchin, *n.* [ukon] Common turmeric [*Curcuma domestica* Valet]. [FOSR]

utchi-n·chun, *vi.* To look downward; cast down one's eyes; hang one's head.

utchintuu, *n.* **1** Lying prone; being in a prone position. **2** Bowing one's head; hanging one's head. **3** One who is in such a position.

utchiri-kubusa·a, *n.* A tumbler; a (*Daruma*) self-righting toy.

·**uti**, *part.* [oite] Attached to nouns, indicates a location of activity: in; at.

uti-bucha·a, *n.* A strong westerly wind. [UKH]

uti-chichi, *n.* [ochitsuki] Composure; self-possession; calmness; serenity; presence of mind.

uti-chi·chun, *vi.* [ochitsuku] To settle down; be self-possessed; become cool; harmonize with.

uti-chiri, *n.* Rubbish; odds and ends; scrap; trash.

u-tiida-ishi, *n.* The sun stone. [ODJ]

utii-daka, *n.* A low-flying falcon. Also **utidaka**. [UKH]

uti·in, *vi.* [ochiru] **1** To fall; drop; drip; crash. **2** To collapse; crumble. **3** To set; sink; go down. **4** To fail; flunk. **5** To be omitted; be left off. **6** To go down. **7** To come off; be removed. **8** To fall short of; be inferior to.

utina, *n.* [utena] A dais; a pedestal; a stand.

utintuu, *n.* [otentoo] The sun; the sun deity; a respectful term for the sun. [UKH]

utintuu-ganashii, *n.* A respectful term for the sun. [UKH]

·utooti, *part.* [oite] Emphatic form of **·uti**.

ut·taa, *pron.* They; those; them.

uttaatu, *adv.* On purpose; intentionally.

uttai, *n.* [uttae] Suit; legal proceedings; a complaint.

uttai-sun, *vt.* [uttaeru] To sue; litigate; take legal steps (against).

uttee·in, *vt.* To sue; go to law.

utti, *adv.* [otte] Later on; afterward; in due course of time.

uttu, *n.* [otooto] A younger sibling.

uttu-kata, *n.* The younger siblings; the younger generation; one's juniors.

uttu-maki, *n.* Lit., defeat by a younger sibling; weakening of nursing infant due to mother's ensuing morning sickness. Also **uttumiimaki**. [UKH]

uttu-mii-maki, *n.* Same as **uttumaki**.

uttu-mii-yoogari, *n.* Same as **uttumaki**. See **yoogariin**.

uttu-ngwa, *n.* The youngest child.

uttu-shiija, *n.* Siblings; brothers and sisters, regardless of age.

utu, *n.* [oto] **1** A sound; a noise; a report (of guns); a din; a roar; a crash. **2** Fame; renown; rumor. **3** News; information.

utugee, *n.* [otogai] The lower jaw; the lower pointed part of the jaw; the submaxilla[e]. See also **kakuji**.

u-tuimuchi, *n.* [otorimochi] Reception; treatment.

utu·in, *vi.* [otoru] To be inferior to; be second to; fall behind.

utu-janda, *n.* Brothers; brothers and sisters; siblings.

u-tumu, *n.* [otomo] An attendant; a companion; a retinue. **-sun**, *v.* To attend on (one's superior); accompany; go with. Also **tumu²**.

utuna·s(h)an, *adj.* [otonashii] Gentle; meek. Also **'wendas(h)an**.

uturi·in, *vi.* [otoroeru] To languish; become weak; lose vigor.

uturus(h)a, *n.* Fear; dread; fright; terror; horror. **-sun**, *v.* To be fearful; be afraid; dread.

uturu·s(h)an, *adj.* Fearful; being afraid of; dreadful; being frightened at; being nervous about.

uturu·u, *n.* One who is to be feared.

utushi-ana, *n.* [otoshiana] A pitfall; a pit; a trap.

utushi-dani, *n.* [otoshidane] An illegitimate child; a love child (of a man of high status). See also **yamana-shingwa**.

utushi-kata, *n.* [otoshikata] An elderly person; the elderly; the senior citizens. Also **utusui**. [UKH]

utushi-mun, *n.* [otoshimono] A lost article; things lost.

utushi-ngwa, *n.* [otoshigo] Same as **utushidani**.

u-tusui, *n.* [otoshiyori] Same as **tusui**. Also **utusuikata**.

utu·sun, *vt.* [otosu] **1** To drop; let fall; throw down. **2** To lose; drop. **3** To remove; omit; miss; leave out; debase; abase. **4** To drive away; exorcise. **5** To force surrender; win a woman's heart.

utu-u·chun, *vi.* [·tan, ·tchi] To be famous; be well known.

u-tuuru, *n.* [otooroo] A lantern for the Buddhist altar.

u-tuushi, *n.* Worshiping from afar; bow to the direction of.

uu¹, *n.* [u] The Hare, the fourth of the twelve calendrical animal signs.

uu², *interj.* Yes (to superior); yes, sir; certainly; all right. See also **oo, ii¹, 'nn, ashi², wuuwuwuu, woooo, yiiyiyii, nnnnn, bee¹, beeru**.

uu³, *n.* Same as **wuu¹**.

uu⁴, *n.* [o] Same as **wuu²**.

uu-ami, *n.* [ooame] A heavy rain; a downpour.

uubi, *n.* [obi] **1** A sash; a belt. **2** A hoop. See also **ufu'uubi, ushinchii, fusu'uubi, china'uubi, minsaa'uubi**. [OBJ, ODJ]

uu-biisa, *n.* Extreme cold (of weather). [UKH]
uubu, *n.* A swelling; a boil; a tumor; an abscess. [GSS]
uu-bui, *n.* [ooburi] A downpour.
uubukka, *n.* A spate of extremely cold weather. [UKH]
uuchi, *n.* [oki] Offshore; off the shore; the offing. See also **uutu**.
uu-chijin, *n.* [oo-tsuzumi] A big drum.
uudu, *n.* Bedding; a quilt; a coverlet. Also **uuru**.
uu-duui, *n.* [oodoori] A main street; a broad street; a highway.
uufa, *n.* Piggyback. **-sun**, *vt.* To carry another person on one's back.
uufa-sari·in, *vi.* [...ri·ran, ...t·ti] To be carried on the back of; get a piggyback ride.
uufa·sun, *vt.* To carry someone piggyback; carry someone on one's back.
uu-fuu, *n.* The use of honorific terms.
uu-gaara, *n.* A big river full of running water.
uu-gurun, *n.* Lit., big darkness, a large rain cloud that darkens the sky. See also **ami**[1].
uu-gutu, *n.* Something to be grateful for; something to be happy for.
uu·in, *vt.* [ou] 1 To drive away; shoo away. 2 To pursue; follow; go after.
uu-jara, *n.* Same as **ufujara**.
uu-kaji, *n.* [ookaze] A typhoon; a storm.
uu-kata, *adv.* [ookata] Probably; perhaps; almost; nearly.
uuku-baa, *n.* [okuba] A molar; a back tooth.
uukui, *n.* [ookuri] 1 A funeral. 2 Sending off of the spirits on the last day of the *Bon* festival. See also **dabi**, **shichigwachi**.
uu-maku, *n.* A naughty person; a naughty child; an urchin. Also **makuu**, **anmaku**.
uu-miji, *n.* [oomizu] A flood; a deluge; an inundation.

uu-nami, *n.* [oonami] A big (heavy) wave; a billow; a big roller.
uunu, *n.* [ono] See **wuunu**.
uu-nuu, *n.* A large field; a large ground. [UKH]
uusari-aasari, *adv.* Prostrated; bowing. **-sun**, *v.* To prostrate oneself (before); go down on one's knees; make obeisance (to); kowtow.
uushee-kurubashee, *n.* Hustling and jostling. **-sun**, *v. colloq.* To hustle and jostle. Also **uusheekurushee**. [GSS]
uushee-kurushee, *n.* Same as **uushee-kurubashee**. [GSS]
uushi, *n.* [usu] A mortar; a hand mill; a stamp mill. See also **chichi'uushi**, **ishi'uushi**. Also **ushi**[2], **ufii**.
uushi-baa, *n.* Same as **uukubaa**.
uushi·in, *vt.* [oosu*] 1 To make (an animal) carry a load. 2 To charge (a person) with (a duty or a crime); blame others.
uu-tigara, *n.* [ootegara] A distinguished service; a great merit; a great exploit.
uu-tootu, *interj.* [ana tooto*] Holy art thou! Thy name be praised! Amen!
uutu, *n.* The open sea; an ocean. Also **ufu'umi**.
uu-wee, *n.* [oiwai] Celebration; felicitation. See **yuuwee**.
uuwee-bukuru, *n.* An envelope for a congratulatory gift of money. [UKH]
uu-yaa-ninju, *n.* A large family.
uuyee-kuyee, *adv. colloq.* Now behind and now ahead; now chasing and now being chased.
uwa·i, *n.* [owari] An end; a close; a conclusion; an expiration.
uwai-juukoo, *n.* The final memorial service, held on the thirty-fifth anniversary of death. See **suukoo**.
uwa·in, *vi.* [owaru] To end; come to an end (close); close; be over; terminate; finish; conclude; expire.
uya, *n.* [oya] A parent; a father; a mother; the parents.

uya-buni, *n.* [oyabune] A mother ship; a tender.
uya-faafuji, *n.* Ancestors; ancestry.
uya-fukoo, *n.* [oyafukoo] Undutifulness to one's parents. **·na,** *adj.* Undutiful; unfilial; disobedient.
uya-fukoo-mun, *n.* [oyafukoomono] An undutiful son or daughter. [UKH]
uya-gaka·i, *n.* [oyagakari] Dependence upon one's parents.
uya-gawa·i, *n.* [oyagawari] Acting in lieu of one's parents. [UKH]
uya-kkwa, *n.* [oyako] Parent and child.
uya-kookoo, *n.* [oyakookoo] Filial piety; filial devotion. **-sun,** *vi.* To be filial to one's parents.
uya-kookoo-mun, *n.* A dutiful son or daughter.
uya-madii, *n.* Losing one's parents. **-sun,** *vi.* To lose one's parents. Also **uyamarii.**
uya-marii, *n.* Same as **uyamadii.** [UKH]
uya-masa·i, *n.* [oyamasari] Surpassing the parent.
uya-masai-ngwa, *n.* A child who has surpassed his/her parents.
uyame·e-kutuba, *n.* [uyamai kotoba] A term of respect; an honorific expression; honorifics.
uya-mutu, *n.* [oyamoto] Parental roof; one's parents' home; one's parents.
uya·nu-kkwa, *n.* A child who is like his or her parent either physically or in personality.
uya·nu-yaa, *n.* [oyano(ie)] 1 Parental roof. 2 One's original home.
uya-shiraji-baa, *n.* [oyashirazuba] A wisdom tooth. [UKH]
uya-uji, *n.* Ancestors; ancestry. Also **uyafaafuji.** [UKH]
uya-umu·i, *n.* Being filial to one's parents.
uya-umuya·a, *n.* Filial child; dutiful son or daughter.
u·yin, *vt.* [oru] To weave.

W———

waa, *n.* 1 Spaciousness; extent; dimensions; width. 2 Nerve; mettle, courage.
waa-, *pref.* My-.
'waa, *n.* A pig; a hog; a swine; a boar; a sow. Also **'waagwaa.**
'waaba, *n.* Excess; extra; surplus; superfluity.
'waaba-gutu, *n.* An unnecessary matter.
'waaba-jikee, *n.* Extra expenses.
'waaba-mun, *n.* 1 An extra thing; a spare; superfluity. 2 One who does useless things; a meddlesome person.
'waaba-shiwa, *n.* An unnecessary worry.
'waabi, *n.* [uwabe] 1 The surface; the exterior. 2 Outward appearance; exterior.
'waabi-biree, *n.* Superficial relationship; superficial friendship.
'waabi-chura·a, *n.* One who is affable on the surface.
'waabi-gaa, *n.* The outer skin; hypodermis; the cuticle; the epidermis; the rind.
'waa-buuru, *n.* Same as **'waafuuru.**
'waa-cha·a, *n.* An affected person; a snob; a prig; a dandy; a dude.
'waa-chi, *n.* [uwaki] Affectation; striking an attitude; giving oneself airs.
'waa-chichi, *n.* The weather; atmospheric conditions.
'waa-chiki-ya·a, *n.* Same as **wuu'waakarayaa.**
'waachi·na-mun, *n. pej.* A conceited (audacious, pert) person. [GSS]
'waa-fa, *n.* A fraction (of figures); an odd sum.
'waa-fuguya·a, *n.* One whose occupation is castrating hogs.
'waa-fuuru, *n.* A pigsty; a pigpen. Also **'waabuuru.**
'waa-gachi, *n.* [uwagaki] An address; directions.
'waagi·in, *vt.* 1 To drive (a person) away; oust. 2 To pursue; chase.

'**waa-gwaa**, *n*. A piglet; a shoat; a young pig; a little pig; a hogling. [ODJ]
'**waagwaa-machi**, *n*. A young pig market; (figuratively) a noisy place.
'**waagwaa-nin·ji**, *n*. Sleeping together in a huddle (esp. of children).
'**waa-hiji**, *n*. A mustache.
'**waai·in**, *vi*. To stand erect (of penis); become stiff.
'**waa-ji**, *n*. [uwagi] 1 One's best clothes; one's holiday suit. 2 A coat.
'**waaji-gin**, *n*. Variant of '**waaji**. [GSS]
'**waaji-jin**, *n*. Variant of '**waaji**.
'**waa-karaya·a**, *n*. A pig farmer or breeder; a swineherd; a hog-raising operation.
waa-mu·chi, *n*. A courageous person.
'**waa-nai**, *n*. [uwanari*] 1 A second wife. 2 Jealousy; envy, especially among siblings. See also **rinchi**. -**sun**, *v*. To be jealous.
'**waa-ni**, *n*. [uwani] The topmost load; the topmost cargo.
'**waa-nu·i**, *n*. [uwanuri] 1 The final coat (of paint, etc.); glazing; finish. 2 Adding to one's loss.
'**waa nu mun kween neenshi**, *phr*. Lit., eating like a pig; making lapping sounds as one eats. [GSS]
'**waa·nu-shishi**, *n*. Pork.
'**waari·in**, *vi*. [owareru] To be chased; be pursued; be ousted.
'**waa-sa·a**, *n*. A butcher (esp. of hogs); a slaughterer.
'**waasaa-machi**, *n*. A meat market (chiefly of pork).
'**waasaa-yaa**, *n*. A butchery; a slaughterhouse.
'**waa-shiba**, *n*. The upper lip.
'**waa·sun**[1], *vt*. 1 To make grow; make larger. 2 To get an erection.
'**waa·sun**[2], *vt*. To add; supplement; meet the demand.
'**waa-'waa**, *n. inf*. A pig.
waa-wuu, *n. inf*. A bugbear; a bogey; a goblin.

'**waa-yuu**, *n*. Thin rice gruel; rice water; the hot, watery part of **ukkeemee**. See also **ukkeemee**.
wabi, *n*. [wabi] Surrender; submission. -**sun**, *vi*. To give up; surrender; submit.
wabiya·a, *n*. A grumbler; a complainer; a querulous person.
wabu-wabu, *adv*. Baggy; puffy (of clothes).
wachaku, *n*. Mischief; a prank; a trick; amusement at another's expense.
wachaku·in, *vt*. To tease; do mischief; make fun of; banter; gibe.
wachara·in, *vt*. [·(r)an, ·ti; wazurau] 1 To be troubled by; be worried about; 2 Be distressed by; be annoyed at.
wachare·e, *n*. [wazurai] 1 Trouble; difficulty; anxiety. 2 An illness; a sickness.
wachi, *n*. [waki] 1 The side of a body; armpit; by the side of. 2 the other way; another place.
wachi-gi, *n*. [wakige] See **wachikuugi**. Also **kuugi**.
wachi-kusa·a, *n*. [waki-kusa*] Offensive armpit odor.
wachi-kuugi, *n*. Underarm hair; hair of the armpit. Also **wachigi**.
wachi-michi, *n*. [wakimichi] A byroad; a bypath; a digression.
wa·chi-miji, *n*. [wakimizu] Springwater; artesian water.
wa·chi-'nji·in, *vi*. To gush out (forth); spout; spurt.
wachi-yaku, *n*. [wakiyaku] An assistant; a deputy; a helper.
wachi-yee, *n*. [wakeai] 1 Meaning; sense. 2 Reason; cause. 3 Circumstance; the case.
wa·chun[1], *vt*. [waku] To divide; halve; split; chop.
wa·chun[2], *vi*. [waku] 1 To boil; grow hot. 2 To grow; breed; be hatched. 3 To spout; gush forth; flow out; flow forth; bubble out. See also **fuchun**[3].
wa-dan, *n*. [wadan] Harmony; friendliness; peace.

wadan-wagoo, *n.* [wadan + wagoo] Peacefulness; harmoniousness.

wa·ga-mama, *n.* [wagamama] Selfishness; egoism. **·na**, *adj.* Willful; selfish; egoistical. See also **jimama**.

wa-goo, *n.* [wagoo] Harmony; concord; unity; friendly relations. See also **wadan**.

waguri-mun, *n.* A person who does not return borrowed items. [UKH]

wa·i-ban, *n.* [wariban] A divided seal or stamp impression.

wa·i-fu, *n.* [warifu] 1 One of two official documents, such as a genealogy or official registry, which have been stamped with a single impression straddling both so that they may be checked later for authenticity. 2 Such an impression made on the leaves of documents.

wa·i-mee, *n.* [warimae] A quota; a share; one's lot.

wa·in, *vt.* [waru] 1 To break; crack; crush; smash. 2 To cut; halve. 3 To dilute; water down.

wai-tui, *n.* A sunken road; a road which has been made by cutting through a hill.

waja, *n.* [waza] Work; a trade; a task. See also **shigutu, shikuchi**.

wajami, *n.* 1 Wrinkles; lines; furrows; a wry face; a grimace. 2 Creases; rumples; folds.

wajami·in, *vt.* 1 To create wrinkles; make lines. 2 To frown (at, on); scowl (at); make a wry face.

waja·mun, *vi.* (Of the face) to frown; (of the face) to become wrinkled.

wajan-kaa, *adv.* Making a wry face.

wajat·tu, *adv.* [wazato] On purpose; intentionally; knowingly. Also **wajatu**.

waja-waja, *adv.* [wazawaza] Expressly; specially; on purpose; purposely.

wajawee, *n.* [wazawai] An evil; a curse; a misfortune; a disaster; a woe.

waji·in, *vi.* To be offended; get angry; be furious; get mad.

waji-waji·i-sun, *v. emph. colloq.* To be enraged; fume; bristle; fly into a passion. See also **kwachikwachii-sun**.

waka-ba, *n.* [wakaba] Young (new) leaves; young foliage; fresh verdure.

waka-gee·in, *vi.* [wakagaeru] To be rejuvenated; be restored to youth; grow young again.

waka-gi, *n.* [wakagi] A young plant (tree); a sapling.

waka·in[1], *vi.* [wakaru] 1 To understand; comprehend; see; follow; make sense of. 2 To know; tell; learn; realize; be known; be identified (to be). 3 To be sensible; have sense. 4 To foretell; tell; know. 5 To appreciate. 6 To be made known; be announced. 7 To find; discover; detect. 8 To recognize; spot.

waka·in[2], *vi.* [wakaru*] To part; branch off; diverge; fork; split; become separated. Also **wakariin**.

waka-jiraa, *n.* A woman in childbed who has not yet rested sufficiently. [UKH]

waka-juukoo, *n.* Lit., the young mass; memorial services held in observance of the third, seventh, and thirteenth anniversaries of a death. See **suukoo**.

waka·ku na·i-misoo·chi, *phr.* Lit., You have become younger, [sir]. New Year's greeting to someone senior to the speaker.

waka-kusa, *n.* [wakakusa] Young grass; fresh grass.

waka-maachi, *n.* [wakamatsu] A young pine tree; pine sapling branch used as a New Year's decoration.

waka-miji, *n.* [wakamizu] The Water of Youth, the first water drawn from a well after the New Year. [OBJ] Also **waka'ubii, sudimiji** .

waka-mun, *n.* [wakamono] A young man; a youth; a youngster; the young.

waka-nachi, *n.* [wakanatsu] Early summer. Also **nachiguchi**.

wakari, *n.* [wakare] **1** Parting; farewell; leave-taking. **2** A branch; an offshoot; a division; an offshore island.

wakari·in, *vi.* [wakareru] **1** To part (from, with); separate; divorce oneself (from); bid farewell; leave. **2** To branch off; diverge; split; part; separate.

waka·sa, *n.* [wakasa] Youth; youthfulness.

wakasaini, *n.* One's youth.

waka·san, *adj.* [wakai] **1** Young; juvenile; youthful. **2** Junior; younger. **3** Immature; inexperienced; raw.

-wakashi, *suff.* [wakashi] Unit of measure for liquor, one *sho*, equivalent to approximately 0.5 US gallon.

waka-shiraga, *n.* [wakashiraga] Gray hair in youth; prematurely gray hair.

waka-shiragi, *n.* Same as **wakashiraga**.

waka-shu, *n.* [< J wakashu] **1** A young man before coming of age. **2** In premodern Okinawa, a young male attendant on nobles. **3** A young male who is the object of homosexual attraction.

waka·sun[1], *vt.* [wakasu] **1** To part; divide. **2** To separate; distinguish. **3** To arbitrate; mediate; intervene; act as a peacemaker.

waka·sun[2], *vt.* [wakasu] To boil (water); heat (the bath); make hot. See also **fuchun**[2].

waka-tuji, *n.* A young wife.

waka-ubii, *n.* Polite term for **wakamiji**.

waka-wikiga, *n.* A young man; a boy; youth. Also **niis(h)ee**.

waka-winagu, *n.* A young woman; a maiden; a girl. Also **miyarabi**, **angwa**.

waki, *n.* [wake] **1** A meaning; a sense. **2** A reason; a cause. **3** The matter; the case; circumstances. **4** Excuse; justification.

waki·in, *vt.* [wakeru] **1** To divide; part; sever; split. **2** To separate; part; isolate. **3** To distribute; divide; share. **4** To distinguish; segregate. **5** To spare. Also **wappuu-sun**.

waki-mee, *n.* [wakemae] A share; a portion; a quota. Also **wappu**.

wakkwa·sun, *vt.* To disassemble; take apart; dismantle; untie; unravel.

wakkwi·in, *vt.* To be disassembled; break down; decompose; become disheveled.

waku-bitchi, *n.* An edible frog. [UKH]

wan[1], *n.* [< J wan] A bay; a gulf; an inlet. Also **magai**.

wan[2], *pron.* [wa] I; myself; self. See also **wattaa**.

wan[3], *n.* [wan] A bowl. See also **makai**.

wan-buu, *n.* A large, deep bowl. See also **sara**[1], **shimudoogu**, **makai**.

wanchamee·in, *vt.* To compensate; indemnify; make up (for loss). See also **hachun**[2].

wanda·in, *vt.* **1** To take care of; look after (the elderly). **2** To take charge of the veneration of the ancestors.

wan·kara-wan·kara, *adv.* Striving. **-sun**, *v. emph. colloq.* To compete; vie with one another; strive to be first. [GSS]

wan·kuru, *adv.* Myself; by myself.

wappu, *n.* [warifu] Allotment; distribution; supply; quota. Also **wappuu**. **-sun**, *v.* To divide; allocate; distribute. Also **wappuu-sun**.

wara, *n.* [wara] Straw.

waraa·ran-ware·e, *n.* A forced laugh or smile; a bitter laugh or smile.

waraari·in, *vi.* [...ri·ran, ...t·ti] To be laughed at; be ridiculed.

waraba·a, *n. pej.* [warabe] A child; children; a youngster; a kid; a tot. See **warabi**[1]. ·**taa**, *n. pl.* of **warabaa**.

warabi[1], *n.* [warabe] A child; children.

warabi[2], *n.* [warabi] A bracken; a fernbrake [*Pteridium aquilinum* var. *latiusculum* (Desv.) Underw. ex Heller.]. [FOSR]

wara-bi[3], *n.* A straw fire.

warabi-achike·e, *n.* [warabe-atsukai] Treating a person like a child; making a fool of a person.

warabi-baka, *n.* A child's tomb. See **haka.**
warabi-dushi, *n.* A friend from one's childhood.
warabi-jimu, *n.* A childish mind.
warabi-naa, *n.* A childhood name (as opposed to the official name given when one reaches adulthood). See also **umi-, ma(a)-, -gani.**
warabi-nchaa, *n. pl.* Children.
wara-boochi, *n.* [warabooki] An indoor broom made of straw. See **hoochi.**
wara-dooshi, *n.* Thin brown paper made of straw, chiefly used for **uchikabi** (or **nchabi**), mock paper money for the after life. See **kabi** .
wara·in, *vt.* [·(r)an, ·ti; warau] 1 To laugh; smile; chuckle. 2 To ridicule; deride; jeer. See also **takawaree, nachiwaree, miiwaree, saawaree, shikawaree, namajirawaree, hanawaree, katakuchiwaree, ufuwaree, waraaranwaree, waraariin.**
wara-jan, *n.* [warazan] A counting device made of straw; an Okinawan *quipu.* Also **warazan.** See also **suuchuumaa, kaidaajii, warashinbuu.**
waraji, *n.* [< J waraji] A straw sandal worn in the sea. See **saba**[1].
wara-jina, *n.* A straw rope.
wara-saba, *n.* Straw sandals. See **saba**[1].
wara-shibi, *n.* [warashibe] The inner core of a rice stalk.
wara-shinbuu, *n.* A straw cord; straw cords as a means of keeping records among illiterate peasants.
ware·e, *n.* [warai] A laugh; laughter; a smile; derision; a sneer; a flattering smile.
waree-banashi, *n.* [waraibanashi] A funny story; a joke.
waree-gau, *n.* [waraigao] A smiling face.
waree-jira, *n.* [waraizura] Same as **wareegau.**
waree-kan·jun, *vi.* [·dan, ·ti] To smile radiantly; beam with delight.

waree-kuji·in, *vt.* To deride; ridicule; mock.
waree-mun-na·sun, *vt.* To make an object of ridicule.
waree-munu·u, *n.* An object of ridicule; a standing joke.
-wari, *suff.* [< J wari] Counter indicating one percent. See also **-bu.**
wari-gaami, *n.* [waregame] 1 A cracked jar; a broken jar. 2 A drunkard.
wari·in, *vi.* To split; cleave; fissure; crack; break apart.
wari-mi, *n.* [wareme] A crevice; a crack; a chasm; a fissure; a split.
wari-mun, *n.* [waremono] A fragile article; a broken article.
waru-mun, *n.* [warumono] A bad fellow; a rogue; a rascal.
wasami·chun, *vi. onom.* To be noisy; be in a commotion.
wasa-wasa, *adv. onom.* [wasawasa*] Noisily; boisterously; with a fuss; with a din.
washi·in, *vt.* [wasuru*, wasureru] To forget; be forgetful of; oblivious to; dismiss from one's mind; think no more of.
washi·nu-tui, *n.* [washi] An eagle. Also **washi.**
washiri-guri·s(h)an, *adj.* Hard to forget.
washiri·in, *vt.* [wasureru] Same as **washiin.**
washita, *n. poet.* We; our. See **wattaa.**
was·sa, *n.* [warusa] An apology; an excuse.
was·san, *adj.* [...ru·ku] 1 Bad; evil; wrong; immoral; wicked; malicious; criminal. 2 Culpable; at fault; wrong. 3 Harmful; injurious; nasty; inadvisable. 4 Indisposed; sick. 5 Inferior; of low grade; deteriorated; stale. 6 Plain; homely; ugly. 7 Poor; weak; feeble. 8 Foul; inclement. 9 Muddy; bad; rough. 10 Ill; unlucky; ominous.
wata[1], *n.* Inner sheath of bamboo.
wata[2], *n.* [wata] Cotton.

wata³, *n.* [wata] **1** The belly; the abdomen; the bowels; the stomach. **2** Heart; mind; intention. **3** (Of animals) intestines; entrails. See also **iiwata, shichawata, ufuwata(a), watabutaa.**

wata-bii, *n.* Small intestines. Also **watabiimun.** See also **watamiimun.**

watabii-mun, *n.* Same as **watabii, watamiimun.**

wata-bonbon, *adv.* Loose, baggy stomach; puffy, bloated stomach.

wata-buta·a, *n. pej.* A person with a big belly.

wata-butu, *n. pej.* The belly; the abdomen.

wata-garasu, *n.* Salted tuna intestines. See also **karasu**¹.

wata·i, *n.* [watari] Same as **tuguchi.** Also **watanji.**

wata·in, *vi.* **1** To go over; pass (over); cross (over). **2** To wade; ford. **3** To be imported; be introduced. **4** To pass into another's hands. **5** To get along; sweep across. **6** To migrate. **7** To be supplied.

wata-irii, *n.* [wataire] Wadded clothes; padded (quilted) clothes.

wata-jin, *n.* [wata-ginu] Lined or padded winter formal wear for both male and female in premodern Okinawa.

watakusa·a, *n.* Pin money. Same as **watakushi.** [OBJ]

watakushi, *n.* [watakushi] **1** Privacy. **2** Secret savings; pin money. Also **watakusaa.**

watakushi-gutu, *n.* [watakushigoto] Privacy.

wata-mii-mun, *n.* The internal organs; the intestines; the entrails. See also **wata, watabii.**

wata-mugee·in, *vi.* To become infuriated.

wata-nakara, *n.* A half-full belly.

watan-ji, *n.* **1** A ferry (crossing). **2** A place name for the ferry dock and nearby red-light district in Naha. Also **watai, tuguchi.**

wata·n-mii, *n.* Satiated state; fullness of stomach. Also **watanumii.**

wata·nu-mii, *n.* Same as **watanmii.**

wata-pon-pon, *adv.* Full. **-soon,** *adj. emph. colloq.* (Of the belly) to be full. [GSS]

wata sagu·in, *v.* Lit., to search one's stomach; to accuse someone; imply (in a negative sense).

watashi-buni, *n.* A ferry boat.

wata·sun, *vt.* [watasu] **1** To pass (a thing or person) over; carry across; ferry (a person) over. **2** Hand (over to); deliver; turn over. **3** To transfer; make over; turn over. **4** To pay; give; provide.

wata-uchi¹, *n.* Same as **hana'uchi.**

wata-uchi², *n.* Heart; mind; intention.

wattaa, *n.* **1** We; we, inclusive of those being addressed. **2** Our house; our family.

wat·taa-, *pref.* Our-.

wattaabii, *n.* Same as **atabichaa.**

wattaa-kuru, *adv.* By ourselves.

wattaa-mun, *n.* Ours.

'weeda, *n.* [aida] **1** An interval; gap; distance. **2** On the way; halfway; midway. **3** A distance; a space. **4** A period of time between two points of time; an intervening period; span. **5** Between; among; amid.

'weeka, *n.* Same as **eeka.**

'weeki, *n.* Same as **eeki.**

'weeki-gumasa, *n.* Same as **eekigumasa.**

'weeki·i, *n.* Same as **eeki·i.**

'weeki-nchu, *n.* Same as **eekinchu.**

'weeku, *n.* Same as **eeku**¹.

'weema, *n.* Same as **eema**¹.

'weeshi-mise·en, *vi.* [exalting] To sleep; go to bed; retire.

wee-wee, *adv. inf. onom.* Weeping and crying (of children).

'we-nchu, *n.* **1** Lit., a person above; a rat; a mouse. **2** *n. slang* A rat, a person who is not fair (not open and honest). [GSS]

'wenchu-yaama, *n.* Same as hanchuu-yaama.
'wenda·a, *n.* A gentle person; a kind person.
'wenda·s(h)an, *adj.* Gentle; mild; meek; quiet; good-tempered; obedient; submissive; modest; well-behaved. See utunas(h)an.
wii[1], *n.* [yoi] Intoxication; inebriation.
wii[2], *n.* [oi] A nephew. Same as wiikkwa.
'wii, *n.* [ue] 1 Upside; topside; the upper part; the surface. 2 The top (of a hill); the summit (of a mountain). 3 Far better. 4 Above (in social status, etc.). 5 Besides; furthermore; in addition.
'wii-baa, *n.* [uwaba] An upper tooth.
wiiba·chun, *vi.* To feel queasy; feel nauseated.
'wii-chi·chun, *vt.* [oitsuku] 1 To overtake; catch up with; gain upon. 2 To chase; pursue.
'wii-dan, *n.* 1 A dais; a footpace; top seats (for honored guests). 2 The upper row (grade, tier, or step); the upper rank. See also shichadan.
wii-furi·in, *vi.* To drink oneself senseless; become dead drunk.
wiigoosan, *adj.* Same as yiigoosan.
wii-gukuchi, *n.* [yoigokochi] Feeling tipsy.
wii-gushi, *n.* [yoiguse] A habit that shows up when one is drunk.
'wii-hoo·in, *vt.* [oi- + hooru] To expel; turn out; drive away; hound out.
'wii·in, *vt.* [ueru] To plant (a tree); grow; raise; sow (seed). Also iiin. See also iikee.
'wii·jun, *vi.* [oyogu] To swim; have a swim.
'wii-kata, *n.* The upper class.
wii-kkwa, *n.* [oi] A nephew. See also miikkwa.
'wii-maa·sun, *vt.* [oimawasu] To pursue; chase.
'wii-muti, *n.* The upper region of a river.

wi·in, *vi.* [you] To get drunk; become intoxicated.
'wii-na·i-shicha-na·i, *n.* Being on top or bottom. -sun, *v.* To be on top or bottom.
'wii-ngwa, *n.* [uigo] The first child. Also iingwa.
'wii-nugari·in, *vi.* [...ri·ran, ...t·ti; oinukareru] To be outstripped; to be outrun.
'wii-nu·jun, *vt.* [oinugu] To outrun; outstrip; pass; surpass; get ahead of; outdo.
wiiri, *n.* [eri] The neck band of a kimono. Also kubi[1].
'wiiriki-dukuru, *n.* A tourist resort; a sightseeing place; a fun place.
'wiiriki·san, *adj.* [? oiroke] Interesting; entertaining; pleasant; enjoyable; amusing; funny. Also iirikisan.
wiiruu, *n.* A cord; a string; a braid; a strap; a tape. Also yiiruu.
'wii-shicha, *n.* [ueshita] Up and down; above and below; high and low; the coat and trousers. Also iihicha.
'wii-ta·chi, *n.* [oitachi] Growing up; growth; development.
'wii-ta·chun, *vi.* [oitatsu] To grow; grow up; be brought up. See sudachun.
wii-tchu, *n.* A drunk person; a drunk; a drunkard. Also witchaa.
'wii-wata, *n.* The upper abdomen.
wikiga, *n.* 1 A man; a male; a gentleman; the male sex; manhood. 2 A fellow; a chap; a guy. 3 An adult male; a mature man. 4 Manliness; manhood; honor. 5 A lover; a paramour.
wikiga-choodee, *n.* A brother; a male sibling.
wikiga-dachi, *n.* A household without a woman; a bachelor household.
wikiga-fuuji, *n.* Male appearance; masculine style.
wikiga-fuuji·i, *n.* A woman who is like a man; a masculine female.

wikiga-gwii, *n.* A male voice.
wikiga-kachimiya·a, *n.* A vamp; a coquette; a jilt.
wikiga-masa·i, *n.* A woman who outdoes men; a heroine; a woman of firm character; an amazon.
wikiga-ngwa, *n.* A boy; a son.
wikiga·nu-uya, *n.* A father.
wikiga-raa·s(h)an, *adj.* Manly; masculine; manful.
wikiga-shitu, *n.* A father-in-law; a husband's father.
wikiga-suga·i, *n.* Masculine attire (worn by a female).
wikiga-uttu, *n.* A younger brother.
wikiga-uya, *n.* Same as **wikiganuuya**.
wikiga-warabi, *n.* A boy; a male child; a boy baby.
wikiga-yagusami, *n.* A widower.
wikiga-yii, *n.* Sitting with one's legs crossed. [UKH]
wikii, *n.* An elder or younger brother (from the standpoint of his sister).
wikii-ukudi, *n.* See **ukudi**.
winagu, *n.* [onago*] A woman; a female; the fair sex; womankind; womenfolk; a mistress; a sweetheart.
winagu-booji, *n.* A nun.
winagu-dachi, *n.* A household without a man.
winagu-fuuji, *n.* A female appearance; female costume.
winagufuuji·i, *n.* A man who is feminine in appearance; a transvestite.
winagu-gwansu, *n.* A female household originator. [ODJ] See also **shijitadashi**.
winagu-gwii, *n.* A female voice.
winagu-kachimiya·a, *n.* A womanizer; a lady killer; an erotomaniac.
winagu-muchiri, *n.* Philandering; lasciviousness.
winagu-ngwa, *n.* A daughter; a girl; a maiden; A young woman.
winagu·nu-kata, *n.* Lit., a woman's side; a wife's side (of the family); maternal.
winagu-nuushi, *n.* A female head of household, business, or institution.
winagu·nu-uya, *n.* A mother.
winagu-raa·s(h)an, *adj.* Womanly; ladylike; feminine.
winagu-shikasa·a, *n.* A philanderer. See **winagukachimiyaa**.
winagu-shitu, *n.* A mother-in-law.
winagu-suga·i, *n.* Female costume.
winagu-uttu, *n.* A younger sister.
winagu-utusa·a, *n. pej.* A lady killer; a philanderer. [GSS]
winagu-uya, *n.* A mother [as a term of reference]. See also **winagunu'uya**.
winagu-warabi, *n.* 1 A daughter; a female child. 2 Women and children. 3 Womenfolk.
witcha·a, *n. pej.* Same as **wiitchu**.
woo, *n.* [oo] A king.
woodan, *n.* [oodan] Jaundice; the yellows.
woo-fi, *n.* [oohi] The queen; official first wife of the king.
woo-fuku, *n.* [oofuku] A round-trip; going and returning; both ways. **-sun,** *vi.* To make a round-trip; go and come back.
woogai, *n.* Highhandedness; oppression; tyranny. **·na,** *adj.* Oppressive; highhanded; tyrannical.
wooji, *n.* [ooji] 1 A prince; sons and brothers of a king. 2 A rank immediately below the king in the Ryukyu kingdom.
woooo, *interj.* No (to one senior in age but inferior in social status).
woo-ree, *n.* [oorai] 1 A road; a street; a boulevard. 2 Comings and goings; traffic.
wubamaa, *n.* An aunt.
wudu·i, *n.* [odori] 1 Dance; formal dance. 2 *arch.* A drama; a play. 3 *Kumiodori* dance-drama; a modern dramatic play in Okinawan. See also **mooi**[1], **shibai**.
wudu·i-suga·i, *n.* Dancing costumes.
wudu-yee, *n.* [odoriai] A dance party

for a male traveler held by the women of his family and relations. See also **kweena, tabisunugusuuji.**

wuga·mun, *vt.* [ogamu] **1** To worship; pray to; adore; bow to. **2** To see; view; watch.

wugan-ju, *n.* A holy place of worship including sacred groves and other places of worship. Also **ugwanju.**

wugari, *n.* Hunger; starvation.

wugari·in, *vi.* To starve; be hungry.

wugari-mun, *n.* One who is famished; a starving or hungry person.

wu·i, *n.* [ori] **1** Time; an occasion; a season; a moment; when. **2** An opportunity; a chance; a time.

wu·i-mi, *n.* [orime] Officially recognized annual events or holidays, often with religious or agricultural significance. Also **shichibi, kijari.**

wu·i-mun, *n.* [orimono] Cloth; fabric; textile; woven goods.

wu·in, *vt.* [oru] See **wuuin**[1].

wujasaa, *n.* An uncle [term of reference].

wu·n[1], *vi.* [oru] **1** [animate] To be; exist; be found; lie; remain; stand; stay. **2** To live; dwell; reside; inhabit; occupy (a room). **3** To happen to be; be present; be around.

wun[2], *n.* [on] Kindness; goodness; a favor; a benefit; a debt of gratitude. See also **unji, wunji, un**[2].

wunai, *n.* A sister, either elder or younger, from her brother's viewpoint.

wunai-gami, *n.* A sister deity, referring to a sister when she is acting in accordance with the traditional belief that she has spiritual power to protect her brother. [OGJ, OBJ, BHEO]

wunai-shitu, *n.* A sister-in-law, sister of one's husband.

wunai-tiisaaji, *n.* A kerchief, made by a sister and presented to her brother to keep him safe while on a journey. [ODJ]

wunai-ukudi, *n.* See **ukudi.**

wunai-wikii, *n.* Brother and sister.

wunchuu, *n.* An uncle; younger brother of one's parents; husband of the younger sister of one's parents.

wunchuu-gwaa, *n.* An uncle (one who is close in age to the speaker).

wunji, *n.* [ongi] A favor; an obligation; a debt of gratitude. Also **unji.** See also **wun**[2].

wusama·in, *vi.* [osamaru] To be governed well; be at peace; calm down; be settled. Also **usamain.**

wusami, *n.* [osame] Control; management; rule; sway; government (exercise of governmental authority). Also **usami, wusamigata.**

wusami-gata, *n.* See **wusami.**

wusami·in, *vt.* [osameru] To rule over; govern; reign over; manage; administer; regulate; order.

wuta·i, *n.* Fatigue; weariness; exhaustion. See also **kutandi, chikariin.**

wuta·in, *vi.* To get tired; grow weary; become exhausted. See also **chikariin.**

wutai-noo·shi, *n.* A drink at supper; an evening drink. Also **kutandinooshi.**

wuttii, *n.* [ototoi] The day before yesterday.

wuttii·nu-naacha, *n.* The fourth day back; four days ago.

wutu, *n.* [otto] A husband. See **sachi-wutu.**

wutu-biree, *n.* Art of getting along with a husband. See **hiree.**

wuu-, *pref.* [o-] Male (of animal); a cock; a bull.

wuu[1], *n.* [u] A fiber banana [*Musa liukiuensis* (Matsum.) Makino]. Also **uu**[3]. [FOSR]

wuu[2], *n.* [wo] A cord; a strap; a thong. See also **wiiruu, china.** Also **uu**[4].

wuu-atai, *n.* A plantain patch. Also **uu'atai.**

wuu-baai, *n.* A male bamboo stick. [UKH] See **haai**[1].

wuu-baara, *n.* A round bamboo basket, about a foot in diameter, used as container for ramie fiber. Also **haara, uubaara.** See also **baaki.**
wuubaara·a, *n.* Same as **wuubaara.** [GSS]
wuu-bana, *n.* A male flower; a staminate flower.
wuubee, *n.* Ramie [*Boehmeria nivea*]. See **maawuu.**
wuubee-gwaa, *n.* Same as **wuubee.** [UKH]
wuu-bingi, *n.* [ohirugi] Male mangrove [*Bruguiera gymnorrhiza* (L.) Lamarck]. [FOSR]
wuu-dui, *n.* [ondori] A cock. Also **wuurui, wuuduyaa.**
wuuduya·a, *n.* Same as **wuudui.** [UKH]
wuu-gaara, *n.* A convex-shaped tile, which makes a pair with a concave tile. See also **miigaara.**
wuu·in^1, *vt.* [oru] **1** To break; snap. **2** To fold double. **3** To bend. Also **wuin.**
wuu·in^2, *vt.* [oru] To shake; swing; joggle; jolt.
wuuji, *n.* [ogi] Sugar cane [*Saccharum officinarum* L.]. See **wuuji'oorasee.**
wuuji-bakuyoo, *n.* A merchant who buys a sugar cane stand before harvesting. [UKH]
wuuji-bataki, *n.* Sugar cane field. [UKH]
wuuji-juku·i, *n.* Sugar cane culture.
wuuji-kasaja·a, *n.* A person who removes the sugar cane leaves. [UKH]
wuuji-kasaji·i, *n.* Removal of the sugar cane leaves. [UKH]
wuuji-katamiya·a, *n.* One who carries sugar cane bundles. [UKH]
wuuji-kwaasa·a, *n.* A person who feeds sugar cane stalks into a press. [UKH]
wuuji·n-gara, *n.* Bagasse.
wuuji·nu-kwee, *n.* Sugar cane fertilizer. [UKH]
wuuji-oorasee, *n.* A game in which boys compete at breaking sugar cane stalks.

wuu-jiru, *n.* The male string of the **sanshin** musical instrument, which produces the deepest and lowest sound of the three strings. See **sanshin.**
wuuji-sani, *n.* Sugar cane saplings.
wuuji-tabaya·a, *n.* A person who ties sugar cane into bundles. [UKH]
wuuji-toosa·a, *n.* A person who harvests sugar cane with a large knife. [UKH]
wuuji-too·shi, *n.* Harvesting of sugar cane. [UKH]
wuu·jun^1, *vt.* To rinse; wash out; shake out.
wuu·jun^2, *vt.* To despise; scorn; disdain; slight.
wuuki, *n.* [oke] A bucket; a pail. See also **taagu, kumiwuuki, kweewuuki, hanjiri, taaree.**
wuuki-jeeku, *n.* A wood bucket maker. See **seeku.**
wuuki-kagan, *n.* A glass bucket; a wooden cylinder with a glass pane at one end so that one can see underwater. [UKH] Also **tamawuuki.**
wuuki-uubi, *n.* A bamboo hoop.
wuu-mun, *n.* [o- + mono] Male (of animals). See also **miimun.**
wuu-muna·a, *n.* Male animal. Same as **wuumun.** See also **miimunaa.**
wuun, *n.* Same as **wuunu.**
wuu-nna, *n.* A male tug in a tug-of-war. See **chinahichi.**
wuunu, *n.* [ono] An axe; a broadaxe with a handle large enough to be held with both hands. Also **wuun, uun, uunu.** See also **yuuchi^2, tiin^2, ishiyuuchi, haa^2, habu^2, niri.**
wuurari·in, *vi.* [orareru] To become broken; be forced to break.
wuuri·in, *vi.* [oreru] **1** To break; be broken; snap; give way; fracture. **2** To be folded; be doubled. **3** To give in; yield to; back down; compromise.
wuu-taka, *n.* A tercel; a male hawk. See also **taka.**

wuu-ushi, *n.* [oushi] A bull; an ox; a steer.
wuu-winagu, *n. pej.* A masculine woman.
wuu-'waa, *n.* A boar; a male pig.
wuu-'waa-karaya·a, *n.* A pig breeder. Also **'waachikiyaa.**
wuu-wu-wuu, *interj.* No (to superior); no, sir; no, ma'am. See also **woooo, yiiyiyii, nnnnn, ashi², bee¹, beeru, uu², oo, ii¹, 'nn.**

Y

·ya, *part.* Topic marker; marks a noun as the sentence topic. See Introduction for alternate forms.
yaa¹, *n.* [ya] 1 A house; a dwelling; a cottage; a residence; a mansion. 2 A home; a family; a household. See also **anayaa, nuchijiyaa, kaarayaa, kayabuchiyaa, kayayaa, yaagwaa, ufuyaa, faafuuyaa, amahaji, ashagi, haaya, hashiru, hinpun, fuuru, ichi², ishigachi, jaa², jashichi, joo³, kaa², kachi², kucha¹, mushiru, tatan, naa⁵, ichibanja, nibanja, nakamee, sanbanja(a), shiiri, nju, shimu¹, tungwa, tinjoo, tuku³, yaajoo, yaanukubi, yashichi, yin¹, 'waabuuru, yaanu'wii, yukasa, ushinuyaa, 'nmanuyaa, meenuyaa.**
yaa², *interj.* Addressing oneself to someone; seeking consent or making sure. You see; you know; I suppose; say; look; listen.
yaa³, *part.* Denotes seeking consent or making sure: …is it?; …isn't it?; …are you?; …aren't you?; …right?
'yaa, *n.* You (to those of equal or lower standing). See also **ittaa, unju.**
yaa-ban, *n.* A house sign or mark.
yaa-bara·i, *n.* A rite of house purification. See **mabui'uui.**
yaa-bushin, *n.* Building a house; house construction.

yaakarasaa

yaachi, *n.* [yattsu] Eight; eight years old. See also **hachi.**
yaa-chuu, *n.* [yaito*] Moxacautery; moxibustion; moxocausis. See also **fuuchi³.**
yaa-doogu, *n.* Household cleaning implements.
yaadu, *n.* [yado] Same as **yadu.**
yaadu-guchi, *n.* [yado + kuchi] The doorway; the doorstep; the door.
yaadui, *n.* 1 A rural settlement for the gentry. 2 A villa; a cottage.
yaa-duu, *n.* A gecko; a house lizard. Also **yaaruu.**
yaa-fuchi-suuji, *n.* Ritual celebration on the completion of a new house. [OBJ]
yaa-gumai, *n.* Confinement at home; secluding oneself at home.
yaa-gumaya·a, *n.* A recluse; one who stays at home; a stay-at-home.
yaa-gunaa, *n.* Members of a family; a family; a household. Also **yaaninju.**
yaa-gwaa, *n.* A little house; a cottage; a hut.
yaa-ija·a, *n.* One who is brave at home but not outside.
yaa-jeeku, *n.* A carpenter; a construction carpenter.
yaa-ji·chun, *vi.* To settle in a house; establish oneself (in a house).
yaa-jiishi, *n.* A funeral urn in the shape of a house. See **jiishigaami.**
yaa-jina, *n.* A family tradition; a family custom.
yaa-jishi·i, *n.* Difficulty sleeping in an unfamiliar environment. See **shishiin¹.**
yaa-joo, *n.* A gate; a roofed gate.
yaa-juku·i, *n.* Construction of a house. See **chukuin.**
yaa-kaja·i, *n.* House and household belongings; household property.
yaa-kaji, *n.* 1 The number of houses. 2 Every house.
yaa·kara-chiya·a, *n.* Everyday wear; weekday clothes.
yaa-karasa·a, *n.* An owner who rents out property; a landlord.

yaa-kaya·a, *n.* A tenant (of buildings).
'yaa-kuru, *adv.* Yourself; by yourself.
yaama, *n.* 1 A spinning wheel. 2 A device; a machine. 3 A trap; a snare.
yaa-madi·i, *n.* A homeless person; a vagrant.
yaa-mucha·a, *n.* A good housekeeper.
yaa-mu·chi, *n.* Housekeeping.
yaamuchi-doogu, *n.* Household effects; household utensils.
yaa-muchi-juku, *n.* Home economics; household management.
yaan, *n.* Next year; the coming year. Also **yani**².
yaa-nare·e, *n.* Training at home; disciplining at home.
yaa-ninju, *n.* 1 A family member. 2 Number of family members.
yaa·n-naa, *n.* A household name; a family name; a surname; a last name. See also **myooji**, **nooji**, **yagoo**.
yaa·nu-baan, *n.* House watching during the family's absence; caretaker.
yaa·nu-kubi, *n.* A house wall; an indoor wall.
yaa·nu-kushi, *n.* The backyard; the back of a house.
yaa-nuu, *n.* The roof of a house. See **yaanu'wii**.
yaa·nu-uchi, *n.* Indoors; the interior of a house.
yaa-nuushi, *n.* [yanushi] A landlord (of buildings); a house owner.
yaa·nu-'wii, *n.* A roof; roofing; covering; the housetop.
yaa-ruu, *n.* Same as **yaaduu**.
yaa·sa, *n.* Hunger; starvation. **-sun**, *v.* To be hungry; be famished.
yaasa-jini, *n.* Death by starvation. See also **gashi**.
yaasa-kurisa, *n.* Pain of hunger.
yaa·san, *adj.* Hungry; starving; famished.
yaasa-noo·shi, *n.* A snack; something to eat to stave off hunger temporarily.
yaasa-shimi·in, *vt.* To make (someone) hungry; leave one to starve.
yaasa-woo, *n.* One who is sensitive to hunger.
yaa-see, *n.* [yasai] Vegetables; greens. See also **oofa**.
yaasee-uya·a, *n.* [yasai + uri] A greengrocer.
yaashi, *n.* [yashi] A palm; any of the *Palmae* family of tropical or subtropical monocotyledonous trees or shrubs. See also **noyashi**, **binroo**. [FOSR].
yaa-shigutu, *n.* Household chores.
yaashi-gwaa, *n.* 1 A coconut. 2 A sake bottle made of a coconut.
yaa-tacha·a, *n.* One who has branched out and established his own household; a branch family.
yaa-tata·a, *n.* Same as **yaatachaa**.
yaa-tiichi, *n.* One household; living in one household.
yaa-uuchi·i, *n.* [yautsuri] Moving from one house to another.
yaa-wakaya·a, *n.* A branch family. Also **yaatachaa**.
yaa-yaa, *n. inf.* Clothes.
yaa-yaa·tu, *adv.* Peacefully; restfully; at rest. [UKH]
yaa-yashichi, *n.* A house and lot; the premises; the estate; a homestead.
yaa-zaree, *n.* The rite of purging a house of a dead spirit after the funeral has been held. See **mabui'uui**.
yabira·a, *n.* A debilitated person; an enervated person.
yabiri·in, *vi.* To weaken; become debilitated; become enervated; become emaciated.
yabiri-mun, *n.* Same as **yabiraa**.
yabuu, *n.* A practitioner of acupuncture and moxibustion.
yachi, *n.* A mean disposition; a vicious character. **·na**, *adj.* Wicked; malicious.
yachiba, *n.* A harrow pulled by a horse; a rake.
ya·chi-doofu, *n.* Broiled tofu (bean curd).

yachi-in, *n.* [yakiin] A brand; a branding iron.
yachi-mun, *n.* [yakimono] Ceramics; porcelain; pottery; earthenware; crockery; chinaware.
yachimun-doogu, *n.* [yakimono-doogu] Pottery.
ya-chin, *n.* [yachin] Rent; a rental.
yachi-nagi·in, *vt.* To burn down; reduce to ashes; sweep away by burning; raze to the ground.
yachiri·in, *vi.* [yatsureru] 1 To become emaciated; be worn out; be exhausted. 2 To be ruined; be reduced; want. 3 To be disguised.
ya·chun, *vt.* [yaku] 1 To burn; fire; set (a house) on fire. 2 To broil; grill; toast; bake; parch. 3 To scorch; bake; fire. 4 To cauterize. 5 To make charcoal. 6 To cremate; incinerate. 7 To print a photo. See also **yakiin**.
yadu, *n.* [yado] An inn; a lodging house; a hotel.
yadu-chin, *n.* [yadochin] The charge for the night's lodging.
yadu-ya, *n.* [yadoya] An inn; a hotel; a lodging house.
yafara·a, *n.* One who has a delicate constitution; a sickly person.
yafara·chun, *vi.* 1 To soften; become tender. 2 To become gentle; become meek. 3 To become weak; debilitate.
yafara-ganju·u, *n.* The sickly-strong; one who looks sickly but is healthy; one who looks frail but is strong; one who is sickly but does not get seriously ill.
yafara-ganjuu-mun, *n.* Same as **yafara-ganjuu**.
yafaraki·in, *vt.* 1 To soften; make soft. 2 To bring to peace with; reconcile; mediate a settlement.
yafara-mun, *n.* Same as **yafaraa**.
yafara·san, *adj.* 1 Soft; tender; pliant. 2 Weak; sickly. See also **yoosan**.
yafat·teen, *adv.* Tenderly; softly; gently; mildly; meekly.
yagama·a, *n.* Same as **yagamayaa**.
yagama·s(h)an, *adj.* [yakamashii] Noisy; clamorous; uproarious; boisterous.
yagama-yaa, *n.* A common gathering house in rural areas for young girls to do night work such as spinning.
yagati, *adv.* [yagate] 1 Soon; in no time. 2 Almost; nearly.
ya-goo, *n.* [yagoo] Name of a household, often dependent on geography, topography, physical or occupational distinctions, last names, or the household's place in the extended family structure. Also **yaannaa**.
yagui, *n.* Same as **yagwii**.
yagu-sami, *n.* A widow.
yagusami-ngwa, *n.* Same as **yamana-shingwa**.
yagwii, *n.* [yagoe*] A shout to mark time; a shout of encouragement; a fighting cry; a fighting spirit.
yahee-gami, *n.* Visitor-deity on the day of the **tantui**, the sowing of the rice seeds on the first day of winter in the Kerama Islands. [ODJ] See also **tantui**.
yai, *n.* [yari] A spear; a pike.
yai-ba, *n. lit.* [yakiba] A tempered blade.
ya·in, *vt.* To tear; rend; rip.
·**yaka,** *part.* Rather than…; better than…; more than….
yakara, *n.* [yakara] 1 A fellow; a guy. 2 A strong man; a man of steady character.
ya-keen, *n.* Eight times.
yaki-atu, *n.* [yakeato] Ruins of a fire.
yaki-chiki·in, *vt.* [yakitsukeru] 1 To glaze; fire (china); plate; stain. 2 To print (photos).
yakii, *n.* Same as **Yeemayakii**. [ODJ]
yaki·in, *vi.* [yakeru] 1 To burn; be burnt; be destroyed by fire; be gutted. 2 To be roasted; be broiled; be baked; be toasted; be grilled. 3 To be scorched; be parched. 4 To be sunburned; be suntanned. 5 To have heartburn. See also **yachun**.

yaki-jiri, *n.* [yakegire] Embers.
yak-kee, *n.* [yakkai] **1** A trouble; a worry; a bother; a burden. **2** Help; care; support; kindness; dependence.
yakkee-baree, *n.* [yakkai-barai] Good riddance (of bad thing).
yakkee-mun, *n.* [yakkai-mono] **1** A dependent; a parasite; a hanger-on. **2** A burden; an encumbrance; a bother; a nuisance. Also **anmasamun**.
yak-kwan, *n.* [yakan < yakkwan] **1** A kettle; a teakettle. **2** A testicle. Also **yakwan**.
yakkwa-na·a, *n.* Lit., one with testicles as big as kettles, often as a result of elephantiasis.
yaku[1], *n.* [yaku] Evil fortune; misfortune; ill luck; disaster.
yaku[2], *n.* [yaku] **1** An office; a post; a position; an appointment. **2** Duty; function; capacity; service; an office. **3** A part; a role. **4** Use; service; good; utility; help; assistance.
yaku-dushi, *n.* [yakudoshi] An unlucky year; a critical year.
yaku-gee, *n.* [yakoogai, yakugai*] A pearl shell [*Lunatia marmorata* (Linnê)].
yaku-joo, *n.* [yakujoo] A contract; a compact; a promise; an agreement.
yakusu, *n.* [yakusho] A government office; a public office.
yakusuku, *n.* [yakusoku] **1** A promise; an engagement; a date; an appointment; a contract; a stipulation. **2** A promise; a prospect. **3** A convention; a rule; regulations. **4** One's destiny; one's fate.
yaku-ta·chun, *phr.* [·**tan**, ·**tchi**, yakudatsu] To be useful; be serviceable; be of use; answer the purpose; do; be helpful.
yakwan, *n.* Same as **yakkwan**.
yama, *n.* [yama] **1** A forest; a woody hill; a knoll; a height. **2** Confusion; disorder; chaos; pell-mell. See **mui**.
yama-, *pref.* **1** Denotes a wild, savage nature, uncouthness, and confusion. **2** Of or pertaining to a wooded hill.
yamaa-gwaa, *n.* Same as **yamanashingwa**.
yamaa-sanka, *n.* Not arranged in order; a state of disarray. [GSS]
yama-atcha·a, *n.* A forester; a woodcutter; a woodsman.
yama-biku, *n.* [yamabiko] An echo.
yama-chi·in, *vi.* To reach a state of confusion.
yama-chira·sun, *vt.* To confuse; cause disorder.
yama-chiri-gutu, *n.* Confusion; disorder; chaos.
yama-chiri·in, *vi.* To become confused; become disorderly.
yama chitchan, *phr.* What a mess! What confusion! See **yama**, **yamachiin**.
yama-dani·i, *n.* Same as **yamanashingwa**.
yama-dumi, *n.* [yamadome] A closed mountain, a taboo on entering the wild fields, wooded areas, and mountainous areas.
yama-gaami, *n.* A land turtle; a tortoise. See also **umigaami**.
yama-gajan, *n.* A wild mosquito (*Stegomyia fasciata*), in contrast to those that are usually found near homes; a striped mosquito.
yama-gakkoo, *n.* Playing truant from school.
yamagan, *n.* A beetle; a coleopteran. [GSS]
yama-guruchi, *n.* [yama + kuro + ki] A wild black tree [J hamasendan; *Evodia glauca* Miquel], used in carpentry. [FOSR]
yamagu, *n.* Cunning; craftiness; craft; unfairness.
yama-gwaa, *n.* A small wasteland; a bush; a thicket.
yama-hija·a, *n.* One whose face is covered with beard.
yama-in[1], *n.* [yamainu] A wild dog; a

masterless dog.
yama-in², *n.* Lit., a wild stamp; a ready-made personal seal with undecipherable character-like design so that anyone can use it.
yama-kaaga·a, *n.* A shy person.
yama-kanda, *n.* [yamakazura*] A wild sweet potato vine [*Stephania japonica* (Thunb.) Miers var. *japonica*]. [FOSR]
yama-mayaa, *n.* A stray cat; an alley cat.
yama-michi, *n.* [yamamichi] A mountain path.
yama-mumu, *n.* [yamamomo] A myrica [*Myrica rubra* Sieb. & Zucc.]; a small sweet round red berry. [FOSR]
yama-naji, *n.* A woodsman's hatchet. [UKH]
yama-nashi-ngwa, *n.* An illegitimate child. See also **yamadanii, yamanumiingwa**. Also **yamangwa, yamaagwaa, guunaingwa, kachinumiingwa, dakinumiingwa, yagusamingwa, utushidani, utushingwa, utushidani, heejuringwa**.
yama-na·sun, *vt.* 1 To confuse. 2 To turn a field into wilderness.
yama-ngwa, *n.* Same as **yamanashingwa**.
yama-nkaji, *n.* [yama + mukade] A scorpion.
yama-'nmu, *n.* [yamaimo] A yam; a wild-stemmed yam [*Dioscorea alata* L.]. Also **yama'umu**. [FOSR]
yama·nu-chiji, *n.* The top of a mountain; a summit.
yama·nu-mii-ngwa, *n.* Same as **yamanashingwa**. [UKH]
yama·nu-naaka, *n.* [yamanonaka] Deep in the hills.
yama-nusudu, *n.* [yamanusubito*] A mountain robber; a bandit.
yama-sa·a, *n.* A forest worker. Same as **yama'atchaa**.
yama-shigutu, *n.* [yamashigoto] Any work in the forest, such as that of the woodsman, charcoal maker, etc.

yama-shishi, *n.* 1 A wild boar [*Sus scrofa riukiuanus* Kuroda]. 2 Wild boar meat.
yama·sun, *vt.* To cause pain; injure; hurt; inflict an injury.
Yamatu, *n.* [Yamato] Japan (in contrast to Okinawa).
Yamatu-achinee, *n.* Trade with Japan.
Yamatu-guchi, *n.* Japanese; the Japanese language.
Yamatu-jiifee, *n.* Japanese alertness; Japanese quickness; the impatience and quick temper characteristic of Japanese. See **chiibeesan**.
Yamatu-mijun, *n.* Fish belonging to the herring family [*Sardinella clupeoides* (Bleeker)].
Yamatu-mun, *n.* Articles made in mainland Japan.
Yamatu-muuku, *n.* A Japanese man married to an Okinawan woman.
Yamatu-naa, *n.* Japanese-style name, in contrast to a traditional Okinawan-style name; Japanese-style names used after 1879, when Okinawa prefecture was established. Also **gakkoonaa**. See also **naa³**.
Yamatu-nchu, *n.* A Japanese; the Japanese. See **naichaa**.
Yamatu-soogwachi, *n.* The Japanese New Year's Day; the New Year's Day according to the solar calendar. See also **Uchinaa-soogwachi**.
Yamatu·u, *n.* A derogatory term for a Japanese person.
Yamatu-yumi, *n.* A Japanese woman who is married to an Okinawan.
Yamatu-yuu, *n.* The Japanese period in Okinawan history, referring to the period from 1879, when Okinawa Prefecture was established under the Japanese government, until 1945, and again from 1972, when Okinawa reverted to Japan after the post-World War Two US administration. See **yuugawai, Uchinaayuu, Amerikayuu**.
yama-uku, *n.* The depths (recesses) of a

yama'umu

mountain. Also **ukuyama**.
yama-umu, *n*. Same as **yama'nmu**. [FOSR]
yami, *n*. [yami] **1** Darkness; the dark. **2** Black-market dealings. **3** Troubled times; chaotic state.
yami·in, *vt*. [yameru] **1** To stop; cease; discontinue; break off; lay off; end; terminate. **2** To give up; quit; abandon; relinquish. **3** To resign (one's post); retire (from office); leave (one's place). **4** To abolish; do away with; discontinue.
yami-wacharee, *n*. [yamiwazurai] Suffering from sickness; being afflicted with a disease.
yami-wandee, *n*. Nursing; tending (a sick person). See **wandain**.
ya·mun, *vi*. [yamu] **1** To feel pain; feel painful; hurt; ache. **2** To be taken ill; suffer from; be afflicted with. **3** To feel sorry; feel regretful.
yamundoo·sun, *vi*. To complain of a pain; be in pain; cry in one's pain.
ya·n, *irreg. cop*. To be; am; is; are; that's right.
yana-, *pref*. Bad, wrong, evil, unjust.
yana·a, *n*. A bad thing; a bad person; an item of low quality.
yana-chi, *n*. Tainted blood; diseased blood.
yana-dakumi, *n*. Wiles; an evil design; a trick; conspiracy.
yana-fuuji, *n*. A bad habit; a bad custom; evil ways.
yana-gata·a, *n*. A perverse person; a disgusting fellow.
yana-gucha·a, *n*. One with an acrimonious tongue.
yana-guchi, *n*. A stinging tongue; abusive language; bad-mouthing.
yana-gukuru, *n*. Malicious intent; an evil thought; a sinister motive.
yana-imi, *n*. A nightmare; a bad dream; an evil dream.
yanaji, *n*. [yanagi] A willow.
yana-jimu, *n*. An evil intention; a sinister motive; an evil thought; a malicious mind; malevolence.
yana-jini, *n*. **1** Abnormal and unnatural death, typically due to a cause such as suicide, drowning, or accident. **2** Death while abroad. See also **dabi, shuukaawatai**. [ODJ]
yana-kaagi, *n*. Uncomeliness; homeliness.
yana-kaagi·i, *n*. A homely woman; a plain-looking woman.
yana-kaja, *n*. Foul odor; ill smell; offensive smell.
yana-kaji, *n*. An evil spirit; an evil wind; an injurious spirit.
yana-kutu, *n*. Wrongdoing; an evil deed; a vice; a crime; a sinful deed.
yana-michi, *n*. A bad road; an evil way.
yana-mii, *n*. A terrible situation; a bad experience.
yana-mun, *n*. **1** A demon; an evil spirit; a ghost; an apparition; a monster. **2** A rogue; a knave; a villain. **3** A bad thing; a thing of poor quality.
yana-munu-ii, *n*. Speaking with evil portent; unlucky way of speaking.
yana-naraashi, *n*. Inciting evildoing; teaching bad ways.
yana-rikuchi, *n*. Cunning; craft; guile; wiles.
yana·san, *adj*. Bad; ugly; nasty.
yana-shimuchi, *n*. A cross temper; perverseness; spite. See also **shimuchi**[2].
yana-tchu, *n*. A bad person; a good-for-nothing; a naughty person. See also **yanaa, yanamun, akunin, yiitchu**.
yana-tinchi, *n*. Bad weather.
yana-'waachichi, *n*. Same as **yanatinchi**.
yana-wachaku, *n*. A practical joke; a mean trick; nasty teasing; a prank.
yana-'wii, *n*. Drunken sickness; drunken frenzy.
yan-ba, *n*. A guide; a sign; a bookmark.
Yanbara·a, *n*. **1** A sailing ship that frequents the Yanbaru region in the north of Okinawa. Also **Yanbaraabuni**,

Yanbarushin. 2 *n. pej.* A person from Yanbaru.

Yanbaraa-buni, *n.* A junk. Also **Yanbaraa, Yanbarushin.**

Yanbaru, *n.* The northern region of Okinawa Island.

Yanbaru-daki, *n.* Yanbaru bamboo [*Pleioblastus linearis* Nakai]. [FOSR]

Yanbaru-kutuba, *n.* The Yanbaru dialect; the dialect spoken in the northern region of Okinawa.

Yanbaru-nchu, *n.* A person from Yanbaru; a native of Yanbaru.

Yanbaru-shin, *n.* Same as **Yanbaraabuni.**

yandi, *n.* [yabure] Damage; breakage; breakdown.

yandi·in, *vi.* 1 To break down; be wrecked; be damaged; be impaired. 2 To fall through; be ruptured; be upset; get out of order.

ya-ngwa, *n.* [yagura] A tree house.

yani[1], *n.* [yani] Resin; gum; nicotine; tar.

yani[2], *n.* Same as **yaan.**

yani·in, *vi.* Be a hindrance to; get in the way; obstruct. [UKH]

yani-shiiyo, *n.* Seed sugar cane. [UKH]

yan·jun, *vt.* [·dan, ·ti; yaburu] To break; destroy; demolish; impair; damage.

-yan·jun, *suff.* To fail (to do).

yanmee, *n.* [yamai] Sickness; a disease; an indisposition; a disorder. Also **byoochi.**

yanmee-mun, *n.* [yamaimono] The sick; a sick person; an invalid; a patient.

yan-muchi, *n.* [yani + mochi] Bird-lime, made from secretions of the bark of the banyan tree. Also **muchi**[3].

yarabu, *n.* A **yarabu** tree; Alexandrian laurel [*Calophyllum inophyllum* L.]. [FOSR]

yarashii-kwaashii, *n.* A plan for tiding over difficulties; tiding over; makeshift. [GSS]

yara·sun, *vt.* To dispatch; send (a person) to (a place).

yari, *n.* [yare] A tear; a rent; a breach; a rupture.

yari·in, *vi.* [yareru] To be torn; tear; rip; rend.

yari-jin, *n.* A torn kimono. See **chin**[3].

yari-mii, *n.* [yareme] A rent; a tear; a split; a crevice; a gap.

yari-saki, *n.* Rips and tears in kimono or other clothing.

yasee, *n.* [yasai] Vegetables; culinary plants. Also **yaasee.**

yashi-agai, *n.* [yasuagari] Being economical; being cheap.

yashichi, *n.* [yashiki] The premises; a residence; a lot; a home site.

yashichi-gami, *n.* Guardian deity of one's premises. [ODJ] See **fuurugami.**

yashichi-ganee, *n.* 1 Ground (land) rent for the premises. 2 Property tax.

yashichi·nu-ugwan, *n.* A prayer for the housing premises. [KCS]

yashiga, *conj.* But; however; nevertheless.

yashi-garu·u, *n.* A skinny person; a mere skeleton of a person. Also **yoogari, yoogaraa.**

yashi-goo·i, *n.* [yassan + kooin] Purchasing at a cheap price.

yashii, *n.* [yasuri] A file; a rasp.

yashi·in, *vi.* [yaseru] To get lean; grow slim; lose weight. See **yoogariin.**

yashima·in, *vi.* [yasumaru] 1 To be able to rest; get rested; be relieved. 2 To endure; be patient; tolerate.

yashimi, *n.* [yasumi] Rest; recess; an intermission; a break; a holiday; a vacation; a day off. See also **yurii.**

yashimi·in[1], *vt.* [yasumeru] To repose; respite; rest (oneself); give rest; let (a thing) idle.

yashimi·in[2], *vt.* To reduce the price; cheapen; make a discount.

yashi-mun, *n.* [yasumono] A cheap article; a bargain; an inferior article.

yashin, *n.* [yashin] 1 Ambition; aspiration. 2 A sinister design; an intrigue.

yashinain

yashina·in, *vt.* [·(r)an, ·ti; yashinau] **1** To bring up; rear; adopt; foster. **2** To support; provide for; maintain.

yashinee-ngwa, *n.* A mock-adopted child; a child who is frail or otherwise unusual without proven reason who is mock-adopted by another couple in the belief that the child is incompatible with its natural parents. See also **yooshi**[1].

yashinee-uya, *n.* Mock-adoptive parents. See **yashineengwa**.

yashin-gutu, *n.* A betrayal; a rebellion; a revolt.

yashit-teen, *adv.* Easily; with ease.

yashi-u·i, *n.* [yasu-uri] Selling cheap; sacrifice; a bargain sale. Also **shitiui**.

yashi-yashi·tu, *adv.* Easily; with ease; without effort. Also **yashitteen**, **duuyashitteen**.

yas·san, *adj.* [...**shi·ku**] Cheap; inexpensive; of low price.

yasunji, *n.* [yasunji] Renunciation; resignation; reconcilement.

yasunji·in, *vi.* [yasunjiru] To be contented with; rest satisfied with; be at ease; have peace of mind.

yatchii, *n.* An elder brother; a big brother. See also **shiija**, **afii**.

yatchii-gwaa, *n.* The (youngest) elder brother.

yatchuku, *n.* [yakkyoku] A pharmacy; a pharmacist.

yatin, *part.* Either; even.

yat-tai, *n.* Same as **hachinin**.

yattu, *adv.* [yatto] At last; ultimately; finally; with difficulty.

yattu-kattu, *adv.* Finally; with difficulty; barely. See also **yattu**.

yatu·in, *vt.* [yatou] To hire; employ; engage.

yatui-ngwa, *n.* Apprenticed child. See **Ichuman-ui**.

Yeema, *n.* Yaeyama Islands, southernmost group of islands in the Ryukyu archipelago. Also **Eema**[2].

Yeema·a, *n. pej.* A person from Yaeyama. Also **Eemaa**.

Yeema-nchu, *n.* A person from the Yaeyama Islands. Also **Eemanchu**.

Yeema-yakii, *n.* Malaria that was indigenous to the Yaeyama Islands. Also **yakii**.

Yeema-yashi, *n.* Same as **binroo**.

Yeigo, *n.* Same as **Eigo**.

yei-saa, *n.* Same as **eisaa**.

yichai-tatchai, *n.* Same as **yitchai-tatchai**.

yida, *n.* [eda] A tree branch; a bough. Same as **yuda**.

yii-, *pref.* [yoi; ii] Denotes good, well.

yii[1], *n.* [i] The Boar as the last of the twelve calendrical animal signs. Also **ii**[2].

yii[2], *n.* [i] A rush [*Juncus decipiens* Nakai], used for making lamp wicks and matting. Also **ii**[3].

yii[3], *n.* [yui] Cooperative labor by means of labor exchange. See **yiimaa-ruu**. Also **ii**[4].

yii[4], *n.* [e] A picture; a drawing; a painting; an illustration. Also **ii**[5].

yii-chiri, *n.* **1** A splashed pattern. **2** Cloth with splashed patterns. Also **iichiri**, **tutchiri**.

yii-daki, *n.* One's sitting height.

yii-data·n, *n.* **Tatan** mats with Ryukyu (rather than **Biigu**) facing. See **yii**[2].

yiifee-jii, *n.* [ihai-ji] A posthumous name.

yii-fudi, *n.* [ehude] An artist's brush.

yii-gaa, *n.* A (water) well; a community well. Same as **kaa**[2].

yiigoo·san, *adj.* [egui*] **1** Acrid; pungent. **2** Itchy; itching. Also **wiigoosan**.

yii·in, *vt.* **1** To play at (dolls). **2** To be especially good at. See also **yiirimun**.

yii-jimu, *n.* A good heart; a good intention; conscience. See **chimu**.

yii-kaagi, *n.* A beauty; a belle; a lovely woman; a pretty girl. Same as **churakaagi**.

yii-kacha·a, *n.* A painter (an artist). Also **yiikachi.** See also **penkiyaa.**
yii-kachi, *n.* Same as **yiikachaa.**
yii-maaru·u, *n.* [yuimawari] A system of cooperative exchange of labor; chipping in on a labor project common to the village such as harvesting rice or building a house. Also **yuimaaru.**
yii-mushiru, *n.* A straw mat covering. Same as **shichimushiru.** See also **mushiru.**
yiin, *n.* [en] Veranda; hallway.
yi·in, *vi.* [·ran, ·chi; iru] To sit; take a seat; be seated; squat down.
yii-niibui, *n.* [inemuri] A doze; a nap; a catnap. **-sun,** *v.* To doze off. See also **yiishinguu.**
yiiri-mun, *n.* [< **yii·in**] A toy; a plaything.
yii-ruu, *n.* Same as **wiiruu.**
yii-saku, *n.* Moderate; temperate; proper; suitable.
yii-shigutu, *n.* A sedentary work.
yii-shinguu, *n.* Same as **yiiniibui.** [UKH]
yiisu, *n.* [isu] A chair.
yiitcha, *n.* Sitting down.
yii-tchu, *n.* A good person; a virtuous person. See also **yanatchu.**
yii-yi-yii, *adv.* No (negative response to an equal or inferior). See also **nba, wuuwuwuu, woooo.**
yin[1], *n.* [en] A veranda, a porch.
yin[2], *n.* [en] **1** A relation; a connection; affinity; ties; bond. **2** Karma; fate; destiny; chance. **3** Love; marriage.
yinjoo-jin, *n.* Betrothal gift money. [UKH] See also **sakimui.**
yinsu, *n.* [miso] Same as **nnsu.**
yin-taka·a, *n.* Same as **yuntaki.**
yin-taki, *n.* Same as **yuntaki.**
yi·nu-gu, *n.* [enogu] Pigment; paint; coloring materials; colors.
yinui, *n.* Same as **yunui.** [UKH] See **ninchi.**
yinui-suukoo, *n.* Same as **yunui.**

yooji

yishi·in, *vt.* To put (something) into position; place; mount.
yi·tchai-ta·tchai, *n.* [itari tattari] Standing and sitting; being restless with joy or sorrow. **-sun,** *v. colloq.* To be restless and keep standing up and sitting down. Also **yichaitatchai.**
yon-naa, *adv.* Slowly; gently; without haste; leisurely; deliberately. Also **yoonnaa.** See also **yoon.**
yoo-baa, *n.* A weakling; a coward; a weak fellow. See also **chuubaa.**
yoo-fuku, *n.* [yoofuku] A suit of Western clothes; Western dress; Western clothes.
yoofuku-danshi, *n.* [yoofuku-dansu] A wardrobe; a dresser.
yoofuku-yaa, *n.* [yoofukuya] **1** A tailor. **2** A tailor shop.
yoogaa, *n.* That which is distorted, crooked, warped, or bent.
yoogaa-hiigaa, *adv.* Meandering; winding; curving.
yoogaa-hiigaa-atchi, *n.* A tottering step; crooked course of walking.
yoogaa-jichi, *n.* Mishearing; hearing incorrectly.
yoogaa-ninji, *n.* Sleeping on one's side. [UKH]
yoogara·a, *n.* Same as **yashigaruu.**
yoogari, *n.* Same as **yashigaruu.**
yoogari-hiigari, *adv.* Being excessively thin. **-soon,** *adj. emph. colloq.* Thin and emaciated.
yoogari·in, *vi.* To become lean; grow gaunt (slim); lose weight; pine away (with anxiety).
yoogari-mun, *n.* A slim person; a skinny person.
yooi, *n.* [yooi] Ease; facility; simplicity; readiness. **·na,** *adj.* Easy; facile; simple; ready.
yoo·in, *vi.* [yowaru] To weaken; grow weak; be enfeebled; languish; be run down.
yoo-ji, *n.* [yooji] A toothpick.

yoo-joo, *n.* [yoojoo] Remedy; medical treatment.
yooka-bii, *n.* 1 The four-day rite of driving out demons, held starting the eighth day of the eighth lunar month. 2 One of the village rites of fortune divining. See **shibasashi**. [ODJ, OBJ]
yoo-mi, *n.* [yowami] A weak point; a vulnerable point; a sore spot.
yoon, *adv.* Lightly; gently; weakly.
yoon-gwaa, *adv.* Very lightly; very weakly; slightly.
yoon-naa, *adv.* Same as **yonnaa**.
yoo-ruu, *adv.* Loose; slack; lax; sagging.
yoo·san, *adj.* Weak; feeble; frail; infirm. See also **yafarasan**.
yooshi[1], *n.* [yooshi] An adopted child; a foster child; a son-in-law. See **chikaneengwa**.
yooshi[2], *n.* [yoosu] 1 The state (aspect, phase, situation) of affairs; things; circumstances. 2 Appearance; looks; an air; a mien; behavior. 3 A sign; an indication; a symptom.
yoosoo·chun, *vt.* To give up and leave things in the status quo; abandon (something) as is; overlook; let go unchallenged.
yootee, *n.* [yootai] The condition (of a patient); the state of health.
yoo-usuma·s(h)an, *adj.* Weird; uncanny; eerie; ominous; unearthly.
yooyaku, *adv.* [yooyaku] Finally; at last; barely; with difficulty; with effort; gradually; by degrees.
yos-saa, *adv.* Even if.
yu-ban, *n.* [yoban] The number four.
yubi-kee·sun, *vt.* To call back. See also **yubimudusun**.
yubi-mudu·sun, *vt.* [yobimodosu] To recall; call back.
yubi-'nja·sun, *vt.* [yobidasu] To call (out); convene; summon; call (someone) to the telephone; invoke.
yubi-suraa·sun, *vt.* To call together; convene; muster; summon.

yubi-yushi·in, *vt.* [yobiyoseru] To call together; summon; send for.
yu·bun, *vt.* [yobu] 1 To call; call out (to); invoke. 2 To send for; send after; summon; call in. 3 To invite; attract.
yuchaa·in, *vi.* [yukiau*] To fit; suit; be suited (to); agree (with); be agreeable (to); congenial.
yuchi, *n.* [yuki] Hail; a hailstone.
yuchi-daki, *n.* [yotsudake] Okinawan castanets, made of bamboo.
yuchifa, *n.* Surplus; superfluity; margin; room; time (to spare); allowance (for).
yu-chii, *n.* [yokei] Abundance; surplus; excess. ·**na**, *adj.* Excessive.
yuchiku, *n.* Abundance; wealth.
yuchiku·na-mun, *n.* A wealthy person; a man of wealth. See also **kuushiimun**, **hinsuumun**.
yuchimi, *n.* Leeway; margin; allowance; room; elbow room; ample room.
yuchira, *n.* Value [used in negative constructions].
yuchi·san, *adj.* Having latitude (literally or figuratively); having a margin.
yu-chiyu, *n.* [yotsuyu] The evening (night) dew.
yuda, *n.* [eda] A branch; a bough; a limb; a twig; a sprig. Also **yida**.
yuda-chi, *n.* A collateral (family) line; a descendant; offspring.
yuda-fa, *n.* 1 Branches and leaves. 2 A side issue; a digression.
yudai, *n.* [yodare, yodari*] Slaver; slobber; saliva; drivel; drool.
yuda-mu·chi, *n.* The branching of a tree; ramification.
yudan, *n.* [yudan] Negligence; remissness; inattention; carelessness; unpreparedness.
yudi·in, *vt.* [yuderu] To boil.
yudi-kuuga, *n.* Same as **yuditamagu**.
yudi-tamagu, *n.* [yudetamago] A boiled egg. Also **yudikuuga**.
yudumi·in, *vt.* [yodomasu] To make

water stagnate; make water stop. See also **tumain, tudumain**.

yudu·mun, *vi*. [yodomu] To stagnate; be stagnant; settle; stop; stay.

yufudu, *adv*. [yohodo] Very; much; highly; considerably; a good deal; far; by far; quite; fairly.

yu-gafuu, *n*. A year of abundance; a fruitful year. See **yuu²**, **kafuumuchi**.

yugami, *n*. [yugami] Contortion; bend; crookedness; distortion; skewed condition.

yugami·in, *vt*. To distort; bend; curve; warp.

yuga·mun, *vi*. [yugamu] To warp; swerve; deflect; be crooked; be misshapen; slant.

yu-gawa·i, *n*. Same as **yuugawai**.

yuguri, *n*. [yogore] Dirt; filth; soil; a spot; a stain; a smudge; a blot.

yuguri-haikara·a, *n*. A person who sports a fashionable style but is not quite immaculate; a person who is not impeccable in spite of high fashion.

yuguri·in, *vi*. [yogoreru] To become dirty; become filthy; be soiled; be smudged.

yuguri-kwenkwen, *adv*. **-soon**, *adj*. *emph*. *colloq*. Indifferent to one's own dirtiness and filthiness. [GSS]

yugu·sun, *vt*. [yogosu] To stain; soil; blemish; defile; debauch; slur; taint; pollute.

yui¹, *n*. [yuri] A lily [*Lilium longiflorum* Thunb.]. [FOSR]

yui², *n*. [yue] A reason; the reason why; a cause; on account of; by reason of; because (of); as; since.

yui³, *n*. [yoi] Early evening; the early hours of the night.

yui⁴, *n*. [yoi] A sieve; a sifter; a chaff-separating basket.

yui-maaru, *n*. Same as **yiimaaruu**.

yui-mun, *n*. [yorimono] Something that has drifted ashore; flotsam; driftage. See also **gireekanee**. [BHEO]

yu·in, *vi*. [yoru; drift] **1** To approach; draw near. **2** To meet together; assemble; congregate; swarm. **3** To drop in; look in; call; stop at, drop by; drift ashore.

yui-uta, *n*. Songs sung while engaged in communal cooperative labor.

yuji·in, *vt*. [yuzuru] **1** To turn over; transfer; part with. **2** To give way; give up. **3** To sell; dispose of. **4** To concede (to someone); be inferior to (someone).

yujiri, *n*. [yuzuri] An inheritance; a legacy.

yuka, *n*. [yuka] A floor; a mattress-covered floor.

yukai, *n*. Fairly; passably; considerably.

yukai-, *pref*. To a considerable extent.

yuka-muchi, *n*. The floor joists.

yukaru-hii, *n*. A lucky day; an auspicious day.

yuka-sa, *n*. Under the floor.

yukasa-mii, *n*. Space under the floor.

yuka-tchu, *n*. A member of the gentry class in the premodern days. Also **samuree**, **bushi**.

yuka·toon, *adj*. Rich (harvest); abundant (harvest). Also **dikitoon**, **yukatuun**. [GSS]

yuka·tuun, *adj*. Same as **yukatoon**.

yu-keen, *n*. Four times.

yuk-ka, *n*. [yokka] Four days; the fourth day.

yukka·nu-fii, *n*. Lit., fourth day; the fourth day of the fifth lunar month, regarded as the unluckiest day of the year.

yukkwa·sun, *vt*. To let the sun set, for instance, before one's work is completed or one reaches a destination.

yuku¹, *n*. [yoku] **1** Avarice; covetousness; greed; cupidity. **2** A desire; a thirst; a hunger; a passion; a wish.

yuku², *n*. [yoko] The side; the flank; width; the breadth; the beam; crossways; broadwise; horizontal; lateral.

yuku³, *adv*. More; further; greater; still

yuku'ana

more; all the more for.
yuku-ana, *n.* [yokoana] A cave; a tunnel.
yuku-bai, *n.* [yokobai] **1** Going sideways; sidling. **2** Diversion; deviation.
yukuba·in, *vi.* [yokobaru] To be greedy.
yukubai-sun, *v.* To stray from the proper path.
yuku-dui, *n.* [yokodori] Usurpation; assumption; seizure; snatching unrightfully. **-sun**, *v.* To snatch; usurp; intercept.
yuku-dushi, *n.* [yokudoshi] The following year; the year after; the next year. Also **naayaan**.
yuku-gau, *n.* [yokogao] The side (half) face; a profile; a silhouette; a sketch.
yukui¹, *n.* [yukue] One's whereabouts; one's traces.
yukui², *n.* A rest; a break.
yukui-dukuru, *n.* A rest house; a room for resting; an anteroom; a lounge.
yukui-maaruu, *n.* A turn to rest.
yuku·in, *vi.* **1** To rest; take a rest (from); repose (oneself). **2** To stop (from work); take a breath; suspend; lay off. **3** To go to bed; retire; turn in; sleep.
yuku-mi, *n.* [yokome] Looking aside; looking away; looking at something else.
yuku-michi, *n.* [yokomichi] **1** A byroad; a bypass; a byway; a pass; a side street; a crossroad. **2** A wrong way; a side issue; digression.
yuku-munu-i·i-sun, *v.* To not speak straight; sidestep the issue.
yukun, *adv.* Furthermore; further; more.
yuku-nami, *n.* [yokonami] A side wave; cross sea.
yukushi, *n.* A lie; a falsehood; a fib; a fabrication; a fake; falsity.
yukushi-munu-i·i, *n.* Telling a lie.
yukushi-munu-ii-sa·a, *n.* A liar; a fibber.
yuku·u, *n.* A grasping person; a miser; a rapacious man. Also **yuukuu**. See **yuku**¹.

yuku-yuku, *adv.* [yokuyoku] Exceedingly; excessively; very; very carefully; closely.
yu-mangwi, *n.* [yuumagure] Evening; dusk.
yumi¹, *n.* [yumi] A bow; archery.
yumi², *n.* [yome] A daughter-in-law.
yumi³, *n.*, *suff.* [yumi] Indicates the density of the warp and the fineness of a textile; seven **yumi** is the coarsest weave. See also **fuduchi**.
yumi-agi·in, *vt.* To read aloud; read off; call out (the names).
yumi-ibira·a, *n.* A parent-in-law or an in-law who abuses a bride.
yumi-kee·in, *vt.* [yomikaeru] **1** To employ another reading (pronunciation) for a Chinese character. **2** To employ one word in place of another.
yu-miji, *n.* [yumizu] Hot and cold water.
yumi-kaki·in, *vt.* To begin to read.
yumi-mun, *n.* [yomimono] Reading matter; literature.
yumi-tu·in, *vt.* [yomitoru] To read (another's mind); understand (a hidden meaning).
yumi-tuu·sun, *vt.* [yomitoosu] To read through (a book) to the end.
yumi-uwa·in, *vt.* [yomiowaru] To finish reading.
yumi-ya, *n.* [yumiya] Bow and arrow; arms.
yumu-, *pref. pej.* [yomo-*] Denotes bad, evil, or hateful to form a pejorative term. See **yumujira**, **yumuwinagu**, **yumuguchi**, **yumuwarabi**.
yumu-guchi, *n.* An evil mouth.
yumu-jira, *n. pej.* An evil face.
yu·mun, *vt.* [yomu] **1** To read; peruse; chant; recite; teach; talk. **2** To guess; divine; read (a person's mind). **3** To compose (a poem).
yumu-warabi, *n. pej.* A naughty child; a terrible kid. See **yumu-**.
yumu-winagu, *n. pej.* A hateful woman;

a bitch. See **yumu-**.
yun-, *pref. pej.* Denotes air of dislike or hatred when attached to adjectives. See **yumu-, yunhagoosan**.
'yu·n, *vt. irreg.* **1** To say; remark; observe. **2** To tell; relate; mention. **3** To talk; speak. **4** To state; pronounce. **5** To express. **6** To call; name. Also **iin**[1].
yuna-, *pref.* [yona] Denotes rice or sand.
yuna-baaki, *n.* A basket for storing rice.
yuna-gata, *adv.* Throughout the night; all night.
yuna-ji, *n.* [< yona + su] Liquid for bleaching ramie and abaca-cloth. See also **shiikwaasaa**.
yu-naka, *n.* [yonaka] In the dead of night; in the night; at midnight.
yunaka-mun, *n.* A late night snack (meal).
yu-nan, *n.* [yonan] The fourth son.
yu-nanka, *n.* A Buddhist memorial service held on the twenty-eighth day after a death. See **nanka**.
yun-chiruma·a, *n.* See **yunchirumii**.
yun-chirumii, *n.* A person who is about the same age. Also **chirumii, yunchirumaa, yunichirumi**.
yun-gutu, *n.* A kind of oral tradition in the Yaeyama Islands.
yun-hagoo·san, *adj.* Very dirty; filthy; foul; unclean.
yuni, *n.* [yone] **1** Rice. **2** *n. poet.* Sand.
yuni-gaami, *n.* A pottery jar to store grains. [UKH]
yunisu, *n.* Grains for storage such as rice, wheat, beans, etc. [UKH]
yun-jichi, *n.* **1** Leap year. **2** Leap month. See also **uruudushi**. [GSS]
yu-nooshi, *n.* [? yonaoshi] A large wooden bowl for holy liquor offered to deities. Also **sara**[1]. [ODJ]
yunta, *n.* A form of ballad in the Yaeyama Islands. See also **yui'uta**.
yunta·a, *n.* **1** Chattering; rattle; chitchat. **2** A prattler; a tattler; a chatterbox.
yuntaka·a, *n.* A prattler; a chatterbox.

yun-taki, *n.* Same height. Also **yintaki, yintakaa**.
yuntaku, *n.* Talking too much; chattering; rattle; idle talk.
yuntaku-hantaku, *adv. emph. colloq.* Chattering; talking incessantly. See also **yuntaku**.
yuntaku-hintaku, *adv. emph. colloq.* Same as **yuntakuhantaku**.
yuntaku·u, *n.* A chatterbox; an idle talker.
yunu-, *pref.* Same; uniform; equal; identical.
yunu-chimu, *n.* The same mind.
yunu-chira, *n.* **1** The same face; like face. **2** An accomplice; a gang; a pack.
yunu-chirumi, *n.* Those of about the same age. Also **chirumii**.
yunu-tchu, *n.* The same person.
yunu-gutu, *adv.* In the same way; similarly.
yunui, *n.* The first annual Buddhist memorial service. Also **yinui**. [UKH] See **ninchi**[1].
yunu-jibun, *n.* Same time.
yunu-mun, *n.* The same; the self-same; the identical thing.
yu·nu-naka, *n.* [yononaka] The world; society; the life; the public; the times; an age. See also **yuu**[2].
yu·nu-nushi, *n.* Lord of a castle; lord of a region; lord of a country.
yu·nu-sachi, *n.* [yonosaki] The future; the time to come.
yunu-tushi-nchu, *n.* People who are about the same age.
yuraa·sun, *vt.* **1** To assemble (people); gather (people) together. **2** To share one portion of food with several.
yurari·in, *vi.* To loiter (tarry) on the way; waste one's time.
yurariya·a, *n.* An idle fellow; a lazybones; a drone; a do-nothing.
yuratii, *n.* Eating from a common bowl.
yure·e-gami, *n.* For a number of people to eat from the same plate or bowl.

yuree·in, *vt*. [yoriaeru] To get (people) together; assemble (people); make (people) meet together.
yuri·in, *vi*. [yoriau] (For people) to gather together; (for people) to meet together.
yurii, *n*. 1 Holidays; a vacation. 2 Leave of absence; furlough. Also **yashimi**.
yuru, *n*. [yoru] Night; nighttime. Also **yuu**[1], **yuuru**.
-yuru, *suff*. A counter for nights.
yuru-hiru, *n*. [yoruhiru] Night and day; day and night; all the time.
yurui, *n*. [yoroi] Armor.
yuruji-na-mun, *n*. [yorozu + na + mono] Various snacks; eating between regular meals.
yurukubi, *n*. [yorokobi] 1 Congratulation. 2 Joy; delight; glee; pleasure; rapture; exultation; gratification.
yuruku·bun, *vi*. [yorokobu] 1 To congratulate; celebrate. 2 To be happy; be pleased; rejoice. See also **uss(h)an, ussa-sun**.
yurumi·in, *vt*. [yurumeru] To loosen; make (something) lax; relax; unfasten; mitigate.
yuru-mikkwa·a, *n*. Night blindness; nyctalopia.
yuru·san, *adj*. Loose; slack; lax; mild; lenient; generous; not strict enough; too indulgent.
yurushi, *n*. [yurushi] Leave; permission.
yurushi-ganee, *n*. Pasturage; grazing.
-sun, *v*. To graze (cattle); put (cattle) to grass. [GSS]
yuru·sun, *vt*. [yurusu] 1 To permit; approve. 2 To license; authorize. 3 To release; acquit; overlook. 4 To confide (in a person). 5 To forgive; pardon; excuse.
yurut·tu, *adv*. [yururito] Leisurely; with ease.
yuru-yunaka, *n*. At midnight; in the middle of the night.
yuru-yuru, *adv*. Leisurely; easily. Also **yuruttu**.

yusandi, *n*. Evening; evening time.
yusandi-akee·i, *n*. An evening glow; a sunset glow; sunset colors; an afterglow (of a sunset).
yusa-yusa, *n*. Complication; commotion; disturbance; unsettled state.
yushi-achimi·in, *vt*. [yose-atsumeru] To gather together; put together at one place; round up; scrape up; rally.
yushi-ashi, *n*. [yoshiashi] Good and evil; virtue and vice; right and wrong.
yushi-bin, *n*. A large pewter liquor bottle with a wide mouth, used on such occasions as weddings or other rituals.
yushi-chiki·in, *vt*. [yosetsukeru] To allow (a person) access; allow (a person) to come near.
yushi-doofu, *n*. Unshaped tofu made by stopping the process of coagulation midway. See also **toofu**.
yushi-gutu, *n*. [yosegoto*] A precept; one's teachings; an injunction; instruction; a lesson.
yushi·in, *vt*. [yoseru] 1 To let (allow to) approach; let (a person) come near; draw near. 2 To advise.
yushi·jun, *vt*. [yusugu] To rinse; wash out.
yu-shimi, *n*. [yosumi] The four corners (of a housing compound).
yushiri, *n*. A small temporary tomb used in the case of unusual, sudden death or the death of an infant. See also **sudigachi, shinkuchi, kariyadu, haka**.
yushiri·in, *vi. formal* To visit; make a call; pay a visit to.
yusu, *n*. [yoso] 1 Another place; strange places. 2 Another person; a stranger.
yusu-mi, *n*. [yosomi] 1 Looking away; looking aside; taking one's eyes off. 2 Another's eyes.
yuta, *n*. A shaman; a medium; a fortuneteller. See also **saadaka'nmari, kamidaari**[2].
yutaka, *n*. [yutaka] Abundance; wealth.

yuta-kooya·a, *n.* A consumer of the services of a **yuta**.
yuta-mancha·a, *n.* A pseudo-**yuta**; one who imitates a **yuta**.
yutami·chun, *vi.* To waver; flicker; sway; shake.
yuta-munu-i·i, *n.* Mystical speech like that of a shaman.
yuta·nu munu ka·mun neen shi, *phr.* Lit., like a shaman eating; eating very, very slowly. [GSS]
yuta·nu shiibai·nu gutoon, *phr.* Lit., like a shaman's urine; weak (of tea). [GSS]
yuta·s(h)an, *adj.* 1 Well; good; all right. 2 All right; may be used to either agree or decline. See also **shimun**[1].
yut-tai, *n.* [yottari] Four people.
yuttai-kwattai-sun, *v. emph. colloq.* 1 (Of water in a vessel) to sway and roll. 2 To waver; vacillate. [GSS]
yuu[1], *n.* [yo; yoru] Night. See also **yuru, yuuru.**
yuu[2], *n.* [yo] A generation; the world; society; life; existence. See also **yununaka, yu(u)gawai.**
yuu[3], *adv.* [yoku] Well; good; nicely; right; rightly; truly; thoroughly.
yuu[4], *n.* 1 Hot water. 2 A hot bath.
yuu-akee·i, *n.* Same as **yusandi'akeei.**
yuu-aki-duu·shi, *n.* Throughout the night; sitting up all night.
yuu-ban, *n.* [yuuban] Supper; evening meal; dinner.
yuuban-manja·a, *n.* Lit., the one eying the evening meal; Venus; the evening star; Vesper; Hesperus. Also **manjaabushi.**
yuubee, *n.* [?yobai] A concubine; a mistress.
yuubee-ngwa, *n.* A concubine's child; an illegitimate child.
yuubi, *n.* [yuube] Last night; last evening.
yuuchi[1], *n.* [yottsu] Four.
yuuchi[2], *n.* [yoki] An axe; a hatchet; a chopper; a hack. See also **wuunu.**

yuu-chi·chun, *vi.* [yoku kiku] To be efficacious; have an effect.
yuu-chiji, *n.* [yutsugi*] A soup server.
yuuchi-wai, *n.* Division into four parts.
yuudu, *n.* [yodo] Stagnation; stopping; staying.
yuu-duri, *n.* Evening lull; an evening calm. See **turi**[1], **asaduri.**
yuu-fiju·i, *n.* Evening chill.
yuu-fuku, *n.* [yuufuku] Affluence; opulence; prosperity.
yuu-furu, *n.* A bath; a bathtub.
yuufuru-yaa, *n.* A public bathhouse.
yuu-gawa·i, *n.* [yogawari] A revolution; vicissitudes; changes and upheavals in the world. Also **yugawai.** See also **Yamatuyuu, Uchinaayuu, Amerikayuu.**
yuugee·sun, *vt.* To get scalded by hot liquid (or steam).
yuu-gumui, *n.* [yogomori] A wake; an all-night vigil over a corpse before burial. Same as **yuutuji.**
yuu-i, *n.* [yooi] Preparation; readiness; provision; arrangement; precaution.
yuu·in, *vt.* [you] To dress the hair; do up (one's hair); bind; tie.
yuu-iri-gata, *n.* Evening; dusk.
yuu-iriyee, *n.* [yuu-iriai] Evening; dusk.
yuu-jin, *n.* A nightgown; nightclothes.
yuu-ju, *n.* [yooji] Things to do; affairs; an errand; engagement.
yuuka·a, *n.* Same as **yuukuu.** [GSS]
yuu-kaagi, *n.* Evening; evening twilight (hours). See also **asakaagi.**
yuuki, *n.* [yooki*] 1 Staying up late at night; keeping late hours; staying up late. 2 To keep vigil all night, usually by relatives at a childbirth or to nurse a patient.
yuu-kui, *n.* A rite practiced in the Miyako Islands to invite a rich harvest or wealth. [ODJ]
yuuku·u, *n.* [yoku] A greedy person; a miser. See **yukuu.**
yuu-maai, *n.* [yomawari] A night watch;

yuuna

a night watchman.
yuuna, *n.* Sea hibiscus [*Hibiscus tiliaceus* L.]. Also **yuunangii**.
yuu-naabi, *n.* [yonabe] Night work.
yuuna-gaasa, *n.* The leaf of a yuuna tree. [UKH]
yuu·nu-ku, *n.* Parched-barley flour.
yuure·e, *n.* [yoriai] A mutual finance association. See **muyee**.
yuuree-baka, *n.* See **muyeebaka**.
yuuree-shidu, *n.* Head of a mutual finance association; one who starts a mutual finance association.
yuu-rii, *n.* [yuurei] A ghost; an apparition; a spirit; a spook. See **mabui**.
yuurii-banashi, *n.* A ghost story.
yuuru, *n.* [yoru] Night; nighttime. Also **yuu**[1], **yuru**.
yuu-sannee, *adv.* Probably; perhaps; maybe.
yuu-shibai, *n.* Bed-wetting; nocturnal incontinence. See also **shiibai**.
yuu-shigutu, *n.* [yoshigoto] Night work.
yuu-shita, *phr.* I told you so! It serves you right!
yuu-shittai, *phr.* See, I told you! You deserve it. Same as **yuushita**.
-yuu-sun, *v. suff.* [...i; yoku suru] To be capable of (doing).
yuu-tu·i, *n.* A bailer. Also **akatui**.
yuu-tuji, *n.* [yotogi] **1** Spending the night with a person to keep him/her company. **2** Keeping someone company; helping a family through the night on such an occasion as childbirth, illness, or a funeral; a wake.
yuu-utee, *n.* Proclamation of political change; revolutionary call; prophecy of change.
yuuwaa, *n.* [yuoo] Sulfur.
yuuwe·e, *n.* [iwai] Celebration. See **uu-wee**.
yuu-yuu, *n. inf.* A chicken.
yuu-yuu·tu, *adv.* [yuuyuuto] Slowly; leisurely; gently; deliberately.

Z

zaa, *n.* [za] A seat. See **jaa**[2].
zai-kin, *n.* [zeikin] A tax; a duty; a charge; dues. Also **joonoo**. [UKH]
zan, *n.* A dugong. See **zannu'iyu**.
zan·nu-iyu, *n.* A dugong; a mermaid; a merman.
zara-mi, *n.* [zarame] Granulated sugar; crystal sugar.
zee-muku, *n.* [zaimoku] Same as **jeemuku**.
zee-san, *n.* [zaisan] Property; fortune; means.
zoo-wudui, *n.* Okinawan dances created for the commercial stage in the modern period (post-1879).

English-Okinawan Glossary-Index

Explanatory Notes

Purpose of the Glossary-Index

The Glossary-Index is a quick guide for finding Okinawan terms by referring to English key words. It is *not*, however, an English-Okinawan dictionary in any reasonable sense of the term. Where there is a close match between the key word and the Okinawan term, the Glossary-Index is indeed like a minimal English-Okinawan glossary, or simple word list. However, in many cases English keys point to Okinawan terms that are semantically related without being exactly equivalent, or that represent a specific item belonging to a category represented by the English key. In the latter cases, the Glossary-Index is clearly more of an index than any sort of dictionary at all.

Symbols and terminology

The ▸ symbol is used to identify Okinawan items that represent either non-exact or partial equivalents of the English key word. For example, the English key 'jealous' (an adjective) points to Okinawan ▸**uramasasun**, a verb meaning 'to be jealous' or 'to envy', and also to ▸**rinchaa**, a noun meaning 'a jealous person'. In the first case, the pointer can be taken as merely indicating the mismatch in parts of speech between the key word and the Okinawan "equivalent"; in the second, the arrow indicates a semantic connection between the key word and an Okinawan term that is somewhat more distant.

Where necessary (and only where necessary) indication of parts of speech is given to disambiguate key words. English 'light', for example, can be variously a verb, noun, or adjective. In the Glossary-Index, such usage distinctions are indicated by appending *n.* for nouns, *v.* for verbs, *adj.* for adjectives, and *adv.* for adverbs, using the same abbreviations as the main body of the *Wordbook*.

In cases where Okinawan items are members of a category named by the key word, the key word is capitalized. Examples of these keys include Clothing, Rites, Weights and Measures, and several others. For the most part, Okinawan items entered for these key words do not correspond well to English terms either because their explanations are encyclopedic in scope or the terms themselves are too highly specialized to have a ready equivalent. The category 'Rites' will yield, for example, **ubiinadii**, a word referring to the use of holy water in homage to well deities, as part of marriage confirmation rites, and in rejuvenation rites, as well as to the priestessly practice of retrieving holy water from sacred springs—none of which encyclopedic descriptions yield reasonable single-word equivalents. Similarly, Weights and Measures will yield, among other items, **shaku**^{1} (a unit of length, roughly 30 cm), **shaku**^{2} (a unit of capacity, roughly 20 ml), **-tu**^{2} (a unit of capacity, roughly 18 l), and **-wakashi** (a unit of volume specifically for liquor, roughly 2 l). Again, no convenient English equivalents correspond to these highly specific terms.

The complete list of category index cues and notes on their scope is below:

- Birds—names of birds that do not have common English equivalents: 'hawk', for example, has an entry, but 'gallinule' does not.
- Clothing—culture-specific items and practices that require without convenient English equivalents.
- Counters—suffixes for numbers used when counting specific types of items.

- Deities—names of gods and semi-divine entities, as well as non-deities of religious significance, such as Buddhist saints.
- Exclamations—both exclamations and interjections.
- Fish—fish that do not have common English names.
- Foods—names of specific dishes that have no ready English equivalent.
- Games—names of games that have no ready English equivalent.
- Months—names of the months in calendar order.
- Plants—domestic and non-domestic plants and trees without common English correspondents.
- Rites—religious and cultural rituals as well as the persons, paraphernalia, and specific practices associated with these when they do not have ready English equivalents. The Rites category has been divided into a number of subcategories as detailed here:
  - Rites (agricultural)—practices associated with planting and harvesting agricultural products.
  - Rites (ancestral)—in general, rites and practices centered on the *Bon* festival.
  - Rites (birth)—practices associated with childbirth and infants.
  - Rites (birthday)—general birthday celebrations as well as ceremonies marking particular anniversaries of birth.
  - Rites (funerary)—both funeral and memorial practices.
  - Rites (housing)—ceremonies associated with houses.
  - Rites (marriage)—ceremonies associated with weddings.
  - Rites (offerings)—items given as offerings to deities and/or ancestral spirits.
  - Rites (paraphernalia)—tools and other items used in various rituals.
  - Rites (seasonal)—rites associated with specific seasons and/or dates.
  - Rites (other)—items, persons, and practices not readily classifiable in any of the other categories.
- Seasons—names of times of year keyed to the lunar calendar.
- Shellfish—shellfish that lack ready English equivalents.
- Tools—names of tools specific to particular jobs, as opposed to generic items such as 'scoop' or 'lever'.
- Weights and Measures—units of capacity, length, and weight.
- Winds—names of various seasonal winds and weather conditions.
- Zodiac—the twelve animals of the Chinese zodiac in traditional order.

Limitations of the Glossary-Index

As noted above, the Glossary-Index is designed to serve as a finder for terms in the *Wordbook*, and not as an English-to-Okinawan dictionary. Its content, therefore, is idiosyncratic in that only English items leading to *Wordbook* entries are included. As the original manuscript on which the *Wordbook* is based was intended as a compendium of the distinctive Okinawan language and culture, it frequently lacks items that afford little intrinsic insight into Okinawa and the Okinawan language. Such items do of course exist for speakers of Okinawan, and some are indeed found in the *Wordbook*, but they are usually fairly recent, overt borrowings from Japanese or English. The reader hoping to find the Okinawan word for 'apple' or 'airplane', for example, will be unable to do so, since neither of these are uniquely or originally Okinawan, and both are represented in the language by transparent Japanese loans.

English-Okinawan Glossary-Index

A

abacus suruban
abandon yamiin
  miishitiin
  miichiin
  umuichiin
  utcharakasun
abate samiin[1]
abdomen shichawata
  'wiiwata
abide mamuin
ability hatarachi
  jinbun
able ▸kanain
  ▸nain[1]
abnormal hijai[1]
abolish yamiin
abortion ▸urusun
about kuru
  atai[2]
  manguru
  -nagii
  namaguru
above 'wii
  ▸ma'wii
abrasion shirikiji
abscess uubu
absconding 'njihangwi
absent kagiin
absentminded
  nurunturun-sun
absentmindedness
  turubaikaabai
  ufuturubai
abstain chichishimun
abstinence chichishimi
abundance juntaku
  yuchii
abundant dikitoon
  ufusan
  yukatoon

abuse iishitarasun
  ijimiin
  kunchikain
  mimijun
abused ▸ijimirariin
academic gakusha
accent kutuba
accented ▸hijaikutuba
accept ukiin[1]
accident bappee
  kutu[1]
  sainan
accidental umiinufuka
accompany hirain
  utumu-sun
accomplice guu[1]
  yunuchira
accomplishment
  tashinami
according to mama
accumulate chimuin
  tamain[1]
accuse wata saguin
accustomed ▸nariin
  ▸shiinariin
achievement dikashi
acidity shiisa
acknowledgment ukidui
  ukitui
acne nikun
acquaintance shiriyee
acquainted ▸chikajichun
acquit yurusun
acrimonious
  kuchigufasan
acrobatics hooka
  karuwaja[1]
act ukunee
actor shibaishii
actual funtoo
acupuncture haai[2]

▸chinbai
acupuncturist yabuu
Adam's apple
  nuudiiguufu
add 'waasun[2]
  shiiin[2]
addition shiibun
address 'waagachi
adept ashibijurasan
  ▸dikiin
adhere chichun[4]
adjoin chijichun
adjust noosun
admire fumiin
admission ▸nugibai
admit iriin
  mitumiin
adopt yashinain
adoptee yooshi[1]
adornment nushi[2]
adult ufutchu
adulterer guunaimun
adulteress guunaimun
adultery ▸guunain
advance n. meegai
  meekaniti
advance v. hakaduin
  iraasun
  shishimun
advancement risshin
advantage ichi[5]
  tuku[2]
adventure hantiwaja
adversity fijaimigui
advice soodan
advise yushiin
affair itchin[1]
affairs munu
  udaasun
affect kajain
affection 'waachi

affected

affected ▶unbuin
affection jooyee
　nasaki
　tchuchimuguris(h)a
affectionate kanas(h)an
　▶jooyeemuchi
affluence yuufuku
afraid uturus(h)an
　▶uturus(h)a-sun
aft matumu
after igu
after (then) urikara
afterbirth iya
afternoon hiruma
aftershock keeshi
afterward utti
afterwards atu
again mata¹
agar tinshiikan
age nindee
　tushi¹
　yununaka
ago mee²
agree aain
　sanshii-sun
　yuchaain
agreement chimujurii
　gattin
　musubii
　sanshii
agriculture harushigutu
　harushikuchi
　mujukui
　taashigutu
　▶chukuimujukui
ahead sachi¹
aid muchinashi
aim miyati
　ningakiin
air fuusun
　tin¹
albino shirutchu
alcohol saki
alcove tukunuma
　tuku³
alga muu
alienate hidatiin
alienation hidati
alight uriin¹
alike niin³
　▶nitakamanta
all mattachi
　muru

nnna
suu-
all day hitchii
all fours ▶ingwaabooi
all night yuu'akiduushi
　yunagata
　yutas(h)an
alley michigwaa
allotment wappu
allow ·sun
　mikumun
　yushichikiin
almost yagati
aloe rugwai
alone duuchui
　duunaakuru
already iina
　naa⁷
also ·n
　mata¹
　naa⁷
altar buchidan
　guriijin
　shichikigwii
　tudana
　ubuchidan
　▶riijin
alteration chukuikee
alternation chigaaruu
although -nagiina
altogether mattachi
always chaa²
　chini
　hijuu
　joohita
Amami Islands Amami
ambition ningaki
　yashin
ambitious chiibeesan
amen uutootu
America Amerika
American Amerikaa
　▶Urandaa
among uchi
amount ikirasa'ufusa
ample ▶mandoon
amulet fuufuda
　keeshi
amuse ▶ashibun
ancestor gwansu
　shinju
　uya'uji
　uyafaafuji

ancestry mutu
　uya'uji
　uyafaafuji
anchor ichai
and ·n
　·tu¹
anshee
and (… etc.) ·tuka²
anger iji
　rippuku
angry wajiin
animal chikushoo
　ichimushi
　inmayaa
　soominaa
animated ▶fichitachun
ankle hisakubi
anniversary ▶miinichi
annotation eejagachi
annoyance
　kakaimachibui
annoyed ▶wacharain
　▶tiiwacharee
annoying kashimas(h)an
annually ninnin¹
another place yusu
answer n. hintoo
　iree
answer (the door)
　tuichijun
answer v. ireein
ant ai¹
　aikoo
antidote dukugeeshi
antiques furudoogu
　furumun
antiquity nkashi
　ufunkashi
anus chibinumii
anxiety chimugakai
　chimusawaji
　munu'umii
　shinroo
　shiwa¹
　wacharee
anxious ▶mujumuju-sun
anyhow nanbun
anyone taa²
anything ▶nuunkwii
anyway maji
　maji
　nanbun
anywhere maagana

maamadin
apartment jashichi
apologize ayamain
apology iiwaki
  wassa
apparition ichijama
appear 'njiin
  arawariin
  miiin[1]
  ▸raas(h)an
appearance bajoo
  chirakaagi
  jintii
  kaagi
  kakkoo[2]
  miiba
  miimayu
  muyoo
  nai[1]
  shigata
  sugai
  yooshi[2]
appetite mununuyuku
  ▸iraa
apply atiin
appoint tuitatiin
appointment sachiguchi
  tuitati
  yakusuku
appreciate chimuin
  mitumiin
  wakain[1]
  minaree
  yatuingwa
apprenticeship
  ichuman'ui
approach chikajichun
  chikayuin
  yuin
approachable
  chikajichiyassan
appropriate soowuu
approve mitumiin
approximate manguru
approximately ·bikee
  atai[2]
  -guru
  kuru
April shingwachi
arbitrariness duugatti
  duukangee
archery yumi[1]
arena shimanaa[1]

argue abiitakkwasun
  aragaain
argument iigaai
argumentative ▸rikuchaa
arm tii[1]
  udi
arm wrestle udikakiin
arm wrestling udikakii
armor yurui
armpit wachi
around -guru
arrange narabiin
  shijimiin
  tuihakarain
  uchaasun
arrest hippain
  subichun
  tukkachimiin
arrival sachimaai
arrive chichun[3]
  tuduchun
arrogance taka'uchagai
arrogant ▸fuuchaa
  ▸gaain
arson chikibi
artery chiijiru
article shina[2]
  ▸soomun
as ·nu gutu
  gutoon
  mama
as is unumama
as soon as -shidee[2]
  -shindee
ascend nubuin
ascent nubui
  nubuibira
ash fee[1]
ashamed chira'afasan
  hajikas(h)an
ashtray feejara
ask chichun[1]
  tajiniin
  tuuin[2]
aspiration ningaki
assemble yuin
  yuraasun
  yureein
assert iitatiin
asserting ▸meenainai
assertion iihai
assessment michimui
assign atiin

assignation shinubi
assist kaashii-sun
assistance kaashii
  muchinashi
assistant hikee
  kaashii
  wachiyaku
associate fireein
associate (with) hirain
association gankoo
  hiree
  tuiyee
  ▸uchigumii
asthma fimichi
asthmatic fimichaa
astonishment
  ufudunmooi
astounded utcheein
astringent shibusan
astrology tinmun
astronomy tinmun
at ·nkai, kai
  ·uti
attach chikiin[1]
  hitchikiin
attack kakain
  shimiin[1]
attacked ▸usaariin
attacking shimiyee
attempt tii neein
attend 'njiin
  atchun
  chimiin
  nnjun
attendance tachiyee
attendant wakashu
attention nin
attentive ▸ichitain
attitude chigaki
  kamee
  shizama
attract fichiyushiin
audacity namajira
audience gusuuyoo
August hachigwachi
aunt wubamaa
  ufu'anmaa
  ufu'ayaa
  ufubaa
aunty baachii
auspiciousness higara
authority chikara
  hikari

autonym

autonym **soonaa**
autumn **achi**
avarice **gooyuku**
  riyuku
avaricious ▸**gooyukuu**
avenue **ufumichi**
average *n.* **namiti**
  narashi[2]
  tchunami
average *v.* **narasun**[1]
  tuunamiin
avoid **dukinain**
  hansun
avoidance **kushi**[4]
awake **miikufain**
  samasun[2]
awaken **ujumun**
awe-inspring **shiidakasan**
awful **dandannu**
awhile **ittuchi**
awkwardness **bukakkoo**
  hijaruu
awning **higataka**
axe **wuunu**
  yuuchi[2]
axis **guchi**[1]
  jiku

B

baby **akangwa**
  chiinumingwa
  ▸**booboo**
  ▸**ufuwikiga**
  ▸**ufuwinagu**
babysitter **kkwamuyaa**
bachelor **duuchuimun**
bachelorhood **chuigurashi**
back *n.* **kusaa**
  kushi[1]
  kushinagani
  nagani
  ▸**maafanachaa**
  ▸**njaichaisun**
back (of the hand) **tiinaa**
back *v.* **hikkumiin**
back and forth ▸**kayui**
back room **uraja**
back up **kaakii-sun**
backbite **nasagasun**
backing **kusati**
  ukaji
backslide **utcheein**

backyard **yaanukushi**
bad **wassan**
  yana-
  yanasan
  yumu-
bag **fukuru**
  kamajii
  kashigaa
  ▸**jiibu**
bagasse **shibuigara***adj.*
  wuujingara
baggy **dabudabuu**
  wabuwabu
bailer **akatui**
  yuutui
bait **mundani**
bake **yachun**
balance **hakai**
  hakainumii
bald **hadaka**
  hagiin
  ▸**hagichiburu**
bald-headed ▸**hagii**
baldness **hagaa**
  ▸**kanpachi**
bale **kamajii**
  taara
ball **maai**[1]
  tama[1]
ballad **fa'uta**
  ▸**ayagu**
ballad ▸**jiraba**
balloon **buukaa**
ballot **fuda**
  irifuda
bamboo **daki**
  chinbukudaki
  deemyoo
  karataki
  maataku
  njadaki
  oodaki
  ubidaki
  wata[1]
bamboo shoot
  dakinukkwa
ban **hattu**
banana **basanai**
  naiwuu
  wuu[1]
bandit **yamanusudu**
bang **ban**[2]
  don

banish **nagasun**
banishment **murabaree**
  tukurubaree
bank **jinkoo**
bank (river) **kaarabanta**
bankrupt ▸**tooriin**
banner **hata**[2]
  hatagashira
banyan **gajimaru**
bar **kamachi**
  kaniin
  kanichi
barb **kakijaa**
barbarian ▸**nanban**
barbershop **danpachiyaa**
bare ▸**akihatakiin**
barefoot **karahisa**
  ▸**karabisaa**
barely **yooyaku**
bargain **kakiyee**
  mitchiri
  yashi'ui
  yashigooi
barge **tinma**
bark *n.* **kaa**[1]
  kiinukaa
bark *v.* **abiin**
barley **hadakamuji**
  ufumujaa
  ufumuji
barmaid
  sakanayaawinagu
barracuda **kamasaa**
barrel **sakitaru**
  taru
barrier **hidati**
  hijami
  jama
base **susu**
bashful **chirahajikas(h)an**
basin **bindaree**
  hanjiri
basis **mutu**
basket **haara**
  tiiru
  hirabaaki
  iidiiru
  maagu
  'nbusaa
  oodaa
  sagijooki
  sanimuntiiru
  sooki[1]

yunabaaki
▸arabaaki
▸magu¹
▸'nmu'areebaaki
▸wuubaara
bastard yuubeengwa
bat kaabuyaa¹
bath yuu⁴
yuufuru
▸ubuyu
bathe amiin
amishiin
bathhouse yuufuruyaa
bathing miji'amii
battle ikusa
bay magai
ura¹
wan¹
be an¹
wun¹
yan
▸imenseen
▸menseen
▸menseebiin
be (not) ▸neen
beach haama
gata
kaniku
kanikujii
namikeeri
shinahama
shirahama
shuubata
tuu'asa
umibata
ura¹
beacon hiitatii
beam haai¹
kita
nuchi¹
nuchigi
bean maami
akamaami
injinmaami
toomaami
bean curd toofu
bean sprouts maaminaa
beanbag oosaaraa
beancake mamikashii
beanstalk maamigaraa
bear n. kuma¹
bear v. kkwanasun
muchun¹

nain²
nasun²
beard hiji
▸hijaa
beardless ▸hijimoo
bearer katamiyaa
beast chikushoo
ichimushi
beat kurusun
beaten ▸makiin
beating hangurushi
▸kitchaikuruchai
beau satu
beautiful churasan
irujurasan
ujiraas(h)an
beautify haneeka-sun
beauty churaa
churakaagi
churakaagii
irujurasa
iruka
because ·kutu
-nu gutu
tami
beckoning tiimanichi
become nain¹
bed jashichi
naashiru
bedding hana'uchi
jashichidoogu
uudu
bedridden ninjun
bed-wetting yuushibai
bee hachaa
beef ushinushishi
beehive hachaanushii
beet nnsunabaa
beetle karajikwee
taa'iifee
yamagan
▸kanibuubuu
before feeku
heeku
mee²
mutu
beforehand meekaniti
beggar kunchaa
munukuuyaa
begin achun
hajimain
hajimiin
kakain

shikakiin
beginning hajimai
hajimi
hakaguchi
-hana⁴
mutu
shikaki
begrudge ▸niitasa-sun
behavior ukunee
yooshi²
being ichimun¹
belief kangee
ninji
believe kangeein
ninjiin
umuin
bell kani³
bell striker kani'uchi
kani'uchaa
bellows fuuchi²
belly fugan
ufuwata
wata³
watabutu
belt china'uubi
kaa'uubi
uubi
bend (back) ▸koogu
magain
bend n. yugami
bend v. magain
magiin
wuuin¹
chinmagain
kagamain
mudiin
nabichun
tamain²
tamiin²
ushimagiin
yugamiin
benefit ichi⁵
rituku
suutuku
tami
benevolence
tchuchimuguris(h)a
bent ▸magai
berth chinba
besides 'wii
·bikeen ya aran
best ichiban
▸masakai

bestow

bestow **kwiin**
bet **kaakii**
betray **uin**
　utcheein
betrayal **yashingutu**
betrothal **sakimui**
better ▸**mashi**[1]
　▸**nooin**[3]
between **eeda**
　'weeda
　uchi
　▸**hasamariin**
beverage **numimun**
bewildered **jaamatiima**
bewitch **mayaasun**
beyond ▸**hatiin**
biased ▸**hijamun**
bid **fuda**
　irifuda
big **magisan**
　dateen
　▸**kuppi**
　▸**magii**
Big Dipper **nanachibushi**
　niibugwaabushi
bill **haree**[2]
　kusuidee
bin **kumiwuuki**
　shiiwuuki
bind **kukuin**
　kunjun
　musubun
bird **tui**
　▸**tuigwaa**
　▸**uguishi**
bird-lime **muchi**[3]
　yanmuchi
Birds
　chinchinaa
　chotchongwaa
　chuutinshi
　kanjuyaa
　kumiraa
birth **'nmari**
　mibun
　nashihanjoo
　sakangwa
　▸**nansan**
birth year **'nmaridushi**
birthday **'nmaribii**
birthmark **sumi**
birthplace **'nmari**
　'nmarijima

bit **chukaki**
bite *n.* **chukuchi**
bite (off) **kwiichiin**
bite *v.* **kanchiin**
　kuuin[1]
bite at **kankuuin**
biting **kankuuyee**
bitten ▸**utariin**
bitter **njasan**
　njami
　▸**kaakaa**
　▸**niitasa-sun**
bitter herb **njana**
black **kurusan**
　kuruu
　▸**kurunboo**
　▸**makkuuruu**
Black Current **kurushuu**
black-and-white
　shiruukuruu
blacken **kurumun**
black market **yami**
blacksmith **kanjaa**
　kanjeeku
　▸**mee'uchi**
bladder **mijibukuruu**
　shiibaibukuru
blade **haa**[2]
　yaiba
blame *n.* **chui'uushi'uushi**
　tugami
blame *v.* **akku-sun**
　sushiin
　tugamiin
　uushiin
bland **afasan**
bleach **sarasun**
　yunaji
blemish **hiikushi**
blend **majiin**
　mankiin
blessed ▸**kafuumuchi**
blessing **fuku**[2]
blight **tachigari**
blind **miikuu**
　shidai
　shirai[2]
blinding **miihicharasun**
blindness **yurumikkwaa**
blindstitch **kukuin**
blink **mii'uchi**
bliss **fuku**[2]
blister **mijibukuruu**

tiimaami
bloat **mukumun**
block **kaniin**
blockhead **namujaa**
blood **chii**[6]
　▸**furuchi**
bloodletting **buubuu**[1]
　kankan[2]
　▸**sakuin**
bloody **chiidarakaa**
bloom **sachun**[1]
　sachichiin
　sachikanjun
blooming **irujurasan**
blossom **hana**[1]
blow **fuchichaasun**
　fuchun[1]
　fuchun[2]
　fuchun[2]
blow (away)
　fuchitubasun
blow (over) **fuchikeesun**
blowfly **oobee**
blowing ▸**puu**
blue **ee'iru**
　massaaraa
　miji'iru
　oosan
　ooruu
blue-black ▸**kunji**
blunderer **soosoobaabaa**
blunt ▸**kamajisaa**
　▸**namariin**
bluntness **bu'eesoo**
　kamajishi
blurry (vision) ▸**kaakanjaa**
blush **akaku nain**
　akamun
boar **wuu'waa**
　yamashishi
Boar **yii**[1]
board **icha**[1]
　ita
　itabu
　marucha
　nuin[2]
　▸**manacha**
boast *n.* **duu'agami**
boast *v.* **fuukasun**
boastful ▸**ibayaa**
boasting **ufuguchi**
　ufumunu'ii
boat **funi**[1]

sabani
fuka'akkisaa
haifuni
inoo'akkisaa
▸chuinuyaa
▸kwaagwaa
▸nakadana
boatman kaku²
bob (hairstyle) akagantaa
kantaa
body duu
duutee
hada
karata
takifudu
boil *n.* uubu
eegasa
niibutaa
boil *v.* fuchun³
fukasun¹
mugeein
niin¹
tajiin
wachun²
wakasun²
yudiin
▸fuchiyuu
▸niikugeerasun
boiled egg yuditamagu
boldly umichitchi
bolt shinbai
bondage ▸duu'ui
bone funi²
guui
kuchi³
bones duubuni
bonito kachuubushi
book kwan²
sumuchi
bookcase funbaku
bookstore sumuchimachiya
bookworm sumuchikweemushi
border hiri
sakee
sakeemii
bore fugasun
bored ▸niriin
born ▸'nmariin
▸shidiin
born again ▸'nmarikaain
borrow irain

kain¹
borrowed ▸kaimun
borrower ▸maguraa
borrowing matagashi
bosom fuchukuru
botch chukuiyanji
chukuiyanjun
both soohoo
▸roohoo
bother yakkee
▸yakkeemun
bothersome ▸anmas(h)an
bottle bin²
sakibin
tukkui
yushibin
bottom chibi
shicha²
suku²
bounce (back) uchikeesun
bound kajiri
boundary murajakee
sakee
bounds dachi
bow (archery) yumi¹
bow *n.* gurii
bow (of boat) fii⁵
meedumu
▸chira
bow *v.* nabichun
bow and arrow yumiya
bowel movement chuuji²
bowels fii⁶
wata³
bowing uusari'aasari
bowing head utchintuu
bowl makai
wan³
aramakayaa
chawan
dunbui
futamakai
haachi
shiimunwan
shirumakai
ubunwan
wanbuu
▸sunkan
▸ushiruwan
▸yunooshi
box *n.* haku
chiibaku
kanabuchi

breath

tibaku
▸bintoojuu
▸juubaku
box *v.* hoochun
boy wikigangwa
boojaa
kkwa
wakawikiga
wikigawarabi
brace (oneself) chimutumeein
braggart ibayaa
shittakaa
tingu
bragging fuukashi
braid amun
kumun²
brains jii'anda
branch wakari
yuda
branching yudamuchi
brand yachi'in
brass chijaku
brave ▸ijaa
▸makuu
bravery ijiri
brawl ooin
brazier fibachi
breadth haba
hirusa
break *n.* yashimi
nakayashimi
nakayukui
break *v.* wain
wariin
chiin²
kudakiin
kuusun¹
wuuin¹
wuurariin
wuuriin
yanjun
break (down) tooriin
wakkwiin
yandiin
break (off) kakiin²
break (promise) tageein
breakfast shitimitimun
breast chii⁷
nniguchi
breasts chiibukkwa
breath iichi
▸ufu'iichi

breathe

breathe **fuchun**[2]
  suuin
breathing **niichi**
breed **chikanain**
  nasun[2]
  sudatiin
  wachun[2]
breeding **sudachi**
breeze **kaji**[1]
  shidakaji
  shirakaji
brew **tariin**[2]
brewery **sakaya**
bribe **shichadii**
  usagimun
brick **ringwa**
bride **miituji**
  miiyumi
  ▸**ainama'ishi**
bridegroom **muuku**
  miimuuku
  ▸**kwiimuuku**
bride-price **duushiru**
bridge **hashi**
  'nma[1]
brief **inchasan**
briefly **chutuui**
bright **aka'akatu**
  ▸**chiradamashi**
  ▸**fichain**
brine **suu**[3]
bring **mutchi chuun**
  chiriin[3]
  'njasun
bring (along) **sooin**
bring down **ushikeerasun**
  toosun
bring (together) **ichaasun**
bring up **ii'njasun**
bristle **kwachikwachii-sun**
broad **hirusan**
broadsides **funabara**
brocade **nishichi**
broker **bakuyoo**
  ▸**ushibakuyoo**
brood **usuin**
broom **hoochi**
  dakiboochi
  suutiichibaaboochi
  waraboochi
  ▸**baranboochi**
broth **dashi**

  shiru
  ushiru[1]
brothel **jurinuyaa**
brothel-hopper
  jurigunboo
brother **afii**
  appii
  niinii
  shiijawikii
  ufu'afii
  ufuuyatchii
  umikii
  utujanda
  wikiga'uttu
  wikigachoodee
  wikii
  yatchii
  yatchiigwaa
  ▸**umi'uttu**
  ▸**umishiija**
brothers-in-law
  muukuchoodee
brow **fichee**
  gappai
brown **chaa'iru**
brows ▸**miimayu**
bruise **shirikiji**
  sumi
  uchichi
brush **fudi**
  haki
  saara
  yiifudi
brutal ▸**chikushoomun**
brute **chikushoo**
bubble **aa**[1]
  aabuku
  mugeein
bucket **taagu**
  wuuki
  ▸**shingweewuuki**
buckteeth **haa'uchagee**
  meebaa
buckwheat **suba**[1]
bud **chibumi**
  kukumui
  miduri
  mii'njiin
  miruri
  mukkuu[1]
Buddha ▸**futuki**
  ▸**kanibutuki**
  ▸**kiibutuki**

build **chukuin**
  kakiin[1]
  tatiin
  ▸**gireein**
building **fushin**[2]
built ▸**kakain**
bulb **tama**[1]
bulge **fukkwiin**
  fukurasun
bulky ▸**kasabain**
bull **ushi**[1]
  wuu'ushi
  ▸**oorasaa'ushi**
bullet **tama**[1]
bullfight **ushi'aashi**
  ushi'oorasee
  kasshin
bullied ▸**ijimirariin**
bullring **ushinaa**
bully **ijimiin**
  mimijun
bump **gaanaa**[1]
bumper year **mirukuyuu**
bumpkin **inakaa**
bundle *n.* **chichin**
  chiiga[1]
  chika
  kana[1]
  tabai
bundle *v.* **tabain**
bungle **chukuiyanji**
  chukuiyanjun
buoy **uki**
burden **'nbushi**
  nii[2]
  niiyakkee
  yakkeemun
burdock **gunboo**
burglar **nusudu**
burn **kugariin**
  meein
  yachun
  yakiin
burn (down) **yachinagiin**
burner **kooru**
burst **hatchiriin**
bury **ujumiin**
  umiin
bush **gumagii**
business **achinee**
  guyuu
  ▸**gumamun'achinee**
  ▸**muyuu**

bustle haneechi
busy hanta²
ichunas(h)an
►hiiraa mooi
but yashiga
butcher 'waasaa
 ushi'waasaa
butchery 'waasaayaa
butt tabakunufeekusu
butterfly haabeeruu
buttocks chibi
 ►chibitai
buy kooin
 tuin
 ►aganeein
buyer kooyaa
buying and selling utaikootai
buzzing bunbun
by ·nkai, kai
 hata¹
by far jooi
by ourselves wattaakuru
byroad wachimichi
byway yukumichi

C ———

cabbage tamanaa
cabinet tanshi
cabinetmaker sashimunjeeku
cage michikumiin
cake kwaashi
 chinpin
 kashitiraa
 ►kujimuchi
 ►'nmukuji'andagii
 ►'nmukujiputturuu
 ►ucha'uki
calculate kajuuin
 nnjun
calculation kanjoo
 sanmin
calendar kuyumi
 shin⁵
calf kunda
call yubun
 yuin
 kakain
 nkeein
 ►menseen
call (back) yubikeesun

yubimudusun
call (out) yubi'njasun
 yumi'agiin
calligrapher jiikachi
callous ►chikushoomun
callousness funinjoo
calm adj. nadayassan
calm n. suuyudun
 turi¹
 yuuduri
calm v. nadamiin
 ►turiin
calm down wusamain
calmly nadayashiku
calmness utichichi
camellia iju
cancel chaasun
 iimudusun
candid ►aarankaa
candies amigwaa²
candle roo
candlestick rootatii
candy ami³
 hachagumi
 koorijaataa
 kuuri
 ►jurinukuuga
cane guusan
canned goods kanjumi
cantankerous
 ►kunjoomun
canteen dachibin
cap futa
capable -yuu-sun
cape hana²
 sachi²
capital miyaku
 mutu
 mutushin
capsize kachikeerasun
captain shinduu
 shinduusuu
capture tuin
car kuruma
card fuda
care chimugakai
 muchinashi
 nin
 nin'iri
 tiinii
 tikaji
career michi¹
careful ►kuguniin

castanets

►kukuriin
►tankiin
carefully tukutu
careless ichitaran
carelessly ukattu
carelessness futuduchi
 sukuchi
 susoo
 yudan
caretaker saji¹
 yaanubaan
cargo chimini
 niiguruma
 niimuchi
carouse kashiin²
carp kuu'iyu
 taa'iyu
carpenter deeku
 seeku
 kiijeeku
 taabajeeku
 ·yaajeeku
carpet shichimun
carriage chakubasa
 kuruma
carried ►uufasariin
carried away ►ukasariin
carrot akachideekuni
 chideekuni
carry muchun¹
 katamiin²
 muchikumun
 mutariin
 nushiin
 uufasun
 ►uushiin
carry (a child) ►kasagiin²
carry over kayaasun
carry-on muchinii
cart basa
 kuruma
 niiguruma
 ►nnaguruma
cartilage gusumichi
carving fuimun
case haku
 itchin¹
 cash jin²
casket haku
 tibaku
cast n. ikata
cast v. channagiin
castanets yuchidaki

casting

casting **imun**
castle **gushiku**
cat **mayaa**
  yamamayaa
  ▸**ankoomayaa**
  ▸**maa'uuu**
  ▸**mikiimayaa**
catalog **mukuruku**
cataract **sukuhi**
  ukufi
catch **kachimiin**
  kakain
  tuin
  ukiin[1]
catch (cold) **uchiin**[1]
catch (fire) **chikain**[2]
catch up **'wiichichun**
caterpillar **kiimushi**
cattle **aka'ushi**
  chikaneemun
  ushi[1]
cattleman **ushichikanayaa**
caught **hamain**
cauldron **saataanaabi**
cause *n*. **iwari**
  mutu
  nii[1]
  yui[2]
cause *v*. ·**sun**
  atiin
caution *n*. **imashimi**
  nin
  nin'iri
caution *v*. **imashimiin**
cave **gama**
  yuku'ana
cavity **kubun**
cedar **shiji**[3]
ceiling **tinjoo**
celebration **iiwee**
  suuji[2]
  uuwee
  yuuwee
  ▸**mee'iwai**
  ▸**meesuuji**
celibacy **chuigurashi**
cemetery **hakaji**
censer **shiichi**
  ukooru
center **mannaka**
  naaka[1]
  nakaba
  nakajin

centipede **mukajaa**
  nkaji
ceramics **yachimun**
ceremony **iyawaree**
  shichi[4]
certainly **danju**
  jifi
  tashika
certificate **suumun**
chafe **shirihajun**
chaff **mumigara**
  'nnagee
chain **kusai**[1]
chair **iisu**
  kushikaki
  yiisu
challenge **shikakiin**
chamberpot **mijikubusaa**
chance **chiidi**
  basu
  hyooshi
  hyooshinamun
  tama[2]
  tuchi
  ujumi
  ▸**man'ichi**
change *n*. **aratami**
  keei[2]
change (of mind)
  kukurugawai
change *v*. **kawain**
  keein[2]
  aratamain
  chiigeein
  nasun[1]
  'njuchun
  noosun
  ▸**kaagigawai**
  ▸**uchikawain**
channel **nju**
chaotic ▸**midariin**
  ▸**njariin**
chapel **tira**
chapping **fibari**
character **jintii**
  muji[1]
  'nmarijichi
  shiishichi
  shimuchi[2]
  shina[3]
  tchu
  ▸**ijijuu**
charcoal **shimi**[3]

▸**uchiri**
charge *n*. **chimidima**
  ukimuchi
  ▸**tai**[2]
charge *v*. ▸**uushiin**
charity ▸**intuku**
charm **fuda**
charming
  chimuganas(h)an
  nzoosan
charms **iruka**
chase **uuin**
  'waagiin
  'wiichichun
  'wiimaasun
chasm **warimi**
chat *n*. **shikinbanashi**
chat *v*. **hanasun**[1]
chatter **furiyuntaku**
  munuyumun
chatterbox **yuntaa**
  yuntakaa
  yuntakuu
chattering **yuntaa**
  yuntaku
  yuntakuhantaku
cheap **yassan**
cheat *n*. **nujun**[1]
cheat *v*. **babakwasun**
  damasun
check **fichaasun**
  fichi'ati
checkerboard **guban**
checkered ▸**guban'aya**
checkers **guu**[2]
cheek **fiijira**
  fuu[1]
  fuujira
cheeks **fuutai**
cheer **haneeka-sun**
cheerful **chibigassan**
  ▸**haneechun**
cheerfully **ihii'ahaa**
  ussa'ussaa
cheering **gaa'ee**
cheerful ▸**chibigaruu**
cherish **ataras(h)a-sun**
  muchun[1]
cherry **sakura**
chest **kee**[3]
  nni[4]
chew **kanaasun**
chic **haikaraa**

cloth

chick piyopiyoo
chicken tui
  haatuyaa
  yuuyuu
chief kashira
  munchuugashira
  teesoo
child kkwa
  chikaneengwa
  eeku[2]
  takarangwa
  umingwa
  'wiingwa
  ▸atubara
  ▸chuingwa
  ▸hadakamuuchii
  ▸kanashingwa
  ▸mishikuuga
  ▸nashichiraa
  ▸nashimunnukkwa
  ▸nashingwa
  ▸uttungwa
  ▸utushidani
child(ren) warabaa
  warabi[1]
childbirth kkwanashi
  nashihanjoo
  san[4]
  ▸kkwanashiyaa
  ▸nashimee
children warabinchaa
chill hijui
chilly hijutteen
  oofijutteen
  shiibiisan
  ▸oofijuruu
chimney hiitatii
china narimundoogu
China Too[4]
Chinese Toonchuu
  ▸kuninda
Chinese (language) Tooguchi
Chinese character jii[2]
  kanji[1]
chip in nuchaasun
chirp fukiin[1]
chisel numi[1]
choke chiichiikaakaa-sun
choose hichinujun
  irabun
  tuin
chop kijamun

ushichiin
chopsticks umeeshi
  chufaashi
  haashi
  meeshi[1]
  'nmeeshi
chores uchigutu
  yaashigutu
chrysanthemum chiku
church tira
cicada asasaa
  giijaa
  jiijaa
  naabikachaa
  sansanaa
circle maru
  maruu
  matteen
  ▸manmaru
  ▸manmaruu
circular marusan
circulation migui
circumference maai[2]
  migui
circumstance wachiyee
circumstances chigoo
  jijoo
  mibun
citrus kunibu
city machi[1]
  machikata
  miyaku
civility eesoo[1]
civilized ▸hirakiin[2]
claim *n.* iibun
claim *v.* hichituin
clam kee[1]
  afakee
  shirunna[2]
clan munchuu
  eekaharooji
  ichimun[2]
clan name uji[2]
clarify shimun[2]
clasp nijiin[2]
class kumi[3]
classes iihicha
clattering gatagata
claw *n.* chimi
claw *v.* kachamun
clay nncha[2]
  ▸akanncha
clean *adj.* churasan

clean (rice) shiragiin
clean up katajikiin
cleaner shintakuyaa
cleaning hoochikachi
  sooji[1]
cleanliness chirii
cleanse churaku nasun
clear *adj.* churasan
clear (away) katajikiin
clear (up) fui'again
  hariin
clear *v.* shinchiriin
  ▸uchagain
clear(ly) sayaka
clearly churaaku
clever ujiraas(h)an
cleverness takuma
cliff fuchi
  fuchibanta
  hanta[1]
climb *n.* nubuibira
climb *v.* again
  nubuin
climbing kiinubui
cling kakaishigain
  shigain
  takkwain
  tuishigain
clinic isanyaa
clip kain[2]
clock tuchii
clod nnchabuku
clogged ▸chimain
clogs ashija
  gita
  tachibaa'ashija
close chichasan
  kuuin[3]
  michiin[1]
close-clipping marubooji
closet kwii[3]
  shichikigwii
  tudana
clot katamain
cloth nunu
  chiri[2]
  mumin
  nuchi'aya
  sawai[1]
  uimun[2]
  wuimun
  ▸basaa
  ▸bingata

clothe
 ▸joofu
 ▸kashi'aya
 ▸kashichi
 ▸katachiki
 ▸kujirigooshi
 ▸sarashi
 ▸shirununu
 ▸uchukwii
 ▸yiichiri
clothe kushiin
clothes chin[3]
 aashi
 chinchirukaa
 ishoo
 yoofuku
 ▸asajin
 ▸chiigeyaa
 ▸chiikaki
 ▸furuji
 ▸furujin
 ▸harukaichiyaa
 ▸keejin
 ▸kurungeei
 ▸miijin
 ▸nachimun
 ▸shigutujin
 ▸ubujin
 ▸ufu'waaji
 ▸ushinchii
 ▸wata'irii
 ▸watajin
 ▸yaayaa
clotheshorse iikaa
Clothing
 dujin
 mee'uubi
 sudichiraa
 tunjifeejii
 uchakki
 uchikaki
 utchakii
 issoochiyaa
cloud kumu
 amigumu
 amigurun
 irichigumu
 ▸uugurun
cloudiness kumui[1]
cloudy ▸kumuin
 ▸kumuyaa'waachichi
cloves chooji
club boo
 bunjiri

clue tigakai
clumsiness hijaruu
clumsy hijaruugisan
clutch nijiin[2]
coach basa
coarse ▸gasaa
coat 'waaji
 fiitaa
 haui
coax shikasun
coaxing shikashiimaashii
coccyx chibigussui
cock tui
 chaan
 niji
 tauchii
 wuudui
Cock tui
cockroach hiiraa
co-conspirators haratiichi
coconut yaashigwaa
coerce chikasun
coffin kwanbaku
 kwancheebaku
coherence chibikuchi
coin akajinaa
 gumajin
 jinnaa
 ▸miifugaajin
cold adj. hiisan
 hijurusan
 oofijutteen
cold (coryza) fuuchi[1]
 kaji[2]
cold n. hijui
 kan[2]
 ▸oofijuruu
 ▸uubukka
cold v. ▸hijuin
coldhearted ▸mujoo
 ▸hijuruu
coldheartedness hakujoo[1]
coldness hijuruu
 uubiisa
 ▸hijuruukookoo
collapse kundiin
 kuuriin
 utiin
collar kubi[1]
 wiiri
collateral tiitoo
colleague eeju
 guu[1]

shinka
collect nuchun[2]
 suraasun
 tabuin
collection nuchishin
collide chichi'atain
colon ufuwata
color iru
column haaya
comb n. kushi[5]
 sabachi
comb v. sabachun[1]
comb box sabachibaku
combination ucheekanee
combine uchain
come chuun
 ▸chaabiin
 ▸menseen
 ▸menseebiin
come (down) uriin[1]
come (off) handiin
come (out) miiin[2]
comet hoochibushi
comfort n. anraku
 nagusami
 raku
comfort v. nagusamiin
comfortable duuyassan
comfortably rakurakutu
comic performance
 manzai
coming ▸njaichai
command n. iichiki
 tujiki
command v. iichikiin
 tujikiin
commerce achinee
common nami[2]
 tada[1]
 tchunami
common sense kani[1]
commoner hyakusoo
 muchii
 shiminchu
commute kayuin
companion dushi
 chiri[5]
 eeju
 utumu
 ▸numidushi
companionship
 dushibiree
company guu[1]

244

hiree
tchunumee
tuiyee
compare kurabiin
tatuiin
comparison fichi'ati
compass jijaku
karahaai
compassion nasaki
compassionate
chimujurasan
compatibility eesoo²
compensate hachun²
hakasun
hakiin
wanchameein
compensation tashimee
compete aragaain
wankarawankara-sun
competitive ▶chiikanain
complacency chimu'amai
complain agaayoo-sun
guchi²-sun
yamundoosun
complainer gujuguju'iyaa
wabiyaa
complaining miijaakoojaa
complaint googuchi
nachigutu
uttai
complete *adj.* akaa
matasan
complete *n.*
▶matashiimun
complete *v.* tujimiin
▶marumun²
completed tujimain
▶naa⁶
completely churaaku
maru-marumaruutu
mattachi
▶naichiin
completion ninchijiri
complexion iru
complicated
▶machibuikaabui-sun
complication yusayusa
compliment *n.*
fumikutuba
meeshi²
compliment *v.* fumiin
compose yumun

compost kajigwee
composure chimu'amai
chimumuchi
compromise wuuriin
compulsion ushi'ushi
concede yujiin
conceit duu'agami
concern chigakai
kangeegutu
concert chichigutu
conclude kukuin
musubun
seekiin²
conclusion chibi
feegattin
hati
kukui
rakuchaku
suukukui
concubine suba²
yuubee
condemn shimiin¹
condensed chijimain
condiments ▶eein¹
condition kagin
condition (of health)
yootee
conditions ▶uchu'u
confectionery kwaashiyaa
confections higwashi
confession hakujoo²
confide uchi'akiin
confidentially neenee¹
confine michikumiin
confined ▶kumirariin
confinement yaagumai
confirm tashikamiin
confront nkain
tachinkain
confuse dumangwasun
mangwasun
yamachirasun
yamanasun
confused yamachiin
yamachiriin
▶awatiin
▶dumangwiin
▶mangwiin
▶midariin
▶soonugiin
▶tiimaamaa-sun
confusion gwasagwasa
jaafee

tiiwoosawoo
yama-yamachirigutu
▶jaamakeeriin
congeal katamain
congratulate yurukubun
congratulation yurukubi
connect chinajun
connected ▶chirugain
connection yin²
connections fichi¹
conquer nabikasun
conscience shin³
yiijimu
consensus suukangee
consent fichi'ukiin
gattin
kukuriin
consequences atu
atusachi
consider kangeein
considerable yukai-
considerate ▶ichitain
consideration munnu'ati
munukangee
consistency chibikuchi
consolidated tujimain
conspicuous ▶uchitachun
conspiracy yanadakumi
constantly hijuu
hitchii
joohita
constipation shibiri
construct kachun³
kumun²
construction yaajukui
yaabushin
▶jiibuku
▶michibushin
consult ii'aasun
kakain
nnjun
soodan-sun
consultation chuugoo
munusoodan
▶uchisoodan
consume kamun
contact fichi¹
container irimun
contempt chui'usee'usee
contents mii³
nakami
contest ▶harusuubu

context

▸haruyamasuubu
context atusachi
continual chaa²
continuance chijichi
continue chijichun
continuously nagiduushi
contract *n.* musubii
  ukiwaja
  yakujoo
  yakusuku
contract *v.* chimain
contract (an illness)
  uchiin¹
contrary angwee
  ura²
  ▸chigain
  ▸handiin
contrast kurabiin
control *n.* kusai²
  tuishimari
  wusami
control *v.* kageein
  kusain¹
  maruchun
  tuishimain
convene yubi'njasun
  yubisuraasun
convenience binri
  chigoo
conversation munu'iikata
cook *n.* muntachaa
cook *v.* niin¹
  shikiin
  tachun²
cooking jooshichi
  ▸maasunii
cool *adj.* shidasan
  sujoosan
cool *v.* hijurasun
  samasun¹
  samiin¹
  shidamun
  sugasun
  sugariin
coolly hiyatteen
coop tuinuyaa
cooperate uchaasun
cooperation chimujurii
  chumichi
co-ownership kaataa
copper akugani
copulate chirubun
copulation chinubi

ukayee
copy *n.* hikee
  tifun
  uchushi
copy *v.* hikeein
  nishiin
  uchusun¹
copying mani
coquette
  wikigakachimiyaa
coral sangu
  umimaachi
cord chiru¹
  wiiruu
  wuu²
cord sash chinnuwuu
core nakaguu
  nakajin
  shin³
cork joo¹
corner kadu¹
  katashimi
  shimi²
  yushimi
  ▸miinukuchi
cornered ▸chimain
  ▸sashichimain
cornerstone ishiji
  nii'ishi
corpse shinin
correct *adj.* mattooba
correct *v.* aratamiin
  noosun
  tadasun
  ▸aain
corrected ▸nooin³
cost 'njirimee
  mutu
costly jin'irimi
costume ishoo
cottage gumayaa
  yaagwaa
cotton wata²
  mumin
couch iisu
cough sakkwii
count kajuuin
counterclockwise
  fijaimigui
counterfeit nishii
  nishimun
Counters
  -baaki

-chibu¹
-chibu²
-kaki
-kara
-kasabi
-keen
-majin
-nin²
-shiji
-taara
-tabai
-tai¹
-tukuru
-yuru
country kuni
▸hiiguni
countryside inaka
couple *n.* chii⁴
  guutumiitu
  miitu
  miitunda
  tujimiitu
couple *v.* chirubun
courage iji
  ijiri
  waa
courageous chimujuusan
course michi¹
  nariyuchi
court saiban
courteous 'nburaasan
courtesan juri
  miimuukujuri
  ▸chimijuri
  ▸juri'agai
courtesy eesoo¹
  jiri
  rii¹
  riiji²
courtyard niwa
cousin ichiku
  ichuku
  ▸ichukuwubamaa
  ▸ichukuwujasaa
  ▸mata'ichuku
cover *n.* futa
cover *v.* hirugain
  kakiin¹
  kakusun
  kanshiin
  kuusun²
  ushiin
  usuin

coveter tchunumunmanjaa
cow ushi¹
　▶moomoo¹
coward shikaa
　shikamun²
　shipitaimun
　yoobaa
　▶anmaa′uuyaa
　▶chimugumaa
cowardly chimuyoosan
　shikasan
cower sukumun
coy chirahajikas(h)an
crab gani¹
　aaman
　gasami
　kaagani
　kanraagani
　umigani
crack fibari
　tabasa
cracker shinbii
craftiness rikuchi
craftsman chinujeeku
　seeku
cramp n. garashimagai
cramp v. ▶kamirariin
crane chiruntui
crawl hooin
crayfish tanagaa
creak gishigishii-sun
crease magui
　wajami
create chukuin
creek ura¹
creel tiiru
creepy hachikoosan
cremate yachun
crematory kwasooba
crepe chijimi
crest kanji²
crevice aaki
　warimi
cricket kamajee
　urumaa
crime yanakutu
criminal tuganin
　wassan
crimson bin¹
　makkaaraa
critical
　kuchiyagamas(h)an

critical (of a patient)
　ukaas(h)an
criticism hyooban
criticize hyooban-sun
criticized ▶uchi′atai-sun
crochet amimun
crook tchudamasaa
crooked ▶chinmagain
　▶magain
　▶yugamun
crop n. naimun²
　▶fudiki
　▶meeninyii
　▶miimee²
crop v. kain²
crop failure fusaku
crops chukuimun
　harunu mujukui
cross ajiin
　kwiiin
　watain
crossbeam tinjoogita
cross-examine tuichimiin
crossing tuguchi
　watanji
cross-knot ajimaamusubi
cross-legged angweeyii
　wikigayii
crossroads kajimayaa
crotch mata²
crouch sukumun
crouching tuntachiyii
crow garasaa
crowbar kanigara
crowd n. burininju
　katamai
　shunin
crowd v. burinain
crowded gwasagwasa
　▶kumun⁴
crown kanmui
　minchaabui
crude jibita
cruel chirinasan
　▶mujoo
crumble kundiin
crumpled ▶maaguu
crush kudachun
cry magi′abiisun
　nachun²
　▶nachi′akasun
cry (of animals)
　nachigwii²

cut

nachun¹
crybaby nachibusaa
crying ▶′ngaa′ngaa
　▶nachigeegee
　▶shiputainachi
　▶weewee
cuckoo inindui
cucumber kii′ui
cuff susu
culprit tuganin
cultivate chukuin
　sudatiin
cultivation ▶meeninyii
cunning rikuchi
　yamagu
　yanarikuchi
　▶rikuchaa
cup chibu¹
　sakajichi
cupboard tudana
cupful ippai
curdle katamain
cure noosun
cured ▶nooin³
curiosity munujichi
curly-haired ▶chijuu
current nagari
　suubi
curse n. kami′arabi
　tatai
　utchakimun
　wajawee
　▶harunu arabi
curse v. ichijama-sun
curve magain
curved ▶magai
curving magayaahigayaa
cushion haaisashii
custom naraashi
　naree
　nari
　kushi²
　kafuu
　yaajina
customer chaku
　▶miiguchi
customs fuu⁵
　juku
cut n. kiji
cut v. chiin²
　chiriin¹
　kain²
　shirichiin

cute
▸ushichiin
cut (off) chiri'utusun
  fitchiin
  kanchiin
cute nzoosan
  ujiraas(h)an
cutlery shiigudoogu
cutting sashiki
cuttlefish icha²
  ika
  kubushimi
  ▸ichagwaa
cycle ▸maai²
cynical kujiin

D———
dad(dy) toochan
dais 'wiidan
damage *n*. kiga
  yandi
damage *v*. arasun
damaged ▸itamun
damned bachikanjaa
damp shiputain
  ▸ndiin
dance *n*. kutin
  mooi¹
  wudui
  zoowudui
  ▸kachaashii
  ▸kuichaa
  ▸oojimee
dance *v*. mooin
dancer mooyaa
dances ▸jii'utee
dancing costumes
  wuduisugai
dandruff irichi
dandy 'waachaa
dangerous abunasan
  ukaas(h)an
  ▸hantigutu
daredevil amashitamun
  hatii
  nuchishitaa
  shitimaku
daring ▸makuu
dark *adj*. kurusan
  ▸kurushibiriin
dark (complexion)
  jiiguruu
dark *n*. kurashin

dark blue oogurusan
darkness kuragai
  yami
darling chimuganas(h)an
date nindee
  yakusuku
  ▸hidui
daughter winagungwa
  winaguwarabi
  chakushiwinagu
  ▸chuiwinagungwa
  ▸gunanwinagu
  ▸ichukumiikkwa
daughter-in-law yumi²
dawn *n*. akachichi
  asa'akeei
  shira'akagai
  shira'aki
dawn *v*. akiin²
day fii⁴
  hiru¹
  hiruma
  ▸ikka
  ▸nannichi
day (next) ▸naacha
day (of rest)
  kushiyukkwii
day after tomorrow asatti
  naa'asatti
  naasati
day before yesterday
  wuttii
day off yashimi
daylight akarahiru
days hikaji
dazed miifaafaa
dazzling miihicharasan
dazzlingly chirachira
dead miigusoo
  ▸shinitchu
deadbeat tchufurubasaa
deadline kajiri
deaf ▸mimaa
  ▸mimikujiriin
  ▸minkujiraa
dealer ▸achinee'anmaa
  ▸maasu'uyaa
death mii'utii
  shigumaashi
  yanajini
  ▸feemaashi
  ▸ichinichi sookwan
  ▸miinichi

▸shinashinaa
debauchery hootoo
debt guwun
  ukka
  wun²
  wunji
decay kusariin
  shiruhain
decayed ▸sabooriin
deceased ▸maasooru tchu
deceive nujun¹
December shiwa'ashi
decide sadamiin
  umitachun
decided ▸sadamain
decision umichiri
  ▸ufusanikatajikiruu
decisively umichitchi
declare iitatiin
decline chijinain
  kutuwain
  sabiriin
decoct shijiin¹
  shinjiin²
decoction shinji
  shinjigusui
  shinjimun
decompose wakkwiin
decorate kajain
decoration kajai
  chukuikajai
  ukajai
decrease *n*. firi²
decrease *v*. hinain
  hinarasun
deed shizama
  suumun
deep fukasan
deer shika
defeat *n*. maki
  fujoomaki
defeat *v*. toosun
  ushimagiin
defeated ▸makiin
defecate main
defect hiikushi
  kushi³
defend fushijun
  mamuin
defense fushiji¹
  mamui
defiance gee
deficit fugi

device

deformed ▸katafichimun
deformity katafa
  katafichi
defy gee-sun
  nkain
degree kagin
Deities
  Akamataa-Kurumataa
  Amanchuu
  Bideetin
  Chinmamun
  fuduunukami
  funadama
  funinukami
  fuudugami
  fuurugami
  hinukan
  hijai[1]
  ibi[2]
  inugan
  jiinukami
  kaanukami
  kamifutuki
  Kwannun
  Makaa
  mijigami
  miruku
  niigan
  nireekanee
  niwoo
  Saakaganashi
  Shaakaganashi
  Shinirichuu
  tinnukami
  tuutiikun
  ubugami
  utintuu
  wunaigami
  yaheegami
  yashichigami
  ▸koojin
  ▸niwoobutuki
  ▸usadami
deity kami
  shiji[1]
  tin[1]
delayed ▸nagabichun
  ▸nubinubi
deliberate kangeein
  umutaikangeetai-sun
deliberately nin'irini
delicate muchikas(h)an
delicious maasan

▸ajikuutaa
delight isoos(h)a
delighted ▸ussakwaataa
delinquent hinjimun
delirious ▸ukasariin
deliver tudukiin
  watasun
  hichiwatasun
  kubain
delivered ▸karumun
delivery kkwanashi
  tiiwatashi
  tuduki
delusion mayui
  chimumayui
demand *n.* iriyuu
  seejuku
  ▸keetuibaakuu
demand *v.* imiin
demeanor munugushi[2]
demon uni[1]
  yanamun
demon possession
  ▸kakaimun
demote urusun
dense fukasan
  ▸maa
dent kubumun
  kubumiin
dentist haa'isa
depart tachun[1]
departing
  ▸naawakaiwakai
departure 'njitachi
  tabidachi
depend on kakain
  kushigaki-sun
  sagai'unbuin
  tayuin
dependable
  ▸matashiimun
dependence kamininji
  tayui
deposit guri
  meejin
  uchiba
depressed ▸kusakusaa-sun
  ▸umuiyamii-sun
depression fumigui
depth mijidaki
deputy deeri
deranged gerengeren

derided ▸useerariin
descend fuin[2]
descendant atu
  yudachi
descending amoori
descent uribira
describe uchusun[1]
design bingata
  chimuyee
  eegata
  gara[2]
  mukurumi
  muyoo
  ▸shima[2]
desire *n.* iruyuku
  kangee
  nigee
  ningaki
  yuku[1]
  ▸iraa
desire *v.* nigain
  nujumun
desirous fuus(h)an
desk suku[1]
desolate ▸sabooriin
despair appangaraa
  chirudai
despise karunjiin
  useein
  wuujun[2]
despised ▸useerariin
destination ikusachi
destiny un[1]
  ingwa
  unchi
  yakusuku
  yin[2]
  ▸akuyin
  ▸usadami
destroy furubasun
  kujusun
  kuusun[1]
destroyed ▸furubasariin
destruction ▸maruyakii
details isee
  kumeeki
detour tuumaai
devastate arasun
development hattachi
  nariyuchi
deviation yukubai
device kufuu
  shikaki

devil

shikumi
yaama
devil **akuma**
  uni[1]
  akagantaa
devote **hamain**
dew **chiyu**
  asachiyu
  yuchiyu
diagnosis **michiki**
dialect **kutuba**
dialogue **ichaihanchai**
diaper **kakkoo**[1]
diarrhea **kudashi**
  kusuhiri
diction **kutubajikee**
die **maasun**
  shinun
  furubun
  kariin[2]
  shigujini-sun
  shinashinaa-sun
differ **chigain**
difference **bichi**
  soo'i
different ▸**kawain**
difficult **muchikas(h)an**
  guris(h)an
  achikaiguris(h)an
  chikajichiguris(h)an
  duuguris(h)an
  fireeguris(h)an
  tachiguris(h)an
  ▸fireegurii
  ▸kamaras(h)an
  ▸kamaras(h)aa
  ▸njaraa
difficulty **jaafeegutu**
  mindoo
  wacharee
dig **fuin**[1]
  fugasun
dig (up) **kujiin**
digest **kanaasun**
  kunasun
dignified **chimudakasan**
  kwankwan
  'nburaasan
dignity **bun**[2]
  minbuku
digression **wachimichi**
  yudafa
  yukumichi

dike **amutu**
dilate **fukkwiin**
diligent **joobatarachi**
  ▸**chitumiin**
dilute **wain**
dim **usugurasan**
dimensions **tatiyuku**
dimple **fuukubu**
dinner **kwatchii**
  yuuban
dip **kumituin**
diplomatic ▸**kanamijooji**
direct **nkiin**[2]
direction **hoogaku**
  kata[1]
  muti[1]
  ▸maamutii
  kukurii
  'waagachi
dirt **aka**[2]
  duru
  hingu
  tii'aka
  yuguri
  ▸chimikusu
dirtiness **buchirii**
dirty **binasan**
  hagoosan
  hagoogisan
  yunhagoosan
  ▸binaa
  ▸hagoomun
  ▸hingaa
  ▸peepee
  ▸yuguriin
disabled ▸**katafaa**
disadvantage **sun**[2]
disagree **chigain**
disagreement **soo'i**
disappointed ▸**atihanriin**
disappointment **chirudai**
  jannin
disarray **yamaasanka**
disaster **nan**
  sainan
discharge ▸**miikusu**
  ▸miishiru
  ▸minjai
discipline *n.* **iinaraashi**
  munnaraashi
  naraashi
  shichiki[2]
  tuishimari

discipline *v.* **iinaraasun**
discomfort **fujiyuu**
discontent **jiigui**
discord **funaka**
  nakatagee
discount **yashimiin**[2]
  ▸makiin
discover **miichikiin**[2]
  wakain[1]
discreet ▸**chichishimun**
discretion **atisoo**
  chichishimi
  funbichi
  tamashi[1]
  tigukuru
  tiikagin
discrimination **bichi**
  hidati
  miwaki
discussion **chuugoo**
  ▸uchisoodan
disease **yanmee**
  ▸miiyami
  ▸muchiyee
disgrace **haji**[1]
  akahaji
  duru
  miiwaku
disgraced ▸**kachun**[2]
disguise **bakiin**
dish **namashi**
  sara[1]
  ▸mimigaasashimi
dish towel **hiichin**
dishcloth **hiichin**
disheartened ▸**shipitain**
dishonor **duru**
dislike *n.* **kushi**[4]
dislike *v.* **chirain**
  nikumun
dismissal **hima**
dismissed ▸**kubi**[1]**nain**
disobedient **uyafukoo**
disobey **sumuchun**
disorder **njari**
  gwasagwasa
  midari
  ▸midariin
  ▸njariin
dispatch ▸**kudasun**[2]
display **kajain**
  mishiin
dispose (of) **katajikiin**

dripping

tuihakarain
tibanasun
disposition 'nmarijishi
shimuchi²
soo¹
dispute *n.* iigaai
kuchigutu
mundoo
dispute *v.* mumun
disrespect busafuu
disrobe hajiin
dissent fugattin
dissolve tukiin
distance *n.* eema¹
distance *v.* hijamiin
distant ▸kaama
▸tuunuchun
distill tariin²
distinction bichi
hidati
hijami
miwaki
distinguish wakasun¹
wakiin
distort iimagiin
distribute hajun²
kubain
district majiri
distrust fushin¹
utagain
disturb kachaasun
kachimingwasun
sawajun
disturbance yusayusa
disturbed ▸njariin
ditch nju
dive shiimi-sun
diver shiimijooji
diverge wakain²
diversion ashibishigutu
divide hajun²
wachun¹
wakasun¹
wakiin
divination hanji
ichi⁶
diviner munushiri
division taachiwai
wakari
yuuchiwai
division (of work) tiwaki
divorce *n.* ribichi
divorce *v.* nuchun³

divorcée tachimudui
divulge abachun
dizziness miikuragan
nubushi
dizzy ▸furafuraa-sun
▸miimaasun
▸nubushiin
do sun¹
do over shiinoosun
doctor isa
document kachimun
kachichiki
waifu
dog in¹
yama'in¹
Dog in¹
dog-god inugan
dogmatism duukangee
doll futukii
futukigwaa
ninjoo¹
dolphin hiitu
done ▸achun
door hashiru
akai
jinkwan
yaaduguchi
▸nakabashiru
door bolt san²
doorkeeper munban
doorstep hashiruguchi
doorway hashiruguchi
jooguchi
dot tin²
dotage rooma
doting ▸kkwa'umii
double bee²
double-dealer
matabashigooyaku
doubt *n.* utagee¹
doubt *v.* fushin¹
utagain
doubtful muchikas(h)an
doughnut andaagii
dove hootu
down fukugii
downhill uribira
downpour uubui
doze *n.* yiiniibui
doze *v.* turumikasun
draft shichagachi
drag *n.* niiyakkee
drag *v.* fichiyushiin

subichun
dragon ruu
Dragon tachi²
dragonfly aakee
aakeejuu
taamaa
drain *n.* kajiramaai
drain *v.* nagasun
nagariin
drainpipe tii²
drama choogin
wudui
▸jii'utee
▸kumiwudui
▸mura'ashibi
▸taafaakuu
draw *n.* hiihiituu
draw *v.* kachun¹
kumituin
nujun²
yushiin
drawer fichijashi
drawing ▸mijikumi
drawing lots kujibichi
drawn ▸hikasariin
dream imi¹
saka'imi
soo'imi
dredge sareein
dress *n.* chin³
churasugai
kakkoo²
nai¹
nishichi
sugai
dress *v.* chiin¹
kushiin
dress (hair) yuuin
dress-up churasugai
drill iri
drink *n.* numimun
ippai
kutandinooshi
wutainooshi
▸amagashi
▸dariyami
▸karajaki
drink *v.* numun
▸nudaikwataisun
drinker sakijooguu
drinking sakigushi
drip tariin¹
dripping chonchon

dripstone

dripstone **amidai'ishi**
drive (away) **'waagiin**
  utusun
  uuin
drizzle **amigwaa**[1]
  guma'amigwaa
  ku'ami
droop **neein**[1]
  neeriin
drop **tain**
  tarasun
  tui'utusun
  urusun
  utiin
  utusun
drop (off) **urusun**
drop in **nubagain**
drought **hyaai**
  hyaaidushi
drown **'nbukkwiin**
drug **dukugusui**
druggist **kusuiyaa**
drum **chigaa**
  teeku
  ▶**paarankuu**
  ▶**uuchijin**
drumstick **bachi**[2]
drunk **saafuufuu**
  ▶**ushijaki**
  ▶**wiin**
  ▶**wiifuriin**
drunkard **wiitchu**
  sakikwee
  warigaami
drunkenness **wii**[1]
dry **abuin**
  fuusun
  hiin[3]
  kaarachun
  kaarakasun
  ▶**kaakiin**
drying **kagibushi**
  ▶**kaagibushi**
duck **ahiraa**
duckweed **muu**
dugong **zan**
  zannu'iyu
dugout canoe **kuibuni**
dull **darusan**
  dunnasan
  turusan
  ▶**namariin**
dullard **dunnamun**

dump **chirishiti**
dumplings **chinsukoo**
  daagu
dunce **jinbunkusaraa**
dung **kusu**
dupe **shikasun**
durability **nagamuchi**
dusk **iri'ee**
dust **chiri**[3]
  fukui
  gumi
  kuu[1]
dust (off) **harain**
duster **gumi'uchi**
dustpan **chiritui**
duty **jiri**
  chitumi
  funbun
  michi[1]
  muchimee
  sukubun
  yaku[2]
dwarf **gunatchugwaa**
dwelling ▶**muchichiriyaa**
dye ▶**feesun**
dye *n*. ▶**sumimun**
dye *v*. **sumiin**
dyeing **sumikata**
dyer **sumimunyaa**
dying **eejumii**
dying (out) **hiihiituu**
dysentery **shibuiwata**

E———

each **-kaji**
  naameemee
  nnna
each day **meenachi**
each other **utagee**[2]
eagle **washinutui**
ear **mimi**
ear (of grain) **fuu**[4]
ear cavity **miminumii**
eardrum **miminukkwa**
earlier **kissa**
  sachi[1]
earlobe **mimigaa**
early *adj*. **feesan**
  chichasan
early *adv*. **feeku**
  heeku
earn **kuchimuchun**

  mookiin
earnestly **hitani**
earnings **hatarachi**
  mooki
ears **mintanba**
earth **jii**[1]
earthquake **nee**[1]
earthworm **mimijaa**
earwax **mimikusu**
ease **raku**
  yooi
easily **duuyashitteen**
  karugaruutu
  yashitteen
  yashiyashitu
  yuruttu
  yuruyuru
east **agari**
  agarinkee
  higashi
easy **duuyassan**
  shiiyassan
  tachiyassan
  ▶**duuyashimun**
easygoing **chimunagasan**
  ▶**nonkaa**
eat **kamun**
  kwain
  tuin
  ▶**kijihooin**
  ▶**kweetoosun**
  ▶**nudaikwataisun**
eat (up) **uchikwain**
eaten ▶**kwaariin**
eating ▶**nusudungwee**
eave **kajira**
eaves **amidai**
ebb **hiin**[1]
ebb tide **hichisuu**
  hiisu
ebony **kuruchi**
eccentric **tanigaaimun**
  tchugawaimun
  ▶**kawaimun**
eccentricity **fuugawai**
  munujichi
echo *n*. **yamabiku**
echo *v*. **fibichun**
economical **yashi'agai**
economize **kumeekiin**
economy **aganee**
eczema **akabee**
  heegasa

edge hanta[1]
hiri
kadu[1]
kataha
educate naraasun
education gakumun
naraashi
▸munnaraashi
eel 'nnaji
taa'nnaji
effect *n.* shin[2]
effect *v.* ▸yuuchichun
effective ▸chichun[2]
effeminacy dajaku
efficacious ▸yuuchichun
effort ▸ganbain
egg kuuga
tamagu
tuinukuuga
▸mishikuuga
▸shimuru
eggplant naashibi
eggshell guru
ego gaa[1]
egoism chimama
duugatti
jimama
egotism duugatti
eight hachi
yaachi
eighteen juuhachi
either ·n
yatin
elapse shijiin[2]
elasticity nubi
elated ▸ameein
elbow hijigee
elder shiija
tusui
elderly utushikata
elders shiijakata
elegant fuuga
eleven juu'ichi
elopement 'njihangwi
elsewhere fuka[2]
embellish kajain
embers hiijiri
uchiri
yakijiri
embezzle fugasun
embrace dachun
mandachun
embroidery nuchimun

embryo tee[3]
emerge 'njiin
emergence shidii
emergency basu
ichideeji
kuuweekutu
man'ichi
emigrant chiruunin
emotional ▸fushigaran
emphasize kajikakiin
employ chikain[1]
tanumun[1]
uchun[1]
employee chikeemun
employment ninjiri
emptiness kara[2]
nna[1]
empty *n.* ▸kararii
▸naakaafuukaa
empty *v.* ▸achun
▸akiin[1]
▸uchiin[1]
empty-handed nnadii
encircle kakumun
enclose kakuin
kanageein
enclosure kakui
encourage chimugaashii-
sun
isamiin
encumbrance
tiihisamachibui
end *n.* uwai
chichi'atai
hanta[1]
hati
ichihati
juu[1]
ooban
rakuchaku
shii[7]
▸oogusu
end *v.* uwain
again
hatiin
shimun[1]
uchinasun
end of mourning imi'aki
endeavor chibain
ending naa[6]
endurance muchidee
nagamuchi
tee[1]

epidemic

endure kuneein
nijiin[1]
shinubun
shinujun
enemy ada[1]
katachi[1]
tichi[1]
energetic chibiraas(h)an
energy ichui
kunchi[2]
saamaki
English Eigo
▸Urandaguchi
engraving fuimun
enjoy tanushimun
enjoyable 'wiirikisan
umussan
enjoying ▸maakumaaku
enlarge hirugiin
enliven haneeka-sun
enough chufaara
juubun
taraain
too[1]
enraged ▸kusamichun
▸kwachikwachii-sun
▸wajiwajii-sun
enraptured ▸chichifuriin
ensure kajikakiin
enter iin[4]
heerinchun
entertain tideein
entertaining 'wiirikisan
entertainment muyuushi
tidee
enthusiasm nin'iri
enthusiastic ▸igumasun
▸nuriin
entirely maru-
muppara
maru
entrails wata[3]
watamiimun
entrance jinkwan
entreat tuishigain
entrust ajikiin
tanumun[1]
entry iriguchi
entwine machibuin
envelope ▸uuweebukuru
envy uramasasun
▸manjun
epidemic fuuchi[1]

epilepsy

epilepsy kukuchi[2]
epileptic kukuchaa
epitaph himun
epoch nindee
equal ▸kanain
equality hiihiituu
  tankaanaa
equinox (autumnal)
  akinuhigan
equinox (vernal) harunu
  higan
equipment sunawai
equipped ▸sunawain
era dee[3]
erase chaasun
erect chukuin
erection ▸'waasun[1]
errand uchikee
  yuuju
error ayamai
  chigeemi
escape *n.* ▸nuchigafuu
escape *v.* hingiin
  nugaain
  ▸nugaasun
essay mungun
establish tatiin
estate chikata
  jeesan
  yaayashichi
estimate chimuin
  michimui
  mikumun
  nnjun
estimation michiki
  miizooroo
  teegeejanmin
etiquette rii[1]
eulogize fumiin
eulogy fumikutuba
Europe ▸Uranda
European nanban
  Urandaa
European (language)
  Urandaguchi
evasion kushi[4]
even ·gan[2]
  ·n
  -nchoon
  yatin
even (if) -teeman
  yossaa
  tatui[2]

evening iri'ee
  yui[3]
yumangwi
yusandi
yuu'irigata
yuu'iriyee
yuukaagi
eventually chaashin
every mee[3]-
  muru
  arumunneenmun
every day meenachi
every other day
  hitchiigushii
every time kaaji
everybody nnna
everything nnna
  ▸nuunkwii
everywhere akkukata
  amankuman
  maankwin
  shirukuchimaakuchi
  ▸hashibashi
evil wassan
  yana-
evil intention kunjoo
exactly chintu
exaggerate fuukasun
  iishijiin
  iitatiin
exaggerated hagoorii
exaggeration fuukashi
  iishiji
examination chinbun
  kinsa
examine nnjun
  tadasun
example hinagata
  tamishi
  tatui[1]
  tifun
excavate fuin[1]
exceed amain[1]
  shijiin[2]
excel masain
  suguriin
excel (at) yiiin
excellence masai
excellent migutu
excerpt nujigachi
excess amaimun[1]
  mushooni
  ▸amain[1]

excessive ▸again
excessively duku[2]
  jikoo
excessiveness usakiinaa
exchange keeruu
Exclamations
  aatootu
  agaa
  agijabee
  ai[2]
  aiyeenaa
  aki
  akisamiyoo
  akkaa
  ari[2]
  ashi[2]
  chee
  daa
  daanaa
  dii[1]
  ee sai
  ee tai
  ee[1]
  hiya
  nda
  'nji
  une
  uri[2]
  uutootu
exclusively muppara
excrete main
excursion ashibi
excuse iiwaki
  kuchimaai
  waki
  wassa
excused ▸nugaain
exercise chiiku
  tinaree
exert (oneself) kunpain
exhaust chikusun
exhausted ▸yachiriin
exhibit mishiin
exhibition mishimun
exile *n.* shimabaree
  shimanagashi
exile *v.* nagasun
exist an[1]
  ichichun
exist (not) ▸neen
exit 'njiguchi
exorcism haree[1]
expand fichinubasun

fukkwiin
fukurasun
expect kangeein
 mikumun
expedience kai
expedient
 ▸ichutanuhanshi
expel 'wiihooin
expenses 'njifa
 jappi
expensive takasan
 ▸deedakaa
experience *n.* chinbun
 ninchi²
 shikarashi
 sujoo²
experience *v.* an¹
 atagain
 kanjiin
 shikarasun
 ubiin
experienced ▸nariin
expert achineejooji
 bushi
 chinchiijooji
 tassha
 ▸kakuribushi
 ▸katti²
explain (oneself) harumiin
explanation iiwaki
exploding ▸pan
exploit ▸uutigara
explore saguin
explosion ▸pachin
explosives kayaku
expose atiin
 hain²
 sarasun
exposed ▸atain²
 ▸marubai
extend fichinubasun
 neein²
 'njasun
 nubasun
 nushikiin
extended nubun
extent hirugai
exterior 'waabi
extinct ▸teein
extinguish chaasun
extinguished ▸chaain
extra 'waaba
extract eesun²

hichinujun
nujun²
extraction nujigachi
extravagance ▸kwabiiti
extravagant ▸kwabiin
extremely ippee
extremes ichishiji
eye mii¹
 katamii
 sagaimii
 ▸agaimii
 ▸miinuchibi
 ▸miikusu
 ▸miimayu
 ▸miishiru
 ▸miiyami
 ▸mintamaa
eye (of a needle)
 haainumii
eye bags ▸miikoogaa
eyeball mintama
 mintami
eyebrow mayu
 mayugi
eyedrops miigusui
 sashigusui
eyeglasses miiganchoo
eyelashes machigi
eyelid miinufuchi
 miigaa
 takaamii
 ▸chukaamii
 ▸niibuimii

F———
fable chukuibanashi
 tatui¹
 tatuibanashi
fabric nunu
 ▸eegata
 ▸minsaa
 ▸rinsu
 ▸shiruji
fabrication chukuibanashi
face *n.* chira
 chiragamachi
 chirakaagi
 minbuku
 umukaji
 ▸naachamiijira
 ▸nabigeejira
 ▸shinigau

face *v.* nkain
 nkiin²
face-to-face mamukoo
fact funnu
factory kooba
facts shimachi
fade (away) samiin³
fail naihansun
 shiiyanjun
 utiin
fail (to catch) ukihansun
fail (to do) hansun
 -yanjun
failure fudiki
 kitchaki
faint *n.* buchigee
 buchikun
faint *v.* miimaasun
 tooriin
 ▸furafuraa-sun
fainting miikuragan
fair *adj.* shirusan
fair *n.* machi¹
fairly yukai-
fairy bunagaya
 kijimun
 seema
fairy tale nkashibanashi
faith ninji
 kamininji
 ninrichi
 ▸ninjiin
faithfulness kadu²
fake *n.* chukuigutu
 nishii
 nishimun
fake *v.* najikiin
faking -najikii
falcon fensa
 sashiba
 taka
 ▸utiidaka
fall chiriin²
 dugeein
 fuin²
 keeriin
 kurubun
 meechintaa-sun
 nugiin
 tooriin
 ukkurubun
 utiin
 ▸mainugasun

falsetto

falsetto **chukuigwii**
fame **utu**
familiar ▸**miinariin**
　▸**nariin**
family **chineeninju**
　chuyaa
　eeka
　tujikkwa
　yaaninju
　▸**niidukuru**
　▸**uchiwa**^{2}
　▸**ufuchinee**
　▸**ufudunchi**
　▸**ufumuutu**
　▸**uuyaaninju**
　▸**yaawakayaa**
family (extended)
　ufuyaaninju
family register **kushichi**^{2}
famine **gashi**
famous **naayuru**
　▸**miishu**
　▸**utu'uchun**
fan *n.* **ooji**^{1}
　uchiwa^1
　▸**oojinufuni**
fan *v.* **oojun**
fang **chiiba**
far **tuusan**
　▸**agatoo**
　▸**ugatoo**
fare **funachin**
farewell **naguri**
　wakari
farm *n.* **haru**^{2}
　hataki
　▸**harushikuchi**
　▸**ufubaru**
farm *v.* **haru atchun**
farmer **chukuyaa**
　haru'atchaa
farming ▸**kaneegakai**
farsightedness **tusuimii**
fart *n.* **hii**^{1}
fart *v.* **hiin**^{2}
farter **fiifiraa**
fashion **feei**^{1}
　▸**feein**
fashionable **haikaraa**
fast *adj.* **feesan**
fast *adv.* **feeku**
fasten **chikiin**^{1}
　chinajun

　kunshimiin
　tumiin
fastidious ▸**kaneegufaa**
　▸**miimiikumagumaa**
fat **anda**
　▸**kweetaa**
fat (of meat) **shirumi**
fate **ingwa**
　tin^1
　tinmii
father **otoo**
　suu^2
　suutaa
　taarii
　wikiganu'uya
　▸**chaachaa**
father-in-law **wikigashitu**
fathom **hiru**^{3}
fatigue **kutandi**
　wutai
fatigued ▸**chikariin**
fatten **muteein**
fatty **andajuusan**
faucet **nijiri**
fault **hii**^{3}
　fusuku
　hiikushi
　kiji
　kushi^3
　machigee
　mii^1
　nan
　tuga
　uchidu
faultfinding **miimiikujii**
favor *n.* **guwun**
　hiichi
　tanumi
　wunji
favor *v.* **fichitatiin**
　▸**utabimisheen**
favored ▸**ayakaain**
favorite ▸**kanain**
　▸**mutiin**
favoritism **hiichi**
　katabiichi
fear *adj.* **uturus(h)a**
fear *v.* **shikamun**^{1}
　ujiin
　usuriin
fearsome ▸**uturuu**
feast **kwatchii**
feat **tigara**

feather **hani**
featherbrain **chakuchakuu**
feathers **kii**^{2}
features **chira**
　ninsoo
February **nigwachi**
feces **kusu**
　▸**'nna**^{2}
fee **dee**^{4}
　kanee
　kaneejin
feeble (mentally)
　uguchiyoosan
feed *n.* **mundani**
feed *v.* **kwaasun**
feel **kanjiin**
　ubiin
　umuin
feel (inclined) **nuriin**
feeling **chimu**
　joo^2
　kukurumuchi
　umii
feelings **ichijimu**
　kukuchi^1
　ninjoo^2
feet **gutee**
fell **toosun**
fellow **guu**^{1}
　wikiga
　yakara
female **winagu**
　miimun^2
　▸**mii**^{1}-
feminine **winaguraas(h)an**
fence *n.* **kachi**^{2}
　kakui
　chinibugachi
　dakigachi
　fiigachi
fence *v.* **kakuin**
feng-shui **funshii**
ferment **amikooin**
ferryboat **watashibuni**
fertile ▸**joobata**
fertilizer **kuugwee**
　kwee^2
fester **eein**^{2}
　'nmun
festival **iiwee**
　umachii
fever **nichi**
feverish ▸**nubushiin**

flat

few ikirasan
fiancé(e) iinajiki
fiber kaji[4]
  kurugaa
  shiji[2]
fickle achihatibeesan
  chimu'asasan
fickleness kukurugawai
fiction chukuigutu
fiddle kuuchoo
fidgetiness
  chimuwasamichi
fief shima[1]
field hachibaru
  hataki
  moo
  moonayaa
  sanya
  taahataki
  ▸joobata
  ▸uunuu
fieldwork harushigutu
fifteen juugu
fifth ichichimii
fifty-fifty gubugubu
fight *n.* ooyee
  ooyeetiiyee
fight *v.* ooin
  tachinkain
fighter ooyaa
figure kaji[5]
filaria kusa[1]
file yashii
filial piety uyakookoo
fill fukkwiin
  mitasun
  ujumiin
filled ▸michun
filling ▸mijikumi
filter shiinoo
filth hingu
  yuguri
filthy yunhagoosan
fin hani
  hira[1]
finally yattu
  yattukattu
  yooyaku
finances ▸muyee
find *n.* kameeimun
find *v.* kameein
  miichikiin[2]
  tumeein

fine *adj.* migutu
  uroosan
  ▸rippa
fine *n.* batchin
fine work joochibai
fineness yumi[3]
finger iibi
  iibinusachi
  iibingwaa
  naka'iibi
  narashi'iibi
  tchusashi'iibi
fingernail chimi
fingerprint tiinu'aya
finish hatiin
  shi'uwain
  shii'uwain
  shiitujumain
  shiitujumiin
  shimasun
  uwain
  ▸neen
fire hii[2]
  ijaibii
  kwaji
  ▸maruyakii
fire irons hiibaashi
firearm tippuu
fireball hiidama
firecracker hanabi
  hoochaku
fired ▸kubi[1]nain
firefighter fiichaasaa
firefighting shooboo
firefly hootanukui
  jiinaa
firewood tamun
  kiiramun
firewood seller
  tamun'uyaa
fireworks hanabi
firmly chuuku
  hashittu
  umichitu
first ara[1]-
  dee'ichi
  hachi-
  maji
  massachi
first (of the month)
  chiitachi
fish iyu
  ▸iyunumii

  ▸mii[6]
  ▸niku
Fish
  ayagachuu
  chiin[3]
  chin[2]
  gachun
  gurukun
  irabuchaa
  kachuu
  kamanta
  kamasaa
  kuu'iyu
  takamaa
  taman
  tontonmii[2]
  toobiraa
  tubuu
  Yamatumijun
  ▸inoo'iyu
  ▸miibai
fish cake kamabuku
fish eggs harami
fish eye iyunumii
fisherman iyukwaasaa
  iyutuyaa
  umi'atchaa
  uminchu
  ▸Ichumanaa
fishhook chiigani
  chiigwaa
fishing fuka'atchi
  tatachaa
  ▸agiyaa
  ▸ijai
fishing line naa[4]
  uminaa
fish market iyumachi
fishmonger iyu'uyaa
fist tijikun
fit aain
  yuchaain
fitting chika
  kanagu
five ichichi
fixed ▸nooin[3]
flag hata[2]
flame hii[2]
flames ▸baabaa
flash fichain
flashy ▸uchagain
flat hirasan
  ▸hirakiin[1]

flatness
   ▸hirapettaa
   ▸shippiraa
flatness too[3]
flat-nose hanabiraa
flatten hirakasun
   narasun[1]
   shippirakasun
   shippiriin
   toomiin
flatterer amaguchaa
   andaguchaa
   meesaa
flattery amaguchi
   meeshi[2]
   ▸juufui
flaw hiikushi
flawless ▸matamun
flax asa[1]
flea numi[2]
   innumi
flee hingiin
fleeing hingimaai
flesh niku
flicker yutamichun
flickering ▸miinuwuu
flinch chijimagain
flip hanchun
flippant gassan
flirt takkwain
   takkwaimukkwai-sun
flirtation meeshi[2]
float *n.* uki
float *v.* ukiin[3]
   nagasun
   uchun[3]
   uchagain
   ukabun
   ukabasun
   ukabiin
flood *n.* uumiji
flood *v.* andiin
flooded ▸chikain[3]
floodgate mijiguchi
floor yuka
   dakiyuka
flotsam yuimun
flour kwaashiguu
   maaminakuu
   mujinakuu
   yuunuku
flow *n.* migui
   nagari
flow *v.* nagariin
   wachun[2]
flower hana[1]
   ▸hanagi
   ▸miibana
   ▸noonoo
   ▸wuubana
flower arrangement
   ichibana
flower viewing hanami
flowerpot hanabachi
fluency pirinparan
flush nagasun
fluster awatiihaatii-sun
flutter dakumichun
   nabichun
   nabikasun
fly *n.* fee[2]
fly *v.* tubun
flyswatter heekurusaa
focus matu
   nakajin
fog chiri[1]
fold takubun
   tatamun
   wuuin[1]
foliage wakaba
folk song shonganee
follow chijichun
   uuin
food mun[2]
   kweemun
   aramun
   hanmee
   munu
   ▸karamun
   ▸manman
   ▸munugushi[1]
   ▸naajiki'ubagii
   ▸nuchigusui
Foods
   achirashikeesaa
   agimun
   andansu(u)
   anmuchi
   chii'irichi
   chiki'agii
   chippan
   gooyaachanpuruu
   habutan'irichaa
   ichagarasu
   inamuduchi
   irichii
   jiijikii
   jiimaamidoofu
   kaakasaa
   kaakasuu
   kaasa
   kachuugwaa
   karasu[1]
   katimun
   koogwaashi
   kunyaku
   kuubu'irichii
   kuubu'nbushii
   maamina'irichaa
   nakaminushiimun
   namamun
   nantuu
   oofa'nbushii
   poopoo
   rafutee
   sabimun
   seefan
   shiimun[1]
   shuunii
   soojiraa
   soomin'irichaa
   sooyuunushiru
   sukkwii
   sunshii
   suunee
   suunii
   tajirashikeesaa
   tunfan
   ufugee
   utchin
   watagarasu
fool *n.* furaa
   furimun
   jinbunkusaraa
   soonugaa
   turubaimun
   ufusoo
   usuu
   usuburimun
   ▸gakuburi
fool *v.* damasun
foolish bakaraas(h)an
   hijaruugisan
foot ashi[3]
   hisa
   katahisa
footprint hisakata
footsteps ashi'utu
footstool ashi'nma
   kii'nma

kudami
kurami
for ·kai, nkai
·nkai, kai
forbid chijiin
tumiin
forbidden muyuu
force *n.* ichui
force *v.* shimiin²
ushichikiin
forcibly shiiti
ford watain
forefathers nkashinchu
forehead fichee
mukoo
foreign country takuku
foremost massachi
forest yama
▸maachuu
foretell igumasun
wakain¹
forewarn igumasun
forfeit nagasun
forfeiture nagari
forge fuuchi²
forget washiin
forgetfulness
munuwashiri
forgetting maruwashii
forgive chimunubi-sun
kuneein
yurusun
fork ▸mata²
form katachi²
formal ▸aratamain
formal verb ending ·biin
former sachi¹
former wife furutuji
fort gushiku
forth ▸njaichai-sun
fortune eeki
fuku²
fuu²
jeesan
zeesan
▸kwafuu
fortune-teller chiitatiyaa
munushiri
sanjinsoo
fortune-telling chii²
uranee
forty shijuu
forward migurasun

foster child yooshi¹
foul wassan
foulmouthed
kuchihagoosan
found 'njiin
foundation ishiji
mutu
nii'ishi
fountain kaa²
four yuuchi¹
fourteen juushi
fowl tui
fraction 'waafa
fragile kuuriyassan
sakusan
fragment chukaki
hamun²
katawari
fragments kumakii
fragrance kabakaja
fragrant kabas(h)an
frail kuuriyassan
freckles feenukusu
free ichanda
tada¹
▸ichandamun
freedom jiyuu
freezing hijurusan
frenzy yana'wii
frequent kayuin
fresh ara¹-
miisan
fret fukkwiin
fretfully jiiguihaagui
friend dushi
chiri⁵
mikata
mutubiree
sakinumidushi
shinka
tayui
▸kubichiridushi
friendliness chimu'iri
wadan
friendly hireeyassan
kanaganaatu
kukuruyassan
friends ▸uchiwa²
friendship hiree
tuiyee
frightened
chimuhijurusan
▸chimuchigeerasun

funny

frightful ▸burigiidachi
fringe fusa
hiri
frivolous ▸afageeriin
▸afageerimun
frizzy ▸mafuyaa
frog atabichaa
wakubitchi
frolic shibeein
from kara¹
from (then) urikara
front mee²
umuti
▸nkain
front (door) meeguchi
frown wajamun
wajamiin
frugal ▸aganeein
▸kumeekiin
frugally sabisabiitu
fruit *n.* nai²
mii³
mukkuu¹
naimun²
niinai
shimunai
fruit *v.* nain²
fruit tree naimungii
fry again
agiin
tashiin
▸irichun
fuel ▸kandabuni
fulfilled ▸kanain
full ippai
wataponpon
▸kumun⁴
▸mii⁴
▸minbui
full moon ▸juuguya
full speed issan
full(y) ufu'ufuutu
fullness mitchakaan
watanmii
fund-raising nuchishin
funeral dabi
sooshichi
uukui
▸dabi'waa
▸dabidoogu
▸dabiyaa
funnel joogu
funny 'wiirikisan

fur

fur **kaa**[1]
furl **takubun**
furlough **yurii**
furnace **funjiruu**
furniture **doogu**
  shichiki[1]
furrow **uni**[2]
further **naahin**
furthermore **yukun**
fuse **hiinaa**
future **atu**
  atu'atu
  gusoo
  igu
  sachi[1]
  yunusachi
fuzz **fukugii**

G ———

gaff **kakijaa**
gain *n.* **ichi**[5]
  marumooki
gain *v.* **kwain**
gain weight **kweein**
gains **rituku**
galaxy **tingaara**
gambling **bakuchi**
game **ashibi**
Games
  ayatui
  buusaa
  chankuuruu
  chiburukami'ee
  chunjii
  giitaa
  giitaamundoo
  iibi'uusee
  iibikakiyee
  ishinaaguu
  ittugayoo
  kaarabuubuu
  kachiminsooree
  kiri'nma
  kwatchiigwaashii
  maai'uuchee
  maainagiyee
  miimiimii
  oosaaraa
  patchii
  tontonmii[1]
  Tooyaamaa
  wuuji'oorasee

gang **yunuchira**
gap **fugi**
  madu
  soo'i
  tabasa
garbage **chiri'akuta**
garbageman **chirituyaa**
garden **hana'atai**
  hataki
  niwa
gardenia **kajimayaa**
  kuchinashi
garlic **hiru**[2]
gasp **feefee-sun**
gate **iriguchi**
  joo[3]
  mun[1]
  turi[2]
  yaajoo
gatekeeper **munban**
gather **achimain**
  achimiin
  kanagiin
  suraasun
  suriin
  yuriin
  yushi'achimiin
gathering **muyuushi**
gaze **miichikiin**[1]
gecko **yaaduu**
gem **tama**[1]
gems **tamakugani**
genealogy **chiiji**[1]
general **namiti**
generally **chutuui**
  teegee
generation **dee**[3]
  ichidee
  yuu[2]
  ▸**uttukata**
generosity **ufujimu**
generous **yurusan**
  ▸**ufujimuu**
genius **dikiyaa**
  suguraa
gentle **'wendas(h)an**
  nadayassan
  ufuyassan
  utunas(h)an
gentleman **meewikiga**
  wikiga
gently **yonnaa**
gentry **chiimuchi**

  samuree
  yukatchu
genuine ▸**soomun**
geomancy **funshii**
  ▸**kaanufunshii**
gesture **tiiyoo**
  tiiyoohisayoo
  timani
get **mutchi chuun**
  ukituin
get (to) **tuduchun**
get along **fireein**
get off **uriin**[1]
get out (of) **uriin**[1]
get over **umichiin**
get up **ukiin**[2]
get well **nooin**[3]
ghost **yanamun**
  yuurii
ghost story **yuuriibanashi**
ghosts ▸**kanabui**
gift **chikituduki**
  chitu
  naagi
  naagimun
  riiji[2]
  shinbichi
  suuji[2]
  ukuimun
  usagimun
  ▸**usudee**
gills **aji**[3]
ginger **soogaa**
girder **haai**[1]
girl **winagungwa**
  kkwa
  miyarabi
  wakawinagu
  ▸**kantaa**
  ▸**kantuu**
girls ▸**jurinukuuga**
girth **migui**
give **kwiin**
  eesun[1]
  'njasun
  turasun
  usagiin
  watasun
  ▸**utabimisheen**
give (in marriage)
  katajikiin
give birth **karumun**
  nasun[2]

260

give up **yujiin**
glad **isoos(h)an**
gladness **isoos(h)a ussa**²
glance **attabajoo chumi iraamii subami**
glare **fichai**
glare at **miifichain**
glass **tamabai**
glasses ▸**miikagan**
glaze *n.* **kusui**
glaze *v.* **yakichikiin**
glazing **'waanui**
gleam **fichai**
glib **kuchibeesan kuchigassan** ▸**kuchifeejuraa**
glimpse **chumi**
glitter **fichain**
glitteringly **chirachira**
glory **myooga**
glossy ▸**haneechun**
glow **akanaa** ▸**jiinaabii**
glue *n.* **nikaa nui**
glue *v.* **chikiin**¹
glum **muchikas(h)an**
glutton **aigami gachi**
gluttony **baakigami**
gnaw **kakajiin**
go **ichun 'njuchun nkain** ▸**menseen** ▸**menseebiin**
go **guu**² ▸**guban**
go (along) **tuuin**¹
go (down) **utiin**
go out **'njiin fuka'atchi-sun**
goal **ati**
goat **hiijaa**¹ ▸**beebee**
goatee **shichahiji**
go-between **nakadachi**
goblin **majimun**¹ **waawuu**
god **kami**

mamun
goddess **kami**
godparent **naajiki'uya**
going ▸**njaichai**
gold **chin**¹ **kugani** ▸**tamakugani**
goldfish **aka'iyu**
goldsmith **chingushi kuganijeeku**
gong **duragani muragani uchigani**
gonorrhea **shiibaiyandi**
good **yutas(h)an yii-** ▸**dikiin** ▸**mashi**¹
good (person) **yiitchu**
good and evil **yushi'ashi**
good-natured ▸**futuki**
goodness **chimu'iri kukuru'iri tuku**¹ **wun**¹
goods **achireemun**
goodwill **chimu'iri**
goose **gaanaa**² **gaatui**
gooseflesh **fukugii irichaa kiiburidachaa kiifukugaa samaa**
gossip **hyooban-sun tchunu kuchi**
gourd **chiburu hyootan shibui**
gourmet ▸**uchuubi**
govern **kageein kusain**¹ **maruchun wusamiin**
governing **shiiji**
government **kuuji**² **kwan**¹ **ukakibusee wusami**
grab **tiijikaan**
grace **bun**² **shina**³ **tuku**¹

great-grandmother
graceful **chimudakasan 'nburaasan**
gracious **fuuga**
grade **dan kuree**
gradually **shideeni tatta yooyaku**
graduation ▸**mii**¹
grain **shina**¹ **toonachin yunisu**
grandchild **'nmaga** ▸**ichukumii'nmaga**
grandfather **tanmee usumee**
grandmother **'nnmee haamee hanshii paapaa**
grandparents **faafuji**
grandson **chakushi'nmaga**
grasp **kachimiin nijiin**²
grass **kusa**² **gushichi ookusa**
grasshopper *see* grassland ▸**kusanumii**
grate **gishigishii-sun**
grateful ▸**nifee**
grater **deekunishirii 'nmukujishirii**
grave *adj.* **'nburaasan**
grave *n.* **haka**
gravel **iifu ishiguruu ishiguu**
graveyard **hakaji**
gray **fee'iru**
grayhaired **shiragaa**
grazing **yurushiganee**
grease **anda**
great **dandannu**
great deal **jooi**
great man **tchugawaimun**
great-grandchild **mata'nmaga**
great-grandfather **ufuutanmee**
great-grandmother **ufu'nmee**

great-great-grandchild
 ficni'nmaga
greed yuku¹
 gooyuku
 riyuku
greedy gooyukuu
 yukubain
 ▸gachimayaa
 ▸kaahain
green *adj.* oosan
 ootteen
green *n.* ooruu
greengrocer yaasee'uyaa
greet nkeein
greeting eesachi
 gurii
 kanami
grievance iibun
 jiigui
grill *n.* abuikuu
grill *v.* yachun
grimace wajami
grind narasun²
grindstone aratushi
 kumatu
 tushi²
grip nijiin²
gristle gusumichi
groaning duunii
groin mata²
 natabashi
groom basahichaa
 'nmatai
groping tiisagui
ground jii¹
group katamai
 kumi³
grove taki¹
 ▸utaki
grow dikiin
 fuchaain
 fudu'waasun
 fudu'wiin
 miiin²
 muteein
 nkain
 shitatiin
 sudachun
 'waasun¹
 wachun²
 ▸arageein
grow (up) 'wiitachun
growth 'wiitachi

chuui
hattachi
sudachi
grudge urami
 ▸uramun
gruel kee²
 'waayuu
 achibii
 juushii
 kugashi
grumble googuchi-sun
 guchi²-sun
grumbler googuchaa
gujuguju'iyaa
 jiiguyaa
grumbling jiiguihaagui
 miijaakoojaa
guarantee fichi'ukiin
 fushoo
guarantor fushoonin
 ukinin
guard baan
guava banshiruu
guess *n.* aatinpuu
 miizooroo
guess *v.* akasun¹
 atiin
 ii'atiin
 yumun
guide annee
 miyati
 yanba
gulp ▸atakunurii
gum gumu
gums hashishi
gun tippuu
gunpowder kayaku
gunwale tana²
gush wachi'njiin
gusset hasa
gutter nju
 shiiri

H
habit kushi²
 kurun
 naraashi
 naree
 nari
habitual fiijii
hail(stone) yuchi
hair karaji

kii²
kantu
karajigii
 mooi²
 shiragi
 ▸'nbugi
 ▸abasaagii
 ▸irigan
 ▸kuugi
 ▸nnigii
 ▸shinigi
haircut danpachi
hairknot kanpuu
hairless ▸kiimoo
hairline aya
 kiimiiguchi
hairpin dakijiifaa
 jiifaa
hairstyle karaji
 ▸maayuui
 ▸meegantuu
 ▸Uchinaakanpuu
hairy ▸kiigataa
half hanbun
 gubu
 nakaba
 nakara
half- han-
half-dead hanbunjini
halfhearted katachimu
half-smile
 katakuchiwaree
halfway 'weeda
 hanmichi
 mannaka
hall ▸niibichijaa
hallway yiin
halo amagasa²
halve wain
halving hanbunwaakii
ham mumu²
hammer *n.* gennoo
 kanajichaa
hammer *v.* uchun²
hand tii¹
 haai²
 ninsuku
 ▸kootu
handcraft tinuja
hand-drum chijin
handhold tigakai
handle mimi
 niri¹

heavy

handmade tijukui
hand-me-down usandee
handmill hichi'uushi
hands gutee
handsome ▶rippa
handwriting tii¹
hang kakain
  kakiin¹
  hikkakiin
  kubiriin
  sagain²
  sagai'unbuin
  tain
  taisagain
  tarasun
hang on kwiisagain
hang onto kakaishigain
hanger narashi¹
hanging ▶kubiraa
hanging death kubirijini
happen ukuin²
  wun¹
happenstance attagutu
happiness karii
  kariyushi
  seewee
  shiyawashi
happy uss(h)an
  ▶sujoo²-sun
  ▶ussagisan
  ▶yurukubun
harass ijimiin
harassed ▶ijimirariin
harassment
  kakaimachibui
harbor nnatu
hard katasan
  kufasan
  duuguris(h)an
  ▶kufaa
hard (to remember)
  ubiiguris(h)an
hard living tachikantii
harden katamain
  kufain
  kufamiin
hardheaded kufachiburu
hardship kuchisa
  kuroo
  nanji
  nanjikunji
hardware kanamun
  ▶kanamunuyaa

Hare ▶uu¹
harelip shibee
harm duku¹
  gee
harmful wassan
harmonious ▶uchain
harmony suriijurii
  uchaishinai
  wagoo
harp kutuu
harpoon tuja
harrow maaga
harsh tii'arasan
harshness aku
harvest ▶fusaku
harvesting ▶'nnikai
haste isuji
hastily isuji
hasty ▶chakkuyaa
hat booshi
  hanagasa
  kabuimun
  kasa¹
  kubagasa
  munjuruu
hatch shidiin
hatchet tiin²
  yamanaji
  yuuchi²
hate chirain
  nikumun
  shikan
hateful mikkwasan
  yumu-
  ▶mikkwasamun
hatred urami
haughty ▶gaain
haul hichun¹
have muchun¹
hawk sashiba
  taka
  wuutaka
hay kaya
hazard hantiwaja
he unchu
  anchu
  ama
  ari¹
  'nma²
  uri¹
head chiburu
  fuu⁴
  kamachi

head cold hanahichi
  hanakaji
head (of cattle) -kara
headache chiburuyan
  katachiburuyami
  namachiburuyan
  ▶anmas(h)an
headband saaji²
headgear kanjimun
headland hana²
headman muragashira
headstrong gaajuusan
  ▶gwankuu
heal nooin³
  noosun
health ganjuu
healthy ganjuugisan
  hashittu
  ▶atchun
  ▶ganjuumun
  ▶kanain
  ▶uganjuu
heap chirishiti
hear chichun¹
hearing mimigani
hearse gan¹
  aka'nmaa
heart chimu
  chimu'uchi²
  fukumaami
  nakajin
  nni⁴
  wata'uchi²
  wata³
heartburn kukuraki
  ▶yakiin
hearth jiiru
heartless chirinasan
heat (for animals) kurii
heat *n.* fumichi
  nichi
  ▶aachuu
  ▶achisakamarasa
  ▶nachimaki
heat *v.* achirasun
  nukumiin
  nukutamiin
  tajirasun
  wakasun²
  ▶kuriin
heaven tin¹
heavy 'nbusan
  katasan

hedge

hedge kachi²
 fukujigachi
 gikijigachi
heel adu
height fudu
 taki²
 tati
 ▸kubidaki
heir atumi
 chakushi
hell jiguku
helmet kabutu
helmsman kajitui
help *n.* tashiki
 fichi¹
 kaashii
 muchinashi
 sukui
 tidashiki
 tiganee
 tii¹
help *v.* tashikiin
 kaashii-sun
 tashimeein
 ukusun
helper kaashii
 taruminchu
 tiganeesaa
helping chuishiijii
hem hiri
 susu
hemorrhoids jii³
 jiiyanmee
hemp asa¹
 surugaa
hen miidui
 haatuyaa
henhouse tuinuyaa
here kuma² ·
 ▸amakuma
 ▸kugata
hereabouts kumakaa
hereafter igu
hermit shinnin
heroine wikigamasai
heron saaji¹
 saajaa
herself funnin
hesitate ukeein
 mutchoohitchoo-sun
 turumun
hesitate (to say) iranpaa-
 sun

hesitation chimumayui
 mutchoohitchoo
 naa²
 ukee'umii
 utamabiikuu
hexagon rukkaku
hibiscus gusoobana
hiccup sakkoobi
hide *n.* kaa¹
hide *v.* kakusun
 kwakkiin
 kwakkusun
 kwakkwasun
 shinubun
 usuin
 ▸kajimiin
hide-and-seek
 kachiminsooree
hiding fukakajimi
high takasan
high price taka'ui
high-pitched kwiidakasan
highway ookwan
 uuduui
hill mui
 hira²
 muigwaa
 saka²
 taki¹
 yama
hilt chika
himself funnin
hinder sawain
hindrance chikee²
 gee
hipbone gamakubuni
hire yatuin
history iwari
hit uchun²
 atain²
 hoochun
 shichikiin
 suguin
 takkurusun
hit (back) uchikeesun
hitting koosaa¹
 patchi
hives kajoorimun
hoarse ▸kashiin¹
hoarseness karigwii
hoe kwee¹
 faa'ishigwee
 hiragwee

ishigwee
kanabai
kanikiibai
kiibai
maagwee
mimatagwee
minta'uchigwee
taa'uchaagwee
tamatagwee
hold muchun¹
 hikeein
 mutariin
 neein²
 uchun¹
hold (meeting) muyuusun
hold (onto) kwiisagain
hole ana
 fugi
 mii¹
holiday yashimi
hollow jii⁴
 ▸naakaafuukaa
home uchi
 chinee
 shimee
 shimeeka
 uyanuyaa
home village 'nmarijima
homeliness yanakaagi
honest ▸mattoobaa
honesty kadu²
 makutu
 shinjichi
 shoojichi
 ▸furimakutu(u)
honey michi²
honor *n.* myooga
 hikari
 jiri
 minbuku
honor *v.* umunjiin
honorable ▸rippa
honorific(s) shishiikutuba
 uufuu
 uyameekutuba
hood jitchin
hoof chimagu
 chimi
 kootu
hook *n.* gakijuu
hook *v.* hikkakiin
hoop daki'uubi
 kani'uubi

illness

ubi²
uubi
wuuki'uubi
hope *n.* nujumi
mikumi
▸nnatarugaki
hope *v.* nujumun
kangeein
nigain
tarugakiin
umuin
hopeless muchikas(h)an
hopelessness tii'ukuri
hopes michimui
horn chinu
hornet hachaa
horrible usumas(h)an
horse 'nma¹
  nui'nma
  onma
  ▸'nma'nmaa
  ▸chikiyaa'nma
  ▸hingi'nma
Horse 'nma¹
horse race 'nmajurii
horseshoe ▸'nmanchimi
hospital isanyaa
hospitality eesoo¹
  tideei
host *n.* shujin
  tiishu
host *v.* nkeein
hostility gee
hot achisan¹
  achikookoo
hot water saayuu
hour jibun
  jikan
house uchi
  yaa¹
  ashagi
  chuyaa
  faafuu
  kaarabuchi
  nuchijiyaa
  ▸hanari
  ▸karashiyaa
  ▸miiyaa
  ▸nnayaa
  ▸ufudunchi
housecoat issoochiya'a
household yaa¹
  chinee

chuyaa
shuutee
suutee
yaagunaa
yaatiichi
▸muutuyaa
▸shuuteedoogu
▸suuteedoogu
▸ufujinee
housekeeper yaamuchaa
housekeeping jooshichi
  yaamuchi
housing ▸muchichiriyaa
how chaa¹
  chaashi
  changutu
  anshi
how many chassa
  iku-
  ikuchi
  nan-
  nandu
how much chassa
  iku-
however ·shiga
  yashiga
howling tachinachi
hug dachun
  mandachun
hull kara³
human ninjin
  tchu
humidity shitchi
humming kuchijanshin
humor chimutuin
humorist namatee
hunchback kooguu
hundred hyaku
hunger wugari
  karawata
  yaasa
  yaasakurisa
hungry yaasan
  ▸wugariin
hunt (for) asain
hurry *n.* isuji
hurry *v.* isujun
  agimaasun
  awatiin
  namanamaasun
hurt sawain
  sukunain
  yamun

yamasun
husband shujin
  tiishu
  wutu
  ▸miitu
  ▸miitunda
  ▸naichaawutu
  ▸tujinukookoo
husk gara¹
hussy abasaa
hut gumayaa
  haruyaa
  kaiya
  yaagwaa
  ▸maasuyadui
hydrometer tamagwaa

I———
I wan²
ice koori²
idea umii
  ati
  kangee
identification miwaki
identify miwakiin
  sujoo¹
idiot furaa
idle ▸ashibun
  ▸keerinkurubin
  ▸tiibuchukuru
idleness ashibingwee
  fuyuu
idler turubaimun
  yurariyaa
if anshee
  mushi²
  mushika
  tatui²
if possible narubichi
ignited ▸teechichun
ignorance mugaku
  ▸shiranfuunaa
ignore chichinagasun
illegitimate child
  yamanashingwa
illiteracy mugaku
illiterate ▸akimikkwaa
illness chibyoo
  chuubyoo
  sawai²
  wacharee
  ▸nagayanmee

illusion

illusion imi[1]
  mayui
image kaagaa
imagination chimu'umii
  kangee
imagine kangeein
  unruin
imitate nishiin
imitation fuunaa
  neebi
  nishii
  nishimun
  tchunu neebi
  uchushi
immature wakasan
immediately chuuchan
  shigu
  soosoo
impatience ashigachi
impatient
  chimu'ichunasan
  tiihagoosan
  ▸ashigachun
  ▸ashigachaa
  ▸awataa
  ▸chiigasagasaa
  ▸nujumuju-sun
impertinent chiidakasan
impoliteness buchoohoo
importance teeshichi
important miidatas(h)an
imported ▸watain
imposter tchudamasaa
impregnate kasagirasun
improper fusoowoona
improve muchinoosun
imprudent ▸ameein
impure ▸chigariin
in uti
  nii[5]
in and out ▸itchai'njitai
in order tami
inactivity fumigui
inapproachable
  chikajichiguris(h)an
inappropriate
  fusoowoona
inappropriateness
  fusoowoo
inattentive ichitaran
inborn 'nmarijichi
incantation
  ▸mabuiwakashi

incense ukkoo
  hira'ukoo
  ippun'ukoo
inchworm hakayaamushi
incivility burii
  guburii
inclination katanchi
incline sakabira
include iriin
  kumiin
incoherent amaiikumaii
income iridaka
  irifa
  irimee
  hatarachi
incoming ▸'nji'iri
incompatible ▸katachi[1]
incompleteness nakatagee
inconvenience fubin
  fuchigoo
  fujiyuu
  jama
  sashichikee
incorrigible ▸namujaa
increase *n.* iimi
increase *v.* ufuku nain
incredible hirumas(h)an
indebted ▸kanjun
indebtedness ukaji
indecent miitoon neen
indecisive ▸annaikannai-sun
  ▸mutchoohitchoo-sun
indeed danju
  danjuka
  nncha[1]
  sattimusattimu
independence chuidachi
indifferent ▸tiitoodaachii-sun
indigestion fumigui
  ▸tudukuuin
indignant ▸kusamichun
indigo ee[2]
  ee'iru
indiscreet atisoonneenuu kuchigassan
individually chuinaa
  ichi'ichi
  naameemee
indoors yaanu'uchi
inept binasan
inexpensive ▸deeyashii

inexperienced oosan
inexpert hita
infamous ▸naa'iruu
infatuation chimumayui
  mayui
infect uchusun[2]
inferior *adj.* chiji[1]
  wassan
  ▸utiin
  ▸utuin
inferior *n.* tiishicha
  ▸gasaa
inflammation ▸miihagi
inflate fukurasun
influence chikara
  haba
  hikari
  ichui
influenza fuuchi[1]
inform shirasun
  moosagi-sun
information chinbun
  kukurii
  sata
  shirashi
infuriated watamugeein
infusion ▸chimushinji
  ▸kuu'iyushinji
  ▸nachoorashinji
  ▸taa'iyushinji
ingredients mii[3]
inhale suuin
inherit fichichijun
inheritance atuchiji
  yujiri
inhibit chijiin
initial ▸nanuigashira
injured ▸itamun
  ▸kijichichun
injury kiji
injustice muhoo
ink shimi[1]
ink (of cuttlefish) kuri[2]
ink pad shimichibu
ink slab shijiri
inking pad inniku
inlet wan[1]
  chiguchi
inn yadu
  yaduya
innocence atinashi
innuendo
  uranuchimunu'ii

inquiry jinmi
  miimee[1]
insane gerengeren
  ▸furiin[3]
insanity shinkee
inscription ▸migachi
insect mushi[1]
  ▸mushi'uturuu
insensitive ▸namajaa
insert hasamun
  sashinchun
inside naaka[1]
  uchi
inside-out urageeshi
  ▸keeshimaa
  ▸urageein
  ▸urageesun
insignificant
  ▸kajinaranmun
insincerity kuchisachi
insist iihain
insomniac miikufayaa
inspect nnjun
inspection aratami
  chinbun
  kinsa
install hichun[1]
  kakiin[1]
instead of kawai
instep hisanaa
instigate teechikiin
instinct kan[1]
instruct iichikiin
  naraasun
instruction furii
  iichiki
  iiwatashi
  naraashi
  yushigutu
insufficiency fusuku
insufficient haganasan
  tara(a)n
insult akahaji
  guchi[2]
intact mama
intelligence sheechi
  suumii
intelligent hashiraas(h)an
  ▸chiradamashi
intend kangeein
  umuin
intensify chuumiin
intention chigaki

chimuyee
kangee
tiinu'uchi
wata'uchi[2]
intentionally uttaatu
  wajattu
intently hitani
intercede tuinoosun
intercourse ▸hoo-sun
  ▸ichain
  ▸ukain
interdependency
  chuitareedaree
interest rii[2]
interest (rate) fibu
  riifii
interesting 'wiirikisan
  umussan
interfere kamain
interlude ▸marumun[3]
interlude (musical) sagu
intermediary chiti
intermediate tuichijun
interrogative naa[8]
intersection ajimaa
interval 'weeda
  eeja
  eeda
  eema[1]
intervene wakasun[1]
interview n. ichee
interview v. ichain
intestine watabii
intestines fii[6]
  iiwata
  nakami
intimate fukasan
  kukuruyassan
  ▸guunain
intractable ▸amasaa
intrigue yashin
introduce fichaasun
intrude sashihankiin
intrude (on) ushikakiin
intruder sashihankaa
intrusion sashihankigutu
intuition kan[1]
invention kufuu
inventory mukuruku
investigate aratamiin
  chiwamiin
  shirabiin
investigation jinmi

shirabi
tuishirabi
  ▸chibisaguin
invitation chikee[1]
  annee
  unchikee
invite nkeein
  yubun
inwardly chimu'uchi[2]
irascibility tanchi
iron tichi[2]
irony uranuchimunu'ii
irrationality ▸kanihandiin
irregular ▸inchaamanchaa
irritability tanchi
irritable ▸mujumuju-sun
island shima[1]
  hanari
  hishi
  wakari
it uri[1]
itch kooshi[1]
  samaa
itchy hachikoosan
  yiigoosan
  ▸mujumuju-sun
itemization tiichigachi
Itoman person
  ▸Ichumanaa

J

jack manrichi
jack-in-the-box
  joojookamiigwaa
jade stone gaaradama
jail ruuya
jailed ▸kumirariin
jam an[3]
janitor kujikee
January ichigwachi
  soogwachi
Japan Yamatu
  ▸naichi
Japanese Yamatunchu
  naichaa
Japanese (language)
  Yamatuguchi
jar kaami
  bin[2]
  dakinchibu
  handuu
  ichigoonuu

jasmine

mirr ichibu
sakigaami
suuchikigaami
yungaami
▸mihautuu
▸nanbangaami
jasmine kajimayaagi
jaundice woodan
jaw iikakuji
  kakuji
  ▸utugee
jaywalk kunchiin
jealous ▸rinchaa
  ▸uramasasun
jealous(y) ▸uragoosa
jealousy rinchi
jelly ami³
  kuuribuutu
jellyfish iiraa
  kureji
jewel ushi
  ▸mitama
jewelry tama¹
jobs ▸kakimuchi
join chijun¹
  chijeasun
  chikiin¹
  hitchikiin
  musubun
  takkwaasun
  tatchikain
joined ▸chirugain
joinery sashimun
joint chigee
  darumi
  fushi²
joist yukamuchi
joke teefa
  sukuchi
  wareebanashi
joker ganmaraa
  namatee
  teefaa
jokester marumun³
jolly fellow fireeyashii
jostling kunkurubaasee
  ▸uusheekurubashee
journey tabi
  doochuu
  michi¹
joy isoos(h)a
  ussa⁻
  ▸tunnooin

▸tunturumooyaa-sun
joyful isoos(h)an
joyous fukuras(h)an
judge miwakiin
  nnjun
  sabachun²
judgment michiki
  funbichi
  miwaki
  tinbachi
  ▸feegattin
jug mijigaami
  tinshiigaami
juggler hookasaa
juice shiru
July shichigwachi
jumble manchaahinchaa
jump tun(u)jun
  tunjiin
jump over tunkwiin
jumping tunjaimootai
junction michiguyaa
June rukugwachi
junior *adj.* wakasan
junior *n.* tushishicha
junk shitigara
junk (boat) Yanbaraabuni
just chintu
  choodu
  gumuttun
  namagata
justice jifi
  jii⁵
  michi¹
  saiban
justifiable gumuttun

K

karate tii¹
  passai
  ▸kuusankuu
  ▸naihanchi
  ▸pin'an
karma ingwa
keel kaara³
keep ajikain
  muchun¹
  tabuin
keep (company) chikajikiin
keep (mistress) kakuin
keep (watch) ▸manjun

▸miimanjun
keepsake katami
  naguri
kelp kijamikuubu
  kuubu
kerchief jitchin
kernel nakaguu
kerosene shichiyu
kettle yakkwan
key saashinukwa
kick kiin
  pattarugeeyaa-sun
kick (away)
  kirikurubasun
  kiritubasun
kick (down) kiritoosun
kidney maami
kill kurusun
kimono iichujin
  itujin
  basaa
  basaajin
  ▸aashimun
  ▸ayamun
  ▸kataruugeei
  ▸koojimaa
kind *adj.* ufuyassan
kind *n.* iru
  kata²
kindhearted
  chimujurasan
kindling fiiteechikiyaa
kindly kanaganaatu
kindness chimu'iri
  guwun
  kukuru'iri
  tchuchimuguris(h)a
  wun²
kinds ikutatii
kinfolk eeka
king woo
  kukuwoo
  ▸Shuitinganashi
kiosk baanyaa
kiss kuchisuuin
kitchen deeju
  shimu¹
  tungwa
  ▸shikubuu
  ▸usumutuu
kite mattakuu
kitten ▸maa'uuu
kleptomania tiigushi

kleptomaniac ▸tiinagasan
knead niin²
knee chinshi
  hija
knife hoochaa
  katahashiigu
  katana
  umiboochaa
knit amun
knitting amimun
knives hamun¹
knocking patchi
knot fushi²
knothole hashirunu mii
know kukuriin
  shitchoon
  ubiin
  wakain¹
  ▸shiin¹
knowledge chinbun
  kukurii
  tishimigakumun
knowledgeable
  ▸munushiri
knuckle fushi²
knucklebone gamakubuni
Korea Chooshin
Korean Chooshinaa
koto kutuu
kumquat chinkan

L
label fuda
  niifuda
labor *n.* hatarachi
  tima
  ▸arashigutu
  ▸yii³
labor *v.* hatarachun
  umiihamain
laborer agachaa
  booshichinaa
  buu
  hiyoo
  hiyoosaa
  jiibuku
  ninsuku
  nja
  shikama(a)
  timatuyaa
lack kagiin
  kakiin²

lacquerware nuimun²
ladder hashi
ladle niibu
  ibira²
  kubaniibu
  mishigee
  nabigee
  saataaniibu
  saragee
  uburu
ladles ▸naabidoogu
lady meewinagu
  ▸ayaamee
lag ukuriin
lake kumui²
lame ▸guunaa
  ▸neejun
  ▸neegaa
  ▸neeguu
  ▸neejaa
lameness guuni
  neegu
lament chimudachun
lamp akagai
  danpu
  shijichi
lamp chimney fuya¹
land jii¹
  tinga
landlord jiinuushi
  yaakarasaa
  yaanuushi
landlubber aginchu
landowner jiinuushi
lane suuji¹
language kutuba
languid darusan
  ▸daruu
  ▸dayaa
lantern choochin
  tuuru
  ▸miguiduuru
  ▸utuuru
lap *n.* chinshi
  hija
lap *v.* kukumun
lard anda
  buta'anda
large hirusan
  magisan
  ufu-
larva uji¹
  boofuyaa

leader

last *adj.* 'njaru
last *n.* ooban
  shiiban
  ▸oogusu
last *v.* tamuchun
  ▸chibinain
last night yuubi
last year kuju²
late niisan
  nikka
  ▸ukuriin
lately chikaguru
later atu
  utti
lattice kooshi²
  tana¹
laugh *n.* hanawaree
  takawaree
  ▸ahaa'ahaa
laugh *v.* warain
laughingstock
  munuwaree
laughter ufuwaree
  waree
launch ukabasun
  ukabiin
  ukiin³
  urusun
launching sura'urushi
launder shintaku-sun
laundering miji'aree
laundry shintaku
  shintakumun
law hattu
  uchiti
lawn ashijiri
lawsuit hiruu
  kuuji¹
lay ninshiin
lay down uchikiin
layer -kasabi
laziness dajaku
  fuyuu
lazy fuyuu
  ▸fuyuunamun
  ▸fuyuunaa
lead *n.* mijikani
  namai
lead *v.* hichun¹
leader kashira
  sachidachi
  shiidu
  shiiduyaa

leaf

leaf teesoo
leaf faa
  kiinufaa
leak muin[1]
leakage ▶namashiibai
lean magain
leap haniin
  tur(u)jun
leap month uruujichi
  yunjichi
leap year uruudushi
  yunjichi
learn narain
  ubin
  miinarain
  ukituin
learning binchoo
  gakumun
  shimisan
  ubi[1]
leather kaa[1]
leatherwork(er) kaajeeku
leave (alone)
  utchannagiin
leave (message)
  iir ukusun
leave *n.* hima
  ituma
leave (over) amasun
leave *v.* 'njiin
  ichun
  keein[1]
  nuchun[4]
  tachinuchun
  uchun[1]
  wakariin
  ▶umuinukusun
leaving (behind)
  utchangiirii
lecher iraa
  naa'iruu
leek chiribira
lees kashi[1]
  ▶andakashi
leeway yuchimi
left hijai[2]
left over ▶nukuin
left-handed hijaigatti
  ▶hijayaa
leftover nukui
leftovers kaminukushi
  nukushi
leg ashi[3]

hisa
  katahisa
  meebisa
  shiribisa
legal hiruu
legend chiteebanashi
  iichitee
  munugatai
  nkashibanashi
leisure hima
leisurely chimunagasan
lend karasun[1]
  tatigeein
  ▶migurasun
length nagi
  tati
  ▶nunudaki
lengthen nubasun
leniency nubi
lens tama[1]
leper kunchaa
leprosy kunchi[1]
let tuusun
let escape
  ▶kachimiihansun
let go hingasun
let go (of) tiiyurusun
let wither karasun[2]
let's... dii sai
  dikka
lethargic ▶dain
letter (character) jii[2]
  muji[1]
letter (correspondence)
  bin[3]
  hagachi
  tigami
lettuce aasa
  chisana
levee amutu
  ▶abushi
level *adj.* hirasan
level *v.* hirakasun
  narasun[1]
  toomiin
  tuunamiin
lever hichi
  tiku
levy kakiin[1]
lewd ▶hoowiigoo
  ▶iraa
liability kumuu
liar hyaku'ichii

yukushimunu'iisaa
liberal chimubirusan
libertine ashibaa
license *n.* kansachi
license *v.* yurusun
lick namiin
lid futa
  kamanta
  naabinufuta
  shinta
lie (down) afanachun
lie *n.* akayukushi
  yukushi
lieutenant ▶kata'udi
life nuchi[3]
  gusoo
  ichimi
  kunuyuu
  kurashi
  nuchikajiri
  shikin
  tchunu nuchi
  ▶ichikaran'ichichi
life of party jaamuchaa
lifelong ▶ichimitutuumi
lifestyle kurashikata
lifetime ichidee
lift agiin
  muchagiin
  sasun
lifted ▶muchagain
light *adj.* gassan
  hissan[1]
  kassan
  ushisan
light (ignite) chikiin[1]
  teechikiin
light *n.* akagai
  fichai
  hikari
lighten karukunasun
lighthouse hiitatii
lightly karugaruutu
  yoon
lightning fudii
like ▶mattachi
like *adj.* gutoon
like (as) ·nu gutu
  -tuui
like *n.* shichi[3]
like *v.* shichun[2]
lily yui[1]
lime (fruit) shiikwaasaa

lotus

lime (mineral) ishibee
limit kajiri
limited ibasan
limits dachi
line michi¹
 shin⁵
 yudachi
lineage 'nmari
 chakushibara
 chatchibara
 chiikaa
 chiishiji
 shiji²
 sujoo¹
 takkwii
 uji²
 ▸magara
linen asa¹
lining ura'uchi
 ura²
lion dance shiishi¹
 shiishimooi
lion-dog shiisaa
 shiishi¹
lip kuchibiru
 shichashiba
 'waashiba
lips kuchishiba
liquid shiru
 duujiru
 mijigusui
 mijigwee
liquor aamui
 numimun
 ▸miki
 ▸muruhaku
 ▸ushaku
listen chichun¹
listener ▸chichijooji
listening ▸chichiburi
listless ▸dain
literature yumimun
litter (palanquin) kagu
 dachikagu
litter (rubbish) chiri'akuta
little *adj.* gumasan
 saa-
little (amount) kunteen
 kuuteen
 kuutengwaa
 ▸miikusunu uppi
little (while) ichuta
 uhee

live *adj.* ▸ichitchu
live *v.* ichichun
 kurasun
 wun¹
live (on) kamun
livelihood chinee
 tachifa
 tachijuku
 ▸kurasun
lively ▸fumichun
liver chimu
livestock chikaneemun
living ichimun¹
lizard andachaa
 andajiraa
 eejaa
 oodoo
load (a firearm) kumiin
load *n.* chimini
 nii²
 niimuchi
load *v.* chimikumun
 chimun¹
loan shark koorigashii
lobby hikeeju
lobster ibi¹
lock hashirunusan
 saashi
 shin¹
lock (up) michikumiin
lockjaw hashoofuu
locust see
lodging tumai¹
log kiiroogu
logic rikuchi
 shiji²
logical muttumu
loincloth hadoobi
 meechaa
 sanaji
loitering michiyurari
lonely shikaraas(h)an
long nagasan
 ▸nagaa
long (in time) nageesan
long life naga'ichi
long stay nagajaa
long time nagadee
 naganin
 nagee
 ▸unnagee
long time no see
 miiduusan

long visit nagajaa
longevity choomii
 naga'ichi
longing ▸kugarijini
look (after) tiijikiin
look (downward)
 utchinchun
look *n.* amamiikumamii
look *v.* nnjun
 saguin
 ▸manjun
 ▸miiin¹
look for kameein
looking away yukumi
 yusumi
looks chirakaagi
 kaagi
 ninsoo
loom jibata
 nunubata
 takahata
 hatamun
 mushiruyaama
 ▸aji²
loose dabudabuu
 yooruu
 yurusan
 ▸teegee
loosen futuchun
 yurumiin
looseness gooruu
lord aji⁴
 yununushi
 ▸udun
lose makiin
 ushinain
 kwaariin
 utusun
lose (argument) iimakiin
lose (money) kabuin
lose (weight) yashiin
 yoogariin
loss firi²
 fugi
 -madii
 maki
 sun²
 sunkabui
lost jaamatiima
 ▸utushimun
lot yashichi
lottery kuji¹
lotus rin

loud

loud ▸magigwii
lounge yukuidukuru
louse shiran
  kiijiran
love (mutual) eenujumi
love (mutually)
  umui'umurariin
love *n.* joo[2]
  kui
  umui[1]
  iru
  jooyee
  nasaki
  shinasaki
  shuushin
  ▸manburi
  ▸umui'umuti
love *v.* kanasa-sun
  umuin
  ▸furiin[4]
  ▸kugariin
  ▸uchifuriin
love child guunaingwa
lovely kanas(h)an
lover kanashii
  ninguru
  satu
  umuyaa
  umuyaagwaa
  wikiga
  ▸kamanta
low hikusan
lower sagain[2]
  sagiin
  urusun
lowlands sagai[1]
luck fuku[2]
  fuu[2]
  karii
  kwafuu
lucky ▸kujiyafaraa
lucky day yukaruhii
luggage niimuchi
lukewarm nurusan
  ▸nuruyuu
lullaby kkwamuyaa'uta
lumber jeemuku
  kiiroogu
lumberyard jeemukuyaa
lump guufu
  gaanaa[1]
  katamai
  murushi

lunch asaban[1]
  ashii
  bintoo
  hiruma
  muchibanmee
lungs fuku[1]
lust hadafuusa
  iru
  iruyuku
lusts bunnuu
luxury hankwa
  kwabi
  ugui
lychee riichi
lye aku
lying yukushimunu'ii
lying (down) nagabooi
lying (prone) utchintuu

M———

machine yaama
madam anmaa
  juri'anmaa
madman furaa
  furimun
magazine ▸chichi'ukuri
maggot uji[1]
magic fushiji[2]
  hooka
magical ▸fushiji[2]
magical formula
  muranukeeshi
magician hookasaa
magnanimous
  chimubirusan
magnet jijaku
maid baachii
  jooshichaa
  muntachaa
  shichabatarachi
maiden miyarabi
  wakawinagu
mail bin[3]
  tayui
main street ufumichi
maintain muchun[1]
  ▸gireein
make chukuin
  kachun[3]
  nasun[1]
make do kuimaasun
make up chukuriin

ujumiin
make-believe choogin
  -gwaasee
maker chukuyaa
makeshift chuteenu
  hanshi
  futu
  kainu
malaria Yeemayakii
malcontent googuchaa
  jiiguyaa
male wikiga
  wuu
  wuumun
malice duku[1]
mallet seejichaa
malt kooji
man tchu
  wikiga
manage kageein
  kuimaasun
  tuihakarain
  wusamiin
management hakaree
  shimachi
  wusami
mane kanji[2]
mangrove wuubingi
manhood wikiga
manner anbee
  munugushi[2]
manners fuu[5]
  juku
manservant jinin
mansion tunchi
  udun
mantis isatuu
manufactured goods
  chukuimun
manufacturer chukuyaa
manure kwee[2]
  kajigwee
  ▸mijigwee
many ufusan
  asakii
  kajikaji
  teebun
  uhooku
March sangwachi
margin ▸yuchisan
mariner shinduu
mark ati
marker chinmaasaa

market machi[1]
machigwaa
▸Chibuyamachi
▸'nmumachi
▸nuimunmachi
▸nunumachi
▸shishimachi
marriage magu[2]
niibichi
risshin
yin[2]
▸aradumeei
▸araniibichi
▸feeniibichi
▸matadumeei
▸matamuchi
▸mataniibichi
marriageable age fudufudu
marrow jii[4]
marry muchun[1]
tumeein
▸kameein
marsh suku[2]
masculine wikigaraas(h)an
mash niin[2]
mask haachiburaa
▸shinigau
mason ishijeeku
massage *n.* anma
massage *v.* mimijun
mumun
masses mannin
shikin'umanchu
masseur anma
masseuse anma
mast hashira
fuubashira
master *n.* nuushi
suutaa
tiishu
master *v.* chiwamiin
mat mushiru
tatan
biigu
Biigumushiru
hanamushiru
yiidatan
mat maker tatanyaa
match (competition) suubu
▸shii'ushi

▸shiijima
match (incendiary) matchi
match *v.* uchiin[2]
matchbox chikijibaku
matched ▸uchaishinai
matchmaker nakadachi
mate eeti
matter deeji
kutu[1]
munu
waki
mattress hiramushiru
adanbaamushiru
kufamushiru
nikubuku
maturity feejuui
May gugwachi
maybe tabun
yuusannee
mayfly sensuruu
meal (grain) kuu[1]
meal (repast) mun[2]
munu
ubun[1]
▸afamee
▸manman
▸mishi'uki
mealtime munujibun
mean asamas(h)an
meandering yoogaahiigaa
meaning imi[3]
wachiyee
waki
means (circumstances) mibun
means (way) doogu
tidan
measles irigasa
measure *n.* hakai
hyooshi
measure *v.* hakain
meat shishi
andajishi
niku
▸kuchikuuyaa
▸mashishi
▸'nmanushishi
▸uchinagani
meat market 'waasaamachi
meats ▸biibii
meddling
▸nana'irumuutii

merchandise

mediation naka'iri
tuinashi
medicine kusui
chikigusui
kuugusui
numigusui
shinjigusui
▸mijigusui
▸nuigusui
medieval age nakamukashi
meditation munukangee
medium (mediation) naka'iri
medium (size) nakatii
medium (spiritual) yuta
medley chaafiifii
manchaahinchaa
meet atiin
ichain
nkain
▸hatchakain
meeting achimai
ichee
muyuushi
surii[1]
▸munchuujurii
melon ui
gooyaa
shibui
melt shirunain
tukasun
tukiin
members ninju
memo hikee
memorandum ubiigachi
memorial kuyoo
memorization ubidee
memorize ubiin
memory ubi[1]
munu'ubii
naguri
ubidee
umukaji
▸uru'ubii
mend chukuriin
noosun
mending chinnukuu
menses akafujoo
chichinumun
juugunichi
juugunichii
merchandise achineemun

merchant

shinamun
uimun¹
merchant achineenchu
  achineesaa
  achoodu
  achooduu
mercury mijigani
merit kunkoo
  ni'uchi
  tigara
  ▸uutigara
merry ▸haneechun
mess jaafee
message dingun
  ii'uchi
  iyai
  tujiki
messenger chikee¹
  uchikee
metal imun
  kani²
metalsmith kuganijeeku
metaphor tatui¹
method shiiyoo
  shikata
  shiyoo
midday hiru¹
middle naaka¹
  mannaka
  nakaba
  nakajin
  tanaka
middleman tuichiji
midnight mayunaka
  yunaka
  yuruyunaka
midsection naka¹
midway hanmichi
  mannaka
midwife kkwanashimiyaa
  sanba¹
midwinter kan²
migrate watain
mild nadayassan
  nukusan
mildew kooji
milepost chinmaasaa
milestone ichirijika
milk n. chii⁷
  ▸ushinuchii
milk v. eesun²
millet awa
  maajin

mimicry tchunu neebi
mind n. chii⁵
  chimugukuru
  kukuru
  shin³
  wata'uchi²
mind v. kamain
mine kanigaa
miniscule ▸chimikusu
minister chikee¹
mint hakka
mirror kagan
misanthrope
  tchukashimas(h)aa
mischief ganmari
  itajira
  tinchama
  wachaku
miser eekigumasa
  gani²
  ibiraa
  ijasaa
  jingunjuu
  kumashiraa
  yukuu
  yuukuu
miserable asamas(h)an
misfortune ingwa
  wajawee
  yaku¹
mishearing yoogaajichi
misjudgment kanchigee
mismatches gumaa'inchaa
miso nnsu
miss atihanriin
  chichi'utusun
  hansun
  handiin
  kachimiihansun
miss (a chance) ushinain
mission chikee¹
misspeak iiyanjun
misspeaking iimachigee
mist chiri¹
  gakayaa
mistake n. ayamachi
  bappee
  hii³
  machigee
  shiiyanji
mistake v. ayamain
  miiyanjun
  ▸bappeein

mistress winagu
  yuubee
misunderstanding
  chichibappee
  kanchigee
mix aasun
  kijun
  majiin
  mankiin
  shirikumun
mix (flour) tukasun
Miyako Myaaku
Miyako person
  Myaakunchu
  ▸Myaakuu
moan nachun²
moaning duunii
model kata²
moderate yiisaku
moderately nadayashiku
moderation uchiba
modern namanuyuu
modest kumasan
modesty kumeeki
  tashinami
moist ▸shimishimi-sun
moisten ndasun
  shimikeein
moisture shimiki
  urii¹
molar uukubaa
molasses shirushita
mold (cast) ikata
mold (mildew) kaabui
  kooji
molding imun
mole aja²
molt ndigara
moment hyooshi
money jin²
  sachi³
  yinjoojin
  ▸hamunjin
  ▸ichandajin
  ▸jindaka
  ▸kujin
  ▸maruchijin
  ▸nchabi
  ▸ufujin
money box jinbaku
moneylender jinkarasaa
money-making
  ▸jinmookijuku

mongoose **manguusuu**
monk **booji**
monkey **saaruu**
  saru
Monkey **saaruu**
monologue
  duuchuimunu'ii
monopoly **muchichiri**
  muchichirishigutu
monster **bakimun**
  majimun[1]
  yanamun
month **chichi**[2]
  ▸**kunchichi**
  ▸**kutachichi**
  ▸**kwitachichi**
  ▸**ningwachi**
Months
  ichigwachi
  soogwachi
  nigwachi
  sangwachi
  shingwachi
  gugwachi
  rukugwachi
  shichigwachi
  hachigwachi
  kugwachi
  juugwachi
  shimuchichi
  shiwa'ashi
month-end **chichishii**
monthly **chichinukaaji**
mood **kukurumuchi**
moon **chichi**[1]
  ▸**akachichijichuu**
  ▸**mikajichi**
  ▸**tootoomee**
  ▸**uburujichi**
  ▸**uchichuu**
moon viewing
  chichinagami
mop *n*. **susui**
mop *v*. **nuguin**
  susuin
mopping **susuikachi**
morality **michi**[1]
morals **fuu**[5]
more **naahin**
  yuku[3]
moreover ·**bikeen ya aran**
morning **asa**[2]
  shitimiti

sutumiti
akookuroo
▸**akachichigurashin**
▸**asakaagi**
▸**mee'asa**
▸**naacha'asa**
morning sickness **saai**
  saaimaki
mortar (grinding) **uushi**
  shiri'uushi
  chichi'uushi
  deefaa
  kii'ushi
  kusui'uushigwaa
  ▸**'nnishiri'uushi**
  ▸**'nnishiyaa'uushi**
mortar (masonry) **muchi**[2]
mosquito **gajaa**
  yamagajan
mosquito net ▸**kacha**
moss **nuuri**
most **ichiban**
  itchin[3]
moth **gaa**[2]
  buun
mother **anmaa**
  ayaa
  okkaa
  winagu'uya
  winagunu'uya
mother (animal) ▸**ahyaa**
motherhood **kkwamuchi**
mother-in-law
  winagushitu
motion sickness **funeei**
motive **shintii**
mountain **mui**
mourn **kuyamun**
mourning **imi**[2]
  kuyami
  ▸**imigakai**
mouth **kuchi**[2]
  ▸**aa**[2]
mouthful **chukuchi**
move **'njuchun**
  duchun
  dukinasun
  nasun[1]
  uchiin[1]
  uchusun[2]
moved ▸**'njuchun**
movie **kwachidoo**
moving **yaa'uuchii**

myself

mower **kusakayaa**
mowing **kusakai**
moxa **fuuchi**[3]
moxibustion **yaachuu**
much **ufusan**
  uhooku
  teebun
  ▸**arubun**
  ▸**aru'ussa**
  ▸**chappi**
  ▸**kuppi**
mucus **hanakusu**
  miikusu
mud **duru**
  iifu
muddiness **duruduru**
  mingwi
muddy **wassan**
  ▸**durubuttaa**
  ▸**mingwasun**
  ▸**mingwiin**
mudflat **katabaru**
muggy ▸**fumichun**
mugwort **fuuchibaa**
multiply **hirugain**
  kakiin[1]
multitude **ufuninju**
mumps **tooshinbai**
Musa **basaanunu**
muscle **kaji**[4]
  udijikara
mushroom **chinuku**
  naba
  shimiji
music **kutin**
  utasanshin
  ▸**jii'utee**
  ▸**kachaashii**
  ▸**kunkunshii**
  ▸**ufubushi**
musical instruments
  naimun[1]
muskrat **biichaa**
must (do) -**too naran**
mustache **'waahiji**
  hanahiji
mustard **naa**[9]
mute **chiigaa**[1]
  chiiguu
muteness **mugun**
my- **waa-**
myriad **man**
myself **wankuru**

mysterious
mysterious **fushiji**²
  hirumas(h)an
mystery **akashimun**
  fushiji²

N———
Naha **Naafa**
Naha dialect **Naafaguchi**
Naha person **Naafaa**
  Naafanchu
nail **kuji**²
  gusunkuji
  kanikuji
  sanjunkuji
nails ▸**kootu**
naked **hadaka**
nakedness ▸**maruhadaka**
name **naa**³
  minjichi
  warabinaa
  yagoo
  yiifeejii
  ▸**futukigwaa**
  ▸**hyaakuugwaa**
  ▸**kaminaa**
  ▸**karanaa**
nameplate **nafuda**
naming ▸**naajiki'ubagii**
  ▸**naajikii**
nap **chuhana**
  hirumaninji
  turumikasun
  yiiniibui
nape **kaji**⁶
  kubigaa
  unaji
  ushiru²
  ▸**ushirukubu**
napkin **hiichin**
narrate **katain**
narrow *adj.* **ibasan**
narrow *n.* ▸**ibamii**
narrow *v.* **ibamiin**
natives **jiinchu**
natural **ataimee**
  gumuttun
naturally **nankuru**
  shijin ni
naturalness **jun**
nature **shijin**
  tin¹
nature (human) **ninjoo**²

naughty ▸**makuu**
  ▸**uumaku**
nausea **funawii**
  fuunee
nauseated ▸**wiibachun**
navel **fusu**
  ▸**tenbusu**
near *adj.* **chichasan**
  chikasan
  ▸**ugachikasa**
near *v.* **chikayuin**
near(by) **hata**¹
nearby **mee**²
nearly **chichasan**
nearsightedness **chikamii**
neatly **churaaku**
necessarily **ataimee**
necessity **kanmuchi**
neck **kubi**¹
  ▸**kubikaji**
neckband **chinnukubi**
nectar **michi**²
need *n.* **iriyuu**
need *v.* **iin**³
  tuin
  ▸**kumain**²
needle **haai**²
  chinbai
  kukuibaai
neglect **ukutain**
  utchannagiin
  utcharakasun
negligence **futuduchi**
negotiation **ukihanshi**
negotiations **kakiyee**
neighbor **tunai**
  chikeetunai
  chinju
  keetunai
  tankaamankaa
neighborhood **chinju**
  mee²
  suba²
  chikeetunai
  chukeetunai
  mangura
  'nmarikaa
  ▸**kurikaa**
neighborliness
  chinjubiree
  tunaibiree
nephew **wiikkwa**
nervous **uturus(h)an**

nervously **sansan**
nervousness **chimusawaji**
nest *n.* **shii**³
nest *v.* **shiigumui-sun**
nesting **shiigumui**
net **ami**²
  agiyaa'ami
  saji²
  ▸**surugaajina**
new **ara**¹-
  miisan
  sara-
  ▸**mii**²-
  ▸**miimun**¹
New Year's (Day)
  gwantan
  shinsoogwachi
  Uchinaasoogwachi
  Yamatusoogwachi
New Year's Eve
  tushinuyuuru
newly **miikuni**
news **ati**
  kwii¹
  shirashi
  tayui
  utu
next **atu**
  tunai
next month **tachichi**¹
next year **akiti**
  yaan
  yukudushi
nibble **kakajiin**
  namiin
nickname **ajana**
night **yuru**
  yuu¹
  yuuru
  ▸**chichuu**
  ▸**meeyuru**
  ▸**uburujichuu**
night and day **yuruhiru**
nightblindness **tuimii**
nightgown **yuujin**
nightingale **chatchaa**
nightmare **yana'imi**
nimble **gurusan**
nine **kukunuchi**
nineteen **juuku**
ninety **kujuu**
nip **nijiin**³
nipple **chiinukubi**

ogling

nirvana **higan**
nit **jichashi**
no **bee**[1]
  nba
  nnnnn
  woooo
  wuuwuwuu
  yiiyiyii
no way **anshinkanshin**
noise **fibichi**
  utu
noisily **gwasagwasa wasawasa**
noisy **minchasan**
  soogasan
  yagamas(h)an
  ▸**wasamichun**
nonpayment **funoo**
nonsense **furimunu'ii taagutu**
noodle **soomin**
noodles ▸**biibii**
  ▸**suba**[1]
noon **mafana**
norm(al) **chini**
normalcy **jun**
north **nishi**
  ▸**manishi**
North Star **niinufabushi**
northward **nishinkee**
nose **hana**[3]
  hananusachi
  hanabukkwa
nosebleed **hanaji**[1]
nostrils **hananu'ana**
not **aran**
not at all **musattu tiichin**
note **chimu'ubii**
  eejagachi
  kachichiki
  ▸**kachi'iriin**
notice **furii**
  tasshi
  tuduki
notice board **tatifuda**
notification **furii**
notify **furiin**[2]
  tudukiin
notoriety **hyooban**
nourish ▸**ujinain**
nourishment
  kunchi'ujinii

kusui
novelty **tanigaaimun**
November **shimuchichi**
novice **oojaaniisee**
now **maji**
  nama[2]
  tadeema
  ▸**namasachi**
nowadays **chikaguru kunuguru**
nucleus **nakajin**
nude **hadaka**
nudity **akahadaka**
  ▸**maruhadaka**
numb ▸**hirakumun**
  ▸**shibiriin**
number **kaji**[5]
  ninju
nun **winagubooji**
nursery **naashiru**
nursing **kanbyoo tunjaku yamiwandee**
nutriment **ujinee**
nutritious ▸**kusuimun**
nymph **tinnin**

O

oar **eeku**[1]
  kee[4]
  kuujaa
oarsman **kuujaa**
obedient **chumama**
obey **chichun**[1]
  nabichun
  shitagain
  ▸**marumiin**
objection **fugattin iibun**
obligation **guwun wunji**
obscene **hagoosan**
observe **mitumiin nnjun**
obsolesce **shitariin**
obstacle **kakaisawai samatagi**
obstinacy **gwanku**
obstinate **shibusan**
  ▸**namujaa**
obstruct **heerinchun yaniin**

obstruction **jama**
obtain **tuin**
obvious **achirakana miiyassan**
occasion **tuchi**
  wui
  basu
  chigoo
  chiidi
  tukuru
  unubaa
occasional **marukeeti**
occident **Uranda**
occur **an**[1]
ocean **'nmi**[1]
  tukee
  ufu'umi
  uutu
  ▸**agarinu'umi**
  ▸**oosuu**
October **juugwachi**
octopus **taku**
odd **ifuuna**
  ▸**hamun**[2]
odor **niwui**
  ifuunakaja
  kaba
  ▸**shiibaikaja**
  ▸**shiikaja**
of course **muttumu**
offend **chimutuihansun**
offense **chimujawai**
  rippuku
  tuga
offensive
  ▸**chichiguris(h)an**
offer **agiin**
  eesun[1]
  'njasun
  usagiin
offering **ukajai**
  usagimun
  ▸**minnuku**
office **murayaa**
  shigutuba
  yaku[2]
official **kwannin**
official duty **kuujigutu**
offing **tunaka**
  tuu[3]
  uuchi
often **tatta**
ogling **iraamii**

oil

oil **anda**
  shichitanyuu
  ▸**saba'anda**
oily **andajuusan**
ointment **chikigusui**
Okinawa **Uchinaa**
  ▸**ufuji**
  ▸**Uruma**
Okinawan **Uchinaanchu**
Okinawan (language)
  Uchinaaguchi
Okinawan islands
  ▸**Urumajima**
old ▸**kooguu**
  ▸**tusui**
omen **bukarii**
  kariinamun
  shirashi
  tamagai
omitted ▸**utiin**
omoro **umui**^{2}
Omoro Sooshi **Umuru**
  Usooshi
on ·**nkai, kai**
on (top of) ▸**ma'wii**
once **chukeen**
  ichika
one **ichi**^{1}
  tiichi
one (of pair) **kataguu**
one after another
  issoonaadii
one and all **issoonaadii**
one's own **duumuchi**
one-legged ▸**hisamoo**
oneself **chui**
  duukuru
  duunaa
one-way **katamichi**
onion **bira**
  niibiru
only ·**bakai**
  ·**bikee**
  tada^2
  uppigwaa
only (that) **ussa**^{1}
ooze **tariin**^{1}
open *adj.* **firubiruu**
open *v.* **achun**
  akihanasun
  fugiin
  furachun

  hajimain
  hirachun
  hirakiin^2
open space **ufumaru**
opening **fugi**
  hajimi
openminded
  chimumagisan
operate **'njuchun**
opinion **kangee**
opponent **eetuu**
opportunist
  matabashigooyaku
opportunity **chigoo**
  jibun
  jishichi
  wui
oppose **gee-sun**
  nkain
opposite **mamukoo**
  nkee
  ura^2
  urahara
  ▸**nkain**
opposition **kuruu**
  rikuchi
  tiinkee
oppression **woogai**
or ·**n**
oracle **mishijiri**
  ushirashi
orange **kaabuchii**
  kuganii
  mikan
  ootoo
orchid **awaran**
order *n.* **achiree**
  chuumun^2
  iichiki
  iiwatashi
  tasshi
order (sequence) **ban**^{1}
  shidee^1
order *v.* **achireein**
  narabiin
ordinal suffix ▸**mii**
ordinary **fiijii**
  nami^2
  shikinnami
organ **watamiimun**
origin **'nmari**
  iwari
  mibun

  mutu
Orion's belt **miichibushi**
ornament **ukajai**
ostracism **chinjubaree**
ostracized ▸**kuruu**
other **tanin**
  yusu
ought **haji**^{2}
ours **wattaamun**
ourselves **duunaa**
outcast **nugimun**
outdo **'wiinujun**
outdoors **joofuka**
outgoing ▸**'nji'iri**
outing **fuka'atchi**
outlaw **amaimun**^{2}
  muhoo
outlook **michiki**
outside **fuka**^{2}
  sutu
  umuti
outskirts **murahajishi**
outstanding
  miidatas(h)an
oven **kama**^{2}
  kamadu
overcharge **kaki**
overcooked ▸**niikuta nain**
overflow **andasun**
  andiin
  ikkeeriin
overlook **miinugarasun**
  yoosoochun
overstatement **iikkwa**
  kwagun
overthrow **furubasun**
overturn **kachikeerasun**
overwork **hatarachikwaa**
owe **tamain**^{1}
owl **chikuku**
  mayaajikuku
own **an**^{1}
  muchun^1
owner **nuushi**
ox **ushi**^{1}
Ox **ushi**^{1}
oxidation **oosabi**
oyster **afakee**

P———

pacify **chimunooshi-sun**
  chimutuin

pack michiin[2]
package uchukwiijichin
packing nijukui
pad haaisashii
paddle eeku[1]
  kee[4]
  mishigee
paddy taa[1]
  asadaa
  taabukkwa
pain n. kuchisa
pain v. hiirachun
  ▸hatahataa-sun
painful duuguris(h)an
  kuchisan
paint n. penki
paint v. kachun[1]
  nuin[1]
painter penkiyaa
  yiikachaa
pair chii[4]
  guu[1]
  guutumiitu
  itchii
palace chifijin'udun
pale ushisan
  ▸irunugaa
  ▸irunugiin
  ▸massaaraa
pale (complexion)
  irushiruu
palm (of the hand)
  tiinuwata
palm (tree) binroo
  biroo
  kuba
  'nnmaagii
  noyashi
  suutiichaa
  yaashi
  ▸maani
palmistry tisoo
palsy chuufuu
pan imunnaabi
  naabi
panic soonugiin
  ▸jaamakeeriin
pans ▸naabidoogu
pant feefee-sun
  fuchun[2]
papaya papaya
paper kabi
  haigami

shirukabi
sugiwara
waradooshi
▸achikabi
▸bashuukabi
▸fugu
▸machikabi
▸minugami
▸mumudakabi
parable tatuibanashi
paradise gukuraku
paralysis chuufuu
paralyzed ▸hirakumun
parasite yakkeemun
parasol higasa
  sashikasa
pare nchun
parent nashi'uya
  soo'uya
  ▸jichinu'uya
  ▸sudati'uya
parent and child
  uyakkwa
parent(s) uya
parent-in-law
  ▸yumi'ibiraa
parents futa'uya
  uyamutu
parents-in-law shitu
  shitu'uya
parlor ichibanja
parody chukuikee
part (from) wakariin
part n. tukuru
part v. nuchun[3]
  wakain[2]
partiality hiichi
  ippoonkee
parting naguri
partner eeti
  eetuu
  eetuu
  guu[1]
part-time job
  katatimashigutu
party sakijaa
  suujijaa
  tankaa'uuwee
  ▸moo'ashibi
  ▸tushiwashiri
  ▸wuduyee
pass fukiin[2]
  kwiiin

pay

shigusun
shijiin[2]
tachun[1]
tuuin[1]
watasun
'wiinujun
passage tukuru
passing ichigachii
passion iruyuku
  joo[2]
  kui
  yuku[1]
paste n. nui
paste v. hitchikiin
pastime ashibi
pasting ▸meenui
patch (garden) atai[1]
  ▸wuu'atai
patch n. chijaahajaa
patch v. chijaasun
patching ▸kuushiikaashii
path michi[1]
  michigwaa
  suuji[1]
  yamamichi
pathetic chimu'ichasan
pathos aakii
pathway tuuimichi
patience chimunubi
  kunchi[2]
patient adj. nijiijuusan
  ▸chitumiin
  ▸kuneein
patient n. byoonin
  yanmeemun
patrol harumigui
patronage hiichi
  ukaji
patronize fichitatiin
pattern gara[2]
  muyoo
  yiichiri
  ▸tutchiri
  ▸ufu'aya
paw tii[1]
pawn kata[2]
pawning shichi[1]
pawnshop shichiya
pay harain
  aain
  fichaain
  iraasun
  'njasun

pay

watasun
pay (in advance) tatigeein
pay attention kumeekiin
payment haree[2]
ninjiri
▸meebaree
pea induumaami
shiru'indoo
peace buji
wadan
▸kuneein
peacefully yaayaatu
peacefulness
wadanwagoo
peach kiimumu
peak nni[2]
▸masakai
peanut jiimaami
peasant chukuyaa
haru'atchaa
naagu
pebble guma'ishi
ishi
pedantic ▸kusabukkwaa
peddler ▸kami'achinee
▸maasu'uyaa
pedestal utina
peek suumi
peel hajun[1]
hagasun
nchun
nkiin[1]
peer chirumii
peg kiikuji
dakikuji
jiifaa
karakui
mudi
pencil ▸ishibanfurigwaa
penetrate nuchun[1]
tuuin[1]
penis hanki
mara
soo[2]
tani
▸chuuchuu
▸hankiin
people umanchu
▸shichakata
pepper kooreegusu
perceive mitumiin
percent -wari
perception kan[1]

perfect *adj.* matasan
mukiji
▸matamun
perfect *v.* shiinasun
performance choogin
▸jiinuu
▸joodiki
performer ▸manzai
perfume kaba'anda
chooji
perhaps uukata
yuusannee
period eema[1]
nindee
'weeda
perishable kusaiyassan
permanency nagachijichi
permission yurushi
permit yurusun
perplexity chimumayui
persimmon shibugaki
persist kunpain
tuusun
persistent ▸ganbayaa
person tchu
funnin
jintii
munu
ninjin
▸arappaa
▸shinitchu
personality jintii
kukurumuchi
persons -nin[1]
persuade shishimiin
perverse ▸magain
pervert ▸magiin
pestle ajin
gappayaa[2]
pestle shirikuji
petroleum shichitanyuu
pharmacy kusuiyaa
yatchuku
philanderer gunboo
winagu'utusaa
winagushikasaa
philandering
winagumuchiri
phlegm kashigui
photograph sashin
▸uchiin[2]
physique fudu
funigumi

soogara
pick (a fight) tii 'njasun
pick *n.* bachi[2]
chimi
pick *v.* chimun[2]
muin[3]
mushiin
pickle *n.* amajuu
chikimun
chikina
yii[4]
pickle *v.* chikiin[2]
piecework ukishigutu
pier sanbashi
tundoo
pierce sasun
pig 'waa
▸'waa'waa
▸chikiyaa'waa
pig breeder 'waakarayaa
wuu'waakarayaa
pig trough tooni
pigeon hootu
piggyback uufa
▸uufasariin
piglet 'waagwaa
pigment yinugu
pigsty 'waafuuru
fuuru
pile *n.* majin
▸'nnimajin
pile (up) chimi'agiin
kasabiin
▸kasabain
pile *v.* chimun[1]
majimun[2]
mui'agiin
muin[2]
pillar haaya
hajibaaya
kakubaai
marubaai
muuyabaaya
nakabaaya
shinbaai
pillow makkwa
kiifuujoo
kiimakkwa
toomakkwa
▸irimakkwa
▸udimakkwa
pillow talk
ninjimunugatai

280

pleased

miitundamunugatai
pimple nikun
pin haai[2]
pin money watakushi
pincers kujinujaa
pinch chinchikiin
  nijiin[3]
pine umuikugariin
pine (tree) maachi
pine needle maachibaa
pinecone maachikasaa
pink mumu'iru
pinwheel kajiguruma
  kajimayaa
pioneer sachibai
pipe chishiri
  ▸fiifuchi
pisser shiibayaa
pit-a-pat dakudaku
pitcher anbin
pitiful chimu'ichasan
  chimuguris(h)an
  ichasan
pivot shinmi
place *n*. baa
  basu
  tukuru
  unubaa
place (on head) kamiin
place (on) nushiin
place *v*. uchikiin
placenta iya
  kkwabukuru
plague fuuchi[1]
plain duuyassan
  toobaru
plan *n*. kangee
  kufuu
  mukurumi
  shikumi
  yarashiikwaashii
plan *v*. ningakiin
  shikumun
  umuitachun
plane kanna
plank icha[1]
plant 'wiiin
  machun[3]
Plants
  achineiku
  adan'ashi
  adaniguchaa
  ahadan

aka'indoo
akabanaa
akabura
akagi
akagusa
akana
baran
bashuu
butan
chaagi
chifafa
chiri[4]
dashicha
diigu
dugwai
fukuji
funui
gikiji
gusoonchunu'aajingii
haameekuugi
hajigi
hirafagusa
ichubi
kabigi
kanda
kunyaku
kusabana
kuukwa
kwaadeesaa
kwaagi
maachinaba
maawuu
magaya
miifukkwaa
mimigui
minna
moo'aasa
mumu[1]
munjuru'ichubi
naabeeraa
nachoora
ringan
rugwai
saataagii
sabangi
sannin
sasaminna
shibaki
shindan
shishidama
sumumu
tabu
taka'ichubi

tiikachi
tinsagu
uchigusa
ukigusa
uru
urushi
usuku
warabi[2]
wuubee
yamaguruchi
yamakanda
yamamumu
yarabu
yuuna
plaster *n*. muchi[2]
  anmaagooyaku
  kooyaku
plaster *v*. nuin[1]
plasterer muchijeeku
plate sara[1]
  chuujara
  gumakee'uchi
  haachi
  ita
  kee'uchi
  kujara
plateau agai
play (a sport) sun[1]
play (an instrument)
  fuchun[2]
  hichun[2]
  narasun[3]
play (drama) kuchidati
  marumun[3]
  shibai
  wudui
play *n*. ashibi
play *v*. ashibun
  ▸uchun[2]
  ▸yiiin
playing fukamaaruu
  ▸mijimutaan
  ▸nnchamutaan
  ▸unjaagii
playmate ashibidushi
pleasant 'wiirikisan
please (request)
  kwimisooree
  tandi
please *v*. chimutuin
pleased isoos(h)an
  uss(h)an
  ▸ussa[2]

pleasure

pleasure **iruyuku**
  sujoo[2]
  tanushimi
  umui[1]
  yurukubi
plectrum **bachi**[2]
  chimi
pledge **kaakii**
plenty **uhooku**
plight **jaama**
  shijama
plot **chikata**
  hakarigutu
  shiji[2]
plover **chijui**
plow *n.* **kiiyama**
  taasuki
plow *v.* **keesun**
pluck **muin**[3]
  mushiin
plucking **iibibanchi**
plug **joo**[1]
  shin[1]
plugged ▸**chimain**
plum **'nmi**[3]
  ▸**'nmibushi**
plunder **kuntuin**
pocket **fuchukuru**
pocketknife **shiigu**
pockmark **kumujaa**
  kumuji
pod **maamigaa**
poem **uta**
  kamiku
  kuika
  ▸**kuduchi**
  ▸**nakafuu**
poetry ▸**ruuka**
point **sachi**[1]
point of view **kangeekata**
pointed **tugain**
poison **deechiree**
  duku[1]
  dukugusui
poisoned ▸**atain**[1]
poisoning **atai**[3]
  hajaa
  ▸**urushimaki**
poke **chichichun**
  nuchun[1]
poker **heekachaa**
pole **kanichi**
  soo[2]

▸**machiwara**
pole bearer **ganmuchaa**
police (station) **kiisachi**
polish **feesun**
  migachun
polite ▸**shishiin**[1]
politeness **tiinii**
polluted ▸**chigariin**
  ▸**chigarimun**
pollution ▸**chigari**
pompous ▸**gaain**
pond **ichi**[2]
  kumui[2]
pool **ichi**[2]
  tamai
poor ▸**hinsuumun**
  ▸**kuushiimun**
  ▸**piipiisoon**
  ▸**soobee**
popping ▸**pan**
populace **mannin**
popular ▸**feein**
  ▸**mutiin**
  ▸**uriin**[2]
popularity **feei**[1]
  hyooban
porcelain **yachimun**
  narimundoogu
porch **jinkwan**
  yin[1]
pork **'waanushishi**
  ▸**boojishi**
  ▸**suujikii**
porridge
  ▸**boroborojuushii**
  ▸**fuuchibaajuushii**
  ▸**kandabaajuushii**
port **nnatu**
  tumai[2]
portion **bun**[3]
  ichininmee[1]
  tamashi[2]
  tuimee
  wakimee
position *n.* **jaa**[2]
  kamee
  mibun
  yaku[2]
position *v.* **yishiin**
positiveness **ugachi**
possess **an**[1]
  mutariin
possessed ▸**taariin**[2]

possession **taari**
post **kwii**[2]
postcard **hagachi**
poster **haigami**
postpone **nubasun**
postponement **nubi**
posture **kakkoo**[2]
  ▸**ninjijama**
postwar **ikusa'atu**
pot **chibu**[1]
  kaami
  naabi
  gungoorachi
  gunmeenaabi
  hagama
  imunnaabi
  saakuu
  ▸**ninmeenaabi**
  ▸**sanmeenaabi**
  ▸**shinmeehannaabi**
  ▸**shinmeenaabi**
  ▸**shirunaabi**
potato **jaga'nmu**
potatoes ▸**fushibii**
potherb **handama**
potluck **nuchaashii**
pots ▸**naabidoogu**
pottage **'nbushii**
  ▸**kuubu'nbushii**
pottery **yachimun**
  anbin
  chibuyayachi
  narimundoogu
  yachimundoogu
pouch **fukuru**
  fuujoo
  kinchaku
poultryman
  tuichikanayaa
pour **chijun**[2]
  kakiin[1]
  nagasun
  uchusun[2]
poverty **hinsuu**
  fujiyuu
  piipii
  piipiikaakaa
powder **kuu**[1]
  ▸**kuufuchun**
power **hikari**
  ichui
  kusai[2]
  saa

powerful chuusan
shijidakasan
powerfully chuuku
pox mijigasa
practice *n.* chiiku
naraashi
tinaree
practice *v.* narain
praise *n.* fumikutuba
praise *v.* fumiin
prank ganmari
wachaku
yanawachaku
prankster ganmaraa
prattler munuyumaa
pray nigain
ninjiin
wugamun
prayer chuumun[1]
gwan
hachi'ugwan
kaminigee
ningwan
ugwan
yashichinu'ugwan
praying chimunigee
precede sachidachun
sachinain
preceding 'njaru
precious ataras(h)an
ichasan
precocious chuuibeesan
feeijuusan
▸kusabukkwaa
▸kusamunu'ii
precocity feejuui
prefabricated nujisachi
pregnancy haramaa
pregnant ▸haramun
▸kasagiin[1]
▸kasaginchu
▸kasagirasun
▸kkwanasaa
▸ufuwata-sun
▸ufuwatamun
prehistoric kamigudee
prelude ▸utamuchi
premature feeijuusan
prematurity hayamaigutu
preparation sugai
shikooi
shikooimukooi
shitaku

sunawai
tigumi
tikubai
yuu'i
prepare chukuin
shikooin
shitaku-sun
shitatiin
sugain
preparedness kakugu[1]
prepayment meebaree
presence mee[2]
present (now) kunuguru
nama[2]
present *v.* kwiin
eesun[1]
'njasun
▸'njiin
presentable miiyassan
present-day namanuyuu
preserve kakuin
tamuchun
press *n.* itabu
press *v.* imiin
usaasun
ushichikiin
press out eesun[2]
prestige hikari
pretend najikiin
pretending -najikii
pretense najiki
pretty churasan
▸futukiinu gutoon
prevent fushijun
samatagiin
previously meekaniti
prewar ikusamee
prey kweemun
price dee[4]
duushiru
nii[3]
sooba
pride duubumii
iji
jiman
myooga
ugui
priest booji
chooroo
jaashi
priestess nuru
chifijin
chinbee

prohibit

kaminchu
kudi
saadakatchu
ukudi
prime banji
primitive (age)
▸kubanufaayuu
prince wooji[2]
princess uminaibi
principal umudatchooru
print (photos) yachun
yakichikiin
priority sachi[1]
prison ruuya
privacy watakushi
watakushigutu
privately neenee[1]
privates haji[1]
privy fuuru
prize fuubi
probably uukata
yuusannee
proceed ichun
nkain
proceedings ubiigachi
proceeds uidaka
procession michijunee
proclamation yuu'utee
prodigal hootoomun
prodigy dikiyaa
produce 'njasun
produced ▸dikiin
producer chukuyaa
product ▸Uchinaamun
profile yukugau
profit *n.* ichi[5]
mooki
marumooki
tuku[2]
▸mookijuku
profit *v.* mookiin
profitable fichaain
profiting aramooki
profits rituku
profound fukasan
progress *n.* dachi
hattachi
hakaduin
progress *v.* habachun
agachun
again
atchun
prohibit sashitumiin

prohibition

prohibition **hattu**
project **mukurumi**
prolong **fichinubasun**
prolonged ▸**nagabichun**
promise *n.* **chijiri**
  mikumi
  yakusuku
promise *v.* **kajikakiin**
promote **fichitatiin**
  fichi'agiin
  tashikiin
  tuitatiin
promotion **tuitati**
prompt **gurusan**
proof **suuku**
prop **chikashi**
propagation **nashihirugi**
proper **ataimee**
  shinnu
properly **chantu**
property **jeesan**
proposal **sagui**
propose **ii'njasun**
  kuuin[2]
  muchikumun
  nujumun
proprietor **shujin**
propriety **riiji**[2]
prosper **dikasun**
  muteein
  sakeein
  ukusun
prosperity **haneechi**
  hanjoo
  hirugai
prosperous **fuchatoon**
  muteeisakeei
prostitute **feejuri**
  juri
  sara'utii
prostrate **uusari'aasarisun**
prostration **uusari'aasari**
protect **mamuin**
  kageein
  kagusamiin
protection **fushiji**[1]
  kakugu[2]
  kataka
  mamui
protrude **tunjiin**
proud **fukuras(h)an**
  ▸**hanafurachun**

▸**ibain**
▸**kuchibuuchaa**
▸**takabuin**
▸**uguin**
proverb **ikutuba**
provided ▸**sunawain**
providence **tin**[1]
provincial **inakanchu**
provincialism
  shimagunikunjoo
provisions **sunawai**
proxy **deeri**
prudent **chimugumasan**
  ▸**chimugumaa**
pry (into) **kujiin**
puberty **juushichihachi**
  tushiguru
public **yununaka**
  tchunumee
  umanchu
public office **yakusu**
publish **'njasun**
published ▸**'njiin**
puddle **tamai**
pull **hichun**[1]
  fichiyushiin
  hippain
  mushiin
  suguin
pull out **hichinujun**
pulse **myaku**
  naaku[2]
pumice **karashi**
pumpkin **chinkwa**
pun(ning) **kakikutuba**
pungent **yiigoosan**
punishment **bachi**[3]
  mukui
  shikkan
pupa **Tooyaamaa**
pupil **miinushin**
puppetry **chondaraa**
puppy **ingwaa**
purchase *n.* **sagai**[2]
  sagaigooi
purchase *v.* ▸**sagain**[1]
pure- m**a***adj.*-
purgative **sagigusui**
purge (the bowels)
  kudasun[1]
purification **haree**[1]
purify **chiyumiin**
  churaku nasun

purity **chirii**
  ▸**'nmarijimu**
purple **murasachi**
purpose **chimuyee**
  umumuchi
purposely **wajawaja**
purse **jin'irii**
  jinbukuru
  kinchaku
pursuit ▸**naga'uui**
pus **'nmi**[2]
push **usaasun**
  ushikiin
push (apart) **ushiwakiin**
push (away) **ushinukiin**
push (down) **ushitoosun**
push (in) **ushikumiin**
push (through)
  ushiwakiin
push (up) **uchagiin**
pushing ▸**meenainai**
put **'njasun**
  uchun[1]
put in **iriin**
put on **kanjun**
  kanshiin
  ▸**utchakiin**
put on (footwear) **kumun**[3]
put (upside-down)
  usubasun
puzzle **munu'akasee**
puzzled **jaama**
pygmy **gunatchugwaa**

Q———

quagmire **durugwettai**
quake **kugeein**
quantity **ikirasa'ufusa**
  ▸**mandoon**
quarrel **ooyee**
  ooyeetiiyee
  kuchigaayee
  miitunda'ooyee
  mundoo
  namikaji
  soodoo
quarter **shibu'ichi**
queen **woofi**
queerness **fuugawai**
question **fushin**[1]
question-and-answer
  ▸**ichaihanchai-sun**

quibble iimagiin
quick feesan
  tiibeesan
quickly feeku
  isuji
  kashikashi
quick-tempered
  chiibeesan
quiet nadayassan
  ufuyassan
quietness shijika
quilt uudu
  kanjimun
  tuku[4]
quilting chijaahajaa
quite yufudu
quotation sooba

R———
rabbit usaji
Rabbit uu[1]
race haarii
  agibaarii
  haayee
  haayeesuubu
  ▶jiibaarii
racetrack 'nma'wii
rack iikaa
radiant miihicharasan
radish deekuni
rafter kichi
rage *n.* rippuku
rage *v.* ariin
rags fukutaa
  kakkoo[1]
rain *n.* ami[1]
  amichibu
  hyaai'ami
  naga'ami
  shimukakiyaa
  tiida'ami
  ▶arachijaa'ami
  ▶attabui
  ▶chirachirabui
  ▶nagabui
  ▶nagashi'ami
  ▶shimu[2]
  ▶uchi'ami
  ▶ufu'ami
  ▶uu'ami
rain *v.* ▶fuchinchun
  ▶uchikumun

rainbow nuuji
raincoat kappa
  ▶nnu
  ▶surugaannuu
rainfall amifui
rainwater tinshii
rainy season suuman
  suumanboosuu
raise chikanain
  fudu'waasun
  karain
  kariin[1]
  shitatiin
  sudatiin
raise (up) muchagiin
  fichi'agiin
  ukusun
raised ▶muchagain
rake heekachaa
  maaga
  yachiba
Ram hichiji
ramie wuubee
ramification yudamuchi
randomly arinkurin
rank dan
  kuree
  mibun
  'wiidan
rape kaamii keesun
rapeseed oil maa'anda
rapid hakaraas(h)an
rapids shii[8]
rare marukeeti
rare (of meat) nama[1]
rarity mari
rascal jaafeemun
  njarimun
rash ashibu
  eegasa
  kajoora
  kajoorimun
rashness hayamaigutu
  namachi
rasp yashii
rat 'wenchu
Rat nii[5]
rate -bu
rates joonoo
rather ·yaka
  keetee
rather (than) tutin
rattan tuu[1]

rattling gatagata
rattrap hanchuuyaama
raven garasaa
ravine saku[1]
raw nama[1]
razor kansui
reach ichain
  neein[2.]
  'njasun
  nushikiin
reach (agreement)
  tujimain
read yumun
  yumikakiin
  yumituusun
read (aloud) yumi'agiin
readiness kakugu[1]
reading, writing, and
  arithmetic hissan[2]
ready too[1]
  ▶chimugakiin
  ▶kangeein
  ▶shiyoomuyoo
real funtoo
reality jintoo
realize satuin
really danju
  danjuka
  funnu
  nncha[1]
realm tinga
rear kushi[1]
  ura[2]
reason waki
  yui[2]
  baa
  basu
  doori
  iwari
  michi[1]
  rikuchi
  shidee[1]
  wachiyee
reasonable gumuttun
  muttumu
  ▶chichiwakiin
reasonableness
  chichiwaki
rebel sumuchun
rebellion mufun
  yashingutu
rebuke nurain
recall umui'atain

recall

recede

recede hiin[1]
receipt ukidui
 ukitui
receive kamiin
 nkeein
 shidiin
 ukiin[1]
 ukituin
recently chikaguru
 kuneeda
reception uchuuji
 ukichiki
 utuimuchi
recess nakayashimi
 nakayukui
recipe chukuikata
reciprocity utagee[2]
recitation hanashibuku
recite utain
 yumun
reckless ▸hatii
 ▸namachaa
recklessness namachi
reclaim seekiin[1]
 umitatiin
reclaimed land kinaa
 seekijii
reclamation kaikun
 seeki
recluse yaagumayaa
recognize miwakiin
 miishiin
 mitumiin
 wakain[1]
recoil hanchigeein
recollect ubi'njasun
recollection ubi[1]
recommend shishimiin
recommendation tuinashi
reconcile kukuin
 yafarakiin
reconciliation nakanooi
reconsider kangeein
 umiinoosun
reconstruct chukuikeein
record nushiin
recount ▸munugatai
recover nooin[3]
 chuuin
 muchinoosun
 noosun
 tuimudusun
recovery chuui

murunooi
red *n.* aka'iru
 akaa
 bin[1]
 ▸makkaaraa
red *v.* akasan
redhead akabusaa
 akagaa
 akagii
red-light district
 hananushima
reduce hinarasun
 ibamiin
re-dye feesun
reed fuduchi
reef faa'uri
 hishi
reel (in) taguin
reel *n.* kashi[2]
 kwan[2]
reel *v.* kuin
reference ukinin
refined chimudakasan
reflect uchusun[1]
reflect (on) kangeein
reflected ▸uchiin[2]
reflection kaagaa
 mijikaagaa
reform aratami
 noosun
refreshed ▸saajaatunain
 ▸tukutu
refrigerate hijurasun
refusal fugattin
 kutuwai
refuse kutuwain
refute iimakasun
regain tuikeesun
regard kangeein
 nnjun
regard (as) umuin
region tukuru
 -kata
register choomin
regress atumudui
regret *n.* jannin
 kuukwee
 kuyami
regret *v.* chimuyamun
 kuyamun
 yamun
regrettable duuguris(h)an
regulation tuishimari

reign *n.* ukakibusee
reign *v.* maruchun
 wusamiin
reincarnate 'nmarikaain
reins tanna
reject fuin[3]
 hanchun
 kutuwain
rejected ▸furariin
rejuvenate wakageein
relapse fuikeesun
relation kakawai
relations naka[2]
 dushibiree
relationship naaka[2]
relative eeka
 shinka
 tayui
relatives eekaharooji
 fichi[1]
 ichimun[2]
 tujikata
 ▸uchiwa[2]
relax kuchirujun
release hanasun[2]
 yurusun
released ▸nugaain
relief raku
relieve tashikiin
relieved ▸saajaatunain
remain nukuin
remainder amai
remainders uinukui
 uinukushi
remains naguri
remarriage matadumeei
 matamuchi
 mataniibichi
remedy *n.* kusui
 yoojoo
remedy *v.* noosun
remember ubi'njasun
 ubiin
 umuin
remembrance chimu'ubii
remove dukasun
 dukiin
 dukinasun
 shiikasun
 tuin
 utusun
removed ▸utiin
renewed ▸aratamain

rice

renovate chukuikeein
renovation chukuikee
rent n. jiganee
  kanee
  yachin
  yashichiganee
rent v. kain^1
rental ▸karashiyaa
rented ▸kaimun
repair n. kuu^2
  muchinashi
  tii'iri
repair v. noosun
  chijun^1
  chukuriin
repaired ▸nooin^3
repay ireein
  keesun
repayment finbin
  ukkabaree
  ungeeshi
repeat kuikeesun
  utcheehitchee-sun
repeatedly juujuu
  -keesaa
  kuikeeshigeeshi
  mata^1
  utcheehitchee
repeater kuikeesaa
rephrase iinoosun
replace irikeein
  kawain
reply hintoo
  ukihintoo
report tuduki
representation deeri
reprimand tugamiin
reprimanded ▸nuraariin
reproduce uchusun^1
reputation hyooban
  kuchishiba
request n. nigee
  tanumi
  unigee
request v. imiin
  tanumun^1
resemble niin^3
resented ▸uramariin
resentful ▸niitasa-sun
residence yashichi
residue nukui
resign akiramiin
  yamiin

resignation akirami
  umichiri
  yasunji
resin yani^1
  ▸maachinu'anda
resist fushijun
  gee-sun
resistance gee
  mufun
  tiinkee
resort 'wiirikidukuru
resources hatarachi
respect n. usuri
respect v. usuriin
  agamiin
  umunjiin
response iree
  ukihanshi
responsibility ▸tai^2
responsible mangatamii
  ▸fichi'ukiin
rest (in peace) ukabun
rest n. yashimi
  yukui^2
rest v. yashimain
  yashimiin^1
  yasunjiin
  yukuin
rest house yukuidukuru
restaurant sakanayaa
restless chimu'ichunasan
  ▸chimu'ashigachi-sun
restore ichigeerasun
  ichigeerasun
  noosun
restored ▸ichigeein
  ▸nooin^3
result hati
  kekkwa
  tami
retinue utumu
retire fichinain
  hikkumun
  yamiin
  yukuin
retract iimudusun
retreat n. atushijichi
  atushinchaa
retreat v. shiichun
retribution mukui
  tatai
  ▸kamidaari^1
return n. keei^1

  keeshi
  mudui
return v. keein^1
  keesun
  muduin
  mudusun
  ukuikeesun
reveal arawasun
  uchi'akiin
revealed bariin
revelation mishijiri
  ushirashi
revenge ada^1
  ▸uchun^2
revenue iridaka
  irifa
  irimee
reverence usuri
reverse n. ura^2
  urahara
reverse v. keein^2
  utcheein
reverse(d) saka^1
revive fuchikeesun
  muchinoosun
revived ▸ichigeein
revolt mufun
revolution migui
  yuugawai
revolve maain
  miguin
reward fuubi
  ireein
rewarded ▸mukuirariin
rhythm hyooshi
rib sooki^2
rice kumi^1
  mee^1
  'nni^1
  yuni
  awamee
  chiifan
  faagusari
  hanmee
  muchigumi
  mumi
  noogumi
  sakugumi
  ubun^1
  ▸akagumi
  ▸ara
  ▸jiimee
  ▸kashichi'i

rice
- ►kufamee
- ►kuukuumee
- ►manman
- ►matabee
- ►miimee²
- ►'nnabi
- ►nuumee
- ►shiragigumi
- ►ukkeemee

rice (grain) **ubunchiji**
rice ball **nijirimee**
  ubunnijirii
rice bowl **meemakai**
rice bran **nuka**
rice cake **muuchii**
  chikaramuuchii
  kaasamuuchi
  ►**fuchagi**
rice cooker **sanjurachi**
rich **dikitoon**
  ►**atta'weeki**
  ►**eekii**
  ►**eekinchu**
richness **eeki**
rickshaw **kuruma**
rickshaw puller
  kurumahichaa
riddle **akashimun**
  akasee
  munu'akasee
ride **nuin**²
  ►**ainui**
ridge **chiji**²
  iricha
ridicule *n.* **ajawaree**
ridicule *v.* **warain**
  wareekujiin
rifle **tippuu**
right **choodu**
right hand **njirintii**
righteousness **jii**⁵
right-minded
  ►**chimugawaimun**
rind **'waabigaa**
ring *n.* **ibai**
  iibinagii
  nii⁴
ring *v.* **nain**³
ringing **minnai**
ringworm **shirabee**
rinse **wuujun**¹
  yushijun
rip *n.* **yarisaki**

rip *v.* **fichisachun**
  sachun²
ripen **'nmun**
rise *n.* **nubui**
rise *v.* **mui'again**
  ukiin²
risky ►**hantigutu**
rite(s) **hooji**
  ukamigutu
  ►**wuimi**
Rites (agricultural)
  abushibaree
  chinahichi
  hachimujukui
  mushibaree
  ningwachi'umachii
  saataashiisuubi
  sangwachi'umachii
  shinugu
  tantui
  ushideeku
  ►**kaaminuhoogai**
Rites (ancestral)
  agarimaai
  anjikabi
  bun⁴
  eisaa
  gusoonu'uchukui
  hatasugashi
  itashikibara
  katachinumee
  shichigwachi
  shichigwachi
  juugunichi
  shichigwachi'eisaa
  sooroomiji
  unkee
  ushiimii
  usooroo
  usooroo'unkee
  usooroo'uukui
  uukui
  ►**manigutu**
  ►**muchimee**
  ►**ubuku**
  ►**uchatoo**
  ►**uchikabi**
  ►**uchikabi'uchaa**
Rites (birth)
  jiirushinchi
  kaa'urii
  mansan
  soojibari

ubagii
ubiinadii
ubuyu
►**ubugamimundoo**
►**ubukaa**
►**ubumiji**
Rites (birthday)
  hariyaku
  tookachi'uuwee
  tushibi
  ►**kajimayaa**
Rites (housing)
  muni'agi
  nni'agi
  tiindatii
  yaabarai
  yaafuchisuuji
Rites (funerary)
  churakunasun
  gireein
  hachinanka
  hakanugusuuji
  harujuukoo
  ichinanka
  mabuiwakashi
  minanka
  munanka
  naachamii
  nanananka
  nanka
  ninchi¹
  nujifa
  sanjuusanninchi
  shijuukunichi
  shindoo²
  shinkuchi
  shiruhirashi
  shiru'iifee
  shuukaawatainu
  wugami
  suugeeshi
  suukoo
  suunuhana
  tamayubai
  tananka
  tingee
  ufujuukoo
  uwaijuukoo
  wakajuukoo
  yaazaree
  yunanka
  ►**asajii**
  ►**kabi'anji**

- ►kabi'anjun
- ►karukunasun
- ►mabuigumi
- ►mabuinugi
- ►mabui'uui
- ►michikumaasun
- ►miigusoo
- ►muimee²

Rites (marriage)
- ubiinadii
- mijimui
- 'nmadima

Rites (offerings)
- hanagumi
- hanajaki
- muimee¹
- ubii
- unsaku
- usandee

Rites (paraphernalia)
- binshii
- butankoo
- fuushugami
- geen
- hana'ichi
- hijainaa
- juubaku
- yunooshi

Rites (seasonal)
- gungwachiyukka
- haarii
- hachigwachi juuguya
- hachika soogwachi
- hachi'ubiinadii
- hachi'unchi
- higan
- ichininchi
- isobaare
- kaamee
- mijinu shidigafuu
- muuchiiwuimi
- sangwachisannichi
- sangwachisannichii
- shimakusarashi
- tanabata
- unjami
- wakamiji
- yookabii
- yunui
- ►unchabi
- ►usagimuchi

Rites (other)
- choojika

fuuchinuwuuwee
hiidamageeshi
hiigeeshi
hoohai
izaihoo
joochijiri
juri'nma
kami'ashibi
shibasashi
shiishimooi
shijikamiin
shimamaai
tabisunugusuuji
utakabi
►binjuru
►hankinu ugwan
►hoohai muuchii
►hoohai utaki
►kanmichi
►munu'uui
►murawuganju
►muuchi
►niitchu
►niiya
►shuunuhana
►tunu
►usakati
ritual iiwee
river kaa²
kaara²
haikaa
kawa
nagarikaa
suukaa
►uugaara
riverside kaarabanta
road michi¹
mutumichi
ookwan
waitui
wooree
►fukajoo
►ichi'atai
roadside michibata
roast abuin
yakiin
rob nusumun
robber nusudu
robbery feeree
robe tanashi
rock *n.* ishi
iwa
buri

roughneck

shii⁵
rock *v.* kugeein
rocket hiitatii
rod buchi
chinbuku
rogue warumun
role yaku²
roll kurubasun
machun¹
yuttaikwattai-sun
roll (of cloth) tan
roll (of paper) machikabi
rolling guruguru
roof yaanu'wii
chiji²
dakibuchi
iricha
nni³
sashika
yaanuu
roof tile kaara¹
room jashichi
jaa²
ichibanja
meenuyaa
nakamee
sanbanja(a)
►irihana
►kucha¹
►nibanja
►ufu'ii
rooster tui
root *n.* nii¹
niigui
root *v.* niijichun
rope china
naa⁴
adan'ashi
sanninjina
warajina
►miinna
►surugaachina
rot kuchun
kusariin
►mijimaain
rotate maain
miguin
rotten ►itamun
►kusarimun
►mijimaayaa
rough ara²-
tii'arasan
roughneck shitatakamun

289

roughness

roughness **tugaifigai**
round **marusan**
  matteen
  ▸**marumun**[1]
  ▸**marumiin**
round-trip **ichimudui**
  woofuku
roundness **maru-**
route **michinaka**
  tuuimichi
row **kuujun**
rub **nashiin**
  mimijun
  mumun
  shiin[2]
rubber **gumu**
rubber ball **gumumaai**
rubbish **chiri**[3]
  gumi
rubella **irigasa**
rudder **kaji**[3]
rude **arasan**
  tii'arasan
rudeness **guburii**
ruin **furubasun**
ruined **saboorikaa**
  ▸**furubun**
  ▸**furubasariin**
  ▸**yachiriin**
rule *n.* **kani**[1]
  sadami
  yakusuku
rule *v.* **kageein**
  maruchun
rumbling **guruguru**
rumor **kuchishiba**
  sata
  tchunu kuchi
run **hain**[1]
  haayeegongon-sun
  'njuchun
run away **'njihangwi-sun**
run over **kwaasun**
running **haayee**
  issanbaayee
rural **inaka**
rush **yii**[2]
  Biiguyii
  sachiyii
rust *n.* **sabi**
rust *v.* **sabikuuin**
rustic **inakaa**
rut (for animals) **kurii**

ruthless ▸**chikushoomun**
rye **hadakamuji**
  ufumujaa
Ryukyu(s) **Ruuchuu**
  ▸**Uruma**
  ▸**Urumajima**

S———

sachet **choojibukuru**
sack **fukuru**
  taara
  ▸**shimiraara**
sacred place **ugwanju**
  wuganju
sacrifice *n.* **migawai**
sacrifice *v.* **usagiin**
sad **nachikas(h)an**
saddle **kura**[2]
  hara'uubi
sadness **umuiyamii**
safety **buji**
saffron **kuukwa**
sail **fuu**[3]
  ▸**mafu**
sailor **funaku**
  funanui
  kaku[1]
  umi'atchaa
saint ▸**shiidu**
sake **saki**
  kuusu
sake lees **kashijee**
sake vessel **karakaraa**
salable ▸**uriin**[2]
salad **eeyaa**
salary **jitchuu**
sales **uidaka**
saliva **chunpee**
  kuchishiru
  yudai
salt **maasu**
salt field **suuhama**
salty **suujuusan**
salve **kooyaku**
same **-tuui**
  yunu-
sameness **tiichimun**
sample **mifun**
sand **yuni**
  niri[2]
  shinaganiku
  shirushina

uru
sandal **saba**[1]
  waraji
  warasaba
sandals **adanbaasaba**
  dakigaasaba
sandbox **shinaba**
sandstone **niibi**
sandwiched ▸**hasamariin**
sanshin **sanshin**
  jahibai
  sanba[2]
  shibubai
  ▸**chiiga**[3]
  ▸**miijiru**
  ▸**nakajiru**
sapling **nee**[2]
  wakagi
sardine **dashi'iyugwaa**
  mijun
sash **uubi**
  ufu'uubi
  ▸**fusu'uubi**
  ▸**minsaa**
  ▸**minsaa'uubi**
sashimi **sashimi**
sassy ▸**kusamunaa**
satin **dunsu**
  ▸**rinsu**
satisfied ▸**michun**
sauce **dashi**
saucer **chataku**
  gumakee'uchi
save **sukuin**[1]
  tamiin[1]
  tashikiin
savior ▸**nuchinu'uya**
savory **kuchinooshi**
saw **nukujiri**
  ▸**arabaa**
  ▸**kumaba**
sawdust **kiikashi**
say **'yun**
  iikkwain
  unnukiin
saying **kuchigushi**
scab **kasa**[2]
  kasabuta
  shishikweegasa
scabies **heegasa**
  kooshi[1]
  ▸**koosaa**[2]
scalded **yuugeesun**

selfishness

scale (measure) hakai
▸mii¹
scale (of fish) irichi
scallion datchoo
scapegoat migawai
scar chimikata
　furukiji
　▸kanpachaa
scarce ikirasan
　▸teein
scare udaasun
scarecrow kakashi
　naashirumabui
scatter chirasun
　chirakasun
　chiriin²
　hooin
　kachihooin
　machun³
　tuichirakasun
scattering naahaibai
scatteringly naachirijiri
scene hakaguchi
scheme takumun
scholar gakusha
school gakkoo
scissors hasan
scold akku-sun
　nurain
　nuraitakkwasun
　shichikiin
　udaasun
scolded ▸nuraariin
scolding ▸mii¹
scoop kumun¹
　sukuin²
scorch kugarasun
　▸niikugasun
scorn miisagiin
scorpion yamankaji
scowl at miifichain
scramble baakee
scratch *n.* chimikata
scratch *v.* kachun²
　kachamun
　sakuin
scream *n.* nachigwii¹
　▸kajichiri'abii
scream *v.* magi'abiisun
screen *n.* akai
　hinpun
　noobu
　sooji²

screen *v.* hidatiin
screw niji
　nijiri
scripture chuumun¹
scroll kakijiku
　kakimun
scrotum fugui
scrounge (for) asain
scrub susuin
scrubbing ▸mijishigutu
scruff ushiru²
　▸ushirukubu
sculpture fuimun
sea 'nmi¹
　▸fuka'umi
　▸nada²
　▸nishinu'umi
　▸uchi'umi
　▸uutu
sea breeze umikaji
sea cucumber shichiraa
sea urchin gachichaa
seacoast ura¹
seahorse umi'nmagwaa
seal han
　in²
　fuu'in
　waiban
　▸yama'in²
seam nooimii
seaman funaku
　funanui
search sageesun
　tajiniin
　tumeein
search (for) asaguin
searching tumeeidumeei
seas namikaji
seashore haama
　umibata
seasick ▸funeei-sun
seasickness funawii
　funeei
　fuunee
season jibun
　jishichi
　wui
season (wood) karasun²
seasoning anbee
　kagin
seasons shichi⁵
Seasons
　boosuu

shiimii
suuman
suumanboosuu
urijin
ushii
seat jaa²
　zaa
seaway funamichi
seaweed kuubu
　muu
　sunui
seclude (oneself)
　▸kumain¹
second niban
　takeenmii
　▸utuin
second floor niikee
secondhand ▸furumun
secret kakushigutu
　kwakkushigutu
　ushiikugani
secretly neenee¹
sediment guri
　iifu
seduce mayaasun
seduced ▸hikasariin
　▸mayaasariin
see nnjun
　nagamiin
　wugamun
　▸miiin¹
seed sani
　mii³
　nai²
seedling nee²
　▸meedani
seem miiin¹
　-raas(h)an
　umaariin
seldom ▸mari
select irabun
selection nujigachi
self duu
　gaa¹
self-amused
　duuchuiwaree
self-defense ▸karati
self-flattery duubumii
self-importance
　duu'agami
self-indulgence fundee
selfish wagamama
selfishness chimama

291

self-respect

duugatti
jimama
katti[1]
self-respect **duu'uyamee**
self-support **duu'agachi**
  duumakanee
sell **uin**
  sabachun[3]
  shiti'ui-sun
  uisabachun
  yujiin
sell (off) **uitubasun**
sell (on credit) ▸**sagain**[1]
semi- **nakaba**
send **'njasun**
  chikain[1]
  ukuin[1]
  yarasun
send (back) **keerasun**
send (message) **tujikiin**
send-off **funa'ukui**
  ▸**mi'ukui**
senile ▸**kanihandiin**
senility **rooma**
  tusuiyooi
senior **tushishiija**
  tusui
sense **funbichi**
sensible **muttumu**
sentiment **umii**
  umui[1]
sentimental **nadayoosan**
separate **fichihanasun**
  hijamiin
  wakariin
  wakiin
separated ▸**akariin**
separately **ichi'ichi**
separation ▸**ichiwakari**
September **kugwachi**
sequel **chijichi**
sequence **maaru**
serious **chamishika**
  chuusan
  'nburaasan
seriously **tukutu**
servant **chikeemun**
  naagu
  shimubatarachi
serve **chitumiin**
  hirain
  iriin
  'njasun
service **guyuu**
  ▸**uutigara**
sesame **shiruguma**
sesame (seed) **uguma**
sesame oil **uguma'anda**
set *n*. **chii**[4]
  chukusai
  guutumiitu
  kumi[3]
set *v*. **chikiin**[1]
  shikiin
  utiin
setback **kitchaki**
setting sun **sagaitiida**
settle **sabachun**[2]
settle (down) **utichichun**
settle (in) **yaajichun**
seven **nanachi**
  shichi[2]
seventeen **juushichi**
severally **naachirijiri**
severe **chuujuuku**
severity **sanjan**
sew **nooin**[1]
sewing **kumanooi**
  nooimun
  ▸**aranooi**
shack **gumayaa**
  anayaa
shade **kaagi**
shadow **kaagaa**
shaft **jiku**
  shinboo
shake **fuin**[3]
  furiin[1]
  futufutuu-sun
  'njuchun
  wuuin[2]
shaking **gatagata**
shaking head ▸**kaabuyaa**[2]
shaky ▸**furafuraa-sun**
shall **haji**[2]
shallow *adj*. **assan**
  asasan
shallow *n*. **gata**
shallows **inoo**
shaman **yuta**
shambles **tutunba**
shame **akahaji**
  haji[1]
  miiwaku
shamed ▸**kachun**[2]
shameful **duuguris(h)an**

shameless ▸**hajichiraa**
  ▸**namajirawaree**
shamelessness **namajira**
shank **shini**
shape **kakkoo**[2]
shapelessness **bukakkoo**
share **ichininmee**[1]
  muchimee
  waimee
  wakimee
sharecrop **kanee-sun**
shark **fuka**[1]
  saba[2]
sharp ▸**chiriin**[1]
sharpen **feesun**
  tujun
sharp-tongued
  kuchiyagamas(h)an
  ▸**kuchigansui**
shatter **kudachun**
shattered ▸**kudakiin**
shattering ▸**pachin**
shave **suin**
shave (off) **hijun**
  kusajun
shavings **kanakudii**
she **anchu**
  ama
  ari[1]
  'nma[2]
  unchu
  uri[1]
shears ▸**ufubasan**
sheath **dakinukaa**
  shii[2]
shed **ndigara**
sheep **meenaa**
sheet **ita**
shelf **tana**[1]
  hijana
shell (conch) **bura**
shell (husk) **kara**[3]
  gara[1]
shell (turtle) **kaaminakuu**
Shellfish
  ajikee
  buragee
  moomoo[2]
  sajee
  shibimoomoo
  yakugee
shelter **kakureyaa**
  kataka

▸amayadui
shield hidatiin
hijamiin
shift noosun
shiikiin
shin karashini
shine fichain
tiin¹
shiny ▸fichain
ship *n.* funi¹
 fuushin
 haifuni
 ▸maaran
 ▸ufubuni
 ▸uyabuni
ship *v.* chimikumun
shipping funabin
 mukoobaree
shipwright funadeeku
shipyard suraba
shitter kusumayaa
shiver futufutuu-sun
 shishiburii-sun
shivering gatagata
shoal inoo
 suubata
shoe kuchu
 kaagutsu
 ▸fuya²
shoo shii⁶
shoot *n.* miruri
shoot *v.* iin²
 uchun²
shop machiya
 sakimachiya
shopping kooimun
shore agi
 haama
 suuguchi
short chichasan
 chikasan
 haganasan
 inchasan
 ▸inchaa
 ▸inchoo
 ▸shippiraa
shortage fugi
 fusuku
shortcut chikamichi
 kunchirimichi
 ▸kunchiin
shorten chijimiin
 inchakunasun

shortened ▸chijimain
shorty fudugumaa
should haji²
shoulder kata³
shoulder blade katabuni
shoulder-breadth
 katahaba
shout *n.* abiisuubu
 yagwii
shout *v.* abiin
 magi'abiisun
show (how to) naraasun
show *n.* mishimun
show (signs) ▸muyuusun
show *v.* mishiin
 miiin¹
 umikakiin
shower amaguri
showy akarakwaara
shrimp ibi¹
 seegwaa
 tanagee
shrine miya
 ugan¹
 kami'ashagi
shrink chijimun
 chijimagain
shriveled ▸kaahain
 ▸kurushibiriin
shrubbery niwagi
Shuri Shui
shut michiin¹
 shimiin³
shuttle fijichi
shy chimugumasan
 chimuguusan
 chira'afasan
 hajikas(h)an
 ▸chimuguumun
sibling niinii
 ▸uttu
siblings choodee
 haratiichi
 harawakai
 uttushiija
 utujanda
 wunaiwikii
 ▸uttukata
sick anmas(h)an
 yamiwacharee
sicken takichikiin
sickle irana
 irara

kama¹
sickly duuyafarasan
sickness yanmee
side hata¹
 -kata
 kata¹
 muti¹
 suba²
 yuku²
side dish sakana
sidelocks binta
sides ▸roohoo
sidesaddle subanui
sideways yukubai
sieve yui⁴
sigh ▸ufu'iichi
sight nagami
sightsee nnjun
sightseeing chinbuchi
sign eeji
 muyuushi
 shirushi
 yaaban
 yooshi²
signal eeji
silence gubusata
 mugun
silent ▸damain
silhouette yukugau
silk ichu
 iichu
 dunsu
 itu
 itumun
 ▸rinsu
silkworm itumushi
 kaigu
silkworm gut tigusu
silliness gudun
silver gin
 nanja
silversmith chingushi
 kuganijeeku
similar gutoon
similarly yunugutu
simple shibusan
 tada¹
 ▸duuyashii
 ▸mattoobaa
 ▸raku
simplicity kumeeki
simplified ▸chijimain
simplify chijimiin

simulation

simulation **najiki**
since then **urikara**
sincerely **juujuu**
sincerity **makutu**
sinewy ▸**kajaa**
sing **utain**
　fukiin¹
　▸**feesun**
singer **utayaa**
　uta'utayaa
　utasaa
singing ▸**jii'utee**
singly **ichi'ichi**
sink *n.* **mintana**
sink *v.* **shijimun**
sip *n.* **chukuchi**
sip *v.* **shishiin**²
sister **'nmii**
　'nnmii
　abaa
　angwaa
　neenee²
　shiijawunai
　ufu'nmii
　uminai
　winagu'uttu
　wunai
　▸**umi'uttu**
　▸**umishiija**
sister-in-law **wunaishitu**
sisters-in-law **eejenda**
sit **yiin**
　hirakiin¹
　▸**hiraku nain**
　▸**hisamanchi**
sitting **tankaayii**
　yiitcha
　▸**maaruuyii**
situation **baa**
　jijoo
　mii¹
six **muuchi**
　ruku
sixty **rukujuu**¹
skein **kashi**²
skeleton **funi**²
　karafuni
skepticism **mayui**
skewer **guushi**
skill **tii**¹
　tiinu'uchi
　tiikagin
　tinami

skillfulness **tiguma**
skim **fukasun**²
skin **hada**
　kaa¹
　'waabigaa
　▸**kaahain**
skirt **kakan**
　hooikakan
skirt (an issue)
　yukumunu'ii-sun
skull **karachiburu**
sky **tin**¹
　akeein
slackness **gooruu**
slag **kanikusu**
slander **kijun**
　sushiin
　sushiri
slate **ishiban**
slaughterhouse
　'waasaayaa
　tutunba
sledge **shiibu**
sleep **ninjun**
　nindariin
　ninrariin
　ninshiin
　▸**ninjibusuku**
　▸**ninshitoochun**
sleeper **miikufayaa**
sleepiness **niibui**
　niibuikaabui
sleeping ▸**asani**
　▸**ninnin**²
　▸**yoogaaninji**
sleep-talking ▸**nigutu**
sleepyhead **asanaa**
　asannaa
　niibuyaa
sleeve **sudi**
slender **uroosan**
slide **shindiin**
slight **kunasun**
　miisagiin
slim ▸**yoogarimun**
slingshot **gomukan**
slip **nugiin**
　shindakasun
　shindiin
　▸**mainugasun**
slippery **nandurusan**
　▸**nanduruu**
　▸**nandurumun**

slob **kachihooyaa**
slope **hira**²
　saka²
　katanchi
　takabira
slouch **daraa**
slough **shidigara**
　shirigara
slow **niisan**
　tiiniisan
　▸**kuchi'nbusan**
slowly **niiku**
　yonnaa
　yuuyuutu
slow-witted **turusan**
slug **andamusaa**
　namimusaa
slut **amasaa**
small **gumasan**
　ibasan
　fuduguusan
　▸**gumaa**
　▸**ibamii**
smallpox **churagasa**
smart **hashiraas(h)an**
smash **kudachun**
　wain
smell **kaja**
　niwui
　yanakaja
　▸**mijikaja**
smile *n.* **waree**
　hanawaree
　miiwaree
　njawaree
　wareekanjun
　▸**nachiwaree**
　▸**shikawaree**
　▸**usuwaree**
smile *v.* **warain**
smirk **chukuiwaree**
smith **kanjaa**
smoke *n.* **kibushi**
smoke (tobacco) **fuchun**²
　numun
smoke *v.* **kibuin**
smoking **paakuu**
smoky **kibusan**
　▸**kibuin**
smoldering **kibusan**
smooth **nandurusan**
snack **ashii**
　kooingwee

yaasanooshi
yunakamun
yurujinamun
snail chinnan
namimusaa
taanna
snail fight chinnan'oorasee
snake jaa¹
habu¹
irabuu
oonajaa
▸akamataa
▸nagamun
Snake mii²
snap hanchun
snap at kankuuin
snatching yukudui
sneer namawaree
saawaree
waree
sneeze hiin²
snivel hanadai
hanashiru
sniveler hanadayaa
snob chiidakamun
taka'uchaagaa
unbuyaa
'waachaa
snore fuchun¹
hanafuchun
snot hanakusu
snout hana³
so an²
anee
kan³
kankan¹
▸an-sun
so much usakii
soak chikiin²
uraakiin
soaked ▸chikain³
soap safun
sobbing miinadasoosoo
▸nachigeegee
sober samiin¹
sociability eesoo¹
sociable ▸eesoomuchi
society shikin
yununaka
yuu²
socks taabi
sod mappaa

soda anchoo
sofa iisu
soft yafarasan
▸raku
▸takkwaimukkwai-sun
soften yafarachun
yafarakiin
softly yafatteen
soil jii¹
kucha³
nncha²
▸jaagaru
▸maaji
▸shinaganiku
sojourner chiruunin
kiryuu
sold out shinajiri
soldier hiitai
sole tada¹
sole (of foot) hisanuwata
solely muppara
solid kufasan
solidify katamiin¹
kufamiin
soliloquy chirani
duuchuimunu'ii
solitary sabisan
solstice (summer) kaachii
solstice (winter) tunjii
solve ireein
katajikiin
someday ichika
somehow chaagana
doodin
someone taa²
taagana
sometimes tuchiduchi
somewhere maagana
son wikigangwa
chakushi
choonan
jinan
sannan
yunan
▸chuiwikigangwa
▸gunan
▸ichukuwiikkwa
song uta
fa'uta
yui'uta
songs ▸ayoo
▸kweena
son-in-law muuku

▸irimuuku
soon chaaki
feeku
nama²
tadeema
tatta
yagati
▸chichasan
▸feesan
▸kunu'uchi
sooner (than) tutin
soot shiishi²
soothe nadamiin
sorcerer ichijama
ichijamaa
sorcery ichijama
sore ▸hagiin
sorrow awari
shiwagutu
urii²
uriigutu
sorrowful nachikas(h)an
sorry ichasan
chimu'ichasan
▸chimuyamun
▸kuyamun
sort iru
sort out sabachun¹
soul chii⁵
chimu
chimukukuru
mabui
▸mandamashi
sound *n.* utu
fibichi
nii⁴
▸pon
sound *v.* fibichun
nain³
▸mikasun
soup shiimun²
ushiru¹
▸ashitibichi
▸kaagaanushiru
▸'nmuwakashii
▸nnashiru
▸nnsunushiru
▸sabijiru
▸shiishinushiru
▸suushiru
source mutu
south fee³
mafee

southerly

▸nanban
southerly **feenkee**
souvenir **chitu**
 naagi
 naagimun
sow *n*. **ahyaa**
 ahyaa'waa
sow *v*. **machun**[3]
 urusun
sowing **tantui**
soy sauce **sooyuu**
soybean **maami**
 toofumaami
 ufuchijaa
soybean meal **mamikashii**
space **eeda**
 eeja
 eema[1]
 'weeda
spacious **firubiruu**
 ▸**yuchisan**
spade **kwee**[1]
spare **'waabamun**
spare time **katatima**
spark **fibana**
sparklingly **chirachira**
sparrow **kuraa**
spatula **hiira**
 iifuyaa
speak **'yun**
 hanasun[1]
speaker ▸**munu'iijooji**
spear **yai**
special **bichidannu**
specimen **mifun**
speech **chichigutu**
 yutamunu'ii
speed up **hayamiin**
speedy **hakaraas(h)an**
spend **akasun**[2]
 chikain[1]
spendthrift **sookibaaki**
sperm **sani**
 subi[1]
sphere **kagee**
spherical **marusan**
spicy **karasan**
spider **kuubaa**
spill **ikkeerasun**
 ikkeeriin
 nagasun
spin **maain**
 miguin

spinach **fuurinnaa**
 unchee
spindle **chimi**
 jiku
spindrift **suubana**
spinning wheel **yaama**
spinster **duuchuimun**
spinsterhood **chuigurashi**
spirit **chii**[5]
 chimu
 chimugukuru
 chimukukuru
 futuki
 ichimabui
 ichui
 jishii
 kijimun
 kukuru
 mabui
 shinimabui
 shii[1]
 tamashii
 ▸**ininbii**
 ▸**nurugami**
spirit possession
 kamidaari[2]
spirits **usooroo**
spit *n*. **guushi**
spit *v*. **hachun**[1]
spite **duku**[1]
spitting ▸**pee**
spittle **chunpee**
splash **kakain**
 kunchakiin
 mijihaniin
 tun(u)jun
splashing **mijihaniyee**
splice **chijaasun**
splinter *n*. **kiijiri**
 nji
splinter *v*. **sugiin**
split *n*. **warimi**
split *v*. **aakiin**
 fichisachun
 wariin
spoil **shiiin**[1]
spoiled ▸**ameein**
 ▸**kusarimun**
sponge **umimayaa**
spontaneously **ubijini**
spoon **kee**[1]
sporadically
 tukurudukuru

sport **ashibi**
sprawl **nagabooi**
spread **hain**[2]
 hirugiin
 maain
 nashiin
 shichun[1]
spread out **habakain**
spring (metal) **bani**
spring (season) **haru**[1]
spring *v*. **hanchigeein**
 haniin
spring (water) **hiijaa**[2]
 ijun
 ▸**kuragaa**[1]
springwater **wachimiji**
sprinkle **hooin**
 kakiin[1]
 machun[3]
sprout *n*. **miduri**
 miruri
sprout *v*. **mii'njiin**
spy **shinubi**
spy (on) **saguin**
 ukagain
squall **amaguri**
 nagashi'ami
square **kaku**
 mashikaku
 shikaku
 ▸**ashibinaa**
squash **chinkwa**
squat **chibitachuuyii**
squatting **nmoo**
squeak **gishigishii-sun**
squeal **moosagi-sun**
squeeze **shibuin**
squid **icha**[2]
 tubi'ichaa
squint **soomi-sun**
stab **chichi**[3]
 nuchikurusun
 sashikurusun
stable **'nmanuyaa**
 ushinuyaa
stack **chimun**[1]
 chimi'agiin
 majimun[2]
stage **banku**
 butee
stagnate **tudukuuin**
 turumun
 yudumun

yudumiin
stagnation fumigui
yuudu
stain *n.* shimi⁴
yuguri
stain *v.* yugusun
stair dan
stairs hashi
stairwell kijai
stake kiiji
kwii²
stale wassan
▸fumichun
▸shiimun¹
stalk funi²
guchi¹
muji³
stamen wuubana
stamina muchidee
stammer anuukunuu-sun
turumun
stammerer 'njanaa
stammering 'njani
stamp han
in²
stand *n.* dee²
kaiya
▸meejiku
stand *v.* tachun¹
tatiin
▸hisadaakaa-sun
stand erect 'waaiin
stand out uchitachun
umudachun
standard hinagata
nami²
standing taatcha
standpoint mii¹
tachifa
star fushi¹
▸akachichibushi
starch kuji³
kuju¹
'nmukuji
nui
stare guruguru-sun
miichikiin¹
miiguruguruu-sun
nagamiin
nnjun
stars buribushi
start (a fight) tii neein
start *n.* hajimai

hajimi
hakaguchi
start *v.* hajimain
hajimiin
hakaguchi'akiin
▸'njiin
starting 'njitachi
starvation wugari
yaasajini
starve wugariin
wugariin
yaasashimiin
starveling wugarimun
state yooshi²
▸muyoo
stature fudu
status bun²
mibun
takibun
stave kuri¹
stay tumain
akiin¹
nukuin
wun¹
yudumun
▸ninshitoochun
steal nusumun
keetuin
tuin
steam *n.* achiki
fuki
steam *v.* 'nbusun
steamed ▸'nburiin
steamer sheeroo
steamer (box) kushichi¹
steel hagani
steering kajitui
steering wheel kaji³
stem funi²
guchi¹
step chuhisa
dan
kii'nma
kudami
kurami
michi¹
step- mama-
step(s) ▸awatibai
stepbrother
mamachoodee
stepchild mamakkwa
stepparent mama'uya
stepsister mamachoodee

stern chira
matumu
tumu¹
steward ▸tunchi
stick *n.* boo
guushi
▸bachi¹
▸bui
▸jinboo
stick *v.* chichun⁴
hitchikiin
mutchakain
tatchikiin
stick out 'njasun
'njiin
sticky muchisan
▸muchamucha-sun
stiff katasan
stiffen katamiin¹
stiffness chiihai
nii¹
still maada
stilts kiibisa
sting sasariin
stingy ▸ibiriin
stinking kusasan
stir kachaasun
kijun
'njuchun
stirrups abui
stitch *n.* nooimii
stitch *v.* nooin¹
stock habu²
stoker shiijoosaa
stomach ii⁶
wata³
fii⁶
▸nniguchi
stone ishi
▸kucha²
stool kushikaki
stoop kagamain
stop kanageein
nain¹
nubagain
tumain
tumiin
yamiin
yukuin
stop (up) kuusun²
stopgap chuteenu hanshi
store *n.* machiya
ufumachiya

store
▸ashijaayaa
▸machiyagwaa
▸magimachiya
▸nuimunyaa
store *v.* kajimifukasun
▸kajimiin
storehouse kura[1]
kumigura
storeroom meenuyaa
storm ufukaji
uukaji
story hanashi
munugatai
stout chimujuusan
stow chimikumun
stow (away) katajikiin
straddle kunpain
straight mamukoo
mattooba
strain hatarachikwaa
straining ▸ninjichigee
strait tuu[3]
strange fin
fushiji[2]
hirumas(h)an
ifuuna
saita
strangeness fushiji[2]
fuugawai
stranger shiranchu
tanin
strangle shimikurusun
strap hanawuu
strategy hakarigutu
straw kaya
munjuru
wara
stray yukubai-sun
stream *n.* kaara[2]
stream *v.* nabichun
street wooree
▸uuduui
streetwalker feejuri
strength chikara
tee[1]
ganjuu
tamashi[1]
udijikara
strengthen chuuin
chuumain
chuumiin
stretch hippain
neein[2]

strew chirasun
stride gongon
strike tatachun
string chiru[1]
strip *n.* chiri[2]
strip *v.* hagasun
stripe aya
strive hamain
umiihamain
striving wankarawankara
strong chuusan
chuujuuku
ganjuugisan
kuusan
▸chuubaa
▸ganjuumun
▸kanain
strongly chujuuku
chuuku
strongman chikaraa
strong-minded chiijuusan
strong-tasting ajiraas(h)an
structure kamee
struggle pattarugeeyaa-sun
tiinkee
stubborn gaajuusan
▸boochiraa
▸gaajuu
▸kaagufaa
stuck hamain
stud chikiyaa'nma
student gakushii
shiitu
▸dikirannuu
▸dikiyaa
studies gakumun
study *n.* binchoo
shimi[1]
tishimigakumun
study *v.* narain
stumble kitchaki-sun
kurubun
stupid bakaraas(h)an
ushisan
stupidity gudun
uruka
stutterer 'njanaa
stuttering 'njani
sty mii'indee
miibuu
mindee
style kamee

stylish haikaraa
▸haikaraa
subdue nabikasun
subject dee[1]
sublease matagashi
submerged ▸chirugain
submissive chumama
submit kubiwuuriin
subscribe tuin
subsist (on) kamun
subsistence kurashi
substance mii[3]
nakami
substitute *n.* migawai
substitute *v.* irikeein
subtract hichun[1]
succeed atiin
chijun[1]
dikasun
dikiin
success dikashi
hanjoo
risshin
succession fichichiji
maaru
successor atuchiji
such angutooru
anneeru
kankan[1]
kungutooru
ungutooru
suck suuin
kukumun
shippuin
suui'njasun
suddenly attani
tachimachi
suddenness atta-
sue hiruu-sun
uttai-sun
utteein
suffer abaichiriin
bachikanjun
kamirariin
kumain[2]
nijiin[1]
ukiin[1]
suffer (from) yamun
suffer (loss) udukiin
suffering kuchisa
nanji
nanjikunji
shiira

suffice tariin[3]
sufficient ▸ninjunu-
  sunawai
  ▸shimun[1]
suffocation iichimadii
sugar saataa
  kurujaataa
  saataananjichaa
  shirujaataa
  teehaku
  zarami
sugar cane wuuji
  saataawuuji
  yanishiiyo
suggest ii'njasun
suit (clothing) 'waaji
  chukusai
suit (legal) uttai
suitable ▸uchain
suitor kuuyaa
sulfur yuuwaa
sulk hin-sun
sultry ▸'nburiin
sum ▸jindaka
summary nujigachi
summer nachi
  ▸nachiguchi
summit 'wii
  chiji[2]
  nni[2]
  yamanuchiji
summon yubun
  yubiyushiin
sun tiida
  fii[4]
  irihi
  utintuu
  ▸agaitiida
  ▸akatiida
  ▸utintuuganashii
sunburn hiyaki
  ▸yakiin
sun-dried fibushi
sundries gumamun
sunset akanaa
  yukkwasun
sunset (colors)
  yusandi'akeei
sunshine fii[4]
superior ▸masain
  ▸tachimasain
superiority jootoo
  masai

tchumasai
supervise kagusamiin
  tuishimain
supervision tuishimari
supper yuuban
supplement tashi
supplication amagui
supply n. wappu
supply v. kwiin
  tareein
support n. chikara
  chikashi
  kaashii
  yakkee
support (oneself) kurasun
support v. fichitatiin
  tamuchun
  tashikiin
  yashinain
suppress chijiin
suppressed ▸usaariin
surely kannaaji
  shikatu
surf nami[1]
surface 'waabi
  umuti
surgeon isa
surname myooji
  yaannaa
surpass kwiiin
  masain
surplus amaimun[1]
  nukui
  yuchifa
surprise udurukasun
surprised ▸awatiin
  ▸uduruchun
surrender n. wabi
surrender v. hichiwatasun
  kubiwuuriin
surroundings maai[2]
survey chinbun
survive ichinukuin
suspect kangeein
suspicion fushin[1]
sutra chuumun[1]
swallow (bird) mattaraa
swallow v. numikumun
  numun
swallowing ▸mannun
swap kuikeein
sway 'njuchun
  yutamichun

syphilis

sweat ashi[1]
  ashimiji
sweep hoochun
sweeping hoochikachi
sweet amasan
  chimuganas(h)an
sweet and sour
  shiisa'amasaa
sweet potato 'nmu
  gungwachaa
  tumaikuruu
  ▸'nmukashi
  ▸'nmunii
  ▸irimusaa
  ▸kuragaa[2]
sweetheart kanashii
  mutubiree
  ninguru
  nzo
  uminzo
  umisatu
  umuyaa
  umuyaagwaa
  winagu
  ▸iibingwaa
  amami[1]
sweets amamun
  kwaashi
  ▸miikufayaa
swell fukkwiin
  muchun[2]
  mui'again
swelling guufu
  uubu
  chiibukki
  gaanaa[1]
swim 'wiijun
swineherd 'waakarayaa
swing n. indaagii
swing v. fuin[3]
  'njuchun
swollen ▸mukumun
sword katana
  tachi[1]
syllabary kana[2]
sympathy joo[2]
  miimee[1]
  nasaki
  shinasaki
syphilis naabaru
  nabangasa
  nanbangasa
  ▸nabaraa

syphilitic

syphilitic **furutchu**
syrup **miji'ami**
  saataayuu

T———

tab **kanjoo**
table **dee**[2]
  taka'ujin
  ujin
  ▸**charagu**
  ▸**jin**[1]
tablet **iifee**
  ▸**riijin**
tablets ▸**nnatootoomee**
tableware **makaidoogu**
taboo **chiree**
  chireemun
  deechiree
  hattu
  san[3]
  ▸**ichukukasabai**
  ▸**munjiree**
taciturn ▸**kuchi'nbuu**
  ▸**'nmunukuchi**
tactful ▸**kanamijooji**
  ▸**tankiin**
tadpole **aataabiinukkwa aminaa**
taffy **appurigwaa**
tag **fuda**
  niifuda
tail **juu**[1]
tailor (shop) **yoofukuyaa**
tail-wagging ▸**juufui**
tailwind **junpuu**
  matumu
  tumukaji
take **hichituin**
  'njasun
  nushiin
  tuin
take (a test) **ukiin**[1]
take (back) **tuikeesun**
  tuimudusun
take (cost) **kakain**
take (down) **urusun**
take along **mutchi'ichun**
take apart **wakkwasun**
take care **wandain**
take charge **ajikain**
  ukimuchun
take off **tubitachun**

tale **munugatai**
  nkashibanashi
  iichitee
talent **jinbun**
  ▸**jiinuumuchi**
talents **takibun**
tale-telling **moosagi**
talisman **fuufuda**
  keeshi
talk *n.* **hanashi**
  furiyuntaku
  munugatai
talk *v.* **'yun**
  hanasun[1]
  munuyumun
  ▸**ihii'ahaa-sun**
talkative **kuchigassan**
talker ▸**kuchibinsaa**
tall **takasan**
  ▸**takaa**
tally **fichi'ati**
tambourine **teeku**
tamper **mutabun**
tan **hiyaki**
tangerine **mikan**
tangled ▸**machibuin**
  ▸**machibuikaabui-sun**
tank **mijigura**
tannin **shibu**
tapioca **kii'nmu**
tardy **nikka**
  ▸**mutchoohitchoo-sun**
target **matu**
taro **'nbashi**
  chinnuku
  miji'nmu
  taa'nmu
tarry **yurariin**
tart **shiisan**
tartar **haakusu**
task **wain**
tassel **fusa**
taste *n.* **aji**[1]
  tashinami
taste *v.* **aji-sun**
  namiin
  numun
taste(s) **chimu**
  ▸**shichibushichi**
tasty **maasan**
tatters **fukutaa**
tattler **abasaa**
  koojinaa

tattling **koojin**
tattooing **hajichi**
taught ▸**narain**
tax **joonoo**
  kanee
  yashichiganee
  zaikin
tea **chaa**[3]
  ucha
  shiimiichaa
  ▸**bukubukuuja**
  ▸**irihana**
  ▸**katajaa**
  ▸**shanpin**
  ▸**usujaa**
tea lees **chaakashi**
tea set **chawandoogu**
tea cake **cha'uki**
  chagwashi
teach **naraasun**
teacher **shinshii**
  shishoo
teachings **michi**[1]
teacup **chawan**
teakettle **imunyakkwan**
teapot **chaanaabi**
  chajuukaa
  chuukaa
tear *n.* **yari**
  yarimii
tear (off) **fitchiin**
tear *v.* **hagasun**
  yariin
  fichisachun
  mushiin
  sakiin
  yain
tearful **nachijira**
tears **nada**[1]
  miinada
  ▸**nachineebi**
  ▸**nadaguruguruu-sun**
tease *n.* **ganmari**
tease *v.* **nabakuin**
  wachakuin
teasing **yanawachaku**
tea-stalk **chaanushin**
teeth **sabachinufaa**
teeth-gnashing **haagishii**
tell **'yun**
  chikasun
  iichikiin
  naraasun

tell (story) hanashi-sun
  katain
tell on moosagi-sun
temper iji
  saku²
temperamental
  ►sakumuchi
temperature nichi
  ►mijikagin
temple tira
  kumikan
temporary futu
  kainu
  ►ichutanuhanshi
tempura tinpura
ten juu²
  tuu²
ten thousand man
tenacious ►kajii
tenant yaakayaa
tender shuuraas(h)an
tendon chiru¹
  ►adujiru
tent tinmaku
tentacle chinu
tenth (day) tuka¹
tepid ►nurumun
termite shirai¹
terrible hagoorii
  shitataka
terribly jikoo
territory kagee
test kukurumi
testicle kuuga
  tama¹
  yakkwan
tetanus hashoofuu
textile sayumi
  uimun²
  ►hana'ui¹
  ►nunudaki
textiles kaji⁴
thank you nifeedeebiru
  shiduugafuudeebiru
thankful ►nifee
thanks kafuushi
  shiduugafuu
that anu
  ari¹
  unu
  uri¹
that (much) uppinaa
  uppi

ussa¹
that (much, many) uhi
thatch n. adan
thatch v. fuchun⁴
thatcher shimiyaa
thatching kayabuchi
theater shibaya
theirs attaamun
themselves duunaa
then anshi
  ansuraa
there 'nma²
  agata
  ama
  amamutii
  ►amakuma
they attaa
  uttaa
thick achisan²
  katasan
  kuusan
thicket yamagwaa
thief nusudu
  gumanusudu
  hijeetiinagaa
  tiinagaa
  ►ufunusudu
thigh mata²
  mumu²
  ►uchimumu
thin hissan¹
  uroosan
  ushisan
  yoogarihiigari
thin hair ►kiibisaa
thin skin ►kaabishii
thing kutu¹
  shina²
think umuin
  kangeein
  umuichichun
think over umuikeesun
think up umichichun
thinking umutaikangeetai
thirsty ►kaakiin
thirteen juusan
thirty sanjuu
this kuri³
this (hard) kansuka
this (many, much) ussanaa
this (much) kansuka
this (sort of) kanneeru
thistle ajama

chibana
  njichaa
thorn nji
thorough-going chukataa
thoroughly marumaruutu
those unu
  uttaa
though -nunjitooti
  tatui²
  -teeman
thought umii
  umui¹
  chimu
  chimuyee
  kangee
  kukuru
  munukangee
  umukutu
thoughtless gassan
  ichitaran
thousand shin⁴
thrashing
  ►kitchaikuruchai
thread iichuu
threads kashinuchi
  nuchi²
threaten ►uraasun
three miichi
  san¹
thresher ininjaayama
  kurumaboo
  senba
threshold shichi⁶
thrifty kumasan
  ►kumeekiyaa
  ►suuteekumasan
thrive fuchaain
thriving fuchatoon
throat nuudii
throw nagiin
throw (down) kurubasun
  utusun
throw away kirishitiin
  shitiin
thrust kamiin
  nuchun¹
thumb ufu'iibi
thumbprint iibiban
thump don
thunder kannai
  hyaaigannai
thundering guruguru
thus kan³

tickle
  kanshi
  kankan[1]
tickle kuchuguin
tickling hagoosan
ticklish hachikoosan
  ▸hagoo'umii
tide suu[3]
  michisu
  ufusuu
  usu
  ▸karasu[2]
  ▸karisuu
  ▸suubanji
tideland katabaru
tidiness chirii
tidy churasan
tidy up katajikiin
tie chinajun
  kukuin
  kunjun
  kunshimiin
  kuntabain
  musubun
  shigiin
tie up shimiin[3]
tiger tura
Tiger tura
tight katasan
tightly chujuuku
  chuujuuku
  hashittu
tile *n.* akagaara
  miigaara
  wuugaara
tile maker kaarayachaa
till uchun[2]
  chukuin
  kunasun
  tageesun
tilled ▸kaneegaki
tilt katanchun
  katankiin
time tuchi
  jikan
  hima
  ittuchi
  jibun
  tukuru
  wui
  ▸kundu
  ▸madu
time being (for the)
  toobun

time-consuming
  himadaari
  timadaari
times jishii
-keen
timid chimuyoosan
timidity munu'uji
timing hyooshi
tin shiji[4]
  shirukani
tinner naabinakuu
tip hanta[1]
  sachi[1]
tipsiness wiigukuchi
tire kutandiin
  wutain
tired darusan
  ▸achihatiin
  ▸hirakiin[1]
  ▸niriin
tissue hanagami
title dee[1]
  minjichi
to ·kai, nkai
  madi
toad atabichaa
tobacco tabaku
tobacco shop tabakuyaa
today chuu
toe iibi
  ▸ufu'iibi
toffee appurigwaa
tofu toofu
  ▸agidoofu
  ▸rukujuu[2]
  ▸yachidoofu
  ▸yushidoofu
together majun
-shiiti
toiler nanjisaa
toilet fuuru
tolerance chimunubi
  nubi
tolerant chimumagisan
  ▸chimunubi-sun
tolerate nijiin[1]
  yashimain
tomato tamatoo
tomb haka
  uhaka
  faafuu
  fuinuchibaka
  hakanujoo

  hakabushin
  haru[2]
  kaaminakuubaka
  shinju
  warabibaka
  yushiri
  ▸munchuubaka
  ▸muyeebaka
  ▸niibibaka
  ▸sudigachi
tomboy sansanaa
tomorrow achaa
tone nii[4]
tone deaf hijainuudii
tongs hiibaashi
tongue shiba
  shicha[1]
tonic kunchigusui
  ▸irabuu shinji
  ▸njanafuuchibaa
tonight chuuyuru
too ·n
  duttu
  mata[1]
  naa[7]
tool(s) doogu
  harudoogu
  kanjaadoogu
  maasudoogu
  seekudoogu
  shimudoogu
  umidoogu
  yaadoogu
Tools
  ajimaa
  banjoogani
  ganjimi
  ibira[1]
  irichi'ukusaa
  kana'ami
  kiishi
  kuda
  kurubashi
  kurubashaa
  kurubashii
  kweefiira
  kweeminkaa
  maaka
  sashi
  shiminaa[1]
  shiminaa[2]
  taanoosaa
  tiibiku

tookachi
toonikachaa
umibaku
tooth haa[1]
▸chinbaa
▸iribaa
▸meeba
▸mushikweebaa
▸shichaba
▸uukubaa
▸uyashirajibaa
▸'wiibaa
toothache haayami
tooth-mark haakata
toothpick yooji
top 'wii
top (toy) kooruu
top and bottom iihicha
topic dee[1]
topic marker ·ya
topknot katakashira
torch tee[2]
  tubushi
  ▸ijaibii
torment kurushimiin
tormented
  ▸kurushimirariin
torn ▸hitchiriin
tornado kajimachi
torso duutee
tortoise yamagaami
toss and turn kugeein
total suudaka
touch n.
  ▸amasaaikumasaai
touch v. saain
touched ▸hikasariin
tough kufasan
  shipusan
toward ▸nkiin[2]
towel tiisaaji
town machi[1]
  machikata
  miyaku
toy nagusamimun
  yiirimun
  ▸joojookamiigwaa
  ▸utchirikubusaa
toy gun ▸kabitippuu
trace ushiigachi-sun
traces atukata
track hisakata
trade (commerce) achinee

▸Too'achinee
trade (swap) tankaageei
trade (vocation) waja
tradition chiteebanashi
  kafuu
traffic njaichai
  wooree
trail tanabichun
training chiiku
  ninchi[2]
  yaanaree
trample kudamiin
  kunasun
transcript uchushi
transfer n. fichichiji
transfer v. hichiwatasun
  uchiin[1]
  watasun
  yujiin
transform bakiin
transmit migurasun
  tuichijun
transplanting iikee
transportation nuimun[1]
transvestite winagufuujii
trap yaama
  aniku
  utushi'ana
trash chiri[3]
  gumi
  utichiri
travel tabi
  doochuu
  ▸funatabi
traveler tabinutchu
travelers tabininju
tray bun[1]
  chabun
  jin[1]
  marubun
  tundaabun
  ubun[2]
  ujin
treading water tachi'wiiji
treason mufun
treasure takara
  atarashimun
treasuring kakugu[2]
treat kwatchii
  ugui
treatment tunjaku
tree kii[1]
  niwagi

▸ufugii
tree house yangwa
tremble furiin[1]
  futufutuu-sun
trembling gatagata
  shishiburii
trend jishii
trial (legal) saiban
trial (test) kukurumi
  tamishi
triangle sankaku
trick hakarigutu
trickle nagariin
tricks hooka
trinkets gumamun
trip ▸naga'atchi
trip (outbound) ichi[4]
tropical ▸achiguni
trouble gee
  kuchisa
  urii[2]
  fuchigoo
  jaafeegutu
  miiwaku
  mindoo
  nan
  nanjikunji
  tima
  wacharee
  yakkee
  ▸kumain[2]
troubled ▸midariyuu
  ▸sukweesun
  ▸wacharain
troubled (with)
  ▸tiiwacharee
troublesome
  muchikas(h)an
  timadaari
trowel hiira
  ▸asangani
  ▸ujunbiira
truancy yamagakkoo
true- ma(a)-
true (of heart) soojimu
truly funnu
truncheon sai[2]
trust n. michimui
trust v. mikumun
  shinjiin[1]
  ▸marumiin
truth funnu
  funtoo

try

jintoo
shinjichi
try kukurugakiin
nnjun
tamisun
tsunami shigaranami
tub taaree
tuck *n.* chibui
tuck *v.* kanagiin
tuft fusa
tug hichun¹
tug-of-war chinahichi
▸tiinna
tumble dugeein
keeriin
ukkurubun
tumbler utchirikubusaa
tumbling keerinkurubin
tumor guufu
uubu
tuna achinu'iyu
kachuu
tune fushi²
-fushi³
tuning chindami
tunnel yuku'ana
turf mappaa
turn (around) tunkeein
turn (inside out) utcheein
turn *n.* maaru
turn (on) kakiin¹
turn (over) keerasun
urageesun
turn *v.* maain
magain
migurasun
turner fichimunjeeku
turnery fichimun
turnip indii
turtle kaamii
garasaagaami
umigaami
twang hanagwii
hanamunu'ii
tweezers shiraginujaa
twelve juuni
twenty ▸hatachi
twice takeen
twig suura
yuda
twilight usu'akagai
twin taachuu
twinkle fichain

twist mudiin
nooin²
twisted ▸machibuikaabuisun
twister kajimachi
two tataachi
typhoon arashi
kaji¹
kajifuchi
teefuu
ufukaji
uukaji
tyranny woogai

U———
ugly wassan
ulcerate eein²
umbilical cord
▸fusuchijun
umbrella kasa¹
amagasa¹
dangasa
uncertainty futashika
uncle ufuusuu
ufuutaarii
wujasaa
wunchuu
wunchuugwaa
unclean hijai¹
uncommonly ▸mari
uncooked nama¹
under shicha
under (the floor) yukasa
yukasamii
undercoating shichanui
undergarment shichaji
hakama
jiban
jiban sarumata
shichabakama
underling shichayaku
undernourished andagaaki
understand kukuriin
numikumun
ubiin
ukituin
wakain¹
yumituin
understanding ubi¹

undertake fichi'ukiin
underwater mijinumii
undo futuchun
undutiful uyafukoo
uneasiness chimuwasamichi
unemployed ▸ashibun
uneven ▸inchaamanchaa
▸inchaanagaa
unexpected umin yuran
umiinufuka
uminchakiran
▸ubirajigutu
unexpectedly angwee
unfasten yurumiin
unfeeling chirinasan
unfilial ▸fukoo
unfit fusoowoona
unfold hirachun
unforgettable washiriguris(h)an
unfortunate ingwa
unfriendly ▸kufain
unhappiness bukukuchi
buseewee
uriigutu
uninjured mukiji
unintentionally ubijini
ubiraji
unique mari
unite aasun
united ▸marumun¹
unity chimutiichi
unjust yana-
unkindness funinjoo
unlock akiin¹
unlucky wassan
unlucky day yukkanufii
unmarried tachimee
▸duuchuimun
unnecessary muyuu
unoccupied ▸nnayaa
unpack futuchun
unreasonableness muri
unreliability futashika
unrequited love kata'umui
unrest midari
unripe oosan
▸oomun
unruly ▸amain²
unsavory niisan
unscrupulous ▸namajiraa

voice

unselfishness muyuku
unsightly miitoon neen
unskilled futassha
unskillfulness fuyiiti
   hita
unsociability kamajishi
unsociable ▸kadu¹
   ▸kamajisaa
unsuitability fusoowoo
untidy
   chikkaamukkaasoon
   nagihoori
untie futuchun
   hansun
   wakkwasun
until madi
unusual mari
unwanted ▸shitigaramun
unwilling -guutuu
unyielding eetiguchi
upbringing iinaraashi
   sujoo²
upheaval yuugawai
uphill nubuibira
upper class 'wiikata
upset ▸chimuchigeerasun
   ▸dumangwiin
   ▸tiimaamaa-sun
   ▸tiiwoosawoo
upside 'wii
upside-down urageeshi
   ▸keerasun
   ▸sakanain
   ▸urageein
   ▸urageesun
urge *n.* muyuushi
urge *v.* isamiin
   ▸muyuusun
urging uriyoo
urinate shiibai-sun
urine shiibai
   ▸shiishii
urn haruyaa
   jiishigaami
   kaaminuchibitiichi
   tirajiishi
   yaajiishi
   ▸udunjiishi
use *n.* chikeemichi
   shin²
use *v.* chikain¹
useful yakutachun
useless ▸daimun

uselessness itajiragutu
   muyuu
usher ukichiki
usual fiijii
usury takariifii
utensils chadoogu
   doogu
   makaidoogu
utmost shippee
uvula nuudii'waagwaa

V———
vacant ▸nnayashichi
vacate duchun
   nuchun⁴
vacation hima
   ituma
   yashimi
   yurii
vaccination jitoo
vagina hoo
vagrant yaamadii
vaguely umuyoo
vain ▸ibayaa
valley suku²
value ataras(h)a-sun
   ni'uchi
   yuchira
vanity ada²
variety iru'iru
   samajama
varnish urushi
vary chigain
   kawain
   'njuchun
vassal shinka
vat ▸eechibu
vegetable naa⁹
vegetables oofa
   yaasee
   yasee
   ▸fushiba
vegetation kusaki
vehicle nuimun¹
vein chiijiru
   ufujiru
velvet tingachuu
venom duku¹
Venus manjaabushi
   yuubanmanjaa
veranda yiin
verification fichi'ati

verify miitudukiin
vertigo nubushi
very yufudu
   duku²
   duttu
   ippee
   njumiti
   yukuyuku
vessel mijikubusaa
via kara¹
vicinity mangura
victim kweemun
victory kachi¹
view *n.* nagami
   ▸miinumee
view *v.* kangeein
   nagamiin
vigil yuuki
villa yaadui
village aja¹
   mura
   shima¹
villager shimaa
   shimanchu
villain akunin
   yanamun
vine chiru¹
vinegar shii⁴
   amajaki
   feei²
   suu¹
violent arasan
   chuusan
   ▸abariin
viper habu¹
virus duku¹
vise manrichi
visible ▸miiin¹
vision imi¹
visit ichun
   nnjun
   yushiriin
   ▸chaabiin
   ▸menseebiin
visit (tomb) hakamee
   uhakamee
vocal cords nuudiijiru
vocals feeshi
vocative interjection tai¹
   tari
   umikii
voice kwii¹
   gumagwii

305

volume

volume
  guna'abii
  nii[4]
  ▸kwiigaai
  ▸magigwii
volume (of water)
  mijidaki
volume (tome) kwan[2]
voluptuous ▸hootunnii
vomit agiin
  hachun[1]
vow chijiri
voyage funatabi
  tukee
vulgar hagoosan
  jibita
  ▸gasaa
  ▸hagoomun
  ▸jibitamun
  ▸kajii

W ———

wage takadima
wage earner timatuyaa
wages tima
  timachin
waist gamaku
wait hikeein
  machun[2]
waiter chuuji[1]
waiting ▸machikantii
waitress chuuji[1]
  sakanayaawinagu
wake (someone up)
  ujumasun
  ukusun
wake (up) samiin[2]
  ukiin[2]
  miikufain
wake (vigil) yuugumui
wakeful ▸kufain
waking miikufai
walk *n.* ▸naga'atchi
walk *v.* atchun
walking kachi[4]
  ▸aatcha
  ▸gongon
wall kubi[2]
  yaanukubi
  ▸hinpun
wallet jin'irii
  jinbukuru
want *n.* iriyuu

want *v.* iin[3]
wanting fuus(h)an
war ikusa
wardrobe yoofukudanshi
warehouse kura[1]
  sakigura
wares gumamun
warm *adj.* nukusan
  nukunukuutu
warm *v.* nukumun
  nukumiin
  nukutamiin
  nurumiin
  ▸nukutamain
warmth nichi
warn imashimiin
warning imashimi
war-playing
  ikusagwaasee
warship ikusabuni
wart kuchubi
wartime ikusayuu
wash arain
  nagasun
wash (rice) tujun
washhouse shintakuyaa
washing ▸mijishigutu
wasp hachaa
waste *n.* itajira
waste *v.* ▸taariin[1]
wasteland arichi
  hagimoo
watch (lookout) baan
watch (timepiece) tuchii
watch *v.* nnjun
  wugamun
watchman yuumaai
water miji
  amamiji
  amidaimiji
  numimiji
  ▸buubuu[2]
  ▸chikeemiji
  ▸jiishiru
  ▸namamiji
  ▸saayuu
  ▸umiji
water (hot) yuu[4]
  achiyuu
water buffalo miji'ushi
water play mijimutaan
waterfall tachi[3]
watermelon shiikwa

watermelon seeds unjani
waterspout ruu
  ruusagai
waterwheel mijiguruma
wave *n.* nami[1]
  miitundanami
  oonami
  shiraginami
  shiranami
  yukunami
  ▸goomichaa
  ▸namikaji
  ▸uunami
wave *v.* fuin[3]
  nabichun
  nabikasun
wavelet sarasaraanami
waver furafuraa-sun
  yuttaikwattai-sun
wavering tunuumanuu
wax roo
way michi[1]
  michinaka
ways ikutatii
we washita
  wattaa
weak yoosan
  binasan
  duuyafarasan
  hissan[1]
  ushisan
  wassan
  yafarasan
  ▸afageeriin
  ▸uturiin
weaken yooin
  neein[1]
  yabiriin
  yafarachun
weakened ▸namariin
weakling biiraa
  nachibusaa
  yoobaa
weakly yoongwaa
weakness fuyiiti
  yoomi
wealth eeki
  yuchiku
  yutaka
wealthy ▸eekii
  ▸eekinchu
weapon ▸nunchaku
wear (last) muchun[1]

wear *n.* firi²
wear *v.* chiin¹
　hachun²
　sugain
　hakiin
weary 'agumun
　▸kutandiin
weather tinchi
　'waachichi
　▸uubukka
weathering hari
weave uyin
weaver hata'uyaa
weaving handi
　hata'ui
wedding niibichi
　niibichisuuji
wedge fundoo
　shikkwa
weed kusa²
　taagusa
weeding kusatui
week ▸higan
weft nuchi²
weigh hakain
weight 'nbushi
　chinmi
Weights and Measures
　andagaami
　chiiga²
　chin⁴
　chooban
　chuwakasaa
　chuyumi
　goo
　gungoochiiga
　gushaakuu
　gushaakunakamui
　hiru³
　ichigoonakamui
　ichigoonuu
　ichinukuhin
　itchin²
　kan⁴
　kanabuchi
　mashi²
　munmi
　munnan
　nakajichi
　nakamui
　nakamuigwaa
　nananukuhin
　ri

shaku¹
shaku²
-su
sun³
-tu²
-wakashi
▸mihautuu
weir kachi³
weird hagoosan
　hirumas(h)an
　yoo'usumas(h)an
welcome *n.* unkee
welcome *v.* nkeein
　tuimuchun
welcomed ▸mutiin
well *adv.* yuu³
well *n.* kaa²
　chiigaa²
　chingaa
　fiijaagaa
　hiijaa²
　ijun
　ijungaa
　kurumagaa
　muragaa
　yiigaa
well-bucket chii³
　kubajii
west iri
　nishi
West (the) Uranda
Westerner Urandaa
wet ndasun
　▸marundii
　▸ndiin
　▸shittain
wet nurse chii'an
whale gujira
wharf sanbashi
　tumai²
　tundoo
what chaa¹
　jinu
　nan-
　nuu
what kind chaaru
　changutooru
　▸changutooruu
what time nanduchi
wheat 'nnamuji
wheedling kuchiguruma
wheel kuruma
　haagaa

when ichi³
　-nunjitooti
　tuchi
whenever kaaji
where maa
whereabouts yukui¹
whetstone tushi²
which jinu
　jiru
　nuu
while ˙gachii
　˙ganaa
　˙giinaa
　eeda
　ichuta
　uchi
whim fundee
　munujichi
whimper nachigutu
whine nachigwii¹
whip buchi
whirlpool machi²
whirlwind machikaji
whisper gumagwii
　guna'abii
whispering
　gumamunugatai
white shirusan
　▸masshiruu
　▸shiruu
white (of an egg) shirumi
white (of the eye)
　shirumii
who taa²
　tanumun²
　tattaa
whole matasan
wholeness maru-
wholly maru-
whore sangwanaa
why nuunchi
wick kakkoo¹
　rooshin
　shin³
　tuujin
wicked yachi
　▸akunin
wickerwork chinibu
　annumii
　sooji²
wide hirusan
　firubiruu
widen hirugiin

widow

widow yagusami
widower wikigayagusami
width haba
  hirusa
  waa
wife tuji
  guniiji
  miituji
  'waanai
  wakatuji
  ▸atudumeei
  ▸atutuji
  ▸miitu
  ▸miitunda
  ▸naichaayumi
wig kajura
wild ara²-
  yama-
  ▸nankurumii
wilderness moo
will chimu
  haji²
  igun
  ninrichi
  tinmii
  ▸usadami
willfulness chimama
  fundee
willow yanaji
willpower ninrichi
wilt neeriin
win *n.* kachi¹
win (over) tiijikiin
win *v.* atain²
  kachun⁴
wind *n.* kaji¹
  fee³
wind *v.* kuin
  machun¹
windbreak kajikataka
winding magayaahigayaa
windmill kajimayaa
window ▸fichidu
Winds
  boosuubee
  feekaji
  fusaagi
  heefuki
  kaachiibee
  kajinunii
  kajimaai
  kuchi¹
  matumu

  miinishi
  namikaji
  ningwachikajimaai
  nishikaji
  nkeekaji
  shiimiinishi
  urijinbee
  utibuchaa
windy kajoosan
wine kuusu
wing hani
wink *n.* mii'uchi
wink *v.* miiyoo-sun
winking miipachipachiI
winnow miijooki
winter fuyu
wipe nuguin
wire shibungani
wisdom jinbun
  soo¹
  suumii
wise hashiraas(h)an
  sooraas(h)an
wise man jinbunaa
  jinbunmuchi
wish *n.* nigee
  ningwan
  nujumi
wish *v.* nigain
  nujumun
  umuin
wishing fuus(h)an
wisteria fuji
wistful nagurinaguriitu
with ·tu¹
  -kaji
  majun
withdraw fichinain
  fichi'agiin
  hikkumun
  hikkumiin
wither kariin²
  neein¹
  neeriin
within mii⁵
  uchi
witness miitudukiin
  nnjun
woe wajawee
woman winagu
  ▸churawinagu
  ▸gijaa
  ▸haamee

  ▸hanshii
  ▸iibingwaa
  ▸nakatagee
  ▸paapaa
womanizer
  winagukachimiyaa
womb kwashii
womenfolk
  winaguwarabi
wonder *n.* fushiji²
wonder *v.* umuin
wonderful hirumas(h)an
  ▸fushiji²
wood kii¹
  jeemuku
wood chip kiijiri
woodpecker kiichichichaa
woodsman yama'atchaa
woof nuchi²
word jii²
work *n.* chitumi
  hatarachi
  shigutu
  shikuchi
  waja
  ▸akachichibaru
  ▸chigakiin
  ▸hiibatarachi
  ▸hitchiibaru
  ▸hitchiishikuchi
  ▸jinmookijuku
  ▸kuchinumee
  ▸mijishigutu
  ▸nuchishitiwaja
  ▸seekushigutu
  ▸tachishikuchi
  ▸tiishigutu
  ▸umishigutu
  ▸yamashigutu
  ▸yiishigutu
  ▸yuunaabi
  ▸yuushigutu
work (someone)
  ▸kunchikain
work *v.* atchun
  hatarachun
  achikain
  agachun
  'njuchun
  tiihisanrasun
worker hatarachaa
  kaneemun
  miguimun

Zodiac

shikuchisaa
►irichirii
world yununaka
yuu²
ichimi
kunuyuu
shikee
shikin
tinga
worm mushi¹
wormwood fuuchibaa
worrier shiwasaa
worries bunnuu
worry *n.* chigakai
chimugakai
kangeegutu
umiishiji
umui¹
worry *v.* shinroo-sun
shiwa¹-sun
umiiyamii-sun
umuiyamii-sun
►umuisugusun
worse chiji¹
worsen chijinain
worship *n.* ►utuushi
worship *v.* wugamun
worth ni'uchi
shin²
tuidukuru
worthless ►kajinaranmun
wound kiga
kiji
wounded ►kijichichun
wounded (person)
kiganin
wrap chichimun
wrestle shimatuin
wrestler shimatuyaa
wrestling shima³
►hijainushi
►machigwaa
►meegaki
►ninjaagwaa
►nushi¹
►Uchinaajima
wretch ►kunuhyaa
wring shibuin
wrinkle *n.* shiwa²
hiija
magui
wajami
►maaguuhiiguu

wrinkle *v.* wajamun
wajamiin
wrinkled ►maguin
wrinkly ►maguihiigui
wrist tiinukubi
write kachun¹
writing kachimun
mungun
►kaidaajii
►suuchuumaa
wrong fuchigoo
wassan
yana-
►chigain
wrong way yukumichi
►michibappee
wrongdoing yanakutu

Y ———
Yaeyama Eema²
Yeema
Yaeyama person Eemaa
Eemanchu
yam yama'nmu
yard fukamaa
naa⁵
niwa
yardstick kani¹
yawn akubi
year tushi¹
ichinin
-nin²
►akiti
►gashidushi
►kuju²
►kundu
►kutushi
►miidushi
►naanchu
►naayaan
►nchu
►ninjuu
►ninnin¹
►yugafuu
yearn (for) kugariin
years naganin
yeast ahyaa
kooji
yell abiin
►hiyamikasun
yellow chiiruu
yes ii¹

'nn
oo
oosaarii
uu²
yesterday chinuu
yet maada
yield wuuriin
yolk akamii
kuuganu'akamii
you 'yaa
ittaa
naa²
nattaa
unju
unjunaa
young wakasan
youngster wakamun
►gafasaawarabaa
your ittaa
yourself 'yaakuru
youth wakamun
niisee
oojaaniisee
wakasaini
wakashu
wakawikiga
youthfulness wakasa

Z ———
zealot chukataa
zinc tutan
zodiac (Chinese) juunishi
►maai²
Zodiac
nii⁵
ushi¹
tura
uu¹
tachi²
mii²
'nma¹
hichiji
saaruu
tui
in¹
yii¹